CAMBRIDGE LIBR

Books of endurir

Ling

From the earliest surviving glossaries and translations to nineteenth-
academic philology and the growth of linguistics during the twentieth
century, language has been the subject both of scholarly investigation and
of practical handbooks produced for the upwardly mobile, as well as for
travellers, traders, soldiers, missionaries and explorers. This collection will
reissue a wide range of texts pertaining to language, including the work of
Latin grammarians, groundbreaking early publications in Indo-European
studies, accounts of indigenous languages, many of them now extinct, and
texts by pioneering figures such as Jacob Grimm, Wilhelm von Humboldt
and Ferdinand de Saussure.

A Comparative Grammar

A founding text of comparative philology, Franz Bopp's Vergleichende
Grammatik was published in six volumes between 1833 and 1852. Bopp
(1791–1867), Professor of Sanskrit and comparative grammar at Berlin, set
out to prove the relationships between Indo-European languages through
detailed description of the grammatical features of Sanskrit compared to
those of Zend (Avestan), Greek, Latin, Lithuanian, Gothic and German.
This translation of Bopp's first three volumes gave British scholars access
to his analytic methodology, at a time when comparative philology was far
advanced in Germany compared to Britain. Translated by Edward Backhouse
Eastwick (1814–1883), the multi-lingual diplomat and scholar, and edited
by Horace Hayman Wilson (1786–1860), Professor of Sanskrit at Oxford,
this work stands as a testament both to Bopp's magisterial research and to
Eastwick's extraordinary skill in translation. This volume continues Bopp's
treatment of the verb, and discusses word formation.

Cambridge University Press has long been a pioneer in the reissuing of out-of-print titles from its own backlist, producing digital reprints of books that are still sought after by scholars and students but could not be reprinted economically using traditional technology. The Cambridge Library Collection extends this activity to a wider range of books which are still of importance to researchers and professionals, either for the source material they contain, or as landmarks in the history of their academic discipline.

Drawing from the world-renowned collections in the Cambridge University Library, and guided by the advice of experts in each subject area, Cambridge University Press is using state-of-the-art scanning machines in its own Printing House to capture the content of each book selected for inclusion. The files are processed to give a consistently clear, crisp image, and the books finished to the high quality standard for which the Press is recognised around the world. The latest print-on-demand technology ensures that the books will remain available indefinitely, and that orders for single or multiple copies can quickly be supplied.

The Cambridge Library Collection will bring back to life books of enduring scholarly value (including out-of-copyright works originally issued by other publishers) across a wide range of disciplines in the humanities and social sciences and in science and technology.

A Comparative Grammar

Of the Sanscrit, Zend, Greek, Latin, Lithuanian, Gothic, German and Sclavonic Languages

VOLUME 3

FRANZ BOPP
EDITED BY H. S. WILSON

CAMBRIDGE UNIVERSITY PRESS

Cambridge, New York, Melbourne, Madrid, Cape Town, Singapore,
São Paolo, Delhi, Dubai, Tokyo

Published in the United States of America by Cambridge University Press, New York

www.cambridge.org
Information on this title: www.cambridge.org/9781108006231

© in this compilation Cambridge University Press 2009

This edition first published 1850
This digitally printed version 2009

ISBN 978-1-108-00623-1 Paperback

This book reproduces the text of the original edition. The content and language reflect
the beliefs, practices and terminology of their time, and have not been updated.

Cambridge University Press wishes to make clear that the book, unless originally published
by Cambridge, is not being republished by, in association or collaboration with, or
with the endorsement or approval of, the original publisher or its successors in title.

A

COMPARATIVE GRAMMAR

OF THE

SANSCRIT, ZEND,

GREEK, LATIN, LITHUANIAN, GOTHIC, GERMAN,

AND SCLAVONIC LANGUAGES.

BY

PROFESSOR F. BOPP.

PART III.

TRANSLATED FROM THE GERMAN

BY

LIEUTENANT EASTWICK, M.R.A.S.

MEMBER OF THE ASIATIC SOCIETIES OF PARIS AND BOMBAY, AND PROFESSOR OF URDU
IN THE EAST-INDIA COLLEGE AT HAILEYBURY.

CONDUCTED THROUGH THE PRESS

BY H. H. WILSON, M.A. F.R.S.

BODEN PROFESSOR OF SANSCRIT IN THE UNIVERSITY OF OXFORD.

LONDON:
JAMES MADDEN,
LEADENHALL STREET.

1850.

COMPARATIVE GRAMMAR.

PART III.

VERBS.

FORMATION OF THE MOODS.

POTENTIAL, OPTATIVE, AND CONJUNCTIVE.

716. In the dialect of the Vêdas the *Lêṭ* mood or conjunctive is also formed by the insertion of an *a*, in cases where, in the corresponding indicative form, an *a* is wanting, by the lengthening of which the mood in question might be formed. Thus, from the aorist *abhût*, "he was," comes the conjunctive *bhuvat*, "he may be;" where, by the augment being dropped, the meaning of past time is also removed, as is likewise the case in the potential and imperative: from *akar*, "he made" (for *akart*, according to §. 94.*), comes *karat*, "he may make;" from *chikêt-ti*, "he recognises" (R. *kit*. Cl. 3.), *chikêtati*, "he may recognise." So in Old Persian, *ahatiy*, "he may be," from *astiy*, "he is" (Behist. IV. 38. &c.), where the Sanscrit स् *s* in Old Persian is retained before *t*, but before vowels becomes *h*.

From the aorists also, in the Vêda dialect, come conjunctive moods with the terminations of the present; hence, *karati*, "he may make" (Rig V. 46. 6.), from *akar*. The Vêda dialect even forms the conjunctive mood by the simple

---

* Aorist of the fifth formation, which in the Vêda dialect is more extensively used than in classical Sanscrit.

annexation of the personal terminations of the present to the base of the aorist, thus *e.g. vivôchati* (*vi* prep.), " he may announce," from *vyavôchat* (Rig V. CV. 4.).

IMPERATIVE.

717. This mood, which, in classical Sanscrit, is formed only from the present indicative, is distinguished from the latter merely by the personal terminations (the first person of the three numbers excepted: see §. 713.), which have been already discussed. The dual and plural, with the exception of the third person plural, have the secondary terminations; so that e.g. *bharatâm*, "let the two carry," is distinguished from *abharatâm*, "the two carried," only by the omission of the augment. In Greek the difference of the termination των of φερέτων, from την of the imperfect ἐφερέτην, is unorganic, as των and την are originally one, and both rest on the Sanscrit *tâm*.

718. The second person singular of the Sanscrit first principal conjugation—*i.e.* that which corresponds to the Greek conjugation in ω, to the Latin fourth conjugation, and to the German strong and weak conjugation — is distinguished from the second principal conjugation, which corresponds to the Greek μι, inasmuch as in the active (parasmâip.) it has lost the personal termination; so that e.g. *bhar-a*, "let him carry" (Zend, *bar-a*) terminates with the class-syllable, to which, in the dual and plural, the personal terminations are annexed (भरतम् *bhar-a-tam* = φέρ-ε-τον, भरत *bhar-a-ta* = φέρ-ε-τε). The loss of the personal termination appears of great antiquity; as in Greek too, φέρ-ε is said for φέρ-ε-θι; and in Latin *leg-e*,* *am-â*, *mon-ê*, and *aud-î*, are likewise devoid of the personal sign.

---

* The *e* of *lege* is, in its origin, identical with the *i* (from *a*, see §. 109ª. 1.) of *leg-i-te*, and rests on the principle, that in Latin, at the end of a word, *e* is preferred to *i*; hence, *e.g. mare* from the base *mari*.

719. In German the strong verbs have, in the second person singular of the imperfect, rejected the class vowel, and terminate, therefore, with the final letters of the root,[*] without, however, in most cases, containing the actual root itself, as the vowel of the root, according to the analogy of the present indicative, appears at one time weakened; as *e.g.* in Gothic, *bind*, from the root *band*, "to bind" = Sanscrit, *bandh*; at another time with Guna, hence, in Gothic, *biug*, "bend," from the root *bug* = Sanscrit, *bhuj*; *beit*, "bite," from the root *bit* = Sanscrit, *bhid*, "to cleave" (see p. 105). The Sanscrit also, and Greek, retain, in the present imperative, the Guna gradations of the present indicative, or, most generally, that of the special tenses; hence, *e.g.* in Sanscrit, *bôdha*, "know" (from *baudh*) from *budh*, and in Greek, φεύγε from φυγ. The German weak verbs retain their class character (see §. 109^a. 6.) corresponding to the Sanscrit *aya*, of the tenth class: the syllable *ya*, however, is contracted to *i* (Gothic *ei* = *î*), as in general the syllable *ya* at the end of a word lays aside its vowel, and changes the *y* into one. Compare, *e.g.* the Gothic *tam-ei*, "tame," from *tamya*, with the Sanscrit causal *dam-aya*; Latin *dom-â*; Greek δάμ-αε. In the second weak conjugation, let *laig-ô*, "lick," be compared with the Sanscrit causal *lêh-aya*, from *lih*, "to lick:" in the contraction of *a*(*y*)*a* to *ô*, however, *laigô* approaches nearest to Latin imperatives like *dom-â*, as the Gothic *ô* = *â* (§. 69.). In the third weak conjugation, compare *hab-ai*, *thah-ai*, *sil-ai*, with the Latin forms of like signification, *hab-ê*,

---

[*] Thus in Latin *dic* for *dice*. With regard to *fer* it is to be observed, that *fero* also, in the indicative, is to be joined rather with the Sanscrit *bhar* (*bhri*) of the third class than with that of the first. Thus, as *fer-s*, *fer-t*, *fer-tis*, corresponds to *bi-bhar-shi*, *bi-bhar-ti*, *bi-bhṛi-tha*, so *fer* answers to *bibhṛi-hi* (from *bibhar-dhi*), the personal termination being suppressed, as in *es* = Greek, ἴσ-θι, Sanscrit *ê-dhi* from *ad-dhi* (for *as-dhi*).

tac-ê, sil-ê, where the ê is a contraction of *ai*, and answers to the Sanscrit *ay* of *aya* (see p. 110). In the second person plural *tam-yi-th* (from *tam-ya-th*) corresponds to the Sanscrit *dam-aya-ta*, Latin *dom-â-te*, Greek δαμ-άε-τε. In Greek and German the imperative second person plural is not distinguishable from the present indicative. In Sanscrit, however, the imperative has the termination of the secondary forms (*ta*) opposed to the *tha* of the primary; thus दमयत *damayata*, "tame ye," opposed to दमयथ *damayatha*, "ye tame." In Latin *domâte* is distinguished from *domâtis*, where the latter form answers to the Sanscrit dual indicative present (दमयथस् *damayathas*, Gothic *tamyats*), the former to दमयत *damayata*, "tame ye" (see §. 444.). The termination *to*, of the second and third person of the so-called future of the imperative, and the Greek termination τω of the third person singular, correspond to the Vêda termination *tât*, which answers for the second as well as the third person;* and in the latter, as has already been remarked, is most correctly retained in the Oscan *tud* (*licitud, estud*.) As in तात the expression of the person is twice contained, so it is in the Latin second person plural *tôte*, for which in Sanscrit तात *tâta* might be expected, which, however, does not occur. In the third person plural *nto* answers to the Greek ντων (*legunto* = λεγόντων), which was before compared with the Sanscrit middle forms in *antâm* (φερόντων = *bharantâm*.)

720. The Sanscrit termination तु, plural अन्तु, is derived from the pronominal base त *ta*, by weakening the *a* to a vowel of middle weight, while in the present indicative, as

---

* See §. 470. The edition of the First Book of the Rig V. by Fr. Rosen, which has appeared since this work was commenced, has confirmed *tât* to be the termination of the second person of the imperative. H. XLVIII. 15. occurs प्र नो यच्छतात् *pra no yachchhatât*, "give us" and CIV. 5. चकृतात् *charkritât* from the intensive of the root कृ *kri*, "to make."

FORMATION OF THE MOODS.

generally in the primary forms the extreme weakening to *i* takes place. We have, therefore, the forms *-ta, -tu, -ti*, as in the interrogative, in the isolated case *ka, ku, ki*. In Zend the *u* of the imperative termination is occasionally lengthened; *e.g.* in the frequently-occurring ‫ﮔﺮاوﺗﻮ‬ *mraotû*, "let him say:" on the other hand, Vend. Sade, p. 142, ‫ﺧﺮﺗﻮ‬ *kharatu*, "let him eat," ‫وﻧﮭﺘﻮ‬ *vanhatu*, "let him put on."

721. The Sanscrit middle termination *sva* (from *tva*, see §. 443.) of the second person singular is in Zend corrupted with a preceding *a* to *anuha* (for *anhva*), where the *v* is changed into the vowel *u*, and has stepped before the *h*; the nasal, however, which, according to §. 56ª., is placed before the *h*, remains, though otherwise ‫ڹ‬ *n* occurs as a guttural nasal, only in *direct* combination with *h*. The combination *nhv* appears, however, too uncouth to be admitted in Zend; and wherever, therefore, it would occur, we find in its stead ‫ﻧﻮه‬ *nuh*: hence, too, ‫وﯾﻮﻧﮭﺘﻮ‬ *vivanuhatô* = Sanscrit विवस्वतस् *vivasvatas*, "of the Vivasvat" (Vendidad Sade, p. 40.). Several examples of imperatives in *anuha* occur in the eighteenth Fargard of the Vendidad, where, however, the text corrected by Burnouf (Yaçna, Note A. p. 17) according to the manuscripts is to be referred to, as the lithographed copy (pp. 457, 458) has, more than once, *anha* faultily for *anuha*: ‫اﯾﻮی وﺳﺘﺮا ﯾﺎوﻧﮭﯿﻨﻮﮬﺎ‬* "put on the clothes;" ‫ﻓﺮا زﺷﺘﮫ ﺷﻨﯿﻨﻮﮬﺎ‬ *frâ zasta snayanuha*, "wash thy hands;"† ‫آ اﺋﺸﻤﻨﻢ ﯾﺎﺷﻨﻮﮬﺎ‬ *â aêsmanm yâsanuha*,

---

* This form is based on the causal of the Sanscrit root यम् *yas* "to strive."

† I take ‫ﺷﻨﯿﻨﻮﮬﺎ‬ *snayanuha* as a passive verb with a middle signification; thus Vend. Sade, p. 331, twice ‫اُش ﺗﻨﻮم ﺷﻨﺎﯾﺌﺘﺎ‬ *uś tanûm snayaêta*, "let him wash his body" (Anquetil, p. 360, "*il lavera son corps*"): on the other hand, p. 330, *uśa* (*uśĕ*?) *tanûm snayâêta*, with a conjunctive vowel between the preposition *uś* (=Sanscrit उत् *ut*) and the

"spread out wood" (compare Sanscrit यम् *yam*, in the special tenses यच्छ् *yachh*, with the preposition आ *â*, "to extend"). So also in the Vend. Sade, p. 39, for ש‍ייו‍)ס‍زد»שש‍‍و *hunvanha* we ought to read ש‍ייו‍)ס‍زد»שש‍‍و *hunvanuha*, according to the manuscripts made use of by Burnouf, and for ש‍ש‍د‍ش‍ز‍ب‍ل‍و *visanha*, "hearken" (Vendidad Sade, p. 123.), perhaps also ش‍ش‍زد‍ب‍د‍ل‍و *visanuha* should be read.

Remark.—In the Latin Edition of my Sanscrit Grammar of the year 1832 (p. 330) I have taken the form ש‍ייو‍)ס‍زد»שש‍‍و *hunuvanuha*, or, as the lithographed manuscript reads, ש‍ייو‍)ס‍زد»שש‍‍و *hunvanha*, as the imperative middle, and translated *frâmaṅm hunvanuha kharêteê* (according to Anquetil, "*qui me mange en m'invoquant avec ardeur*,") by "*me celebra ad edendum*." The root *hu* is, as is remarked *l. c.*, added to the conjugational character of the first class, besides that of the fifth class *nu*, for without this unorganic adjunct the form would be *hunushva* (= Sanscrit सुनुष्व *sunushva*). It is certain that the Zend root *hu* must in Sanscrit be *su*, and the opinion which Burnouf ascribes to me (Journal Asiatique, 1844, Dec. p. 467), that the Zend *hu* rests on the Sanskrit हु़ *hu*, "to offer," has been neither expressed by me at p. 781, nor in my Critical Grammar, p. 330, nor anywhere else. That a Zend ש *h* never corresponds to the Sanscrit ह़ *h* has been expressly remarked in §. 57.; and it is also remarked in §. 53. that ש *h*, in an etymological respect, never corresponds to the Sanscrit ह़ *h*, but always to the pure or dental स़ *s*. Had I wished to compare, therefore, *l. c.* its Sanscrit type with the Zend *hu* I could only have referred to one of the roots सु *su*, of which one, like the

---

the following word (see §. 518. p. 737). The transitive meaning of the root *snâ* is, on the other hand, usually represented by ס‍و‍زد‍ש *snâdh* in the active; *e. g.* Vendidad Sade p. 233, 8. : ש‍ס‍ש‍ع‍ב‍ש‍ש‍ס‍ل‍و ש‍س‍ש‍ש‍ع‍ש‍ש‍ש‍ש‍ש‍ש‍ש‍ש‍ב *aêtâo vastrâo frasnâdhayên* "let them wash these clothes."

FORMATION OF THE MOODS. 959

Zend *hu*, belongs to the fifth class. On the meaning "*celebrare*," which I have given to the Zend *hu* (according to Anquetil " *invoquer avec ardeur* ") I did not desire to lay any particular stress; for my chief object was to settle the value of the grammatical forms which Anquetil mistook, and I wished to recognise, in the interrogative form, an imperative termination based on the Sanscrit *a-sva*, and in *kharĕteĕ*, the dative of an abstract substantive, while, according to Anquetil's translation ("*qui me mange*") it might be taken for a third person present. In both respects I now find myself supported by the Sanscrit translation of Neriosengh, which is given (*l.c.*) by Burnouf, which renders ᴀᴠᴇꜱᴛᴀɴ *hunvanuha* by परिसंस्कारं कुरु *parisanskâram kuru*,* and ᴀᴠᴇꜱᴛᴀɴ *kharĕteĕ* by खादनाय *khâdanâya* ("for the eating," or "the food.") The explanation of the appended commentary is आहारार्थं सन्मानय *âhârârtham sanmanaya*,† *i.e.* "on account of the food honour (me)."‡ The root ᴀᴠᴇꜱᴛᴀɴ *hu* occurs several times in the ninth Ha of the Izeschne, from which our passage is taken; and indeed in the third person of the imperfect *hunûta* (once *hunvata* with the addition of the character of the first class), which Anquetil everywhere paraphrases by "*ayant invoqué et s'étant humilié*," I have translated it (*l.c.*) by "*laudabat*," and regret that Burnouf has not given us Neriosengh's trans-

---

* Burnouf remarks, "Nos manuscrits sont très-confus en cet endroit: celui de Manakdji a सस्कारश्चरु *sanskâraścharu*, mais je ne suis par sûr du श्च *śch*; le numero II. F. lit. संस्कारंकु *sanskâranku* avec श्च *śch* au-dessus de la ligne." However, I have no doubt that Burnouf is right in reading कुरु *kuru*.

† So Burnouf reads for the सन्मारय *sanmâraya* of the manuscripts, which is unmeaning.

‡ Burnouf translates "*honore-moi comme nourriture*," in which I cannot agree with him; for *âhârârtham*, can only mean "on account of the food," not "as food;" and in *khâdanâya*, as the translation of *kharĕteĕ*, the relation of cause is apparent.

lation of this expression also. Undoubtedly, however, the circumstance that the verb derived from *hu* everywhere refers to ‍‍‍ *haoma*, the personified Sôma-plant, speaks in favour of Burnouf's opinion, that the Zend *hu* has the same signification as the Sanscrit root सु *su*; viz. "to press out the sap," where it is to be further remarked, that in Sanscrit the verb from this root is especially used in relation to the Sôma-plant. I avail myself of the occasion which has led me to speak of the ninth Ha of the Izeschne, to correct an error to which I was led by a false reading of the lithographed manuscript of the Vendidad Sade. Four times in this Ha the masculine nominative of the interrogative occurs before the accusative of the pronoun of the second person. The lithographed manuscript reads once ‍‍‍ *kasê thwanm* (p. 42), once ‍‍‍ *kasê thwanm* (*s* ‍‍ for ‍‍ *s̀*, p. 40, by mistake), once ‍‍‍ *kasêthwanm* (p. 41), and once ‍‍‍ *kas̀ithawanm* (p. 39). Here, therefore, two readings support the separation of the two pronouns, and two their combination; and at first I supposed that the form of writing in which they were separated was the right one, where, in the *ê* or *i* of *kasê* and *kas̀i*, was to be recognised an appended pronoun, like the Greek demonstrative ι (οὑτοσί, ἐκεινοσί: see §. 157*., and Gram. crit. Add. ad r. 270). The *s̀*, however, I regarded as the sign of the nominative, and this it really is; for though the Sanscrit termination *as* in Zend regularly becomes *ô*, but *s* in the middle and beginning of a word before vowels *h*, there might, however, be an exception in the case of the termination *as* occurring before an enclitic, where *as* might retain its original form; for in Zend ‍‍ *s̀* is not so much the palatal sibilant as the श in Sanscrit is, for the latter occurs before no other mutes but palatals only; while ‍‍ occurs before mutes of all organs (see §. 49.), and before mutes which are not palatals always corresponds to

FORMATION OF THE MOODS. 961

the Sanscrit स् *s*, except before *p*, where this springs from the Sanscrit *v*, as *e.g.* in ᭣᭣ *spâ* = Sanscrit स्व *sva*. As, however, we learn from the notice of the various readings of the Paris manuscripts, which have been in the meantime published by Burnouf (Yaçna, Note R. p. 134), that ᭣᭣᭣ *kaśĕ*, and the combination of the interrogative with the following ᭣᭣᭣ *thwanm*, "thee," is the prevailing reading (we find the words joined seven times, and separated only five times, and seven times *ĕ* occurs—for *i* twice, and for *ê* three times) it admits of scarce any doubt that the vowel which stands between *kaś* and *thwanm* is inserted only to assist the utterance, and that we must regard *kaśthwanm* as the original form; so that, as is the case before the enclitic particle *ka*, the sibilant of the nominative has maintained itself under the protection of the following consonant, and remained too when a conjunctive vowel was inserted to aid the pronunciation.* I shall not decide whether this vowel must necessarily be an ᭣ *ĕ*, and could not be either *i* or *a*. Let, however, the quite similar case be considered, where, between the preposition ᭣᭣ *uś*, and the verb ᭣᭣᭣᭣ *histâmi*, in the lithographed manuscript at least, at one time ᭣ *ĕ*, at another ᭣ *i*, at another ᭣ *a* occurs as the vowel of conjunction (see §. 518. p. 737). We may indeed expect, that in all places where the lithographed manuscript has *i* or *a* some one or other of the manuscripts has *ĕ;* and undoubtedly this, the shortest of all the vowels, is best adapted for insertion as a mere vowel of conjunction, as, too, it is regularly used for this

---

* Thus, as ought to have been remarked at §. 47., the forms ᭣᭣᭣᭣᭣ *bitya*, "of the second," and ᭣᭣᭣᭣᭣ *thritya*, "of the third," point to a time when the *i* of the Sanscrit *dvitîya*, *tritîya*, was still present, on which account the *y* has not communicated an aspiration to the preceding consonant, as is the case *e. g.* in *mĕrĕthyu*, where the combination of the *T*-sound with the semi-vowel is primitive.

purpose, to prevent the direct combination of *r* with a following consonant (§. 30.), without any other vowel being used for this object. Here, too, the question might be started, why no interposed vowel is to be found in the combinations *kaśtê*, "who to thee," and *kaśnâ*, "which man?" (for "who" generally: see p. 281,) mentioned by Burnouf *l. c.* (p. cxxxix), while *kaśthwañm* nowhere occurs? The reason of this, I doubt not, lies herein, that *thwañm*, on account of its double consonant, less easily unites with a preceding *ś*, than *tê* and *nâ*; while ᨦᨯᨯ *śt* and ᨯᨯ *śn* are quite favourite and usual combinations. On the other hand, *histâmi*, though its initial sound is one of weak consonants, required the interposition of a vowel when combined with *uś*, because *śh* is an impossible combination in Zend. At the beginning of the twenty-first Fargard of the Vend. (Vendidad Sade, p. 498) we five times find *nĕmaśĕ tê*, i.e. "adoration to thee!" (= Sanscrit नमस् ते *namas tê*,)* each time written separately, though the two words evidently ought to be joined, as the vowel of conjunction *ĕ*, and the retention of the termination *aś*, for which *ô* would otherwise be substituted, sufficiently demonstrate. It appears, however, that on account of the polysyllabicalness of the word, to which in this case the enclitic *tê* is attached, the phonetic combination appears less intimate, and this may also be the reason why the *t* cannot, as in *kaśtê*, follow the *ś* without an intermediate vowel. We may see how much the Zend inclines to use monosyllabic pronominal forms enclitically, in that it attaches them even to prepositions, which have become detached from the verbs to which they belong: hence, ᨦᨯᨯᨦᨯᨯᨦᨯᨯ *frâmañm hunvanuha* in the passage cited above; so ᨦᨯᨯᨦᨯᨯ *âmañm yâśanuha*, which

---

* That Anquetil's translation "*addressez votre prière*" is incorrect requires no proof.

FORMATION OF THE MOODS. 963

Neriosengh translates by मां समीहस्व, *i.e.* "wish or obtain me ;" and Burnouf (Journ. As. Dec. p. 465) by "*invoque-moi.*"* We may also here preliminarily remark that, for the first time, we have learned, through Rawlinson's late ingenious discoveries, that in Old Persian also the pronouns readily attach themselves as enclitics to the preceding word, and that if we read without the *a* (which in old Persian is sometimes contained in the consonants, and sometimes not), *y*, which is regularly added to the *i* at the end of a word, as well as to the diphthong *ai*, the old Persian enclitics will, in like manner, be all monosyllabic. For this, as for other reasons, I read *auramazdâmaiy*, "Auramazda to me," for Rawlinson's -*maiya* (former reading *miya*).

722. The first person of the three numbers of the imperative follows in Sanscrit and Zend a peculiar principle of formation, which, as has already been remarked, corresponds rather to the conjunctive or *Lêṭ* than to the other persons of the imperative. An *â* is prefixed to the

---

* Anquetil altogether omits to translate this expression, for which, in the lithographic manuscripts (p. 39), occurs by mistake *yâsanha*. Burnouf thinks he recognises in the root *yâs*, the Sanscrit याच् *yâch*, "to demand, ask ;" but a difficulty arises in the ᛯ *s* for Sanscrit च् *ch*, of which I have elsewhere met with no example. The root यछ् *yachh*, as substitute of यम् *yam*, answers better, on account of its final consonant, as छ् *chh* in Zend is regularly represented by *s*; on which account I have above (§. 721.) preferred *âyâsanuha*, "spread out," to this root. Here, however, the meaning of the Sanscrit यम् *yam*, यछ् *yachh*, preposition आ *â*, does not suit. Perhaps the *â* (*mânm*) *yâsanuha* in question is radically identical with the frequently-occurring *âyêsê*, "I praise" (or "invoke"?) which leads to a Sanscrit root *yas*, which is only retained in यशस् *yasas*, "glory." With regard to the Zend *ê* for the Sanscrit *a* or *â* see §. 42. It is probable, however, that in *âyêsê*, as also in genitives in *yêhê* for *yahê*, and in present forms in *yêmi*, besides the preceding *y* the vowel also of the following syllable has an assimilating influence in the change of *a* or *â* to *ê*: hence we find, indeed, *âyêsê*, but not *âyêsanuha*, but *âyâsanuha*.

personal terminations, the terminations of the present indicative middle which end in *ê* lengthen this diphthong to *âi*, and the verbal theme keeps, in the second principal conjugation, the strengthened form, which elsewhere enters only before the light personal terminations. The first person singular has *ni* for its ending, where *n* is clearly a corruption of *m* and is suppressed like the latter in the Sanscrit middle, while the Zend maintains this decided advantage over the Sanscrit, that it for the most part retains the personal character, and presents *ânê* to match the Sanscrit *âi*. This ݮݛݡ *ânê* therefore bears the same relation to the active ݛݡ *âni*, that, in the Greek present indicative, μαι does to μι. In order to exhibit the principle of formation of the Sanscrit first person imperative I here present the said person of the three numbers of the two active forms of the root द्विष् *dvish*, "to hate," compared with the corresponding forms of the present indicative.

	ACTIVE.		MIDDLE.	
	INDIC.	IMPERAT.	INDIC.	IMPERAT.
Sing.	*dveshmi*,	*dvêsh-â-ṇi*.*	*dvishê*,	*dvêshâi*.
Dual	*dvishvas*,	*dvêsh-â-va*.	*dvishvahê*,	*dvêsh-â-vahâi*.
Plur.	*dvishmas*,	*dvêsh-â-ma*.	*dvishmahê*,	*dvêsh-â-mahâi*.

So in Zend, Vendidad Sade p. 477, several times ݛݡݫݜݛ *jan-â-ni* (= Sanscrit *han-â-ni*) "I will smite, destroy,"†

---

* The lingual *ṇ* occurs on account of the euphonic influence of the preceding lingual sibilant according to §. 94³. of my Sanscrit Grammar.

† In Sanscrit also the first person imperative sometimes occurs in the sense of the future or present indicative, to express a decided volition of a positive impending action, *e. g.* Sunda and Upas. I. 26. Anquetil takes *janâni* as the third person of a preterite, and renders it (p. 413.) by "*il frappa*," and once by "*seront anéantis*." It needs, however, no proof that *janâni* is really the first person imperative, for Zoroaster speaks to Ahriman the words ݛݡݜݛ ݫݛݓݛݩ ݲݡݫݟݛݩ ݲݡݫݓ ݛݠݡݟݛ *duschda aṇrô mainyô janâni dâma daêvô dâtĕm*, &c., "Vicious Ahriman,

FORMATION OF THE MOODS.   965

pp. 132, 479. ͪ͏ͪͪͪͪ *kĕrĕnav-â-nê* "I should make,"
(= Sanscrit *kṛiṇ-avâni* from *karnav-â-ṇê*).

723. In verbs of the first principal conjugation and of the ninth class, as also in roots in *â* of the second or third class, the modal *â* combines with the preceding *a* or *â*; hence *e.g.* भराणि *bharâni*, "let me carry;" Zend ͪͪͪͪ *barâni*, middle ͪͪͪͪ *barânê* (Vendidad Sade, p. 480). So ͪͪͪͪ *viśânê*, "I will obey;"* ͪͪͪͪ *yazânê* (see p. 278), "I should offer;" ͪͪͪͪ *pĕrĕnânê*, "I should destroy" (Vendidad Sade, p. 335, compare Burnouf, Yaçna, p. 530, ff.); ͪͪͪͪ *yaoschdathânê*, "I should purify" l.c. p. 480).†

Ahriman I will destroy the Daêva-created people." Upon which (p. 478) Ahriman says to Zoroaster,

ͪͪͪͪͪͪͪͪͪͪͪͪͪͪͪͪͪͪͪͪͪͪͪͪͪͪ
mâmê dâma mĕrĕchaṇuha ashâum Zaratustra
"Slay not my people, O pure Zoroaster!

* Vendidad Sade, p. 124. ͪͪͪͪ ͪͪ ͪͪ *azĕm tê viśânê*, "I will obey thee," so *l. c.* are other imperatives in the sense of the future, as ͪͪͪͪ ͪͪ ͪͪ *azĕm tê gaêthão varĕdhayêni*, "I will make thy lands increase" ("make fruitful," Anquetil p. 271. "*je rendrai votre monde fertile et abondante*").

† See §. 637. I am now, however, of opinion, in departure from what has been remarked at p. 112, that the *th* of *dath* is a substitute of *dh*, and I take *da* as the syllable of reduplication, as in the Sanscrit *dadhâmi*. The ͪͪͪͪ *nidaithyaṅn*, "deponant," mentioned at p. 112, corresponds to the Sanscrit निदध्यम् *nidadhyus*, ͪͪͪͪ *ni-daithîta* to the Sanscrit निदधीत *ni-dadhîta*. (§. 702.) In the genitive of the participle of the reduplicated preterite ͪͪͪͪ *dathushô* corresponds to the Sanscrit *dadhushas;* while in the nominative ͪͪͪͪ *dadhvão* (= Sanscrit दधिवान् *dadh-i-vân*) and in the accusative ͪͪͪͪ *dadhvãoṇhĕm* (= Sanscrit *dadh-i-vânsam*), the alteration of *dh* to *th* does not take place, an alteration which most probably is found only in the weak cases. Perhaps in Zend *th* is considered weaker than *dh* and *d*, and this may be the reason that the interrogative verb, where it appears without a preposition or other incumbrance of composition, or even with compositional incumbrance, but without reduplication, also exhibits no *th* in the examples

with

After ‫جج‬ *y* comes *ê* for *â*; hence *e.g.* ‫باﯾﺬر۔ﻋﺪججرﺳى‬ *varĕdhayêni*,
"I will make to grow" (Vend. Sade, p. 124); ‫ﺪﻟﻠﺴﻮﺳﻠججرسﻢ‬
frahârayênê.* In the production of this *ê*, however, the *i*
or *ê* of the termination bears the most important part, for
if the *y* alone was the efficient cause, it would also influence
the following vowel, if *i* or *ê* did not occur in the termination; this, however, is not the case, hence *e.g.* ‫باﯾﻊ۔ﺳﻮﺟججﺳ‬
varĕdhaya, "make to grow" (Vend. S., p. 124); ‫رﻟﻠﺴﻮﺳججﺳ‬
raôchaya, "make to give light, kindle" (p. 457); ‫ﻋﺳجرﺳججﺳﺻر‬
yaṡnayata, "*sacrificio colite*" (Burnouf, Yaçna, Note A. p. 13.)†
So in the second person plural middle, ‫باﺳﺪرﺳﺪﺟﺟﻌﻮﻋﺪع‬
vârayadhwĕm, "defend ye;" ‫۔ﻣﻮﺳﻠﺠﺠﺳﻮﻋﺪع‬ *dhârayadhwĕm*,
"preserve ye" (Burnouf, l. c. Note D. p. 38.)

---

with which I am acquainted; while, where the reduplicated verb is
burthened by composition, *th* almost universally occurs in the base-syllable,
though *dh* also is occasionally found, *e. g.* in *yaoshdadhâiti* (Burnouf,
Yaçna p. 360.) In cases where the forms with *th* follow the analogy of
the Sanscrit first class, as *e. g.* in *nidathĕm*, "I have made," (Burnouf l. c.)
I regard the vowel which follows *th* not as the class vowel, but, as in the
conjugation of the root स्था *sthâ*, ‫ﺳﻮﻧﺠﺳ‬ *s'tâ*, as the shortening of the radical
vowel (see §. 508.) I also now consider the verbal-theme *snâdha*, "to wash,"
as a compound of the root *s'nâ* and *dhâ*, the radical vowel of the latter
being shortened (compare Benfey Wurzel lex., II. 34.) The perhaps not
numerous forms may appear surprising in which the vowel of the syllable
of reduplication of the Zend root *dhâ* (without a vowel preceding, *dâ*) is
long, as in the example mentioned by Burnouf (l. c.) *nidhâthayĕn*, "they
may lay down." Here either the lengthening of the syllable of repetition
is a compensation for the shortening of the base-syllable, or the genius of
the language takes *dâth* for a secondary root, without being conscious that
the *d*, with its vowel, is in fact a syllable of reduplication, as in Sanscrit
the forms *dĕ-hi*, "give," (from *dad-dhi*, Zend *daz-di*) and *dhĕ-hi*, "place,"
(from *dhad-dhi*), no longer give the impression of reduplicated forms.

* Vendidad Sade, p. 82. ‫ﺳﻮﻋع‬ ‫باﯾﺴﻮرﻋﻮع‬ ‫۔ﺳﻮﺳﺳﻋ‬ ‫ﻋع‬
‫ﺪﻟﻠﺴﻮﺳﻠججرﺳﻢ‬ *hê urvânĕm vahistĕm ahûm frahârayênê*, " I will
make his soul go to the most excellent place;" Anquetil, p. 139, "*je ferai
aller librement son ame aux demeures célestes.*"

† *Yaṡnayêmi* is a denominative from *yaṡna* = Sanscrit *yajna*, "offering."

FORMATION OF THE MOODS.

Remark.—An explanation—and I am now much inclined to adopt it—might be given of the *a* of the terminations *âni, âva,* &c., in the first principal conjugation, as follows; viz. by recognising in it only the lengthening of the short *a* of the class-syllable, while only *ni,* &c. is regarded as the personal termination. There is a twofold occasion, however, for the lengthening of the *a* of the class-syllable; first, that in the *Lêṭ* mood, or conjunctive, to which, according to its principle of formation, the first person of the imperative belongs, the *a* of the class-syllable is lengthened (see §. 713.); and secondly, that especially before pronominal-consonants of the first person, in case of their being followed by vowels, an *a* originally short is lengthened; and hence forms like *ami, avas, avæ,* &c. nowhere occur, wherefore *ani* also is not to be looked for. On the latter principle may be explained the *â* of *dvesh-â-ṇi, bibhar-â-ṇi, yunaj-â-ni, kinav-â-ni,* and *karav-â-ṇi;* so that we may assume that the *a,* which, according to §. 716. is added in the conjunctive, is lengthened simply on phonetic grounds. It is certain that the first person plural of the l. c. cited, भुवत् *bhuvat,* "let him be," can only be *bhuvâma,* and this is at the same time the imperative of the fifth aorist-formation (see §. 573.). The first person plural of the Old Persian *ahaty,* "let him be," quoted in §. 716., is most probably *ahâma,* which would correspond to the Sanscrit imperative असाम *as-âma.* If this view be correct, then in the ninth class also the words *yu-nâ-ni, yu-nâ-va,* &c., must not be divided into *yu-nâ-âni,* &c., but we must assume that, as here, an *â* in the original word precedes the personal termination, no further *a*-sound could be added. The ninth class already meets the requirement for fulness of form in the first person in this way, that the syllable *nâ* is not, as in the weak forms, weakened to *nî*. The roots *dâ* and *dhâ,* which reject their *â* before the heavy terminations, retain the same in the imperative by reason of their inclination to fulness of form; thus e. g. *da-dâ-ma, da-dhâ-ma,* not *dad-ma, dadh-ma* (compare §. 481.).

724. Besides the middle termination *ânê,* which surpasses the Sanscrit in correct retention of the original form, the Zend also recognises the abbreviated form *âi,* of which, however, it makes but unfrequent use. An example is بازدسس *vîśâi* in the fourth Card of the Visperéd (Vend. S., p. 55), where سرع بازدسس *azĕm vîśâi,* occurs seven times, which Anquetil renders by "*j'obeis.*" With the preceding imperative *âśtâya,* "bring,"* the present indicative accords best; so that, in the want of positive examples, we might believe بازدسس *vîśâi,* to be only a more energetic form for the present indicative *vîśê.* The form سـسـسع *yazâi,* which occurs several times in the twenty-second Fargard of the Vend., is rendered by Anquetil "*rendez hommage;*" and the context requires also the second person, for *yazâi,* &c., expresses the command of Ormuzd directed to Zoroaster, to whom he promises, as the reward of the reverence required of him, that which follows, *dathâni,* "I will give" (=Sanscrit ददानि *dadâni,* first person imperative). I see also no reason to assent to Burnouf in placing (Yaçna, p. 495) the words سـسـسع *yazâi,* &c., in the mouth of Zoroaster; and I take *yazâi* to be the imperative active of the causal form, and, indeed, as a contraction of *yazaya;* whether it be that this expression really has a causal signification, and means "let honour," or that the causal form has here the same meaning as the primitive form, as in Sanscrit also is not unfrequently the case. In a phonetic view, the relation of *yazâi* to *yazaya* resembles that of سـسج *nâi,* "conduct," to the Sanscrit नय *naya.* With regard to *yazâi,* as well as to *nâi,* we must assume that, in compensation for the suppres-

---

* Literally, "make to come," the causal of *itâ,* "to stand," with the preposition *â.* Anquetil takes the adjoining accusative as a nominative, and *âśtâya* as the third person.

sion of the final *a*, the *a* of the preceding syllable is lengthened, or, which comes to the same thing, the *a* of the final syllable is transposed, nearly as in the change of *ashavan* "pure," into *ashâum* (with *m* for *n*) in the vocative. The form ꜱꜱꜱ *nâi*, "conduct," occurs six times at the end of the ninth Ha of the Izeschne in combination with *nâśem**[*] (Vend. S., p. 47). Anquetil (p. 112) renders ꜱꜱꜱꜱ ꜱꜱꜱ *nâsemnâi kĕhrpĕm* by "*enseignez-moi le moyen d'anéantir son corps*." The literal meaning, however, is "conduct the body to destruction," (e. g. *azôis*, "of the snake," = अहेस् *ahês*.) Here, perhaps, the composition of the imperative with the accusative *kĕhrpĕm* may have given occasion for the contraction of *naya* to *nâi*. This, however, does not prevent the assumption that, without any special occasion, a transposition of the *a* of the syllable *ya* may also take place, since the Zend is particularly fond of transposing the *a* of the syllables *ya* and *va*, and forming them into a diphthong with the vocalized semi-vowel. I shall return to this subject in the emendations to §. 42.

725. In respect to Syntax, it deserves notice that the first person of the imperative in Zend not only, as has been already shewn by some examples, sometimes supplies the place of the future indicative, but is also used as the conjunctive, governed by ꜱꜱꜱ *yatha*, "that." Thus, in a passage quoted by Burnouf (Yaçna, p. 427) with a different object from the fourth chapter of the Yescht de Gosch, ꜱꜱꜱ ꜱꜱꜱ ꜱꜱꜱ *yatha azĕm bandayêni*, "that I bind;" ꜱꜱꜱ ꜱꜱꜱ *uta bastĕm vâdhayêni*, &c., "and (that I) beat those who are bound;" ꜱꜱꜱ ꜱꜱꜱ *uta bastĕm upanayêni*, "and (that I) conduct those who are bound." On passages of this kind Burnouf's

---

[*] This word is not once written quite correctly in the lithographed manuscript; the correct reading, however, may be easily found by a comparison of the several erroneous ones.

opinion may be based, that the forms in *âni* (or *êni*), in point of sense, belong as well to the imperative as to the potential, while he denies in toto that the middle form in *ânê* (or *ênê*), which was first brought to light by Fr. Windischmann (Jenaische Allgemeine Litt. Z. July 1834, p. 138), belongs, in point of signification, to the imperative, and explains the forms in *âi* according to their meaning as genuine imperatives middle of the first person (Yaçna, p. 530, Note). I cannot assent to this opinion, as *e. g.* ܝܙܕܢܐ *yazânê*, "offer," in the passage quoted above (p. 278), has as imperative a meaning as the first person for the most part admits of, while *visâi* (§. 724.), according to its signification, is rather a present indicative, and *yazâi* (l.c.) is explained as the second person imperative active of the causal.

726. Among the European sisters of the Sanscrit, the Gothic alone presents a first person of the imperative, but only in the plural, where, e.g., *visam*, "*simus*," (Luc. xv. 23.) corresponds to the Sanscrit *vasâma*, "*habitemus*," without, however, being formally distinguished from the present indicative; as the Sanscrit terminations *mas* and *ma* in Gothic are represented by mere *m*, except in the conjunctive, where *ma* corresponds to the Sanscrit म *ma* of the secondary forms. It has been already remarked that, according to its formation, the imperative of the Sclavonic and Lithuanian does not belong to the proper imperative (see §§. 677. 699.).

I here give a general view of the points of comparison which have been arrived at for the imperative present.

	SANSKRIT.	ZEND.	GREEK.	LATIN.	GOTH.
1. p. sg. act.	*han-â-ni*,	*jan-â-ni*,	. . . . .	. . . .	. . . .
	bhar-â-ṇi,	*bar-â-ni*,[1]	. . . . .	. . . .	. . . .
1. p. sg. mid.	*karav-âi*,	*karav-â-nê*,	. . . . .	. . . .	. . . .
	bar-âi,	*bar-â-nê*,	. . . . .	. . . .	. . . .

[1] *Barâni* cannot be supported by quotation, but is clearly deduced from the middle *barânê* (§ 723.) and the plural *barâma* (V. S. p. 208).

FORMATION OF THE MOODS.

	SANSCRIT.	ZEND.	GREEK.	LATIN.	GOTH.
1. p. pl. act.	bar-â-ma,	bar-â-ma,	. . . . .	. . . . .	bair-a-m.
2. p. sg. act.	dê-hi,[2]	dazdi,[3]	(δίδο-θι),	. . . .	
	ê-dhi,[4]	. . . . .	ἴσ-θι,	. . . .	
	bhar-a,	bar-a,	φέρ-ε,	. . . .	bair.
	vah-a,	vaz-a,	ἔχ-ε,	veh-e,	vig.
	vah-a-tât,[5]	. . . . .	. . . . .	veh-i-to,	. . . .
2. p. sg. mid.	dat-sva,[6]	. . . . .	δίδο-σο,	. . . .	
	bhar-a-sva,	bar-aṅ-uha,[7]	{ φέρου, from φέρ-ε-σο, }	. . . .	
2. p. du. act.	bhar-a-tam,	. . . . .	φέρ-ε-τον,	. . . .	bair-a-ts.
2. p. pl. act.	bhar-a-ta,	bar-a-ta,	φέρ-ε-τε,	. . . .	bair-i-th.
	bibhṛi-ta,	. . . . .	. . . . .	fer-te,	. . . .
	vah-a-ta,	vaz-a-ta,	ἔχ-ε-τε,	veh-i-te,	vig-i-th.
2. p. pl. mid.	bhar-a-dhvam,	bar-a-dhwĕm,	φέρ-ε-σθε,	. . . .	
3. p. sg. act.	vas-a-tu,	vaṅh-a-tu,	. . . . .	. . . .	
	vah-a-tât,	vaz-a-tât,[8]	ἔχ-ε-τω,	veh-i-to,	. . . .
3. p. du. act.	bhar-a-tâm,	. . . . .	φερ-έ-των,	. . . .	
3. p. pl. act.	bhar-a-ntu,	bar-a-ntu?	. . . . .	. . . .	

[2] *Dê-hi* from *dad-dhi* for *dadâ-hi* from *dadâ-dhi*, See §§ 450. 481.

[3] وَدَزْدِى *dazdi* from *dad-di*, See § 450., where for *dazdhi* read وَدَزْدِى *dazdi*, as ذ *dh* occurs only between two vowels. Thus we twice read in V. S. p. 50, وَدَزْدِىمِى *dazdi-mê*, "give to me," with *mê*, "to me," enclitic, where we must remember, that in Sanscrit, also, the forms मे *mê*, "*mei, mihi*," and ते *tê*, "*tui, tibi*," are used only enclitically; just as in Old Persian *maiy* and *taiy*. We must therefore take the (in V. S. pp. 505, 507, 508) frequently recurring وَدَثَانِى ته *dathâni tê*, "I will give to thee," as = *dathânitê*, since composites in Zend are frequently separated in writing. If, however, *dathânitê* is to be taken as one word, I should then explain the *th* as being for *dh*, on the same principle as that by which the root *dâ*, "to lay," in the reduplicated forms, when they appear in composition, regularly exhibits *th* for *dh* in the radical syllable. (See p. 964, Rem. **.)   [4] From *ad-dhi* for *as-dhi*.   [5] 956 Rem.
[6] For *dadâ-sva*. (See § 481.)   [7] See § 721.   [8] See p. 653, Note †.

727. In the Vêda dialect and Zend occur forms also which correspond to the imperative of the aorist in Greek,

972   VERBS.

and, like the latter, have with the augment, which is the true symbol of past time, also laid aside the past signification. To the Greek first aorist corresponds भूष bhúsha, "be" or "become" (see Westerg. r. भू, pref. आ) euphonic for $bh\hat{u}$-$sa = \phi\bar{v}$-$\sigma o\nu$. The ν of the termination $\sigma o\nu$, if organic, may be deduced from ς*, and this from θ, as, e.g., δός

---

* See § 97. With regard to the transition of final s into ν compare also ἦν, "he was," with the Doric ἦς and आस ás of the Védas: moreover the suff. θεν = Sanscrit tas, Latin tus (§§ 421. 531.). The form -θεν, as it approaches closer to the Sanscrit tas and Latin tus than θε does, must be regarded as more organic than the latter, which, as Buttmann remarks, (§ 116. 4. Rem. 1.), is of frequent occurrence only in certain particles, in which the original meaning ("whence") is not so perceptible, and is found elsewhere but seldom where the metre requires it (ἀντρόθε Pind., Κυπρόθε Calimm., Λιβύαθε, πάντοθε Theocrit.). Observe, also, the complete rejection of the ν in the acc. of bases ending in a consonant (πατέρα=Sanscrit pitaram, Latin patrem), as well as, in particular, the abundantly demonstrated fact, that final letters are the most exposed to weakening and complete extinction. The weakening of s to n is too, in itself, not more remarkable than that of s to another liquid, viz. r; which, in Sanscrit, so frequently takes place according to settled laws, and occurs dialectically also in Greek (see §. 22.), and is found in several kindred languages in certain parts of Grammar; as, e.g., in Irish the termination mar of the 1st p. pl. represents the Sanscrit mas, Latin mus, Doric μες, which latter, in the common dialect, is corrupted to μεν. The Sanscrit secondary termination ma, which also occasionally occurs in the present, is very probably an abbreviation of mas (see §. 439.), which first appeared after the separation of dialects; an abbreviation which enters more extensively into Old Persian, since there the final s after a and â has become the weakened form of all terminations. Therefore I cannot agree with Pott (Etym. Forsch. II. 306.)—to whom G. Curtius (Formation of the Tenses and Moods, p. 27) assents—in deriving only μες from mas, but μεν from ma, as if the ν were only a later suffix or echo. Why, it might be asked, have similar enduring resonant letters (not used like the ν ἐφελκυστικόν to prevent the hiatus) not been suffixed to distinct vowel-ending forms, e.g. to the ε of the voc. of the 2d decl. (§. 204.), or to that of the dual (§. 209.)? The Doric termination ντω in the 3d p. pl. imper. (λεγόντω, ποιούντω, ἀποτισάντω) may be regarded with

at

FORMATION OF THE MOODS. 973

from δόθι. We should therefore have to regard -σαθι as the original form, and from that -σας, and afterwards -σον, with the change of α to ο, which is preferred before nasals (see p. 104). In this manner, if the ν of τύπ-σο-ν appears to be the personal termination, and, in fact, in a place where the Vêda dialect has lost the personal termination (bhû-sha from bhû-sha-dhi), then it must be remarked that, in Prâkrit also, the termination hi, which is a mutilated form of dhi, is much more extensively used than in Sanscrit (see Lassen, p. 338. Höfer, p. 185). From σαθι a middle termination σασθι may be developed, according to the principle of τυψάσθω from τυψάτω, τύψασθε from τύψατε; for as all terminations, which in the active begin with τ, are preceded in the middle by σ, where τ passes into θ (see §. 474.), so it cannot be matter of astonishment, if, from the to-be-presupposed τύψαθι is formed τύψασθι, and hence, by rejecting the σθ, τύψαι, which presents an accidental agreement with the infinitive active of the aorist,

---

at least equal justice as an abbreviation of ντων; as, vice versâ, ντων may be looked on as a lengthened form of ντω, for the Doric dialect has not in all cases preserved the most ancient forms. Pott (l. c.) finds, in a physiological view, the interchange between s and ν difficult to comprehend; as, though both are dentals, yet the difference in their pronunciation is vast. Still greater, however, is the difference between that of a mute and the nasal corresponding to its organ; and yet, in Sanscrit, final mutes, if they occur before a nasal, pass into the nasal of their organ (atishṭhan mûrdhni, " he stood at the top," for -tm); and in Latin somnus stands for sopnus; in Greek σεμνός for σεβνος: while reversedly, in Lithuanian and Sclavonic, without its being occasioned by the neighbouring letters, the n of the number nine (Sanscrit navan) has become d (see §. 317.); and in Greek the n of the suffix मन् man, Latin men, has become τ (ὀ-νοματ=नामन् nâman, nomen). I am also of opinion that the Vêda termination tana, in the 2d p. pl., has arisen from tata, and therefore is only a reduplication of the common termination ta, and rests, therefore, on the principle of the Latin imperative-ending tôte, and the Vêda tât of the 2d and 3d pers. singular.

as in Latin also, *ama-re*, "be loved" (the last syllable of which is only a fuller form of the reflexive, which we, see §. 476., have recognised in *amo-r*, &c.) is in sound identical with the active infinitive. If, however, the imperative τύπ-σαι has arisen from τύπ-σασθι, the abbreviation is only one degree greater than, in the indicative, that of ἐτυπ-σα-σο to ἐτύπ-σω. We return to the Vêda dialect to remark, that to forms like τυπ-σά-τω, irrespective of the personal termination, corresponds the नेषतु *nê-sha-tu* (*sh* euphonic for *s*, see §. 21.), which is cited by Pânini (III. 1. 81. Schol.) "let him conduct." In the second person dual भूषतम् *bhúshatam* (उपभूषतम् *upabhúshatam*, see Westerg., r. भू *bhû*, prefix उप *upa*), corresponds admirably to φύσατον, and in the third person plural, श्रोषन्तु *śrô-sha-ntu*, "they shall hear" (Rig. V. I. 86. 5), in respect of the aoristic suffix, to forms like λυ-σά-ντων.

728. In Zend as yet no imperatives have occurred, which, like the Vêda भूष *bhúsha*, &c., would correspond to Greek imperatives of the first aorist; on the other hand, دَيـدِ *dâi-dí*, "give" (Vendidad Sade, p. 311 twice, pp, 421, 422), corresponds to δό-ς, from δο-θι, داتا *dâ-ta*, "give ye" (Vendidad Sade, p. 224)* to δότε, and *dâ-ta* "do ye," "make ye," (in comp. یَوشچداتا *yaoschdâta*, "purify ye," Vendidad Sade, p. 367, frequently) to θέ-τε. I think I discover a middle imperative aorist in داؤنها *dâonhá*, "give thou" (Vendidad Sade, p. 222, l. 1 from the bottom); but we require to understand the passage where this expression occurs by the aid of Neriosengh's Sanscrit translation, as well as a comparison of manuscripts. It is probable that we ought to read داؤنُها *dâonuhâ*, where the long *â* would present no difficulty, as in this passage other originally short *a*'s at the end of a word are found lengthened. In the Vêda

---

* I write *dáta* for *dâtâ*, as in this passage long *a* stands for short *a* everywhere at the end of a word.

FORMATION OF THE MOODS. 975

dialect the forms are very numerous which answer to the Greek imperative of the second aorist; thus, *śrudhi*, "hear thou," = κλῦθι,* from *srinômi* (R. *śru*, Cl. 5, irreg.); *śag-dhi*, "be able," from *śaknômi* (R. *śak*, Cl. 5); *pûr-dhi*, "fill thou," from पिपर्मि *piparmi* (R. पृ *pṛi*, i.e. *par*, Cl. 3). To अभूत् *abhût*, "he was" (aorist of the fifth formation, §. 573.), corresponds *bhû-tu*, "*esto.*" Forms like मुमुग्धि *mumugdhi* "loose thou" (R. *much*, third person, *mumôktu*), strongly resemble the Greek like κέκραχθι. The Sanscrit form, however, as appears (see Westerg.) from the indicative form *amumuktam*, distinctly belongs to the aorist, which in the Vêda dialect also exhibits similar reduplicated forms, combining the personal terminations direct with the root, which therefore stand in the same relation to the fifth formation (see §. 573.), which in the Vêda dialect is used also in roots ending in a consonant, as that in which forms of the seventh formation (§. 579.) do to those of the sixth (§. 576.). The वावृधस्व *vâvṛidhasva*, "grow thou" (Rig. Veda, I. 31. 1.), which has been differently explained above (§. 709. Note), is perhaps an imperative middle of the seventh aorist formation: it would then stand for *vavṛidhasva*, as from *mṛig*, in the aorist indicative active, comes *amamṛigam*. The lengthening of the syllable of reduplication would, according to §. 580., be more authorised in the aorist referred to than in the Vêda perfect indicative *vâvṛidhê* (Rig. Veda, 52. 2.), for *vavṛidhê* of the common dialect. The circumstance that no

---

* So long as a pres. of the 2d cl. *śrômi* does not occur, I am inclined to regard the forms of the indicative cited by Westergaard, *aśravam*, "I heard"; *aśrôt*, "he heard," as aorists of the 5th formation, with Guna of the short radical vowel, which appears lengthened in the Greek κλῦθι; as, in forms like δείκνῦμι, the ῡ corresponds to the Sanscrit *u* with Guna. Remark, that also in the Vêda aorist *akar*, "he made," *akaram*, "I made," the broader and here the original, but according to Indian Grammar the Gunized, form of the root occurs, while the imper. *kṛidhi*, "make thou," has the shorter form.

indicative occurs corresponding to *vávṛidhasva*, when regarded as an aorist, would not be a sufficient reason for rejecting this view; for hitherto no indicatives *abhúsham*, *anêsham*, *aśrôsham*, have been found to correspond to the aorist imperatives mentioned in §. 727., *bhúsha*, *bhúshatam*, *mêshatu*, *srôshantu*. If, however, with Westergaard, we assume potentials and imperatives of the perfect, we can then, with him, derive *vávṛidhasva* from the perfect indicative *vávṛidhê*. But, according to the signification, the reduplicated imperatives and potentials, which all have a present meaning, are better derivable from the aorist (which in its moods lays aside its past signification together with its augment) than from the perfect, where the reduplication expresses past time, and which, therefore, must remain in the moods likewise; as, *e. g.*, in Gothic, *haihaityau* signifies " I was called," not " I am called." If, however, in the Vêda dialect the reduplicated modal forms spring, in part at least, from the perfect, we must then assume that they have, through a perversion, surrendered the past signification, which belonged to them, so that the German conjunctives of the preterite in this respect stand on older ground. The explanation of the reduplicated modal forms from the intensive, attempted in §. 709. Note, is now far from satisfactory to me; and I now hesitate between the derivation of them from the perfect, and their deduction from the reduplicated aorist. To the latter might be referred *ni . . sêda*, " seat thyself " (see Westerg. pp. 177, 179.), as अनेशम् *anêśam* (see §. 582.) presents an analogous indicative. To the *avôcham* mentioned in the said §. belongs the imperative *saṅvôchâvahâi* (1 p. du. mid. Rig. V. I. 25. 17.).

729. Traces of an imperative of the auxiliary future occur in classical Sanscrit. But the few examples hitherto found all belong to the 2d person pl. of the middle; viz. प्रसविष्यध्वम् *prasavishyadhvam*, " shew ye " (Bhagavad-Gîtâ,

FORMATION OF THE MOODS.

3. 10.); भविष्यध्वम् *bhavishyadhvam,* "be ye" (Mahâ-Bhârata, III. 14394. Râmâyana, ed. Schl. I. 29. 25); and वेत्स्यध्वम् *vétsyadhvam,* "find ye," "obtain ye" (Mahâ-Bhâr. I. 1111.). The conjecture elsewhere expressed, that by *sanvakshyata* (in Stenzler's Brahma-Vaivarta-Purani Specimen I. 35.) a future imper. act. of the 2d p. pl. is established, I must now retract; as, by repeated examination of the passage, I find, by the context, that for संवक्ष्यत *sanvakshyata,* which Stenzler renders "*alloquimini,*" we should read *sanraxhata* (*i.e.* "*arcete*").*

CONDITIONAL.

730. The Sanscrit conditional bears the same relation in respect of form to the auxiliary future that the imperfect does to the present, *i.e.* the augment is prefixed to the root, and the secondary personal terminations supply the place of the primary: hence, *e.g.,* अदास्यम् *adâsyam,*" I would give," and also "I would have given," answering to *dâsyâmi,* "I will give." We may therefore, as in departure from my former opinion I am now inclined to do, regard the conditional as a derivative from the auxiliary future; so that, although the substantive verb is contained in it, there is no necessity for assuming the existence of an obsolete

---

* Observe, that in manuscripts written in Bengal, and especially in the manuscript used by Stenzler, the *r* is frequently not distinguishable from the *v*, as is remarked l. c. p. 10. The य *y* after the क्ष *ksh* is added by Stenzler as an emendation. The meaning *alloquimini,* however, does not agree with the context, whilst *arcete principem* corresponds to the sense of the preceding Sl. In Sl. 32 of the same Spec. occurs a form worthy of notice in respect of syntax, viz. the imperative *brûta* as representative of the conjunctive governed by *yadi*: *yadi satyam bruta,* "if ye speak the truth." So in the fifth book of the Mahâ Bhâr. the second person plural middle of the imperative *prayachchhadhvam* governed by *chét*: *nachét prayachchhadhvam amitraghatinô yudhishthirasyâ 'nsam abhîpsitan svakam,* "if ye do not give the fiend-slaying Yudishthir his required share." In the Rig Vêda (I. 27. 12) we find the first person plural of the imperative, or *Lét,* after *yadi*: *yadi śaknavâma,* "if we can."

ásyam, "I would be," or "I would have been;" and even though such a form should have existed, we might still regard *ásyam* as a derivative of *asyâmi*, "I will be" (= Lat. *ero, eris*, see. §. 650.), which has disappeared from use; just as *adâsyam* as a derivative from *dâsyâmi*. The circumstance, that in none of the European kindred languages a mood analogous to the said one in Sanscrit is to be found, might lead us to the conjecture, that it is of comparatively late origin, as in Latin the imperfect conjunctive (see §. 707.), which resembles it most, but has evidently sprung up on Roman ground. Compare *da-rem* from *dâ-sem*, for *dâ-saïm* with अदास्यम् *a-dâ-syam*.

731. The Sanscrit employs but seldom its conditional, which, in the earlier period of the language, is commonly supplied by the potential: a few examples, therefore, may be given here (manuscript vii. 20.), *yadi na praṇayêd, râjâ daṇḍan daṇḍyêshv atandritaḣ ι śûlê matsyân ivâ 'pakshyan durbalân balavattarâḣ*, "If the king did not indefatigably punish those worthy of punishment, then the stronger would roast the weak on spits." But here follow four potentials, all standing in the same relation, which are nevertheless explained by the Scholiast by conditionals; viz. *adyât*, "would eat," by *akhâdishyat*; *avalihyât* "would lick," by *avâlêkshyat*; *syât*, "would be," by *abhavishyat*; and *pravartêta*, "would become," by *prâvartishyat*. In the eighth book of the Mahâ Bh. (Sl. 1614) we read, *vrijinaṅ hi bhavêt kiñchid yadi karṇasya pârthiva ι nâ 'smâi hy astrâṇi divyâni prâdâsyat bhrigunandanaḣ*, "If any fault attached to Karnas, O Prince, the son of Bhrigu would not have given him the heavenly weapons." The conditional occurs as well in the antecedent as in the relative sentence, and, in fact, the first time in the sense of the pluperfect conjunctive, *l. c.* Sl. 709, *nachêd arakshishya* imañ janam bhayâd dvishadbhir êvam*

---

* For *arakshishyas* on account of the *i* following,

FORMATION OF THE MOODS.

balibhir prapíditam ι tathâ 'bhavishyad dvishatâm pramôdanam
"If thou hadst not freed from danger this band assailed by powerful fiends, then they would have been the joy of their enemies." Thus, in the Naishadha-Char. 4. 88, *api sa vajram adâsyata chêt tadâ tvadishubhir vyadalishyad asâv api*, "If he (Brahmâ) had given also the thunder-bolt (to thee, the God of love, as a mark), so would even this have been rent in twain (have been split) by thy darts."

Remark—In Zend I know of no instance of the conditional; some resemblance to it, however, may be traced in the form ꝏꝏꝏ *fravacsyaṅm*, at the end of the 44th Ha of the Izeschné (V. S. p. 359), which Anquetil translates "*je parle clairement.*" I consider this form to be the first person of the auxiliary future, which, in the absence of examples, I formerly thought must end in *yèmi* (see §. 664.). The fact, that the first person of the future is very frequently replaced by that of the imperative, is perhaps the reason of the rare occurrence of the former. If, however, I am right in explaining the form *fravacsyaṅm* as the first person of the future, it has lost the *i* of the termination; as in Prâkrit, where, except in the form in *himi* (see §. 615.), the termination *mi* of the future auxiliary has everywhere dropped the *i*, whereby, however, the preceding *a* has been shortened; hence, *e. g.*, सुमरिस्सं *sumarissaṅ*, "I will call to mind," corresponding to the Sanscrit *smarishyâmi*. In Zend, through the loss of the final *i* an occasion also for the mutation of the *â* preceding the *m* to *ê* has disappeared; the termination *âm*, however, must, according to §. 61., become ꝏ *aṅm*; thus, ꝏꝏꝏ *fravacsyaṅm* = Sanscrit प्रवक्ष्यामि *pravakshyâmi*. In the same Ha, at the end of which occurs the form ꝏꝏꝏ *fravacsyaṅm*, occurs also six times the form *fravacsyâ* (V. S. p.356), which Anquetil, in like manner, translates by "*je parle clairement*" or "*je vous parle clairement.*" Then follow the words which Zoroaster (not Ormuzd, as Anquetil supposes) speaks. If, however, *fravacsyâ* is really a first person, it must still belong to the future only; and it would then, in this form, as compared with that in *aṅm*, be an abbreviation similar to that of the dual case-termination *bya*—for which, in accordance with the Sanscrit *bhyâm*, we should expect *byaṅm*—and to that of the feminine pronominal locative termination *a* (see §. 202.) for the Sanscrit *âm*. The occurrence in *fravacsyâ* of a long *a* is in agreement with the fact that, in the Ha above mentioned, particularly at the end of a word, *â* is found for an originally short *a*; *e. g.* in ꞏꞏꞏ *sraotâ*, "hear ye." If, however, ꞏꞏꞏ *fravacsyâ* is not the first person of the future, it can only be taken as the second person of the future imperative, and must then be regarded as a command addressed by Ormuzd to Zoroaster.

DERIVATIVE VERBS.

732. The appellation "derivative verbs" strictly belongs only to denominatives; for passives, causals, desideratives, and intensives, stand quite as near the root as the ten classes of the so-called primitive verbs, excepting the second class (see §. 109ᵃ. 3.), which latter may be regarded as the base-form of all the rest. The passive, also, is identical in form with the middle of the fourth class, and the causal with the tenth class; while that form of the intensive which joins the personal terminations direct to the root is distinguished from the third class only by the strengthening of the syllable of reduplication, and in that this extends also to the universal tenses. And here we must observe that the tenth class also extends a part of its class character to the universal tenses. We might—as the passive agrees with the middle of the fourth class, and the causal with the tenth class—reckon in all twelve classes of verbs; so that, perhaps, the intensives would fall under the eleventh class, and the desideratives under the twelfth. It is, however, certain

that the verbs called derivative in idea, and as regards their origin, must be classed under those which express only the simple verbal notion along with the relations of person, time, and mood; and must also be regarded as later, and originating in the first place from these latter. For before there could exist a verb signifying, *e. g.*, "I cause to hear," or "I wish to hear," or "I am heard," there must have existed one more simple with the meaning "I hear;" and though श्रावयामि *srávayámi*, *śuśrushámi*, and *śrúyê*, may be derived from the root itself, *śru*, more readily than from *sriṇômi*, "I hear," or its theme *sriṇu* (a contracted form of *śruṇu*), still *śruṇu* may stand as the base form from which the so called derivative and secondary verbs have proceeded, by the suppression of the class-syllable *mi* before the characteristic affix of the derivative base referred to; just as the causal bases, when passives are formed from them, lose their characteristic affix *ay* before the passive character *ya*: as, *e. g.*, from *śráv-aya-ti*, "he causes to hear," comes *śráv-ya-tê* (for *śráv-ay-yatê*), "he is made to hear." According to this scheme the derivative verbs have, in point of fact, only the bare root at bottom as formative material; but the sole reason of this is, that from the primitive verbs, whose offspring they are, all ingredients are removed which do not belong to the expression of the radical idea, in order that the derivative form should not be too unwieldy; just as certain comparatives and superlatives spring, not from the full base of the positive, but from it abbreviated by the removal of the formative suffix (see §. 298. pp. 395, 396.)

733. Let us now consider the formation of derivative verbs severally, beginning with the passives. These in Sanscrit, in the special tenses, annex the syllable य *ya* to the root, and join thereto the personal terminations of the middle. The conjugation agrees exactly with the middle of the fourth class (see §. 500.), so that in the present,

982 VERBS.

in the example given at p. 696, we have only to annex the middle terminations (see §. 512.) in the place of the active. I give below the 3d per. sing. and pl. with the corresponding persons of the middle (for the class peculiarities of which refer to §. 109ª.) of the roots *budh*, Cl. 1, "to know" (Goth. *ana-bud*, "to command"); *tud*, Cl. 6, "to push" (Lat. *tud, tundo*); *vas*, Cl. 2, "to dress oneself" (Goth. *vasya*, "I put on" = caus. *vâsayâmi*);* *bhar* (*bhri*, see §. 1.), Cl. 3, "to bear;" *yuj*, Cl. 7, "to bind" (Lat. *jug*, Gr. ζυγ); *star* (*stri, strī*, see p. 680. Note), Cl. 5, "to spread," "to deck;" *prî*, Cl. 9, "to gladden," "to love" (Goth. *friyô*, "I love").

ROOT.	3D PER. SINGULAR.		3D PER. PLURAL.	
	PASSIVE.	MIDDLE.	PASSIVE.	MIDDLE.
budh, Cl. 1,	*budh-ya-tê*,	*bôdh-a-tê*.	*budh-ya-ntê*,	*bôdh-a-ntê*.
tud, Cl. 6,	*tud-ya-tê*,	*tud-a-tê*.	*tud-ya-ntê*,	*tud-a-ntê*.
vas, Cl. 2,	*vas-ya-tê*,	*vas-tê*.	*vas-ya-ntê*,	*vas-atê*.[1]
bhar (*bhr*), Cl. 3,	*bhri-ya-tê*,[2]	*bibhri-tê*.	*bhri-ya-ntê*,[2]	*bibhr-atê*.[1]
yuj, Cl. 7,	*yuj-ya-tê*,	*yunk-tê*.	*yuj-ya-ntê*,	*yuñj-atê*.[1]
star (*stri*), Cl. 5,	*star-ya-tê*,[2]	*stri-nu-tê*.	*star-ya-ntê*,[2]	*stri-nv-atê*.[1]
prî, Cl. 9,	*prî-ya-tê*,	*prî-nî-tê*.	*prî-ya-ntê*,	*prî-na-tê*.[1]

[1] See §. 459. [2] Roots in *ar*, which in the pure or light forms contract this syllable to *ri*, when only a single consonant precedes the radical vowel, exhibit the syllable *ri* before the passive character *ya*, which *ri* I consider to be a transposition of *ir*, and the latter a weakening of the old form *ar*, which has remained after a double consonant; hence, *star-ya-tê* corresponding to *bhri-ya-tê*. With regard to the protection which two combined consonants afford to the primitive syllable *ar*, compare the circumstance, that the imperative termination *hi* (from *dhi*) remains in verbs of the 5th class after two combined consonants, but cannot be supported by a single consonant; thus, *chinu*, "collect," opposed to *âpnuhi*, "obtain" (see §. 451.). By this principle I would also explain the fact that, the Latin root *stâ* (=Sanscrit स्था *sthâ*, "to stand") has, almost in every case, preserved the original length of the base-vowel in opposition to *da* (=Sanscrit *dâ*). The transposition of भिर् *bhir* to

---

* See §. 169ª. 6.

भृ *bhri*, reminds us of Greek forms like πατράσι, which has been explained above as a transposed form of παταρ-σι: I am also now of opinion that in Gothic plural bases like *bróthru, dauhtru* – whence come *bróthryu-s*, "brother;" *dauhthryu-s*, "daughter"—we must assume a transposition of *ur* to *ru*; so that the to-be-presupposed bases, *brtóhur, dauhtur*, correspond, as weakened forms of *bróthar, dauhtar*, to the Sanscrit genitives *bhrâtur, duhitur*, which are deprived of their case-termination (see §. 191. Note).

734. It must be observed, that the incumbrance which the root receives in the passive by affixing the syllable *ya*, occasionally introduces irregular weakenings of the root; as, *e. g.*, the contraction of *vach* to *uch* (*uch-ya-tê*, "*dicitur*"), analogously with some anomalous forms of the active (*úchima*, "we spoke," from *u-uchima*): so, too, the contraction of the syllable *ra* to *ri* in the root प्रछ् *prachh*, "to ask;" पृच्छ्यते *prichchhyatê*, "*interrogatur*;" as, पृच्छामि *prichchhámi*, "I ask;" *paprichchhima*, "we asked," compared with *paprachcha*, "I asked;" *prashṭum*, "ask ye." This principle also explains the fact, that some roots in *â* change this vowel in the passive to the lighter *í*; hence, *e.g.*, *díya* is the passive base of the root *dâ*, "to give" (*díyatê*, "*datur*"). The Zend, on the contrary, as a consequence of the same principle, shortens the long ᴡ *â* to ᴀ *a*, at least in the examples which occur to me: ⁕⁕⁕ *nidhayêintê*, "*deponuntur*"[*] (= Sanscrit *nidhíyantê*); ⁕⁕⁕ *snayanuha*, "be washed"[†] (= Scr. *snáyasva*);

---

[*] Vendidad Sade p. 246: (? ⁕⁕⁕) ⁕⁕⁕ ⁕⁕⁕ *yamnya narô irĕsta* (*irista?*) *nidhayêinchê*, "in quâ (*terrâ*) *homines mortui deponuntur;*" according to Anquetil (p. 325), "*dans les quels on a mis des hommes morts*," see Note [†].

[†] With middle meaning, "wash thyself" (*zaśta*, "the hands") (see p. 957, Note **). Burnouf (Yaçna, p. 361, Note) takes the syllable *ya* of this form not as the passive character, which according to him (l. c. p. 359) must be looked for in Zend little more than in Greek and Latin. It appears to me, however, that we may be very nearly right in regarding the

ڬڜڛڛڎڛڎڜڞ *snayaêta*, "let him be washed," or "wash himself" (see. p. 957, Note). In support of the view, that the forms *snayanuha* and *snayaêta* may be taken as passives with a reflexive signification, it may here also be adduced that in Old Persian a similar phenomenon occurs; viz. in 𒀸𒈨𒉌𒋾𒁹 *patipayanvâ** (Beh. IV. 38.), which Benfey, in my opinion rightly, renders "guard thyself" (Rawlinson by "*te expeditum habe*"), and refers to the Sanscrit root पा *pâ* (with the preposition *pati = prati*,) which, therefore, in agreement with the Zend, has shortened the long *â* before the passive character.

735. If, with the Indian Grammarians, we regard the Sanscrit *jâyê* (irregular for *janyê*) "I am born," as a middle of the fourth class (see §. 500.), then the corresponding Zend verb may be explained in the same manner. As, however, the meaning "to be born" is strictly passive, and

---

the syllable *ya* in the form above mentioned as the passive character, and the whole as a by-no-means-surprising change of the passive into a reflexive or middle meaning, while in Greek, Gothic, Latin, Lithuanian, and Sclavonic, the reverse is the case. If the form ڜڞڎڞڛڛڎڛڎڜڞ *nidhayênti*, "*ils deposent*," which Burnouf has mentioned at p. 361, and which I am unable to quote, be only a different reading of the *nidhayêinté* mentioned above in the lithographed manuscript, I would also then recognise in it a passive, and draw attention to the fact, that in Sanscrit also, in the passive, the active terminations not uncommonly take the place of the middle, so that the passive relation is to be discerned only in the syllable *ya* (see Lesser Sanscrit Gram., 2d Edit. §. 446). If, however, we take *nidhayênti* as active, we must then explain "they lay down" in the sense of "one lays down," and consider *narô irista* as the accusative (see p. 247). Constructions of this kind, as far as I know, are not confirmed by unmistakeable forms, and I therefore prefer explaining the verb as passive.

* Rawlinson and Benfey read *patipayuwâ*; I doubt not, however, that the *a* inherent in 𒅀 *y* must be here read in conjunction with it. The termination *uvâ*, for *huvâ* (euphonic for *hvâ*), corresponds to the Sanscrit imperative termination *sva*.

the form of the middle of the fourth Class is identical with that of the passive, I prefer to explain in both languages the forms with passive signification as really passives; and I adopt for the Sanscrit a middle *jan* of the fourth Class, a kind of deponent with the active meaning "to bring forth," of which, however, but few examples occur, as, *e.g.*, Râmây. ed. Schl. I. 27. 3. पुत्रं व्यजायत *putraṇ vy-ajâyata*, "she bore a son" (with the prep. *vi*). The Zend root ju͜s *zan*, the passive of which frequently occurs in combination with the preposition ju͜s *us* (= Sanscrit उत् *ut*), likewise rejects the final *n* before the passive character *ya*: the preceding *a*, however, is not lengthened, or the long *â*, which had been introduced, is again shortened; which cannot surprise us, as from the first the long *â* at the end of a root is shortened before the passive *ya*. Hence, *e. g.*, ju͜sju͜sju͜sju͜sju͜s *uš-zayêintê*, "they are born,"* corresponds exactly to the before-mentioned *nidhayêintê* (§. 734). Of the imperfect we find the second and third person singular; viz. ju͜sju͜sju͜sju͜s *ušazayanha*, "thou wast born," (see §. 466. and §. 518.), and *ušzayata*, "he was born".†

736. As the middle of Sanscrit verbs of the fourth Class is identical in form, and, as I believe, in origin also, with the passive, and therefore म्रिये *mriyê*, "*morior*," म्रियते *mriyatê*, "*moritur*," may also stand for the passive, it may here be remarked, that the corresponding verb in Zend, the conjunctive of which, *mairyâiti*, frequently occurs (Vendidad

---

* Vend S., p. 136, ju͜sju͜s ju͜sju͜s ju͜sju͜sju͜s ju͜sju͜sju͜s ju͜sju͜sju͜sju͜s ju͜sju͜sju͜sju͜s ju͜sju͜sju͜s ju͜sju͜sju͜s ju͜sju͜sju͜sju͜s ju͜sju͜sju͜s *dvaêibya hacha nĕrĕbya dva nara ušzayê intê mithwana štricha nairyaścha*, "*duobus ex hominibus duo homines nascuntur, par, feminaque masque.*" Anquetil (p. 278), translates "*de deux hommes naquirent deux hommes distingués, le mâle s'étant uni à la femelle.*"

† Vend. S., p. 39, *yaṭ hê* (so I read for ju͜s *he*) *puthrô ušzayata*, "that a son was born to him."

Sade, p. 24ª), has replaced the middle termination by the active, as also in Sanscrit the active termination frequently takes the place of the middle in acknowledged passives. The above-mentioned *mairyâiti* is so far older than the corresponding Sanscrit verb, in that it has experienced neither the transposition of *ir* to *ri* mentioned at §. 733. Note 2. (*mri-yatê*, like *bhri-yatê*) nor the weakening of *a* to *i*, but *mairyâiti* "*moriatur*" stands for *maryâiti*, in consequence of the assimilative power of the *y* (see §. 41.), and affords us a new proof of the unoriginality of the Sanscrit ऋ *ri*; and shews that in Sanscrit not *mri*, but *mar*, is the true root, whence comes, in Latin, *mor*, which presents to us in the *io, iu*, of *morior, moriuntur*, a fine remnant of the Sanscrit passive character *ya* य. Compare *iu* in *mor-iu-ntur* with the Sanscrit *ya* of *mri-ya-ntê*. The conjunctive *mor-ia-r, mor-iâ-ris*, gives us still more exactly the character of the Sanscrit passive, only that here the Latin *â* appears long, inasmuch as it has absorbed the modal exponent *i*. The Lithuanian also has, in the said verb, preserved the passive character, which we have already (§. 500.) recognised in *gemmu* from *gem-yu*, "I am born," *gim-yau*, "I was born."* So we have *mir-iau*, "I died," while the present *mir-sztu*, "I am dying," belongs to a different conjugational form. In Latin, too, may be mentioned *fio* as a remnant of the old passive. I divide the word thus, *f-io*, and regard it as an abbreviation of *fu-io*, (just as in Old Persian *b-iyâ*,† "let him be" = Sanscrit *bhûyât*), and therefore analogous to the Sanscrit

---

* The Gothic also presents a remarkably analogous form to the Sanscrit *jâ-yê*, "I am born," in the isolated form *us-kiyanata*, "*enatum*" (Luc. viii. 6.), which presupposes in the present *us-kiya*, "*enascor*," and therefore a simple verb, *ki-ya*, "*nascor*," for *kin-ya*, as in Sanscrit, *jâ-yê* for *jan-yê*.

† Euphonic for *byâ*, as *y* unites very often with a preceding consonant without a preceding *i*.

bhûyê*, exclusive of the middle personal termination of the Sanscrit. Compare, therefore, *f-iu-nt*, with *bhû-ya-ntê*, *f-ie-t* with *bhû-yê-ta*, *f-iê-mus* with *bhû-yê-mahi*. As the Sanscrit passive is frequently used impersonally in expressions like श्रूयताम् *srúyatâm*, "let it be heard," instead of "hear thou," आस्यताम् *âsyatâm*, "let it be placed," मम्रे *mamrê*, "let it be dead," I will also here further observe, that in Georgic, whose grammatical relations with Sanscrit I have elsewhere pointed out†, such modes of expression are very common, viz. in the verbs or tenses called by Brosset "indirect," whose element of formation, *ia* or *ie*, presents an unmistakeable resemblance to the passive character; compare, e. g., მგონია *m-gon-ia*, "it is thought by me" (= Sanscrit मया ज्ञायते *mayá jñá-ya-tê*, "it is known by me") for "I think," შემიყვარებია *shê-mi-qwareb-ia*, "it was loved by me" = "I had loved" (see "The Caucasian members," &c., p. 59). But the common Georgic passive also, where it is retained, corresponds, in its principle of formation, to the here mentioned य *ya*, and most clearly in the third person plural, e. g., in შეიყვარებიან *she-i-qwarebian*, "amantur," answering to the active შეიყვარებენ *she-i-qwareben*, "amant," the termination of which, in its abbreviation, corresponds to our German forms, as *lieben* (from *liebent*) l. c. p. 56.

737. Originally the Sanscrit passive character *ya* may perhaps have extended over the universal tenses; and in roots ending in *â* or a diphthong I think, even in the pre-

---

* The passive of *bhû* "to be," must be looked for as impersonal only in the 3d per. sing., as we also find the neut. of the part. fut. pass. in constructions of this kind; *e.g.* (Hit. ed. Bonn. pp. 17. 20.), *tavâ 'nucharêṇa mayá bhavitavyam*, "mine is it to be thy attendant" = "I must be thy attendant." The idea "to be" is expressed by the active of *bhû*, as *bhavâmi* means as well "I become," as "I am."

† "The Caucasian members of the Indo-European family of languages."

sent state of the language, I recognise a remnant of it, viz. in the *y*, which, in the aorist, the two futures, the precative, and the conditional, precedes the conjunctive vowel *i*; *e. g.*, in *adâyishi*, "I was given," *dâyitâhê* and *dâyishyê*, "I shall be given," *dâyishíya*, "may I be given," *adâyishyê*, "I might be given." I am led to this view principally by the circumstance, that that form of the intensive which, on account of its passive form and active signification, I term deponent, retains the passive character in the said tenses and moods after vowels other than *â*; hence, *e. g.*, *achêchíyishi*, "I collected," *chêchíyitâhê*, *chêchíyishbyê*, "I will collect," from चि *chi*.* If the यु *y* occurred only after आ *â*, it might be assumed, as was formerly my opinion, to be a mere euphonic insertion (see smaller Sanscrit Gram. §. 49ᵃ.), as, *e. g.*, in यायिन् *yâ-y-in*, "going," from *yâ* with the suffix *in*. The reduplicated preterite of the passive is in all verbs, like the corresponding tense in Greek, exactly like that of the middle; so that, *e. g.*, ददृशे *dadṛisê* signifies, as middle, "I or he saw," and as passive, "I or he was seen." Moreover, the reduplicated preterite or perfect is that one of the universal tenses of the passive, which, with the exception of the third person singular of the aorist, is the only one in common use. I cannot recollect to have seen in any author other universal tenses, or other persons than the third singular of the aorist.†

---

* Before the *y* of the passive character *i* and *u* are lengthened, as generally the *y* exerts a lengthening power over *i* and *u* preceding it, except when the *iy* is only a euphonic developement of *i* or *î*, as, *e. g.*, in *bhiyas*, "*timoris*," from *bhi+as*. Observe, with respect to the lengthening influence of the Sanscrit यु, that in Latin also *j* within a word alone produces for itself length by position.

† This ends in *i*, and wants the personal sign, *e.g.*, *ajani*, "he was born." In this *i* might be recognised a contraction of the passive character यु *ya*: to this view, however, are opposed forms like *adâyi*, "he was

738. With respect to the origin of the passive character य ya, a very satisfactory explanation, I think, is given of it by Sir G. Haughton,* wherein he mentions that in Bengálí and Hindústání the passive relation is expressed by an auxiliary verb, which signifies "to go": जाना jând (from yând, see §. 79.), in Hindústání, and या yâ in Bengálí; in the latter, e. g., करा याइ karâ yâi signifies "I am made," as it were "I go in making." Now in Sanscrit both इ i and या yâ, Class 2, signify "to go"; but of these it appears best to keep to the latter root, which, in Bengálí, also expresses the passive relation: and I believe that the shortening of the syllable या yâ to य ya is to be ascribed to the root being burthened by composition, which rendered a diminution of the weight of the auxiliary verb desirable. The a of the passive ya is therefore radical, and not, as in the first and sixth Class, a conjugational affix: it follows, however, the analogy of the class syllable a, just as, according to §. 508., the root स्था sthâ, "to stand," after its abbreviation to स्थ stha subjects its final a to the analogy of verbs of the first and sixth Class. Through the middle terminations combined with the appended auxiliary verb, and expressing the reflexive relation, the auxiliary keeps the meaning "to go oneself"; and while the Bengálí karâ yâi signifies simply "I go in making," the Sanscrit composite implies more, viz. "I go (betake) myself in making." Compare the Latin constructions like *amatum iri*, "to be gone in love": remark, also, *veneo* in opposition to *vendo;* as also the expressions of such common occurrence in Sanscrit, like "to

---

was given," because here y is the passive expression: the i, however, most probably is identical with that of *adây-i-shi*, "I was given," *adâyi-shma*, "we were given:" *adâyi*, therefore, would be an abbreviation of *adâyishta*.

* In his edition of Manu, B. I. p. 329, and in his Bengálí Grammar, pp. 68 and 95.

go in joy," "to go in anger," for "to be rejoiced," "to be angered": we even find *grahaṇaṅ samupâgamat* "he went in seizure," for "he was seized," in the Râm. (of Schl. I. i. 73.).

CAUSALS.

739. The Sanscrit and Zend causal is, in its formative character, identical with that of the verbs of the tenth Class (see §. 109ª. 6.). In explanation of the affix अय् *ay*, in the special tenses अय *aya*, the Sanscrit furnishes the roots इ *i*, "to go," and ई *î*, "to wish," "to demand," "to pray": from both arises, by Guna, before vowels अय् *ay*, and in combination with the character of the first Class, अय *aya*. The meaning "to wish," "to demand," appears, perhaps, adapted to represent the secondary notion of the causal verbs, in which the subject completes the action, not by the deed, but by the will: thus, *e.g.*, *kârayâmi*, "I cause to make," would properly mean "I require the making," whether it were intended that "any one made," or "any thing was made." But if the causal character springs from a root which originally signifies "to go," we must then observe, that in Sanscrit several verbs of motion signify also "to make"; *e.g.*, *vêdayâmi* might properly signify "I make to know."

740. Although, as has been remarked (p. 109), all German weak verbs are based on the Sanscrit tenth Class, still that form alone, which has most truly preserved the Sanscrit *aya*, viz. that which in Gothic, in the 1st per. sing. pres., terminates in *ya* (Grimm's first weak conjugation), is used in the formation of causal verbs, or of transitive from intransitive verbs, but not in such a manner that the language, like the Sanscrit, could form a causal from every primitive verb, but rather so that it is content with those handed down from old time. These, in Gothic, agree with the Sanscrit causals also in this point, that the radical vowel always appears in the strongest form that the primitive verb has

developed*. Hence, the weakening of *a* to *i*, which the primitive or strong verbs have frequently experienced in the present, is not admitted in the causal; and the vowels *i* and *u*, which are capable of Guna, are Gunized; and, in fact, through the original heavy Guna-vowel *a*, not as in the present of the primitive through *i* (see §. 27.). Generally, in Gothic, the causal exhibits the vowel of the monosyllabic forms of the preterite of the primitive, yet without its being possible to say that it is derived from the latter; but the causal and the singular of the preterite of the primitive stand, with respect to their radical vowel, in a sisterly, not in a derivative relation. Compare, *e. g.*, *satya*, "I place," (R. *sat*) with *sita*, "I sit," *sat*, "I sate," and with the Sanscrit causal *sâdayâmi*, from the root *sad*, perf. *sasâda*; thus, *lagya*, "I lay," from the root *lag* (*liga*, "I lie," *lag*, "I lay"); *nasya* "I make whole," "I heal," from the root *nas* (*ga-nisa*, "I recover," pret. *ga-nas*); *sagqvya*, "I sink, make to sink," from the root *sagqv* (*sigqva* "I sink," pret. *sagqv*); *dragkya*, "I drank," from the root *dragk* (*drigka*, "I drink," pret. *dragk*); *ur-rannya*, "I cause to go up," from the root *rann* (*ur-rinna* "I go up," pret. *ur-rann*). Examples of Gunized *u* in the Gothic causal form are the following: *ga-drausya*, "I make to fall down," "I throw down," from the root *drus* (*driusa*, "I fall," pret. *draus.*, pl. *drusum*; compare Sanscrit *dhvaṅs*, "to fall," §. 20.); *lausya*, "I loosen," from the root *lus* (*fra-liusa*, "I lose," pret. *-laus*, pl. *-lusum*; compare Sanscrit *lû*, "to tear away," "to cut off"). So in Sanscrit, *e. g.*, *bôdhayâmi* (*ô = au*), "I make to know," "I awaken," from the root *budh* "to know," "to wake up." The following are examples of the Gunizing of *i* to *ai*: *ur-raisya*, "I set up," from the root *ris* (*ur-reisa*, "I stand up,"

---

* Those forms only are admitted which have arisen from the contraction of reduplicated preterites (see §. 606.): in Sanscrit, however, the *â*, *e.g.*, of *sâdayâmi* is heavier than the *ê* (*=a+i*) of *sêdima*.

pret. *ur-rais*, pl. *ur-risum*); *hnaivya*, "I lower," from the root *hniv* (*hneiva*, "I bow myself," pret. *hnaiv*, pl. *hnivum*). So in Sanscrit, *e. g.*, *vêdayâmi* (ए ê = ai) "I make to know," Zend. ڊۼﺳﺟﮋﺳﻌﺠﻠﻳﮋ *vaêdhayêmi**, from *vid*, "to know." Our new High German causal remains, such as *setze*, "place," *lege*, "lay," *senke*, "sink," are, by reason of abbreviations of their endings, no longer to be distinguished from their primitives, and furnish a remarkable proof of a corruption of form gradually reaching a point where it becomes imperceptible. Without the fortunate preservation of Gothic forms like *satya*, and other formations of the Old German dialects, corresponding more or less, it would have been impossible to trace in the *e* of *setze* a relation to the Sanscrit *ayâmi* of *sâdayâmi*, and hence an agreement in the principle of formation of the German and Sanscrit causals. So early as the Old German the causal character appears much defaced; *e. g.*, in *nerent*, "*alunt*" (*vivere faciunt*) to be found in Notker, for *neriant*, Gothic *nasyand*; *lego* "*pono*," for *legio*, *legiu*, Gothic *lagya*; *legent*, "*ponunt*," for *legiant*, Gothic *lagyand*, l. c.

741. In Old Sclavonic that conjugation corresponds in which we, in §. 505., have recognised the Sanscrit tenth Class: it therefore corresponds also to the Indo-Germanic causal formation: it also contains the verbs which by their signification alone rank as causals, and to which, as primitive, corresponds a non-causal or intransitive verb. In accordance with the Sanscrit-Gothic principle noticed in the preceding §. these casual verbs exhibit a heavier vowel than the primitive, or they contain a vowel, while the primitive has lost its radical vowel. Thus, as in Sanscrit, from the

---

* It often occurs in combination with the prep. *ni*; ڊۼﺳﺟﮋﺳﻌﺠﻠﻳﮋﺑﮋ *nivaêdhayêmi*, according to Anquetil, "*je prie*;" according to Neriosengh, निमन्त्रयामि *nimantrayâmi*, i. e. "I summon" (see Burnouf, Yaçna, p. 419). With regard to the foundation of the *ê* of the termination *êmi* see p. 963, Note.

root *mar,* "to die" (in its abbreviated form, मृ, which Grammarians regard as the primitive), comes the causal *máraydmi,* "I kill," "I make to die"; so in Sclavonic, from the radically abbreviated мрѫ *mrú,* "I die," comes a causal, морѫ *moryú,* "I cause to die" (Dobr. p. 361), which perhaps no longer admits of citation in Old Sclavonic, but is confirmed by the Russian морю *moryú*. The same is the case with варити *var-i-ti,* "to cook" (trans.), compared with врѣти *vr-ye-ti* (intrans.), with бѫдити *búd-i-ti,* "to wake," compared with бъдѣти *bhd-ye-ti,* "to awake" (Sanscrit *bodhayámi,* "I wake," *budhyê,* "I awake"). For the *e* of the primitive the causal receives the heavier *o*; hence, *e.g.,* положити *po-losch-i-ti,* "to lay," compared with лежати *lesch-a-ti,* "to lie." The *a* of *sad-i-ti,* "to plant," properly "to set," corresponds to the Sanscrit *á* of *sád-ayá-mi* (Goth. *satya,* "I set"), while the ѣ *ye* of сѣсти *syes-ti,* "to place oneself" (euphon. for *syed-ti,* see §. 457.), has probably first weakened the short *a* of the root to *e,* and then (as is commonly the case in Sclav.) prefixed a *y.* Compare the Lithuanian *sêdmi,* "I sit," answering to *sodinù,* "I plant," with the remark that the Lithuanian *o* frequently supplies the place of the long *á,* as, *e.g.,* in the nom. pl. of feminine bases in *a* (*aszwos* = Sanscrit *asvás,* "the mares"). Here may also be noticed the Irish *suidiughaim,* "I set," "plant" (answering to *suidhim,* "I sit"), where *gh,* as generally happens in the Irish causal verbs, represents the Sanscrit *y* (compare p. 110, and Pictet, pp. 148, 149). Of Sclavonic causals notice also растити *rast-i-ti,* "to increase," properly, "to make to grow," (*rast-ye-ti,* "to grow"),*

---

* Sanscrit *vardhayâmi,* Zend *varêdayêmi,* "I make to grow," "I increase." The Sclavonic verb has retained the affix *t,* whence the radical *d* must become *s*. As, however, the primitive verb had already an *a,* an augmentation of the vowel in the causal was impossible. Compare also the Sanscrit *ṛidh* (from *ardh*), "to grow," which is probably an abbreviation of *vardh.*

вѣсити *vyes-i-ti* "to suspend," (*vis-ye-ti*, "to hang"), *na-po-i-ti*, "to give to drink" (*na* prep., *pi-ti*, "to drink"), *po-ko-i-ti*, "to quiet," (*po-chi-ti*, "to rest"). As the Sclavonic ѣ *ye* is the usual representative of the Sanscrit ए *ê=ai* (see §. 255. e.), so is the vowel relation between *vyes-i-ti*, "to suspend," and the root *vis*, "to hang," like that of the Sanscrit *vêś-ayá-mi*, "I make to enter," to *viśâmi*, "I go in." The Sclavonic root *vis* is also probably identical with the Sanscrit *viś*, which, in combination with the prep. नि *ni* in the causal, signifies, among other things, "to adjoin," "to annex," and brings us, therefore, very near the signification of the Sclavonic causal, viz. "to suspend," as generally the Sclavonic and Sanscrit roots meet one another in the idea of "approaching" (आविश् *âviś* means "to approach," उपविश् *upaviś*, "to place oneself"). The formal relation of (*na*)*poiti*, "to give to drink," to *piti*, "to drink," cannot be correctly measured without taking in the Sanscrit; for from a Sclavonic point of view it would seem as if *poiti* had arisen from *piti* by the insertion of an *o*, while, in fact, the *o* of *poiti* rests on the Sanscrit *â* of the root *pâ*, to which corresponds the Greek ω of πῶ-θι, πέπωκα, and the *o* of ἐπόθην, as also the Latin *ô* of *pô-tum*, *pô-turus*, and the Old Prussian *uo* of *puo-ton*, "to drink": the *i* of *piti* is based, like the ῖ of the Greek πῖ-θι, πίνω, on the weakening which has already occurred in Sanscrit of *pâ* to *pî*, whence the passive *pî-yatê*, "*bibitur*," the perf. pass. part. *pî-ta-s*, "drunken," and the gerund *pî-tvâ*, "having drunk." The Sclavonic causal has, according to the general principle, preserved in *po* the heavier vowel of the root, and that which stands nearer to the original *â*. The relation of *po-koiti*, "to quiet" (*po-ko-i-ti*, *po* prep.), to *po-chi-ti*, "to rest," is, however, of a different kind. For if, as I doubt not, Miklosich is right (Radices linguæ Sclav. p. 36) in comparing the Sclavonic root чи *chi* with the Sanscrit *śî* (from *kî*), "to lie," "to sleep," it must then be observed that the said Sanscrit root, as also the kindred Greek root κεῖμαι, assumes an irregular Guna augment, which extends throughout, and which appears in Greek either in the form of κει, or in that of κοι (κοίτη, κοί-τος, κοιμάω, see §. 4.). To the latter form corresponds the Sclavonic *ko* of *po-ko-i-ti*, where, however, the radical vowel is lost, for the following *i* is the expression of the causal relation.

742. The form *i*, in which, in Old Sclavonic, the causal character for the most part appears, corresponds exactly to the form into which, in Gothic, the causal *ya* contracts itself before the appended auxiliary verb of the preterite (see §. 623), and before the suffix of the pass. participle; therefore, as we have in Gothic, *sat-i-da*, "I placed," *sat-i-th'-s*, "placed" (Gen. *sat-i-di-s*); so in Sclavonic, *sad-i-ti*, "*plantare*," *sad-i-ty*, "*plantat*," *sad-i-shi*, "*plantas*," *sad-i-m*, "*plantamus*," *sad-i-te*, "*plantatis*." In the 1st per. sing. and 3d per. pl. of the pres. ѭ *yû* (from *yo-m*), ıѧть *yaty* (from *yanty*), corresponds to the Gothic *ya*, *yand*, Sanscrit *ayâ-mi*, *aya-nti*, provided that euphonic laws do not introduce an alteration, as is the case, *e.g.*, in сѧждѫ *saschdû* for *sadyû*. In the imperative (see §. 626.) the causal character is lost in the mood exponent; hence *sadi*, "*plantes*," "*plantet*" (Goth. *satyais*, *satyai*), сѧдѣмъ *sadyem*, "*plantemus*," сѧдѣте *sadyete*, "*plantetis*" (Goth. *satyaima*, *satyaith*), as *nesi*, "*feras*," "*ferat*." With regard to the preterite of the Old Sclavonic causal, corresponding to the Sanscrit aorist see §. 561., where, however, the *i* of възднх *bûd-i-ch*, "I did wake," corresponds, not to the Sanscrit *i* of *abódh-i-sham*, "I did know," but, as has already been remarked (§. 562.), to the exponent of the causal relation; while in Sanscrit the aorist is, with the exception of the precative active corresponding to the Greek aorist optative, the sole tense in which the Sanscrit divests itself of the character *aya* (in the universal tenses *ay*). As, however, all causals assume the reduplicated form of the aorist (see §. 580.), so the incumbrance of the

root by the reduplication, combined with the augment, is perhaps the reason of the loss of the causal character: perhaps even the reduplication is held as compensating for the causal expression, just as, in Latin, *sisto*, opposed to the unreduplicated and intransitive *sto*, or as in *gigno* = Sanscrit *jajanmi*, "I beget," opposed to *nascor* from *gnascor*.

743. The Lithuanian very seldom uses for the formation of causals from primitive verbs the forms contrasted in §. 506. with the Sanscrit अय *aya*. The only examples which occur to me are *źindau*, "I cause to suck," from *źindu*, "I suck," and *gráu-yu*, "I pull down (make to fall in) a house," from *grúw-u*, "I fall in like a house." The *w* of *grúw-u* appears to be only a developement from the *ú*, as, in Sanscrit, forms like *babhúva*, "I was," "he was," from *bhû*. If we take *grû* as the root, the causal form *gráu-yu* corresponds in its vowel increment to Sanscrit causals like *bhâv-ayâ-mi*, "I make to be," "I bring into existence," from *bhû*, "to be." The usual termination of Lithuanian causals is *inu* (pl. *ina-me*), by which, as in Sanscrit by *aya*, are formed denominatives also, as *e.g.*, *ilg-inu*, "I make long," a denominative causal from *ilga-s*, "long." The *n* of these forms, in departure from that mentioned above (§. 496.), extends over all tenses and moods, as well as to the participles and the infinitive; for I cannot agree with Mielcke (p. 98. 10.), in considering it to be a deviation from this rule, that before *s* (according to Sanscrit principles) it passes into the weakened nasal sound, which I express, like the Sanscrit *anusvâra*, by *ṅ* (see §. 10.); thus, *e.g.*, *laup-siṅ-su*, "I will praise."

744. The Lithuanian formations in *inu* agree with the Sanscrit, Zend, German, and Sclavonic causal verbs in this, that they love a heavy vowel in the root; so that many have preserved an original *a*, while the primitive has corrupted that vowel to *i* or *e*; whence they appear to us exactly in the light of the German Ablaut system (see p. 38, Note).

Thus, as *e.g.*, in Gothic, to the intransitive *sita*, "I sit" (which is a weakened form from *sata*), corresponds a preterite *sat*, and a causal *satya*, "I place"; so in Lithuanian, to the neuter verb *mirsztu*, "I die," answers a causal *marinu*, "I cause to die" (Scr. *máraydmi*, Sclav. *moryû*); and to the *gem-mu* (from *gem-yu*), "I am born," represented above (§. 501.) as passive, corresponds a causal *ga-minu*, "I beget." The following are causals, with *a* answering to the *e* of the corresponding intransitive: *gadinu*, "I ruin," "kill," opposed to *gendu, nagendu*, "I am ruined"; *kankinu*, "I vex," opposed to *kenchiu*, "I suffer." In the Lithuanian causals also, in place of the organic *a*, *o* is found answering to the *e* of the intransitive (as in Sclav., §. 742.); for example, in *sodinu*, "I plant," answering to *sĕdmi*, "I sit." There is much that is interesting in the vowel relation of *pa-klaidinù*, "I mislead," "bring into error," to *pa-klystu*, "I mislead myself" (euphon. for *pa-klyd-tu*), for the *y* is, in pronunciation, identical with *i*; so *pa-klaidinu*, in respect to its Guna form, corresponds very well to the Gothic causals like *hnaivya*, "I humble," and Sanscrit, as *védayámi* (= *vaidayámi*), "I make to know" (see 109.[a] 16.). The same is the case with *at-gaiwinu*, "I quicken" (properly "I make to live," compare *gywas*, "living," Sanscrit *jív*, "to live"), the primitive of which, "I recover myself," "become fresh again," "lively," is probably an abbreviation of *at-giwjù*; *waidinù-s*, "I shew myself" (see §. 476.), contains a stronger Guna vowel than *weizdmi*, "I see," and corresponds to the just-mentioned Sanscrit causal *védayámi*. An example of the manner in which a Lithuanian causal has, just like its corresponding intransitive, corrupted an original *a* to *e*, is *deginu*, "uro," answering to the intransitive *degu**, "ardeo."

---

* In Sanscrit the fourth Class of the root *dah* (*dahyámi* "ardeo") represents the intransitive meaning, and the first Class (*dahámi* "uro") the transitive. On the latter is based the Irish *daghaim* "uro."

998   VERBS.

745. The circumstance that the Lithuanian formation *ina*
(1st per. sing. *inu*), like the Sanscrit *aya*, forms as well causals
as denominatives, and that the causals so formed, like the
Sanscrit, German, and Sclavonic, prefer a powerful radical
vowel, gives us ground, (in variance from the assertion set
forth at the end of §. 495. which I gladly retract), for seeking
to compare the Lithuanian *ina* and Sanscrit *aya*. We might
in the *i* of *ina* recognise the weakened form of an original
a, as it appears also in the forms mentioned at §. 506. in
iyu, iya. The *n*, then, as semi-vowels are easily interchanged, must be held to be a corruption of य् *y*[*]. The *i*,
however, of *ina, inu*, as in the forms in *iu*, plural *i-me*
(*myl-i-me*, "we love" §. 506.), might correspond to the Sanscrit *y* of the derivative *aya*; so that, *e.g.*, the syllable *in*
of *sod-in-ti*, "to plant," would be identical with the *i* of the
Sclavonic *sad-i-ti* of the same meaning, and with the Gothic
i of *sat-i-ta*, "I placed," (compare §. 743.). The *n* of the
Lithuanian form would then be an unorganic affix, like a rind
which has grown upon the vowel termination of the verbal
theme, according to the same principle by which, in German, so many nominal bases have received the affix of *n*;
so that, *e.g.*, to the Sanscrit base *vidhavâ*, "a widow" (at
the same time a nominative, see §. 137.), to the Latin *vidua*,
and Sclavonic *vdova*, corresponds a Gothic base *viduvôn*
(Nom. -*vô*, §. 140.); and to the Sanscrit feminine participial
bases in *antî* respond Gothic bases in *andein* (Nom. *andei*).
If this view be taken, we must then assume that the verbal
theme of *sodi* (Sanscrit *sâdaya*), extended to *sodiu*, has taken
up the character of the Sanscrit first conjugational Class, and

---

[*] See §. 20. As regards the transition of the *y* into another liquid, remark the relation of the German *Leber* (labial for guttural, as in Greek
ἧπαρ, see Graff, II. p. 80) to the Sanscrit *yakrit* (from *yakart*) and Latin
jecur. With respect to the transition of *l* to *n*, observe, *e. g.*, the relation
of the Doric ἤνθον to ἤλθον.

CAUSALS. 999

has thus entered into the Lithuanian first conjugation; thus *sodin-a-me*,* " we plant," as *suk-a-me*, " we turn," In favour of the first mode of explanation might be adduced the circumstance that, together with *szlowinu*, " I praise," " extol," exists a *szlówiyu*,† which latter is clearly identical with the Sanscrit *śrávayámi*, " I make to hear," and Russian славлю *slavlyú*, " I laud." Since in Latin, as I think I have clearly proved, three conjugations—the first, second, and fourth—correspond to the Sanscrit tenth Class, we have reason to look among these for the Latin causals, as already (p. 110.) *moneo* has been compared with the Sanscrit *mánayámi* and Prâkrit *mạnêmi*, " I make to think." The causal meaning, however, is no longer apparent in the Latin *moneo*, as it has not any primitive verb corresponding to it, from which it might have been derived in a regular way, and one, as it were, often trodden for similar purposes; for *memini* may be regarded as a sister form connected with it, both in sound and sense, but not as the parent of which it is the offspring. *Sedo*, which corresponds to the Sanscrit causal *sádayámi* and its German-Sclavonic sister forms (*sed-â-s* = सादयसि *sâd-a*(*y*)*a-si*), might, according to the sense, be regarded as the causal of *sedeo;* but the latter is in form likewise a causal, and there is a want of other analogous cases for the formation of causals by the change

---

* Ruhig doubles the *n* of *laupsinu* in both the plural numbers and in the third person singular of the present and perfect. Mielcke, on the other hand, makes no remark, p. 98, 10. with regard to the necessity of such a reduplication, where it does not already occur in the first person singular of the present. For the rest it may be remarked, that liquids especially are easily doubled, and that, *e.g.*, in Sanscrit a final *n*, if preceded by a short vowel, is doubled in case the word following begins with a vowel.

† The kindred *klausau*, " I listen," has, like the Greek κλύω, preserved the original guttural, which in *szlawiyu*, as in the Sanscrit *śru*, has been corrupted to a sibilant.

from the second to the first conjugation. In Latin, therefore, the three verbs *sido, sedeo,* and *sedo,* can only be regarded as three kindred verbs, which, each in its own way, are referable to the Sanscrit root *sad*. To the Sanscrit *trâsayâmi,* (Prâkr. *tâsêmi*), "I make to tremble," "to fear," "I terrify," corresponds *terreo* by assimilation for *terseo,* from *treseo*. The fourth conjugation presents *sôpio* as a form fairly analogous to the Sanscrit causal *svâpayâmi,* "I make to sleep," (*svapimi,* "I sleep," irregular for *svapmi*), Old Northern *svepium,* "*sopimus,*" (singular *svep*), Old High German *in-suepiu,* Russian усыпляю *usyplayu*[*]. The causal notion, however, is lost in this *sôpio* also, as there is no intransitive *sŏpo* of the third conjugation corresponding to it as a point of departure. The German dialects have, indeed, preserved the primitive (Old High German *slâfu*). but it has become estranged from the causal by the exchange of the semi-vowel *v* for *l* (see §. 20.). In Russian, on the other hand, сплю *splyu,* "I sleep" (euphonic for *spyu*), corresponds, as verb of the Sanscrit fourth Class (see §. 500.), to the causative *u-syplayu* (*u* preposition), the *y* of which is based on the Sanscrit *u* of contracted forms like *sushupima,* "we slept," *supta,* "having slept;" with which, also, may be compared the Greek ὑπ of ὕπνος. I here place opposite to one another the corresponding forms of the Latin and Old High German languages for comparison with the Sanscrit *svâpayâmi* and its potential *svâpayê-y-am* (see §. 689.):

svâp-ayâ-mi,	*sôp-io,*	*in-suep-iu.*
svâp-aya-si,	*sôp-î-s,*	*in-suep-i-s.*
svâp-aya-ti,	*sôp-i-t,*	*in-suep-i-t.*
svâp-ayâ-mas,	*sôp-î-mus,*	*in-suep-ia-m.*
svâp-aya-tha,	*sôp-î-tis,*	*in-suep-ia-t.*
svâp-aya-nti,	*sôp-iu-nt,*	*in-suep-ia-nt.*

---

[*] The *l* is only a euphonic affix required by *p*; *ayu* therefore=*ayâmi*

CAUSALS.

svâp-ayê-y-am,*	sôp-ia-m,		in-suep-ie.‡
svâp-ayê-s,	sôp-iê-s,†	sôp-iâ-s,	in-suep-iê-s.
svâp-ayê-t,	sôp-ie-t,	sôp-ia-t,	in-suep-ie.
svâp-ayê-ma,	sôp-iê-mus,	sôp-iâ-mus,	in-suep-iê-mês.
svâp-ayê-ta,	sôp-iê-tis,	sôp-iâ-tis,	in-suep-iê-t.
svâp-ayê-y-us,	sôp-ie-nt,	sôp-ia-nt.	in-suep-iê-n.

746. In the Latin first Conjugation, which has preserved the two extremes of the Sanscrit causal character *aya* in the contraction *â*, the verbs *necâre, plôrâre, lavâre* and *clamâre*, as well as the above-mentioned *sedâre*, present themselves as genuine causals, both in signification and in origin, though they are no longer perceived to be such by the genius of the language, since their primitive has either been lost or estranged in form. *Necare*, which, specially regarded from a Roman point of view, must be taken as the denominative of *nex* (*nec-s*), corresponds to the Sanscrit *nâś-ayâ-mi* "*perire facio*," causal of *naś-yâ-mi*, Cl. 4. *pereo*. Another form of नाशयामि *nâśayâmi*, with softened meaning, is *noceo*. In Greek νέκυς and νεκρός are to be referred to the Sanscrit root *naś*, from *nak*. I believe I am right in regarding *plôro* as a corruption of *plôvo* for the reason mentioned at §. 20. It would consequently correspond to the Sanscrit *plâvayâmi*; properly "I make to flow," from the root *plu*, "to flow," which, in the Latin *fluo*, has experienced an irregular phonetic modification; while in *pluit*, which belongs to the same root, the original tenuis is retained. In *lavare* (Greek λούω) one of the two combined initial consonants is lost; in other respects, however, *lavo* corresponds still better than *plôro* to the Sanscrit *plâvayâmi*, "to wash," "to sprinkle" (in middle "to wash oneself,") on which also is based the Old High German *flewiu*,§ "I

---

* See §. 689.   † See §§. 691, 692.   ‡ See §. 694.

§ This is, like *lavo* when compared with its intransitive *fluo*, estranged from the primitive *fliuzu*, "I flow," in that it has kept itself free from the inorganic *z* (see p. 114).

wash." In Carniolan *plev-i-m,* "I water," "I dissolve" (Metelgo, p. 115.), is the regular causal from *plav-a-m,* "I swim" (=Sanscrit प्लवामि *plav-â-mi). Clamo* properly signifies (if I am right in explaining its *m* as a hardened form of *v* (see p. 115.), "I make to hear," and possesses, therefore, a concealed affinity to *cluo,* κλύω and is identical with the Sanscrit *śrâv-ayâ-mi* (*ś* from *k*), "I make to hear," "I speak," with the Zend *śrâv-ayê-mi* of the same meaning, the Carniolan *slav-i-m,* "I praise," (*sluyem* "I hear"), the Old Sclavonic словлѭ *slovlyû* (from *blagoslovlyû,* "I bless"), the Russian *slavlyu,* "I praise," and the Lithuanian *szlôwiyu,* id. (see §. 745.).

747. Roots, which in Sanscrit end in *â,* or in a diphthong to be changed into *â,* receive before *aya* the affix of a *p*; hence, *e.g., sthâp-ayâ-mi,* "I make to stand," from *sthâ; yâp-ayâ-mi,* "I make to go," "I set in motion," from *yâ*. As labials in Latin are not unfrequently replaced by gutturals*, I believe, with Pott (Etymol. F. p. 195.), that the Latin *jacio* should be deduced fron *japio,* and be identified with the above-mentioned *yâp-ayâ-mi;* though properly only the *io* of the fourth, and not that of the third Conjugation (=Sanscrit य of the fourth Class), corresponds to the Sanscrit causal character. The agreement of forms like *capio, capiunt, capiam,* &c., and the analogous forms of the fourth Conjugation, might, however, easily favour a transition of the latter into the third. The same appears to me to be the case with *facio,* which I compare with the Sanscrit *bhâvayâmi,* "I make to be," "I bring into existence;" but in so doing I assume that the *e* is a hardening of the radical *v*† (see §. 19.), as roots in *û* in the Sanscrit causal never assume a *p*. The Gothic gives us *bau-a,* "I

---

* Compare, *e.g., quinque* with *pañchan,* πέντε; *coquo* with *pachâmi,* πέσσω, Servian *pechem,* "I roast."

† From *û*—for *âu,* before vowels *âv,* is the Vriddhi form of *û;* see §. 39.

build" (from *bau-ai-m*), as the kindred form to the Sanscrit *bháv-ayá-mi* and Latin *facio*: in the second and third persons, therefore, the character *ai* of *bau-ai-s*, *bau-ai-th*, answers to the Sanscrit *aya* of *bháv-aya-si*, *bháv-aya-ti*. From a German point of view, however, we could as little perceive the connection between our *bauen*, "to build," and *bin*, "I am," as recognise in Latin the affinity of the roots of *fac-io* and *fu-i*. If, however, I am unable to compare the *c* of the said form with the Sanscrit causal *p*, still I think I can shew in Latin one more causal in which *c* takes the place of a Sanscrit *p*, viz. *doceo*, which I take in the sense of "I make to know," and regard as akin to *di-sco* (properly "I wish to know") and the Greek ἐδάην, διδάσκω. If the *d* of these forms has arisen from *g* (compare Δημήτηρ from Γημήτηρ), then *doceo* leads to the Sanscrit *jñáp-ayámi*, "I make to know" (*já-ná-mi*, "know," for *jñá-ná-mi*), and to the Persian *dá-ne-m*, "I know". As an example of the Latin causal, in which the original *p* has remained unchanged, let *rapio* be taken, supposing it to correspond to the Sanscrit *rápayámi*, "I make to give,"* from the root रा *rá*, "to give," which, in my opinion, is nothing but a weakening of *dá*. There also occurs, together with *rá*, in the Véda dialect, the form *rás*, just as, together with *dá*, exists a lengthened form *dás*. In its origin the root *lá*, to which are ascribed the meanings "to give," and "to take," appears to be identical with *rá* and *dá*.

748. To the roots which, in Sanscrit, irregularly annex a *p*

---

* The derivation (elsewhere admitted as possible) from *lup* (*lumpámi*), "to rive," "break," "destroy" (compare Pott. I. 258), to which *rumpo* belongs, is less satisfactory, as *a* in this explanation must be taken as the Guna vowel, with the loss of the proper vowel of the root. The Latin, however, avoids the use of Guna, and generally retains the radical vowel rather than that of Guna; *e.g.* in *video*, which is based on the Sanscrit causal *védayámi*, "I make to know," from the root *vid*.

3 T 2

in the causal, belongs ऋ *ri*, i.e. *ar* (see §. 1.), "to go," whence *arp-ayâ-mi*, "I move," "cast," "send" (*śarân arpayâmi*, "*sagittas mitto*"), with which, perhaps, the Greek ἐρείπω is connected,* which, however, as causal, should be ἐρειπέω, or ἐρειπάω, or ἐρειπάζω (see. §§. 19. 109ª. 6.). Inasmuch as the theme ἐρειπ has lost the true causal character, this verb has acquired quite the character of a primitive verb, just like ἰάπτω, which Pott has referred, in the same way as the previously mentioned Latin *jacio*, to the Sanscrit *yâp-ayâ-mi*, "I make to go." If ῥίπ-τω does not belong to *kship*,† "to throw," but, like the others, to *arpayâmi*, it is then a transposed form of ἰρπ-τω,

749. The Sanscrit root पा *pâ*, "to receive," "to rule," assumes, in the causal, *l*; hence *palâyâmi*. So, in the Greek βάλλω, στέλλω, ἰάλλω, the second λ of which appears to have arisen by assimilation from *y*, as ἄλλος from ἀλyος = Gothic *ALYA*, Latin *alius*, Sanscrit *anya-s* (see p. 401). Βάλλω, therefore, is for βάλyω, from βᾱ (see §. 109ᵇ. 1.), the radical vowel being shortened (ἔβᾰλον), which, however, in the transposition βλη (βέβλη-κα) has preserved its original length;

---

* Ρειπ might be taken as a transposed form of εἰρπ, and the ε as a vowel prefix, as, *e.g.*, in ἐλαχύ-s = Sanscrit *laghu-s*. Observe, also, that the π of σάλπιγξ, which Sonne (Epilegomena to Benfey's Gr. Roots, p. 24), identifies with the Sanscrit causal *p*, belongs to a root, which in Sanscrit ends in *ar* (*ri*), viz. to *svar* (*svṛi*), to which Pott also (Et. F. p. 225) has referred it: σάλπιγξ, therefore, properly = "making to sound." Should, too, the Lith. *szwilpinu*, "I whistle," notwithstanding its *sz* for *s*, belong here, then remark the shorter form adduced by Ruhig of the 3d per. sing. *szwilpya*, "the bird whistles," where *pia* corresponds to the Sanscrit forms in *payati*, such as *arpayati*, "he makes to go," "he moves."

† The derivation of *kship* pre-supposes an abbreviation of ῥίπτω from κρίπτω; so that ρ would have taken the place of the Sanscrit sibilant, as in κρείων, which Fr. Rosen has compared with the Sanscrit root *kshi*, "to rule"; see his Rig Vêda Sanhita, Annot. p. xi., where, too, κραιπνός is compared with *kshipra*, "swift" (from *kship*, "to cast"), and the Latin *crepusculum* with *kshapâ*, "night" (better with *kshapas*).

CAUSALS. 1005

στέλλω, from στελγω (ἔσταλκα), for σταλγω, from στᾶ (ἵστᾱμι, ἵστημι)=Sanscrit *sthâ*, which, in combination with various prepositions, obtains the notion of movement*; ἰάλλω, from ἰαλγω, is to be referred, in a manner different from ἰάπτω, to the Sanscrit root या *yâ*, " to go," to which also belongs ἵημι, as reduplicated form for γιγημι (fut. ἥσω=यास्यामि *yâ-syâmi*, compare Lithuanian *yó-su*, " I will ride "). Perhaps κέλ-λω from κελ-γω=Sanscrit *châlayâmi*, " I move," causal of the root चल् *chal*, " to move oneself;" perhaps, also, πάλ-λω, from παλ-γω, for παδγω=Sanscrit *pâdayâmi*, causal of *pad*, " to go," to the causal of which may be referred also the Latin *pel-lo* as by assimilation from *pel-yo*. All these forms, therefore, if our explanation of them be correct, have lost the initial *a* of the Sanscrit causal character *aya* of the special tenses, and are hereby removed, as it were, from the Sanscrit tenth Class to the fourth (compare Pott II. 45.). As in Greek, verbs in εω, αω (for εγω, αγω), αζω, are the proper representatives of the Sanscrit causal form or tenth Class; and as these extend their character also over the present and imperfect; so here, too, may καλέω be considered as a concealed causal, which, like the Latin *clamo*, properly signifies " to make to hear," and answers to the Sanscrit *srâvayâmi* (*s* from *k*). Accordingly I take καλέω as a transposition of κλα-έω for κλαϝ-έω.

750. The Zend, it appears, has no part in the use of the *p*, which, according to §. 747., is, in the causal, to be added to roots in *â*; at least I know of no example where it is found: on the other hand, we find evidence of the discontinuance of the addition of a *p* in ⟨Zend⟩ *âstâya*, " make to come," " bring " (Vend. S. p. 55. several times)

---

* Observe, also, that together with *sthâ* there exists a root *sthal*, and with *pâ* a root *pal*. To *sthal* belongs our *stelle*, "place," Old High German *stella*, from *stelyu*; properly, " I make to stand"=Sanscrit *stâlayâmi*.

= Sanscrit *âsthâpaya*, from स्था *sthâ*, "to stand," with the preposition *â*, "to approach." In 𐎠𐎿𐎫𐎠𐎹 *âstâya*, from *âstâ-aya*, the *a* of derivation has coalesced with the radical vowel; so in Old Persian 𐎠𐎺𐎠𐎿𐎫𐎠𐎹𐎡𐎹 *avâstâyam* (from *ava-astâ-ayam*), "I restored" (Beh. I. 63. 66. 69.), In Prâkrit, on the other hand, those roots also which end in a consonant frequently take, in the causal, the said labial, in the softened form of *b*, where, however, the root is previously lengthened by the addition of an *a*; e. g., *jîvâbêhi*, "make to live," *jîvâbêdu*, "let him make to live" (see Delius, Radices Prâkrit s. r. *jîv*). In Sanscrit also, in the unclassical language of popular tales, forms of this kind occur; and indeed *jîvâpaya*; for the just-mentioned *jîvâbêhi* (Lassen's Anthol. Sanscrit, p. 18), which latter surpasses the Sanscrit in the preservation of the imperative termination *hi* from *dhi*. In the 1st. per. sing. pres. is found, *l. c., jîvâpayâmi* (Prâkrit *jîvâbêmi*), and in the part. perf. pass. *jîvâpitah* = Prâkrit *jîvâbidô*. Lassen, in mentioning these forms, remarks (Institut. linguæ Prâkrit, pp. 360, 361), that causals of this kind still exist in Mahratta; and I was surprised at finding myself able to trace the analogy of these formations even to the Iberian languages[*]; since in Latin, as G. Rosen remarks, the affix *ap* (only *p* after vowels) always gives a transitive meaning to verbs. Thus *gnap*, "to unveil," "to make evident," corresponds to the Sanscrit *jñâpayâmi*, "I make to know," while *gna*, "to understand," agrees with the Sanscrit root ज्ञा *jñâ*, "to know." In Georgian the said causal affix appears in the form *ab, eb, ob, aw, ew, ow,* without, however, the very numerous class of verbal bases which so terminate being regarded as causals in meaning, which cannot sur-

---

[*] See "*The Caucasian members of the Indo-European family of languages.*"

CAUSALS. 1007

prise us, as in Latin also, and German, the form of the Sanscrit causals, or tenth Class, is so prevalent as to extend over three Conjugations in Latin, and the three Classes of the weak Conjugation in the German dialects (see §. 109ª. 6.).

DESIDERATIVES.

751. We now betake ourselves to the examination of the Sanscrit desideratives, which, as has been already elsewhere remarked,* are retained also in Greek; if not in signification, at least in form, in verbs like βιβρώσκω, γιγνώσκω, μιμνήσκω, διδάσκω, διδράσκω, τιτρώσκω, πιπίσκω, πιπράσκω, πιφαύσκω, where the guttural is most probably, as in ἔσκον and the Old Latin future *escit*, only a euphonic accompaniment of the sibilant, which in all Sanscrit desideratives is appended to the root, either directly, or by means of a vowel of conjunction, *i*. The roots beginning with a vowel repeat the entire root, according to the principle of the seventh aorist formation (§. 585.); *e.g.*, *ásis-i-sh*,† "to wish to sit," as a weakened form of *ásâsish*; *arir-ish*, "to wish to go," for *ararish*, from अर् *ar* (ऋ *ṛi*). So, in Greek, ἀραρίσκω. Roots which begin with a consonant repeat it or its euphonic representative, with the radical vowel, where, however, a long vowel is shortened, and the heaviest vowel *a* weakened to *i* (see §. 6.),‡ according to the same principle by which, in Latin, the *a* especially is excluded from syllables of repetition (see §. 583.). On this account the *i* prevails in repeated syllables, and the agreement

---

* Annals of Oriental Literature (London, 1820), p. 65.

† The appended sibilant is originally the dental (स् *s*), but, according to §. 21., subjected to a mutation into *sh*.

‡ Though roots with *ṛi* in their middle receive an *i* in the repeated syllables, still this is based on the original form *ar*.

with the kindred forms in Greek is thus the more striking. We find, *e.g.*, *yuyutsâmi*, "I wish to contend" (R. *yudh*), *bubhúshâmi*, "I wish to adorn" (R. *bhush*), but not *jagadishâmi*, but *jigadishâmi*, "I wish to speak"; not *jajñâsâmi*, but जिज्ञासामि *jijñâsâmi*, Mid. *jijñâsê*, "I wish to know," "to learn," "to inquire." To जिज्ञासामि *jijñâsâmi* corresponds in form the Greek γιγνώσκω, and Latin (*g*)*no-sco;* which latter, like all similar Latin formations, has lost the reduplication. To *mimnâsâmi*, desiderative of *mnâ** (*memorare, nunciare, laudare*), corresponds μιμνήσκω, and the Latin *reminiscor*. In the special tenses the Sanscrit places an *a* by the side of the desiderative sibilant, which, according to the analogy of the *a* of the first and sixth Classes, is liable, in the first person, to production (see §. 434.), and also in Greek and Latin, in the same way as the said class-vowel is represented (see §. 109.ᵃ 1.). I give, for comparison, the present and imperfect active of जिज्ञासामि *jijñâsâmi* over against the corresponding forms of Greek and Latin.

PRESENT.

	SANSCRIT.	GREEK.	LATIN.
Sing.	*jijñâ-sâ-mi*,	γιγνώ-σκω,	*no-sco.*
	jijñâ-sa-si,	γιγνώ-σκει-ς,	*no-sci-s.*
	jijñâ-sa-ti,	γιγνώ-σκει,	*no-sci-t.*
Du.	*jijñâ-sâ-vas*,	. . . . .	. . . .
	jijñâ-sa-thas,	γιγνώ-σκε-τον,	. . . .
	jijñâ-sa-tas,	γιγνώ-σκε-τον,	. . . .
Plur.	*jijñâ-sâ-mas*,	γιγνώ-σκο-μες,	*no-sci-mus.*
	jijñâ-sa-tha,	γιγνώ-σκε-τε,	*no-sci-tis.*
	jijñâ-sa-nti,	γιγνώ-σκο-ντι,	*no-scu-nt.*

---

* Clearly only a transposed form of *man*, "to think," with the radical vowel lengthened, as, *e.g.*, in Greek, βέβληκα from βαλ, πέπτωκα from πετ.

DESIDERATIVES.

IMPERFECT.

	SANSCRIT.	GREEK.	LATIN.
Sing.	ajijñá-sa-m,	ἐγίγνω-σκο-ν,	....
	ajijñá-sa-s,	ἐγίγνω-σκε-ς,	....
	ajijñá-sa-t,	ἐγίγνω-σκε,	....
Du.	ajijñá-sâ-va,	.....	....
	ajijñá-sa-tam,	ἐγιγνώ-σκε-τον,	....
	ajijñá-sa-tâm,	ἐγιγνω-σκέ-την,	....
Plur.	ajijñá-sâ-ma,	ἐγιγνώ-σκο-μεν,	....
	ajijñá-sa-ta,	ἐγιγνώ-σκε-τε,	....
	ajijñá-sa-n,	ἐγιγνώ-σκο-ν,	....

In the universal tenses Sanscrit desideratives lay aside only the vowel which is added to the sibilant; while in Greek and Latin the whole formation extends only to the special tenses; and, *e.g.*, γνώ-σω springs from the simple unreduplicated root, and hence stands in no closer analogy to the Sanscrit *jijñás-i-shyâmi*. That in Latin the future *noscam* departs from the Greek arises from this—that the future of the third and fourth conjugations, according to its origin, is only a mood of the present; and hence, *e.g.*, *noscês* corresponds to the Sanscrit *jijñásês*, and Greek γιγνώσκοις.

752. It may reasonably be conjectured that the desiderative form is no stranger in Zend, but I am unable to furnish satisfactory examples. Perhaps the forms ﺳﻮﺟﻴﺠ *jijisanuha* and ﺳﻮﺟﻴﺠ *jijisâiti*, in the Fifteenth Fargard of the Vend. (Vend. S., p. 431, Anq., p. 393), are to be referred here. The first-mentioned form, which Anquetil translates "*est vivante*," is evidently, like the ﭘﺮﺳﻨﻮﻫ *pĕrĕsanuha*, "ask," which follows it, an imperative middle; and ﺟﻴﺠ *jijisâiti*, which Anquetil renders "*on s'approchera*," is, like the ﭘﺮﺳ *pĕrĕsâiti*, "*interroget*," which follows it, the 3d per. sing. of the conjunctive active. Perhaps ﺟﻴﺠ *jijisanuha* may correspond to the Sanscrit जिज्ञासस्व *jijñâsasva*, "inform thyself," and ﺟﻴﺠ *jijisâiti* be based on a to-be-pre-

supposed Lêṭ-form जिज्ञासाति *jijñâsâti?* I will not venture to decide this point, any more than as to the forms which occur in the same page of the Vend. S., ꜱᴏɢᴅɪᴀɴ *mimaresanuha*, and ꜱᴏɢᴅɪᴀɴ *mimarēcsâiti*, which likewise have the appearance of desideratives. As regards the origin of the desiderative character *s*, it is probable it springs, like the *s* of the auxiliary future and of the aorist of primitive verbs, from the root *as* of the verb substantive. Compare, *e. g.*, *didik-shâmi*, "I wish to shew," with *dêkshyâmi*, "I will shew," and *adidik-sham*, "I wished to shew," with the aorist *adik-sham*, and the imperatives of the aorist mentioned above (§. 727.) like *bhûsha*, *nêshatu*.

INTENSIVES.

753. Besides desideratives, there is in Sanscrit another class of derivative verbs, which receive a reduplication, viz. intensives. These require a great emphasis on the syllable of reduplication, and hence increase the vowels capable of Guna, even the long ones, by Guna, and lengthen *a* to *â*; *e. g.*, *vêvêśmi* (or *vêviśími*), plural *vêviśmas*,* from *viś*, "to enter;" *dêdípmi* (or *dêdipími*) from *dîp*, "to shine;" *lôlôpmi* (or *lôlupími*) from *lup*, "to cut off;" *bôbhûshmi* (or *bôbhûshími*) from *bhûsh*, "to adorn;" *śâśakmi* (*śâśakími*), from *śak*, "to be able." As in Greek ω is a very frequent representative of long α (see §. 4.), so, as has been elsewere remarked Glossarium, Sanscr. a. 1830, p. 113), τωθάζω has quite the build of a Sanscrit intensive, only that it is introduced into the ω conjugation. In παιπάλλω, δαιδάλλω,

---

* After the analogy of verbs of the third Class, regard being had to the weight of the personal terminations (see §. 486.). To the light terminations, beginning with a consonant, *i* may be prefixed as conjunctive vowel, when, however, the Guna of the base syllable is dropped; hence, *e.g.*, *vêviśími*.

παιφάσσω, μαιμάζω, μαιμάσσω, the insertion of an ι in the syllable of repetition supplies the place of the lengthening of the fundamental vowel; so in ποιπνύω (R. πνυ, πνέω, from πνεϝω, fut. πνεύσω), μοιμνάω, μοιμύλλω, where the υ of the root is, in the syllable of repetition, replaced by ο, since υι does not form a convenient diphthong. On this analogy rests also δοίδυξ and κοικύλλω.

754. Roots beginning with a vowel, of which only a few possess an intensive, repeat the whole root twice, in such a manner that the radical a is lengthened in the second place; hence aṭâṭ from aṭ, "to go," aśâś from aś, "to eat." I believe I recognise a clear counterpart to these intensive bases in the Greek ἀγωγ, though this forms no verb, but only some nominal forms, as ἀγωγός, ἀγωγεύς. The case of the ω for ᾱ is just the same as in the above-mentioned τωθάζω. On the other hand, in ὀνίνημι, ὀπιπτεύω, ἀτιτάλλω, the base syllable has experienced a weakening of the vowel, like that which enters into Sanscrit desideratives (§. 751. ad init.), which does not, however, prevent me from referring these forms, according to their origin, rather to intensives than to desideratives (compare Pott II. p. 75); so also ἀλαλάζω and ἐλελίζω exhibit the same weight of vowel in the base and in the syllable of repetition.

755. Roots, also, which begin with a consonant and end with a nasal, in case they have a as the base vowel, repeat the whole root twice in the Sanscrit intensive, but lengthen the radical vowel neither in the syllable of repetition nor in that of the base. The nasal, in accordance with a universal rule of sound, is influenced in the former syllable, so as to conform itself to the organ of the following consonant; and in roots which begin with two consonants, only one enters into the syllable of repetition; hence, e.g., dandram from dram, "to run;" bambhram from bhram, "to wander about;" जङ्गम् jangam from gam, "to go." So in Greek, παμφαίνω from φαίνω, the ν of which, though not be-

longing to the root, is nevertheless reflected in the syllable of repetition (see §. 598.). On जङ्गम् *jangam* is based, I believe, the Gothic *gagga* (*i.e. ganga*, see §. 89. 1.); so that therefore *gam*, in the syllable of the root, has lost the termination *am**, and *gagg* has entirely assumed the character of a root, which in High German has produced a new reduplication (Old High German, *giang* from *gigang*, our *gieng*, see §. 592.). And in the formation of the word, *gang* holds as an independent root; whence, in Gothic, *gah-ts*†, "gait" (*inna-gahts, fram-gahts*). The Lithuanian presents *żengiu* "I step," as analogous form ‡.

756. Some Sanscrit roots also, which do not end in a nasal in the intensive, introduce a nasal into the syllable of repetition; *e.g.*, *chañchal* (or *châchal*) from *chal*, "to move oneself;" *pamphul* from *phal*, "to burst," with the weakening of the *a* to *u* in the base syllable; so *chañchur* from *char*, "to go." As liquids are easily interchanged, it may be assumed that here the nasal of the repeated syllable is only a changed form of the radical liquid *l* or *r*. So in many Greek reduplicated forms; as, πίμπλημι, πίμπρημι, γιγγραίνω, γίγγλυμος, γαγγαλίζω, γάγγραινα, τονθορύζω, τανταλεύω, τενθρηδών, πεμφρηδών. The following are examples in which the liquids remain unchanged in the syllable of repetition: μαρμαίρω, μορμύρω, μέρμερος, μερμαίρω, μερμηρίζω, καρκαίρω, γαργαίρω, βορβορύζω, πορφύρα, πορφύρω. Compare with these the intensives of those Sanscrit roots in *ar* which contract this syllable in the weakened forms to ऋ *ri*: these, in the active of the intensive, repeat the whole root twice, except when this begins with two consonants, in

---

* The final *a* is the class syllable; 3d per. pl. *gagg-a-nd*.

† Euphonic for *gag-ts*, the nasal being rejected. With respect to the suffix, compare the Sanscrit *ga-ti-s*, "gait," for *gan-ti-s*, see §. 91.

‡ In Lithuanian *ż* often stands for the Sanscrit *g* or *j*. Compare, *e. g.*, *żadas*, "speech," with the Sanscrit *gad*, "to speak."

which case only one enters into the syllable of repetition;
e.g., dar-dhar-mi, pl. dar-dhṛi-mas, from dhar, dhṛt, "to stop,"
"to carry;" but sâsmarmi, according to the universal principle, from smar, smṛi, "to remember." To dardharmi, potential dardhṛiyâm, 3d. per. dardhriyât (from dardharyâm, dardharyât), corresponds the Zend. darĕdairyât* in a passage of the Vendidad (Vend. S. p. 463.). ڶڼۑڮۑ . ڽۑڻڗڎ -ڎڼۑۑۑ . ڤۑۑڎۑۑ . ڤۑۑڎڤ . ڮۑڽۑۑۑڎۑۑۑ . ڶۑڝۑۑۑۑۑۑڎۑۑۑ ۑۑڤۑۑۑۑڎۑۑۑۑڎۑۑۑ yatha vĕhrkó chathwarĕzangró barĕthryât hacha puthrĕm nischdarĕdairyât "as the fourfooted wolf tears away (carries off) the child (the son) of her who bore him (the mother?): according to Anquetil (p. 407), "comme le loup à quatre pieds enleve et déchire l'enfant de celle qui a porté (cet enfant)". If, however, ڶۑۑۑۑۑۑڎۑۑۑۑ nischdarĕdairyât does not come from the Sanscrit root dhar, dhṛi, it springs from दर् dar (दृ dṛi), "to split," "tear asunder" (Gr. δέρω, Gothic taira); whence, in the Vêda dialect, the intensive dardar (see Westerg. R. दृ dṛi), in classical Sanscrit dâdar. The first derivation, however, appears to me far the more probable: at all events, the form in question is a sure proof that in Zend also intensives are not wanting.

757. Some Sanscrit roots, which have a nasal as their last letter but one, take this in the syllable of repetition; hence, e.g., bambhanjmi from bhanj, "to break;" dandaṅṡmi from daṅṡ, "to bite" (Gr. δακ); chan-î-skandmi from skand, "to mount" (Lat. scando); the latter with î as vowel of conjunction between the syllable of reduplication and that of the base, as also in some other roots of this kind, and at will, also, in those roots in ar which admit a contraction to ṛi, and which nevertheless may assume a short i instead of a long one; hence, e.g., char-î-karmi, or char-i-karmi, with char-karmi, from kar, kṛi "to make."

---

* With regard to the ĕ inserted in darĕdairyât, see §. 44.

758. The intensive forms *pan-î-pad* and *pan-î-pat*, from *pad*, "to go," and *pat*, "to fall" (Pân. VII. 4. 84.), appear obscure. In explanation of these it may be assumed, that together with पद् *pad* and पत् *pat* there have existed also the forms *pand* and *pant* with a nasal, as together with many other roots which terminate in a simple mute there exist also those which have prefixed also to their mute the nasal corresponding to their organ; as, *e.g.*, *panth* with *path*, "to go."* Together with *dah*, "to burn," exists also a root दंह् *daṅh*; and hence may be deduced the intensive form *dandah* (Pan. VII. 4. 86.), to which the Gothic *tandya*, "I kindle" (with the causal character *ya*, see §. 741.), has the same relation, as above (§. 755.) *gagga* = *ganga*, "I go," to *jangam*.†

759. In Latin, *gingrio* has the appearance of a Sanscrit intensive, and is by Pott also referred here, and radically

---

* With *panth* are connected the strong cases of *pathin*, "way," as also the Latin *pons, pont-is*, as "way over a river," and the Slavonic пжть *puty*, "way" (see §. 225ᵍ.): with *path* is connected, amongst other words, the Greek πάτος (see Glossarium Sanscr. a. 1847, p. 206).

† With regard to the *t* for *d* of *tandya*, see §. 87. The retention of the second *d* of the Sanscrit form *dandah* is to be ascribed to the influence of the *n* preceding it (compare §. 90.). Remark, also, the form *sandya*, "I send," in which I think I recognise the causal of the Sanscrit root *sad*, "to go," (*sâdayâmi*, "I make to go,") with a nasal inserted. Graff sets up (IV. p. 685) for the Old High German a root *zand* (*z* for Gothic *t*, and *t* for *d*, according to §. 87.), which he likewise endeavours to compare with the Sanscrit *dah*, but without finding any information as to the *n* and *t* through the intensive form दन्दह् *dandah*. On the primitive root *dah*, if not on the causal form *dâhay*, is based also the Old High German *dâh-t* or *tâh-t* (our *Docht, Dacht*), which by more exact retention of the radical consonants is completely estranged from the intensives (in meaning causals) *zand* or *zant*. Initial Mediæ remain in German frequently unaltered, *e. g.*, in the above-mentioned *gagga*, "I go,"=*jangam*; while the Gothic root *qvam*, "to come" (*qvima, qvam*), which is based on the primitive *gam*, has experienced the regular change of Mediæ to Tenues.

INTENSIVES. 1015

compared with *grī*, i. e *gar, gir* (whence *gir*, "voice"). The syllable of reduplication exhibits *n* for *r*, as in Sanscrit *chañchur*, and similar Greek forms (§. 756.). To *girâmi* (also *gilâmi*), "*deglutio*," belong, amongst other words, the Latin *gula* and *gurgulio*, which latter, in its repeated syllable, replaces the liquid *l* by *r*.

760. The passive form of the Sanscrit intensive has usually an active meaning, and then, by Indian Grammarians, is regarded according to its formation, not as passive, but as a particular form of the intensive, which I nevertheless call deponent, as in its origin it is evidently nothing else than passive. This appears more frequently in classical Sanscrit as the form without *ya*, yet still seldom enough. I know of no examples besides चञ्चूर्यन्ते *chañchûryantê*, "they convey" (Mah. I. 1910.), from चर् *char* (see §. 756.), *lêlihyasê*, "thou lickest," from *lih* (Bhagavad-G. 11. 30.); *dêdîpyamâna*, "shining," from *dîp* (Nal. 3. 12. Draup. 2. 1.). In *dôdhûyamâna* (l. c.), from *dhû* or *dhu*, the passive form has also a passive signification. Of the form without *ya* there occurs the participle present *lêlihat*, Mid. *lêlihâna* "licking," Mah. III. 10394, 12240. The Vêda dialect makes more frequent use of the active form of the intensive: the following are examples: *nânadati*, "they sound,"[*] Rig. V. I. 64. 8. 11.; *abhipra-nônumas*, "we praise," from *nu* (prep. *abhi, pra*, l. c. 78. 1.); *jôhavîmi*, "I summon," with *î* as vowel of conjunction (see §. 753. note), from *hu*, as contracted form of *hvê*, l. c. 34. 12.; *â-navînôt*, "he moved," "stirred," from *nud*, "to move," "to drive" (prep. *â*), Rig. V. V.[†]

---

[*] All reduplicated forms, which combine the personal terminations direct with the root, suppress the *n* of the 3d per. pl. (compare §. 459.). To the root *nad* corresponds the Welch *nadu*, "to cry."

[†] See Westerg., Radices, p. 45, and root *nu*, to which *ânavînôt* likewise, according to its form, might belong; the meaning, however, in the passage

VERBS.

DENOMINATIVES.

761. Denominatives are not so frequently used in Sanscrit as in the kindred languages of Europe. Their formation is effected either by the addition of the character of the 10th Class, or by the affix *ya*, *sya*, and *asya*; both which latter ought probably to be divided into *s-ya* and *as-ya*, so that in them the root of the verb substantive *as* is contained, either entire or after dropping the vowel (compare §. 648.). As the Latin verbs of the 1st, 2d, and 4th conjugations are based on the Sanscrit 10th Class (§. 109^a. 6.), forms like *laud-â-s*[*], *nomin-â-s*, *lu-min-â-s*, *color-â-s*, *fluctu-â-s*, *æstu-â-s*, *domin'-â-s*, *regn'-â-s*, *sorori'-â-s*[†], *cœn'-â-s*, *plant'-â-s*, *pisc-â-ris*, *alb'-ê-s*, *calv'-ê-s*, *can'-ê-s*, *miser'-ê-ris*, *feroc-î-s*, *lasciv'-î-s*, *lipp'-î-s*, *abort'-î-s*, *fin'-î-s*, *sit'-î-s*, correspond to Sanscrit forms such as *kumâr'-aya-si*, " thou playest," from *kumâra*, " a boy;"[‡] *sukh'-aya-si*, " thou

---

sage cited leads to the root *nud*: the *t*, therefore, of the form in question is not a sign of the person, but radical (euphon. for *d*), since the personal character of the 2d and 3d pers. sing. of the imperf., according to §. 94., cannot combine with roots ending in a consonant; hence, *e. g.*, *ayunak*, " thou didst bind," and " he bound," for *ayunaksh*, *ayunakt* (see smaller Sanscrit Grammar, §. 289). With respect to the syllable of reduplication, the form *â-nav-î-nôt* for *ânônôt* is remarkable on account of the insertion of an *î*, as, according to grammatical rules, such an insertion occurs only after *r* and *n*, see §. 757., and smaller Sanscrit Grammar, §§. 500. 501. 508.

[*] I give the 2d per., as the 1st exhibits the conjugational character less plainly, and presents the least resemblance to the other persons.

[†] From *sororius*, not from *soror*; for from the latter would have come *sororo*, not *sororio*.

[‡] The Indian Grammarians wrongly exhibit a root *kumâr*, " to play "— which, if only for the number of syllables, is suspicious—and thence derive *kumâra*, " a boy;" in which I recognise the prefix *ku*, which usually expresses " contempt," but here " diminution," and *mâra*, which does not occur by itself, but is joined with *martya*, " man," as " mortal." In general there occur, among the roots exhibited by Indian Grammarians, many

DENOMINATIVES. 1017

rejoicest," from *sukha,* "contentment;" *yŏktr'-aya-si,* "thou encirclest," from *yŏktra,* "band" (R. *yuj* "to bind"); *kshamaya-si,* "thou supportest," from *kshama,* "patience." From these examples we see that in Sanscrit also the final vowel of the base word is rejected before the verbal character; for otherwise, *e.g.,* from *yŏktra-aya-si* would come *yŏktráyasi.* That in Latin forms like *coen'-á-s* the *á* does not belong to the base noun is seen from this, that the final vowel of bases of the second declension is rejected before the verbal derivatives *á, é,* and *í*; hence, *regn'-á-s, calv'-é-s, lasciv'-í-s.* As to the retention, however, of the organic *u,* viz. that of the fourth declension before *á* (*aestu-á-s, fluctu-á-s*), I would remark, that in Sanscrit also *u* shews itself to be a very firm vowel, inasmuch as it maintains itself before the vowels of nominal derivative suffixes; and, indeed, it moreover receives the Guna increment, while *a* and *i, i.e.* the heaviest and lightest vowel, are dropped; hence, *e.g., mánav-a-s,* "man" (as derived from *Manu*), from *manu*; शौचम् *sauch-a-m,* "purity," from शुचि *súchi,* "pure;" *dásarath-i-s,* "Son of Daśaratha," from *daśaratha.* Before *í,* however, in Latin, the *u* of the fourth declension disappears in denominative verbs, as in the above-mentioned *abort'-í-s.*

762. As a consequence of what has been said in the preceding §., I believe that a suppression of the vowel of the base noun is also to be assumed in Greek denominatives in αω, εω, οω, αζω, ιζω. I therefore divide, *e. g.,* ἀγορ'-άζω*, ἀγορ'-άο-μαι, μορφ'-όω, κνισσ'-όω, πολεμ'-όω, πολεμ'-έω,

---

many denominatives, amongst them also *sukh,* "to rejoice," which contains the prefix *su* (Gr. εὐ), as certainly as दुःख *duḣkh,* "*dolore afficere,*" (from *duḣkha,* "smart,") contains the prefix *dus*=Greek δυς. By the Indian Grammarians, however, *duḣkh* likewise is considered as a simple root.

* I have already, in §. 502., pointed out another mode of viewing the forms αζω and ιζω, but in §. 503. I have given the preference to the above

πολεμ'-ίζω, and recognise in the α of αζω the Sanscrit a of *ayâ-mi*, and in the ζ the corruption of य् *y*, as in ζεύγνυμι compared with the Sanscrit युज् *yuj* and Latin *jungo* (see §. 19.); while in forms in αω, εω, οω, the semi-vowel is suppressed; and, moreover, in the two last forms the very common corruption from α to ε, ο has taken place (§. 3.). It admits of scarce any doubt that in forms in ιζω also the ι is only a weakening of α; for though the weakening of *a* to *i* is not so frequent in Greek as in Latin and Gothic, still it is by no means unprecedented, and occurs, to quote a case tolerably similar to the one before us, in ἵζω, ἵζομαι, compared with the Sanscrit root *sad*, "to place oneself," Gothic *SAT*. (*sita*, "*sat*").

763. The lightness of the vowel *i* may be the reason why the form in ιζω has become more used than that in αζω, and that those bases which experience no abbreviation before the denominative derivative element by the relinquishment of their final letter admit scarce any letter but ι before ζ; hence, *e.g.*, ποδ-ίζω, ἀγων-ίζομαι, ἀκοντ-ίζω, ἀνδρ-ίζω, αἱματ-ίζω, ἀλοκ-ίζω, γυναικ-ίζω, θωρακ-ίζω, κυν-ίζω, μυωπ-ίζω, κερατ-ίζω, κερματ-ίζω, ἑρματ-ίζω; ἑρμ'-άζω, ὀνομ'-άζω, γουν'-άζομαι*, which, I think, ought not to be divided ἑρμά-ζω, ὀνομά-ζω; so easy is it, from the point of view of the Greek in particular, to identify the α of ἑρμάζω, ὀνομάζω, ἀγοράζω, ἀγοράομαι, and the like, with the α of the base noun. For then the analogy of these verbs with ἱππ'-άζομαι, λιθ'-άζω, εἰκ'-άζω (from the base εἰκοτ), ἐνδι'-άω, γενει'-άω, πελεκ'-άω, νεμεσ'-άω, and with the Sanscrit denominatives in *aya*, would be unnecessarily destroyed; for as ο and η, and occasionally υ and ι, are dropped

---

above, and do so now with the greater confidence, as the other members also of our family of languages, the denominatives of which I had not then considered, follow the same principle.

* Not from γονυ, but from the base γουνατ, whence γούνατ-ος, γούνατ-α.

before the derivation αω, αζω*, there is nothing more natural than that α also should give way before the same. But as bases in α and η (from ā, see §. 4.) produce principally denominatives in άω, άζω, and those in o principally such as end in όω, ίζω, from this the influence of the final vowel of the base noun on the choice of the vowel of the derivative may be inferred; α and η favour the retention of the original α, while o, which is itself a corruption of α, readily permits the α of the derivative to be weakened to o, in which it seems to re-appear unchanged, but which (if we wish to allow in its full extent the transmission of apparently autochthonic Greek forms from the time of the unity of language) presents no obstacle to our placing on the same footing as regards their principle of formation, verbs like πολεμ(o)-όω, χρυσ(o)-όω, ἀγκυλ(o)-όω, and such as αἱματ-όω, ἀρρεν-όω, πυρ-όω, κατοφρυ-όω, θαλασσ(α)-όω, κνισσ(α)όω, and to our recognising such verbs as ἀγορ(α)-άο-μαι, τολμ(α)άω, διψ(α)-άω, νικ(η)-άω, as analogous with κυν-άω, γενει(o)-άω, λοχ(o)-άω, ἀντι(o)-άω, νεμεσ(ι)-άω, πελεκ(υ)-άω. The proposition appears to me incontrovertible that the Greek denominatives in αζω, αω, εω, οω, ιζω, correspond to the Sanscrit in aya (1st per. ayâ-mi, Zend ayê-mi); and that, as in Sanscrit, Zend, and Latin, so also in Greek, the final vowel of the theme of the base noun is, for the most part, suppressed before the vowel of the derivative†: where, however, it is retained, which is only at times the case with ι and υ, the vowel of the verbal derivative also remains after it (δηρι-άο-μαι, ὀφρυ-όω, ἰχθυ-άω). Forms like δηρί-ο-μαι, μητί-ο-μαι, μηνί-ω, μεθύ-ω, δακρύ-ω, belong to another class of denominatives, which exists also in Sanscrit, of which hereafter.

764. In German, also, the final vowels of nominal bases

---

* Examples, in which ι and υ are retained, are κλαυσι-άω, ὀκρι-άω, δηρι-άομαι, ἰχθυ-άω.

† G. Curtius is of a different opinion ("*Contributions to the Comparison of Language*," pp. 119, 120).

are suppressed before the vowel or *y* (for *ay*) of the verbal derivative, which is based on the Sanscrit *aya*; hence, in Gothic *audag'-ya*, "I account happy," from the base *audaga* (nom. *audag'-s*, see §. 135), "happy;" *gaur'-ya*, "I sadden," from *gaura*, nom. *gaur'-s*, "sad;" *skaft'-ya*, "I make," from *skafti*, "creation," nom. *skaft'-s*;"* *manv'-ya*, "I prepare," from *manvu*, nom. *manvu-s*, "ready;" *maurthr'-ya*, "I murder," from *maurthra*, nom. *maurthr* (see §. 153.) "murder;"† *tagr'-ya*, "I weep," from *tagra*, nom. *tagr'-s*, "a tear," (Greek δάκρυ, Sanscrit *aśru*, from *daśru*). Among those Gothic denominatives which have retained in the present the last syllable of the Sanscrit derivative *aya*, the verb *ufárskadv-ya*, "I overshadow," stands alone, since this verb has retained the final vowel of the base *skadu* (nom. *-us*) before the verbal derivative (with euphonic change into *v*), while other bases in *u* follow the general principle; hence, *thaurs'-yan*, "to thirst" (impers. *thaursyith mik*, I thirst," literally, "it is a thirst to me,") from *thaursu* (nom. *-us*), "dry;" *dauth'-ya*, "I slay," from *dau-thu-s*, "death;"‡ as in Greek, θανατ'-όω from θανατο. The following are derivatives belonging here, and springing from bases ending in a consonant: *namn-ya*, "I name," from *naman* (nom. *namô*, see §. 141.); and *aug'-ya*, "I shew," from *augan* (nom. *augô*), "an eye." The former, like the Latin *nomin-o*, and Greek forms like αἱματ-όω, αἱματ-ίζω, preserves the final consonant of the base, but has, however, admitted an internal abbreviation, like that of the Sanscrit weakest

---

* This does not occur in the simple form, but compounded: *ga-skaft'-s*, "creation," "creature;" *ufar-skaft'-s*, "commencement."

† Compare Sanscrit *mâr-ayâmi*, "I make to die;" the Gothic suffix *thra*=Sanscrit *tra*, of which hereafter.

‡ Scarcely from *dauth(a)-s*, "dead," for the Old High German clearly comes from *tôd* (theme *tôda*), "death," not from *tôt* (nom. masc. *tôtêr*), "dead."

DENOMINATIVES. 1021

case (nâmn-as, "nominis"): on the other hand, aug-ya (for augan-ya or augin-ya) follows the principle already mentioned in §. 503., by which Sanscrit denominatives are governed, such as varm'-ayâ-mi, "I harness," for varman-ayâ-mi, from varman. Compare, besides the Greek formations discussed l. c., also derivatives from comparatives; as, βελτι(ον)-όω, μει(ον)-όω, ἐλασσ(ον)-όω, κακι(ον)-όω.* In Greek, also, bases in Σ reject their final consonant, together with the vowel preceding it, which is the less surprising, as this class of words has in the declension, too, preserved but few traces of the σ of the base (see §. 128.). Hence, πληρ (εσ)-όω, from πληρες (see §. 146.); ἀλγ(εσ)-έω, from ἀλγες; ἀσθεν(εσ)-έω, from ἀσθενες; τευχ(εσ)-ίζω, from τευχες; γηρ-(ασ)-άω, from γηρας (§. 128.).

765. We return to the Gothic, in order to adduce some denominatives from Grimm's second and third conjugations of weak verbs. The second conjugation, which exhibits $ô = â$ (§. 69.) for the Sanscrit aya, and has therefore, like the Latin, first rejected the य़ y of aya, and then contracted into one long vowel the vowels which, by the loss of the y, touch one another, yields, e.g., fisk'-ô-s, "thou fishest," for comparison with the Latin pisc'-â-ris. The Gothic base fiska (nom. fisk'-s, see §. 135.) has abandoned its a, as the Latin pisci its i, before the vowel of the derivative (see §. 761.). The Gothic thiudan'-ô-s, "thou reignest," from the base thiudana (nom. -n'-s), "king," resembles, in its principle of formation, the Latin domin'-â-s, as the Gothic first strong declension masculine and neuter and the Latin second on one side, and the Gothic second weak conjugation and the Latin first on the other side, are in their origin fully identical. To Latin denominatives from the first declension, like cœn'-â-s (see §. 761.), correspond Gothic

---

* On the other hand, πλεον-άζω, not πλε'-αζω.

verbs of the same class; as, *fairin'-ô-s*, "thou blamest," from the base *fairinô* (nom. *-na*), "blame." To *aestu-â-s, fluctu-â-s*, corresponds *lust'-ô-s*, from the base *lustu*, "desire," "longing," with the rejection of the *u*, however, of the nominal base. Bases in *an* weaken their *a* to *i*, as in the genitive and dative; hence, *frauyin-ô-s*, "thou reignest," from *frauyan*, "lord" (nom. *frauya*, gen. *frauyin-s*), as in Latin, *nomin-â-s, lumin-â-s* (§. 761.); so *gudyin-ô-s*, "thou administerest the priest's office," from *gudyan*, nom. *gudya*, "priest." Some bases terminating in *a* add *n* before the formation of a denominative, and likewise weaken the *a* of the base to *i*; thus, *skalkin-ô-s*, "thou servest," from *skalka*, nom. *skalk'-s*, "servant," gen. *skalki-s* (see §. 191.); *hôrin-ô-s*, μοιχεύεις, from *hôra*, nom. *hôr'-s*, "adulterer;" *reikin-ô-s*, "thou rulest," from *reikya*, nom. *reiki* (see §. 153.), "rich." That class of weak verbs which has contracted the Sanscrit *aya* to *ai*, and stands on the same footing with the Latin second conjugation (Grimm's third weak conjugation), presents, *e.g.*, *arm'-ai-s*, "thou commiseratest," from *arma*, nom. *arm-s*; as, in Latin, *miser'-ê-ris* from *miseru* (*miser* for *miseru-s*); *ga-hveil'-ai-s*, "thou stayest," from *hveilô*, nom. *hveila*, "time," "delay."

766. The Sclavonic uses, for the formation of denominatives, that conjugational form which corresponds to the Sanscrit tenth Class. But, as has been remarked in §. 505., not only Dobrowsky's third conjugation belongs to the Sanscrit verbal class just mentioned, but also the greater portion of those verbs which, in §. 500., I wrongly classed all, without exception, under the Sanscrit fourth Class; whilst I can now recognise as sister forms of the Sanscrit fourth Class, of Latin verbs like *capio*, and Gothic like *vahs-ya*, "I grow," only such verbs of Dobrowsky's first conjugation as combine the formative elements commencing with a consonant; for example, the *ch* of the preterite, the *l* and *v* of the participle preterite active, and of the

DENOMINATIVES. 1023

gerund preterite, as also the suffixes ти *ti* and ть *t* of the infinitive and supine, direct with the root, a circumstance which occurs only with respect to a few roots terminating in a vowel; *e.g.*, from пи, " to drink " (Sanscrit *pí*, Class 4, middle), comes пиѭ *pi-yû*, "I drink" (Sanscrit *pí-yê*), пикши *pi-ye-shi*, " thou drinkest " (Sanscrit *pí-ya-sê*), пихъ *pi-ch*, " I drank," пилъ *pi-l*, " having drunk," пивъ *pi-v* (gerund), пити *pi-ti*, " to drink," sup. питъ *pi-t*. Those verbs, however, in ѭ *yû* or аѭ *ayû*, which, in the said forms, interpose an *a* between the root, or the verbal theme, and the formative element which follows (Paradigm B. of Dobrowsky), I am now of opinion must be compared with the Sanscrit tenth Class; so that *yû*, and more fully *ayû*, of the 1st person, corresponds to the Sanscrit *ayâ-mi* and the Lithuanian *oyu*, *ûyu*, *iyu* (see §. 506.). Compare, *e.g.*, рыдаѭ *ryd-ayu*, " I lament," with the Sanscrit causal *rôd-ayâmi*, " I make to weep " (R. *rud*, " to weep"), and the Lithuanian *raud-oyu**, " I lament."

SINGULAR.

SANSCRIT.	OLD SCLAVONIC.	LITHUANIAN.
rôd-ayâ-mi,	*ryd-ayû*,	*raud-oyu*.
rôd-aya-si,	*ryd-aye-shi*,	*raud-oyi*.
rôd-aya-ti,	*ryd-aye-ty*,	*raud-oya*.

DUAL.

rôd-ayâ-vas,	*ryd-aye-va*,	*raud-oya-wa*.
rôd-aya-thas,	*ryd-aye-ta*,	*raud-oya-ta*.
rôd-aya-tas,	*ryd-aye-ta*,	*raud-oya*.

---

* As the Sanscrit *ô* is a contraction of *au*, so in this respect the Lithuanian form corresponds still more than the Sclavonic to the Sanscrit causal. The Sclavonic ы *y* corresponds (according to §. 225. c.) to the Sanscrit radical *u*.

1024   VERBS.

	PLURAL.	
SANSCRIT.	OLD SCLAVONIC.	LITHUANIAN.
rôd-ayâ-mas,	ryd-aye-m,	raud-oya-me.
rôd-aya-tha,	ryd-aye-te,	raud-oya-te.
rôd-aya-nti.	ryd-ayûty*,	raud-oya.

767. Both in Sclavonic and in Lithuanian the *y* of this conjugational class is dropped before the formative elements which begin with a consonant, and then, in Lithuanian, only the *o* is left, and, in Sclavonic, the more ancient *a*, which corresponds to it; hence, the infinitive in Lithuanian is *raud-o-ti*, in Sclavonic *ryd-a-ti*, and the future in Lithuanian *raud-o-su*. The Sanscrit, on the contrary, preserves the य *y* before formations beginning with a consonant, by the insertion of a vowel of conjunction, viz. *i*; hence, *rôd-ay-i-shyâmi* corresponding to the *raud-o-su* just mentioned; and in the infinitive *rôd-ay-i-tum* answering to *raud-o-ti*, *ryd-a-ti*†, sup. рыдать *ryd-a-t*. The verbs under Paradigm B. in Dobrowsky and Kopitar have lost, in the present and the forms connected therewith, the *a* of the class character, and retain only the *y* (*glagol-yû*, "I speak," for *glagol-ayû*) before formations beginning with a consonant, but exhibit the *a* in other places, in accordance with the verbs which have *ayû* in the present; thus, *e.g.*, глаголахъ *glagol-a-ch*, "I spoke," *glagol-a-ti* "to speak," like рыдахъ *ryd-a-ch*, рыдати *ryd-a-ti*. The Lithuanian presents no forms analogous to verbs like *glagol-yû*, since forms like *myl-iu*, plural *myl-i-me*, correspond to Dobrowsky's third conjugation (*e.g.*, *vol-yû*, plural *vol-i-m*, see §. 506.), while forms like *penu*, *laikau*, plural *pen-a-me*, *laik-o-me* (see §. 506.), exhibit the Sanscrit *aya* in the abbreviated form,

---

* From *rydayo-nty*, see §. 255. g.

† I do not mean by this comparison to assert that the Lithuanian and Sclavonic infinitive suffix is connected with that of the Sanscrit language.

which in *raud-oyu*, рыдаѭ *ryd-ayû*, enters, save in the present indicative and its derivatives, only before suffixes beginning with a consonant.

768. The Lithuanian and Sclavonic nominal bases, like those of the kindred languages already mentioned, when they terminate with a vowel, which is generally the case, reject this before the verbal derivative; hence, in Lithuanian *balt'-oyu*, "I appear white," *balt'-inu*, "I make white,"* from *balta*, nom. *-ta-s*, "white;" *dŭwan'-oyu* "I bestow," from *dŭwana* fem. "gift;" *czyst'-iyu*, "I purify," from *czysta*, nom. *-ta-s*, "pure;"† *gataw'-oyu* and *gataw'-iyu*, "I make ready," from *gatawa'-s*, "ready;" *dal'-iyu*, "I divide," from *dali-s*, "portion;" *apyok'-iu*, "I deride," from *apyoka-s* "jest;" *didd'-inu*, "I enlarge," from *diddi-s*; *brang'-inu*, "I render dear," from *brangu-s*. The following are examples of denominatives in Old Sclavonic: дѣлаѭ *dyel'-ayû*, "I make," дѣлахъ *dyel'-a-ch*, "I made," from дѣло *dyelo*, "work;" подобѣть *podob'-ye-ty*, "it is fitting," infin. подовати *podob'-a-ti*, from *podoba*, "use;" знаменаѭ *znamena-yû*, "I denote," from знамен *znamen*, nom. *znamya* (see §. 264.), "mark" (Kopitar Glagol. p. 73.); глаголѭ *glagol'-yû*, "I speak," infin. *glagol'-a-ti*, from *glagolo*, nom. *glagol*, "word." In forms in ȣѭ *ûyu*, infin. *ov-a-ti*, the ȣ *û* appears to me, in departure from what has been remarked at §. 255. h. as a contraction of *aʋ* or *ou* (§. 255. f.), and the *v* of *ov-a-ti* as the euphonic alteration of the final element of the diphthong ȣ *û = ov*. The corresponding form in Lithuanian is *auyu*, the first *u* of which, before vowels, likewise changes into its equivalent semi-vowel; hence, *e. g.*, *naszl'-áuyu*, "I live in widowhood," from *naszlẽ*

---

* Denominatives in *inu* have all a causal signification, compare §. 744.

† With the formations in *iyu* compare the Greek in ιζω = ιγω, see §. 762; *iyu* and *oyu* have the same relation to one another as ιζω and αζω have to one another in Greek.

"widow," pret. *naszl'-aw-au*, fut. *naszl'-au-su*. So in Old Sclavonic; вдовѵю *vdov'-ŭ-yŭ*, pret. вдововахъ *vdov'-ov-ach*, infin. вдововати *vdov'-ov-a-ti*, from вдова *vdova*, "widow" = Sanscrit *vidhavá*. именѵю *imen-ŭ-yŭ*, "I name," infin. именовати *imen-ov-a-ti*, from the base имен *imen*. Other examples of this kind occur in Dobrowsky, p. 372. We may regard the *ŭ*, *ov*, of these forms as a lengthening of the theme of the base noun, and divide, therefore, as follows: *vdovŭ-yŭ*, *vdovov-a-ti*, *imenŭ-yŭ*, *imenov-a-ti*, where we must recall what has been observed at §. 263. regarding the unorganic introduction of Sclavonic bases into the declension in ъı *y*. In denominatives in ѣю *yeyŭ*, as, *e.g.*, богатѣю *bogat'-yeyŭ*, "I am or become rich," infin. богатѣти *bogat'-ye-ti*, from the base *bogato*, nom. *bogat*, ѣ *ye* corresponds to the Sanscrit *a* of *ayâmi*, which will not appear surprising when we consider the peculiarity of the Sclavonic in constantly prefixing to vowels a *y*. The following are examples of denominatives from Dobrowsky's third conjugation (see §. 505.): женюся *schen'-yŭ-sya* "I marry," infin. женитися *schen'-i-ti-sya*, from жена *schena*, "woman;" готовлю *gotov'-lyŭ* (euphonic for *vyŭ*), "I prepare," infin. готовити *gotov'-i-ti*, from готово *gotovo*, nom. m. готовъ *gotov* "ready;" цѣлю *zyel'-yŭ*, "I heal," infin. цѣлити *zyel'-i-ti*, from цѣло *zyelo*, nom. цѣлъ *zyel*, "healthy."

769. I have already, in §. 502., compared the Greek denominatives in σσω, as αἱμάσ-σω from αἱματ-yω (see §. 501.), with those in Sanscrit formed with य *ya*. While, however, in Sanscrit, the final vowel of the base noun, if short, is lengthened, the same in Greek, according to the analogy of §. 762., is dropped; hence, *e. g.*, ἀγγέλλω from ἀγγελ(ο)-yω, ποικίλλω from ποικιλ(ο)-yω, αἰκάλλω from αἰκαλ(ο)-yω, μαλάσσω from μαλακ(ο)-yω, μειλίσσω from μειλιχ(ο)-yω. Bases in ρ, ρο, and ν, transfer the *y*, vocalized to *i*, to the preceding syllable, instead of assimilating it to

DENOMINATIVES. 1027

the preceding consonant; hence, τεκμαί-ρ-ο-μαι from τεκμαρ-
γο-μαι, from τέκμαρ; καθαίρ-ω from καθαρ(ο)-γω, from κα-
θαρο; μεγαίρ-ω from μεγαρ-γω, not from μέγα-ς, but from the
base of the oblique cases μεγαλο, the λ being exchanged for ρ
(see §. 20.); μελαίνω from μελαν-γω, from the base μελαν; ποι-
μαίνω, πεπαίνω, τεκταίνω, ἀφραίνω, εὐφραίνω, from ποιμαν-γω,
&c., from the bases ποιμεν, πεπον, τεκτον, ἀφρον, εὔφρον, with
the retention, however, of the original α, instead of the unorganic vowels ε, ο (see §. 3.). In denominatives from substantive bases in ματ, as ὀνομαίνω, κυμαίνω, σπερμαίνω, σημαίνω,
χειμαίνω, the ν probably springs from the original form of the
suffix ματ, as this is a corruption of μαν, and answers to the
Sanscrit *man*, and Latin *men*, *min*.* It appears, however, to
me impossible to determine with certainty as to the case of
the preponderating number of denominatives in αινω, whose
base nouns terminate neither in ν, nor in a letter which can
have proceeded from ν. I cannot, however, believe that the
Greek language has produced such formations independently,
and that, therefore, they are entirely unconnected with the
kind of forms handed down from the period of the unity of
language. Perhaps the bases in ν, and those which terminate in a consonant which is a corruption of ν, have only
supplied the type for the formations in αινω; and verbs like
ἀλεαίνω, ἀκταίνω, γλυκαίνω, θερμαίνω, ἐριδαίνω, κηραίνω, have
followed the beaten path, in the same way as, in German,
many bases have pressed into the so-called weak declension, in that they have extended the original limits of the
base by the addition of *n*, or the syllable *an*. Perhaps,
too, αινω, in a portion of that class of verbs which have
this termination, viz. those which have sprung from other
verbs, is some way connected with the Sanscrit formation
aya, with which we have before compared Lithuanian

---

* See §. 497., and compare G. Curtius *De nominum Græcorum formatione*, p. 40.

causals and denominatives in *inu* (see §. 745.). If the ν in those denominatives which have not proceeded from bases in ν, or ματ for μαν, is a corruption of the *y* (compare §. 745.), then the αι preceding might be regarded as representing the *â* (compare §. 753.), which, in most Sanscrit denominative bases in य *ya*, precedes the semi-vowel; for though this *â* belongs to the nominal base, and is in general a lengthened form of short *a* (*chirâ-yati*, "he delays," from *chira*, "long"), still the same, in course of time, might come to be regarded as a portion of the derivative, and be suppressed before its Greek representative αι, as in the formations in αω, αζω, &c. Those verbs in αινω which appear to spring from more simple verbs, might, in their principle of formation, be contrasted in a different manner with the Sanscrit; as, *e.g.*, αὐαίνω (ἀύω), δραίνω (δράω), κραδαίνω (κραδάω), χαλαίνω (χαλάω), stand in the same relation to the corresponding short forms, as, in the Vêda dialect, *charaṇyâmi*, "I go,"[*] does to *charâmi*. The broader forms come from the noun of action चरण *charaṇa*, "the going" (euphonic for -न -*na*, on account of the *r* preceding). Some Sanscrit verbs, however, of this kind do not exactly correspond to the noun of action, from which they spring, but exhibit a weakening or contraction of the vowel, or the pure radical vowel instead of the gunised one of the base word, seemingly on account of the incumbrance caused by the verbal derivative; thus, *bhuraṇyâmi*, "I receive" (Rig. V. 50. 6. *bhuraṇyantam anu*), from *bharaṇa*, "the bearing," "receiving" (R. *bhar, bhṛi*); *turaṇyâmi*, "I hasten" (Rig. V. 121. 1. *turaṇyan*) from *tvaraṇa*, "the hastening" (R. *tvar*); *churaṇyâmi*, "I steal" (see Westerg. Radices p. 337.), from *chôraṇa*, "the stealing" (R. *chur*). As, according to rule, a noun of action in *ana*

---

[*] It occurs in combination with the preposition *ut*, "out," in the Yajur-Vêda, see Westergaard Rad. p. 337.

DENOMINATIVES.

may be formed from every root, and on this, too, are based all the German and Ossetian infinitives*, it cannot surprise us that, in Greek, a few denominatives of this kind remain, whose base nouns have been lost; and thus, e. g., αὐαίνω, from αὐανγω, would come from a lost nominal base αὐανο, or αὐανη. Μαραίνω, which has no short verb corresponding to it, reminds us of the Sanscrit noun of action mara-ṇa-m, "the dying," from mar, mṛi, "to die," causal mârayâmi. Let attention be given to the Greek feminine abstracts in ονη, which correspond to the Sanscrit in anâ, or aṇâ.† Verbs in ανω may, in part, owe their origin to obsolete nominal bases in ανο.

770. How necessary it is, in the explanation of denominatives, to look back to an earlier state of language, and at the same time to examine the kindred dialects, is shewn by an interesting class of Gothic denominatives, in which the n likewise plays a part, though it is no way connected with that of Greek verbs in αινω, in whatever way these latter may be explained. I rather recognise, as already stated in my " Conjugational System," (pp. 115, 116), a connection in Gothic verbs like ga-fullna, " impleor," us-gutna, " effundor," distaurna, " disrumpor," and-bundna, " solvor," ga-hailna, " sanor," fra-qvistna, " perdor," ga-vakna, " excitor," us-lukna, " aperior," dauthna, " morior," with the Sanscrit passive participles in na; as, bhug-na, " bent," to which the Greek verbals in νο-ς correspond (στυγ-νός, σεμ-νός &c.), and from which the Gothic passive participles have somewhat diverged, in that they do not append the suffix na direct to the root, but retain the class syllable; thus, biuga-n(a)-s, " bent," answering to भुग्नस् bhug-na-s; while the verbs just mentioned point to a period of the language,

---

* E. g., Gothic bindan, Osset. bathin, " to bind "=Sanscrit bandhana, " the binding."

† Examples are: yâchanâ, " precatio;" arhaṇâ, " honoris testificatio."

when the suffix was still, as in Sanscrit and Greek, added direct to the root; so that, *e. g.*, *ga-skaidna*, "I separate myself" (1. Cor. vii. 11. *yaba gaskaidnai*, ἐὰν χωρισθῇ), answers better than *skaid-a-ns*, "separated," to the Sanscrit छिन्न *chhin-nas* (euphonic for *chhid-nas*), "cleft." Compare, also, and-*bund-na*, "I am loosed (set free)," with *bund-a-n(a)-s*, "bound;" *bi-auk-na*, "I am enlarged," with *bi-auk-a-n(a)-s*, "enlarged;" *fralus-na*, "I am dissolved, destroyed, lost," with *lusa-n(a)-s*, "loosened" (Sanscrit *lû-na-s* "cut off," "torn off"); *galuk-na*, "I am closed," with *ga-luk-a-n(a)-s*, "closed;" *and-lêt-na*, "I am unloosed," with *lêt-a-n(a)-s*, "tranquil;" *af-lif-na*, "I am left remaining," "I remain over" (περιλείπομαι), with the to-be-presupposed *lib-a-n(a)-s*, "left remaining" (*laibôs*, "remnant"), for *lif-a-n(a)-s*, as the law for the transposition of sounds (§. 87.) would lead us to expect, in answer to the Greek λείπω*, from the lost verb *leiba, laif, libum* (Old High German, *bi-lîbu*, "I remain," *bileib*, "I remained," *bi-libumês*, "we remained"); *ufar-haf-na*, "I raise myself above" (ὑπερ-αίρομαι), with *ufar-haf-ya-n(a)-s*, "raised over," "elevated;" *dis-taur-na*, "disrumpor*," with *dis-taur-a-n(a)-s*, "diruptus;" *ga-thaurs-na*, "I dry up" (ξηραίνομαι), with *ga-thaurs-a-n(a)-s*, "ἐξηραμμένος," from the non-existing verb *ga-thairsa, ga-thars, gathaursum*. *Dis-hnaup-na*, "dirumpor," from the root *hnup* (*hniupa, hnaup, hnupum, hnupans*), is so far irregular as it has the radical vowel gunised, whilst otherwise denominatives in *na*, like the passive participle with the same termination, attach themselves to one of the lighter forms of the verbal theme. *Us-geis-na*, also, "*percellor*," "*stupeo*," from the to-be-presupposed *geisa, gais, gisum* (Grimm. II. p. 46.), is con-

---

* In departure from what has been remarked at p. 441, I now agree with Benfey (Greek Wurzellexicon II. p. 11) in taking the Sanscrit root *rich* (from *rik*), "to separate," "to leave," as the root akin to the Latin *lic* (*linquo*), Greek λιπ, and Gothic *lif, lib*.

DENOMINATIVES. 1031

trary to the common analogy, and should be *us-gisna*. But *dis-skrit-na*, "*findor*," and *tundna*, "*uror*," the base verbs of which are likewise lost (*skreita, skrait, skritum, tinda, tand, tundum*), exhibit the regular vowel.

771. After that *na* in Gothic, as in the above-mentioned instances, had once raised itself to be the exponent of the passive relation, it might also extend itself to the adjective bases, and thus denominatives in *na* and *ya* (for *ya* also *ai*, see §. 109.ª 6.), as passives (or verbs neuter) and transitive active verbs, stand mutually answering to each other. The final vowel of nominal bases are dropped as well before *na* as before *ya* (=Sanscrit *aya*, see §. 674.); hence, *e. g.*, from the base *fulla* (nom. masc. *full'-s*), "full," *full'-na*, "*impleor*," *full'-ya*, "*impleo*;" from *mikila*, "great" (nom. *mikil'-s*), *mikil'-na*, "*magnificor*," *mikil'-ya*, "*magnifico*" (compare μεγαλίζω); from *veiha* (*veih'-s*), "holy," *veih'-na*, "*sanctificor*," *veih'-a* (*veih'-ais*) "*sanctifico*;" from *ga-nôha* (*ganôh'-s*), "enough," *ga-nôh'-na*, "*expleor*," *ganôh'-ya*, "*expleo*;" from *managa* (*manag'-s*), "much," *manag'-na*, "*abundo*" ("I am made much"); *manag'-ya*, "*augeo*;" from *gabiga* (*gabig'-s*), "rich," *gabig'-na*, "*locupletatus sum*," *gabig'-ya* "*locupleto*." It cannot surprise us that the base words of denominatives in *na* cannot be all cited from the lingual sources which have been preserved to our time, nor that some were already obsolete in the time of Ulfila, but survive only in the denominatives, of which they were the parents. Thus, *e. g.*, an adjective base *drôba* (*drôbs*), "troubled" (Anglos. *dróf*), does not occur; whence comes *drôb'-ya*, "I trouble," "excite," "shake," and *drôb'-na*, "I am troubled." Inseparable prepositions precede the denominatives, as they do the primitive verbal themes, though the base word be simple; as, *e. g.*, from *blinda* (*blind'-s*), "blind," comes *ga-blind'-na*, "I am blinded," and *ga-blind-ya*, "I blind," "dazzle;" from *dumba* (*dumb'-s*), "dumb," *af-dumb'-na*, "I become dumb," "grow speechless" (Mark

iv. 39. *afdumbn* πεφίμωσο). It is possible, that from the simple adjective bases at first simple denominatives proceeded, and from these, which no longer exist, or cannot be cited, compound denominatives; thus, from *dumbn* came, at first, *dumbna*, and thence *afdumbna*; as, in Latin, from *mutu-s, mutesco*, and thence *obmutesco*.

772. To return to the Sanscrit, we must remark that denominatives formed with य *ya* partly express a wish; as, *e. g.*, *patí-yâmi*, "I wish for a spouse," from *pati*; *putrí-yâmi*, "I wish a son, or for a son, or children," from *putra*. These forms lead us to the Greek desiderative denominatives in ιαω, which, however, in departure from the Sanscrit, reject the final vowel of the base noun, while the latter lengthen it, but in doing so weaken *â* to *í*; thus, *putrí-yâmi* for *putrâ-yâmi*.* And Greek forms like θανατ'-ιάω, στρατηγ'-ιάω, κλαυσ'-ιάω, are properly based on the causal form of the just-mentioned Sanscrit denominatives in *ya*; thus, θανατ'-ιάω, θανατ'-ιάο-μεν = Sanscrit forms like *putrí-yayâ-mi, putrí-yayâ-mas*, while *putrí-yâ-mi, putrí-yâ-mas*, would lead us to expect Greek forms like θανατ'-ιω, θανατ'-ιο-μεν, or, according to §. 502., θανασσω, θανασσομεν. It deserves, however, notice, that, in Sanscrit, denominatives in *ya* occasionally adopt the causal form without a causal signification; thus we find, without a causal meaning,† the gerund *asûyayitvâ*, which belongs to the causal form, but is used as coming from the denominative *asû-yâmi*, "I curse," "execrate" (intrans. "I am wrath," from *asu* "life").

---

* But we find in the Vêda dialect *aśva-yâmi*, "*equos cupio*," from *aśva*, "a horse" (S. V. II. 1. 1. 11. 2.).

† Nal. 14. 17.: *krôdhâd asûyayitvâ tam*, "*irâ exsecrando eum.*" On the other hand, *dhûmâyayâmi*, the causal of *dhûmâ-yâmi*, "*fumo*," has also a causal meaning: *dhûmâyayan diśati*, "causing the regions of the world to smoke."

773. With the causal form of denominatives in य ya may be compared also the Latin in igâ. The i would then be the final vowel of the base noun, either in an unaltered form, as in *miti-gâ-s, levi-gâ-s, navi-gâ-s*[*]; or the weakening of a heavier vowel (see §. 6.), as in *fumi-gâ-s* (for *fumu-gâ-s*, or *fumo-gâ-s*), *remi-gâ-s, clari-gâ-s, casti-gâ-s* (but *pur-gâ-s* with i suppressed); or the unorganic extension of a base ending in a consonant, as in *liti-gâ-s* opposed to *jur-gâ-s*. The g must be taken as the hardening of y, which indeed occurs, perhaps, nowhere else in Latin, but is not uncommon in the kindred languages (see pp. 110. and 993.), and with which is connected the fact, that in Greek ζ often stands as the hardened form of an original y (see §. 19.). The â of the forms in question, as generally of those in the first conjugation (except where it is radical), must be the contraction of the Sanscrit a(y)a; and thus *fumi-gâ-s* would be, as it were, the Latinization of the Sanscrit *dhûmâ-ya(y)a-si*, "thou makest to smoke"[†]. If, however, we agree with the common opinion, which, however, is opposed by Düntzer, ("Doctrine of the Latin Formation of Words" p. 140,) in recognising in the verbs in *igo* composites with *ago*, we must then divide thus, *mit'-igo, fum'-igo*, &c., and assume a weakening of the radical a of *ago* to i, and a transfer of *igo* from the third conjugation to the first, both of which things occur in *facere*, which, at the end of compounds, becomes *ficare*.

774. Bases which, in Sanscrit, end in n, reject that letter as well in desideratives as also in other denominatives in ya. Other consonants, also, are occasionally dropped before the denominative suffix य ya; hence, *vṛihâ-yê*, "I become great" (Mid.), from *vṛihat*, in the strong cases *vṛihant*, pro-

---

[*] I retract the conjecture expressed at §. 109^b. 1.
[†] See p. 379 and §. 772. note **.

perly a participle present from *varh, vrih,* "to grow." Thus *tripâ-yê, rôhâ-yê,* from the participles *tripant, tripat, rôhant, rôhat* (see Westergaard Rad. pp. 337, 339). We might consequently expect from the participle of the auxiliary future forms like *dâ-syâ-yê* for *dâs-yat-yê*, or *dâsyant-yê;* and it follows that we may regard the Greek desideratives in σείω as denominatives, *i. e.* derive them from the participle, and not from the indicative future. The ε, for instance, of παρα-δω-σείω must then be looked upon as the thinning of the ο of the suffix οντ, and παρα-δωσε'-ίω must therefore be derived from παραδωσο(ντ)-ιω; just as above, §. 503., ἀεκ'-αζόμενος from ἀεκοντ. But if Greek desideratives in σείω spring from a future participle, then Latin desideratives in *turio,* as *cœnaturio, nupturio, parturio, esurio* (from *es-turio,* see §. 101.), may be placed by their side as analogous forms* in which the *i* appears to correspond to the Sanscrit suffix य *ya,* though usually the *í* of the Latin fourth conjugation corresponds to the Sanscrit *aya,* while the simple *ya* is represented by the *i* of the third conjugation. As, however, the *i* of the third conjugation is occasionally altered to the *í* of the fourth†, it cannot surprise us that some denominatives of the Latin fourth conjugation should, in their origin, belong, not to the Sanscrit formation *aya,* but to *ya;* and so *equ'-io, equ'-is,* both as regards its base word and its derivation, might be compared with the Vêdian *aśvâyâmi,* "*equos cupio,*" mentioned above (§.772. Note*).

775. Denominatives with a desiderative meaning are

---

* The short *u* of verbs in *turio* occasions me no difficulty in deducing them from the participle in *tûru-s.* The incumbrance of the verbal derivation appears to have occasioned the shortening of the vowel, as in denominatives like *colŏro, honŏro,* compared with *color, colô-ris, honor, honôr-is.*

† See §. 500., and Struve *On the Latin Declension and Conjugation,* p. 200 (from *fodio,* in Plaut., *fodîri;* from *gradior, aggrediri;* from *pario,* in Enn., *parîre;* from *morior, morîmur*).

DENOMINATIVES. 1035

also formed in Sanscrit by the suffixes *sya* and *asya*; *e. g.*, *vṛishasyâmi*, "to long for the bull;" *aśva-syâmi*, "to long for the stallion" (*equio*); *madhv-asyâmi*, "to wish for honey." We have already noticed the agreement of these forms with that of the auxiliary future, as also, as respects the sibilant, with the desideratives which spring from verbal roots. From Latin may be adduced imitatives in *sso*, as has already been done by Düntzer ("Doctrine of the Latin formation of words" p. 135). Whence, *e. g.*, *patri-sso* would stand by assimilation for *patri-syo* (compare the Prâkrit futures, §. 655.), with *i* as the extension of the base noun, as in *patri-bus*. The *i* of *attici-sso, grœci-sso*, is the weakening of the final vowel of the base noun. The first conjugation, however, does not admit of comparison with Sanscrit desideratives like *aśva-sya-ti*, which leads us to expect the Latin third conjugation, as in derivatives from verbs like *cape-sso, incipi-sso, lace-sso, peti-sso*, which admit of comparison with Sanscrit verbal desideratives in *sa*—in so far as their *s* really stands for *sy*—or also with the auxiliary future. The *e* or *i* of Latin forms is, however, most probably the class vowel of the third conjugation, though usually this does not extend beyond the special tenses. *Incesso*, from *cedo*, is probably an abbreviation of *incedesso*; and *arcesso*, if it comes from *cedo*, of *arcedesso*.

776. Outwardly a similarity presents itself between the Sanscrit nominal desideratives in *sya* or *asya*, and the Latin inchoatives in *asco* and *esco*: these, however, as respects their principle of formation, are scarcely transmitted from the time of the unity of language, but most probably first originated on Roman ground, by the annexation, as it appears to me, of the verb substantive with the meaning "to become" to nominal bases, which, when they terminate in a vowel, drop this before the vowel of the auxiliary verb (compare §. 522.). Thus, as *pos-sum* from *pot-sum* for *poti-sum, pot-eram* for *poti-eram*; so, *e. g.*, *puell'-asco, ir'-*

ascor, puer'-asco (from the base *pueru,-rŏ*), *tener'-asco,* and *tener'-esco, acet'-asco, gel'-asco* (from *gelu*), *herb'-esco, exaqu'-esco, plum'-esco, flamm'-esco, amar'-esco, aur'-esco, clar'-esco, vetust'-esco, dulc'-esco, juven'-esco, celebr'-esco, corn'-esco.* Whether we ought to divide *long'-isco, vetust'-isco,* or *longi-sco, vetusti-sco,* may remain undecided. In the former case the *i* of the auxiliary verb might be compared with that of the Greek imperative ἴσ-θι: in the latter *i* is the weakening of the final vowel of the adjective base, as in compounds like *longi-pes* and derivatives like *longi-tudo.* Bases ending in a consonant experience no abbreviation, thus, *arbor-esco, carbon-esco, lapid-esco, matr-esco, noct-esco, dit-esco,* but *opul-esco* from *opulent-esco,* which reminds us of the Sanscrit denominatives from abbreviated participial bases in *nt* mentioned above (§. 774.). The verb substantive, which I think I recognise in these formations, answers to the obsolete future *esco* (*escit, superescit, obescit*), which, however, in composition, has occasionally retained the original *a*; as in Old Prussian, also, in its simple state, *as-mai, as-sai, as-t,* corresponds to the Lithuanian *es-mi, es-si, es-ti.* How close the notions of futurity and of becoming, as of future existence, approach one another needs no mention. With respect to the guttural which has attached itself to the root of the verb substantive, *asco, esco* and the isolated future *escit,* resemble the Greek imperfect ἔσκον, which, with the rejection of the radical vowel, enters also into combinations with attributive verbs (δινεύε-σκε, καλέε-σκον, ἐλάσα-σκε).* The Latin *esco,* also, when added to

---

* I have no hesitation in ascribing the vowel which precedes the σ to the temporal base of the simple verb; for the ο of ἐκάλεον is, in its origin, identical with ε, and stands in place of the ε of ἐκάλεες, ἐκάλεε, only on account of the nasal which follows: the ε of the 3d person of the 1st aorist is identical with the *a* of the other persons, which is everywhere retained where an ending follows it.

DENOMINATIVES. 1037

verbal bases, relinquishes its initial vowel; for the a (ă), e (ĕ), and i (ĭ) of forms like laba-sco, ama-sco, consuda-sco, genera-sco, palle-sco, vire-sco, rube-sco, senti-sco, obdormi-sco, are clearly the characters of the first, second, and fourth conjugations; on which account we here divide differently than above, in puer'-asco, clar'-esco, dulc'-esco &c. In compounds with bases of the third conjugation the i of gemisco, tremi-sco, must be regarded as by nature short, as it is identical with the i of gem-i-s, trem-i-s (see §. 109ª. 1.), which leads us back to the Sanscrit a. The i of profici-scor, concupi-scor, is identical with that of faci-s, profici-s, cupi-s; nanci-scor presupposes a simple nanco, nanci-s; frage-sco exhibits ĕ for the ĭ of frangi-s (compare §. 6.), and has lightened itself by the rejection of the nasal of the root. To Latin forms like laba-sco, ama-sco, palle-sco, correspond, in their principle of formation, Greek forms like γηρά-σκω, ἡβά-σκω, ἱλά-σκομαι, ἀλδή-σκω; where, however, it is not asserted that the Latin ē of the second conjugation is connected with the Greek η of forms like πεφίλη-κα, φιλήσω, though both lead us back to the Sanscrit aya; but of this the Latin contains the two first letters in the contraction of ai to ē (see §. 109ª. 6.), while the Greek η of φιλήσω and εε, εο of φιλέετε, φιλέομεν, contain the first and third letter of the Sanscrit aya, either separate (in εε, εο), or united in η. The ι of forms like εὑρί-σκω, στερί-σκω, ἁλί-σκομαι, ἀμβλί-σκω, is scarcely a vowel of conjunction, but, in my opinion, only a weakening of a heavier vowel; thus, εὑρίσκω, στερί-σκω, for εὑρήσκω, στερή-σκω; ἀμβλι-σκω, ἁλί-σκομαι for ἀμβλω-σκω, ἁλω-σκομαι; to which, among other things, the futures εὑρή-σω, ἁλώ-σομαι, &c., point. We must remark the weakening of o to ι in ὀνί-νημι for ὀνόνημι, ὀπιπτεύω for ὀποπτεύω*; and, moreover, the forms ἀληθή-σκω

---

* See §. 754., and compare ὀπωπή and ὀπωπέω, which forms, by the lengthening of the radical vowel in the second syllable of the root, which

is

and ἀλθί-σκω which exist together. I am now inclined, in departure from what was remarked at §. 751., to assume that the Greek reduplicated forms in σκω, in spite of their striking resemblance to Sanscrit verbal desideratives like *jijñâsâmi* (compare γιγνώσκω), are nevertheless not historically connected with them, but, as comparatively younger formations, have arisen from the junction of the verb substantive in a form analogous to the imperfect ἔσκον and Latin future *escit*, but deprived of the radical vowel, to roots repeated according to the principle of the Sanscrit third class (see §. 109ª. 3.). Thus, γιγνώσκω, μιμνήσκω, presuppose simple verbs like γίγνωμι, μίμνημι, according to the analogy of δίδωμι, τίθημι, βίβημι, or such as γιγνόω, μιμνέω. And ἔγνων and γνώσω bear the same relation to the probably existent γίγνωμι that ἔδων and δώσω do to δίδωμι. If, however, the Greek reduplicated forms in σκω must, with regard to their principle of formation, be looked on as distinct from Sanscrit verbs like *jijñâsâmi*, the same must hold as regards Latin forms like *no-sco*, *di-sco* (perhaps from *dida-sco*), *pa-scor*, *na-scor* (*gna-scor* by transposition from *gan-scor*), which correspond to Greek unreduplicated forms like βά-σκω, θνή-σκω.

777. In Sanscrit, denominatives may also be formed by annexing simply an *a* to the theme of nominal bases in the special tenses, which *a*, like that of the first and sixth classes of primitive verbs (§. 109ª. 1.), is suppressed in the universal tenses. A final *a* of nominal bases is dropped; hence, *e. g.*, *lôhit'-a-ti*, "he is red," from *lôhita*. I am unable to quote from authors instances of such denominatives: there occur, however, among the roots exhibited by Indian Grammarians of the first or sixth class, several in which I think I recognise denominatives from bases in

---

is twice repeated in its full form, correspond admirably to the Sanscrit intensives there mentioned.

DENOMINATIVES. 1039

a; thus, among others, *bhâm*, "to be angry," *bhâm-a-té*, "he is angry," which I derive from *bhâm-a*, "anger:" this latter, however, which also signifies "light," "splendour," clearly comes from the root *bhâ*, "to shine." As the Latin *i* of the third conjugation corresponds to the Sanscrit *a* of the first and sixth class, so *metu-i-t, tribu-i-t, statu-i-t, minu-i-t*, correspond to the Sanscrit denominatives here mentioned. In Greek correspond denominatives, which in the special tenses add ο and ε to the nominal base; thus, e. g., μηνί-ο-μεν, μηνί-ε-τε, δηρί-ο-μαι, μητί-ο-μαι, δακρύ-ο-μεν, μεθύ-ο-μεν, ἰθύ-ο-μεν, ἀχλύ-ο-μεν, βασιλεύ-ο-μεν, βρα-βεύ-ο-μεν. What, however, are we to say of that rather numerous class of denominatives in ευω, which are not founded on any nominal base in ευ; e.g., κορ'-εύο-μαι, "I am a maiden;" πολιτ'-εύ-ω, "I am a citizen;" ἀθλ'-εύ-ω, "I contend," properly, "am in strife;" ἰατρ'-εύ-ω, "I am a physician;" κρατιστ'-εύ-ω, "I am the best;" κολακ-εύ-ω, "I am a flatterer, flattering;" δουλ'-εύ-ω, "I am a servant;" ἀληθ'-εύ-ω, "I am true"? If the verb substantive, which in most of these formations is more or less evidently present in spirit, be also contained therein bodily, we must then have recourse to the root φυ (see p. 115), which therefore, in these compounds, has preserved the original notion, while in its simple state the causal meaning of bringing into existence, "making to be," prevails. The ε of -ευω would therefore be the Guna vowel, corresponding to the *a* of the Sanscrit *bhav-â-mi*, "I am," "I become;" and, with respect to the dropping of the radical labial ευω, would stand on the same footing with *ui, vi*, of Latin forms like *pot-ui, mon-ui, ama-vi, audi-vi*, (see §. 556.).* In Gothic the verbs

---

* The Ossetian also has, in its simple state, lost the labial of the auxiliary verb under discussion, and gives, e.g., *wa-d*, "he must be," *wonth*, "they must be," corresponding to the Sanscrit *bhavatu, bhavantu*: see "*The Caucasian Members of the Indo-European Family of Languages,*" pp. 43

in *na* (as *fullna*, "*impleor*"), mentioned above (§. 770.), belong to the class of denominatives here mentioned. These verbs in *na* come from participial bases with the same termination, which, like the Sanscrit bases in *a* (*rôhit'-a-ti*), reject their final vowel before that of the class; thus, *fulln'-i-th*, "*impletur*," from *fullna-i-th*, for *fullna-a-th* (see §. 67.), plural *fulln'-a-nd*, as in Sanscrit *rôhit'-a-ti, rôhit'-a-nti*. But this kind of formation holds, in Gothic, only for the present and its derivatives, while in the preterite an *ô* takes the place of *a* or *i*; so that, e. g., *fulln'-ô-da*, "I was filled," in its principle of formation agrees with Latin forms like *regn'-â-vi*, the base noun also of which, *regnu* ("kingdom as ruled"), with respect to its derivative suffix, is connected with the to-be-presupposed Gothic base *fullna* (Sanscrit *púrna*, "filled").

FORMATION OF WORDS.

778. With regard to the formation of verbs there remains nothing to be added to what has been already said regarding the structure of roots and the classes of verbal bases (§. 109[a].) which proceed thence, and subsequently respecting the formation of derivative verbs. The primitive pronouns, and the appellations of numerals, do not follow the ordinary rules for the formation of words (see §. 105.), and, with their derivatives, are discussed in the paragraphs allotted to them. We shall now discuss simply the formation of substantives and adjectives; and, first, those which stand in close connection with the verb, and, both in the organization and in the application of language, play a very important part: we allude to the participles and the infinitive. It might be said that we ought to treat of

---

pp. 43 and 82, Rem. 43. In Persian the present of the verb substantive may be combined with any substantive, adjective, as well as with the personal pronoun; *e.g., piram*, "*senex sum;*" *manam*, "*ego sum.*"

the formation of nouns before treating of their inflection, because words must be formed before they are inflected. But for practical considerations it appeared more useful, at first, only to lay down the principle of the formation of words generally, as is done in §§. 110. 111., and to defer the more full investigation of the subject to this place. At all events, the theory of the formation of tenses must precede that of the participles, as the latter, for the most part, irrespective of their nominal suffixes, rest on a principle of formation similar to that of the corresponding tenses of the indicative, and bear a sisterly, if not a filial relation to them. It will, however, be clearly seen from the following paragraphs how requisite an acquaintance with the forms of cases, and with the distinction of genders, is to the understanding of the theory of the formation of words.

779. The participle present active forms a point of observation as regards the representation of the original unity of the Indo-European languages; and it is here worthy of notice, that several of the still living tongues of our quarter of the world have, in some cases, preserved the original formative suffix in a more perfect form than the Sanscrit in its most ancient sources. The full form of the suffix is *nt*; the Sanscrit, however, exhibits the *n* only in a few cases, which in all places, where a division of the theme into stronger and weaker forms occurs, has retained the original and full form of the base (see §. 129.); hence, *e.g.*, *bharan*, *bharantam* = φέρων, φέροντα, *ferentem*, dual *bharantâu*, Vêda *bharantâ* (nom. acc. voc.) = φέροντε, plural *bharantas* (nom. voc.) = φέροντες, *ferentes*; but in the accusative we find *bharatas*, by the loss of the *n* in the latter part of the word, opposed to φέροντ-ας, and so in all the other cases of the three numbers the *n* is dropped in Sanscrit; and in the genitive singular *bharatas* stands, from this loss, in an inferior position when compared with the Greek

φέροντος, Latin *ferentis*, Gothic *bairan-din-s* (see p. 138), and our German strong participial genitives, as *stehendes, gehendes*.*
The Lithuanian also has till the present time retained the nasal of the participle present through all the cases of the three numbers in both genders: it extends the theme, however, in the oblique cases, by the addition of *ia*; and, according to a universal law of sound, changes the *t* before *i*, when this is followed by any vowel but *e*, into the sound *tsch*, which Ruhig writes *ch*, Mielcke *cz*; hence, *e.g.*, *degans*, "the burning" (= Sanscrit *dahan*), according to the analogy of Zend forms like *barans*, Latin like *ferens*, Æolic as τιθένς, accusative *degantin* (for *degantien*, from *-ian*), genitive *deganchio*.

780. The Old Prussian, differing from the Lithuanian, extends the participial base in the oblique cases by the simple addition of *i*, and so far agrees entirely with the Latin, which, *e.g.*, forms simply *ferens* from the base *ferent*, which has not exceeded its original limits, but which, in all the other cases, follows the analogy of bases in *i*. *Ferenti-a* and *ferenti-um* belong as decidedly to the *i* declension as *facili-a, facili-um*. We are therefore right in dividing *ferente-m* just as *facile-m* (from *facili-m*), though from a base, *ferent*, the accusative could be in no case other than *ferentem* = Zend *barĕnt-ĕm*. The participles present masculine which remain to us in Old Prussian are, *dilants*, "the worker," "working;"† *sidans*, "*sedens*;" *empriki-sins*, "*præsens*;" dative *empriki-senti-smu*, according to the pro-

---

* Verbs of the third class, in Sanscrit, owing to the incumbrance of the syllable of reduplication, have lost the nasal in the strong cases also; hence, *e.g.*, *dadatam* compared with διδοντα, *dadatas* with διδοντες (compare §. 459.).

† According to the mode in which the two following examples are written we should expect *dilans*; but as respects the retention of the T-sound, *dilants* corresponds to Gothic forms like *bairands*.

FORMATION OF WORDS. 1043

nominal declension (see §. 170.); *niaubillìnti-s*, "of the under age," "not speaking" (*infantis*);* *ripinti-n*, "*sequentem ;*"† *empriki waitiainti-ns* (acc. pl.), "*contradicentes ;*" *warguseggienti-ns*, "*maleficos*." The following are adverbial datives, *giwantei*, "living," and *stanintei* (also *staninti*) "standing," from the bases *giwanti* (Sanscrit *jìvant*), *staninti* (see Nesselmann, pp. 52 and 76).

781. Before the feminine character *ì*, the Sanscrit, according to the difference of conjugation of the respective verbs, either retains the nasal of the participial suffix or rejects it, and in such a manner as that verbs of the first principal conjugation regularly retain it, and but rarely reject it, while conversely those of the second ordinarily reject it, and only occasionally retain it; while the Gothic and Lithuanian have constantly preserved it. Compare, *e.g.*, with the Sanscrit *vasantì*, "the inhabiting" (also *vasatì*, Nal. 13. 66.), from *vas*, Class 1, the Gothic *visandei* (Them. *visandein*, see §§. 120. 142.), "the abiding or being;" and with the Sanscrit *dahantì*, "the burning," the Lithuanian *deganti* (gen. *deganchiôs*, see p. 174, Note *). In Greek, θεραπόντις is in form a solitary participle present feminine with ιδ = Sanscrit *ì*, according to the analogy of the feminine bases in τριδ = *trì*, Latin *trì-c*, mentioned in §. 119. The root अस् *as*, Class 2, of the verb substantive, forms in Sanscrit *satì*, "the being," never *santì*; the Lithuanian *esanti* therefore surpasses the Sanscrit both in the retention of the radical vowel and in that of the *n* of the suffix.

---

* *Billi*, "I speak." The inseparable preposition *au*, combined with the negation *ni*, corresponds to the Sanscrit *ava*.

† Also *ripintinton*, in the last syllable of which I think I recognise an appended pronoun or article=Sanscrit *tam*, Lithuanian *tan*, Greek τόν. As regards the *o* for *a*, compare the accusative of the participle perfect passive *dâto-n*, "*datum*"=Sanscrit *dattam*, from *dadâtam*, irregularly for *dâtam*.

In the masculine nominative, also, the Lithuanian *esans* has two points of superiority to the Sanscrit *san*, the retention of the radical vowel, and of the nominative sign: the latter is shared also by the Latin *sens*, of *præ-sens*, *ab-sens*, to which the abovementioned (§. 780.) Old Prussian *sins*, of *emprīki-sins*, admirably corresponds. The Greek, for the most part, with its ὤν, contrasts disadvantageously with the Lithuanian *esans*; for while the latter has, together with the case sign, preserved the complete root, we miss in ὤν both the entire root and the expression of the nominative relation. The epic and Ionic form ἔων, however, leads us to conjecture a formerly existing ἔσων, and the suppression of the σ in this position is not surprising according to §. 128. It is, however, not less marvellous that a form which, in Greek, has been corrupted for thousands of years, quite up to remote antiquity, and which has been tolerably accurately retained by the Latin only under the protection of the prepositions *præ* and *ab*[*], should have remained quite perfect in the Lithuanian up to the present day.

782. The Indian Grammarians assume *at*, in the strong cases *ant*, as the suffix of the participle present. I cannot, however, attribute to the suffix the *a* of forms like *bharant*, any more than the *o* of the Greek φέροντ : the vowel belongs in both languages to the class syllable; *i. e.* the *o* of φερ-ο-ντ is identical with that of φέρ-ο-μεν, φέρ-ο-ντι, and with the ε of φέρ-ε-τε, ἔφερ-ε-ς, &c. That the Greek participial suffix is simply ντ, not οντ, is clear from the conjugation in μι, where ντ attaches to the final vowel of the root or of the verbal theme (διδο-ντ, τιθε-ντ, ἱστα-ντ, δεικ-νυ-ντ) : the Sanscrit, however, in accordance with a peculiarity, which, in my opinion, first arose after the separation of languages

---

[*] On the other hand, in *potens*, just as in the simple *ens*, the sibilant is lost.

FORMATION OF WORDS. 1045

in cases, where the *nt* or *t* of the suffix would be added to a letter other than *a* or *â*, prefixes to the suffix an *a* (compare §. 437. Remark, and §. 458.), or extends the verbal theme by the addition of an *a*; hence, *e. g.*, *strinvant*, "strewing" (for *strinunt*), answers to the Greek base στορνυντ. The *e* of Latin participles of the third conjugation, *e.g.*, of *veh-e-ns*, *veh-e-ntem* (= Sanscrit *vah-a-n*, *vah-a-ntam*, Zend *vaz-a-ns̀*, *vaz-a-ntĕm*), is in origin identical with the class vowel *i* (from *a*, see §. 109ª. 1.) of *veh-i-s*, *veh-i-t*, &c. (see §. 507.), and is based on the circumstance that before two consonants the Latin language prefers *l* to *i* (see §. 6.). In the fourth conjugation, *ie*, *e. g.*, in *aud-i-ens*, represents the Gothic *ya* and Sanscrit *aya* of forms like *sat-ya-nds*, "placing" = Sanscrit *sâd-aya-n*, "making to sit" (compare §. 505.). It does not require mention, that in verbs of the first and second conjugation the *a* and *e*, as in *am-a-ns*, *mon-e-ns*, belong to the conjugational syllable; the *a*, however, of *da-ns*, *sta-ns*, *fa-ns*, and *fla-ns*, to the root: and as little does it require notice, that in German and Lithuanian the vowel which precedes the *n* of the participle present is identical with that of the class syllable. Compare, in Gothic, *bair-a-nds*, "the carrying," *vahs-ya-nds* (Zend *ucs-ya-ṅs̀*), "the growing" (see §. 109ª. 2.), *sat-ya-nds*, "the placing," "making to sit,', *salb-ô-nds*, "the anointing,," with *bair-a-m* (Sanscrit *bhar-â-mas*), "we carry," *vahs-ya-m*, "we grow," *sat-ya-m*, "we place" (Sanscrit *sâd-ayâ-mas*), *salb-ô-m*, "we anoint;" and in Lithuanian, *weź-a-ṅs*, "the conveying," with *wez-a-mé*, "we convey;" *myl-i-ṅs*, "the loving," with *myl-i-me*, "we love." With regard to the non-correspondence of the Lithuanian *es-a-ṅs*, "being," to *es-mi*, "I am," *es-me*, "we are," we must observe, that here an auxiliary vowel is necessary in the participle, which in the Sanscrit *s-a-n* (accusative *s-a-ntam*) occurs in the same form, while the Latin *-sens* places in its stead an *e*, and the Old Prussian *-sins* an *i*.

783. In Old Sclavonic, the so-called gerundives correspond to the participles of the kindred languages, and that of the present to the participle present active here under discussion. In the nominative singular masculine, where, *e.g.*, вєзꙑ *veźy*, "*vehens*," answers to the Sanscrit *vahan*, Zend *vazanś*, Lithuanian *weźans*, and Gothic *vigands*, we should scarce observe the analogy of the Sclavonic form to those of the kindred languages, as, according to a universal law of sound, all final consonants in Sclavonic are suppressed*, but in the dual, вєзѫщѧ *veźunshcha*†, corresponds to the Vêdian *vahantâ* and Zend *vazanta*; and in the plural, вєзѫщє (*veźunshche*) answers to the Sanscrit *vahant-as*, and Greek ἔχοντ-ες (see p. 618, Note 3.); where it is to be observed, that щ *shch* more frequently occurs as the euphonic alteration of *t* (Dobrowsky, p. 39, Kopitar, p. 53), just as *d*, under similar circumstances, becomes жд *schd*: a sibilant, therefore, is prefixed to the *T*-sound, and, besides, the original *t* is changed into *ch*, as in Lithuanian likewise the latter is used before *i*, with a vowel following.

---

* See §. 255. 1. I now think that the monosyllabic words also must be subjected to the universal law, as I no longer recognise in the forms нас *nas* and вас *vas* of the genitive and locative plural of the two first persons the Sanscrit secondary forms *nas* and *vas*, but I refer the с *s* of the genitive to the Sanscrit pronominal genitive termination *sâm*, and that of the locative to the Sanscrit locative termination *su*. The fact that the *s* of these terminations is elsewhere changed into χ *ch* (see §§. 255. m. 279. and p. 355, Note 6.), and that in Sanscrit the genitive termination *sâm* occurs only in pronouns of the third person plural, conceals the causal nature of the ending of the forms насъ *na-s*, васъ *va-s*; but in Old Prussian also the ending साम् *sâm*, in the form much nearer to the Sanscrit *son*, has made its way into the pronouns of the first and second person; hence here are found *nou-son*, ἡμῶν, *iou-son*, ὑμῶν, after the analogy of *stei-son*, των=Sanscrit *te-sham*, answering to the Sclavonic насъ *na-s* and васъ *va-s*.

† As to ѫ=*uṅ*, see the Remark at the end of the preceding §.

FORMATION OF WORDS. 1047

Compare, therefore, in this respect, the dual вєӡѫщА *veżuńshcha* with the Lithuanian *weżanchiu*. It is probable that in Sclavonic also, as well as in Lithuanian, a *y*, or the syllable *ya*, has, in the oblique cases, mingled with the *t* of the participial suffix, and under the influence of the *y* the preceding *t* has become щ *shch*. So in Dobrowsky's third conjugation, in which, in the first person present, a *y* is found before the termination *uń*, forms occur like мѫщѫ *muńshchuń*, "*turbo*," euphonic for *muńtyuń*, infinitive *muńt-i-ti*[*]. In the feminine singular the gerundive spoken of is вєӡѫщи *veżuńshchi* = Lithuanian *weżanti*, "the conveying" (genitive *weżanchiôs*), Sanscrit *vahantí*.

Remark 1. Dobrowsky, to whose grammar I was circumscribed in treating (§. 155.) of the Old Sclavonic alphabet, makes neither an orthographical nor a phonetic distinction between ѫ and оу, or ъ, and never uses the first-mentioned letter, as he everywhere writes ю for ѭ. It is now, however, generally supposed, and I think with good reason, that the vowels ѫ (with *y*, ѭ) and ѧ (with *y*, ѩ) contain a nasal, as was first discovered by Vostokov, but still held by Kopitar (Glagolita, p. 52) to be doubtful. It is, however, certain that the vowels ѫ, ѭ, ѧ, ѩ, in the Old Sclavonic Grammar, as Kopitar has informed us, occur scarce anywhere but where the Polish has vowels with a nasal; and comparison with the ancient allied languages leads us to expect a nasal, for which reason I have before assumed a corruption of *on* (from *an*) to *û* (see §. 155. ᵍ.). On the other hand, however, оу, or ъ, and the *û* contained in ю (*yû*), wherever these letters occur in Old Sclavonic in their proper place, in forms which admit of comparison usually, according to etymology, represent the Sanscrit औ *ô* (for *a+u*), or its resolved form *av;* hence, *e.g.*, оуѕтА *ûsta* (neuter plural), "mouth"=*ôshtha*," "lip" (Theme); сроути *srû-ti*, "to hear"= '*rôtum* (irrespective of the infinitive suffix); воудити *bûd-i-ti*, "to wake"=*bôdayitum;* шоуи *shûi*, left"=*savya*. So in the termination of the genitive locative dual, where, *e.g.*, обою "*amborum, in ambobus*," answers to the Sanscrit *ubhayôs*, and Zend *ubóyó* (see §. 273.). Now let us examine the cases in which nasalized vowels, the nasal of which I now

---

[*] Miklosich compares the Sanscrit root *manth*, "to shake;" and ѫ *uń* therefore stands for the Sanscrit *an*. See the note to the preceding §.

express, as in Lithuanian, by *ṅ* (see §. 10.), in grammatical terminations or suffixes, correspond to a Sanscrit *n* or *m* with a preceding vowel (*a* or *â*). There appear, therefore, if I have not overlooked any thing, the following:—

1. Accusative singular of feminine bases in *a*; *e.g.*, ВДОВѪ *vdovuṅ*, "*viduam*"=*vidhavâm*.*
2. Accusative singular of pronouns of the first and second person: МѦ *maṅ*, ТѦ *taṅ*=Sanscrit *mâm, tvâm*; like the reflexixe СѦ *saṅ*.
3. Accusative plural of masculine pronominal bases of the third person in *ya*, and therefore also of definite adjectives compounded with the base *ya*. Compare ІѦ *yaṅ*, "*eos*," with the corresponding Sanscrit *yân*, "*quos*," and Old Prussian accusatives like *scha-ns, schi-ns,* "*hos*," *wira-ns,* "*viros*," Gothic *vaira-ns* (see §. 236.).
4. First person singular present, where Ѫ *uṅ*=Sanscrit *âmi*; *e.g.*, *veçuṅ*=*vahâmi*; АІѪ *ayuṅ*=*ayâmi*, e.g., *rydayuṅ*=*rôdayâmi* (see §. 766.).
5. Third person plural of the present, where ѪТЬ *uṅty*=Sanscrit *anti*; *e.g.*, ВЕЗѪТЬ *veçuṅty*=*vahanti*; and in Dobrowsky's third conjugation (see Kopitar, p. 61), ІѦТЬ *yaṅty*=Sanscrit *ayanti*.
6. The above-mentioned gerundive or participle present.

The nasal vowel in the genitive singular and nominative accusative plural of feminine bases in *ya*, *e.g.*, in ВОЛІѦ *volyaṅ*, "*voḷuntatis*," and "*voluntates*" (nom. acc.), appears surprising. If we consider, however, that in the three cases spoken of the Sanscrit grammar exhibits a final *s*, which is also contained in the Lithuanian and Lettish, which approximate closely to the Sclavonic languages, as also in Gothic in all the words which cor-

---

* Compare §. 266. The Polish also, in the corresponding forms, has a written nasal vowel, though now, at the end of a word, the nasals, though written, are no longer pronounced; just as in the instrumental, where I regard the Sclavonic *vdo-voy-uṅ*=Sanscrit *vidhavay-â* as joining to the old instrumental termination the new also, with a corruption of the *my* (Dobr. gives only *m*) to the now probably very weak nasal sound *ṅ*. Remark, that in the plural instrumental, the feminines, especially rather than the masculines and neuters, have the termination *mi* (see p. 349); for which, in Lithuanian, both in masculine and feminine, stands *mis*, only that the masculines in *a* have contracted *a-mis* to *ais*.

respond to the Sanscrit feminine bases in â*, we are led to infer the nasalization of a final *s*, as in the Prâkrit instrumental termination *hiṅ* = Sanscrit *bhis* (see §. 220.). The *y* especially appears to have protected the nasalized vowels which follow it, as we may conclude from No. 3. and the gerundives mentioned below (Remark 2.). A place where the Old Sclavonic has a nasal vowel at the end of a word, while the Sanscrit has a simple vowel, occurs in the nominative and accusative singular of neuter bases in *n*; in има *imaṅ*, "*nomen*" (from the base *imen* from *iman*), answering to the Sanscrit *nâma*, from *nâman*. Here, however, the nasal of the Sclavonic nominative and accusative cannot surprise us, as it belongs to the base word, and the Latin also has firmly preserved the *n* of the base in the nominative and accusative singular neuter. Thus, as in Latin, *nomen, semen*, opposed to *homo, sermo*, &c., so има *imaṅ*, сѣма *syemaṅ*, opposed to камы *kamy*, " stone," from *kamen*.

Remark 2. The verb substantive gives сы *sy* = Sanscrit *san*, Lithuanian *seṅs*, and in the feminine сѫщи *suṅshchi* = सती *sati* (for *santî*), *sentî*. After the *y* in the nominative masculine the nasal and the old *a* remains; hence бия *biyaṅ*, "*cædens*," feminine биѫщи *biyuṅshchi*. In Dobrowsky's third conjugation the я extends also to the other forms with щ; hence воля *volyaṅ*, "*volens;*" волящe *volyanshche*, "*volentes;*" волящи *volyaṅshchi*, ἐθέλουσα. As regards the use of the gerund, it is limited to those constructions in which the participle present stands as predicate, and in German the uninflected form of the participle is used; hence (Luc. xxiv. 13.) бѣста идѫща *byesta iduṅshcha*, " they (two) were going," is the translation of the Greek ἦσαν πορευόμενοι, only with this point of difference, in which the Greek is inferior, that the Sclavonic has the dual of the verb as well as that of the participle. Where the participle stands as epithet or substantively, the Sclavonic uses the definite form of the participle (see §. 284.), and in this the participle is fully declined; thus, l. c., κώμην ἀπέχουσαν is rendered вьсь отьстоящѫѭ *vysyotstoyaṅshchuṅyuṅ*.

784. The same suffix that forms the present participle

---

* So, in Lettish, *akka-s* is both the genitive singular and the nominative and accusative plural of *akka*, " spring of water " (compare Latin *aqua*, Gothic *ahva*, " stream," genitive singular and nominative, accusative plural *ah-vô-s;* Lithuanian *uppé*, " stream;" Sanscrit *ap*, " water").

is added in Sanscrit and Zend to the theme of the auxiliary future; just as in Greek and Lithuanian, where δώ-σω-ν, δώ-σον-τα, dů-se-ṅs, dů-se-ntiṅ, correspond to the Sanscrit dâ-sya-n, dâ-sya-ntam. In the feminine the Lithuanian dů-se-nti, "the (woman) about to give," answers admirably to the Sanscrit dâ-sya-ntí ; deg-se-ṅs, "the (man) about to burn," accusative deg-se-ntiṅ, answers to the Sanscrit dhak-shya-n, dhak-shya-ntam ;[*] and in the feminine, deg-se-nti to dhak-shya-ntí. The Lithuanian root bu, "to be," gives bu-se-ṅs, "futurus," bu-se-nti, "futura," as analogous to the Zend bû-sya-ṅs, bû-syai-nti. Somewhat further off lies the Sanscrit bhav-i-shya-n, bhav-i-shya-ntí, on account of the Guna of the radical vowel, the insertion of the vowel of conjunction, and the suppression of the nominative sign in the masculine. As regards the e of Lithuanian future participles like dů-se-ṅs, bu-se-ṅs, I see in it, not a corruption of the i of indicative forms like dů-si-me, "dabimus" (see §. 652.), but a corruption of the a of Sanscrit bases like dâ-sya-nt : it is therefore identical with the o of the Greek δω-σο-ντ; and the Lettish also gives an o for this Lithuanian e, as to the a, also, of the present participle it opposes an o, while for the i of the future indicative it has, in like manner, i ; e. g. buhschots, "futurus" = Lithuanian busens ; buhschoti, "futura" = busenti; as essots, "being" = esaṅs, feminine essoti = esant.[†]

---

[*] See §§. 21. and 104.

[†] The future participle in Lettish occurs only in paraphrasing the conjunctive, and the present participle also has the feminine form in ti only in this kind of phrase, but elsewhere scha, which, in my opinion, comes from schia, and this from schi ; so that under the influence of the i, with a vowel following it, the t is changed into sch, as in Lithuanian into ch (genitive esanchios = Lettish essochas). Refer to what has been said before (§. 783.) regarding the origin of the щ shch in the Sclavonic gerund. The coincidence of the Lettish feminine termination scha with the Greek σα,

785. The aorist tenses in Sanscrit have left us no participles; and the Greek language, by forms like λύσας, λιπών, φυγών, τυπών, maintains a superiority over the Sanscrit. As, however, the first aorist in Greek contains the verb substantive (see §. 542.), we may compare σας, σαντα, σαντες, &c., with the Sanscrit *san, santam, santas*. The forms which appear in composition maintain a similar superiority over the simple ὤν, ὄντος, with respect to the more true preservation of the ancient form, to that which the Latin *sens* of *præsens, absens*, does over the simple *ens*. In respect to the accent, and the pure radical vowel, Greek participles of the second aorist like λιπών, φυγών, opposed to λείπων, φεύγων, answer to Sanscrit participles of the sixth class like *tudán*, "the pushing," accusative *tudántam*. As in the Vêda dialect many verbs occur in conjugational classes other than those which they follow in the common dialect, I still hesitate to concur with Benfey in considering participles like *vridhánt*, "increasing," *dhrishánt*, "daring," in the weak cases *vridhát, dhrishát*, as aorist participles, though in no other case have the roots in question been shewn to belong to the sixth class. If, however, they are really aorist participles, then *dhrishamána-s* (Rig. V. I. 52. 5.; probably to be accented *dhrishámána*), also a middle aorist participle of the sixth formation, though in the common dialect, having no middle voice, belongs to this formation in the indicative. The root *pá*, "to drink," whence *pivámi* (Vêd. *pibámi* from *pipámi*), in the Vêda dialect follows also the second class, as is clear from *pátha*, "ye drink" (Vêd. *thá* for *tha*, Rig. V. I. 86. 1.); whence I cannot concur with Benfey in ascribing the participle *pántam*, "bibentem," to the aorist, and just as little can I allot to it the imperative

---

σα, in forms like τύπτουσα, τύψουσα, is also remarkable. This σα was probably preceded by a form σια (compare τρια=Sanscrit *trî*, §. 119.), so that the σ was produced from τ by the influence of the ι following.

pâhí, "*bibe*," which likewise belongs to the present of the second class. With respect to the accentuation of the participle present active, I must draw notice to the fact that the Greek conjugation in μι agrees with the corresponding Sanscrit conjugation in this (the reduplicated verbs excepted), that it accents the second syllable of the participle in question, and that therefore, in this respect, στορνύς, στορνύντα, stand in the same relation to φέρων, φέροντα, as, in Sanscrit, *stṛinván, stṛinvántam,* to *bháran, bhárantam.* The Sanscrit, however, differs from the Greek in allowing, in the weakest cases (see §. 130.), the accent to sink down to the case syllable; hence in the genitive singular and accusative plural *stri-ṇva-tás* opposed to στορ-νύ-ντος, στορ-νύ-ντας. The Sanscrit differs from the Greek also in this, that in the accentuation of the participle present (the theory of the weakest cases excluded) it is governed by that of the corresponding tense; thus, *bódh-a-n, tud-á-n, shúchyan, chór-áya-n,* according to *bódh-á-mi, tud-á-mi, śúch-yá-mi, chôr-áyá-mi.* In the second conjugation (see §. 493.) the participle present is governed with respect to its accent by the heavy terminations, especially by that of the third person plural, and, in irregular verbs, participates also in the abbreviations, which the root experiences before heavy terminations: hence from *váśmi*, "I will," comes not *váśant*, but *uśánt*, "willing," according to the analogy of *uśmás, ushṭhá, uśánti.* The third class has, as well in the entire singular (with few exceptions) as in the third person plural and in the participle present, the accent on the syllable of reduplication; hence *dádámi*, "I give," *dádati*, "they give" (see §. 459.), *dádat*, "the giving" (see §. 779. Note), the latter opposed to the Greek διδούς, τιθείς, while *dádámi, dádhámi,* agree with δίδωμι, τίθημι.

Remark. The principle of Sanscrit accentuation appears to me to be this, that the farther the accent is thrown back, the graver and more

FORMATION OF WORDS. 1053

powerful the accent; and I believe I may assert the same principle in Greek also; only that here, out of regard for the harmony and euphony of the word, the accent in polysyllabic words cannot overstep the limit of the third syllable, while the Sanscrit places the accent on the first syllable, without reference to the extent of the word, and contrasts *bárâmahê* with the Greek φερόμεθα. A very striking proof of the dignity and energy of the accentuation of initial parts of words, and, at the same time, a very remarkable point of agreement between Sanscrit and Greek accentuation, is afforded by the circumstance, that both languages, in the declension of monosyllabic words in the strong cases (see §. 129.), which, with respect to their accentuation, are, as it were, pointed out by the genius of the language as the most important, lay the accent on the base, but in the weak cases allow it to fall on the case termination. Here, however, the accusative plural, though in respect to sound it belongs to the weak cases, yet passes, as regards accent, in most monosyllabic words in Sanscrit, as in Greek, for a strong case *; which cannot surprise us, as this case in the singular and dual belongs, in each respect, to the strong cases. Compare the declension of *vâch*, fem., "speech," "voice," with the Greek ὄπ (from Ϝοπ for Ϝοκ, Latin, *voc*).

	SINGULAR.				PLURAL.		
	SANSCRIT.		GREEK.		SANSCRIT.		GREEK.
N. V.	vák		N. V. ὄψ	N. V.	váchas		N. V. ὄπες
Acc.	vácham		Acc. ὄπα	Acc.	váchas		Acc. ὄπας
Instr.	váchá		. . .	Instr.	vâgbhís		. . .
Dat.	váché		. . .	D. Abl.	vâgbhyás		. . .
Gen. Abl.	váchás		Gen. ὀπ-ός	Gen.	váchám		Gen. ὀπῶν
Loc.	váchi		D. ὀπ-ί	Loc.	vákshú		Dat. ὀψί

	DUAL.		
	SANSCRIT.		GREEK.
N. A. V.	váchâu	Vêd. váchá	N. A. V. ὄπε
I. D. A.	vâgbhyắm		D. G. ὀποῖν
Gen. Loc.	vâchós.		. . .

I consider as a consequence of the emphasis, which lies in the accentuation of the beginning of a word, the circumstance that active verbs, to

---

* See the exceptions in Böhtlingk, "*A first attempt as to the Accent in Sanscrit*" (St. Petersburg, 1845), §. 14.

which the middle verbs also belong, in Sanscrit principally accent the first syllable, so that, therefore, the energy of the action is represented by the energy of the accentuation; and I perceive an agreement of the Greek accentuation with the Sanscrit in this, that Greek verbs throw back the accent as far as possible. In dissyllabic and trisyllabic forms, therefore, the two languages usually agree most fully in their accentuation of verbs. Compare εἶμι with *émi*, δίδωμι with *dádámi*, τίθημι with *dádhámi*, φέρομεν with *bhárámas*, ἔφερον with *ábharam*. In forms of more than three syllables the Greek approaches the Sanscrit as closely as, without a violation of the fundamental law of its system of accentuation, is possible; hence the already-mentioned φερόμεθα compared with *bhárámahê* (from -*madhê*, see §. 472.), and also ἐφερόμεθα compared with *úbharámahi*. A quite similar agreement, together with a similar contrast, appears between the Greek and Sanscrit accentuation in cases in which the Greek, in accordance with the Sanscrit principle, throws back the accent of the base word in the vocative.* This evidently happens, in both languages, in order to give emphasis to the name of the person called, and to bring it prominently forward by the voice; and in the vocative, in the three numbers of all words, the Sanscrit (where this case is specially accented) always accents the first syllable, however long the word be, and wherever the accent may fall in the other cases. To the nominatives *pitá́*, *mátá́*, *duhitá́* (acc. *pitáram*, *mátáram*, *duhitáram*), correspond the vocatives *pitar*, *mátar*, *dúhitar*, with which the corresponding Greek vocatives πάτερ, μῆτερ, θύγατερ—as compared with πατήρ, πατέρα, μήτηρ (for μητήρ), μητέρα, θυγάτηρ (for θυγατήρ), θυγατέρα,—stand in surprising agreement; and this is the more remarkable, as the words denoting affinity in our family of languages belong also, in another respect, to those expressions which have preserved the ancient stamp with astonishing fidelity. While, however, the Sanscrit also exhibits vocatives like *vishvamitra*, the Greek, owing to accentual limits prescribed to it, can only shew such as Ἀγάμεμνον, which, however, does not prevent us from recognising, even in forms of this kind, the agreement of the Greek and Sanscrit vocative theory; and just as little, in my opinion, could forms like φερόμεθα compared with *bhárámahê* cause us to overlook the affinity of Greek and Sanscrit verbal accentuation. The principal part of the Sanscrit first conjugation (see §. 493.) is formed by the first class, which comprehends almost one half of the whole number of roots, and to which,

---

* Compare Benfey in the "*Halle Journal of General Literature*," May 1845, p. 907.

with few exceptions, all the German strong verbs belong (see §. 109ª. 1.): these in the special tenses throughout accent the first syllable. The sixth class, which is properly only an offshoot of the first, and contains, as it were, the diseased members of that class (about 140 roots), has, with the Guna, put off also the accenting of the radical vowel, and accents instead the class vowel, only that the augment, as well in the imperfect as in the aorist in all classes of verbs, has the accent; hence, *tudámi,* "*tundo,*" *tudási,* "*tundis,*" opposed to *bódhámi,* "*scio,*" *bódhási,* "*scis.*" The passive accents its characteristic *ya,* and therefore the second syllable instead of the first, undoubtedly because in it the energy of self-exertion is lost: this is evident from the fact, that verbs of the fourth class, though their middle is literatim the same as the passive, nevertheless accent the first syllable ; hence, *śúchyaté,* "*purificat,*" opposed to *śuchyáté,* "*purificatur.*" It is also of some importance for the support of my view of the meaning of Sanscrit accentuation, that when the passive is used as reflexive, the accent may be thrown back on the radical syllable, though only in roots terminating in a vowel, or which drop their final consonant. Desideratives and intensives, excepting the deponent of the latter, as is natural from the energy inherent in them, hold fast to the general principle of throwing back the accent as far as possible; hence *pípásámi,* "I wish to drink;" *bébhédmi,* "I cleave" (intens.). As to the fact, however, that verbs of the tenth class, though they Gunise the radical syllable, still throw the accent on the second (*chóráyámi,* "I steal," not *chóráyámi*), we may suppose that these verbs feel themselves to be compounds, and in a measure determinatives; and as such, in accordance with the prevailing principle of compounds, accent the last member of the compound,* but the first syllable of it in order to comply with the fundamental rule of verbal accentuation. The same syllable, in my opinion, is accented in denominatives formed by *ya* for the same reason (*putriyáti*). I consider it as another consequence of the composition that the auxiliary future accents not the first syllable of the whole compound, but the auxiliary verb, whether it begins with the second or the third syllable of the whole expression; while the Greek, through all tenses, retains the fundamental principle of verbal accentuation; hence, δώσω, δώσομεν, compared with *dásyámi, dásyámas,* and forms like *tanishyámi* ("*extendam*"), *tanishyámas.* So in Sanscrit the auxiliary verb, which is added in the potential (optative) and precative (aorist of the potential=optative), viz. the syllable *yá,* draws the accent upon itself; hence, *dadyát,* "*det*" (διδοίη), precative

---

* See Aufrecht "*De Accentu compositorum Sanscriticorum,*" p. 5.

1056   FORMATION OF WORDS.

déyát (δοίη), *bhúyáma,* "*simus.*"* On the other hand, in cases where the modal element coalesces with the preceding class vowel into a diphthong, the accent remains on the same syllable as is accented in the indicative; thus, *bhárês, bhárêt, bhárêma*=φέροις, φέροι, φέροιμεν: on the other hand, *tudés, tudét,* &c., according to the analogy of *tudási, tudáti*. The analogy of the sixth class is followed by the potentials of the aorist of the sixth formation peculiar to the Vêda dialect; hence, *śakéma,* "*possimus.*"

In the six classes of verbs belonging to the Sanscrit second conjugation (see §. 493.), as also in the perfect of all verbs, the heavy personal terminations exercise a similar influence on the attraction of the accent to that manifested in Greek in all classes of words by the length of the final syllable, only that the heavy personal terminations in Sanscrit not only attract the accent, but appropriate it, and, if dissyllabic, to their first syllable. In this way *émi* (=εἶμι), *dádámi* (=δίδωμι), *jáhámi,* "abandon," are in the plural *imás, dadmás* (for *dadâmás*, middle *dadmáhi*,† *jahîmás*. In the fifth, seventh, eighth, and ninth class, as also in the perfect, the Guna syllable, or the heavier class affix or insertion, exercises an influence in throwing back the accent; hence, *chinómi,* "I collect" (plural *chinumás*); *yunájmi,* "I bind" (plural *yuñjmás*); *tanómi,* "I extend" (plural *tanumás*); *yunámi,* "I bind" (plural *yunîmás*); *tutóda,* "I did thrust" (plural *tutudimá*), instead of the forms *chinômi, yúnajmi,* &c., which, according to the fundamental principle of verbal accentuation, would be looked for. The heavy suffix of the participle present (*nt, ant*), the *a* of which, just like that of the third person plural, is viewed, with respect to the accentuation, as an essential portion of the termination, or of the suffix, follows, in the just-mentioned verbal classes, the analogy of the heavy personal terminations, especially that of the third person plural; but in the weak cases (with the exception of verbs of the third class) allows the accent to fall down to the case termination; and the feminine *î*, in case the suffix loses its *n*, follows the analogy of the weakest cases. The same principle is followed by the participle present of the sixth class.

---

* Sâma Vêd. II. 6. 2. 16. 2. Remark the dropping of the *s* of the common dialect (*bhâyâsma*), as in Zend, see §. 701.

† Reduplicated roots accent only those heavy terminations which begin with a consonant, and accord to those commencing with a vowel no influence in casting back the accent. The vowel *a*, which precedes *n* in the third person plural, holds as regards the accentuation as belonging to the personal termination. Hence *yánti,* "they go," compared with *éti;* but *dádati,* "they give" (see §. 459.) not *dadáti,* like *dádáti,* "he gives."

FORMATION OF WORDS. 1057

I annex the nominative, accusative, and genitive singular masculine (the neuter also of the genitive), and the feminine nominative in *î*: *dvishán, dvishántam, dvishatás, dvishatî'; dádat, dádatam, dádatas, dádatî ; yuñján, yuñjántam, yuñjatás, yuñjatî ; chinván, chinvántam, chinvatás, chinvatî ; tanván, tanvántam, tanvatás, tanvatî ; yunán, yunántam, yunatás yunatî ; tundán, tundántam, tundatás, tundántî.*—As in Greek, participles present active of the conjugation in μι, in agreement with the prevailing principle in the corresponding Sanscrit conjugation, accent the vowel which precedes the ν, instead of the first of the base-word, and στορνύς, στορνύντα, στορνύντε, στορνύντες, stand for comparison with the Sanscrit *strinván, strinvántam, strinvántá* (in the Vêda dialect) *strinvántas*, it might be conjectured that originally the heavy personal terminations, as they exercise (see §. 480.), as in Sanscrit, a shortening influence on the preceding syllable, have also, in like manner, attracted to themselves the accent. Then the Doric forms διδόντι, τιθέντι, ἱστάντι, δεικνύντι, might be regarded as remnants of an older system of accentuation. In the opposite case, we must look upon Sanscrit forms like *strinumás*, compared with the Greek στόρνυμεν, as the consequence of an influence upon the accentuation exercised by the heavy personal terminations, and first accorded to them by the genius of the language after the separation of languages. I have no doubt that forms like *strinómi* (from *starnómi=* στόρνυμι), *yunájmi*, through the influence of the weight of the second syllable, first, after the separation of languages, transferred the accent from the first to the second syllable. This takes place also in some verbs of the third class, which we find, therefore, in this respect, as it were, in the period of transition from the original system of accentuation to that more recent, in which, in the second principal conjugation, the weight, of the second syllable has made its influence on the accentuation effectual. However, in the Vêda dialect, in those roots also which admit the accentuation of the radical syllable, the accenting of the syllable of reduplication seems principally to prevail. Benfey (*Glossary to the Sáma-Vêda*, p. 139.) cites from *bhar, bṛi*, Class 3, the forms *bíbharshi,* "*fers," bíbhratê*, "*ferenti," bibhratí,* "*ferentes*," (as Vêda pl. fem. for *bíbhratyas*), opposed to *bibhárti,* "*fert.*"*

---

* We must not infer from *bibhárti*, and similar forms, that *ar* is really the Guna of *ṛi :* it is natural, however, that in parts of grammar where vowels capable of Guna receive it, that those verbs which admit of weakening should preserve the full form of the root, as *vaś*, "to will," becomes contracted to *uś* only in places which do not allow of Guna; hence,

A strong proof of the emphasis of the accentuation of the beginning of words (in Sanscrit always of the first syllable) is afforded in Sanscrit and Greek by the suffixing of the degrees of comparison, ईयांस् *íyâns* (in the weak cases *íyas*), ιον, इष्ठ *ishṭha*, ιστο, which, where they are added, always require the accent to be thrown back as far as possible. Thus, in Sanscrit, from *svâdú*, "sweet"=ἡδύ, comes the comparative *svádîyâns*, nominative masc. *svádîyân*, and the superlative *svádishṭha-s*. To the latter corresponds the Greek ἥδιστο-ς, and to the nominative and accusative neuter of the comparative *svádîyas* the Greek ἥδιον; while ἡδίων, ἡδίονος, for well-known reasons, do not exhibit an agreement of accentuation with *svádîyân*, *svádîyasas*. The Greek degrees of comparison in τερο, τατο, follow essentially the same principle, *i. e.* they throw the accent as far back as possible, by which, however, only the syllable preceding the suffix is reached, so that the accent is often necessarily transferred from the beginning to the middle of a word, as in βεβαιότερος, βεβαιότατος, compared with βέβαιος. In Sanscrit, on the other hand, the degree suffixes, corresponding to the Greek τερο, τατο, exercise no influence at all on the accent; and the positive base retains the accent on the base in whatever part of the word soever the same may occur; thus the

---

hence, *uśmás*, "we will," opposed to *vásmi*, "I will" (Comp. Vocalismus, p. 158). When Benfey, who, in the "*Halle Journal of General Literature*" (May 1845, p. 944) contrasts the Greek ὄρνυμι with the Sanscrit *riṇómi*, remarks, that in Greek *ri* is Gunised, because it is accented, and that *u* is for the same reason Gunised in Sanscrit, I cannot assent to him in either point. In the first place, I recognise in forms like ὄρνυμι, στόρνυμι (the latter = *striṇómi*), no Guna, but only the discontinuance of the abbreviation of *ar* to *ri*, which was admitted in Sanscrit, just as in τρίτος compared with the Sanscrit *tritîyas* (Latin *tertius*, transposed from *tretius*, for *tritius*), the abbreviation of the syllable *ri* has ceased. In the second place, I cannot admit that forms like *riṇómi*, *striṇómi*, have, for this reason, Gunised the second syllable because it is accented; for if the accent occasioned the Guna, we should also expect for *bibharshi* and *vivakti* (in the Vêda dialect), *bébharshi*, *vévakti*, and for desideratives like *pipâsâmi*, *pépâsâmi*. To me, therefore, the principle set forth above, viz. that the accenting of the first syllable belongs to the verb, but that heavy syllables have often destroyed the original accentuation, and appropriated the accent to themselves, appears far more natural. The Greek replaces the Guna of *riṇómi*, *striṇómi*, by the lengthening of the vowel (στόρνῡμι opposed to στόρνῠμεν), but nevertheless preserves the original accentuation.

comparative and superlative of *mahát* (in the strong cases *mahânt*) are in the nominative masculine *mahattaras*, *mahattamas*; and the superlative of *vṛishan*, "liberal," "giving freely" (in the Véda dialect), *vṛishantama-s*, genitive *vṛishantamasya* (Rig. V. I. 10. 10.). The reason that *tara* and *tama*, in Sanscrit, exercise no influence on the accentuation lies, in my opinion, in this, that these suffixes are rather enclitic in their nature, and have not grown up so inwardly united with the principal word, as the other more rare suffixes of comparison; as appears, also, from the circumstance that the feminine accusative *tarâm*, *tamâm*, may be added to verbs adverbially also; *e. g. vádatitamâm*, "he speaks very much."

A consequence of the emphasis which lies in accenting the beginning of a word is this, that abstract substantives, which frequently are merely intensifications of adjectives, affect, in Sanscrit and in Greek, this kind of accent. Thus the suffix *as*, in Sanscrit, is used especially in forming abstracts, and requires an accent on the first syllable of the word; as in *yáśasu*, "glory," compared with *yaśás*, "glorious" (the latter only in the Véda dialect, see Benfey's Glossary), whence the comparative *yaśástara-s*, superlative *yaśástama-s*; thus, *ápas*, nominative "activity," "work," "offering" (Latin *opus*), compared with *apás* masculine "the active," "the warrior," "the sacrificer." As to Sanscrit neutral bases in *as* correspond the Greek in ος, ες, ε(σ)-ος (see §. 128.), Benfey draws our notice, as regards the paroxytone accent of the abstracts spoken of, and the oxytone accent of the adjectives, to the relation of the Greek ἄγος to ἀγής. It may also be observed, that Greek bases in ος, ες, when they form possessive compounds in combination with preceding words, usually throw the accent on the suffix, while other compounds of this kind accent the first member of the compound, or, at least, throw back the accent as far as possible; thus εὐρυσθενής, μεγαλοσθενής, μεγαθαρσής, δυσκλεής, εὐκλεής, compared with forms like μεγάθυμος, μεγάδωρος, μεγαλόδωρος, μεγαλόδοξος, αἰολόμορφος, αἰολόπεπλος, αἰολοχαίτης.

786. The suffix of the participle of the reduplicated preterite or perfect (see §. 588.) is, in Sanscrit, in the parasmâipadam or active (see §. 426.), according to the difference of case, *vâns*, *vat*, and *ush*, and in all these forms, according to the analogy of the heavy terminations of the indicative (see p. 1057), has the accent. Indian Grammarians, however, consider *vás* as the true form of the suffix, though it does not appear in this form in a single

1060   FORMATION OF WORDS.

case, but the strong cases spring from *vâns**, the middle from *vát*, and the weakest from *úsh* (euphonic for *us*). From *úsh* comes also the feminine theme *ushí*, to which the Lithuanian *usi* is an admirable counterpart; hence *degusi*, "the having burned" = Sanscrit *dêhúshí*, for *dadahushí* (see §. 605.). The oblique cases of the Lithuanian feminine participle spring, for the most part, from an extended base *usia*; hence the genitive singular *degusiô-s*, as *rankô-s*, from *ranká*, "hand." Compare herewith the Greek υια of τετυφυῖα, which has been already elsewhere compared with the Sanscrit *tutupúshí*.†

787. With the weakest form of the Sanscrit participial suffix above mentioned are connected also, in Lithuanian, the oblique cases of the masculine, but with the same unorganic affix of *ia*, which, too, the participle present has retained; thus, genitive *degusio* (as *wilko* from *wilka-s*) corresponding to the Sanscrit *dêhúsh-as*, dative *deg-usia-m*‡, accusative *deg-usi-ṅ* for *deg-usia-ṅ*. The nominative *degeṅs* is based on the Sanscrit strong theme *dêh-i-váṅs* (*i* as conjunctive vowel); but the *s* of the Lithuanian form scarcely belongs to the base, but is the sign of case, and extends, as in

---

* The vocative singular, which in general disclaims long vowels (see §. 205.), shortens the long *á*; hence, *van* compared with the nominative *vân*, since anusvâra (*n*) after the *s* is dropped (see §. 9.) becomes *n*. I am not inclined with Böhtlingk (Decl. p. 10) to represent *vans* as the original form of the suffix; for if, as we ought to be, we are guided by the strong cases, which in general, where different modifications of the theme occur, have preserved the original form, we must then take *váns* to be the ancient form, and allow that the vocative, as is its wont, has shortened the vowel, which perhaps is only a consequence of the emphasizing the beginning of the word in the vocative by accenting it. Böhtlingk also, in his zeal for the vocative, represents *íyaṅs* as the theme of the comparative suffix *íyâṅs*, *íyas* (see §. 298.), the long *á* of which, in Latin, takes the form of *ó* in all the oblique cases.

† "*On the Influence of Pronouns in the Formation of Words*," p. 4.

‡ According to the analogy of the adjective declension, see § 281.

FORMATION OF WORDS. 1061

the participle present, to the vocative also; while the Sanscrit, as it cannot bear two consonants at the end of a word (see §. 94.), in both cases abandons both the nominative sign and the final consonant of the base; thus, nominative *dêh-i-ván*, vocative *dêh-i-van*, corresponding to the Lithuanian *deg-eṅs*.* The Zend, on the contrary, has retained

---

* In the Old Prussian Catechism there occur two perfect participles in *wuns* very deserving of notice, viz. *klantîwuns*, "having cursed," and *murrawuns*, "having murmured," which stand nearer to the Sanscrit *váṅs* than any other European kindred form. The *u* of *wuns*, as also that of the common form *uns* (after consonants also *ons*, and sometimes *ans*), is evidently, like the *e* of the Lithuanian *eṅs*, a weakening of *a*, originally *â;* as in *widdewu*, "widow"=Sanscrit *vidhavâ*, Latin *vidua*, and some similar feminine nominatives. The *u* of the plural *-usis*, accusative *usins*, and of the accusative singular *usin*, is, on the other hand, organic, and identical with the Sanscrit *u* of the base of the weakest case and of the feminine, as also with that of the corresponding forms in Lithuanian. Nesselmann ("*The Language of the Old Prussians*," p. 64) represents the participles in *uns* (*ons, ans, wuns*) as indeclinable, and takes *usis* as an independent form with declinable terminations. I, however, consider *wuns, uns, ons, ans*, as the singular nominative masculine, with *s* as the sign of case, as in Lithuanian *eṅs*. This participle seldom requires declension, as it is principally used for a periphrasis of the perfect indicative, and thus occurs in the nominative relation; *e.g.*, *asmai murrawuns bhe klantîwuns*, "I have murmured and cursed" (literally, "I am the person having murmured and cursed"). The nominative singular usually takes the place of the plural, as also in Lithuanian the present and perfect participles have lost the termination of the plural nominative, and in this case only have rejected the *s* of the nominative singular: hence, from *sukeṅs*, "having turned," comes the plural *sukeṅ*. Where, however, in Old Prussian, the plural relation of the participle perfect is really expressed, it ends in *usis*, probably from a lengthened base in *usi* (compare §. 780.); so that *i-s* of the Lithuanian plural termination corresponds to the *y-s* of bases in *i* (*awy-s*, "sheep," from the base *awi*). The examples occurring in the Old Prussian Catechism may be found in Nesselmann, p. 31, n. 84.: *madliti, tyt wirstai ious immusis; laukyti, tyt wirstai ious aupallusis*, "ask, and ye shall receive (be having received); seek, and ye shall find (be having found)." The future, which is wanting in Old Prussian,

the nominative sign in its participles; as, ܘܗܝܣܘ *dadh-vâo*, "having made," *víd-vâo*, "knowing" (εἰδώς), which it has also done in the participle present, a point in which it is superior to the Sanscrit, and agrees with the Lithuanian, Latin, and Gothic; for from वान् *vân* is formed in Zend, not ܒܘܣ *vâo*, but ܝܘܢܒ *vańn*. It is clear, however, that the *o* of *vâo* does not represent the *s* of the theme of the strong cases, as the suffix *vant* also, in the nominative, forms *vâo* (compare Burnouf Yaçna, Note R. p. 128). In the accusative, ܡܗܢܘܣܘܗܣܘ *dadhvâonhĕm* corresponds to the Sanscrit *dadh-i-vánsam*; in the weakest cases, and before the feminine character *î*, the Zend suffix is contracted, like the Sanscrit suffix, to *ush*[*]; hence, in the genitive ܘܗܫܘܗܬܕ *dathushô* (Vend. S. p. 3. for *dadhushô*, see p. 965.

---

sian, is always periphrastically expressed by the auxiliary verb signifying "to be," with the participle perfect; hence, p. 12, n. 15., *pergúbons wyrst*, "he is come" (is the person having come). The oblique cases of the perfect participle, from being little required, seldom occur, and spring likewise from the theme increased by *i*, while the Lithuanian adds *ia* to the base. The only instances that occur are, *au-lau-ûsi-ns*, "the slain" (*mortuos*, for which, also, *aulausins* and *aulauwussens*), and *ainan-gimm-usi-n*, "to those born in" (the place), the latter with passive signification, which, except in the root *gem*, *gim*, does not occur in this participle. If we should not admit a nominative plural in *usis*, the above-mentioned forms might then be taken as singular nominatives, with a plural signification. The circumstance, however, that the real and frequently-occurring singular nominative always terminates in *ns*, and that, too, the participle present leaves the old base (in *nt*) in the nominative singular unlengthened, and in the other cases lengthened only by *i*, is much opposed to this view.— The single feminine form of this participle which occurs deserves mention; viz. the nominative singular *aulausé*, "*mortua*," for *aulauusé*, as above *aulau-sins* together with *aulauusins*. The final *é* corresponds, therefore, to the Sanscrit *î* and Lithuanian *i* of feminine forms in *ushî*, *usi*.

[*] The lithographed Codex of the Vendidad Sadé has, almost in all places, ܣ *s* for ܫ *sh*: I, however, agree with Burnouf in reading ܫ *sh* as probably the sole correct reading.

FORMATION OF WORDS. 1063

Note*); in the dative ڊٞوِدُوشْێ *vídushê*, "to the knowing" (l. c. p. 214.) = विदुषे *vidúshê* (εἰδότι); in the genitive plural ږٞاِرِرِتھُشانم *irírithushanm*, "of the dead" (l. c. p. 101); in the genitive singular feminine ږٞجَغمُوشیَاو *jaghmûshyâo* (l. c. p. 91. twice, and 304. twice)* = Sanscrit *jagmushyás*, from *gam*, "to go"; in the accusative feminine ږٞوِتھُشيم *víthushîm* = Sanscrit *vidúshîm*, from *vid*, "to know" (l. c. p. 469).

788. With the contracted form उष् *ush* of the suffix here spoken of is connected a word which appears in Gothic as a solitary remnant of an obsolete participial gender, and corresponds in a remarkable manner with Sanscrit forms like *dêhúsh* (theme of the weakest cases) from *dah*; I mean, *bêrusyôs*, "the parents," occuring only in the nominative plural masculine, and which, I have no doubt, properly signifies "the having given birth to;" and, with respect to its radical vowel, corresponds to the polysyllabic forms of the preterite of *baira* (*bar*, plural *bêrum*, conjugational singular *bêr-yan*, plural *bêr-ei-ma* (see §. 605.). The theme is *bêrusya*, which corresponds in its unorganic affix *ya* to the above-mentioned (§. 787.) Lithuanian *ia*; *e. g.* of *deg-usia*, dative *deg-usia-m*. The nominative singular, according to §. 135. would be *bêr-useis*, and the accusative *bêrusi*, the latter like the Lithuanian *degusi-ṅ*.

---

* With regard to the long *û* of *jaghmûshyâo*, let it be noticed that the sibilant is here followed by a semi-vowel, since, as it appears, a lengthening of the *u*, which is, in Sanscrit, always short, occurs especially before two consonants; hence, also, Vendidad Sadé, p. 515, ږٞجَغمُوشتێمو *jaghmûshtĕmô* (with ش *s̈* for س *s*), a superlative formed from the weakest theme; and p. 525, *dadúschbís*, an interesting form; whence it is clear that in Zend also the middle cases (see §. 130.) of this participle spring from the weakest theme. There occurs, however, a long *û* in *pipyûshîm*, without the occasion of two following consonants, as also in its negative *apipyûshîm* (Vend. S. p. 429), from *pê*, "to drink," with a causal meaning ("the having sucked"). Perhaps the circumstance that two consonants precede has its influence.

789. To the form *vát,* whence come in Sanscrit the middle cases of the perfect participle[*], belongs the Greek ότ, which has preserved the ancient accent (see §. 786.); but after losing the digamma, which is generally lost in the middle of words, in case it does not assimilate with a preceding consonant (see τέσσαρες, §. 312.), as, for instance, also in the suffix εντ = Sanscrit *vant* (of the strong cases): thus, the same relation that ἀμπελό(F)εντ has to Sanscrit forms like *dhána-vant* ("endowed with riches," see §. 20.), τετυφ-(F)ότ has to *tutupvát,* to which, as nominative, accusative, and vocative, in Greek, τετυφός corresponds (see §. 152.). To the plural locative *tutup-vát-su* corresponds the Greek dative τετυφ-ό(τ)-σι. Mention has already been made of the feminine form in υῖα, as abbreviation of υσια, and of the affinity, as regards formation, of τετυφυῖα with the Sanscrit *tutupúshí* (see §. 786.). The Latin, perhaps, in *secûri-s* presents a remnant of these feminine participles in *ushí* (euphonic for *usi*), and the proper translation, therefore, is, perhaps, "the cutting" (instead of "the having cut"), the *u* being lengthened, and the sibilant being changed between two vowels into *r*.[†] As several participial suffixes are often used also in the formation of derivative words, there is, therefore, ground for comparing the suffix *ôsu* in words like *lapid-ôsus, lumin-ôsus, fructu-ôsus, form'-ôsus, pisc'-ôsus,* with the Sanscrit *váns* of the strong cases, to which it has nearly the same relation that the comparative suffix *iór* has to ईयांस् *íyáns* (see §. 298.),

---

[*] See §. 130., where it must be also noticed that the nominative, accusative, and vocative singular of neuters in the threefold theme gradation always are connected with the middle form.

[†] See §. 22. In the Véda dialect there are abstract substantives in *ushí,* with the accent on the radical syllable (see p. 1059); as, *tápushí,* "ire" (properly, "the burning"), from *tap,* "to burn;" *tárushí,* "strife," from *tar* (*tṛi* तृ), "to overstep."

only that the original sibilant is retained, though the *v* is lost, just as in *sopio=svapimi; soro, sorôrem=svasâr, svasâram; sol=svar*, "heaven" (from *sur*, and this from *svar*, "to shine"), Zend *hvarĕ*, "the sun." With respect to the prolongation of the suffix by a vowel affix, compare the relation of the suffix *tŭru* to *tôr*, Sanscrit *târ* (see §. 647.).

790. In Old Sclavonic the gerundive preterite corresponds to the participle here spoken of, as is most clearly apparent in the feminine singular form, in which, in verbal bases ending in a vowel, въши *ŭshi* corresponds to the Sanscrit-Zend *ushî*, and Lithuanian *usi*. Compare бывъши *by-ŭshi*, "having been" (feminine) with the Sanscrit बभूवुषी *babhûv-ŭshî*, and Lithuanian *buw-usi*. In the nominative plural masculine (used also for the feminine), въшЕ *ŭshe*—with *e* as the termination of case = Sanscrit *as*, Greek ες—answers to the Sanscrit *vánsas*, and therefore бывше *by-ŭshe* to *babhû-vánsas*; on the other hand, in the singular the sibilant is lost in the nominative masculine; thus, бывъ *by-ŭ* corresponding to the Sanscrit *babhû-ván* and Lithuanian *buw-ens* (see §. 787.), where it must be observed that generally the Sclavonic has lost the original final consonant, so that the *s* also of the Lithuanian *buw-ens* belongs not to the suffix, but to the case sign. After consonants the *v* of the gerundive suffix is suppressed; hence, *e.g.*, несъ *neś*, "having carried" (for *nes-ŭ*), plural несъше *neśshe* (for несвъше *nesŭshe*), feminine singular несъши *neśshi* (for *nes-ŭshi*).

Remark. In the Sclavonic that tense of the indicative is wanting whence the past participle or gerundive has proceeded: on the other hand, I am now of opinion that the Lithuanian perfect (also aorist), which I formerly compared with the Sanscrit first augmented preterite (Greek imperfect), must be compared with the Sanscrit reduplicated preterite, Greek perfect and Gothic preterite of the strong conjugation. I assume, therefore, that in *buwau*, "I was," or "I have been," instead of the augment, the syllable of reduplication is dropped, as in Gothic preterites like *baug*, "I bent," *bugum*, "we bent"=Sanscrit *bubhója, bubhujimá;* and I compare it with the Sanscrit *babhúva*, to which, with regard to its medial *u*, it corresponds better than to the imperfect *ábhavam*. *Buwau* does indeed closely resemble also the Sanscrit aorist *ábhúvam*, but in the third person *buw-o* answers better to *babhúv-a* than to *ábhút* ; and in both the plural numbers the forms given above (p. 762) answer better to *babhúv-i-vá* (from -*a-va*) *babhúv-a-thús* (from -*thas*), *babhúv-i-má* (from -*a-ma*), *babhúv-a-*(*ta*), than to *ábhútam, ábhú-ma, ábhú-ta*. The conjecture that the Lithuanian perfect belongs to the universal tenses, and not to the imperfect, is also confirmed by the consideration that the imperfect in Sanscrit and Greek always takes part in the base of the present, *i.e.* in the class peculiarities, while the Lithuanian preterite, which is called perfect, does not; hence the perfect of *gáu-nu*, "I am acquainted with," which corresponds to Greek verbs like δάκ-νω, Latin like *ster-no* (see p. 718), is not *gau-nau*, but *gaw-aù* (future *gáu-su*). In the perfect, too, *t* or *st* of the present base is dropped, which formerly, when we sought to compare this tense with the Sanscrit-Greek imperfect, appeared a difficulty (see §. 498.). As to the circumstance that the *y* or *i* (see p. 722) compared with the Sanscrit fourth class is retained in the perfect, and that from *liepyu*, "I order," comes the perfect *liepyau* (future *liepsu*); from *traukiu*, "I draw," the perfect *traukiau* (future *trauk-su*), this may be explained from the near resemblance in form of the fourth class to the tenth, in which the retention of the *y* or *i* in the universal tenses is regular. In general the perfect loves a *y*, and often adds one in verbs which do not exhibit one either in the present or in any other tense; as from *dŭmi* (for *dŭdmi*), or *dŭdu*, "I give," comes *daw-yau* (future *dŭ-su*); from *demi* (for *dedmi*), "I lay," *dĕ̆-yau* (future *dĕ̆-su*=*dhâ-syâmi*, θή-σω)*; from *eimi*, or *einu*, "I go," *ĕ̆yau* (future *ei-su*=Sanscrit *é-shyámi*). In every case the form of the participle may be safely inferred from that of the perfect indicative; but when the *y* of the first person singular indicative disappears in the other persons, it is lost in the participle also; thus, from *daw-yau*, second person *daw-ei*, participle *daw-eńs*, feminine *daw-usi;* but from *dĕ̆yau*, second person *dĕ̆yei*, participle *dĕ̆y-eńs*, feminine *dĕ̆y-usi;* from *ĕ̆yau*, "ivi," second person *ĕ̆yei*, participle *ĕ̆y-eńs*, feminine *ĕ̆y-usi*. It is beyond doubt, therefore, that as

---

* If the Lithuanian perfect belonged to the Sanscrit-Greek imperfect, then the perfect of *dŭdu* and *dedu* would most probably be *dŭdau, dedau* =Sanscrit *ádadâm, adadhâm*, Greek ἐδίδων, ἐτίθην.

FORMATION OF WORDS. 1067

the participle is based on the Sanscrit in *vâṅs*, feminine *ushî*, so the preterite indicative, which is most intimately connected with it, must also be connected with the Sanscrit reduplicated preterite and its European kindred forms. The Old Prussian simple preterite also, which in signification usually appears as aorist, appears to me to be a sister form of the Sanscrit reduplicated preterite, with the loss of the reduplication: hence, *dai*, "he gave," for *da**=Sanscrit *dadâu*, for *dadâ*. The present *dast*, from *dad-t*, is, on the other hand, like the Lithuanian *dûs-ti*, a reduplicated form (see p. 661). The *ts* which often terminates the third person singular preterite; as in *daits*, "he gave," a form used together with *dai*; *immats*, "he took," with *imma*; *billats*, "he spoke," with *billa*: this *ts* I regard as an appended pronoun, and abbreviated for *tas* (compare Lithuanian *tas*, "that," and the Sanscrit base *ta*, "he," "this," "that"). Let it be observed, that in general bases in *a* for the most part suppress this vowel before the nominative sign *s*; hence, *deiws*, "God"=Lithuanian *diewa-s*, Sanscrit *dêva-s* (see Nesselmann, p. 49). That the *ts* spoken of is not characteristic of the preterite is clear from this, that it also occurs sometimes in the present; for example, in *astits*, "he is,"† and *po-quoitêts*, "he desires." The former occurs twice, and once in the sense of the conjunctive: Nesselmann, p. 23, n. 51, *nostan kai tans sparts astits*, "on which he may have power." Here, therefore, the idea "he" is three times expressed, once by *tans*, then by the ancient personal termination *ti*, of the meaning of which the language is no longer conscious, and lastly by the appended *ts*. This *ts*, however, can scarcely be admitted in reference to feminines: there are no neuter substantives in Old Prussian; and in one place, where *astits* appears to mean "he is," it refers to the masculine *unds*, "water" (Nesselmann, p. 17): *adder sen stesmu wirdan Deiwas astits ainâ Crixtisnâ*, "but with the word of God is a baptism." Here, therefore, the appended pronoun, as the subject of the proposition, is correctly in its place.

791. The middle and passive participles in Sanscrit, in

---

* *Ai* frequently stands in Old Prussian for *a*; as in the nominative singular feminine, where both *a* and *ai* correspond to the Sanscrit *â*, see Nesselmann, p. 48; and compare *quai*, "which?" with the Sanscrit *kâ*, Lithuanian *ka*, and Latin *quae*; so *stai* (also *stâ*), "this," "the"=Lithuanian *ta*.

† Compare Sanscrit *asti*, Lithuanian *esti*, the *i* of which in Old Prussian is contained only in this compound (simply *ast*)

so far as they attach themselves to any tense of the indicative, have the suffix *mâna* or *âna*. I consider the latter to be an abbreviation of the former, as it is represented in Greek, just like *mâna*, by μενο: nor is it probable that the Sanscrit should have originally appropriated to the participle present of the middle voice two suffixes which resemble one another so closely as *mâna* and *âna*; and which, in use, are so distributed, that the former belongs exclusively to the first principal conjugation—only with the exception, that the tenth class, probably on account of its greater fulness of form, admits also *âna*—while the latter is fixed in the second conjugation; and, moreover, in the perfect, to which, as it appears to me, on account of its incumbrance with the syllable of reduplication, the shorter form is more agreeable, where we must remark, that in the present participle active also the reduplication has an influence on the weakening of the participial suffix (see §. 779. Note). The auxiliary future has everywhere preserved the complete suffix *mâna*; hence, *dâ-syâ-mâ-na-s*, both middle and passive = δω-σό-μενος. With this agrees the Lithuanian *dū̆-se-ma-s* (feminine -*ma*), "qui dabitur," since in Lithuanian the said participial suffix has been abbreviated to *ma*, which nevertheless does not cause us to overlook its connection with the Sanscrit *mâna* and Greek μενο. In the participle present *dū̆d-a-ma-s*, "qui datur," corresponds to the Greek διδό-μενος, and Sanscrit *dádh-âna-s* (for *dadh-mâ-nas*, and this for *dadâ-mâna-s*): the latter, however, is middle only, and the passive participle is दीयमानस् *dí-yá-mâna-s*.[*] The Old Prussian, which approaches the Lithuanian very closely, has, in one of the two examples of the said participle which remain to us in the translation of Luther's Catechism, preserved the origi-

---

[*] Several roots in *â* (among them *dâ*) weaken this vowel before the passive character *ya* to *i*.

nal form of the suffix with astonishing fidelity, it may be said, in its perfect Sanscrit form, unless, perhaps, the *a* of the first syllable be short. The example I mean is, *po-klaus-î-mana-s*, "heard," or rather "being heard," ἀκουόμενος :* in form, however, ὑποκλυόμενος would be the corresponding word, as *klaus* or *klus* is the Prussian form of the Greek root κλυ (Sanscrit *śru*, from (*kru*), and *po* corresponds to the Greek ὑπό, Sanscrit *úpa*. Besides *poklausímanas*, the Prussian Catechism presents one more form, which, with respect to its suffix, evidently belongs, in like manner, to the participle passive present; viz. *eni-m-u-mne*, "agreeable," properly "becoming accepted," as the participle perfect passive also signifies both "accepted" and "acceptable."†

---

* The participle present passive suits the passage where the expression occurs better than the perfect participle (Nesselmann, p. 16), *stawidas madlas ast steismu tâwan en dangon enimmewingi bhe poklausîmanas*, "such prayer is acceptable to and becoming heard (=is heard) by the Lord in heaven."

† Nesselmann (p. 104) takes *enimumne* to be a typographical error, though he gives no reason for this opinion. The termination *mne* does not appear to me doubtful: the internal vowel is omitted, as in the Latin *al-u-mnus*, *Vert-u-mnus* (§. 478.), and as in the Zend forms *bar-a-mněm*, *vaz-a-mněm*, of which hereafter. So in Old Prussian, from *kermen-s*, "body," comes the accusative *kermnem* (also *kermenen* and *kermenan*). This *kermens* for *kermenas* is, according to its formation, probably, in like manner, a passive participle; so that, properly, its meaning is equivalent to "created," "made" (Sanscrit *karômi*, "I make," compare Latin *creo, creatura*). Pott refers the Latin *corpus*, and Zend *kěrěf-s* (accusative *kěhrpěm*, to the root *klṛip, kalp;* which, however, is itself connected with *har* (*kṛi*), as Pott also assumes (see my *Sanscrit Glossary*, a. 1847, p. 84). As regards the final *e* of *enimumne*, it is either an adverbial or a neuter termination. The passage wherein the expression occurs requires properly the nominative singular neuter (Nesselmann, p. 24, n. 56, *sta ast labban bhe dygi enimumne prîki Deiwan nousesmu pogâlbenikan*, "this is good and acceptable before God our Saviour"), as *labban* also is really a neuter,

792. With respect to accent in Sanscrit, the participles, middle and passive, in *mána*, *ána*, follow the same principle as the active participles (see p. 1057), *i.e.* they are governed by the accent of the corresponding tense in the indicative; so that the suffix receives the accent only in cases in which the indicative has it on the personal termination, which happens in the heavy terminations of the present of the second principal conjugation (with the exception of the third class, see p. 1056) and of the perfect of all verbs. The Greek corresponds, in forms like τετυμ-μένος (opposed to τυπτόμενος), to the accentuation of the Sanscrit cognate forms, only that the latter have the accent on the final syllable of the suffix, so that *tutup-ánás* corresponds to the Greek τετυμ-μένος.*

---

neuter, according to the analogy of Sanscrit neuters in *am* (see §. 152.). If, however, *enimumne* is a neuter, in that case the *e* stands, as frequently happens in Old Prussian, for *a*, and the case-sign is suppressed, as in the pronominal neuters, *sta*, "this," *ka*, "what" (accusative *ka* and *kan*), and in Lithuanian neuters, as *géra*, "*bonum*" (§. 135.). If, however, there is a typographical error in this word, which is an isolated one of its kind, we might perhaps conjecture *enimumnem*=*mnan*. As regards the vowel *u*, it is probably like the Latin *u* of *al-u-mnus*, *Vert-u-mnus*—for which we might have expected *al-i-m(i)nus*, *Vert-i-m(i)nus*—the corruption of an original *a*, and corresponds to the Sanscrit *a* of the first and sixth class (§. 109ª. 1.).

* At the time when the Sanscrit suffix *ána* had not yet lost its *m*, it will probably have had, like the Greek -μένος of τετυμ-μένος, the accent on the first syllable; for that the circumstance of the suffix beginning with a consonant or a vowel may have an influence on the accentuation is clear from this, that the verbs of the third class in the present indicative have the accent only on those heavy terminations which begin with a consonant, while in cases where the heavy termination begins with a vowel, the syllable of repetition is accented (see p. 1088): hence, *bibhri-váhé*, "we two carry" (Mid.), but second person *bibhr-áthé*, third person *bíbhr-áté*, so also in the participle present middle *bíbr-ána*, not *bibhr-áná*: it is highly probable, however, that *bibhri-máná* would be said if the *m* of the suffix were retained.

FORMATION OF WORDS. 1071

793. In Old Sclavonic the participial suffix in question has experienced the same abbreviation as in Lithuanian : it is in the nominative masculine мъ *m'*, feminine мА *ma*, neuter мо *mo*, and, as in Lithuanian, has only a passive signification, but occurs only in the present. Compare везомъ *vez̧-o-m'*, "the being conveyed," feminine везома *vez̧-o-ma*, neuter везомо *vez̧-o-mo*,* with the Lithuanian *wez-a-ma-s*, feminine *-ma*, the Sanscrit *váh-a-mána-s, -á, -a-m*, the Greek ἐχ-ό-μενο-ς, -η, -ο-ν, and the Latin *veh-i-mini* (see §. 478.). In the German languages this participle, as such, has disappeared, but the Gothic *lauh-móni*, "the lightning," properly, "that which lights," from the feminine base *lauh-mónyó*,† is a substantive remnant of the participle present middle, and, therefore, the *y* is an unorganic affix, otherwise *mónó* would correspond admirably to the Sanscrit feminine suffix *máná*, as *ó* is the most common representative of the *á*, which is wanting in Gothic (see §. 69.). The nominative form *-móni*, of *mónyó*, is to be explained according to §. 120.‡

794. The Zend has either shortened or rejected the middle *a* of the Sanscrit suffix *mána*, and weakened the preceding class vowel *a* usually to ę *ĕ*. The form *mana* (*mna*) becomes, as it were, the step of transition to the Greek μενο, and Latin *minu* §. 478), and is identical with

---

* It needs, perhaps, no remark, that the vowel which precedes the *n* in all the languages here compared belongs to the class syllable, and is therefore not to be referred to the participial suffix (see §. 507.).

† Sanscrit *róch-a-máná*, "the shining," from the root *ruch* (from *ruk*), which is only used in the middle, according to the first class (see §. 109ª.). The Latin *luceo* is based on the causal form *rócháyámi* (see p. 110).

‡ It may also be assumed that the Gothic *mónyó, moni*, is based on a to-be-presupposed Sanscrit form *mání*, as bases in *a*, especially in substantives, form their feminines frequently in *î* ; as, *dêvî*, "a goddess," from *déva*, "a god." This *î* must, in Gothic, according to §. 120., take the form of *yó* or *ein*, nominative *i, ei*.

the Old Prussian *mana*, of the (§. 791.) above-mentioned *po-klaus-î-mana-s*; while the form *mna*, which has lost its internal vowel, finds an accidental countertype in the Latin *mnu*, of *al-u-mnus*, *Vert-u-mnus*, and the Old Prussian *mne*, of *en-im-u-mne* (§. 791.). In Zend, also, this suffix, as in Greek, has, beginning even with the present, both a middle (or purely active) and passive signification, while the Sanscrit in the passive prefixes the character *ya* to the participial suffix. Thus we find in the Vendidad Sade, p. 203, *barĕmanĕm*, "being carried" (= φερόμενον), and *vazĕmnem*, "being conveyed," as adverbial accusatives in reference to the nominative plural *mazdayaṡna*.* At times the final vowel, also, of the suffix *mana* is suppressed, together with the middle vowel; so that thus only *mn* is left, to which are affixed the case terminations. Thus, in *nyâsĕmn-ô*, "*celebrantes*," *yêzimnô*, "*venerantes*," which indeed, according to their termination, might also be singular nominatives of bases in *a*, but in the passage where they occur clearly shew themselves to be plurals of bases in *n*.† We might,

---

* [Zend text] *yaṭ aêtê yôi mazdayaṡna pâdha ayantĕm vâ tachĕntĕm vâ barĕmanĕm vâ vazĕmnĕm vâ tachi aipya naṡdum frajaṡaṅn*, "If those, who being worshippers of Ormuzd, going on foot, or ..... or carried, or riding ..... approach a corpse." Anquetil (p. 312) translates: "*Si un Mazdéiesnan allant à pied, ou en bateau, porté (dans une voiture), ou élevé de quelque façon que ce soit (aperçoit) un mort.* In a similar passage (l. c. p. 279) occurs *barĕmnĕm*, and likewise *vazĕmnĕm*.

† Vendidad Sade, p. 482: *Narô aṅhĕn ashavanô havôyazasta nyâsĕmnô yêzimnô Ahuramazdahm;* "*Viri sint puri, lævam manum habentes (lævâ manu tenentes), celebrantes, venerantes Ahuramazdam.*" Anquetil translates (p. 416): *Qu'il n'y ait que l'homme pure qui coupe le Barsom; et que, le tenant de la main gauche, il fasse izeschné à Ormuzd.* I consider *myâsĕmnô* as an abbreviation of *ni-yâs*, and refer, on this hand, to the root *yâs*, p. 963, Note.

FORMATION OF WORDS. 1073

therefore, also distribute the forms barĕmnĕm and vazĕmnĕm into barĕmn-ĕm and vazĕmn-ĕm, as bases which end in a consonant have, in the accusative, ĕm as their termination. That, however, in general in Zend the suffix spoken of has not lost its plural a, is shewn by forms like vazĕmna (Vend. S. p. 521), which, as nominative plural, can belong only to a base in a (§. 231. Note); thus, csayamana (l. c. p 543.) = Sanscrit ksháyamânâs, from kshi, "to rule," csayamnâo plural feminine (l. c. p. 550); frây(a)zĕmnananm, genitive plural = Sanscrit prayajamânânâm, from यज् yaj, "to honour," "to sacrifice." An example of a form in âna (for mâna) in the second principal conjugation is uś-âna (l. c. p. 543), as nominative plural for the Sanscrit uśânâs, from vaś, "to wish," with an irregular contraction of the syllable va to u. The following are examples of participles of the future passive : ᴀᴊᴀᴠᴊᴊᴡᴀᴠᴊ zanhyamana or -mna, "about to be born" (Vend. S. pp. 28 and 103)*, and ᴀᴊᴄᴀᴊᴊᴡᴘᴀᴜᴡᴄᴊ uzdâkhyamna, "being about to be raised up" = Sanscrit uddhâsyamâna (Vend. S. p. 89, see §. 669.).

795. In close connection with the participial suffix mâna stands the Sanscrit suffix man, the original form of which appears to be mân, which has remained in the strong cases. The words formed with it have, like the kindred participles, either an active or a passive signification: some are abstract substantives, like the Greek formations in μονή (φλεγμονή, χαρμονή, πεισμονή, πλησμονή, πημονή, φεισμονή), which, in form, are essentially identical with the participial feminines in μενη, as ε and o are originally one (§. 3.);

---

* See §. 668., where, however, we should read ᴀᴊᴊᴡᴀᴠᴊ zanhya, for ᴀᴊᴊᴡᴈᴡᴄ zanhya; and the remark at the end of the §. on the incorrectness of the way in which the word is written must be cancelled, and the ṅ of the participial forms referred to be really regarded as an euphonic alteration of the n of the root ᴊᴀᴠᴊ zan.

—and with regard to the accentuation of the last syllable of the suffix, they agree with the Sanscrit ânấ, anấ (for mânấ, mânấ), of the second conjugation (see §. 792.).* But few masculines in *man* remain to us in Sanscrit, and these, too, are, for the most part, but rarely used. The following are examples: *śúsh-man*, "fire," as "that which dries;" *úsh-man*, "the hot time of year," as "the burning;" *véman*, "weaver's loom," as "weaving or apparatus of weaving;" *sī́man*, "border," as "binding," from सि *si*, "to bind," with the *i* lengthened; *pā́p-man*, "sin," as "that which is sinned" (*peccatum*), from a lost root. Some masculines in *man* have a vowel of conjunction *i*; as, *har-i-mán*, "time," as "carrying away," "destroying;" *sar-i-mán*, "the wind," as "moving itself," "blowing;" "*dhar-i-mán*," "form," as "borne," "sustained" (thus the Latin *forma*, from the root *fer*); *star-i-mán*, "bed," as "spread out" (compare *stramen*). Thus, also, the two abstracts *ján-i-man*, "birth," and *már-i-man*, "death," which are likewise masculine, but are distinguished from the other forms in *man* by accenting their first syllable; *ján-i-man*, *már-i-man* — like *śúshman*, &c. — opposed to *harimán, sarimán, starimán, dharimán, bharimán*.†

---

* Compare φλεγμονή with Sanscrit middle participles like *yuñjânấ*, "the binding," from *yuñjmânấ*.

† See Böhtlingk, "*The Unâdi Affixes*," p. 58. Wilson renders *bharimán* by "nourishing," "cherishing;" Böhtlingk by "maintenance." I think, however, I may venture to deduce from the accentuation that it is not an abstract substantive; for otherwise, like *máriman*, "death," and *jániman*, "birth," it would have the accent on the radical syllable (see p. 1091). The expression कुटुंब *kuṭumba*, by which, in the Unâdi Book of *Kâumudî*, *bharimán* is explained, according to Wilson also, signifies, not "nourishing," "cherishing" (though to the root *kuṭumb*, an instance of which has not yet been met with in books, the meaning "supported" (*dhṛityâm*) is ascribed), but, amongst other things, "family;" and I conjecture that *bharimán* signifies "family," in the sense of "that which is maintained

796. In Sanscrit the masculine bases in *man* are much more numerous than the neuter: they all have the accent on the last syllable, and express partly a passive, partly an active relation, or are abstracts. The following are examples: *dhámaṇ*, "a house," as "that which is made or built," from *dhá*, " to place " (*vi-dhá* " to make "); *vártman*, "way," as "that which is gone upon," from *vart, vṛit,* "to go;" *véśman*, "a house," as "that which is entered," from *viś*, "to enter;" *sádman*, "a house," from *sad*, "to go," and "to sit;" *kárman*, "deed," "*factum*;" *várman*, "harness," as "that which covers;" *róman*, "hair" (abbreviated from *róhman*), as "growing;" *dáman*, "band," as "binding;"* *sthámaṇ*, "strength," as "having continuance," from *stá*, " to stand;" *jánman*, "birth," from *jan*, " to bear;" *préman*, "love," from *prí*, " to love." The Zend furnishes the neuter bases جسودومج *dámaṇ*, "people," as "created" (= Sanscrit धामन् *dhámaṇ,* "house;") جسودسومج *maéśman*, "urina" (*quod mingitur*, Sanscrit *mih*, "*mingere;*") and جسوجسومج *chashman*, "an eye," as "telling," "announcing." The last is radically connected with the Sanscrit *chakshus*, from *chaksh*, "to say."

797. Adjective bases in *man* are rare in Sanscrit: one example is, शर्मन् *śarman*, masculine, feminine, neuter, "happy" (as neuter substantive, "happiness,") the con-

---

maintained or supported," as the wife, *bháryá,* implies " she who is to be supported," and the husband *bhartár, bhartṛi,* "he who supports." Wilson and Böhtlingk also regard शरिमन् *śarimán* as an abstract substantive, and the latter renders it (l. c. p. 149) " to bring forth," " to bear." The explanatory Sanscrit expression (*prasava*) is, however, ambiguous: I have, in my Glossary, assigned to it the meanings *partus, partura,* and *proles, progenies, suboles ;* and here, where *śarimán* is explained by it, I would adhere to the last signification, on account of the oxytone accentuation of the just-mentioned expression.

* Without any root corresponding in idea. Compare the Greek δέω, δέσματ, from δεσμαν, of which hereafter.

nection of which with its apparent root (शर् *śar*, शृ *śṛi*, "to break,") is, as regards meaning, by no means clear. In Greek, adjective bases in μον correspond, both as to accent and as to the non-distinction of the feminine base from that of the masculine neuter; as, μνῆμον, τλῆμον, λῆσμον, ἴδμον, φράδμον, ἐπιστῆμον. To the paroxytone masculine substantive bases mentioned in §. 795., like *śúshman*, "fire," as "drying," correspond in Greek such as πνεῦμον (" lung," as " breathing "), γνῶμον, δαῖμον (" god," " goddess," properly "shining,"* στῆμον. With the there-mentioned tri-syllable oxytone masculine bases like *harimán*, "time," as "taking away,"- compare κηδεμόν, ἡγεμόν. Here, too, belong—as ε, like ο, is a corruption of *a* —some bases in μέν; viz. ποιμέν (" herdsman," as " causing to feed," compare *pasco* and the Sanscrit root *pâ*, "to support," "to nourish "), ἀϋτμέν,† λιμέν, πυθμέν (the two latter from roots now obscured). The suffix μών, μῶν-ος, of κευθμών, θημών, χειμών, λειμών (from λειβ-μών), has preserved, through all the cases, the long vowel, which, in the corresponding Sanscrit suffix, is retained only in the strong cases: so, too, the corresponding Latin *môn* of the bases *sermôn, termôn* (=*terminus*, see §. 478.) *têmôn*, and *pulmôn*.‡—

---

* It belongs to the Sanscrit root *div*, "to shine;" whence *déva*, "a god;" *div*, "heaven; *divasa*, "day," &c. (See Benfey, *Gr. R. L.* II. p. 207.)

† With respect to the T-sound in ἀϋτμήν and σταθμών, and which is often added to the root before the suffix μο, remark a similar circumstance in Sanscrit, where, before the suffixes *van, vara*, and the gerundial suffix *ya*, a euphonic *t* is always added to roots which end with a short vowel; as from *ji* comes *jitvan* and *jitvara*, "conquering;" *jitya* (with prepositions preceding), "after the conquest."

‡ Compare Pott, *Etym. Inq.* II. 594. and I. 270., where *té-mo*, as well as *tig-num*, is compared with the Sanscrit *taksh*, "*frangere, findere, fabricari;*" whence, also, *takshan*, "a carpenter;" and our *Deichsel*, " a chip-axe" (Old High German *dihsila*, and Anglo-Saxon *dhixl*), and the Old High German *dehsa* and *dehsala*, feminine, "axe" (Graff, V. 125.), as "cleaving."

It is also highly probable that to the Sanscrit formations in *man* belongs the Latin *ho-min*, for *ho-môn* (in the old language *he-mo*, *he-mônis*). I take the *h*, as has been already remarked elsewhere ("*Berlin Annual Reg. of Lit. Crit.*" Nov. 1830. p. 791; compare Pott, "*Etymological Inquiries*," I. p. 217; and Benfey, "*Gr. R. L.*" II. p. 105), to be the representative of the *f* of *fui*, &c., and therefore *hŏ* as =*fŏ*, in *fŏ-re, fŏ-rem*. Let reference be made to the Prâkrit *hômi* and *havâmi*, "I am," for the Sanscrit *bhavâmi*, and the dative termination *hi*, of *mihi*, compared with the Sanscrit *hyam*, from *bhyam* (see §. 215. and §. 23. at the end). Man, therefore, according to the Latin expression, is simply "the being," as in Sanscrit *jana*, "the born" (root *jan*, "to produce," "to bear"). There is also in Sanscrit an appellation of man, from भू *bhû*, "to be," viz. *bhuvana* (see Wilson); and two appellations of the earth, viz. *bhû* (the simple root) and *bhûmi* (compare Latin *humus*). I am, however, not aware that *bhavat*, "being," also signifies "man," as Benfey l. c. asserts. The resemblance of the Gothic base *gu-man*, "man," Old High German *go-mon*, *ko-mon* (nominative *guma, gomo, komo*), on which is based our *gam*, of *Bräutigam*, "bridegroom" (Old High German *brût-gomon*, properly *Braut-Mann*) to the Latin *ho-min*, *he-môn*, is surprising: the relationship, however, I am now of opinion, is confined to the suffix, and the German expression in reference to its root belongs to the above-mentioned Sanscrit *jana* (compare Graff, IV. p. 198), with the retention of the old medial (see §. 92.), and with the loss of the *n*, as in the radically, and, by suffix, related *kí-mon*, "germ" (see §. 799. Note), and in the Latin *gê-minus* (see §. 478. at the end). Properly, therefore, *gu-man, go-mon*,

---

"cleaving." With the active signification among Latin formations in *môn* only remains *pulmón*, "lung," as "breathing," by transposition from *plumón* (Ionic πλεύμων).

signify "the born." The circumstance that we have already the Sanscrit root *jan* contained in Gothic in the forms *kin* (*keina, kain, kinum,* whence our *Kind,* "child"), *kun* (*kuni,* "sex") and *qvin* (*qveins,* "lawful wife," as "she who bears," compare γυνή), need not prevent us from admitting a form which has preserved the original medial. I would recall to mind the fact that both the Gothic *qvam,* "to come" (*qvima, qvam*), and *gagga,* "I ġo," are derived from the Sanscrit root *gam,* "to go" (see §. 755.). But to return to the Latin suffix *môn*—from it arise the forms *mônia, môniu,* by the addition of *ia* or *iu*; as, *tôria,* from *tôr* (*victôria,* from *victor*), with this difference, that the primitives in *môn* of derivatives like *quer-i-mônia, al-i-mônia, al-i-mônium, cer-i-mônia* (root *cer* = Sanscrit *kar, kri,* "to make") have disappeared. From adjective and substantive bases also spring, by this double suffix, abstracts like *acri-mônia, ægri-mônia, casti-mônia, miseri-mônium, tristi-mônium, testi-mônium, matri-mônium.* I consider the *i* of forms like *casti-mônia, ægri-mónia,* to be a weakening of the final vowel of the base-noun (see "*Vocalismus,*" pp. 132, 162, and 223), and the *i* of *matri-mônium* to be an extension of the base, which, in the generality of cases, is added to all bases ending in a consonant. I therefore now regard the *ê* in the nominative plural as a contraction of *ai,* and as = the Sanscrit *ay* (from *ai*), of *ay-as*: *ovê-s,* for example, therefore, has the same relation to the Sanscrit *avay-as* that *mon-ê-s* has to *mân-aya-si,* Prâkrit *mân-ê-si* (see p. 119); and thus *pedê-s, amantê-s,* come from the extended bases *pedi, amanti.* Remark that bases in *u* also, in the nominative plural, have simple *s* for their termination, and that here the lengthening of the *u* represents the Sanscrit and Gothic Guna; *e. g., fructû-s,* as in Sanscrit *sûnav-as,* and in Gothic *sunyu-s,* "son," from *sûnu, sunu* (see §. 230.). Compare, also, what has been said before (§. 780.) regarding the Old Prussian present participle.

FORMATION OF WORDS. 1079

798. In Greek there are some bases in μῑν which preserve the long vowel in all cases, and resemble the Sanscrit strong cases with mán, to which, with respect to their í, they bear the same relation that, in Sanscrit, the plural kri-ní-más, " we buy," has to the singular kri-ná-mi (see §. 485.). Compare the accusative singular ῥηγμῖν-α, and the nominative plural ῥηγμῖν-ες, with analogous Sanscrit forms like súshmán-am, súshmán-as; while in the genitive singular, which belongs to the weak cases, the Sanscrit súshman-as (with short a) stands in disadvantageous contrast with the Greek ῥηγμῖν-ος. The suffix μῑνο, feminine μῑνη, is connected with the Sanscrit participial suffix mána, and, with reference to the retention of the long vowel, stands nearer the latter, than the usual μενο. Here belong κάμῑνο-ς, " oven," as " burning," " glowing," from καίω, κᾱω, with the radical vowel shortened; ὑσμῑνη, " strife," for which no root occurs in Greek, but which Pott (II. p. 594) rightly traces to the Sanscrit yudh, " to strive " (whence yudhma-s, " strife," which would lead us to expect, in Greek, ὑσμος); κυκλάμῑνος, κυκλάμῑνον, properly " rounded."

799. To the Sanscrit masculine substantive bases in मन् man, mentioned in §. 795., correspond the just-mentioned masculine bases ahman, " spirit," as " thinking " (ahya, " I think "); hliuman, " ear," as " hearing " (Sanscrit root śru, from kru, " to hear,' Greek κλυ); blôman, " a flower," as " blowing " (Old High German bluot, " floret ;" bluont, " florent "); milhman, " a cloud " (probably like the Sanscrit mégha, originally "mingens," see §. 140.) ; skeiman, " a lamp," as " shining," " lighting" (Sanscrit kan, " to light")* ; and

---

* I have no scruple in deducing skeiman from the root skin, " to shine," " to light " (skeina, skain, skinum), with the suppression of the final consonant of the root, as nm is a combination unsuited to the German ; hence, also, in Old High German, kí-mon, chí-mon (nominative -mo), "germ," from

with passive signification, *mal-man*, "sand," as "triturated," also neuter (nominative masculine *malma*, neuter *malmô*, see §§. 140. 141.); and *hiuh-man*, "heap," as "heaped up," from the root, lost as regards the verb, *huh* (euphonic *hauh*, see §. 82.), to which also belongs *hauhs*, "high" (Grimm, II. p. 50). The Old High German places over against the Gothic-Sanscrit *man* the form *mon* (nominative *mo*), and in this form corresponds to the Greek μον. The following are examples: *wahs-a-mon*, and *wahsmon*, "vegetables," "fruit," as "growing," or "having grown;"* *glíz-e-mon*, "lustre;" *ka-smag-mon*, "taste;" with passive signification; *sâ-mon*, "seed," as "sown" (Latin *se-men*).† As in Sanscrit the suffix *man* also forms abstract substantive or adjective bases, as *prath-i-mán*, "breadth," from *prithú*, "broad" (from *prathu*, compare Greek πλατύ); *krishn-i-mán*, "blackness," from *krishná*, "black;"‡ we may also here mention the Old High German *rôta-mon* (also *rôto-mon*, *rôte-mon*),

---

from the roots *kin*, *chin* (*chin-i-t*, "*pullulat*," *ar-kin-i-t*, -*chini-t*, "*gignit*," "*germinat*," see Graff, IV. 450.) = Sanscrit जन् *jan*, "to produce," "to bear" (Latin *gen*, Greek γεν), whence *ján-man* neuter, and *ján-i-man* masculine, "birth," which agrees with *kímon* in root and suffix. *Ger-men*, for *gen-men*, corresponds in Latin. With respect to the rejection of the final consonant of the root before the *m* of the suffix, compare the (§. 796.) above-mentioned Sanscrit *rô-man*, "hair of the body," as "growing," for *rôh-man*; and Latin forms like *fulmen*, for *fulg-men*; *lû-men*, for *luc-men*; as well as *gê-minus* (see §. 478. conclusion), which is probably, in root and suffix, connected with *kí-mon*. To *lû-men* corresponds, in root and suffix, the Anglo-Saxon *lëo-man* (nominative *lëoma*), "light," for *lëoh-man*, compare Gothic *lauh-môni*, "lightning" (§. 793.).

† The kindred Sanscrit root *vaksh*, "to grow," would, in the middle, form *vákshamána* as participle present.

* This has been already explained in the above sense in my Review of Grimm's German Grammar ("*Berlin Ann. Reg. of Lit. Criticism*," Feb. 1827, p. 757; "*Vocalismus*," p. 131).

‡ The final vowel of the base word is rejected before the vowel of conjunction *i*.

FORMATION OF WORDS. 1081

"redness," from the adjective base *rôta*, as a very remarkable analogous form. The Latin uses for this object the suffix *môniu*, or feminine *mônia* (see §. 797. conclusion), extended from *môn*.

800. In Lithuanian the suffix spoken of appears in the form *men*, nominative *mů̃*; and thus, from a Lithuanian point of view, the obscure *piemen*, nominative *piemů̃*, "shepherd's boy," corresponds to the Greek ποιμέν, ποιμήν (see §. 797.); and *akmen*, —*mů̃*, "stone," to the Sanscrit, also obscure, *áśman*, —*mâ*. From a Lithuanian point of view, the bases *aug-men*, *źel-men*, "sprout," "shoot," as "growing," (*augu* and *źelu*,"I grow"); *yos-men*, "apron-string," "girdle" (*yós-mi*, "I have a girdle on;" *ap-si-yós-mi*, "I gird myself"); *sto-men*, "stature" (*stowyu*, "I stand," compare Sanscrit *sthâ-man*, "strength, from *sthâ*, "to stand"), are quite intelligible. *Semenys*, "linseed," properly only "seed" (*sĕyu*, "I sow," future *sĕ-su*), is a nominative plural, as *akmeny-s*, "stones," from the extended base *akmeni*,* and leads us to expect a singular *semů̃*; and therefore corresponds to the Old High German base *sâ-mon* (§. 799.), and to the Latin *se-men*. The Old Sclavonic presents a few masculine bases in мен, which, in the nominative, contrast мы *my* with the Lithuanian *mů̃* and Sanscrit *mâ* (see §. 260. at the end, and p. 348), but prefer, however, the form *meny*, from the prolonged base *meni* (Dobrowsky, pp. 287 and 289, under ЕНЬ *eny*). From a Sclavonic point of view, however, only *pla-men* (nominative *plamy*, or *plameny*, "flame," as "burning,"

---

* The suffix *men* forms the entire plural, with the exception of the genitive (*akmen-û*, "*lapidum*"=Sanscrit *aśman-âm*), from the extended *meni*. In some cases of the singular the suffix is extended by the addition of *ia*; thus, in the genitive, *ákmenio* (like *wilko*, §. 169.), together with the organic *ákmen-s*; instrumental *ákmeniu* (like *wilku*), together with *akmeni-mi*; accusative *ákmeni-ǹ*; locative *ákmeniye*, according to the analogy of *awiye*, from the base *awi*, "a sheep."

4 A

is etymologically intelligible (планѫтица *planuṅti-saṅ*, "*comburi*;" палити *pal-i-ti*, "*urere*," &c.; see Miklos. p. 62); камен *kamen*, "stone" (nominative *kamy*, or *kameny*) answers to the Lithuanian *akmen, akmů*, and Sanscrit *áś-man, áśmá*.

801. To the Sanscrit neuter bases in *man* (nominative *ma*, see §. 139.), mentioned at §. 796., correspond the Latin in *min* (*men* in the cases having no termination beyond the base), the Greek in ματ, for μαν (see §. 497), and the Gothic and Sclavonic in *man*, мен *men*. The Latin and Greek formations which come under this class have, like their Sanscrit sister forms, either a passive signification, which, indeed, is generally the case; as *praefamen, stramen, sêmen, agmen, segmen, germen*,* πραγματ, ποιηματ, ῥηματ, ἀκουσματ, γραμματ, γλυμματ, δοματ, βρωματ; or an active signification, as *flûmen, lûmen*, (from *lucmen*), *fulmen* (from *fulgmen*), *tegmen, teg-i-men*,† *teg-u-men, reg-i-men* ("helm," as "guid-

---

* *Germen*, from *genmen*, is founded on the frequent interchange of liquids (§. 20.).

† The *i* of *teg-i-men, reg-i-men*, is identical with the class-vowel of the third conjugation, and leads us, therefore, to the Sanscrit *a* of the first and sixth class, which in Latin has been weakened to *i* or *u* (*veh-i-mus, veh-u-nt*, see §. 507.): this is clear from the long *i* of the fourth conjugation (*mol-î-men, fulc-î-men*, as *mol-î-mini, fulc-î-mini*), and the *â* of the first (*certâmen, levâmen*, &c.). Forms like *agmen, fragmen, tegmen*, on the contrary, belong to that period of Sanscrit which combines the suffix *man*, without reference to the conjugation of the verb, almost invariably direct with the root. In the Latin second conjugation we should expect *ê* before the said suffix, and the *mentu* derived from it: for it, however, we find, where the suffix is not combined direct with the root, according to the analogy of the third conjugation, *i* or *u*; hence, *sed-i-men, doc-u-men, doc-u-mentum, mon-i-mentum, mon-u-mentum*. In general, the Latin *ê* of the second conjugation does not keep its place so firmly as the two other representatives of the Sanscrit tenth class (see p. 110); hence, also, *doc-ui, doc-tum*, opposed to *am-â-vi, am-â-tum, aud-î-vi, aud-î-tum*.

ing "), δεσματ, ρυματ, πνευματ, ἀηματ, βροντηματ, εἱματ, ἐσθηματ ; or are abstracts, as *solamen, certamen, levamen, tentamen, regimen, molimen,* βληματ, βοηματ, βρυχηματ, δειματ, χαρματ. At the end of compounds, the original ν of the suffix ματ, which is corrupted from μαν, either remains in its original form, or is entirely suppressed: in both cases, however, the α is corrupted to ο (nominative masculine and feminine μων); probably because the heavy sounds τ and α are found, through the incumbrance of composition, less appropriate than the lighter ν and ο; hence, πολυπραγμον, ἀπραγμον, ἀναιμον, and ἀναιμο, ἀκυμον and ἀκυμο, ἀνωνυμο, συνωνυμο. The form νωνυμνο is interesting, because here we find intact the old *n* of the Sanscrit *náman,* Latin *nómen,* &c., which, in ὀ-νοματ, has become τ, but elsewhere, in the compounds of this word, is suppressed: along with its retention, however, we find the base prolonged by ο, and the vowel of the suffix suppressed (νωνυμνο, from νωνυμανο, or νωνυμονο); in the latter respect compare the weakest cases of the Sanscrit *náman,* the genitive *námn-as,* dat. *námn-ê,* and the Gothic plural *namn-a.** Ἀπαλαμνο points to a lost substantive παλαματ, from παλαμαν (of which, also, παλαμναῖος is a proof), which apparently has been disused for παλάμη. I would also rather regard κρηδεμνο, " head-band,"

---

* In §. 235. *namóna* is given incorrectly, though this form would be the regular one (compare *hairtóna*), and would correspond well to the Sanscrit *namân-i* (from *namân-a,* see §. 234.). The form *namna,* on the other hand, answers to the Sanscrit weakest cases, while the nominative, accusative, and vocative plural of Sanscrit neuters always belong to the strong (see smaller "*Sanscrit Grammar,*" §. 177. Note). It appears, however, that in Gothic it is necessary, for the protection of the full form *óna,* that it be preceded by a vowel long in itself or by position, or by more than one syllable; hence *augóna, ausóna, barnilóna, ubilóna,* but not *namóna,* and probably, also, not *vatóna,* from *vatan,* "water," as the dative is *vatnam,* not *vata(n)-m*; compare Grimm, I. p. 609, Gabel. and Löbe, p. 67.

with respect to its concluding element, as a form analogous to -ωνυμνο (and, therefore, as a derivative from δεματ, from δεμαν), than as a participle for δεμενο: on the other hand, I look upon δίδυμνο, which Passow takes to be analogous to νώνυμνο-ς and ἀπάλαμνο-ς, as a participle (properly, therefore, "doubled") from a reduplicated verbal base δίδυ, which has sprung from δύο, and from which a present indicative δίδυμι might have been expected; thus, δίδυμνο-ς, like διδόμενο-ς, only with the suppression of the middle vowel of the suffix, as in the Latin *al-u-mnu*, and in the above-mentioned (§. 791.) *en-im-u-mne*. Compare, also, the participial substantive bases in μνο, feminine μνα, as, βελεμνο, μεδιμνο, μεριμνα, which have been already discussed by Pott (*E. I.* II. p. 594.) under this view, and which have no corresponding verb, any more than the above-mentioned δίδυμνο, though βελεμνο, just like βελος, is visibly connected with βάλλω.

802. The Old Sclavonic neuter bases in мен *men* have in the cases, which in Sanscrit and Gothic drop the final *n*, retained the original *a* with a resonant nasal; hence, има *iman*, "names" (see §. 783. Rem. 1. conclusion), from the base *imen* = Sanscrit *nâ-man*. Here belong, also, the bases сѣмен *sye-men*, "seed," as "sown" (*sye-ya-ti*, "to sow") = Latin *semen*, Old High German *sâmon* masculine (see §. 793. Note 3), писмен *pis-men*, "letter of the alphabet," as "written" (*pis-a-ti*, "to write");* знамен *zna-*

---

* I cannot refrain from drawing attention here to the strong agreement between the Sclavonic root *pis* and the Old Persian *pish*, with the preposition *ni*: *ni-pish*, "to write down," "to describe," properly, "to hew in." Rawlinson (Beh. IV. 47. 48.) translates 𐎴𐎡𐎱𐎡𐏁𐎫𐎶 *nipishtam* by "*scriptum*;" and, IV. 71., 𐎴𐎡𐎹𐎱𐎡𐏁. ▶𐏐. *niyapisha(ya)m* by "*inscripsi.*" I think, however, that we must, with the 𐎱 *p*, read also the *a* contained in it; thus, *niyapaishayam*: for whether this form be taken as a causal—thus, "I have caused to describe" — or as a verb of the tenth class, in both cases Guna is indispensable.
The

men, "a sign," as "making to know" (*ǧna-ti* "to know"), and a few words from obscure roots (Dobrowsky, p. 288). The Gothic furnishes besides *na-man*, "names" (nominative accusative *namô*, see §. 141.), which, in the other German languages, has become masculine, only *aldô-man*, "age," if this word really be, as Gabel. and Löbe suppose, a neuter, which cannot be discerned from the but once occurring dative *aldômin* (Luke i. 36). As the neuter abstract of an adjective it would correspond to the above-mentioned (§. 799. conclusion) Sanscrit neuter bases like *kṛishṇ'-i-mán*, "blackness," from *kṛishṇá*, "black;" while the there-mentioned *rôta-mon*, "redness," like *namon*, "names" (nominative *namo*), has perhaps first become neuter as it was gradually corrupted. The *ô* of the Gothic *aldô-man* I take to be the lengthening of the *a* of the base *alda* (see §. 69.), "old," which, indeed, does not occur, but may be inferred from the cognate dialects (see Graff, I. 192). If, however, *aldô-man* is derived, not from an adjective, but from a verb, we must suppose a lost denominative *aldô-m*, "I grow old" (see §. 765.); and *aldô-mon* would then correspond to Latin formations like *certâ-men* (§. 801.). We can hardly imagine any similarity of formation between the above and the Old High German compounds *alt-duom, alt-tuom* (see Grimm, II. 151.).

803. From the suffix *men, min*, an extended form *mentu* has proceeded in Latin (*argu-mentu-m, mon-u-mentu-m, incre-mentu-m, co-gno-mentu-m, sed-i-mentu-m* &c.), in which I do not agree with Pott (*E. I.* II. 594.) in recognising the affix of a participial suffix *tu* (*tus, ta, tum*), but one that is simply phonetic; just as, in Gothic, the base *hun-da* (nominative *hunds*) stands over against the Sanscrit *śun* of the weakest

---

The causal form of the Sanscrit *pish*, Class 7, "to beat down," "to bruise," whence the meaning "to engrave," "to hew in," is easily deducible appears to me the most probable.

cases, and Greek κυν (κύων, κυνός), or as, in Latin, the Sanscrit roots *tan*, "to extend," and *han* (from *dhan*), "to smite," "to slay" (Greek θαν), has become extended to *tend, fend* ($f=dh$, θ, see §. 293.), and, in Sanscrit itself, *kan* and *chand* (from *kand*), "to shine," are originally one. A mute is readily attracted to the side of a nasal, and the former as easily annexes a vowel; and thus, for the Latin extended suffix *mentu*, without reference to gender, we find a parallel in the Old High German *munda* (from *manda*), nominative *mund*, but only in the solitary base *hliu-munda*, nominative *hliu-mund* (abbreviated *liu-mund*, our *Leumund*, "renown"), "fame," as "that which is heard," as in Gothic *hliu-man*, "ear," as "hearing" (compare Grimm, II. p. 243). The Greek base ἐλμινθ, "worm," as "winding itself," has added to the suffix μῖν, mentioned above (§. 798.), only a θ, but in this respect stands as isolated as, in Old High German, the just mentioned *hliu-munda*. The form ἐλμιγγ (ἔλμιγγες) exhibits, instead of the *T*-sound, a guttural, and thus reminds us of the relation of our *yung*, "young" (Gothic *Yugg-s*, theme *yugga = yunga*), to the Sanscrit *yuvan*, in the weakest cases *yûn* (genitive *yûn-as*), and Latin *juvenis, junior*. Thus the Old High German suffix *unga* (our *ung*) of abstract substantives, as in *ar-find-unga*, "invention," *warn-unga*, "warning," may be identical with the Sanscrit feminine form of the suffix *ana* (*anâ*); so that the first *a* has become weakened to *u*, as in the polysyllabic forms of the preterite, as *bunti*, "thou didst bind," compared with the monosyllabic *bant*, "I bound," "be bound." In the same way our root *sang*, "to sing," (Old High German *singu*, "sang," second person *sungi*), may be compared with the Sanscrit root *svan*, "to sound" (compare Graff, VI. p. 247).

804. I think I discover the origin of the medio-passive participial suffix *mâna*, and of the cognate nominal suffix *man*, in the combination of two demonstrative bases *ma*

and *na* (see §§. 368. 369.); the vowel, therefore, being lengthened in *mâna*, and in the strong cases of *man*, and the final vowel in the last-mentioned form being suppressed. We must here observe that *na* readily combines with other pronominal bases, and then always takes the last place; hence अन *ana*, एन *êna*, in Greek κεῖνος, and in Old Prussian *ta-ns*, for *ta-na-s*, "he,"* opposed to the Lithuanian simple *ta-s*, "the." If the medial relation be really expressed formally in the suffix *mâna*, μενο, in that case the final element must express the nominative relation, or that relation which, from time to time, belongs to the position of the participle; and the unchangeable *mâ*, με, the dative or accusative (*sibi, se*); so that, therefore, न *na*, νο, denote the person acting, and मा *mâ*, με, the person acted upon, which, however, in the middle, are one and the same. The suffixes of participles, as in general those of adjectives and substantives, represent the personal terminations of verbs, *i.e.* those of the third person; and I thus consider the *t* of the participle present and future active as identical with the termination of the third person, and, like the latter, a derivative from the pronominal base *ta*, the vowel of which, in the participial suffix, is dropped. The *n* of the active participial suffix probably serves only for the phonetic intensification and more emphatic designation of the agent; while, in the third person plural, plurality is symbolically denoted by the same nasalization (see §. 536.): hence the coincidence of *bhárant*, φέροντ, *ferent* Gothic *bairand*, "bearing," with *bháranti*, φέροντι, *ferunt*, *bairand*, "they bear."

805. We recognise the simple pronominal base *ma* in the Sanscrit suffix म *ma*, which in adjectives or substantives denotes the person or thing which completes the action

---

* Feminine *tanna*, with the favourite repetition of the liquid.

expressed by the root, or on whom that action is accomplished. Abstracts, also, are formed by this suffix, which, however, is seldom adopted in that state of the language which has descended to us; while the corresponding suffixes of the Lithuanian and Greek (*ma*, μο) are of very frequent use. The following are examples in Sanscrit: *rukmá-m*, "gold," as "glittering" (*ruch*, from *ruk*, "to shine"); *yugmá-m*, "pair," as "bound together;" *tigmá*, adjective (*-má-s, má, má-m*), "sharp" ("sharpened"), "hot" (root *tij*, from *tig*, "to sharpen"), substantive neuter (*tigmá-m*) "heat;" *bhîmá*, "fearful" ("feared," root *bhî*, "to fear"); *dhûmá-s*, "smoke," as "being moved" (root *dhû*, "to move"); *yudh-má-s*, "combatant," "contest," "arrow" (*yudh*, "to fight"); *gharmá-s*, "heat," apparently as "moistening," by sweat (root *ghar*, *ghri*, "to sprinkle"); *ishmá-s*, "tone" (root *ish*, "to wish"); *idhmá-s*, "wood," as "being burned" (root *idh*, "to burn"). To the latter corresponds the Zend ‌‌‌‌ *aêsma* (nominative *mô*). Remark the agreement of the above-mentioned Sanscrit words in the accentuation of the suffix with Greek formations like στολμό-ς, παλμό-ς, κορμό-ς, ὀδυρμό-ς, κομμό-ς, τριμμό-ς, φλογμό-ς, ἀγμό-ς, ῥυμό-ς, χυμό-ς, κλαυ-θ-μό-ς, μυκη-θ-μό-ς. In Sanscrit, also, there are a few words formed with *ma*, which, like πότμο-ς, οἶμο-ς,* ἄνεμο-ς, ὄλμο-ς, and some others of obscure origin in Greek (Buttmann, II. p. 315), have the accent on the radical syllable. Here belong, for example, *bhấma-s*, "the sun," as "giving light," *śúshma-m*, "fever," as "drying." To the masculine nominatives in *ma-s* correspond numerous Lithuanian abstracts in *i-ma-s*, or, with *m* doubled, *i-mma-s*,†

---

* οἰ is the Guna form of the root *i*, "to go" (compare §. 609). Thus, in Sanscrit, *vártman*, "way," from *vart*, *vṛit*, "to go."

† With regard to the doubling of the *m*, compare the doubling of liquids so common in Old Prussian. I believe I have discovered it to be a fixed law in Lithuanian, that the doubling of the *m* in the said suffix is only

FORMATION OF WORDS. 1089

the *i* of which, as in Sanscrit forms like *ján-i-man*, " birth " (see §. 795.), is only a vowel of conjunction. The following are examples: *gimm-i-mma-s*, " birth;" *ey-i-mma-s*, "going" (*ei-mi*, " I go ;" *ey-au*, " I went "); *pa-gadinn-i-ma-s*, " ruin " (*pa-gadinu*, "I mar"). In this manner, in Lithuanian, abstract substantives are formed from adjective bases also, in which formation a final *a* of the adjective base is weakened to *u*, while bases in *u* have their vowel unchanged. The following are examples: *gûdu-mma-s*, " avarice," from *gûdù-s*, "avaricious ;" *gra-źu-mma-s*, " beauty," from *graźù-s*, " beautiful ;" *darku-mna-s*, " ugliness," from *darkù-s*, " ugly ;" *drasu-mna-s*, " boldness," from *drasù-s*, " bold " (compare Greek θρασύς, θαρσύς, Sanscrit *dharsh*, *dhṛish*, " to dare "); *rietu-mna-s*, " hardness," from *rieta-s*, " hard ;" *auksztu-mma-s* " height " from *aukszta-s* " high ;" *ilgu-mma-s* " length," from *ilgi-s* (for *ilgia-s*, see §. 135.), " long."*

806. The Latin has but a few words in *mu-s*, and those of obscure origin and etymology, to offer in comparison with the Indo-Lithuanian in *ma-s* and Greek in μο-ς ; as, *an-i-mus*, which, like the Greek ἄν-ε-μο-ς, has originated from the Sanscrit root *an*, " to breathe," " to blow " (see 109[b]. 2.); *fu-mus* = θυμός, Sanscrit *dhû-más*, " smoke " (root *dhû*, θυ, see §. 293.); perhaps *pô-mu-m*, " apple," as " nourishing," or " being tasted " (Sanscrit *pâ*, " to support," and " to drink," compare *pa-bulum*, *pa-sco*, *pâ-vi*, *pô-tus*, *pô-*

---

only then permitted or required when, exclusive of prefixes in combination with the verb, the verbal base is monosyllabic. If, however, it be polysyllabic, the *m* is not doubled; hence, indeed, *gimm-i-mma-s*, "birth," and also *uz-gimm-i-mma-s*, idem. ; *su-gruw-i-mma-s*, " circumstance" (*gruwu*, " I occur "); but not *graudén-i-mma-s*, " warning," but *graudén-i-mas* (*graudenu*, "I admonish").

* Bases in *ia*, nominative *is*, drop their *i* before the *u* of their abstracts which has arisen from *a*; hence *middu-mmas*, "greatness, from *middis*, "great."

tûra); and the adjectives *for-mus* (compare *ferveo, fer-mentum*), *fir-mus* (compare *for-tis, fero*), *al-mus*. In the German languages, also, the formations of this class are, for the most part, no longer conscious of their origin: they occur in Grimm, II. p. 145, where, however, the bases in *ma* and those in *mi*, which have both lost their final vowel in the nominative singular, are not distinguished. I regard the suffix *mi*, which exists also in Sanscrit and in Greek,* as merely a weakened form of *ma*, as in the Greek pronominal base μι (accusative μίν) = Sanscrit *ma* (see §. 368.). The Gothic *bag-ms*, "tree" (theme *bag-ma*), probably means originally "the growing" (Sanscrit *barh, bṛih*, "to grow"): the adjective base *ar-ma*, nominative *arms*, is perhaps an abbreviation of *ard-ma*, and a shoot from the Sanscrit root *ard*, "to vex," with which I would compare, also, the Sanscrit *ár-ma* (nominative masculine *árma-s*, neuter *árma-m*) "a malady of the eyes:" *bar-mi* (nominative *barms*), "lap," springs evidently from the root *bar* (*baira, bar*) "to carry." In Old High German *dau-m, dou-m* (theme *-ma*, or *-mi*?) "vapour," corresponds to the Sanscrit *dhû-má-s*, "smoke;" *trau-m*, theme *trau-ma* (Old Saxon *drô-m, drô-ma*), leads us to the Sanscrit root *drâ* "to sleep;" *sau-m* (theme *sau-ma*), "seam," to सिव् *siv*, "to sew" (Old High German *siwu*, "*suo*"); *hel-m*, "helm," as "covering," springs from the root *hal*, "to conceal" (*hilu, hal, hulumês*).

807. The feminine form of the suffix, viz. *mâ*, does not occur in Sanscrit in substantives; but the Greek in μη, as γνώμη, μνήμη, στιγμή, γραμμή, correspond to it; as do the Latin, like *flamma*, from *flagma, fâma, spûma, strûma, glûma*

---

* *E.g.* दलिमस् *dal-mí-s*, masculine, Indra's "thunderbolt," from *dal*, "to cleave;" भूमिस् *bhû-mí-s*, "earth," feminine, from *bhû*, "to be," "to become;" δύνα-μι-ς, φῆ-μι-ς, θέ-μι-ς (Ion. genitive Θέμι-ος).

FORMATION OF WORDS. 1091

for *glubma*; and the Lithuanian in *ma*, *mẽ*;* as *waźmà*,
"riding;" *túźmà*, "grief" (*túźio-s*, "I grieve"); *sluźmà*,
"service" (*sluźiu*, "I serve");† *giesmẽ*, "song" (*giĕdmi*,
"I sing"); *báimẽ*, "fear" (*biyau*, "I fear" Sanscrit root
bhî, "to fear," *bhímá-s*, "fearful," and nominative preterite, whence the patronymic *bháima-s*, feminine *bháimî*);
drausmẽ,‡ "prohibition." To this class probably belong,
also, the Lithuanian and Sclavonic abstracts in *ba*, *bẽ*, ва
ba; so that the medial stands in place of the organic
nasal, as in *dewini*, дєвать *devañty*, "nine" (see §. 783.);
and as in Greek βροτός, βραδύς = Sanscrit *mritá-s*, *mridú-s*.
Thus, in Lithuanian we find the forms *túźbà*, "grief,"
slúźbà, "service," side by side with *tuźmà*, *sluźmà*, which
have the same meaning. *Garbẽ*, "honour," "fame" (*gir-
riu*, "I praise"), corresponds in its root to the Sanscrit
gar, *gri* (in the Vêda-dialect, "to praise"). Abstracts in
bẽ from adjective bases, whose final vowel has been weakened to *y* (= *i*), are numerous; as, *silpny-bé*, "weakness,"

---

* *Mẽ* from *mia* (see p. 174, Note *).

† Thus *drutu-mà*, "strength," together with *drutu-ma-s*, from the adjective base *drúta*, "strong."

‡ For *draud-mẽ* (*draudziu*, "I forbid"), according to the analogy of
the infinitive *draus-ti*, in which the change of the *d* before *t* into *s* is regular (see §. 457.). In *ei-s-mẽ*, "going" (*ei-mi*, "I go"), the *s* is euphonic,
as in Greek forms like δε-σ-μή, δε-σ-μός. A euphonic *s* of this kind sometimes precedes the masculine suffix also, but, I imagine, only after gutturals, and then the insertion of the vowel of conjunction *i*, mentioned at
§. 805., does not take place; hence, *dźaug-s-mas*, "joy" (*dźaugio-s*, "I
rejoice"); *werk-s-mas*, "weeping;" *rêk-s-mas*,"clamour." Hence it appears that, in Lithuanian, *ksm* or *gsm* is a more favourite combination
than *gm*, *km*. Compare, in this respect, the insertions of consonants
mentioned in §§. 95. 96., from which, however, is to be excepted the *s* of
the Old High German *tarst*, "thou venturest," *torsta*, "I ventured," as
here the *s* belongs rather to the root (Sanscrit *dharsh*, *dhrish*, "to dare"),
see *Sanscrit Glossary*, a. 1847, p. 186.

from *silbna-s*, "weak;" *byaury-bĕ*, "ugliness," from *byaurù-s*, "ugly." The following are examples of Russian abstracts in *ba*: мольба *molyba*, "begging" (молю *molyu*, "I beg"); служба *sluschba*, "service" (служу *sluschu*, "I serve"); стражба *straschba*, "watching" (стрегу *steregu*, "I watch"); алчба *alćba*, "hunger" (алчл *alću*, "I am hungry"). Perhaps, as we have seen in Gothic *m* take the place of *b* in the dative plural (see §. 215.), so we may assume the converse mutation of *m* to *b*; and, in fact, in the formations in *u-bni* (theme *u-bnya* neuter, *u-bnyô* feminine, see Grimm, II. p. 184), occasionally *u-fni*. If we retrace the *b*, which is evidently the more genuine form, to *m*, then *vit-u-mni* (*vit-u-bni*, "knowledge," would resemble Latin formations like *al-u-mnus* (see §. 478. conclusion); and in my opinion the Gothic like the Latin *u* is only a class vowel, and therefore a weakened form of *a*, or, in Grimm's weak form of the second conjugation, of *ô*; and therefore *vund-u-fni*, feminine, "wound," is for *vund-ô-fni*, from *vund-ô*, "I wound." It deserves notice, that, together with *fraist-u-bni*, feminine, "attempt," there occurs also the form *fraist-ô-bni* (genitive plural *fraist-ô-bnyô*, Luke iv. 13.), evidently from a weak verb *fraistô* (compare the Old Northern *freista*, "tentare," see Graff, III. 830.), which cannot be cited; for the strong verb *fraisa* gives no authority to the *t*, and would make us expect only *frais-u-bni*. In *fast-u-bni*, "fasting," the *u* represents the *a* sound of the diphthong *ai* of the third weak conjugation, where we must observe that the *i* element of this diphthong is dropped also before personal terminations beginning with nasals; thus, as *fast-a-m*, "we fast," *fast-a-nd*, "they fast," for *fast-ai-m*, *fast-ai-nd*, so *fast-u-bni*, from *fast-u-mni* for *fast-ai-mni*.

808. In order to exhaust the presumptive cognates of the Sanscrit participial suffix *mâna*, the Latin suffix *mulu* must also be here mentioned, the *l* of which, perhaps, like that of *alius* = Sanscrit *anya-s*, "the other," rests on the

favourite interchange of the liquids (see §. 20.). We divide, therefore, *fa-mulus*, properly "the making" (for *fac-mulus*); or if, as Ag. Benary conjectures, it belongs to the Sanscrit root *bhaj* "to honour," "to serve" (compare Gothic *and-bah-ts*, "servant," "he who serves ;" *sti-mulus* (for *stig-mulus*), "sting," as "sticking" (compare, according to Vossius, στίζω, στίγμα, &c.). Compare the Irish suffix *mhuil*, in *fas-a-mhuil*, "growing" (*fasaim*, "I grow")= *váksh-a-mána-s*.* If, however, the *a* of *fasa-mhuil* is not a class vowel, as in *fas-a-mar*, "we grow"= Sanscrit *váksh-á-mas*, but to be included in the suffix (to be divided, therefore, *fas-amhuil*), in that case the last portion of the word properly means "like," and is most probably an abbreviation of the adjective *samhuil*,† which occurs uncompounded. Words like *fear-amhuil*, "manlike," can scarcely be explained otherwise than as compounds of *fear* and *amhuil*. The Latin suffix *mulu* might, however, be also connected with the Sanscrit *mara*; whence, *admara* and *jasmara*, "voracious," from *ad*, *jas*, "to eat," *srimara* (Wilson), according to some authorities, "a young deer," from *sar*, *sri*, "to go," This suffix, however, as *v* and *m* are easily interchanged, is originally one with the more usual *vara*; whence *nasvara*, "transitory," from *nas*, "to be ruined ;" *bhásvara*, "shining," from *bhás*, "to shine ;" *sthávara*, "standing," "immoveable," from *sthá*, "to stand."

809. Before we pass on to the consideration of those participles which do not, like those already discussed, belong to any tense of the indicative, and make no distinction between active, passive, and middle, we must mention one other participle peculiar to Latin, viz. the participle future passive in *ndu*. I have already, in my *Conjuga-*

---

* It being taken for granted that *vaksh* is used in the middle. *F* for Sanscrit *v* is, in the Irish dialect of the Celtic, very usual.

† Compare the Sanscrit *sama*, "like," Latin *similis*.

tional System (§. 109ᵃ. 1.), considered this, with regard to its form, as a modification of the participle present active, and think I must continue to support this view, though it may be objected that, in this manner, the passive and future signification of the said participle will have no foundation as respects form. But words seldom express in form those relations, to denote which they are destined by the use of language; and grammatical forms often change their original meaning, as, in Persian, the forms in *târ* or *dâr* (*faref-târ*, "deceptor," *dâ-dâr* "dator,"*), which are based on the Sanscrit nouns of agency in *târ*, Greek in τηρ, and Latin in *tor*, *tôr-is*, are used, contrary to their original intention, with a passive meaning; also, *gi-rif-târ*, "*captus, captivus, præda*;" *res-târ*, "*liberatus*;" *kush-tár*, "*occisus*;" *guf-târ*, "*sermo*" (see Vuller's *Inst. L. Pers.* p. 166); while conversely the participles in *tah* or *dah*, which are based on the Sanscrit passive participles in *ta*, have generally an active signification, and retain their original passive meaning almost only when in combination with the auxiliary verb *shudan* (" to be "); hence *burdah*, "*qui tulit* " = Sanscrit *b̲ritá-s* (from *bharta-s*), "*latus*;" but *burdah míshavam*, "*feror*," properly "*latus fio*." The Latin *ferendus* approaches very closely the Persian present participle *barindah*, "bearing;" and, like the latter, has weakened the original tenuis (of *ferent*) to a medial, and extended the base by the addition of a vowel, both which changes take place also in Prâkrit and Páli (see p. 301)†. This opinion that

---

* The choice of *d* or *t* in the suffix depends on the preceding letter. Compare §. 91. conclusion.

† The Sanscrit also has a few words which, in their origin, are evidently present participles, but have added to the *nt* also an *a*, or have preserved the *a* of the base *ta* (see §. 804.). They accent the suffix; hence, *bhâsantá-s*, "sun," as "lighting," opposed to *bhấsant* (see §. 785.); *rôhantá-s*, " a certain tree," as "growing," opposed to *rôhant*; *gadayantá-s*,

the future passive participles have proceeded from the active present participles is confirmed by the circumstance, that the class peculiarities, which do not extend over the present and imperfect, and the forms which spring from the present, are preserved in the form in *ndu*; *e. g.* the *n* of *sterno* (see §. 496.), the *t* of *pecto, plecto,* the reduplication of *gigno* (*gen-ui, gen-i-tum*); the gerunds also, which are in form identical with the future passive participle, point to an original active and present signification of the participial form; *docendi,* "of teaching," *docendo,* "by teaching," speak for the signification "teaching," which "*docendus*" must originally have had; for such abstract substantives, especially those which, like the Latin gerunds, express only the exercise of an action, spring naturally from active present participles; as *abundantia* from *abundant, providentia* from *provident,* and not from passive participles. Participles in *tûru,* when they form abstracts, or rather raise their feminine form to an abstract, abandon their future meaning, and then pass as present participles or nouns of agency; thus, *ruptura,* "tearing," as the personification of "to tear," properly "the person who tears;" *junctura,* "joining;" *mistura,* "mingling;" *genitura,* "producing;" "having." It must be noticed that in Gothic, also, from adjectives spring feminine forms which are used as abstracts, as *mikilei,* "greatness" (theme *mikilein*), from the adjective base *mikila,* to which it bears the same relation that, in Sanscrit, *sundarî,* "*pulchra*" does to the masculine neuter base सुन्दर *sundara* (see §. 120.); so, among others, also *managei,* "a multitude," from *manag(a)s,* "many;" *siukei,*

---

yánta-s, "cloud," as "making to flow," opposed to *gadayánt,* from *gad,* "to flow," in the causal. So in Latin *unguentum,* if it be not an extended form of "*unguen*" (compare §. 803.), and perhaps *argentum,* "silver," as "shining" (Sanscrit *raja-tá-m*), apparently from *ráj,* "to shine," with the vowel shortened.

"sickness," from *siuk(a)-s* "sick," (see Grimm, I. p. 608). In Greek, too, there are a few adjectives, the feminines of which represent abstracts; in such a manner, however, as that the latter is distinguished from the feminine adjective by throwing back the accent, in agreement with what has been before remarked on similar phænomena in Sanscrit; hence, θέρμη, "heat," κάκη, "wickedness," opposed to θερμή, κακή; as above, *yáśas*, "fame," opposed to *yaśás*, "famous" (see §. 785. Remark); *jániman*, "birth," *máriman*, "death," opposed to words like *sarimán*, "wind," as "blowing" (§. 547.). But to return to the Latin participles in *ndu*, *secundus*, "the following one," has correctly retained the original design of the suffix; and the conjecture, therefore, that it is a contraction of *sequebundus* is unnecessary: yet, in my opinion, words in *bundus* in so far belong to this class, as most probably the verb substantive is contained in them in the same way as we have recognised it in the imperfects and futures in *bam*, *bo* (see §§. 526. 663.). When, however, Voss derives the forms *bundu* from the imperfect, as, *errabundus* from *errabam*, *vagabundus* from *vagabar*, *gemebundus* from *gemebam*, he appears to be in error, as this derivation is not supported by the sense; as *gemebundus* signifies, not "*qui-gemebat*," but "*gemens*." I allow, therefore, between *gemebam* and *gemebundus* only a sisterly relation, and take *bundu-s* rather as the participle present of the root *fu*,* with the extension of the suffix *nt* to *ndu*, as in the future passive participle under discussion. In Persian the participle present of the root *bú*, "to be," would probably be *bavandah* (for *bu-andah*, compare *bavam*, "I may be"); and in Sanscrit from *bhú* really comes *bhávant*, "being" (base of the strong cases), to which the Latin *bundu*, exclusive of the suffix *u*, has nearly the same rela-

---

* Regarding *b* for *f*, see §§. 18. 526.

tion as *bam* (*ama-bam*) has to *á-bhavam*. The first *u* of *bundu* I take to be not the radical vowel of *fu*, but the corruption of an original *a*, as in the third person plural (*veh-u-nt* = Sanscrit *váh-a-nti*). As a proof that the forms in *bundu-s* are, in their origin, participles, may be adduced also the circumstance that they occasionally govern the accusative; thus, in Livy, *vitabundus castra*, *mirabundus vanam speciem*. But should these forms originally belong to a tense other than the present, we might recognise in them obsolete future participles, and assume that the use of the participle in *turus* has caused them to be less freely employed, given room for their being dispensed with, and changed their signification. An especial corroboration of this view is to be found in the fact that the majority of forms in *bundus* belong to the first conjugation, and that in old Latinity futures in *bo* occur also in the third and fourth conjugation, a form which may originally have belonged to all classes of verbs; as, as has been shewn, forms like *legam* and *audiam* are nothing but present tenses of the subjunctive mood, and used as a compensation for the lost futures (see §. 692.). We should consequently regard *lascivibundus* and *sitibundus* as analogous forms of old futures like *scíbo*, *dormíbo*, only with the vowel shortened, as before the suffix *bundu-s*, with the exception of the *á* of the first conjugation, only short vowels are found, and, therefore, we have *gemĕbundus*, *fremĕbundus*, opposed to *dicêbo*, and *pudibundus* opposed to *pudêbit*.

810. Let us now betake ourselves to the consideration of those participles which, without any formal designation of any temporal or lineal relation, have retained their destination in this respect merely by the use of language. These are in Sanscrit the future participle in *tár*, *tri*, the perfect passive participle in *ta* or *na*, and the future passive participle in *ya*, *tavya*, and *aníya*. The first-mentioned participle, which is, at the same time, a noun of agency, has

been already discussed in §§. 646, 647; somewhat, however, remains still to be observed on the subject. And first must be noticed the coincidence in accent which exists between the Sanscrit and Greek, since the formations in तृ *tăr*, like the Greek in τηρ, regularly accent the suffix; thus, *dâtăr*, nominative *dâtá* (see §. 144.) *dator* and *datúrus*, as in Greek δοτήρ; *janităr*, nominative *janitá* "*genitor*," and "*geniturus*" = γενετήρ. On the other hand, the suffix τορ, which in origin and signification is identical with τηρ, and the long vowel of whose nominative τωρ, is to be regarded only as a compensation for the want of the case-sign, has lost simultaneously its organic length and its accent: it admits, too, of scarce any doubt, that, in Sanscrit, the weight of the suffix *tăr* is the cause of its being accented, according to the same principle by which, in the second principal conjugation, the heavy personal terminations assume the accent (see §. 785. Remark). The Greek formations in τη-ς, which in §. 145. have likewise been compared with the Sanscrit in *tăr*, have, in part, remained true to the old accentuation, since in forms of more than two syllables a vowel long in itself by position, with σ generally, and occasionally also with κ, ρ, ν, and λ preceding the suffix, serves like a dam to the accent which belongs to the suffix, and prevents it from receding farther back; hence, indeed, δότης opposed to δοτήρ, *dátá*; but μαχητής, ποιητής, ζηλωτής, δικαστής, ἀκοντιστής, βαστακτής, φορμικτής, λυμαντής, εὐθυντής, ποικιλτής, καθαρτής, opposed to forms like γαμέτης, γενέτης, πανδακέτης. The ε of forms like γεν-έ-της, γεν-ε-τήρ, πανδακ-έ-της, is most probably a corruption of ι; for it corresponds to the *i*, which often occurs in Latin, and still oftener in Sanscrit, between the root and the suffix; e. g. γεν-ε-τήρ and γεν-έ-της correspond to the Sanscrit *jan-i-tăr* and Latin *gen-i-tor*.

811. In the weak cases the Sanscrit suffix *tăr* suppresses its vowel, and the accent then falls on the case terminations

FORMATION OF WORDS.

beginning with a vowel; while before consonants the *r* becomes *ri*, and the accent abides on the suffix; hence *dâtr-é*, "to the giver," as in Greek πατρ-ός, πατρ-ί, for πατέρ-ος, πατέρ-ι, but *dâtrí-bhyas*, "to the givers." The analogy of the weak cases is followed also by the feminine of the noun agent, inasmuch as before the feminine suffix *í*, which usually receives the accent, the vowel of the principal suffix is suppressed; hence *dâtrí*, "the female giver." The Greek and Latin, which possess over the Sanscrit the superiority of retaining the vowel of the masculine suffix (τηρ, τορ, *tôr*) through all the cases, follow notwithstanding the analogy of the Sanscrit in suppressing, in the feminine forms τριδ, τρια, *trí-c* (see §. 119.), the vowel of the principal suffix, and the Greek τριδ agrees with the Sanscrit *trí* also in the retention of the accent, which the form τρια (perhaps on account of its increase of syllables) has abandoned; thus, ληστρίδ, ἀλετρίδ, αὐλητρίδ, σημαντρίδ, λαλητρίδ, ὀρχηστρίδ, στεγαστρίδ, as in Sanscrit *dâtrí*. The base γάστρι deserves especial notice, which, though also masculine, is properly nothing but the feminine of γαστερ, nominative γαστήρ*, in which I think I recognise the Sanscrit root *jas*, "to eat," whence might be expected a noun of agency *jastâr*, feminine *jastrí*; thus γαστήρ, properly "the male eater," and γάστρι-ς (properly "the female eater") has indeed experienced a transposition of the accent, but has kept clear from the inorganic affix of a δ. The feminine bases in τιδ seem to me, where they appear as nouns of agency, to be abbreviations of τριδ: they correspond, as respects the loss of the ρ, to their masculines in τη(ρ)-ς, but have throughout displaced the accent, even where the masculine has retained it in its original site;

---

* In shortening the vowel of the suffix, as also in declension, γαστέρ follows the analogy of the words denoting affinity, see §. 813.

thus, not only ἱκέτι-ς compared with ἱκέτη-ς, but also εὑρέτι-ς opposed to εὑρετή-ς.

812. The words denoting affinity in तर् *tár, tri*, are evidently, in their origin, nouns of agency (see "*Vocalismus*," p. 182); for *pitár*, weakened from *patár*, and this again from *pâtár*, means properly "nourisher," or "ruler," from the root *pâ*; and *mâtár*, "mother," I regard as "she that brings forth;" while I dissent from the Indian Grammarians who derive it from *mân*, "to honour," and prefer deducing it from the root *mâ*, "to measure," which, with the preposition *nis*, "out of" (*nir-mâ*), signifies "to make," "to produce," and even without a preposition is capable of this interpretation.* *Duhitár*, "daughter," signifies properly "suckling," from *duh*, "to milk;" *náptâr*, "grandchild," is in its final element essentially identical with *pitár*, "father" (this, however, is perhaps opposed to my former opinion, see p. 387, Note †), here not in the sense of "father," but to be taken in its primitive meaning, while we regard the compound not as a possessive but as a determinative; so that *naptâr*, in opposition to *pitár*, as "ruler," or "family chief," would signify the "not ruler," or "subject," and thus it might mean any member of a family but the father; as also in the Vêda dialect, *napât*, which has preserved the original

---

* I now find a strong confirmation of this opinion, which is elsewhere expressed ("*Vocalismus*," p. 182) in the Vêda dialect in the First Book of the Rig. Vêda (Hymn 61. 7.), which has been edited in the interim by Fr. Rosen, where the genitive *mâtur* occurs as masculine, with the meaning "*creatoris.*" The Old Persian furnishes the noun of agency *framâtâr* (*fra* preposition), which is connected in root and suffix with *mâtar*, the accusative of which, *framâtâram*, occurs repeatedly in the inscriptions with which we are acquainted, and is rendered by Lassen, "*imperatorem.*" I have no doubt that the above-mentioned Vêdian *mâtur* has an accusative *mâtâram* (not *mätäram*), and that, therefore, the theme is properly *mâtâr*, not *mâtär*, as the *â* is shortened only in words denoting affinity.

length of the root *pâ*, signifies in the passages cited by Fr. Rosen (on the Rig. V. I. 22. 6.) "son," though in form it corresponds to the Latin base *nepôt*, as also its feminine *naptî*, "daughter," to the Latin base *nepti**, Old High German *nifti* (nominative accusative *nift*). *Bhrâ-tar*, "brother," has clearly lost a consonant before the suffix, for there is no root *bhrâ*. If, as the Indian Grammarians assume, the root is *bhrâj*, "to shine," we must then observe that the *râj*, which is probably related to it, and from which Pott deduces *bhrâj* (for *abhi-râj*), signifies besides "to shine," also "to rule," and, therefore, "the brother" may be so designated as "ruler" in the family, which, according to Indian manners, the eldest brother after his father's death really is (see "*Vocalismus*," p. 182). But *bhrâ*, in *bhratâr*, may also have sprung from the root *bhar*, *bhṛi*, "to carry," "to support," by the transposition and lengthening of the radical vowel, just as in Greek from βαλ: βλή-σω, βέβλη-κα, βλῆ-μα, &c., from πετ = Sanscrit *pat*, "to fall," "to fly" (πίπτω from πιπετω): πτω and πτη (πτῶσις, πτῶμα, πτῆσις), and in Sanscrit from *man*, "to think," *mnâ*, "to mention,"

---

* This feminine form leads to the conjecture that the masculine *napât* in the weakest cases (see §. 130.) rejects its *â*; that, therefore, the genitive would be *napt-as*, for *napât-as*, since feminine bases in *î* generally follow the analogy of the weakest cases; as, *râjñ-î*, "a queen," follows that of *râjñê*, to the king," *râjñ-as*, "of the king," &c. Before terminations beginning with a consonant, where *napt* would be impossible, I should expect *napât*; thus, *napad-bhyas*, "to" and "from the sons." If such forms were confirmed, I still could not assent to Benfey's (Glossary to the Sâma Véda, p. 106) conjecture, that *â* in *napât*, as also the *ô* of forms like *datór-is*, &c., is a lengthening that originally belongs only to the strong cases, which, in Latin (*nepôt*), has entered into all cases. It is more natural to suppose the theme of the Sanscrit strong cases to be the original one, and therefore, also, in the classical languages, for the most part, carried through all the cases, as is the case in the example before us with the suffix *tôr*, τηρ, contrasted with the Sanscrit strong *târ* (shortened in the vocative to *tar*) and with the participle present in *nt*.

which is regarded by the Indian Grammarians as a distinct root. If, as now appears to me more probable, this is the derivation of *bhrâ-târ*, viz. from *bhar*, in that case the "brother" is properly "the supporter," as the stay of the mother, sisters, and younger brothers after the father's death.* So the husband, also, in relation to the wife, who is termed *bhâryâ* ("the female to be supported, to be cherished"), is "the supporter," and as such is called *bhartâr*, nominative *bhartá*; a word, the creation of which still lies within the clear recollection of the language, and which, therefore, in departure from its supposed cognate *bhrâtar*, follows the ordinary declension. The appellation of "sister," in Sanscrit *svásâr*, has still preserved the long vowel in the strong cases, but has, on that account, like the Latin *sorôr* from *sostôr*, lost a *t*, which has remained in the German and Sclavonic languages (Gothic *svistar*, English "sister," Old Sclavonic *sestra*), and in the Lithuanian *sesser* (nominative *sessŭ*, genitive *sesser-s*, see §. 144.), has assimilated itself to the preceding *s*. *Svá-s(t)âr* is properly "the wife belonging" (regarding the pronoun *sva*, see §. 341.), and is, in its final element, akin to *strî*, "woman," which Pott is undoubtedly right in deducing from the root *su*, *sû*, "to bear a child" (E. I. I. p. 126); so that, like *fe-mina* (see §. 478. conclusion), it originally signifies "the parturient," and is a regular feminine noun of agency up to the loss of the radical vowel.

813. The shortening of *â* to *a*, which most words denoting affinity have experienced in Sanscrit and Zend in the strong cases, appears to have existed so early as the time of the unity of language, as it is scarcely fortuitous that *pitáram, pitar-âu* (Vêda *-râ*), *pitáras*, stand in the same

---

* So in a passage of *Sâvitrî* (p. 16 of my translation of "*The Deluge*"): "When the husband (of the mother) is dead, that son is culpable who is not the protector of his mother."

relation to *dátáram, dátáráu (-rá), dátáras*, as, in Greek, πατέρα, πατέρε, πατέρες, to δοτῆρα, δοτῆρε, δοτῆρες, particularly as the Latin makes a distinction between the declension of words like *pater, patris,* and such as *dator, datór-is*.

814. In the Vêda dialect, formations in *tár, tri,* occur also in the sense of the participle present or future governing the accusative; and in this case the accent invariably is thrown back from the suffix to the radical syllable; hence *dátár,* "giving," opposed to *dátár,* "giver;" *pátár,* "drinking," opposed to *pátár,* "drinker" (Latin *pótór-*); *hántár,* "smiting," "slaying," opposed to *hantár,* "smiter," "slayer;" *ástár,* "casting," opposed to *astár,* "caster." These participles serve principally to represent the present indicative; so that, as in the participial future of the classic Sanscrit, the verb substantive is either to be supplied or is formally expressed. The former is the case if the participle refers to the third person; the latter if the first or second person is the subject. The forms of this kind which occur in the Sâma Vêda are all in the masculine singular nominative: and it is matter for future investigation, whether the feminine also occurs in constructions of this kind, or whether, as in the participial future of the classic Sanscrit, the nominative masculine represents the other genders.* I annex a few examples from Benfey's edition of the hymns of the Sâma Vêda: *Hántá yó vritrán sánitó'tá (-tá utá) vájan dátá maghâni,* "who (Indra) striking (cleaving) *is* the cloud, and distributing *is*

---

* That in Zend, also, the form in *tár* occurs in the sense of a participle present, and governing the accusative, is proved by a passage in the beginning of the 1st Farg. of the Vendidád (V. S. p. 498), where ᚵᛖᚱᛟᚢᛗ *bactĕm* is governed by ᛞᚨᛏᚺᚱᛟ *dáthró,* "to the giving" (genitive in the sense of dative, as is frequently the case in Sanscrit): *nĕmaś été dáthró bactĕm,* "worship to thee the giver of happiness (riches)."

food, giving is riches"="who strikes," &c. (I. 4. 1. 5. 4.); *yá ádṛityá śaśamânâya sunvaté dâtâ jaritrá* (euphonic for .... *tré*) *ukthyám*, "who is giving that which is commendable to the praise singer, who slays with care, and expresses the juice of the (Sôma)" (II. 1. 1. 14. 2.); *tváshṭâ nó dâivyañ váchaḥ parjányó bráhmaṇaspátiḥ*, "Parjanyas Brahm *is* creating for us godlike speech"* (I. 4. 1. 1. 7.); *ástâ 'si śátravé vadhám*, "thou art hurling death at the foe" (II. 9. 1. 13. 3.). I take *pâtâ* as a future participle in the following passage: *pâtâ vṛitrahá sutám â ghâ gamat*, "*poturus Vritri occisor sômæ succum adeat*" (II. 8. 2. 1. 3.). † As regards the cause of the retrogression of the accent in these expressions, I have no doubt that the aim which the language has in view is most emphatically to express, by the accentuation, the energy of the action, which, in the case where the form in *târ* as a participle governs the accusative, appears in its full force; and I am of this opinion, as, as has already been remarked (see §. 785. Remark, at the beginning), the accenting the initial syllable of a word in Sanscrit is the most emphatic.

---

* *Tváshtâr* is paroxyton also as a noun of agency.

† According to Benfey's translation, "let the Vritra-slayer drink the juice," &c., *pâtâ* would=*pâtâ syât*, "*bibens sit.*" I doubt, however, that these participles can, without an auxiliary verb, represent the potential or imperative; for the indicative only of the verb substantive is, in Sanscrit, very frequently omitted, as being by the sense itself understood. The enclitic *ghâ* (for *gha*), which stands in the text in the common dialect *ha*, which, as well as *hâ*, occurs in the Vêdas, and attaches itself to pronouns especially (see F. Windischmann's Sankara, p. 73; and Benfey's Glossary to the Sâma Vêda, p. 206), gives me occasion to remark, that I now, in departure from my former explanation (§. 175.), regard the Gothic *k*, and our *ch* in *mi-k*, *thu-k*, *si-k*, *mi-ch*, *di-ch*, *si-ch*, as well as the Old High German *h* in *unsi-h*, ἡμᾶς, *iwi-h*, ὑμᾶς, as a particle which has grown up with the base, and as identical with the Sanscrit *ha*, *gha*, and Greek γέ (Dor. Æol. γά), and therefore *dich* as=Sanscrit *tvâṅ-ha*, Greek σέγε, as, in a phonetic point of view, *ich*, Gothic *ik*=*aham*, ἐγώ.

815. As to the origin of the suffix *târ*, it may be regarded as springing from the verbal root *tar* (तृ *tṛi*).* This root properly signifies "to overstep," "to transgress," but also "to accomplish," "to fulfil;" *e.g. pratijñâm*, "a promise." And it must be observed that several verbs of motion express also "to transact," "to do;" as, *char* signifies (1) "to go," (2) "to pass through," (3) "to do," "to practise," "to arrange." Thus, *dâtâr*, "*dator, dans, daturus*," may be taken as "the accomplisher," the "exerciser of giving," or, also, if we keep to the primitive signification of the root, as, "the man who passes through the action of giving;" as, *pâraga*, properly "going to the farther shore," is used in the sense of "perusing." The verbal roots, therefore, in combination with the suffix *târ*, are to be taken as abstract substantives, which cannot surprise us, as some of them appear as such without any annexation of a formative suffix; as, *bhî*, "fear," from *bhî*, "to fear;" *hrî*, "shame," from *hrî*, "to fear;" *yudh*, "strife," from *yudh*, "to strive." It may be requisite here to observe, that in Latin several formative suffixes beginning with *c* can be traced back to the Sanscrit root *kar*, *kṛi* (with which *creo* is connected). Thus, for example, *cri* for *ceri*—nominative masculine *cer*, feminine *cri-s*—and *cru* in *volucer*, "flying," properly "fulfilling the action of flying;" *ludicer, ludicru-s*, "sport," "pleasure," "causing enjoyment;" *involu-cre*, "that which envelopes or serves thereto;" *lava-cru-m*, "that which makes to bathe," "to bathe;" *ambula-cru-m*, "that which makes to walk out, gives occasion thereto," hence "promenade;" *sepul-cru-m*, "that which makes to inter," "a grave;" *lu-cru-m*, "that which causes to pay," "gain;" *ful-cru-m*, for *fulc-cru-m*, "that which makes to support," "a support." As *r* and *l* are easily

---

* Compare Benfey, "*Greek Etymology*," II. p. 257.

interchanged, I have no hesitation in referring to this class also the suffix *culu*, and comparing it with the Sanscrit *kara*, "making;"* thus, *ridicu-lu-s*, properly "making to laugh;" *pia-culu-m*, "that which makes to atone;" *specta-culu-m*, "that which makes to see," "gives to see;" *vehi-culu-m*, "that which makes to ride;" *pô-culu-m*, "that which makes to drink;" *mira-culu-m*, "that which makes to wonder;" *ba-culu-s*, "that which makes to go" (βίβημι, ἔβη-ν).

816. From *târ* springs, in Sanscrit, by the affix of an *a*, and with the suppression of its own vowel, as in the weak cases, and before the feminine character *î*, the neuter suffix *tra*, and thence the feminine *trâ*. The neuter form is principally used, and, like the feminine *trâ*, of rare occurrence, forms substantives which express instruments, which are, as it were, the inanimate accomplishers of an action. They Gunise the radical vowel, and, for the most part, in accordance with the Greek analogous forms in τρο, θρο, τρα, θρα,† accent the first syllable of the word. The following are examples: *né-tra-m*, "an eye," as "conducting," or "instrument of conducting" (root *nî*); *śrô-tra-m*, "ear" (root *śru*, "to hear"); *gá-tra-m*, "limb" (root *gâ*, "to go"); *vás-tra-m*, "garment" (root *vas*, "to put on"); *śás-tra-m*, "arrow" (root *śas*, "to slay"); *yók-tra-m*, "band" (root *yuj*, "to bind"); *dánshtrâ*, "tooth" (root *danś*, "to

---

* At the end of compounds *bhâs-kara-s*, "making brilliance," "the sun;" *bha-yan-kara-s*, "making fear," "formidable."

† It is a question whether the θ of θρο, θρα, is produced by the influence of the ρ, in analogy with the law of sounds in force in Zend (see §. 47.), or whether independently of the ρ a change or weakening of the tenuis to the aspirate has taken place, as has become the rule in Germanic languages (see §. 87.). The latter appears to me more probable, as the combination τρ is very usual; but θ for an original τ occurs also before vowels, as in the suffix θεν=Sanscrit *tas*, Latin *tus* (§. 421.), and in the personal terminations of the middle and passive which begin with σθ (see §. 474.).

bite"); *yâtrâ*, feminine, "provisions" (root *yâ*, "to go").
So in Greek, νίπτρο-ν, πλῆκτρο-ν, μάκτρο-ν, λέκτρο-ν ("bed," as
"means of lying"), βάκτρο-ν ("stick," as "means for going"),
ζῶ-σ-τρο-ν, ἄροτρο-ν, θέλγητρο-ν, φίλητρο-ν, ἔλυτρο-ν, θήρα-
τρο-ν, ἄρθρο-ν, βάθρο-ν, λείβηθρο-ν, μάκτρα, πί-σ-τρα, καλύπ-
τρα, βάθρα, κρεμάθρα. The suffix in the class of words under
discussion is, in Sanscrit, seldom accented, and still more
rarely in Greek: the most common Sanscrit word of this
kind is *vaktrá-m*, "mouth," as "speaking," or "instrument
of speaking;" so *paktrá-m*, "holy fire," properly "that
which cooks" (root *pach* from *pak*); *dhartrá-m*, "house,"
as "holding," "receiving" (root *dhar, dhṛi*); *vêtrá-m*, "a
reed," as "moving itself" (root *vî*). In Greek, λουτρό-ν
and δαιτρό-ν belong to this head. The latter, by its passive signification, corresponds ("the distributed") to the
Vêdian *dâtrám*, "gift," as "that which has been given," or
"is to be given."* As respects its base syllable, however, δαιτρόν (δαίω) belongs to the Sanscrit root *dô=dâ*,
"to cut off," whence *dâtra-m*, "a sickle." As the suffix
târ, in Sanscrit, is occasionally preceded by an *i* as conjunctive vowel, so also is *tra*, and then either the conjunctive
vowel or the base syllable is accented: the former in *khan-
i-tra-m*, "a spade" (*khan*, "to dig"), the latter in *vâd-i-
tra-m*, "a musical instrument," properly "that which
causes to speak or utter a sound" (root *vad*, "to speak,"
in the causal); *gâr-i-tra-m*, "rice," properly "that which
causes to eat," "nourishes" (root *gar, gṛi*, "*deglutire*," in
the causal). As we have above (§. 810.) compared the
Greek ε of forms like γεν-ε-τήρ with the Sanscrit-Latin
vowel of conjunction *i* of the corresponding *jan-i-târ, gen-i-
tôr*, so may also the ε of φέρ-ε-τρο-ν be taken as the cor-

---

* Benfey quotes in his Glossary to the Sâma Vêda, p. 88, the following passage of the Rig. Vêda: *ási bhágô ási dâtrásya dâtá*, "thou art the
Lord: thou art the distributor of alms."

ruption of ι, and the said word be contrasted with Sanscrit formations like *khan-i-tra-m* and *vád-i-tra-m*. It may, however, be the case, that the ε of φέρ-ε-τρον is identical with the class-vowel ε of φέρ-ε-τε, φέρ-ε-τον, &c.; then φέρ-ε-τρον would correspond to Sanscrit formations like *pát-a-tram*, "wing," as "instrument of flying;" *vádh-a-tra-m*, "weapon," as "slaying;" *krínt-a-tra-m*, "plough," as "cleaver" (root *krit* from *kart*, in the special tenses *krint*, compare κείρω): for which, indeed, the Grammarians assume a suffix *atra*, the *a* of which, however, appears to me identical with the inserted vowel of the first and sixth class; thus, *pát-a-tra-m*, like *pát-a-ti*, "he flies;" *krínt-a-tra-m*, like *krínt-a-ti*, "he cleaves."* Thus in Greek the η of forms like φίλη-τρο-ν and κόρη-θρο-ν evidently belongs to the verbal base, and is identical with that of φιλή-σω, κορή-σω. The same is the case with the *â* and *ê* of the corresponding class of words in Latin *arâ-tru-m*, *fulgê-tru-m*, *fulgê-tra*, *verê-tru-m*, where it must be observed, that, according to §. 109ª. 6., the *â* of the first as well as the *ê* of the second conjugation are identical in their origin with the η of the above-mentioned Greek forms. As, however, the *ê* of the second conjugation is less permanent than the *â* of the first and the *í* of the fourth (see §. 801. Note), we cannot be surprised to find, not *mulgê-tra*, *mulgê-trum*, but *mulc-tra*, *mulc-tru-m;* not *monê-tru-m*, but *mon-s-trum*. The *s* of *monstrum* corresponds to the euphonic *s* mentioned in §. 95. A similar one is also to be found in *lu-s-trum* and *flu-s-trum*. *Vi-trum*, "glass," as it were, "instrument of seeing," or "making to see," has lost the *d* of the root. We should have expected *vis-trum* (see §. 101.) according to the analogy of *ras-trum*, *ros-trum*, *claus-trum*, *cas-trum*. In the third con-

---

* The Indian Grammarians include the *i* of the above-mentioned words in *i-tra* in the suffix.

jugation, the class syllable of which has, from the time of the unity of language, as a rule not extended itself beyond the present, with its derivatives, and the imperfect, the suffix is joined, for the most part, direct to the root, *e.g.* *ru-trum, spec-trum*. In the fourth conjugation we should expect *í-trum*, in accordance with *â-trum* in the first, and *ê-trum* in the second; but *haus-trum*, from *hauris*, is in conformity to the other anomalies of this verb.

817. The Zend has, according to §. 47., changed the *t* of the suffix *tra* into *th*, but leaves it unaltered after sibilants, which, in general, do not admit of *th* after them; hence ‎‎‎‎‏‎‎ *yaoschdâthra*, "means of purification" (V. S. p. 263), nominative accusative *-thrĕ-m* (see §. 30.): *dôithrĕ-m*, "eye" (as "seeing"), is connected in its root and suffix with the Greek θέατρον, although the meaning of the latter has taken a different direction, since it signifies the place which affords the spectacle. The corresponding Sanscrit root is most probably *dhyâi*, with which Pott ("*E. I. I.*" p. 231) has been the first to compare the Greek θεάομαι, although *dhyâi* signifies not "to see" but "to think," where it is to be observed that बुध *budh*, "to know," has, in Zend, received the meaning of "to see," as विद् *vid*, "to know," has in Latin, while the Greek root ἰδ (εἴδω, οἶδα) unites the two meanings. Remark, also, with Burnouf ("*Yaçna*," p. 372), the New Persian root *dí*, "to see" (infinitive *dí-dan*),* and the contraction which the Sanscrit root *dhyâi* has experienced in the substantive *dhí* (nominative *dhí-s*), "understanding," "insight." The following are examples in which the suffix spoken of has preserved its original tenuis under the protection of a preceding sibilant: *vastrĕm*, "robe," feminine *vastra* (see §. 137., Sanscrit *vástra-m*, see §. 721.

---

* The present *bínam* belongs probably to a different root, and, in fact, to the Sanscrit *vid*.

Note **), and ⟨Zend⟩ *vâstra* (as theme), "the willow," as "growing"* (connected in its root with the Old High German base *wahs-a-mon*, "shrub," "fruit," see §. 799.), whence the often occurring *vâstravat*, "willowy," as also *vâstrya* (nominative *-yô*), "farmer." The Zend uses the formations in *thra, tra*, also in the sense of abstract substantives, which, according to what has been said (§. 809.) regarding the radically connected Latin formations in *tûra*, cannot surprise us. The following are examples: ⟨Zend⟩ *dar-ĕ-thrĕ-m*, "possession," "reception," "retention" (Sanscrit root *dhar, dhṛi*, "to keep"); ⟨Zend⟩ *mar-ĕ-thrĕm*, "mention" (Sanscrit root *smar, smṛi*, "to remember"); ⟨Zend⟩ *khâthrĕm*, "splendour;"† ⟨Zend⟩ *khâś-trĕm*,

---

* I doubt not that this expression comes from the Sanscrit root *vaksh*, "to grow," which, in Zend, in the devoid of Guna special tenses of the fourth class, is contracted to *ucs*. With respect to the suppression of the guttural in the above form, compare the relation of the Sanscrit *chash-tê*, "he says," to the root *chaksh*, and the Zend *chashman*, "eye" (as "saying," "announcing"), to the same root, and to the cognate Sanscrit word *chákshus*.

† At the end of compounds *pôuru-khâthra*, "having much lustre" (see Burnouf, "Yaçna," p. 421). I consider *khâthra* to be an abbreviation of *kharthra* (*kharĕthra*, according to §. 44.), and derive it from the root *khar*, "to shine," whence, also, ⟨Zend⟩ *kharĕnô*, "lustre." The root *sur* (from *svar*, see §. 36.) corresponds in Sanscrit. The loss of the final consonant of the root appears to be compensated by lengthening the vowel, as in the Sanscrit *jâtâ*, "born," from *jan*; *khâtâ*, "engraven," from *khan*. Observe, also, the relation of the Zend ⟨Zend⟩ *zazâmi*, "I produce," to the Sans. *jájanmi*. Burnouf gives another derivation of *khâthra*, "lustre" (l. c. p. 419) dividing it into *kha*, "*suus*," and *âthra*, according to which its literal meaning would be "*suum ignem habens*," and therefore *âthra* would be connected with the word *âtar*, "fire," which is used in its uncompounded form, and the *a* of which is suppressed in the weakest cases; hence *âthr-at*, "*igne*;" *âthr-aṅm*, "*ignium*." Burnouf touches also on the possibility of the prefix सु *su, hu*, "fair," being contained in *khâthra*, in which case its proper signification would be "*pulchrum ignem habens*."

A

FORMATION OF WORDS. 1111

"taste." The latter Burnouf (" *Yaçna*," p. 220) derives, undoubtedly with justness, from the Sanscrit root *svâd* : the transition of *d* into *ś* is here quite regular (see §. 102. conclusion); and *khâstrĕm* therefore resembles, both in the euphonic treatment of the radical *d* and in the suffix, the (§. 815. conclusion) above-mentioned Latin formations, as *claus-trum*.

818. As regards the formation of abstract substantives through the suffix under discussion, the German languages admit of comparison with the Zend in several interesting forms. The Gothic furnishes us with the neuter base *maur-thra* (nominative accusative *maurthr*, see §. 153.), "murder," properly "the killing," the obscure root of which leads us to the Sanscrit *mar*, *mri*, "to die," causal *mârâyâmi*, "I slay." * Besides the above, J. Grimm (II. p. 123) deduces from *blôstreis* a neuter *blôstr*, "oblation" (theme *blôstra*), which I should be glad to admit did it anywhere occur. Nevertheless, I think its existence must be assumed, and I derive from it the existing masculine *blôstrei-s*, the base of which, *blôstrya* (see §. 135.), has the same relation to its presupposed primitive base *blôstra* that the previously mentioned Zend *vâstryô* (theme *vâstrya*), "countryman," has to its primitive base *vâstra*, "pasture."† The root of the Gothic base *blôs-tra* is *blôt*, "to sacrifice," "to

---

A derivation, however, in which *khâthra* would etymologically also signify what the sense requires, and according to which it would be radically identical with a word (*kharĕnô*) literally meaning "lustre," appears to me the most natural.

* The *u* of the Gothic form is a weakening of *a*, to which, according to §. 82., an euphonic *a* is prefixed. As most of the German languages have lost the *r* of the Gothic *maurthr*, and consequently the agreement between them in suffix with the primitive suffix *tra*, *thra*, is no longer recognisable, we should remark with care the English "murder."

† It is a rule in Sanscrit that verbal bases terminating with a vowel reject their final vowel before vowels or *y* in an annexed derivative suffix.

worship," whence, according to §. 102., *blôs-tra*, in analogy with the Zend *khâs̄-tra*, "taste," from *khâd-tra*; so *gils-tra*, "tax," nominative accusative *gilstr*, from *gild-tra*, *gild-tr*, from the weakened form of the root *gald*, with the preposition *us* and *fra*, "to repay."* The *a* of the Old High German *gels-tar*, *kels-tar*, *ghels-tar* (Graff, IV. 194.), I take to be an auxiliary vowel inserted to remedy the harshness of an accumulation of consonants at the end of a word, and which, on the annexation of the case-terminations in these and similar words, is again dropped, hence genitive plural *ghels-tro*; so from *bluos-tar*, *blos-tar*, "oblation," dative *blos-tre*; from *hlah-tar*, "laughing," "laughter," dative *hlah-tre.*† We have, therefore, in the common German expression *Ge-läch-ter*, as also in the English "laugh-ter," analogous forms to the Zend abstract neuter bases in *thra*, *tra*, as also to the Sanscrit formations in *tra*, Greek in τρο, and Latin in *tru*. Thus in English also "slaugh-ter," which in its radical part, graphically at least, is more perfectly retained than the cognate verb "slay." Probably, also, "thun-der" and "wea-ther" are to be included in the class of words which are formed in Sanscrit by the suffix *tra*, though the *t*-sound of the suffix is lost in the appellation of "thunder" in the older dialects (Old High German *donar* masculine, Old Saxon *thunar*, Anglo-Saxon *thunor*); on the other hand, in Latin we have *ton-i-trus*, *ton-i-tru*, where the *u* of the fourth declension is matter of surprise, as the Sanscrit *a*

---

* With respect to the interchange of *t*, *th*, and *d* (*blôs-tra*, *gils-tra*, compared with *maur-thra*), in suffixes originally commencing with *t*, I refer the reader to §. 91.

† Whether the gender be masculine or neuter is not to be determined from the cases which occur (accusative *hlahtar*, dative *hlahtre* and *hlahtere*); as, however, the perfectly analogous *blôstar* shews itself, by the accusative plural *blôstar*, to be neuter, I agree with Graff (IV. 1112.) in considering *hlahtar* also as neuter, in accordance with the analogous Gothic and Zend forms.

would lead us to expect only the unorganic *u* of the second declension (see §. 116.). The corresponding Sanscrit root is *stan*, "to thunder," whence *stan-ayi-tnú-s*, "the thunder."* "Weather" belongs to the Sanscrit root *vâ*, "to blow," whence also the Lithuanian *wĕ-tra*, "storm." To return to the Gothic; *fô-dr*, "sheath" (theme *fô-dra*), and *huli-s-tr*, "veil" (theme *huli-s-tra*), belong to the class of words here discussed. The latter proceeds from the verbal base *hul-ya;* its *i*, therefore, is the contraction of the syllable *ya*, as in the preterite *hul-i-da*. I regard the *s* as an euphonic affix, as in the Latin *lu-s-tru-m*, *flu-s-trum* (see §. 815. conclusion), *capi-s-trum*. The following nominal derivatives are analogous: *avi-s-tr*, "sheep-cote," as "place of the sheep," from the lost primitive base *avi* (=Sanscrit *avi*, Lithuanian *awi*); and *navi-s-tr*, "grave," as "place of the dead," from *naus*, theme *nava*, with the weakening of the *a* to *i*, as in the genitive *navi-s* (see §. 191.) Observe that the Greek and Latin languages very frequently transfer the suffixes of verbal derivatives to nominal derivatives. *Fô-dr*,

---

* *Ay* is the character of the tenth class, and *itnu* the suffix, which forms adjectives with the signification of the participle present and masculine appellatives; as, *harshayitnús*, "rejoicing," and as a substantive masculine "son," as "the causer of rejoicing" (so *nandana*, "son," from *nand* "to rejoice"). The *i* is evidently merely a vowel of conjunction, as in the future *stan-ay-i-shyáti*, "it will thunder:" there also exists, as well as *i-tnu*, a more simple suffix *tnu*, as in *hatnú-s*, masculine, "sickness," and "a weapon," as "slaying," from *han*, "to slay." The *t* of *tnu* and *itnu* may be regarded in the same light as the euphonic *t* mentioned above (§. 797. Note); so that, therefore, only *nu* would be left as the true suffix, as appears in *bhánú-s*, "sun," as "giving light." The circumstance that the Latin *ton-i-tru-s*, *ton-i-tru*, stands in the class of words under discussion in a very isolated position, owing to its *u* of the fourth declension, may lead us to compare it, with respect to its suffix also, with the Sanscrit *stanayitnú-s*, by assuming an exchange of the liquids; so that *tru* would stand for *tnu*, just as in the Latin *pul-mô* (for *plu-mô*) an *l* stands over against the Greek nasal of πνεύμων (compare §. 20.)

1114   FORMATION OF WORDS.

"sheath," theme *fô-dra*, in its obscure root corresponds to the Sanscrit *pâ*, "to receive," and in its entire form to *pâtra-m*, "vessel," as "keeping." With respect to the Gothic *d*, for the *th*, which was to be expected, compare *fa-drein*, "parents," with the Sanscrit *pi-tárâu* (for *pa-*), which is also radically connected with *fô-dr* (see §. 812.). The Old High German *fô-tar, fuo-tar*, "fodder" (for *fô-tr*, Anglo-Saxon, *fô-dr, fô-dher, fo-ddar, fo-ddur*) is identical in root and suffix with the appellation of "sheath," which "supports," but only in a different manner from that in which "fodder" does. To this class of words may be added, with more or less certainty, a few other Old High German neuters which end, in the nominative and accusative, in *tar* or *dar*: viz. *flu-dar*, "float," from the root *flu* ($=$ Sanscrit *plu*), which has generally assumed the affix of a *z* (see 109^b. 1.); *flô-dar*, "*fluor*,"* from the same root; *ruo-dar*, "rudder," apparently as "making to flow or navigate," in root and suffix akin to the Latin *ru-trum*, and Greek ῥέ-θρον (ῥέω from σρε(F)ω, Sanscrit *srávâmi*, from the root *sru*, "to flow," causal *srâvay*), and radically, perhaps, also with *re-mus*.† Perhaps, too, we ought to class here *wundar, wuntar*, "wonder," and *wuldar*, "glory,"‡ as derivatives from roots now unknown.

819. To the Sanscrit feminine suffix *trâ*, as in *dánshtrâ*, "tooth" (see §. 815.), corresponds the Gothic *thlô*, in *nethlô* (nominative and accusative *nêthla*), "needle," as "instrument of sewing;" as in the Greek ακέστρα, but with *l* for *r*; which, according to §. 20., cannot surprise us, particularly as the Greek suffixes τλο, θλο, τλη, θλη (see Pott, II. p. 555), are

---

* The Sanscrit form for *flu-dar, flô-dar*, would be *plô-tra-m* (*ô=au*).

† Graff, II. p. 493, presupposes a root *rad*; but the Anglo-Saxon *rovan, reovan, revan*, "*remigare*," mentioned by him, proves the contrary, and answers to the Sanscrit causal base *sravây*.

‡ Gothic *vulthus*, probably with *thu*, = Sanscrit *tu*, as suffix.

likewise evidently to be referred to the Sanscrit *tra, trá*; as in ὄχ-ε-τλο-ν, χύ-τλο-ν, θύ-σ-θλο-ν, ἐχ-έ-τλη, γεν-έ-θλη. Ὄχ-ε-τλο-ν, in a Sanscrit form would be perhaps *vah-i-tra-m*, or *vah-a-tra-m*. With regard to γενέθλη as an abstract substantive, I must remark, that in Sanscrit also the feminine suffix *trá* is occasionally used to form abstract substantives; thus, the *yátrá* mentioned above (§. 815.) means also "gait." In Old High German the word for "needle" exhibits in the nominative and accusative, in different writers, *ná-dla, ná-dila, ná-dela*, and *ná-dal*: the Anglo-Saxon form is *næ-dl*. We have further to mention, in Gothic, *hleithra* (theme *-thró*), "a tent," which has retained the old *r*, though its root is obscured: it belongs, in my opinion, to the Sanscrit *śri* from *kri*, "to go" (compare *véśman*, "house," from *viś*, "to enter"), whence *á-śraya-s*, "asylum," "house," and in Gothic also *hliya*, masculine, (theme *-yan*), "a tent." To this root belongs also, among other words, the Old High German *hlei-tara* (for *hleitra*)*
(which, on account of its suffix, also belongs to this class), Anglo-Saxon *hlœdre, hlœ-der*, German *Lei-ter*, "ladder," as "instrument of mounting."

820. Let us now consider somewhat more closely the perfect passive participle, which we have already had occasion to mention more than once.† Its suffix is, in Sanscrit and Zend, usually *ta* (masculine and neuter), feminine *tá*, and is, I have no doubt, identical with the demonstrative base *ta* (see §. 343.). There is no ground, therefore, in the word itself for a passive signification, except, perhaps, in the accent; for while, according to §. 785. Remark, the ac-

---

* Graf (IV. p. 1115.) quotes for the nominative the forms *leitra, hleitar, leitera, leiter*, genitive *hleitra*. It admits of no doubt, that the forms in *r* have lost a final *a*, and that they cannot be classed with *muotar, tohtar, suestar*, of which the proper termination is *r*.

† See §§. 513. 588.

tive forms require the most powerful accentuation, *i.e.* the accent on the first syllable; in the passive participle under discussion the suffix receives the accent: hence we have *paktás*, "*coctus*," accusative *paktám*, standing similarly opposed to *páchan*, "*coquens*," *páchantam*, "*coquentem*," as above (§. 785. Remark) *śuchyátê*, "*purificatur*," is opposed to *śúchyatê*, "*purificat*." Greek verbals in τό-ς, which, as scarce needs to be noticed, are identical with the perfect participles passive of the cognate languages, have retained the old accentuation, and thus we have ποτό-ς, ποτή, ποτόν,* standing in the same relation to πότος, "the drinking" (compare §. 785. Remark, near the end), that, in Sanscrit, *píyátê*, "*bibitur*," has to *píyatê* (Class 4, middle), "*bibit*." The paroxytone or proparoxytone accent of abstracts in το appears to be preserved principally where, together with the abstract, the passive verbal is actually in use, and where, consequently, there is the more ground for bringing the abstract meaning prominently forward by the accent; whilst otherwise the abstract follows in its accentuation the prevailing example of verbals with passive signification; hence, indeed, πότος, ἄροτος, ἄμητος, τρύγητος, ἔμετος, ἄλετος, opposed to ποτός, ἀροτός, ἀμητός, τρυγητός, ἐμετός, ἀλετός (ἄλητον); but not κόπετος, κώκυτος, ἀλόητος, but κοπετός, κωκυτός, ἀλοητός, as these abstracts have no oxytone passive verbals to match them. There are, however, some isolated abstracts, or words which express the time of an action, which have the accent thrown back, as βίοτος, δείπνη-σ-τος.

821. The participial suffix त *ta* is either joined direct to the root or by a vowel of conjunction *i*. To the first kind of formation belong *jñâ-tá-s*, "known" = Greek γνω-τό-ς,

---

* Compare the Sanscrit *pítás*, *pítâ*, *pítám*, from the root *pá*, "to drink;" which, in the passive, has the *â* weakened to *i*. There is also a middle root *pi* of the fourth class.

FORMATION OF WORDS.

Latin (g)nô-tu-s, i-gnô-tu-s; dat-tá-s, "given,"* Zend dâ-tô (theme dâta), Latin da-tu-s, Greek δο-τό-ς; śru-tá-s, "heard," Greek κλυ-τό-ς, Latin clu-tu-s; bhû-tá-s, "been," "being," Greek φυ-τό-ς; bhri-tá-s (from bhartas, see §. 1.), "borne," Zend bĕrĕtô (theme -ta), Greek (φερ-τό-ς) ἄ-φερ-το-ς, Latin fer-tus, "bearing," "fruitful;" stri-tá-s, "extended" (from startás), Zend fra-stárĕtô (fra preposition), Greek στρα-τό-ς, (transposed from σταρ-τός), Latin strâ-tu-s; pak-tá-s, "cooked," Greek πεπ-τό-ς (root πεπ from πεκ, Sanscrit pach, from pak, Latin coc, from poc), Latin coc-tu-s; uk-tá-s, "spoken" (irregular for vaktás), Zend uctô (hûctô, "well-spoken" (from hu-uctô); yuk-tá-s, "bound," Greek ζευκ-τό-ς, Latin junc-tu-s; bhrish-tá-s, "roasted" (from bhrashtás, and this from bhrak-tás), Greek φρυκ-τό-ς, Latin fric-tus; bad-dhá-s, "bound" (euphonic for badh-tá-s, root bandh), Zend bas-tô;† lab-dhá-s, "obtained" (euphonic for labhtás), Greek ληπ-τό-ς; jâ-tá-s, "born" (root jan), Zend zâ-tô, Greek γε-τό-ς, in the compound τηλύγετος;‡ matá-s, "thought" (root man), Zend matô, (compare μεν-ε-τός); dish-tâ-s, "shewn" (euphonic for dish-tás, from dik-tás, see §. 21.), Greek (δεικτός) ἀναπόδεικτος, χειρόδεικτος, &c., Latin dic-tus; dash-tá-s, "bitten" (euphonic for daś-tás, from dak-tás), Greek (δηκ-τό-ς), ἄδηκτος, καρδιό-δηκτος; drish-tá-s, "seen" (from darshtás, and this from

---

* From dadátas, with irregular retention of the reduplication of the special tenses.

† See §. 102., and compare Greek analogous form, as κεστός, πιστός. With regard to the Latin form of this participle in roots with a T sound see §. 101.

‡ It is a rule in Sanscrit that before formative suffixes beginning with t, which require no Guna augment, the n and m of the root are rejected; jan, "to produce, to bear," and khan, "to engrave," lengthen their vowel in doing this. From han, "to smite, to slay," comes hatás, with which we may compare the Greek -φατος, as ΦΕΝΩ (φόνος, ἔπεφνον), like θνήσκω, most probably belongs to the Sanscrit root han, from dhan (nidhana, "death").

dark-tás), Greek (δερκτός), ἐπίδερκτος; *ush-tá-s,* " burnt," Latin *us-tu-s.* The following are examples with the conjunctive vowel *i*: *prat-i-tá-s,* "*extensus*" (root प्रथ् *prath,* whence *prithú-s,* " broad," from *prathú-s,* Greek πλατύ-ς, Lithuanian *pla-tù-s*); *añch-i-tá-s,* "*erectus,*" *pat-i-tá-s,* "*qui cecidit,*"* So in Latin, *dom-i-tus, mon-i-tus, mol-i-tus, gen-i-tus.* In Greek the ε of forms like μεν-ε-τός, σκελ-ε-τός, ἑρπ-ε-τός, corresponds, where we again leave it undecided whether this *t* be a corruption of an *i* or an *a*.†

822. The Latin forms in *idus,* springing from neuter verbs, and for the most part of the second conjugation, as *pall-i-dus, ferv-i-dus, frig-i-dus, torr-i-dus, tim-i-dus, tep-i-dus, splend-i-dus, nit-i-dus, luc-i-dus, fulg-i-dus, viv-i-dus, sap-i-dus, flu-i-dus,* correspond to the participles in *tá* in Sanscrit, which spring from neuter verbs, and have an active signification, and especially to those which have a present meaning; as, *tvar-i-tás,* " hastening," *sthitás,* " standing," *suptás,* " sleeping " (also " having slept "), *śaktás,* " being able," ‡ *yat-tas,* " striving," *bhí-tás,* " fearing," *hrí-tás,* " being

---

* Regarding the active signification of this participle in neuter verbs see §. 513. conclusion; so, in Greek, στατός, " standing," = Sanscrit *sthitás* (weakened from *sthâtás*), which likewise signifies present time: on the other hand *pra-sthitás* means both "*proficiscens*" and "*profectus.*"

† Compare §. 815., and Curtius "*De Nominum Græcorum formatione,*" pp. 38, 60. Indian Grammarians assume a suffix (*uṇâdi*) *atá,* the *a* of which, however, is most probably only a class-vowel, with which the Greek ε might be compared; thus, ἑρπ-ε-τός (compare ἕρπ-ε-τε) like *pach-a-tás,* " fire," as " cooking." The abstracts θάν-α-τος, " death," and κάμ-α-τος, " fatigue," have preserved the conjunctive vowel in its original form, and thus correspond to the Sanscrit *mar-a-tá-s,* " death ;" where, however, we must observe that the Sanscrit root *mar, mṛi,* " to die," in its verbal conjugation, does not belong to the first or sixth class any more than the Greek roots θαν and καμ.

‡ The form with the conjunctive vowel (*śak-i-tás*) has a passive signification, so *yat-i-tás,* " obtained by efforts, sought for," compared with *yat-tás,* " striving." In Latin, *vice versâ, rap-i-dus,* active, opposed to *rap-tus,* passive.

ashamed;" and to the Greek στατός, "standing;" μενετός, "remaining;" ἑρπετός, "creeping." The opinion, therefore, elsewhere stated, appears probable, that the *d* in the Latin forms just mentioned is only the weakening of an original tenuis,* just as in *quadraginta, quadruplus, quadruplex*, for *quatraginta*, &c. An active and present meaning, though in a transitive verb, and with the retention of the old tenuis, occurs in the participle spoken of in *fertus*, "bearing," "fruitful," which corresponds in form with the Sanscrit *bhritás*, from *bhartás*, "borne," Zend *bĕrĕtô*, and Greek -φερτος (see §. 818.).

823. The Sanscrit verbs of the tenth class, and the causals identical with them in form, have all of them the conjunctive vowel *i*; hence *pid-i-tás*, "pressed," "pained;" *vêś-i-tá-s*, "made to enter." The circumstance, however, that the said verbs extend their character *ay* (in the special tenses *aya*) to the universal tenses also, and a great part of the formation of words, gives room for the conjecture that the *i* of forms like *pid-i-tás, vêś-i-tás*, is not the ordinary vowel of conjunction, but a contraction of *ay*; or that such forms in *i-tá-s* have been preceded by older ones in *ay-i-tas*, according to the analogy of the infinitives, as *pid-áyi-tum*. As, then, Latin supines like *am-á-tum, aud-í-tum*, are related to *pid-áyi-tum*, just such is the relation of *am-á-tus, aud-í-tus*, to the presupposed *pid-áyi-tas*. Although the Latin second conjugation also belongs here, and, for example, *moneo* corresponds to the Sanscrit causal *mân-áyâ-mi* and Prâkrit *mân-ê-mi* (see p. 110), I would nevertheless prefer to identify *mon-i-tus* with *mân-i-tás* in such a way

---

passive. Observe, also, the active *cup-i-dus* together with the passive *cup-i-tus*. These, however, are only arbitrary usages, which rest on no general principle.

* *Influence of Pronouns in the Formation of Words*, pp. 21, 22. Pott is of a different opinion, E. I. M. p. 567.

that I could thence infer the existence of similar forms in the time of the unity of language, while I would prefer assuming a casual coincidence in the similar abbreviation of a common element. In Greek the η or ω of forms like φιλ-η-τός, τιμ-η-τός (from τιμ-ᾱ-τος), χειρ-ω-τός, corresponds to the character of the Sanscrit tenth class, and therefore to the Latin *â* and *î* of *am-â-tus, aud-î-tus*. In Gothic, where, as generally throughout the German languages, this participle remains regular only in the so-called weak conjugation, the old tenuis, instead of, in accordance with §. 87., becoming an aspirate, has sunk down to a medial, in suchwise, however, as that before the *s* of the masculine nominative, and in the accusative, which has lost the final vowel of the base and the case termination, a *th* for *d* enters (compare §. 91.). According to the difference of the conjugational class, an *i* (from *ya*), *ô*, or *ai*, *i.e.* the three different forms of the Sanscrit character of the tenth class (*ay*, see §. 109ª. 6.) precedes; hence the bases *tam-i-da*,[*] "*domitus*;" *friy-ô-da*,[†] "*amatus*;" *ga-yuk-ai-da*, "*subjugatus*;" nominative masculine *tamiths, friyôths, gayukaiths*; accusative *tamith*, &c.; genitive *tamidi-s*, &c. (see §. 191.). The direct annexation of the participial suffix occurs in Gothic only in certain irregular verbs, and in such a manner that, according to the measure of the preceding consonant, either the original tenuis is preserved, or has become *d* (see §§. 626. 91.). Thus the base *bauhta*,[‡] "purchased" (*bugya*,

---

[*] Compare Sanscrit *dam-i-tás* (from *dam-ayi-tás*?) from *damâyâmi*, causal of the root *dam*, "to tame," but of the same meaning as the primitive and the Latin *dom-i-tus*.

[†] It may be regarded as the denominative of the Sanscrit *priya*, "dear," "beloved;" and it is also, radically and in its formation, akin to the Greek φιλ-η-τός (from φιλέω, denominative of φίλος, transposed from φλιος), the η of which has sprung, like the Gothic *ô*, from *â*.

[‡] Euphonic for *buhta* (see §. 82.), and this from *bukta*, from the root *bug*.

"I purchase"), corresponds to Sanscrit forms like *bhuktá*,*
"eaten" (root *bhuj* from *bhug*), Greek like φρυκτό, and Latin
like *junctu* ; *mun-da*, "believed," answers to the Sanscrit
ma-tá, "thought," "believed," for *man-tá*, as the feminine
substantive base *ga-mun-di* (nominative *-n-ds*) does to the
Sanscrit base *má(n)-ti*, "meaning."

824. In Lithuanian the participial suffix spoken of is retained quite unaltered in form, and, indeed, in all verbs, so far as they have a passive. In the nominative masculine *ta-s* corresponds to the Sanscrit *tá-s* ; e.g. *sekta-s* "followed" = Sanscrit *saktá-s* (root *sach*, from *sak*, "to [G. Ed. p. 1156.] follow," compare Latin *sequor*); *seg-ta-s*, "fastened" = Sanscrit *sak-tá-s* for *sag-tá-s* (root सञ्ज् *sañj*, from *sang*, "to fasten"); *deg-ta-s*, "burnt" = Sanscrit *dag-dha-s*.† In the nominative feminine *sekta, segta, degta,* correspond to the Sanscrit *saktá́, dagdhá́*, only with the *a* shortened, as in Gothic, Latin, and Zend forms like *bauhta* (genitive *bauhtô-s*), *juncta*, ᭢᭢᭢᭢ *basta* (see §. 137.): to the Latin *juncta* corresponds literatim the Lithuanian *junkta*, from *jungiu*, "I yoke (the oxen)": *hept-as*, *hepta* (from *heppù*, "I bake," see §. 501.), corresponds to the Sanscrit *pak-tú-s, tá,* Greek πεπτό-ς, τή, Latin *coctu-s, ta*. Forms like *wes-ta-s,* "conducted" (root *wed*), correspond in a euphonic respect to Zend like *baṡ-tô*, "bound" (root *bandh*(, *iriṡ-tô*, "dead" (root *irith*), and Greek like πισ-τός, κεσ-τός (see §. 102.). To the Gothic participles of the weak conjugation correspond the participles of those Lithuanian conjugations, which we have above

---

* In the former parts of this work the accent is not given to Sanscrit words, as the subject of Sanscrit accent had not then been investigated. In 1843, Böhtlingk published a treatise on Sanscrit accentuation (as the Author of this work tells us in the Preface to his Fifth Part), which opened up a new field of inquiry. The mark over the *a* then, in *bhuktá*, is the accent, and does not denote vowel length.

† *Dh* euphonic for *t*, see §. 104. In Irish, *daghaim*, "I burn," corresponds to the Sanscrit *dahámi* ; and *dagte*, "burnt," to the passive participle *daghda-s*, Lithuanian *degtas*.

4 D

(§. 506., p. 704) compared with the Sanscrit tenth class; thus, *myl-i-tas*, "beloved;" *pen-ē-tas*, "nourished;" *laih-y-tas*, "held."

825. The Sclavonic languages have, if the opinion expressed in §. 628. be well founded, transferred to the active voice the passive participle here spoken of—with the retention, however, of the meaning of past time—and have weakened the original *t* to *l*, probably by changing it in an intervening stage to *d*. In the former point they correspond to the New Persian, where the participle in question has, at least generally, an active signification: in the latter point they agree with the Georgian, where ჭამული *jam-u-li* signifies "eaten" (Sanscrit *jam*, "to eat"), and თბობილი *thbob-i-li* "warmed" (Sanscrit *tap*, "to burn").

[G. Ed. p. 1157.] The suffix ло *lo* (n. m. лъ *l'*, neut. *lo*, f. *la*) is joined, in Old Sclavonic, either directly to the root or to the class-syllable, the latter in the verbs which correspond to the Sanscrit 10th class and the German weak conjugation; hence, *e. g.* былъ *byl'*, была *byla*, было *bylo*, "been" = Sanscrit *bhútás, tā́, tám* (pers. *búdeh*); пилъ *pi-l'*, пила *pi-la*, пило *pi-lo*, "having drunk" = Sanscrit *pī-tás, tā́, tám*, "drunk;" неслъ *nesl'*, несла *nesla*, несло *nes-lo*, "having borne;" воудилъ *búd-i-l'*, воудила *búd-i-la*, воудило *búd-i-lo*, "having waked" = Sanscrit *bódh-i-tás, tā́, tám*, "waked."*
Should, however, these Sclavonic participles not be connected with the Sanscrit participles in *ta*, it appears to me almost impossible to compare them with forms in the cognate languages; at least I do not believe that the suffix *la*, which occurs in Sanscrit only in a few words, *e.g.* in *chap-a-lá-s*, "trembling," or the suffix *ra*, the use of which is in like manner but rare, *e. g.* that of *dip-rá-s*, "shining," can have served as the source from which the Sclavonic participial suffix *lo* is derived.

---

* With regard to the change of the old *t*-sound into *l*, compare also the Gipsy *mu-lo*, "dead," from *mudo*, Prâkrit *mudo* (nom. masc.).

826. The Sclavonic languages, however, are not deficient in forms also which have preserved the old *t* and the passive signification of the participle under discussion, although in all the Sclavonic dialects this participle is generally formed by the suffix *no* (fem. *na*)= Sanscrit *na*, of which hereafter. In the Old Sclavonic we find an example in *to* (nom. masc. тъ *t'*, fem. та *ta*, neut. то *to*) in отатъ *otan-t'*, "*ademtus*" (prep. *ot'*, "from"), which in root and formation corresponds to the Sanscrit *yatá-s* (for *yan-tá-s*, from *yam-tá-s*) and Latin *emtus*.* In Slowenian [G. Ed. p. 1158.] or Carniolan the passive participles in *t* are very numerous; *e.g. ster-t*, "extended" (compare Zend *starĕta*, Sanscrit *stritá*), *der-t*, "flayed," *bi-t*, "struck," *slu-t*, "famed" (Sanscrit *śru-tá-s*, "heard," *vi-śru-tá-s*, "famed," Greek κλυ-τό-ς).† In Russian the following are examples: пишыЙ *pi-tyĭ*, "drunk" (Sanscrit *pí-tá-s*); пролишыЙ *pro-li-tyĭ*, "spilt," *po-vi-tyĭ*, enveloped," *po-bi-tyĭ*, "smitten, slain," *kolotyĭ*, "stuck;" шанушый *tanutyĭ*, "drawn."‡ The opinion, however, that the suffix *l'*, *la*, *lo* is based on the Sanscrit *ta-s*, *tá*, *ta-m*, is not refuted by these forms, as it is by no means uncommon in the language to find together with the new and corrupted form the original also existing, with regard to which I will here only refer to the division of the suffix here treated of into *tu* and *du* (see §. 822.), which, in my opinion, made its first appearance in Latin.

Remark.—A. Schleicher, who, in his work, "The Languages of Europe," p. 261 *passim*, opposes the opinion that the Sclavonic participle referred to is, in its origin, identical with the Sanscrit in *ta*, finds it inexplicable that from the to-be-presupposed forms like *nest* the favourite combination of consonants *st* should be changed into the much rarer *sl*.

---

* "Kopitar Vocab.," p. 78; and Miklosich, "Doctrine of Forms," p. 47.

† See Metelko, p. 105, *passim*.

‡ See Reiff, "Grammaire Russe," p. 188. The termination *yĭ*, or rather the simple *ĭ* (from *yo*), fem. *ya*, is the affix mentioned above (§. 284.) of the definite declension.

I, too, believe, that had the to-be-presupposed form *nest* stood alone, it would, owing to the firmness of the combination *st*, and its being such a favourite, never have become *nesl*. And though I assume *d* as a middle point between *t* and *l*, and allow the language, in its corruption of the suffix referred to, to have proceeded from *to* to *do*, and thence to have arrived at *lo*, I nevertheless do not think that in every individual verb this process has been *de novo* and independently carried on; nor do I imagine that there ever existed in Sclavonic a participle *nesd', nesda, nesdo*; but I assume that the *t* of the suffix under discussion has, in the different [G. Ed. p. 1159] conjugations, and the majority of verbs, gradually been corrupted to *l*. Were, however, *lo*, in the majority of Sclavonic verbs, once substituted for the suffix *to*, it might, as it appears to me, be transferred by the force of analogy to those verbs also with whose final letters a *t* agrees better than *l*. Only in the case that the combination *sl* had been unendurable in Sclavonic would the roots in *s* and those in *d*, which, according to a general euphonic law in Sclavonic (see §. 457.), change this letter before *s* into *t*, have necessarily retained the elder form of the suffix. I must here recal attention to the fact, that the Bengālī also possesses a preterite, which appears to be of participial origin, and has *l* for its most essentially distinguishing feature; *e.g. kŏrilâm*, "I made" (*kŏr-i-lâ-m*), 2d pers. *kŏrili*. It is highly probable that, as Max Müller ("Report of the British Association for Advancement of Science for 1847," p. 243) assumes, the *l* of these forms has arisen from *t*, through the intervention of a middle point *d*, and that the entire form owes its origin to the Sanscrit perfect passive participle in *ta;* so that, therefore, *kŏrilâm* would equal the Persian *kardam*, from which it is materially distinguished only by the further weakening of the *d* to *l*, and the insertion of the vowel of conjunction *i*, which, also in Sanscrit, is very common in the participle referred to. In the 2d pers. sing. *kŏrili* answers to the Persian *kardi*. With regard to the use in Bengālī of the Sanscrit passive perfect participle without alteration of form and signification, it is to be remarked that this is avowedly borrowed at a later period (see Haughton, §. 241.); and so, in general, in the Bengālī lingual Thesaurus one has to distinguish between the words which have been, as it were, moulded and remodelled in the lap of the daughter language, and those which have been adopted newly from the Sanscrit. Should we, however, be desirous of seeking out in order to explain Bengālī preterites like *kŏrilâm*, a class of words in Sanscrit to which they would in external form correspond better than to the passive past participles in *ta*, we must then betake ourselves to the suffix *ila* (properly *la*, with *i* as conjunctive vowel), which has left behind only a very small family of words, to which belong among

FORMATION OF WORDS.

others *an-i-lá-s,* " wind," as " blowing ;" *path-i-lá-s,* " traveller " (from *path,* " to go "). One does not, however, see how this rare suffix with a present signification has arrived at the destination of forming a preterite in Bengālī from every root. Another modern Indian dialect which furnishes a corroboration to the Sclavonic languages with [G. Ed. p. 1160.] respect to the participle under discussion is the Marāṭhī.* Here a perfect passive participle in *lă* (m.), *lĭ* (f.), *lŏ* (n.),† springs from every verbal root;

---

* It is very much to be regretted that the learned Professor has been guided in his remarks on the Marāṭhī language by Carey's Grammar, which was published half a century ago, and at a Presidency where the Marāṭhī language is not so well known as at Bombay. Hence he gives a past participle in ल to transitive verbs, the fact being that this participle is never separated from the vowel which marks the gender, and must be, *e. g.* पाहिला *pâhilâ,* पाहिली *pâhilî,* पाहिलें *pâhilen̆,* never पाहिल *pâhil.* The sentence म्या बायकोस पाहिल *myâ bâyakôs pâhil,* " I saw the woman," is altogether incorrect. It should be मीं ती बायको पाहिली *mîn̆ tî bâyakô pâhilî,* or मीं त्या बायकोला पाहिलें *mîn̆ tyâ bâyakôlâ pâhilen̆.* With reference to the termination स *s* and ला *lâ* in this case (be it the dative, or, as I regard it, the accusative), Dr. Stephenson rightly lays down the following rule: " When motion to a place is intended, then स *s* is preferred; but when the dative is the object of a verb, then ला *lâ* is more common; as, तो गांवास गेला *tô gân̆wâs gelâ,* 'he is gone to the village;' त्याने त्या बायकोला मारिलें *tyâne tyâ bâyakolâ mârilen̆,* 'he beat that woman.' " I am at a loss to guess where the learned Professor found authority for stating that the Sanscrit short ă is pronounced in Marāṭhī like ŏ; for so far from this being the case, I do not believe that that sound of *o* exists in any of the modern languages of India, except Bengālī, save, perhaps, before *r.*—[Note by the Translator.]

† The Sanscrit short *a* is pronounced in Marāṭhī and Bengālī like ŏ; so that the neuters of the participle under discussion in that language correspond exactly to those of the Sclavonic, as *neslo* (see §. 255 *a.*). The long *â* in the masculine of the Marāṭhī adjectives is probably based on the Sanscrit nominatives in *as,* so that for the suppression of the *s* compensation is made by lengthening the preceding vowel. On the other hand, the pronominal nominatives तो *tô,* " he," and जो *jô,* " which" (*j* from *y,* see §. 19.), are based on the corruption which the termination *as* has everywhere experienced in Zend, Pali, and Prâkrit (see §. 56 *b.*). Adjectives, as such, are not declined in Marāṭhī.

e.g. pâhilâ, "having seen,"* *kelâ,* "having made," the latter being, as it seems, from *kaïlâ* for *karilâ*. Compare the Bengālī *kŏrilâm*, "I made," and the Prâkrit *kada* from *karda,* "made." The active construction of other languages is, in the Marāṭhī, changed into the passive by a periphrasis in the past tenses, which are wanting in that language, as in most of the Sclavonic dialects; and thus, *e.g.* myâ † *kêlâ, myâ kêli, myâ kêlŏ,* which Carey translates by "I did," is literally nothing else than "*a me factus, facta, factum;*" although Carey, in this and analogous tenses, appears in reality to recognise an active form of expression: for he remarks (p. 67), "It must be observed that the gender of the verb, in the imperfect, perfect, and pluperfect tenses, varies, to agree with that of the object." That which, however, is here called the object, is, in fact, the grammatical subject, and the participle is governed by this, not only in gender, but also in number. At p. 129 it is remarked, "It must be observed, that when the verb is used actively, viz. when the object is expressed in the accusative, the form of the neuter singular only is used. When the object is in the nominative case, the verb is passive, and varies with the gender of the subject." Ex. म्यां बायकोस् पाहिलॢ *myân bâyŏkôs pâhilŏ,* "I saw the woman;" म्यां बायकॊ पाहिली *myân bâyŏkô pâhilî,* "the woman was seen by me." I am convinced, however, that the first construc-

[G. Ed. p. 1161.] tion is quite as much passive as the second; for were it active, the pronoun must have stood in the nominative, and have sounded therefore मीं *mîn,* and not *myân,* ‡ as in the second. The difference between the two constructions is only this, that in the first the neuter passive participle stands impersonally, or contains the subject in itself, and governs an accusative; while in the second the participle is the predicate of the subject, expressed by *bâyŏkô,* "woman." Could the first construction be imitated in Latin it would be literally rendered by "*a me feminam visum (est).*" In Greek, constructions such as τοὺς φίλους σοι θεραπευτέον correspond to this. In neuter verbs, *i.e.* the substantive verb in combination with various ideas, the Marāṭhī participle in *lâ, li, lŏ,* like its Sanscrit prototype in *ta-s, tâ, ta-m,* has an active signification, and has therefore also the pronominal or substantive subject placed before it in the nominative; and thus we have, *e.g. mîn gêlô-n,* "I went," properly "I am having gone;" since the substantive verb, in spirit at least, is contained therein (see §. 628. Rem. 1.), fem. *mîn gêli-n;* 2d pers. masc. *tûn gêlâ-s,*

---

* *H* for Sanscrit *sh* of the defective root *pash (pashyâmi,* "I see").

† *Myâ* corresponds to the Sanscrit instrumental *mayâ*.

‡ Evidently only an inorganic extension of the above-mentioned *myâ*.

FORMATION OF WORDS. 1127

fem. *gĕli-s*; 3d pers. masc. *tŏ gĕlá*, fem. *ti gĕli*, without a personal termination. So in the verb substantive, *min jhâlô-n*, " I was " (" I am having been"), fem. *jhâlê-n*, 2d pers. *jhâlâ-s*, *jhâli-s*, 3d pers. *tŏ jhâlâ*, *ti jhâli*. The Marāṭhī, therefore, here appears almost in the dress of the Polish, which in like manner, in the 3d person, gives the bare participle, but in the 1st and 2d appends to it the personal terminations: masc. *byt-em*, *byt-eś*, *byt*, fem. *byta-m*, *byta-ś*, *by-ta*, neut. *byto-m*, *byto-ś*, *byto* (see §. 628. Rem. 1.). Irrespective of the passive participles newly borrowed from the Sanscrit, and which for the most part remain entirely unchanged, as *dŏttŏ*, "given," *yuktŏ*, "bound," *grŏstŏ*, "swallowed," *sŏmâptŏ*, "ended," there is in Marāṭhī perhaps only one solitary participle of this kind which has preserved the old *t*, viz. *hôtî*, fem. *hôtî* (or *hôtê*), neut. *hôtŏ*, "having been"=Sanscrit *bhūtá-s*, *â*, *â-m*, (see Prâkrit *hô-mi*, " I am"), whence *hôtô-n*, "I was," as above, from another root, and with a corrupted suffix झालों *jhâlô-n*. According to this analogy one should expect *hôlôn* from *hô*. The participle, which is found in the so-called 2d aorist present, e.g. the form *min kortô-n*, " I do " (" I am doing," see Sanscrit *kartâsmi*, "*facturus sum*"), fem. *min karti*, I derive from the Sanscrit participle future, or noun of agent in *târ*, *tṛi*, [G. Ed. p. 1162.] nom. masc. *tâ*, which frequently occurs in the Vêda dialect in the sense of the participle present (see §. 814.).* The 2d pers. masc. *kŏrtâs*, "thou doest," answers to the Sanscrit *kartâsi*, "*facturus es*," or "*factor es*," but the substantive verb is not contained in the Marāṭhī form, but only the character of the 2d person; and this participle is treated in Marāṭhī as if it had been formed in Sanscrit by the suffix *ta* (not by *târ*, *tṛi*). In the substantive verb, both the Sanscrit *bhūtá-s*, "been," and *bhav-i-tâ*, "*futurus*," are represented in Marāṭhī by *hôtâ*. The said language, however, is not wanting in forms in which the form corresponding to the Sanscrit noun of agency, or participle future, appends its suffix by a conjunctive vowel *i*, e.g. इच्छितो *ichchhitô*, "wishing" (Carey, p. 80), fem. *ichchhitê*. As regards the *ô* of the masculine form *ichchhitô*, it corresponds to the before-men-

---

* That the participle which appears in the 2d aorist present is not, perhaps, formally based on the Sanscrit passive participle in *ta* is evinced in the case before us, by the circumstance, that not only does *kartô-n* answer better to *kartâ* than to *kṛitá-s*, but also, that beside the genuine Marāṭhī *kĕlâ*, "made," mentioned above, there exists in Marāṭhī a second borrowed form *krŏtŏ* (see Carey, p. 36, *isvŏrŏkrŏtŏ*, "God-formed"), which, like the Prâkrit *kada* (for *karda* or *kṛada*), is based on the original form *karta*, of which *kṛita* is a contraction (see §. 1.).

tioned (p. 1125, Note †) pronominal nominatives, as *tô*, "he," *jô*, "which;" while *tâ* in *hôtâ*, "being,"* answers to the ordinary adjective-nominatives in *â*. Carey, in the different verbs and auxiliary verbs which his garmmar exhibits, gives, in the 3d pers. masc. of the 2d aorist present under discussion, pretty indifferently either *tâ*, or *tô*, or *tôṅ*, only in *hôtâ* he gives only *tâ*, but elsewhere either *tôṅ* or *tô*. The nasal of the former is most probably only an inorganic affix, which the Marāṭhī occasionally adds also to some other forms which end in a vowel; as, *e.g.* in the instrumental म्यां *myâṅ*, "by me" (with *myâ*), mentioned above (p. 1126), and the analogous *tvâṅ*, "by thee" (Carey, p. 127), together with the *tvâ* from the base *tva* (see §. 158.) corresponding to the Zend Grammar. We must similarly regard, I doubt not, the Anusvâra of the repeated participle in तां *tâṅ*, as *kŏrtâṅ, kŏrtâṅ*, "doing, continuing to do," since this participle [G. Ed. p. 1163]. is only by its repetition distinguished in formation from that by which the 2d aorist present is periphrastically denoted. The case is different with the termination *tôṅ* of the 1st person, in which the never-failing *ṅ* is the expression of person=Sanscrit *mi*, and the preceding portion of the word is the masculine nominative. The feminine allows in the 1st person the suppression of the *ṅ*; hence *kŏr-tê*, "I make," opposed to *sŏk-tê-ṅ*, "I can" (Carey, p. 79), with *ê* for *î*, which appears in the 2d person *kŏrti-s*, while the masculine form retains its *ô* (*kŏrtô-s*).

827. By *ta* with the conjunctive vowel *i* in Sanscrit are formed, from substantives, also adjectives, which can be taken as the passive participles of to-be-presupposed denominative verbs; as, *e.g. phal'-i-tá-s*, "furnished with fruit," from *phalá*, "fruit;" whence might spring a denominative *phal'-ayâ-mi*, "supplied with fruits," which would form a passive participle *phal-i-tá-s*. Corresponding forms in Latin are such as, *barbâ-tus, alâ-tus, fimbriâ-tus, cordâ-tus, aurî-tys, turrî-tus, versû-tus, verû-tus, astû-tus, cinctû-tus, jus-tus, nefas-tus, sceles-tus, robus-tus*, (*robur, roboris* from *robus, robos-is*), *hones-tus* (*honôr-is* from *-s-is*); and in Greek, forms like κροκω-τός, ὀμφαλω-τός, αὐλω-τός, φολιδω-τός, ἀνανδρω-τός. Let attention be directed to the inclination towards a long

---

* Carey, p. 92, *tô hôtá*, "he is" (literally, "he being").

vowel before the suffix, evinced as well in Latin as in Greek. In like manner as the originally short *u* of the 4th declension, and the *ĭ* of the 3d, is lengthened, so also is the inorganic *u* of the 2d in *nasû-tus*, and so is, in themes terminating in a consonant, the *i* which extends the base (see p. 1078), *e.g.* in *marî-tus*, *patrî-tus*, which, according to form at least, belong here; so also in Greek is the *o* which extends the base; hence, *e.g.* φολιδ-ω-τός. The word ἁμαξ'-ι-τός stands alone, properly, "furnished with a wagon," which, by the suppression of the final vowel of the base, and the assuming a vowel of conjunction *ι*, corresponds admirably to Sanscrit formations like *mudr'-i-tás*, "sealed," from *mudrá*, "a seal." [G. Ed. p. 1164.] Here belong also the Latin formations in *ê-tu-m*, *arborê-tum*, *quercê-tum*, *fimê-tum*, *pomê-tum*, which, as Pott too assumes ("Etym. Inqui." p. 546), as it were presuppose denominatives of the 2d conjugation, in which we might well expect participles like *monê-tus* (see pp. 1107, 1108).

828. In Lithuanian and Sclavonic also adjectives spring from substantive bases, which in form and signification correspond to the passive perfect participles here treated of. Examples in Russian are рогашый *rog'-a-tyĭ*, "horned" (Lithuanian *ragútas*), from рогъ *rog'*, theme *rogo*, "horn;" волосашый *volos'-a-tyĭ*, "like hair," from *volos'*, theme *voloso'*, "hair;" горбашый *gorb'-a-tyĭ*, "humpbacked," from *gorb'*, theme *gorbs*, "hunch;" именішый *ime-ni-tyĭ*, "named," from імя *imya*, theme *imen* "name;" шресновішый *tres-nov-i-tyĭ*, "embroidered," "covered with embroidery," from *tresna*, "embroidery;" *domov-i-tyĭ*, "domestic," from домъ *dom'*, "house" (see p. 348).* The words which belong

---

* The above examples, according to Dobrowsky (p. 529), apply in part also for the Old Sclavonic: compare, therefore, the formations beginning with a consonant from the denominatives treated of in §. 766, *e.g.* the infinitives in *a-ti*, *i-ti*, *ov-a-ti* (§. 768.), with which the insertions *a, i* (*ov-i*) (based on the Sanscrit *aya*) of the nominal participles above are identical.

here have, part of them, inserted an *s* before the *t* of the participial character, according to the manner of the Greek verbals like ἀκε-σ-τός, ἀκου-σ-τός, and of the Lithuanian abstracts in *stẽ*, opposed to the Sanscrit in *tá*, and Latin in *ta, tât, tút*, of which hereafter. Thus, *e.g.* in Russian, каменисшый *kamen-i-styĭ*, "stony" (Lith. *akmen-ŭ̊-tas*); шернісшый *tern'-i-styĭ*, "thorny" (*tern'*, theme *terno*, "thorn" = Sanscrit *triṇa* from *tarṇa*, "grass"); бородасшый *borod'-a-styĭ*, "bearded, provided with a beard," (*boroda*, "beard," compare Sanscrit *vardh*,
[G. Ed. p. 1165.] *vṛidh*, "to grow," Lith. *barzda*, "beard," *barzd'-ŭ̊-tas*, "bearded"). In Lithuanian an *o* usually precedes the suffix *ta* of this class of words (occasionally instead of it *ŭ̊* = *uo*), after the analogy of the denominatives treated of in §§. 766, 767, in the formations beginning with a consonant (§. 767); and in fact so that here also the final vowel of the base noun is dropped before the vowel which forms the denominative verbal base; thus, *e.g. migl'-o-tas*, "misty," "attended with mist," from *migla*, "mist;" *plauk'-o-tas*, "hairy," from *plauka-s*, "hair;" *plunksu'-o-tas*, "feathery," from *plunksna*, "feather;" *dumbl'-o-tas*, "slimy," from *dumbla-s*, "slime." In forms like *akmen-ŭ̊-tas*, "stony," *rag'-ŭ̊-tas*, "horned," from the bases *akmen*, *raga*, *ŭ̊* is only a substitute for the simple *o*; as, *e.g.* in *waźŭ̊-yu*, "I drive," opposed to *dumoyu*, "I think" (see p. 704). The verbs, however, in *ŭ̊yu* for *oyu*, do not retain their *ŭ̊* in the formations beginning with a consonant, but here exhibit simply *o*; whence *waź-o-tas*, "driven," not *waź-ŭ̊-tas*. In forms which admit of comparison in Sanscrit a long *â* fills the place of the Lithuanian *ŭ̊*; as, *e.g.* in *dâdâmi*, "I give," *áśmâ*, "stone" (nom. of *áśman*) for the Lithuanian *dŭ̊mi*, *akmŭ̊*.* The simple *o* also is often, in Lithuanian, the

---

* I see, therefore, no reason to compare the forms in *ŭ̊ta-s, ota-s*, with the possessives in Sanscrit like *dhana-vant, -vat*, "rich," from *dhana*, "riches," which are formed by the suffix *vant* (in the weak cases *vat*). Cf. Pott, II. p. 546.

FORMATION OF WORDS. 1131

etymological representative of a Sanscrit long *â*; *e.g.* in the feminine plural-nominatives like *aszwos*, " mares " (sing. *aszwà*), contrasted with the Sanscrit *ásvâs*, and Gothic forms like *gibôs* (see §. 227). We may therefore identify both the $\overset{\circ}{u}$ of forms like *akmen-ŭ-tas*, and the preponderating *o* of such as *migĺ-o-tas*, *plauk-o-tas*, with the *â* of Latin forms like *cord-â-tus*, as with the *o*, too, of Mielcke's 4th conjugation; *e.g.* that of *yeszk-o-me*, " we seek," *yeszk-ó-* [G. Ed. p. 1166.] *tas*, " sought," is essentially identical with the Latin *â* of *am-â-mus*, *am-â-tus*.* The forms in *ĕ-ta-s*, in Lithuanian, stand alone; as *dulkĕ-tas*, " covered with dust," " dirty," from *dulkês*, " dust " (nom. pl. from the base *dulkê*);† as here the *ĕ* of the base takes the place of the derivative *o*, which is found, *e. g.* in *raukzĺ-o-tas*, " wrinkled," from *raukszlĕ̃*, " wrinkle."

829. The feminine of the suffix त *ta*, viz. *tâ*, forms, in Sanscrit, also abstract substantives from adjectives and substantives. They accent the final syllable of the primitive base; *e.g. śuklá-tâ*, " whiteness," from *śúkla*, " white ;" *samá-tâ*, " levelness," from *samá*, " level ;" *prithútâ*, " breadth," from *prithú*, " broad ;" *vadhyátâ*, abstract from *vádhya*, " occidendus ;" *strí-tâ*, " womanhood," from *strí*, " woman." In Greek correspond the abstract substantive-bases in τητ, and in general, in the matter of accentuation also, with the addition of a τ (see §. 832.), which shews

---

* Above, also (§. 506.), Mielcke's 4th conjugation ought to have been identified with the Sanscrit 10th class: it is distinguished from the 3d by this, that it retains the *o* in places where the latter exhibits *y* (=*i̯*) in the class-syllable; hence, *e. g. yeszk-o-tas*, " sought," *yeszk-o-su*, " I will seek," compared with *laik-y-tas*, " held," *laik-y-su*, " I will hold."

† Feminines in *ĕ̃*, like *giesmĕ̃*, " song " (Mielcke, p. 33), presuppose an older *ia*, hence in the genitive plural *iû* or *yû* (*żwákiû, giesmyû*), as *rankû*, " *manuum*," from *rankà* (see §. 157. Note 3.). Remark, also, that to the masculine adjective-nominatives in *i-s* (from *ia-s*) belong feminines in *ĕ̃*; *e. g.* the feminine of *didi-s*, " great," is *didĕ̃* or *didi* (Mielcke, p. 47).

itself also in the corresponding Latin suffixes *tât and tût*;*
hence, *e.g.* ἰσό-τητ, κακό-τητ, ἀγριό-τητ, πλατύ-τητ(=p̣rithúlâ);
[G. Ed. p. 1167.] *facili-tât, habili-tât, levi-tât, celeri-tât, civi-tât, puri-tât, veri-tât, anxie-tât, ebrie-tât, socie-tât, liber-tât,* (for *liberi-tât*, as *liber* for *liberu-s*), *puber-tât, majes-tât,* (from *majus*), *vetus-tât, venus-tât, eges-tât, potes-tât,*† *felic-i-tât, virgin-i-tât, hered-i-tât, juven-tût, senec-tût, vir-tût, servi-tût.* In *senec-ta, juven-ta, vindic-ta,* (from *vindec-s, vindic-is*) the suffix appears without the addition of a *t*. The German, too, as has already been shewn, l. c., is not wanting in analogous formations. Their theme ends in Gothic in *thô*, which corresponds as exactly as possible to the Sanscrit *tâ* (see §§. 69. 87.), and in the noun is abbreviated to *tha* (§. 137.); hence, *e.g. diupi-tha,* "depth," *hauhi-tha,* "height," *gauri-tha,* "mournfulness," *niuyi-tha,* "novelty," in the *i* of which I recognise the weakening of the *a* of the adjective primitive-bases *diupa, hauha, gaura, niuya,* in agreement with the principle observed in Latin, which, in like manner, weakens the inorganic *u* of the 2d declension, which corresponds to the Gothic 1st, to *i* (see §. 6.), or to *e* in case that another *i* precedes it (*puri-tât* for *puru-tât, varie-tât* for *variu-tât*). The organic *u* also of Grimm's 3d adjective-declension is weakened before the suffix under discussion to *i*;‡ hence,

---

* See "Influence of the pronouns on the formation of words," pp. 22, 23; where, however, from the classical tongues only *tât*, τητ, are contrasted with the Sanscrit *tâ*. It, however, admits of no doubt that *tût* also belongs here, as the weakening of the *â* to *û* can no more surprise us, than that of *a* to *u* (cf. *tûrus*=Sanscrit *târ*, p. 647).

† *Eges-tât* and *potes-tât* come from the participial-bases *egent, potent,* and, indeed, so that the nasal is thrown out, and the *t* changed to *s* before the *t* following (see §. 102.). On the other hand, *volun-tât* for *volen-tât* (from *volent*) has preserved the *n* in preference before the final consonants. This is also Pott's view (E. I., II. p. 562), who here refers to the Greek χαριέσ-τατος, from χαρίεντ; he, however, admits the possibility of *potes-tât* being derived from *potis.*

‡ Regarding the weight of the *u*, see §. 584., and "Vocalismus," p. 227.

FORMATION OF WORDS. 1133

aggvi-tha, "narrowness," from *aggvu*, "narrow ;" *manvi-tha*, "readiness," from *manvu*, "ready ;" *afgrundi-tha*, "abyss," from the base *grundu*, "ground ;" belongs, at least as regards formation, here. The bases in *ya*, with a [G. Ed. p. 1168.] consonant preceding, reject their *a* before the suffix *thô*, and vocalise the *y* to *i*: hence, *niuyi-tha*, "novelty," from the base *niuya;* but not *fairnyi-tha*, but *fairni-tha*, "age," from the base *fairnya*, nom. masc. *fairnei-s* (see Gabelentz and Löwe, Grammar, p. 75 c.); so *unhraini-tha*, "impurity," from the base *unhrainya*, "impure." The following are examples of this class of words in the Old High German (where *d* occurs for the Gothic *th*, according to §. 87.): *hreini-da*, "purity ;" *herdi-da*, "hardness ;" *samfti-da*, "softness ;" *sterchi-da*, "strength" (see Grimm, IV. 242). In English the following words belong here: *heal-th*, *heig-th*, *leng-th*, *dep-th*, and some others. The New High German exhibits these formations only in local dialects, as in the Hessian; *e.g. Läng-de, Tief-de, Breite-de*, the latter answering to the Sanscrit *prithú-tâ*, and Greek πλατυ-τητ. With the suffix under discussion the German languages form also abstracts out of the themes of weak verbs; *e.g.* in Gothic, *svegni-tha*, "joy, exultation" (*svegnya*, "I exult"); *mêri-tha*, "notice, rumour" (*mêrya*, "I announce"); *vargi-tha*, "condemnation" (*ga-vargya*, "I condemn."). Here the *i* is the contraction of the class-syllable *ya* (=Sanscrit *aya*, see §. 109^a. 6.), as in the preterite and passive participles; as, *sôk-i-da*, "I sought," *sôk-i-ths*, "sought." So in Old High German; *e.g. hôni-da*, "scorn" (*hôniu*, "I scorn"); *hôri-da, ga-hôri-da*, "hearing" (*hôr-iu*, Gothic *haus-ya*, "I hear"). The Gothic *gaunô-tha*, "mourning, complaint" (*gaun-ô*, "I sorrow," preterite *gaun-ô-da*), is the offspring of a verb of Grimm's 2d weak conjugation. This, a solitary example of its kind, which first came to light by the publication of the translation of the Pauline Epistles (2 Cor. vii. 7.), confirms the opinion that the *i*, which in all other places precedes the *th*, belongs not, as is commonly supposed, to the derivative suffix, [G. Ed. p. 1169.] but to the primitive base, as I should have assumed even without the form *gaunô-tha*, " to know."*

830. Bases ending in a consonant add, in order to lighten the combination with the consonant of the suffix, in some words in Latin, an *i* ; in Greek universally an *o* ; hence, *e.g.* *virgini-tât, capâci-tât, felîci-tât,* μελανό-τητ, χαριεντό-τητ, in opposition to such words as *juven-tât, juven-ta, juven-tût, volun-tât, senecta, senec-tût, vetus-tât.* To the latter corresponds, in Gothic, the solitary specimen of its kind, *yun-da,* " youth," =Latin *juven-ta,* with the contraction, however, which the Sanscrit sister-word *yuvan* has experienced in the weakest cases (*e.g.* gen. *yûn-as,* Latin *yûn-ê,* see §. 130.), and the Latin in the comparative (*jun-ior*). With regard to the inorganic affix *ga* of the base *yugga* (=*yunga*), whence we might have expected *yuggi-tha,* see §. 803. The *d* for *th* in *yun-da* must, I believe, be ascribed to the influence of the preceding *n,* although this liquid admits also of the combination with *th.*†

831. In no province of European languages has the type of Sanscrit abstracts, as *śuklá-tâ,* "whiteness," *bahú-tâ,* "plurality," been retained so truly as in Sclavonic. In order to see this, we must not, with Dobrowsky (p. 299.), assume a suffix *ota* for words like *dobrota,* " goodness," but must place the *o* on [G. Ed. p. 1170.] the side of the primitive base, to which it in fact belongs ; therefore *dobro-ta,* not *dobr-ota.* So among

---

* " Influence of the Pronouns on the formation of Words," p. 22. I had in view there only the forms in which the *i* exhibits itself as the weakening of the *a* of the primitive base, as in *diupi-tha* from *diupa.* The explanation of the *i* as the contraction of the syllable *ya* in forms like *fairni-tha,* " age," for *fairn-ya-tha,* is here given for the first time.

† See §. 91. The feminine Sanscrit suffix *ti,* which is there spoken of, shews itself three times in the shape of *di* after *n* (*ga-mun-di,* "money," *ana-min-di,* "conjecture," *ga-kun-di,* "persuasion"), and twice in the form of *thi* (*ga-kun-thi,* " appearance," *ga-main-thi,* " community ").

others also слѣпота *slyepo-ta,* "blindness," теплота *teplo-ta,* "warmth," тѣснота *tyesno-ta,* "narrowness," нагота *nago-ta,* "nakedness," from the indefinite adjective-bases *slyepo* (nom. masc. слѣпъ *slyep'*, f. *slyepa,* n. *slyepo*), *teplo, tyesno, nogo,* the final *o* of which is the legitimate representative of the Sanscrit *a* (see §. 257.). For comparison with the *nago-ta,* just mentioned the Sanscrit would present the form *nagná-tâ,* if *nagná,* "naked," did not prefer another suffix for its abstract. The adjective-bases in *yo* (see §. 258.), which, according to §. 255. n, change this syllable to *ye* or *e,* form abstracts in *ye-ta* or *e-ta*; *e.g.* суєта *sûye-ta,* "vanity," from the base *sûyo,* nom. суй *suĭ,* "empty." Dobrowsky (p. 300) assumes for this class of words a suffix *eta.*

832. In the Vêda dialect there is a suffix *táti,* which is used for the formation of denominative abstracts of the feminine gender just as much as *tâ,* and these agree with those in *tâ* also in this, that they accent the final syllable of the primitive base; *e.g. arishtátáti-s,* "invulnerableness," from *árishta,* "unwounded" (here with a meaning equivalent to "invulnerable"); *ayakshmátáti-s,* "health," from *ayakshmá,* "healthy;" ("void of illness," *yákshma* and *yakshman,* "consumption"); *vasútáti-s,* "riches," from *vásu,* "treasure, wealth;" *dêvátáti-s,* "sacrifice," (originally "godhead, divinity"), from *dêvá, sarvátáti-s,* "allness, entireness, the whole,"* from *sárva,* "every, all;" *sántáti-s,* "luck," from [G. Ed. p. 1171.]

---

* On this *sarvátáti* is based the above-mentioned (p. 221, §. 207. Note †, and p. 229, §. 214. Note) Zend *haurvatát,* which I there, without knowing its Sanscrit prototype, and especially the Vêdic suffix *táti,* have translated "entireness;" and, in fact, for this reason, because I thought I recognised in its suffix, as also in that of *amĕrĕtát,* an affinity to the Sanscrit *tâ,* Greek τητ, and Latin *tât,* regarding which, however, I had no occasion l. c. to deliver my sentiments more closely, because this circumstance belongs to the doctrine of the formation of words (see Burnouf, "Yaçna," p. 162, Note). As, according to Pânini, IV. 4. 142., *sarvatâti* has the same

sam of the same meaning. As regards the origin of the suffix *táti*, I have scarce any doubt of its connection with the more simple *tá* (§. 829), whether it be, as Aufrecht conjectures ("Journal of Comparative Philology," p. 162), that in the appended *ti* the suffix is contained, which is employed for the formation of primitive, *i.e.* verbal abstracts, of which hereafter, or that the *táti* is a simple phonetic extension of *tá*; so that *ti* is properly only the repetition of *tá*, with the weakening of the *á* to *i*, according to the principle of aorists, like *ápipam* for *ápápam*, from *áp* (see §. 584.), and of reduplication-syllables like *ti*, *pi*, for *tá*, *pá*, in *tíshthámi*, "I stand" (§. 508); *pípásámi*, "I wish to drink," from *pá* (§. 750.). It might be also possible that at first only a *t* was added to the suffix *tá*, in the same way as to roots with a short final vowel, and in Greek to those with a long final vowel, where they are found at the end of composites a *T*-sound is added as a support.* The *i* of *táti* would, under this view of the subject, which pleases me best, be only an off-shoot of later growth; and the forms in *tát*, which occur occasionally in the Vêdas† must consequently

[G. Ed. p. 1172.] be recognised as the oldest. The analogous Zend abstracts in *tát* would not, therefore, have lost any *i* belonging to the base, but only dispensed with a more modern affix, which would also have remained aloof from the Greek and Latin, in case that the final *T*-sound of the suffixes τητ,

---

same signification as its primitive *sárva*, we may regard the "entireness, totality" as tantamount to "the all, the whole."

* Of this more hereafter. With regard to the Greek compounds like ἀγνώ-τ, ὠμοβρώ-τ, and especially with regard to the inclination of the Greek to extend bases ending in a vowel by the addition of τ, see Curtius, "*De nominum Græcorum formatione*," p. 10.

† Benfey (Glossary to the S. V.) quotes several cases of *dêvátát*; and Aufrecht (l. c. p. 163) adduces from the 2d book of the Rigvêda the locative of *vṛikátát*, "persecution," which presupposes for the primitive *vrika* (commonly "wolf") the meaning "following, pursuer."

tât, tût, is an heir-loom brought from their original Asiatic home, and has not first sprung up on European soil. It would, however, be surprising if the suffix under discussion, in Greek, Latin, and Zend, had sprung from the form *tâti*, but the final *i* in the three languages just named had been lost without leaving a trace, as this vowel elsewhere, in Greek and Zend at least, has never allowed itself to be displaced in the classes of words in *i*, which are common also to the Sanscrit. The abstracts in ⲣⲙⲱⲡ *tât* (ⲣⲙⲱⲡ *tât* according to §. 38.), which have hitherto been discovered in Zend, are, besides the frequently-mentioned *haurvatât*, "entireness," and *amĕrĕtât*, "immortality;"* *uparatât*, "supériorité," (see Burnouf, Yaçna, p. 285), from *upara*, "*superus,*" (see Sanscrit *upari*, "over," Gothic *ufar*, &c.); *drvatât*, "firmness," (Burnouf, Études, p. 261.), from *drva* "firm," = Sanscrit *dhruvá* (Old High German *triu*, "true"); *paourvatât*, "antériorité," (Yaçna, p. 285 Note 141), from *paourva*, "anterior," = Sanscrit *pûrva;* *ustatât*, "greatness," (Aufrecht, Journal, p. 162), from *usta*, "high, great," = Sanscrit *uttha*, "standing up, raising oneself," (see §. 102.), for *utstha*; ⲣⲙⲱⲡⲣⲉⲃ̇ⲩⲗ *vanhutât*, "riches," (Aufrecht l. c.) = Sanscrit *vasútâti* (see beginning of this §.); *yavatât*, "duration," from *yava*, idem (Burnouf, Études, p. 9); ⲣⲙⲱⲡⲙⲱ̇ⲗⲉ *arstât*, perhaps the Vêdic *arishtâtâti* (see beginning of this §., and Brockhaus, Glossary); *rasanstât,* according [G. Ed. p. 1173.] to Anquetil, "droiture," of uncertain derivation, whence the signification also is uncertain.†

---

* I regard *amĕrĕ* as = Sanscrit *amara*, "immortal." The word, therefore, in Vêdic form, would be *amarátâti* or *amarátât.* Regarding *haurvatât*, see beginning of this §. Note.

† *Rasans* is, according to the form, a participle present, and signifies, perhaps, "shining," and its abstract "lustre." Compare *raś*, which lies at the root of the Sanscrit *raśmi*, "beam of light," which does not elsewhere occur, but is probably related to *las*, "to shine."

1138 FORMATION OF WORDS.

833. If the Sanscrit suffix *tâti* or *tât*, as a formative of denominative abstracts, is really old, and if it existed in the period before the separation of languages, we may then refer to it another suffix from the province of the European sister-languages, and one which is likewise feminine, viz. *duthi*, nom. *duth-s*, the use of which, on the presupposition that it is short, would be to be so regarded as that the long *â* had first been shortened and then weakened to *u*; as, *e.g.* the *u* of Anglo-Saxon nominatives of Grimm's first strong feminine declension (*gifu*) answers to the Gothic short (*giba*) and Sanscrit long *â* (§. 137.). As regards the consonants, the law of the mutation of sounds in Gothic would lead us to expect *thuthi;* but in accordance with what was remarked at §. 91., we cannot be surprised that in the former place the old tenuis has been changed to a medial instead of to an aspirate. Formerly in this class of words *ayuk-duth*(*i*)-*s*, "eternity" (see Grimm, II. 250), from a to-be-presupposed adjective base *ayuka*, nom. masc. *ayuk-s*,[*] stood quite isolated. But now the sources of language which have been lately discovered supply us with the bases *manag-duthi*, "a crowd" (nom. *-duths*, 2 Cor. viii. 2.), and *mikil-duthi*, "greatness" (gen. *mikil-duthai-s*, acc. *mikil-duth*, Skeir.). From the final *i* of the Gothic suffix, in case of [G. Ed. p. 1174.] its being really connected with the Vêdic *tâti, tât*, one must not, however, deduce the inference that *tâti* is necessarily the elder form, for the Gothic could easily further add to the *T*-sound, as the original final letter of the suffix, an *i;* as the declension of consonants, with the exception of *u* in Gothic, and generally in German, is not a favourite, and the lightest vowel *i* is readily applied to transfer a

---

[*] After removing the suffix *ka*, we may so compare *ayu* with the more simple base *aiva*, nom. *aiv-s*, as supposing that the syllable *va* has been contracted to *u*, and then that the *i*, on account of the vowel following, has passed into its semi-vowel.

FORMATION OF WORDS. 1139

theme terminating in a consonant to a more convenient order of declension; hence, *e.g.* to the Sanscrit base *chatvår*, 4 (see §. 312.) answers, in Gothic, *fidvôri* (dat. *fidvôri-m*); and the bases *shash*, 6, *saptan*, 7, *navan*, 9, *daśan*, 10, in Old High German form their declension from *sehsi, sibuni, niuni, zehani*. If Grimm (II. 250.) is right, as I am much inclined to believe, in conjecturing an affinity between the Gothic suffix under discussion and the Latin *tûdo, tûdin-is*, we should also be able to compare this suffix with the Sanscrit-Zendian *tât* or *tâti*. We must therefore regard *tût* (in *servitût*, &c.) as = the Vêdic-Zendian *tât* (see §. 832.), and lengthened to *tûdo, tûdin*, with the weakening of the second *t* to *d* (see §. 822.). The addition *ôn, in-is*, would be less surprising, as the Sanscrit suffix *ti* also, of which hereafter, is lengthened in Latin by a similar inorganic addition, and, *e.g.*, the base *pak-ti* has become *coc-tiôn*. From *tûdô* we should expect in the genitive *tûdôn-is*, but the *ô* = Sanscrit *â* (see §. 139.), has, with the increase of the form, been weakened to *i*, as in *homin-is* (old *hemôn-is*, see p. 1077).

Remark.—The Vêdic suffix *tâti* forms not only abstracts, but has at times also the signification "making, maker" (Pânini, IV. 4. 142.), and, indeed, it likewise accents the syllable preceding the suffix. An example is afforded in the Rigv. I. 112. 20., where the masculine dual *sântâtî*, "happiness maker," or perhaps "augmenter of happiness," is explained by *Sáyana* by *sukhasya kartârâu*, "*gaudii factores.*" In words of [G. Ed. p. 1175.] this kind, on whose age a doubt is cast by their not being represented in the European sister languages, *tâti* is perhaps from a different origin from that whence it springs when it appears as a formative of abstract substantives. We might recognise in it a derivative from the root *tan*, "to stretch," without, on that account, extending, as Benfey does, this explanation to the suffix of abstracts also, although the accentuation of both kinds of words is the same; since, perhaps, the accentuation of the preponderating abstracts has exerted an influence on that of the concretes, after that the feeling with reference to the difference of origin had been extinguished. But if in the concretes in *tâti* a derivative of the root *tan*, "to extend," be contained, I would then, in certain cases, prefer to recognise a noun of agency rather than an abstract: for although *ti* be no

4 E 2

regular suffix for the formation of nouns of agency, it nevertheless forms several appellatives, which, according to their fundamental signification, are nouns of agency; as, *e. g. tantí-s,* "weaver," properly "stretcher;" *krishtí-s,* "man," as "plougher" (Vêda). According to this, the beforementioned *sántáti-s* would properly mean "extender," *i. e.* "augmenter," or "grounder, creater of happiness," which gives a more satisfactory sense than if it be taken, instead of as dependent compound, as possessive, according to which it would signify "having the augmentation of happiness," which sense is not suitable in the passage of the Rigvêda that has been cited. But when, in a passage of the Yajurvêda (VII. 12.), the Scholiast Mahîdhara takes *jyêshthátátim* as an actual possessive (which, however, is not confirmed by the accentuation), in that he explains *táti* as being a derivative from *tan,* "to extend," and therefore, according to the sense, as = *vistára,* "extension," we cannot thence infer that he recognises in the words formed by the suffix *táti* in general, or in any particular branch of them, possessive compounds with *táti,* "extension," as the last member of the compound; for he adds to the explanation above given another and a more satisfactory one, and explains *jyêshthátáti* as a simple word formed by the suffix *táti,* when he refers to Pânini, V. 4. 41.; according to which the suffix under discussion, in combination with *jyêshtha,* produces only a strengthening (*prasansá,* properly "extolling") of the meaning of the original word, and therefore *jyêshthátáti-s* would be equivalent to "the best of all," or "the notoriously best." If we wish to confirm this signification of the (according to Pânini) isolated in its kind *jyêshthátáti,* by the circumstance of its being in its origin a possessive
[G. Ed. p. 1176.] compound, we must then assign to it the meaning, "the extension" (as it were, "most highly potent"), including "the best."

834. We may here at once notice another suffix, which in Sanscrit, just like *tá, tát, táti,* forms abstracts from adjectives and substantives, viz. the neuter suffix *tva,* which is probably an extension of the infinitive suffix *tu* by *a; tva* therefore, from *tu-a,* as the hereafter-to-be-discussed suffix *tavya* is from *tu,* with Guna, and *ya.* The abstracts in *tva* are oxytone; *e.g. amritatvá-m,* "immortality," from *amṛíta; nagna-tvá-m,* "nakedness," from *nagná; bahu-tvá-m,* as *bahú-tá,* "multitude," from *bahú.* This class of words has been retained with all possible exactitude, exclusive of the insertion of a euphonic *s* before the *t* of the suffix (see

FORMATION OF WORDS. 1141

§. 825.), in Sclavonic, as т *tva*, according to §. 257., in Old Sclavonic could take no other form than *tvo;* and the nominative *tva-m*, in like manner, could be nothing but *tvo*. The final vowel of the primitive base is rejected in Sclavonic; hence, *e. g.* дѣвство *dyev-stvo*, "maidenhood," from дѣва *dyeva*, "maiden;" вдовство *vdov-stvo*, "widowhood," from вдова *vdova*, "widow;" лоукавство *lûkav-stvo*, "cunningness," достоинство *dostoin-stvo*, "worth," from the adjective bases *lûkavo*, "cunning," *dostoino*, "worthy" (see Dobrowsky, p. 303). The Gothic, in the only word which belongs here, has changed the old tenuis of the suffix त *tva* to *d* instead of into *th*, as in *fidvôr*, "four" = चत्वार् *chatvâr* (§. 312.)—I mean the neuter base *thiva-dva*, "serfdom," nom. acc. *thiv-dv*, from the primitive base *thiva*, nom. *thiu-s*, "serf."

835. In the Vêda dialect *tva* occurs also as primary (Krit-) suffix in the sense of the cognate *tavya*, and forms from *kar, kri*, "to make," the paroxonytised *kártva = kartavya*, "*faciendus*," as neuter substantive (nom. acc. *kártva-m*), "work," as "being to be done." So in Zend [G. Ed. p. 1177.] ꞵꞵꞵ *běrěthwa*, "*ferendus*."* Here belong, in my opinion, the Old High German masculine substantive-bases in *don* (nom. *do*), for the most part abstracts; as, *e. g.* suep-i-do (or -du), "*sopor;*" *irr-a-do, err-i-do, irr-e-do*, "*error;*" *yuch-i-do, yuk-i-do*, "*prurigo;*" *hol-ô-do*, "*foramen;*" the intermediate vowel of which I assign to the class syllable of the verb. The *v* of the Sanscrit suffix *tva* is dropped in the Old High German, with reference to which we may note also the still more marked abbreviation of the numeral *fior* compared with the Gothic *fidvôr* and Sanscrit *chatvâr-as*. The Gothic has retained the semi-vowel in the suffixes which belong here: *tva*, neut. (nom. *tv*), from *vaurs-tv*,

---

* Comparative with the prep. *upa, upa-běrěthwôtara* (V. S. p. 255, see Burnouf, Études, p. 215).

"work;"* *thvô*, fem. (nom. *thva*, see §. 137.), from *fri-a-thva*, "love;"† *fi-a-thva* (for *fiy-a-thva*), "enmity;"‡ *sal-i-thvôs*, pl. "harbour" (*sal-ya*, "I turn in, remain," pret. *sal-i-da*), Old High German *sal-i-tha, sal-i-da, sel-i-da*; *tvôn*, fem. (nom. *tvô*, see §. 142.), from *vah-tvô*, "watch," *ga-tvô*, "street" (Sanscrit root *gâ*, "to go"), Old High German *ga-za* (*gâ-m*, "I go"); *uh-tvô*, "morning, twilight," (Sanscrit *ush*, "to burn, to give light," *ushás*, "aurora"). Here belong also, I have no doubt, some Sclavonic abstract feminine-bases (together with nominatives) in *tva*, which Dobrowsky (p. 286.) reckons with the formations in *va*, since he derives them, not from the root, but from the infinitive in *ti*; *e.g.* жатва

[G. Ed. p. 1178.] *schan-tva*, "mowing, harvest," (жьнѫ *schynun*, "to cut down") клатва *klan-tva*, "execratio," (кльнѫ *klynun*, "execror"); ловитва *lov-i-tva*, "venatio," (*lov-i-ti*, "captare"). I now prefer to deduce also the above-mentioned (§. 807.) Lithuanian abstracts in *ba, bĕ*, and the abstracts in *ba*, which so frequently occur in the Sclavonic dialects, from the Sanscrit suffix *tva*, *i.e.* from its feminine *tvâ*, and, in fact, so as to assume, after the *t*-sound is dropped, a hardening of the *v* to *b*, with regard to which I would recall attention to the relation of the Latin and Zend adverb of number *bis*, and that of the *bi*, which appears in both languages at the beginning of compounds, to the Sanscrit *dvis, dvi* (see p. 424.). From adjective-bases spring, in Slowenian, among others, the following feminine abstracts: *sladko-ba*, "sweetness," from *sladek(o)* "sweet;" *gerdo-ba*,

---

* It springs, perhaps, from *varth*, "to be" (*vairtha, varth, vaurthum*), with *s*, therefore, for *th*, according to §. 102. p. 102.

† From *friyô*, "I love," might be expected *friy-ô-thva*; yet the shortening of *ô* (=*â*) to *a*, according to §. 69., cannot surprise us.

‡ We might have expected *fiy-ai-thva*; but only the first part of the diphthong of the class-syllable *ai* has remained, as in *fiy-a*, "I hate," *fiy-a-m*, "we hate," for *fiy-ai, fiy-ai-m*.

"ugliness," from *gerd*(o), "ugly ;" *gnyilo-ba*, "rottenness," from *gnyil*(o), "rotten ; *tesno-ba*, "narrowness," from *tesen*,* "narrow."

836. The perfect passive participle is, in a comparatively small number of roots, formed by the suffix *na*, which is always united directly to the root, and, like the more prevalent *ta*, has the accent. The following are examples: *lû-ná-s*, "disengaged forcibly ;" *bhug-ná-s*, "bent," (root *bhuj*); *bhag-ná-s*, "broken," (root *bhañj*); *bhin-ná-s*, "cleft," (from *bhid-ná-s*); *stîr-ná-s*, "spread," (root *star*, स्तृ *strî*); *pûr-ná-s*, "filled up," (root *par*, पृ *prî*).† To these correspond, in respect of accentuation also, the likewise few in number Greek formations in *νο*, feminine *νη*; as, στυγνό-ς, στεγνό-ς, [G. Ed. p. 1179.] σεμνό-ς, (for σεβνός), ἀλαπαδνό-ς, ἰσχνό-ς, σπαρνό-ς, φερνή, σκηνή (Sanscrit छन्न *chhanná-s*, from *chhadná-s*, "covered," (see §. 14.), τέκνο-ν, which has the accent thrown back. In Latin belong here, besides *ple-nu-s*, *eg-e-nus* (with active signification), *regnum*, several words which, from a Roman point of view, are of obscure origin (see Pott, II. p. 570.); as, *magnu-s*, properly "grown," (Sanscrit *mah*, *maṅh*, "to grow," whence *mahánt*, *mahát*, "great,"); *lignu-m*, as "kindling," (Sanscrit *dah*, "to burn"); *tignu-m*, as "hewed," (Sanscrit *takṣh*, "to break, to cleave,"); *dignu-s*, properly "shewn, marked out," (Sanscrit *diś*, from *dik*, "to shew," Greek δεικ). Perhaps *signu-m*, is connected with the Sanscrit root *sañj*, Lithuanian *sej*, "to affix," so that it would properly signify the "affixed."

837. In German this suffix has extended itself over all the strong verbs; but in such a manner that it is not, as

---

* See Metelko (p. 44), who, however, in imitation of Dobrowsky's example, assigns the *o* (*o* stroked through) of the adjective base to the derivative suffix (*oba*).

† In the two last examples *ṇ* stands for *n* through the influence of the preceding *r*.

in Sanscrit, Greek, and several Latin expressions which belong here, joined directly to the root, but by the intervention of a conjunctive vowel *a* (later *e*, Old Northern *i*); hence, *e.g.* in Gothic, *bug-a-n(a)-s*, "bent," (for Sanscrit *bhug-ná-s*, (from the root *bug*,* (*biuga, baug, bug-u-m*). The denominatives discussed above (§. 770.) point to an older period in which the *n* of this passive participle plays an important part, [G. Ed. p. 1180.] but is joined direct to the root.† In the Sclavonic languages the suffix beginning with *n* of the perfect passive participle has obtained still wider diffusion than in the German dialects. The old Sclavonic verbs which are based on the Sanscrit 1st class, exhibit, in the place of the original अय *aya* before the participial suffix under discussion, either а (*a*), or ѣ (*ye*), or е; *e.g.* ГЛАГОЛАНЪ *glagol-a-n'*, "said;" зрѣнъ *ʒyrye-n'*, "seen;" ВОЛѤНЪ *vol-ye-n'*, "willed," (see §. 767.). The verbs which are based on the Sanscrit 1st class add to the root, as in most of the persons of the present, an е. Compare НЕСЕНЪ *nes-e-n'*, "borne," fem. *nes-e-na*, neut. *nes-e-no*, with *nes-e-shi, nes-e-ty, nes-e-m', nes-e-te, nes-e-va, nes-e-ta*. Perhaps, however, in this class of verbs the *e* is not the old class-vowel, but an insertion of later date, like the *a* of the corresponding Gothic participles. It is to be noticed, with regard to the

---

* It is an oversight, that, in §. 770., the *a* preceding the *n* is identified with the class-vowel; for were the class character retained in the passive participle, in that case the verbs (see §. 109ª. 2.) belonging to the Sanscrit 4th class would retain the syllable *ya*; the passive participle of *haf-ya*, "I raise," would be *haf-ya-ns*, not *haf-a-ns*. Thus, from *vahs-ya*, "I grow," the participle under discussion is *vahs-a-ns*, not *vahs-ya-ns*, where it is to be observed, that in neuter verbs this participle has in the German languages, as in Sanscrit, an active meaning; thus, *vahs-ya-ns*, "qui crevit."

† A direct junction of the suffix is found also in the adjective *us-luk-na-s*, "open," properly "unlocked;" so the neuter substantive-base *bar-na*, nom. *barn*, "child," as "born" (like τέκ-νο-ν), compared with the actual participle *baur-a-ns*.

FORMATION OF WORDS. 1145

verbs belonging to the Sanscrit 1st class, that, in Sanscrit also, the character *aya* (dropping only the final *a*) extends over the special tenses. This, too, is the case in German with the corresponding affix of the weak conjugation. It is surprising that the Lettish languages, although they border next on the Sclavonic, are nevertheless distinguished in the case of the participle under discussion, that they employ the suffix *ta* more constantly than the latter do the suffix *no*, fem. *na*. In the Lettish languages, however, analogous forms in *na-s* are not altogether wanting: they are, however, no longer conscious of their origin, and pass for ordinary adjectives; as, *e.g.* the Lithuanian *silp-na-s*, "weak" ("weakened," see *silpstu*, "I become weak," pret. *silpau*); *pil-na-s*,(Lithuanian *pil-n'-s*),"full," [G. Ed. p. 1181.] properly "filled," = Sanscrit *pûr-ṇá-s*,* Zend *pĕrĕnô*, fem. *pĕrĕnê* for *pĕrĕná* (see §. 137.).

838. Just as the passive participial suffix *ta*, in Sanscrit, forms from substantives possessive adjectives, like *phal-i-tá-s*, "gifted with fruit" (see §. 824.), so for a like purpose is used the suffix *na*, in like manner, with the insertion of a conjunctive vowel *i*, which the Indian Grammarians include in the suffix. Examples are, *phali-ná-s*, "gifted with fruit;" *mal-i-ná-s*, "covered with dirt." With these agree, in respect of accentuation also, Grecian formations like πεδ'-ι-νό-ς (Buttmann, II. §. 119. 74.), properly "endued with evenness," hence (1) "flat, even," (2) "living in the plain;" σκοτεινό-ς (from σκοτεσ-ι-νό-ς, see §. 128.), "endued

---

* The *û* of the Sanscrit form owes its origin to the labial preceding; otherwise its place would be filled by *i*, as, *e.g.* in *stîr-ṇá-s*: the old form, however, is evidently *par-ṇa-s*, and the true root is *par*, whence *píparmi*, "I fill." On *parna* is based also the Zend base *pĕrĕna*, of which the first *ĕ* is founded on the original *a*, while the second is explained by §. 44. The *i* of the Lithuanian *pil-na-s* is a weakening of the original *a*, as that of *wilka-s*, "wolf," compared with the Sanscrit *vṛika-s* from *varka-s*, see §. 1., and "Vocalismus," p. 100.

with darkness;" φαεινό-ς (from φα-εσ-ι-νό-ς), "endued with light;" ὀρεινό-ς (from ὀρεσ-ι-νό-ς), "gifted with mountains." The ε of εὐδιεινό-ς is the weakening of the α of εὐδία, where it is necessary to recall attention to the fact, that the suffix ων also is very frequently preceded by an ε as a weakening of the final vowel of the primitive base; e.g. ῥοδεών from ῥοδο-ων. In words which express a time, as e.g. in χθεσ-ι-νό-ς, ἡμερ-ι-νό-ς, ὀρθρ᾽-ι-νό-ς, the fundamental signification lies more concealed; but χθεσινό-ς properly means no more than "with yesterday," "combined with yesterday," "belonging thereto," as our German expressions also, like "*gestrig, heutig,*" contain a possessive suffix. In spite of the difference of accentuation, I be-
[G. Ed. p. 1182.] lieve that adjectives, too, like ξύλινος, λίθινος, ἀδαμάντινος, are not distinguished in their formative suffix from the oxytone forms in ι-νό-ς, but that the language only aims at bringing these expressions prominently forward with more emphasis, and therefore gives the more energetic accentuation (see p. 1052). There occurs also, in Sanscrit, a word among the formations in *ina* which accentuates not only the suffix but the primitive word, viz. शृङ्गिणस् *śring-i-ṇa-s*, "horned," from शृङ्ग *śringa*, "horn." In Gothic the conjunctive vowel has been lengthened in the corresponding class of words to *ei* ($=i$, see §. 70.) before which the final vowel of the base word is likewise dropped; hence, e.g. *silubr-ei-n*(*a*)*-s*, "*argenteus*" (also *silubrius*, Math. 27. 3.); *fill-ei-n*(*a*)*-s*, "*pelliceus;*" *liuhad-ei-n*(*a*)*-s*, "*lucidus;*" *suny-ei-n*(*a*)*-s*, "*verax;*" from the bases *silubra* (nom. *silubr*), &c.; *sunyó* (nom. *sunya*). The following are examples in Old High German: *hulz-î-n*(*a*), "*ligneus;*" *stein-î-n*(*a*), "*lapideus;*" *boum-î-n*(*a*), "*arboreus;*" *rôr-î-n*(*a*), "*arundinaceus;*" *eihh-î-n*(*a*), "*quernus;*" *ziegal-î-n*(*a*), "*lateritius.*" In New High German the vowel of conjunction *i* has been weakened to *e*, and, after *r*, altogether dislodged; hence, e.g. *eich-e-n, tann-e-n, gold-e-n, tuch-e-n, leder-n.* From plurals in *er* (out of *ir*, see §. 241.) spring forms like *hölzer-n,*

hörner-n, gläser-n, which have given occasion to misshapen forms like *steiner-n* for *stein-e-n* (Grimm, II. p. 179). From the Old Sclavonic here belong, in respect to their suffix, words like огнєнъ *ogn-e-n'*, "fiery" ("fire-gifted"), from огнь *ogny*, "fire;" вредєнъ *vrede-n'*, "pernicious," from вредъ *vred'*, "injury;" миренъ *mir-e-n'*, "peaceful, pacific," from миръ *mir'*, "peace;" the *e* of which is evidently only a vowel inserted to combine the words, and is not to be referred, with Dobrowsky (p. 224), to the derivative suffix. In Lithuanian the conjunctive vowel of the suffix under discussion has been retained unaltered; and thus words like *sidabr'-i-na-s*, "silvery," *auks'-i-na-s*, "golden," *milt'-i-* [G. Ed. p. 1183.] *na-s*, "mealy," with the suppression of the final vowel of the primitive base (*sidabra-s*, "silver," *auksa-s*, "gold," *miltar*, "meal"),* answer admirably to the above-mentioned (see beginning of this §.) Sanscrit formations like *phal'-i-ná-s, mal'-i-ná-s*. From the bases in *-na* comes, by the addition of a secondary suffix, the form *i-nia* (*ia* = Sanscrit य *ya*, of which hereafter), nom. *ini-s* for *inia-s* (see §. 135.), gen. *inio*; hence, *e.g. auks-i-ni-s* = *auks-i-nia-s*, "a florin," from *auks-i-na-s*, "golden." This derivative form, however, in general replaces the primitive, whereby the *n* is usually doubled.† Of the same signification with *sidabr-i-na-s*, "silvery" (also *sidabr-i-n'-s*), is *sidabr-i-ni-s* (see Ruhig, s. v. "*silbern*"). From *wara-s*, "copper," comes *war'-i-nna-s*, "made of copper;" from *yowara-s*, "beech," *yowar'-i-nni-s*, "beechen;" from *szikszna*, "leather," *szikszn'-i-nni-s*, "leathern." We find also the vowel of conjunction lengthened and written *y* (= *i̯*), and, indeed, in words which denote the place filled with a number of the things ex-

---

* Plural of a to-be-presupposed singular *milta-s*.

† Regarding the doubling of consonants, which often has no other meaning than that of pointing out the shortness of the preceding vowel, see Kurschat, "Contributions," &c., II. p. 32.

pressed by the base noun; as, *e.g.* from *osi-s*, "ash," *os'-y-na-s*, "ash-wood;" from *ŭga*, "berry," *ŭg'-y-na-s*, "a place where many berries are;" from *akmŭ* (theme *akmen*), *akmen-y-na-s*, "heap of stones." Words like *bĕd'-na-s*, "miserable" (properly "gifted with misery"), from *bĕda*, "misery," *dyw'-na-s*, "wonderful," ("gifted with wonder"), from *dywa-s*, "wondrous work," appear to have lost a vowel of conjunction; for else the final vowel of the primitive base would hardly be suppressed before the suffix. Compare Russian formations like *pyly-nyĭ*, "dusty," from пыль *pyly*, "dust;" *muchh-nyĭ*, "mealy," from *muka*; *bolot'-nyĭ*, "marshy," from [G. Ed. p. 1184.] *boloto*, "marsh." There are, in Lithuanian, also formations in *na-s*, with *o* as conjunctive vowel, which run parallel to those above mentioned (§. 825.) in *o-ta-s; e.g. wiln'-o-na-s*, "to will," from *wilna*, "will;" *raud-o-na-s*, "red" ("endued with a red colour"), from *raudà*, "red colour."

839. In Latin the denominative formations in *nu-s*, fem. *na*, which answer to the Sanscrit and Lithuanian forms in *i-na-s*, stand in multifarious relations to their base word, which do not require a detailed explanation here. The originally short conjunctive vowel *i* has been lengthened, as in the older German languages, and the final vowel of the base word is suppressed, as in the sister languages. The following are examples: *sal-í-nu-s, Vejent-í-nu-s, reg-í-na, carnific-í-na, doctr-í-na* (for *doctór-í-na*), *textr í-nu-s, tonstr-í-nu-s* (from *tonstor*, whence *tonsor*, see §. 101., cf. *tonstrix*); *stagn'-í-nu-s, gall'-í-na, discipl'-í-na* (for *discipulína*), *orc-í-nu-s, fer'-í-nu-s, tabul'-í-nu-s, pisc'-í-na, mar'-í-nu-s, ali'-é-nu-s, lani'-é-na,** *pecu-í-nu-s,*† *bov-í-nu-s*. The conjunctive vowel

---

* *é* for *i*, to avoid two *i*-sounds following one after the other.

† The retention of the organic *u* of the 4th declension, in opposition to the suppression of the other vowels, agrees with the phenomenon, that in Sanscrit also *u* is retained before the vowels of the derivative suffix in preference to the other vowels, and, indeed, with Guna increment, and with euphonic change of the *ó* (=*au*) into *av*.

FORMATION OF WORDS. 1149

is most commonly suppressed after *r* (as in German, see §. 818.),; hence, *e.g. ebur-nu-s, pat*ɛ*r-nu-s, mater-nu-s, ver-nu-s, veter-nu-s, quer-nu-s, int*ɛ*r-nu-s, exter-nu-s, infer-nu-s, super-nu-s*. Also after *g* (from *c*); *salig-nu-s, ilig-nu-s, larig-nu-s*, if we ought not here to divide thus, *sali-gnu-s*, and assume the dropping of the final consonant of the primitive base (see *abie-gnu-s, privi-gnu-s*), when *gnu-s* (for *g*ɛ*nus, ginus*) would signify "produced" (cf. Pott, II. 586.). The Indian Grammarians assume also a suffix *ína*, the *í* of which is probably, in like measure, only a lengthened conjunc- [G. Ed. p. 1185.] tive vowel, so that *í-na* would be identical with the above-mentioned *i-na*. Examples are: *sam'-í-na-s*, "yearly," from *samá*, "year;" *kuĺ-í-na-s*, "noble" ("gifted with good family, good descent"), from *kulá-m*, "race." The Latin *â* also, in words like *mont-â-nu-s, urb-â-nu-s, sol-â-nu-s, veter-â-nu-s* (see *veter-í-nu-s, veter-nu-s*), *Vejent-â-nu-s* (*Vejent-í-nu-s*), *oppid'-â-nu-s, insul'-â-nu-s, Rom'-â-nu-s, Afric'-â-nu-s*, is probably only a vowel used to connect the words; so that here also only *nu* is the true suffix, as *e.g. tu* in *cord-â-tu-s, sceler-â-tu-s* (see §. 824.), where we would recal attention to the disposition which the secondary suffix *tu* also has to be borne by a long vowel. We might, however, also so regard the forms *â-nu-s* as though they bore the class-character of the 1st conjugation and presupposed verbal-themes like *montâ, veterâ*, after the analogy of *amâ, laudâ*.

840. As the Sanscrit bases in *a* produce not only feminines in *â*, but some also in *í*, we may also regard such feminines as *indrấní*, "the wife of Indra," *rudrấní*,[*] "the wife of Rudra," *varuṇấní*, "the wife of Varuna," *mâtulấní*, "the wife of an uncle by the mother's side" (from *mâtula*), *kshatriyấní*, "wife of the kshatriya caste," as productions of the suffix न *na*, and bring them into relationship with the Latin, Lithuanian, and German formations which have

---

[*] ṇ for *n*, through the influence of the preceding *r*.

been described; but in this class of Sanscrit words I hold the â, not, as in Latin forms like *mont-â-nu-s*, for a conjunctive or class-vowel, but for the lengthening of the *a* of the primitive base, which in all the words which belong here ends in

[G. Ed. p. 1186.] *a*. I divide, therefore, thus, *e.g. mâtulâ-nî*, for which we might also expect *mâtulâ-nâ*.* To these feminines correspond in Greek θέαινα, λύκαινα, ὕαινα, ἄκαινα, μολύβδαινα, δέσποινα,† from θεανι-α, &c. (see §. 119.). Feminine patronymics also, Ἀκρισιώ-νη, admit of being referred here, with the lengthening, therefore, of the final vowel (*o* = Sanscrit *a*) of the primitive base, as in Sanscrit, in case we ought not rather to distribute it Ἀκρισι-ώ-νη, and look on the ω as the conjunctive vowel. The latter view is corroborated by Latin forms like *Mell-ô-nia*, together with *Mell-ô-na* (as it were, "the honey-bound"), *Vall'-ô-nia*, *matr-ô-na*, *patr-ô-na*. We divide, therefore, also *Pom'-ô-na*, *Bell'-ô-na*, *Morb'-ô-nia*, *Orb'-ô-na*, although the 2d declension, in which the *u* and *o* are interchanged at the end of the base, authorises the referring the *ô* to the primitive base.

841. In Lithuanian the feminine suffix *ĕnĕ̃*‡ corresponds to the Sanscrit *â-nî*, Greek αινα, ωνη, and Latin *ô-nia*, *ôna*. With respect to signification also, *e.g. brol'-ĕnĕ̃*, "brother's wife,"§ corresponds admirably to Sanscrit formations like *mâtulânî*, "wife of an uncle by the mother's side." Other Lithuanian formations of this kind are: *bern'-ĕnĕ̃*, "the serf's wife," from *berna-s*; *kalw'-ĕnĕ̃*, "the smith's wife," from *kalw-si*

---

* Indian Grammarians regard *ân* in these words as an affix inserted between the base-noun and the feminine *î*, which they call *ánuk*, where the *k* probably denotes the accentuation of *ân*.

† Δέσποινα presupposes for δεσπότη-ς a nominative masculine δεσπο-ς, the final syllable of which we may compare with Sanscrit compounds like *nṛipa-s*, "ruler of men" (from *pâ*, "to rule").

‡ From *ĕnia* (see p. 174, note).

§ From *broli-s*, "brother," from *brolia-s*.

FORMATION OF WORDS. 1151

(for *kaluya-s*); *awyn'-ěně*, " the uncle's wife," from *awyna-s*; *asil'-ěně*, " she-ass," from *asila-s*; *wilk'-ěně*, " she-wolf," from *wilka-s*. In Old Sclavonic corresponds ынıa *ynya*, or, with suppression of the *a* in the nominative, *ini* [G. Ed. p. 1187.] (see Miklosich, " Doctrine of Forms," p. 12); *e.g.* рабынıa *rab'-ynya* or рабыни *rab'-yni*, " maid," from рабъ *rab'*, theme *rabo*, " servant ;" богынıa *bog'-ynya* or богини *bogini*, "goddess," from *bog'*, theme *bogo* (Dobr., p. 291). In Old High German the suffix *inna* corresponds, probably by assimilation, from *inya*** for *inia*, so that to the Sanscrit feminine character *í*, the common feminine termination *a* (from *â*, Gothic *ô*), has also been added (see §. 120.). The following are examples: *gut'-inna*, " goddess ;" *kuning'-inna*, " queen ;" *meistar'-inna*, " mistress ;" *wirt'-inna*, " landlady ;" *aff'-inna*, " she-ape ;" *esil'-inna*, " she-ass ;" *hen'-inna*, " hen ;" *hund'-inne* (for *-inna*), " a bitch." In the nominative and accusative singular exist abbreviated forms in *in*, as *gutin, kuningin* (together with *gutinna, kuninginna*), on which are based our new German forms like *Göttin, Königin* (Grimm, II. 319.), which extend over all the oblique cases of the singular; while the plural (*Göttinnen, Königinnen*) point to a more full singular, like *Göttinne, Königinne*. So far, however, as one cannot cite a genitive, dative singular, or nominative accusative plurals, as *gutini*, I see no reason to refer the forms under discussion in *in* to Grimm's 4th declension, according to which they would belong to bases in *ini*, the *i* of which must be suppressed in the nominative and accusative singular. The Anglo-Saxon genitive-dative forms, also quoted by Grimm (II. 319.), as *gyd-enne*, " *deæ*," can be as well explained from the 1st strong declension as the 4th: I prefer to refer them to the 1st, and take *gyden*, " goddess," as the abbrevia-

---

* Compare the assimilation in forms like *quellu* from *quelyu* (Grimm, I. 870), which so frequently enters into the 1st weak conjugation, and similar phenomena in Lithuanian (§. 501.).

tion of *gydenu*,* from which Bosworth ("Dictionary of the Anglo-Saxon language") quotes the form *gydene* (*e* as the weakening of *u*). Important are the Old Northern forms, as *apynya*, "she-ape," *vargynya*, "she-wolf,"† for the support of the view, that the doubled *n* of the forms spoken of stand by assimilation for *ny*. The *y* comes by "*Umlaut*" from *u*, which approaches closer to the Sanscrit *â* of *ânî* than the *i* of *inna*, which probably springs from it by still further weakening. For *wirtin*, in Old High German, *wirtun* actually occurs (Graff, I. 932.). In the circumstance that bases in *on* before the suffix *inna*, *in*, drop the final consonant of the base, together with the preceding vowel (*e.g. aff'-inna*, *aff'-in* for *affon-inna*, *affon-in*), the German agrees with a similar phenomenon in Sanscrit, where bases in *n* generally reject this consonant with the vowel preceding it before vowels and य *y* of the derivative suffixes; hence, *e.g. râjhyá-m* (or, with the weaker accent, *râjhyà-m*), "kingdom," from *râjan*, "king."

[G. Ed. p. 1188.]

842. We return to the primary suffix *na*, in order to remark, that by it and its feminine *nâ*, in Sanscrit, some oxytone abstracts also are formed direct from the root; as,

---

* Observe that also the above-mentioned (§. 803.) formations in *unga*, in Anglo-Saxon, and even in Old High German (in Kero and Is.), have lost the final vowel of the base in the nominative (see Grimm, II. 362.), just as in New High German, through which, however, they nevertheless do not fall under Grimm's 4th strong declension, *i.e.* the bases in *i*. In Anglo-Saxon, on the other hand, the real feminine bases in *i* have nearly all passed into that declension, the final vowel of which ends originally in *â* (Gothic *ô*), *i.e.* into Grimm's 1st declension, feminine of the strong form; and thus *dæd*, "deed," presents no single case, which we must necessarily derive from a base *dædi*; and the nominative accusative plural *dæda*, and dative *dædu-m*, belong decidedly to the 1st declension; just so the accusative singular *dæde* (like *gefe*), as the final *i* has already been dropped in the accusative in Gothic (*anst*, "*gratiam*," for *ansti*).

† According to the weak declension, see Grimm, II. 319. Compare the masculine *varg'-r*, "wolf," with the Sanscrit *vṛika-s* from *varka-s*.

FORMATION OF WORDS. 1153

e.g. यज्ञस् *yaj-ñá-s*, "worship, sacrifice" (Zend ▽⟩ⵊⵊⴰⵙ *yas'-nó*, theme *-na*); *yat-ná-s*, "effort;" *praś-ná-s*, "question" (Zend ⵊⵊⴰⵙ⟩⟩ *fraś-na*, neuter, *fraś-nĕ-m*, see Brockhaus, Glossary, p. 378); *raksh-ná-s*, "protection, support;" *yách-ñá*, "the request, entreaty;" *triṣh-ṇá*, "thirst." An exception as regards the accent is to be found in *svápna-s*, "sleep" (Zend *khaf-no*, see §. 35.), to which the Lithuanian *sáp-na-s*, "dream," very well corresponds, only with the rejection of the *w*. In Greek ὕπ-νο-ς corresponds, in Latin *som-nu-s* (see §. 126. Note). To Sanscrit feminines like *yách-ñá* corresponds, irrespective of the accentuation, the Greek τέχ-νη. In Latin we may perhaps refer here *ru-í-na* and *rap-í-na*, which, therefore, have retained the class vowel *i* (see §. 109ª. 1.), and, indeed, lengthened it, as in general this suffix, in Latin, loves to have long vowels before it (*í-nu-s*, *á-nu-s*, *ó-na*). The Old High German *loug-na*, "falsehood, lying" (see Graff, II. 131), and the Old Saxon *hóf-na*, "to weep, to lament," undoubtedly belong here. To the masculine abstracts in न *na* I refer the Old High German *loug-i-n* or *loug-e-n*, "*negatio*" (Graff, l. c.), theme *loug-i-na*, *loug-e-na*, with a vowel of conjunction inserted (cf. §. 837.).

843. There is a close affinity in Sanscrit between the participial suffixes त *ta*, न *na*, and the suffixes ति *ti*, नि *ni*, which are used principally for the formation of feminine abstracts, in the *i* of which I recognise the weakening of the *a* of the pronominal bases *ta, na*. The suffix नि *ni* appears only in those abstracts whose roots in the perfect passive participle replace the suffix *ta* by *na*; thus, *e.g. lú-ni-s*, "tearing apart," *glá-ni-s*, "exhaustion," *jír-ṇi-s*, "old age," *há-ni-s*, "abandonment," compared with the passive participles *lú-ná-s*, "torn asunder," *glá-ná-s*, "exhausted," *jír-ṇá-s*, "aged, old," *hí-ná-s*, "abandoned" (irregu- [G. Ed. p. 1190.] lar for *há-ná-s*), to which, with regard to accentuation, they bear the same relation as in Greek, *e.g.* πότο-ς to ποτός (see §. 820.). The comparison of σπά-νι-ς with σπα-νό-ς, from an

4 F

FORMATION OF WORDS.

obscured root σπα, is closer. In Lithuanian *bar-ni-s*, "quarrel" (*baru*, "I quarrel"), is a fine remnant of this kind of formation of feminine abstracts: in Old Sclavonic this class of vocables is somewhat more richly represented by words like дань *da-ny*, "impost" (for *dani*, see §. 261.), брань *bra-ny*, "war," properly "the contesting" (борю *boryuṅ*, "I contend"), by transposition from *bar-ny* = Lithuanian *bar-ni-s* (Dobrowsky, p. 290). In Gothic here belong the feminine bases *lug-ni*, "a lie;"* *ana-bus-ni*, "command" (*s* for *d*, *ana-biuda*, "I command," root *bud*); *vaila-viz-ni*, "subsistence," properly "welfare" (*z* from *s*, see §. 86. 5., root *vas*; *visa, vas, vêsum*); *taik-ni*, "sign" (originally "the shewing," *e.g.* δείκνυμι, Sanscrit *diś*, from *dik*, "to shew"); *siu-ni*, "the looking, viewing;" nominative *liugn'-s*, &c. (see §. 135.). Moreover, the suffix *ni*, in Gothic, is a common means for the formation of feminine abstracts from weak verbs, the character of which is retained before the suffix, with contraction, however, of the syllable *ya* of the 1st conjugation to *ei*, as in the 2d person singular of the imperative. The following are examples from the 1st conjugation, which is here most richly represented: *gôl-ei-n(i)-s*, "*salutatio;*" *hauh-ei-n(i)-s*, "*exaltatio;*" *haus-ei-n(i)-s*, "*auditio;*" *gamêl-ei-n(i)-s*, "*scriptura.*" The 2d conjugation furnishes us only with *lath-ô-n(i)-s*, "*invitatio;*" *mit-ô-n(i)-s*, "*cogitatio;*" *salb-ô-n(i)-s, unctio:*" the 3d only *bau-ai-n(i)-s*, [G. Ed. p. 1191.] "*œdificatio;*" *at-vit-ai-n(i)-s*, "*observatio;*" *midya-sveip-ai-n(i)-s*, "*diluvium;*" *lib-ai-n(i)-s*, "*vita;*" *lub-ai-n(i)-s*, "*spes*" (the verb is uncited).

844. To the Sanscrit oxytone passive participles in *ta*

---

* It being presupposed that the only citable accusative with two meanings, *liugn*, actually belongs to a feminine base *liugni* (see Grimm, II. p. 157); otherwise the neuter of the passive participle mentioned above (§. 837.) has most claim to this word, and then *liugn(a)* would properly signify "the lied," and correspond to Sanscrit forms like *bhugná-m*, "the bent."

correspond abstracts in *ti*, which have also the accent in the radical syllable; compare *e. g. yúk-ti-s*, "joining," *pák-ti-s*, "cooking," *úk-ti-s*, "speech," *sthi-ti-s*, "state," with *yuk-tá-s*, "joined," *pak-tá-s*, "cooked," *uk-tá-s*, "spoken," *sthi-tá-s*, "standing" (see §. 821.). The following are examples of analogous abstracts in Zend: ꮯꮯꮯ *kars-ti-s*, "the ploughing" (*karsta*, "ploughed"); ꮯꮯꮯ *kharĕ-ti-s*, "the eating" (see p. 182.); ꮯꮯꮯ *yaôschdâi-ti-s*, "purification" (see §. 637.).* In Gothic this feminine suffix takes, according to the measure of the preceding letters of the root, either *ti*, or *thi*, or *di* (see §. 91.), but with *i* regularly suppressed in the nominative (see §. 135.); hence, *e.g. ga-skaf-t*(*i*)*-s*, "creation," gen. *gaskaf-tai-s* (see §. 185.); *fra-lus-t*(*i*)*-s*, "loss;" *ga-baur-th*(*i*)*-s*, "birth;" *gamun-d*(*i*)*-s*, "memory" (cf. Sanscrit *má-ti-s*, "understanding, meaning," for *mán-ti-s*). For examples in Old High German see §. 91. p. 80.† In the present condition of our language, at this day, too, there are tolerably numerous remains of this class of words; as, *e.g. Brun-s-t, Kun-s-t, Gun-s-t* (see §. 95), *An-kun-f-t, Zu-kun-f-t, Zun-f-t* (see §. 96.), *Mach-t, Zuch-t, Fluch-t, Sich-t, Fahr-t, Schrif-t, Schlach-t*, which have partly lost their plural, or introduced it into the *n*-(weak) declension, partly, however, retained it on the grade of the Old High German, corrupting, however, the *i* of the base to *e*, the power of whose *Umlaut* (vide p. 38, Note), however, points to its predecessor *i*; hence, [G. Ed. p. 1192.] *e.g. Brünste, Künste, Zünfte, Mächte*, compared with *Fahrten, Schriften, Schlachten*. In Lithuanian here belong *pyú-ti-s*,

---

* There is a misprint in the German text here in the word ꮯꮯꮯ where ꮯ is given for ꮯ. So, too, in §. 637. in the German, ꮯ is given five times for ꮯ, a mistake which I have inadvertently followed.

† Where, however, in the First Edition, the word should be divided *ki-walt*, as its *t* belongs to the root (whence *waltu*, pret. *wialt*). The fault is corrected in the Second Edition.

"the mowing" (*pyauyu*, "I mow"); *s-mer-ti-s*, "death" ("the dying"); *pa-źin-ti-s*, "knowledge, agnition, acquaintance" (*źinnau*, "I know"); *pri-gim-ti-s*, "nature" (*gemu*, "*nascor*"). The Old Sclavonic has corrupted the *i* of the suffix under discussion in the nominative accusative singular to ь y (see §. 261.); and, in general, the abstract feminine bases which belong here follow the declension of *kosty* (theme *kosti*, see p. 348). The base *pa-mya-ti* (ПАМѦТИ, "memory") I now read, according to p. 1048, *pa-man-ti*, as ѧ is an *a* with a nasal sound; the Sclavonic *man-ti*, therefore, has this superiority over the Sanscrit *má-ti*, that it has not entirely lost the nasal of the root before the suffix. Compare, also, the above-mentioned Gothic base *ga-mundi*, nom. *ga-mund'-s*. The following are other Old Sclavonic abstracts belonging here, which I annex in the nominative: БЛАГОДАТЬ *blago-daty*, "benefit;"* СЪМРЬТЬ *s'-mry-ty*, "death" (see Mikl., "Radices," p. 52) = Sanscrit *mri-ti-s*, from *mar-ti-s*; ВЛАСТЬ *vlas-ty*, "dominion;"† СТРАСТЬ *stras-ty*, "suffering" (root *strad*); *vyes-ty*, "information" (root *vyed*, compare Sanscrit causal *védáyámi*, "I make to know, I inform," from the root *vid*, "to know"). To this class of verbal abstracts belong most probably also the Sclavonic and Lithuanian infinitives in *ti*, of which hereafter.

[G. Ed. p. 1193.] 845. In Greek the *t* of this suffix, except in χῆ-τι-ς, μῆ-τι-ς, (=Sanscrit *má-ti-s*, Sclavonic *man-ty*), φά-τι-ς (together with φά-σι-ς), ἄμπω-τι-ς (with ἄμπω-σι-ς, compare Sanscrit *pí-ti-s*, "the drinking"), has been retained unaltered only under the protection of a preceding σ. The protecting

---

* *Dat-y* answers admirably to the Zend *dáiti-s*, mentioned above (p. 1155), from *ya-ósch-dáitis*, properly "making pure," and to the Gothic base *dé-di* (*é*=*á*, see §. 69.), Old High German *tâ-ti*, nom. *tât* (our *That*). The Sanscrit leads us to expect *dhá-ti-s*, from the root धा *dhá*, "to place, to make."

† Miklosich (Rad., p. 10) rightly compares the Sanscrit root *vridh* (from *vardh*), "to grow," from which *vríd-dhis* (euphonic for *vridh-ti-s*), "growth, increase, success."

sibilant, however, as in the just-mentioned Sclavonic formations, is the euphonic representative of an original t-sound ; hence, e.g. πίσ-τι-ς (together with πεῖ-σι-ς), πύσ-τι-ς (with πεῦ-σι-ς), λῆσ-τι-ς. With respect to the weakening of the τ to σ, which generally takes place after vowels, compare the same phenomenon in the 3d person singular of the conjugation in μι, and of the 3d person plural of all verbs: as, therefore, δίδω-σι, τίθη-σι, so also δό-σι-ς, θέ-σι-ς. After gutturals and labials, with which the σ unites itself in writing to ξ, ψ, the weakening of the t-sound to the sibilant is of most frequent occurrence; hence, e.g. ζεῦξι-ς (=ζεῦκ-σι-ς, euphonic for ζεῦγ-τι-ς) compared with the Sanscrit *yúk-ti-s*, Latin *junc-tio*; πέψι-ς* (=πέπ-σι-ς) for Sanscrit *pák-tis*, Latin *coc-tio*. It admits of no doubt, that, in Greek, the ι has obtained an influence on the τ preceding, which does not, indeed, prevail completely throughout, but is shewn in its preferring an σ to the τ; hence e.g. the opposition between ζευκ-τό-ς, πεπ-τό-ς, and ζεῦκ-σι-ς, πέπ-σι-ς; while in Sanscrit, *yúk-ti-s*, *pák-ti-s*, *trip-ti-s* (" satiating"=Greek τέρπ-σι-ς), with respect to the initial consonants of the suffix, agree with the passive participles *yuk-tá-s*, *pak-tá-s*, *trip-tá-s* (Greek τερπ-νό-ς for τερπ-τό-ς, see §. 836.). Observe, that the Sanscrit, in accordance with the Greek, has retained the more energetic accentuation for the abstract (see §. 785, p. 1052), while the participle has allowed the accent to sink down upon the final syllable; thus, *yúkti-s* [G. Ed., p. 1194.] compared with *yuktá-s*, as ζεῦξι-ς compared with ζευκτό-ς.

846. In Greek, from σι, by the inorganic addition of an α, the form σια has developed itself, in similar wise as above (§. 119. p. 130) we saw -τρια, e.g. in ὀρχήστρια, answer to the Sanscrit *trí*. The extended form σια appears, as has already been elsewhere remarked,† to be most inclined to unite itself with forms which, by derivative letters or com-

---

* Πεπ from πεκ =Sanscrit *pach* from *pak*, Latin *coc*.

† " Influence of Pronouns on the formation of Words," p. 23.

position, have enlarged themselves; while it rather avoids monosyllabic roots. We find, indeed, θυσία, but not λυσία, φυσία, ρυσία. On the other hand, we find, e.g. δοκιμασία, ἱππασία, θερμασία, σημασία, ἐπιβασία (with ἐπιβασι-ς). Externally these forms approximate to nominal abstracts, which are formed by the suffix ια from adjective or substantive bases, in so far as these change a τ which occurs in the final syllable into σ; as, e.g. ἀκαθαρσ'-ία from ἀκάθαρτο-ς, ἀθανασ'-ία from ἀθάνατο-ς.

847. In Lithuanian, also, there occur verbal abstracts, which, like the Greek in σια, have given an inorganic affix to the suffix *ti* under discussion, and presuppose bases in *tia*, whence, in the nominative, comes *tẽ* (see p. 174. Note). Thus, together with the *pyú-ti-s*, "the mowing," mentioned above (p. 1192 G. ed.), there exists a *pyút-ẽ* of the same signification, and at the same time a masculine *pyúti-s* (for *pyutia-s*, genitive *pyuchio*, euphonic for *pyutio*, see §. 783. p. 1046): another example is *beg-tẽ*, "the running." The nominal abstracts in *y-stẽ*, as *bagot'-y-stẽ*, "riches," from *bagota-s*, "rich," *yaun'-y-stẽ*, "youth," from *yauna-s*, "young," "*diẽw'-y-stẽ*, "godhead," from *diẽwa-s*, "God," *merg'-y-stè*, "maidenhood,"
[G. Ed. p. 1195.] from *mergà*, "maiden," represent the abovementioned (§. 829.) Sanscrit abstracts in *tâ* (compare *diew'-y-stẽ* with *dêva-tấ*, "godhead"), but appear, with regard to their suffix, to belong to *ti*, and, like Sclavonic formations, as юностъ *yuno-sty*, "youth," горестъ *gore-sty*, "bitterness," have inserted before the *t* a euphonic *s*.* Irrespective of this, they already answer to the Latin nominal abstracts in *tia* or *tie-s* (see §. 137.), as *cani-tia*, *cani-tie-s*, *pigri-tia*, *pigri-tie-s*, *justi-tia*, *amici-tia*, *pueri-tia*, *pueri-tie-s*, the *i* of which (before the *t*) I regard as the weakening of the final vowel of the primitive base (cf. p. 1167 G. ed.). An example of a neuter belonging here is *servi-tium*. In

---

* See Dobrowsky, p. 302, and compare the formations in *stvo*=Sanscrit *tva* (§. 834.)

Latin the suffix *ti* here discussed has received, as a means of formation of verbal abstracts, a further extension by the addition of *ôn;* thus *tiôn,* nom. *tiô,* with the euphonic alterations required by §. 101. = Sanscrit *ti.* Compare *e.g. coc-tio* with *pák-ti-s, frac-tio* with *bhák-ti-s, junc-tio* with *yúk-ti-s, fis-sio* (from *fis-tio,* and this for *fid-tio,* see §. 101.), with *bhít-ti-s* (from *bhid-ti-s*), *sta-tio* with *sthí-ti-s, i-tio* with *i-ti-s*. The latter hardly occurs in its simple state, but exists in *sám-iti-s,* " fight," properly " the coming together, the conflict." In Latin occurs, together with *i-tio,* also *i-tiu-m,* in the compound *in-i-tiu-m,* which, in its formative suffix, answers to the nominal abstract *servi-tium.* Remarkable remains of the older formation of this class of words are supplied to us by the adverbs in *tim* (or *sim,* according to §. 101.), which I elsewhere (which Pott, E. I., I. 91., has overlooked) have represented as adverbial accusatives of lost abstracts;* thus, *e.g. trac-ti-m,* properly " with drawing;" *cur-si-m,* " with running ;" *cæ-si-m,* " with [G. Ed. p. 1196.] hewing, smiting;" *confer-ti-m,* "with pressing together" (Sanscrit *sám-bhri-ti-m* (from *sam-bhar-ti-m*), acc. from *sámbhriti,* "bringing together, crowd"). *Passim,* from *pas-ti-m,* I derive not from *pando,* but with *pas-sus,* " step" (from *pas-tu-s*), from a lost root " of going ;" and I would bring to remembrance the Sanscrit *pad,* " to go" (whence *pada-m,* " step"), as also *path* id., whence *pathín, pánthan,* " path " (Latin *pons,* see §. 255. (g.) p. 319). The following are declinable words of the older formation : *mes-si-s,* from *mes-ti-s,* " the mowing," *tus-si-s,* from *tus-ti-s,* " cough," whether the latter be connected with the Sanscrit root *tus,* " to sound," or with *tundo,* when it would properly signify " the thrusting ;" *semen-ti-s* is probably derived from a noun,† but is

---

* " Influence of Pronouns on the formation of Words," p. 24.

† From *semen;* for from the denominative verb *semino* we should expect *semin-â-ti-s* (compare *nomin-â-tim*).

to be remarked on account of the pure retention of the suffix. *Mor-s* and *men-s* have probably lost an *i* belonging to the base (therefore from *morti-s, menti-s*): the former answers to the Sanscrit *mrí-ti-s* (from *mar-ti-s*) "death," the latter to *má-ti-s* for *mán-ti-s*.

848. With the suffix *ti*, in Sanscrit, masculine substantives also are formed, which, according to their fundamental signification, denote the person acting; as, *e.g. yá-ti-s*, "tamer, binder (of the senses)," from the root *yam*; *pá-ti-s*, "lord (ruler), husband," for *pā́-ti-s* (root *pâ*, "to support, to rule"); *sáp-ti-s*, "horse," as "runner;"* *jñā́-ti-s*,† "relation." To [G. Ed. p. 1197.] *páti-s* answers the Lithuanian *pati-s* in *wiesz-pati-s* (usually *-pat'-s*), the Gothic *fa-di*, nom. *fath-s* (see §. 90.), the Greek πό-σι-ς, Latin *po-ti-s*. To this class of words belong, further, among other words, the Greek μάν-τι-ς, the Latin *vec-ti-s* (from *veho*), the Gothic *ga-drauht(i)-s*, "soldier" (root *drug*, "doing military service," pret. *drauh*, pl. *drugum*); *gas-t(i)-s*, "guest," as it appears to me, as "eater,"‡ Sclavonic *gos-ty*. Here belong, further, in Lithuanian, *gen-ti-s*, "relation," and the following with a

---

* The root *sap*, "to follow," akin to *sach*, id. (from *sak*), the Latin *sequor*, Lithuanian *seku*, "I follow," Greek ἕπομαι, probably denoted originally "rapid motion," as also other terms used to denote a horse, are based on the notion of rapidity. Compare Weber, "Vâjasanêya-Sanhitæ Specimen," II. 54.

† Perhaps from *jan* ("to bear, to produce"), transposed to *jñâ* (compare *dhmâ* with *dham*). In the Vêda dialect this suffix forms also adjectives with the signification of the participle present; *e.g. vríddhi* (euphonic for *vrídh-ti*), "growing;" *júshthi* (euphonic for *júshti*), "loving" (Rigv. I. 10. 12.).

‡ Compare Sanscrit *ghas*, "to eat," to which the Latin *hos-ti-s* also appears to belong, as, in Sanscrit, ह *h* and घ *gh* are often interchanged, and ह *h* is represented in Latin also by *h*. In Lithuanian, *gas-padà*, "house-keeping," appears, in respect to its initial syllable, to belong here, and *padà* seems to be radically akin to the Sanscrit *padá-m*, Greek πεδό-ν. Compare also the Latin *hos-pes*.

lengthening of the base by an inorganic *a*, which, however, is wanting in the nominative (see §. 135.): *kwes-ti-s,,* "inviter" (gen. *kwechio*, root *kwet*, whence *kwetu* and *kwechiu*, "I invite"); *rais-ti-s*, "head-band" (*riszu*, "I bind"); *kamsz-ti-s*, "stopple" (*kamszau*, "I stop"); *ram-ti-s*, "support" (properly "the supporter," *pa-remyu* and *ramstau*, "I support"); *yau-ti-s*, "ox" (Sanscrit *yu*, "to couple," "*yáu-mi*, "I bind"), compare Latin "*jumentum*." Perhaps, also, in the Latin nominal derivatives *cœle-sti-s, agre-sti-s,* only *ti* is the true suffix, and *s* a euphonic prefix,* as in the Lithuanian formations like *yaun-y-ste*, "youth," and the Slavonic in *s-tvo* (see §§. 834. 847.). So the *s* of *campe-stri-s, terre-stri-s, silve-stri-s*, might owe its introduction only to the inclination a *t* has to lean on a preceding *s*; [G. Ed. p. 1198.] so that here *tri* would present itself as the true suffix, and as a development from the above-mentioned (§. 810.) *tôr* = Sanscrit *târ*, fem. *trí*. If any one, however, would desire, with Pott (l. c.), to recognise in the syllable *sti* of *agre-sti-s, cœle-sti-s*, the root of "to stand," according to the analogy of Sanscrit compounds like *divi-shthá-s*, "standing in heaven," "heavenly," I still see no reason to recognise in the above-mentioned Lithuanian and Sclavonic classes of words compounds with derivatives from the said verbal root, as a euphonic *s* in the forms spoken of does not surprise us more than in the Greek words ἀκου-σ-τός, ἀκου-σ-τής, ἀκου-σ-τικός.† The *e* of the Latin formations in *e-sti-s* and *e-stri* I regard as a corruption of *i* (see §. 6.), occasioned by the following combination of consonants.

849. The Indian Grammarians assume a suffix *ati* to

---

* *Dome-sticus* presupposes a more simple *dome-sti-s* (compare Pott, Et. I., II. 543.); and thus, too, *rus-ti-cus* a more simple *rus-ti-s*.

† -τι-κος presupposes abstract bases in τι, as σι-μο-s (βά-σι-μο-s, κρί-σι-μο-s, πτώ-σι-μο-s) presuppose such bases in σι. See Pape, "Etymol. Lexicon," p. 140 *b*.

1162   FORMATION OF WORDS.

explain some rare words; as, *aratí-s*, m., "wrath," and with the accent on the root, *árati-s*, f., "fear, care" (from the root *ar*, *ri*, "to move oneself," compare Latin *ira*); *ramatí-s*, m., "the God of Love," as "sporter" (root *ram*, "to sport"); *vahatí-s*, m., "wind," as "blower." I believe, however, that in this class of words *ti* only is the true suffix, and *a* the retained class-vowel (see p. 1108). The Lithuanian presents as analogous forms *gyw-a-sti-s*, "life," and *rimm-a-sti-s*, "rest," the *s* of which is therefore euphonic. The latter answers also radically to the Sanscrit *ram-a-tí-s*, as *ram*, with the prep. *á* (*áram*), signifies "to rest." On the other hand, from *gyw-a-sti-s* ($y = i$) we had to expect *jiv-a-ti-s*. The circumstance that the said Lithuanian words form in the genitive *gywaschio, rimmaschio*, from *gywaschia*

[G. Ed. p. 1199.] and *rimmaschia* (*chia* euphonic for *-tia*, see §. 783., p. 1046), and are become masculine, which the Sanscrit abstracts in *ti* never are, need not deter us from recognising the affinity of formation of the words spoken of in both languages, as similar extensions of the limits of words, as also changes of gender, are not uncommon in the Indo-European stock of languages. I refer, with respect to both these points, to the Latin *in-i-tiu-m* for *in-i-ti-s* above mentioned (§. 847.). Together with *gyw-a-sti-s*, "life," and *rimm-a-sti-s*, there exist also, in Lithuanian, some analogous masculine abstracts which exhibit *e* for *a* as the middle vowel; thus, *luk-e-sti-s*, "the writing;" *mok-e-sti-s*, "paying;" *rup-e-sti-s*, "care;" *gail-e-sti-s*, "penitence;" *pyk-e-sti-s*, "rancour" (*pykstu*, "I am wrath," pret. *pykau*). In Greek we find a few analogous forms which admit of comparison with the above-mentioned Sanscrit abstract *ár-ati-s*, "fear, anxiety," in which ε has been inserted: νέμ-ε-σι-ς, λάχ-ε-σι-ς, εὕρ-ε-σι-ς (see p. 1098), where the agreement in accentuation is also to be noticed.

850. The suffix *ni*, moreover, is, in Sanscrit, not only a means of forming feminine abstracts, but produces also

some similar appellatives, which accentuate, some the root, some the suffix: *e.g.*, *vrish-ní-s*, "rain," as "impregnator" (*n* euphonic for *n*);* *ag-ní-s*, "fire," is perhaps an abbreviation of *dag-ni-s* (compare *dág-dhum*, "to burn," root *dah*), which reaches back beyond the time of the separation of languages, as *áśru* is a more recent one of *dáśru* (Greek δάκρυ); *váh-ni-s*, in the Vêdas, among other things, "horse," as "bearing" or "drawing" (see Benfey's Glossary), in classic Sanscrit "fire;" *yó-ni-s*, masc. fem., "*vulva*" (root *yu*, "to join together"). An accurately-re- [G. Ed. p. 1200.] tained analogous form to *agní-s* is to be found in several of the European sister languages: in Latin, *ig-ni-s*, in Lithuanian, *ug-ni-s*, which latter, however, has become feminine; while the Sclavonic огнь *og-ny* (theme *ogni*) has preserved the gender handed down to it. In Lithuanian *ni* appears in some other feminine bases, the root of which is obscured; thus, *us-ni-s*, "thistle," is perhaps originally "the sticking," and radically akin to the Sanscrit *ush*, "to burn" (Latin *us*, *ur*);† *szak-ni-s*, "root," may be named from "to grow," and be akin to the Sanscrit *śak*, "to be able;" as, conversely, the Gothic *mag*, "I can," and *mah-t*(*i*)-*s*, "might," conduct us to a Sanscrit root which signifies "to grow" (*mah*, *manh*). In Latin we may perhaps further refer here *crî-ni-s*, *pâ-ni-s*, *fi-ni-s*, *fû-ni-s*, and the adjectives *lê-ni-s* and *seg-ni-s*, which, however, are all of them more or less obscured as to their roots. *Crî-ni-s* may, like the Sanscrit *rô-man* for *rôh-man* (see §. 796.), and *śirô-ruhá*, "hair of the head" ("growing on the head"), be named from "to grow" (*cre-sco*, *cre-vi*), inasmuch as it

---

* Root *varsh*, *vrish*. The Latin *verres*, which is probably akin, takes its form perhaps by assimilation for *verne-s*.

† Thus, in all probability, *dygulis*, "prickle, thorn," *digsni-s*, "stitch with the needle," and *deÿiu*, "I stick" are connected with *degu*, "I burn."

does not spring, as *capillus* from *caput*, from another term for the head (Sanscrit *śiras* from *kiras*, " head," Greek κάρα); *pâ-ni-s* signifies, perhaps, " the nourishing" (Sanscrit *pâ*, " to support, to nourish," compare *pa-sco*), but might also have lost a final radical consonant (as, *e.g.* lu-*na,* lu-*men,* for luc-*na,* luc-*men,* ful-*men* for fulg-*men*), and may be named from " to bake;"* *fĭ-ni-s,* perhaps for *fid-ni-s,* from *fid, findo; fû-ni-s* [G. Ed. p. 1201.] is referred by Pott (Et. I., I. 251.), and I believe rightly, to the Sanscrit *bandh*, " to bind," with which he also compares *fido, fœdus*, and the Greek πείθω (root πιθ); consequently, in the latter forms, the old *a*, as in our pres. *binde* (see p. 106), has been weakened to *i;* while the *û* of *fû-ni-s* for *fud-nis* is closer to the old *a*, and compensates by its being lengthened for the consonant that has been dropped.† But if *fûnis* belongs to *bandh*, the *n* might also be radical, which, however, I do not believe, as *fído* also, and πείθω, have lost the nasal, and roots which terminate in a mute with a nasal preceding dispense rather with the less important nasal than with the mute: hence, in Sanscrit, *e.g. baddh-á-s*, " bound." *Seg-ni-s* I hold to be akin to the Sanscrit root *sajj*, " *adhærere;*" *sañj*, " *affigere*" (*sak-tá-s*, " *affixus*"): it may originally sig-

---

* The *p* of the Sanscrit *pach* (from *pak*), Greek πέπω, has been changed into a guttural in *coquo*, which does not prevent the assumption that the original labial has not been entirely lost.

† Regarding the origin of the aspirates of *funis* and *fido*, opposed to the Greek πείθω, see §. 104., and Ag. Benary, " Doctrine of Roman Sounds," p. 190. As regards the Greek π for Sanscrit *b*, we find the same relation in πυθ, compared with the Sanscrit root *budh*, " to know." The circumstance, that in Sanscrit, together with *bandh*, there exists another root which cannot be cited, *bundh*, cannot instigate me to refer the Latin *fŭ-ni-s* rather to this *bundh* than to *bandh;* but I believe that the weakening of the *a* to *u* (see §. 604.), which, for the reason given above, has been lengthened in Latin, has found its way into the Sanscrit *bundh*, Latin *fŭ-ni-s*, and Gothic *bund-um*, " we bound," for the first time after the separation of languages, from a principle common to the three languages.

FORMATION OF WORDS. 1165

nify "held fast, held in," hence "slow, inactive." In Lithuanian, *segu* means " I fasten," the original *a* of which has maintained itself in *sak-ti-s* (gen. *-tes*), "clasp, buckle." *Lê-ni-s*, if it be akin to λεῖος, can have *ni* only as formative suffix. In Sanscrit, *lí*, cl. 1., signifies "*liquefacere, solvere*," whence *lí-ná-s*, "*solutus, extinctus;*" *lí*, cl. 9., "*adhærere, inhærere, insidere.*"

[G. Ed. p. 1202] 851. The intermediate vowel-weakening of the pronominal bases त *ta*, न *na*, exhibited by the suffixes *tu, nu*, shew that they stand in the same phonetic relation to the forms *ta, na, ti, ni*, as that in which, in the interrogative, the form *ku* stands to *ka, ki* (see §§. 386. 389. 390.). The suffix *tu* is particularly important in Sanscrit as a formative of the infinitive, and of a gerund in *tvá*. I have already, in my System of Conjugation (pp. 39, 43), represented the former as an accusative, with *m* as the sign of case, and the latter as an instrumental, and will not repeat here the grounds which induce me to regard the infinitive in all languages as an abstract substantive, with the privilege of governing, like the so-called gerunds and supines, the case of the verb, and to employ several other freedoms in construction. The Indian Grammarians assign the *m* of the infinitive in *tum* to the suffix, which they call *tu-mun*, in order to express by *n*, which is joined by means of the conjunctive vowel *u* to the *tum*, which they view as the true suffix, the denial of the accent, which rests on the radical syllable; hence, *e.g. dá-tum*, "to give;" *sthá-tum*, "to stand;" *pák-tum*, "to cook;" *trás-tum*, "to tremble;" *át-tum*, "to eat;" *vét-tum*, "to know." That the Indian Grammarians regard the final *m* of these forms not as the sign of the accusative, and therefore as alien to the true suffix, must surprise us the more, as in the Véda dialect, of which I was ignorant when I first began to treat of this subject, the abstract substantive in *tu* occurs also in other cases, and, indeed, in the dative with the termination *tavé* or *taváı*, and in the genitive-ablative with the termination *tôs*. In these forms, however, the Indian Grammarians refer the case-terminations *ê* or *âi*, and *s* likewise, to the suffix (Pânini, III. 4. 9.); yet we can hardly imagine it possible that Pânini, when he, [G. Ed. p. 1203.] *e.g.* III. 4. 13., says, *îsvarê tôsun-kasunâu*, *i.e.* that in construction with *îsvará*, "lord, capable," the unaccented suffixes *tôs* and *as* may supply the place of the infinitive suffix *tum*, he can therein have overlooked that here *tôs* is the genitive of the suffix *tu*, and *as* the genitive termination of abstract substantives without any suffix. It is, however, certain that the practical Grammarians often overlooked that which was not far to find, if it was no longer clearly perceptible in the usances of the ordinary language of the day; and if Pânini has made a mistake here, we cannot wonder that Colebrooke also, who, in his Grammar, keeps strictly to the rules handed down by the native Grammarians, should assign the formations in *tôs*(*un*), (*k*)*as*(*un*), *tum*(*un*), and (*k*)*tvâ*, to the "aptotes" ("Grammar of the Sanscrit language," p. 122);[*] and, *e.g.* place *kártum*, "to

---

[*] As regards the infinitive in *tum*, and the gerund in *tvâ*, A. W. v. Schlegel, too, has, in noticing my view of these forms (Indische Bibliothek," I. p. 125), so far assented, as to say that the assertion that the infinitive in *tum* is the accusative of a verbal noun in *tu* "has a certain speciousness," for the supine of the Latin has undoubtedly the appearance of a verbal noun of the 4th declension. As regards, however, the form in *tvâ*, Schlegel very decidedly denies the justness of viewing in a gerund of the same (*i.e.* according to his idea) any oblique case whatever of an abstract substantive governing the case of the verb; but he will have the form in question called "an absolute participle," perhaps because it, as he remarks at p. 124, when it governs an accusative, can be aptly rendered into Latin by the ablative absolute; *e.g. tan drishtvâ* by *eo viso*. Though, however, *tan drishtvâ* might aptly be so rendered, yet this does not prevent its properly signifying "*post-actionem videndi eum*, "after seeing him:" for the instrumental, which I recognise in *drishtvâ*, expresses also, where it refers to a time, the relation "after;" hence, *e.g. achirêna kâlêna*, "after a short (not long) time;" consequently this gerund

make," *kṛitvâ*, "after making," in the same [G. Ed. p. 1204.] class with adverbs like *kútas*, " whence ?" *yátra*, " where ?"

gerund case, where it expresses the relation "after," is fittingly translated into other languages by a preterite participle; thus, *e.g. ity uktvâ* ("after so speaking") may be rendered into Latin by "*ita locutus*," and into German by "*so gesprochen habend.*" We must, however, be on our guard, if we would understand the nature of a form of speech, against disposing of it according to the fashion in which it can be most conveniently rendered into another dialect without injury to the general import. As the instrumental also expresses the relation "with," the gerund under discussion may also be employed where a present participle might be expected, and where, in translations into other languages, we might aptly avail ourselves of such a part of speech; as, *e.g.* Nal. IX. 24., "he spake to *Bhâimî* with explanation," *i.e.* "explaining" (compare W. v. Humboldt in Schlegel's I. Bibl., II. 127.); where, indeed, in the original, we do not find the gerund in *tvâ*, but another, of which hereafter, which, however, in its constructions, agrees exactly with that in *tvâ*, and in which, too, an instrumental may be recognised, though not, indeed, as clearly. Our gerund expresses the relation "with" also there, where it comes after *alam*, "enough," in which position, however, we more commonly find the instrumental of other abstract substantives. The forms *alam bhuktvâ* and *alam bhôjanêna*, *i.e.* "enough with eating," signify the same; and I have appealed already, in my Conjugation-System (p. 52), to this kind of construction as to a decisive proof of the instrumental and gerundial nature of the form in *tvâ;* and will only further add here, that Forster also, whose Grammar was then unknown to me, regards the form in *tvâ*, in this particular case, as a gerund ("Essay on the principles of Sanscrit Grammar," p. 463), without, however, entering into any explanation of its origin, and of the case-relation denoted by it. The use of gerunds with *alam* is very rare in authors, in that, as it appears, the abstracts in *ana*, which will be discussed hereafter, and on which our German infinitive is based, have almost entirely supplanted the gerunds in *tvâ* and *ya* in this position. I am able at present to quote only one solitary example of the gerund in *ya* with *alam;* viz. Mah. III. 869. 1., *alan kṛishnâ' vamanyâi' nam*(-*ya ênam*), "Enough, Kṛishṇa, with despising him" (*i.e.* "despise him no further"). Schlegel grounds a principal objection against the formative affinity of the form in *tvâ* and the infinitive in *tum* on the circumstance that the two forms do not stand in such exact accordance with one another in all roots as in *páktum* and *paktvấ*;
but

táthâ, thus." As regards the infinitive in *tum*, the circumstance that this form does not in all places express the

---

but I had myself before, in my Conjugation-System, pp. 57, 58, drawn attention to the difference; as, *e.g.* between *vaktum*, from the base *vaktu*, and *uktvâ*, from the contracted base *uktu*: and, moreover, W. v. Humboldt (Indische Bibl., I. 433., II. 71.), in a copious and profoundly penetrating examination of the disputed point, whether the form in *tvâ* be an indeclinable participle or a gerund, has not been deterred by such differences from recognising in the infinitive and the form in *tvâ* a formative affinity and common suffix, and from uniting with me in representing the latter as a gerund invested with the termination of the instrumental and expressing the relations of this case (l. c. II. p. 127). On the other hand, Lassen (l. c. III. p. 104) consents indeed to recognise in the form in *tvâ* a gerund, but denies it to be an instrumental. His objection against the original identity of the infinitive and the gerund (which, as is evident from what has been said, I have never asserted) is from the "older forms of the gerund" which occur in Pânini (VII. I. 47.). Before I mention these forms, I must repeat, that, as Lassen lays down in other places, that alone is to be considered as ancient which the Vêda dialect exhibits differing from the classical Sanscrit; otherwise we must (to keep to the instrumental) regard the Vêdic instrumentals, mentioned in the Scholiast to Pânini, VII. I. 39., *dhíti*, *matî*, *sushṭutî* (for *dhíty-â*, *maty-â*, *sushṭuty-â*), which have dropped the case-terminations—as well as locatives like *charman* for *charmani*, l. c.—as older than the forms of the classic language which are provided with the case-termination. After the analogy of the said Vêdic instrumentals may also be explained the Vêdic gerunds in *tví* (*e.g.* *vṛitví*, Rigv. I. 52. 6.), if we, with Kuhn ("Journal of Lit. Crit.," 1844, p. 114), compare these forms with Vêdic instrumentals like *dhṛishṇuyâ*, "with courage," which I now readily do, without, however, assuming, with the said learned man, that such instrumentals come from bases in *vî*; but I hold the *y* of *dhṛishṇuyâ*, *uruyâ*, for a euphonic insertion (see § 43.); and I refer to the analogous feminine pronominal instrumental *amu-y-â* ("through that") of the common language opposed to the masculine neuter *amu-n-â*. The feminine theme of the pronoun spoken of has indeed a long *û*, except before the euphonic *y*; as, however, adjectives also can lengthen a final *u* in the feminine, so may *dhṛishṇu-y-â* and *uru-y-â* be derived from *dhṛishṇú*, *urú*. Were it, however, preferred to derive them from *dhṛishṇvi*, *urvî*, because adjectives in *u* can annex an *î* (see §. 119.), we should still feel no slight ground for
assuming

FORMATION OF WORDS. 1169

accusative relation, but is also found expressing relations otherwise far removed from the [G. Ed. p. 1206.]

assuming, together with the pronominal base *amû*, a base *amvi*, simply in order to annex thereto the terminations beginning with a vowel, especially as from *amvî*, according to the only rule which prevails in Sanscrit, must come *amvy-â*, *amvy-ô-s*. If we, however, choose to consider the *y* in *amu-y-â*, *amu-y-ôs*, as an insertion, the inference of this recoils also upon the said Vêda forms *dhrishnu-y-â*, *uru-y-â*, which in the Scholiast to Pânini (l. c.) are represented as=*dhrishnu-n-â*, *uru-n-â*, and belonging to the masculine or neuter, which can hardly be established by the Vêda text. In the substantively-used *dhrishnuyâ*, "with courage," the gender cannot be discovered from the passages of the Rigv. which lie before me. I regard it, however, as feminine, until I find proof to the contrary. The Vêdic gerunds in *tvî*, if we derive the *tvî* from *tu-y-â*, accord with the above-mentioned Vêdic instrumentals (*dhíti* from *dhíty-â*, &c.), in so far that they, in like manner, have, after dropping the termination, changed the preceding semi-vowel into the corresponding long one. But if the termination *tvî* do not rest on this principle, I would explain, as I have before done, *tvî* from *tvâ* as the consequence of the weakening of the vowel, according to the principle of forms like *yu-nî-mâs* for *yu-nâ-mâs* (see §. 485.).—The Vêdic gerunds in *tvâ-ya* have the appearance of datives from bases in *tva*: as they, however, have not a dative, but, in like manner, an instrumental meaning, and also in their formation, exclusive of the affix *ya*, approximate to the usual form in *tvâ*, but not to the above-mentioned (§. 835.) abstracts in *tva*, e.g. *gatvâya* (Schol. to Pân. VII. I. 46.) to *gatvâ*, *vrittvâya* (Yajurvêda XI. 19.) to *vrittvâ*, *kritvâya* (l. c. 59.) to *kritvâ* (cf. *kártva-m*, §. 835.), I would rather, with Pânini, regard *tvâya* as a lengthened form of *tvâ* with the affix *ya*, than conversely, with Lassen (l. c. p. 106), look upon *tvâ* as an abbreviation of *tvâya*. The lengthening of the instrumental termination *â* to *âya* is like that by which, in bases in *a*, the dative termination *ê* has prolonged itself to *aya* (from *ê* + *a*, see §. 165.), only the *y* here is the representative of the *i* contained in the diphthong *ê*, while the *y* of *tvâya* is perhaps an euphonic insertion (see §. 43.); as, e.g., in *yâ-y-in*, "going" (root *yâ*, suffix *in*); and in the Vêdic *dhá-y-as*, "the carrying, supporting" (root *dhâ*, suffix *as*).—Besides *tvî* and *tvâya*, *tvínam* also (Pân. VI. I. 48.) is named as the representative of the termination *tvâ*, occurring, however, as added to the root *yaj*, "to honour" (*ishtvínam* for *ishtvâ*); and in the scholium on the said Sûtra we find also a form in *tvânam*, viz. *pîtvânam*

4 G   for

accusative, may have chiefly occasioned the overlooking its *m* to be the sign of the accusative, for *pîtvâ*. If these forms, of which I know no examples that can be cited, are really equivalent in meaning to those in *tvâ*, and therefore expressive of instrumental relations, I can but recognise in their termination *nam* an enclitic; and I could only join with Lassen in conjecturing a suffix *tvan*, and deriving from it *pîtvânam*, after the analogy of *râjânam*, and in regarding *ishtvínam* as a weakened form of *ishtvânam*, if the forms *ishtvínam* and *pîtvânam* were shewn, according to this signification, to be accusatives; but I could in nowise be induced to look upon the form in *tvâ*, which is also the prevailing one in the Vêdas, as an abbreviation of that in *tvânam*. M. Professor Lassen, in his polemic against my theory with regard to the form in *tvâ*, has kept the principal point of my argument quite in the back ground; viz. this, that the forms which terminate in *tvâ*, if we regard them, as Lassen does, as gerunds, express in all places, as is well demonstrated by W. v. Humboldt's copious investigation, only such case-relations as are denoted by the instrumental, but which are quite and entirely removed from the accusative, as also from the dative; and were this not the case, the mere form would never have led me to recognise in the formations in *tvâ* the instrumental of feminine substantives in *tu*, which, with regard to their gender and their suffix, find a good support in the Greek abstracts in τύ-ς (as ἐδητύ-ς), to which I first drew attention in my treatise "On the influence of Pronouns on the formation of Words" (p. 25). However, Lassen further remarks (l. c. p. 105), that if we compare the lingual use of this gerund, the instrumental " or ablative" were perhaps better adapted for expressing the notional relation of this verbal form, than the accusative, which is never suited for that purpose. Into the province of the ablative, however, in my opinion, this gerund never enters, unless one thinks of the Latin ablative, which, at the same time, represents the Sanscrit instrumental; hence, *e.g.* in a passage of the Bhag. (II. 37.), *jitvâ* may be aptly translated by the ablative of the gerund (*vincendo*), thus, " *vel occisus cœlum es adepturus, vel vincendo possidebis terram.*" If need be, however, I would regard here also the instrumental gerund as expressing the relation " after," " after conquering thou wilt possess the earth." A Sanscrit ablative, perhaps *jayât*, "from the victory," or "on account of the victory," could hardly be expected in this and similar passages. Still more decisively than in the passage just quoted, is the genuine instrumental relation, or that of the Latin ablative of the gerund expressed in a passage of the Hitopadês,
already

the relation of which the infinitive evidently there expresses, where it is governed by verbs, or verbal-substantives, or adjectives, which express, "to [G. Ed. p. 1208.] will," "to wish," "to know," "to strive," "to be able," "to begin," "to command," "to determine;" where it is to be observed, as regards the verbs of mo- [G. Ed. p. 1209.] tion, that the object of every motion in Sanscrit is regularly expressed by the simple accusative. As to the accusative nature of the infinitive a passage of the Śakuntalâ, already cited by Hofer ("Of the Infinitive" p. 95), is very characteristic, in which, of two actions influenced by a verbal expression denoting "beginning," the one is expressed by the accusative of an abstract substantive in *a*, and the other by the infinitive: *bâhútkshêpan rôditun̄-cha pravrittâ*, "she began outstretching arms and to weep."

---

already cited by me in my Conjugation-system (p. 45): *tvam uchchâih śabdan kritvá sváminan kathan na jâgarayasi*, "*tu clarâ voce clamorem faciundo dominum cur non evigilas.*" When Lassen (l. c. p. 105) studiedly calls the gerund under discussion "indeclinable," I have nothing to say against it, inasmuch as one may term any case, *as such*, indeclinable, and so much the more those which are only the remains of the originally perfect declension of a certain class of words. When, however, the said learned person refuses to see what can have induced me to blame those who have preceded me for calling the gerund indeclinable, I must be allowed to remark, that my censure chiefly consists in this, that my predecessors have called this "gerund," not "a gerund," but "a participle." One might very well be content with an indeclinable gerund, though perhaps no one would see the necessity of making especial mention of the incapability of further declension in a form which had been admitted to be a gerund. As, however, in the form in *tvâ* a participle was recognised, by which one had reason to expect a capacity for declension (cf. W. v. Humboldt, l. c. II. 134.), Wilkins expressly called this putative participle "indeclinable," and Carey "adverbial:" on the other hand, Lassen, in that he acknowledged the gerundial nature of the form under discussion, supported the one moiety of my assertion, and, in the same manner as myself, blamed the clothing the formations in *tvâ* and *ya* with the name of indeclinable or adverbial "participles."

FORMATION OF WORDS.

Such passages, too, require especial notice where one and the same verb simultaneously govern the accusative of the infinitive and that of a person, in exact agreement with the construction of the Latin and Greek accusative with the infinitive, and with similar constructions in German; as, "*Ich sah ihn fallen*" "I saw him fall" (cf. Conjugation-system, pp. 75, 107, and Hofer's Infinitive, p. 122). Thus, Sâvitrî, V. 100. (Diluvium, p. 39), *yadi mâñ jîvitun ichchhasi,* "*si me vivere cupis;*" Râm. ed. Schl. II. 12. 106., *na jîvitun tvâṅ vishahê,* "*non vivere te sustineo;*" Vṛihatkathâ, p. 314, sl. 172, *kam api râjânaṅ snâtun tatra dadarśa,* "he saw a certain king bathe there." In verbs of motion the infinitive expresses at the same time the place to which the motion is directed. As one, however, moves toward an action in order to execute it, the accusative termination of the infinitive here enters upon the province of the dative, which latter case, in Sanscrit, most usually expresses the causal relation, while the proper dative relation is for the most part expressed by the genitive, which in Prâkrit and Páli has indeed quite supplanted the dative. Thus, *e.g.* Hidimba I. 34., *âgatô hantum imân sarvân,* "arisen in order to destroy all these;" Râm. ed. Schl. I. 20. 2., *abhyayâd draṣhṭum*
[G. Ed. p. 1210.] *ayôdhyâyân narâdhipam,* "he came to see the prince of men in Ayôdhyâ;" II. 97. 18., *âvâṅ hantum abhyêti bharataḥ,* "Bharat draws near to slay us both." Hence the language may have arrived at expressing, through the accusative of the infinitive, the causal relation also, in places where it is not the object of any verb of motion, or where the direction of the motion is immediately towards a distinctly-expressed place, and the infinitive only expresses the reason of the motion; thus, *e.g.* Mah. I. 2876., *muniṅ virajasan draṣhṭun gamishyâmi tapôvanam,* "to see the immaculate hermit I will go into the wood of penitence;" Hitôp. (Bonn. Ed.) p. 47. 17., *pânîyam pâtum yamunâkachchham agamat,* "He went to the shore of the

Yamunâ to drink water." Without a verb of motion, Draup. 4. 20., *alan tê pânḍuputrânâm bhaktyâ klêśam upâsitum*, "Away with thy love to the sons of Pâṇḍu, in order to bear distress;" Indralôka, I. 15. 16., *âruhasva rathôttamam . . . . sudurlabham samârôdhum*, "ascend the best of chariots, which to ascend (on account of the ascending) is hardly to be attained." I now, too, regard the infinitive as expressing the dative relation where it is by the side of words which express a time, or by other substantives, and at the same time it appears to represent the genitive or the Latin gerund in *di;* as, *e.g.* Nalas, 20. 16., *nâ yan kâlô vilambitum*, "this is not the time to hesitate" ("to the hesitating, for the hesitating"); thus Urvaśî (Lenz, p. 10., Bollensen, p. 12), "this is not the time to see Śatakratus (*drashṭum*); Draupadî III. 7., "The time has approached for these most excellent heroes to come here" ("to the, or for the, approach"); Hitôp. ed. Bonn. p. 59, line 6, *sthâtum ichchhâ*, "the wish to stay" (not "of staying"); Râm. ed. Schl. II. 9. 7., *śrôtuñ chhandaḥ*, "the wish to hear;" Mah. 1. 422., [G. Ed. p. 1211.] *pâṇḍavân hantum mantraḥ*, "the plan to slay the Pâṇḍavas" (for the slaying, on account of the slaying, not, " of the slaying"); Hitôp. ed. Bonn. p. 119. Sl. 40, *yôddhuṅ śaktiḥ*, "the power to fight;" Arjun's return, 9. 6. (Diluvium, p. 111), *antaram . . . padâd vichalitum padam*, "room to move foot from foot." Observe that the ordinary accusative also occasionally expresses the relation of the cause or of the object; as, Bhagavad Gîtâ, XVI. 3. 4. 5., *sampadan dâivîm abhijâtô 'si*, "to a god-like destiny art thou born." Conversely we sometimes find the dative of common abstracts in constructions where the infinitive was to be expected in its genuine accusative function. I have already, in a Note to "Arjuna's journey to Indra's heaven" (p. 79), drawn attention to such a use in *upa-kram*, "to begin, to commence." We read, viz. Hiḍimba, I. 22., *gamanâyô 'pachakramê* "he began to go" ("to the going," or "on account of the going," instead of "the going;" so Râm. ed. Schl. I. 29. 26.).* Still more important is another passage of this kind (Mahâ-Bhâr. III. 12297.), where the dative dependent on *upa-kram* governs the accusative exactly after the manner of an infinitive, *astrâṇi* . . . . *darśanâyô 'pachakramê*, "he began to survey the arms." Similarly we find *abhirôchay* (causal of अभिरुच् *abhiruch*), " to be pleased, to will, to wish," with the dative of abstract substantives instead of the infinitive standing in the accusative relation ; *e.g.* Râm. ed. Schl. I. 36. 2., *gamanâyâ 'bhirôchaya*, " be [G. Ed. p. 1212.] pleased to go" (to the going, instead of, "the going," *actionem eundi*). So also *utsah*, "to be able," in which again the remarkable circumstance occurs, that, in the example before me the dative governed by the said verb, viz. *paribhôgâya*, "to enjoy" ("to the enjoying"), like the ordinary infinitive *paribhôktum*, governs an accusative, Mah. III. 16543., "Thee, O Maithilî, I cannot enjoy" (*tvâm* . . . . *nô 'tsahê paribhôgâya*). So we sometimes find the dative expressing the place towards which a motion is made, for which purpose the accusative is altogether and specially employed ; *e.g.* Mah. II. 2613., *vanâya pravavrajuḥ*, "they went forth to the wood;" III. 10076., *âśramâya gachchhâva*, "we go (both of us) to the hermitage." On the other hand, we find precisely in its place the dative of abstract substantives as representative of the infinitive in the causal relation ; *e.g.* in a passage ("Arjuna's Journey to Indra's heaven," p. 74) of the 12th part of the Mah., already elsewhere quoted, "in order to dwell (*vâsâya*) twelve years in the wood (went he);" Draup. 8. 20., "Suratha sent to slay Nakula (*vadhâya nakulasya*), the most excellent of the elephants;" Schol. to Pâṇini, II. 3. 15.,

---

* We find, however, also the infinitive in construction with *upakram*; *e.g.* Indralôka, I. 21., *tam âpraṣhṭum upachakramê*, "he began to take leave of him."

FORMATION OF WORDS. 1175

pákáya vrajati, "he goes to cook" (in order to cook)·
Urvaśî (Lenz, p. 4., Boll. p. 5.), *yatishyê vah' sakhípratyána-
yáya*, "I will strive to bring back your friend." It deserves notice, that the abstract substantives, which in
classical Sanscrit intrude upon the functions of the infinitive, are all, except the proper infinitive in *tu-m*, formed
by the suffixes *ana* or *a*, to which I particularly draw attention for this reason, that we afterwards meet with the
same suffixes slightly corrupted in the European languages
also.

852. We very often find the abstracts, [G. Ed. p. 1213.]
which are formed with *ana*, in order to express the causal
relation of the infinitive, in the locative, which, in Sanscrit
especially, very frequently stands for the dative. Such infinitive locatives, after the manner of ordinary substantives,
regularly govern the genitive; as, *e.g.* Sâvitrî, I. 33., *bhartur
anvêshanê tvara*, "hasten to seek a spouse" ("in the seeking
of a spouse," or "on account of the seeking"); Nal. 24. 29.,
upáyah .... *ánayanê tava*, "the means of bringing thee
hither" ("to the bringing hither of thee"); 17. 29., *nalasyá-
nayanê yata*, "strive to bring Nala here;" 34., *yatadhvan
nalam árjanê*, "strive ye to seek Nala" ("in the searching
of Nala");* Mah. 3. 14798., *na tv abhyanujñán lapsyámi
gamanê yatra pándaváh*, "I shall not, however, obtain per-
mission (thither) to go, where the Pândavas." As the
dative of abstract substantives is found representing the
accusative relation, so is also the locative of the form in
ana, and, indeed, in the example before me, it is governed by
śak, "to be able," with which in general usage we find the
infinitive in *tum*; but Râm. ed. Schl. I. 66. 19., *na śêkur
grahanê tasya dhanushah*, "they could not receive this bow"
("in the receiving this bow"), with which may be com-

---

* On the other hand, the same verb with the form in *tum*, Nal 15. 4.,
sarvan yatishyê tat kartum, "all this will I strive to do."

pared the above-mentioned (G. ed. p. 1212.) *nô 'tsahê paribhôgâya*. As in the passage mentioned this *paribhôga* governs an accusative, so also is the form in *anê* occasionally found with an accusative; but hitherto I know of no parallel example to place by the side of that already quoted elsewhere ("Arjuna's Journey," &c., p. 80). It [G. Ed. p. 1214.] occurs Nalus 7. 10., *tam* .... *suhridân na tu kaśchana nivâraṇê 'bhavach chhaktô dívyamânam*, "but none of his friends was capable of restraining him (in the restraining) playing." It is more rare to find the locative of a substantive formed by the suffix *a* as representative of the infinitive. One example occurs, Râghuvanśa, 16. 75., where, however, it is uncertain whether *tadvichayê* be to be taken as a compound, or whether *tad* be an accusative neuter, governed by *vichayê*, "to seek." I annex the whole passage: *samajñâpayad âśu sarvân ânâyinas tadvichayê* (or *tad vichayê*) "he commanded therewith all fishermen to seek* that (bracelet," *valaya* masc. neut.). It may be considered as a point in favour of the view which regards *tad* as the accusative governed by *vichayê* that both the dative and accusative of abstracts formed by the suffix *a* occur as substitutes for the infinitive in construction with the accusative. As regards the dative, I recall attention to *tvâm paribhôgâya*, "to enjoy thee," in the passage quoted above (p. 1212 G. ed.). An instance of the accusative of this class of words governing the accusative as substitute for the infinitive is afforded us in the Kriyâyôgasâra, of which we have to expect an edition from Wollheim: *chakrê vivâhan tân kanyâm*, i. e. lit., "he made to marry that

---

* The commentary takes *tadvichayê* as compound, and explains *tad* by *tasyâ "bharaṇasya*. I, however, do not doubt that *tad*, whether it be taken as the first member of a compound in the genitive relation, or as an accusative governed by *vichayê*, certainly refers to *valaya*, "bracelet," and not to *âbharaṇa*, "ornament," which, in the preceding Ślôka, stands at the end of a Bahuvrîhi (*tulyapushpâbharaṇaḥ*).

maiden." Here we must return to the feminine form of the suffix *a*, viz. *â*, isolated accusatives of which are employed in Zend for the infinitive, where it expresses the accusative relation (see §. 619.). I now [G. Ed. p. 1215.] prefer to translate the *varayâm prachakramuh*, mentioned at §. 619. p. 842, and which remains, as yet, a solitary example, by "they made to gain," than by "they made gaining."* To this form in *âm* may also be referred the Marātha infinitives in *ûṅ*, e.g. करूं *kŏrûṅ*, "to make, to do," so that *û* would be to be taken as a corruption of an original *â*, as in the first persons; as, इच्छूं *ichchhûṅ*, "I wish" (=Sanscrit *ichchhâmi*); करूं *kŏrûṅ*, "I make;" सकूं *sŏkûṅ*, "I can;" for which, in Sanscrit, we should expect, according to the 1st class, *karâmi, śakâmi*. It appears to me, however, more probable, that the said infinitives have lost a *t*, just as in *bhâû*, "brother," for *bhrâtâ*. If this view be just, still the Marātha infinitive cannot therefore be compared with the Sanscrit in *tum*, because there is no reason apparent why the *u* should have been lengthened; but I would rather explain कं *ûṅ*, from तूं *tûṅ*, for *tvam*, in the same way as *tvam*, "thou," in Marāthī has become तूं *tûṅ*. In the Marātha infinitive, therefore, the suffix त्व *tva* would be contained, which in classical Sanscrit forms denominative abstracts (see §. 834.), and in the Vêdic dialect also verbal abstracts (see §. 835.). From this suffix I should prefer also to deduce the Marātha gerund in अन् *ûn*; thus, e.g. करून् *kŏrûn*, "after the making" ("having made"), from the instrumental *kŏrtvâna*,† with the suppression of the final *a*, which is left in the Prâkrit gerunds as

---

* If *prakram* be not confirmed in the meaning "to make," we must translate "they began to obtain," which does not prejudice the infinitive nature of the form in *âm*.

† Cf. देवानो *dêvânŏ*, or देवाने *dêvânê*, "by the God"=Sanscrit *dêvê-n-a*.

1178   FORMATION OF WORDS.

[G. Ed. p. 1216.] *pâúṇa, ghêúṇa, lahiúṇa, vilôhiúṇa, ágantúṇa, ghêttúṇa.** The Prâkrit, however, is not wanting also in

---

* The *t* of the gerundial suffix appears to be preserved principally, if not solely, under the protection of a preceding consonant. The first *t* of *ghêttúṇa* (Sanscrit root *grah*) evidently rests on assimilation, be it that the *n* or the *h* of *ghêṇh* (inf. *ghéṇhiduṅ* and *ghêttuṅ*) has assimilated itself to the *t* following. In *hattúṇa*, from *han*, the first *t* stands decidedly for *n*. Lassen also (Inst. p. 367) compares these Prâkrit gerunds with those in Marāṭhī, but traces them both back to the above-mentioned (G. ed. p. 1207), but as yet unciteable, gerund in *tvânam*. Against this explanation, even if the gerund in *tvânam* were better established than it is, as accusative, the objection would present itself, that the Prâkrit has nowhere else allowed the accusative sign *m* to be lost, but has everywhere retained it in the form of an anusvâra. Lassen (l. c. p. 289) also deduces the Prâkrit nominal abstracts in *ttaṇa* (by assimilation from *tvaṇa*) from the already-mentioned *tvan*; but since then, in the edited Vêda text an actual secondary (*taddhita-*) suffix *tvana* has been found, which, as such, as also by its form, has a much stronger claim to be regarded as the origin of the Prâkrit *ttaṇa*. The following are examples: *mahitvaná-m*, "greatness" (from the Vêdic *mahi*, "great"); *sakhitvaná-m*, "friendship;" *martyatvaná-m*, "mortality or humanity"(?). I cannot, however, see the reason why Benfey (Glossary to the Sâma-Vêda, s. v. *mahitvá*) calls the suffix *tvana* more organic than *tva*: for the broader form might as well be an extension of the shorter, as conversely the shorter be an abbreviation of the broader. They both appear to be of primitive antiquity. The former we have already recognised in Gothic and Sclavonic (see §§. 834. 835.); on the latter is based very probably the Greek σύνη; *e.g.* in δουλοσύνη, δικαιοσύνη, σωφροσύνη, which has passed into the feminine. With regard to the syllable συ, for the Sanscrit *tva*, compare the relation of σύ to *tva-m*, "thou" (§. 326.) In Marāṭhī we meet with the Vêdic suffix *tvana* in the rather obscured form of *pŏnŏ* in abstract neuters; as, *bâlŏpŏnŏ*, "childhood" (see Vans Kennedy, "Dictionary," II. p. 16), with *p* for *tv* (cf. §. 341.; Schluss and Hoefer, "de Prâcrita dialecto," p. 165). Carey (Gramm., p. 32) writes पण *pŏn* for पण *pŏnŏ*, and suppresses also, in his dictionary, very frequently the final vowel of Sanscrit neuter bases in *a*: he writes, *e.g.*, पाप् *pâp*, "sin," दशन् *dŏsŏn*, "tooth," पायस् *pâyŏs*, "milk," चंदन् *chŏndŏn*, "sandal-wood," वाहन् *vahŏn*, "vehiculum," for पाप *pâpŏ*, &c.

gerunds, which are based on the Sanscrit [G. Ed. p. 1217.] in *tvâ;* as, *e.g. gadua* = Sanscrit *gatvâ*, with the final vowel shortened. The Marāthī also uses, to express the infinitive, abstract substantives in *ŏnŏ*, and, indeed, especially to express the nominative relation, in which the form in ऊं *ûṅ* is scarcely to be found. Thus, in Carey (Grammar, p. 76), *molâ kŏrŏnŏ pŏdŏtŏ,* " to me to do (the doing) (is) beseeming :" on the other hand, p. 78, *mîṅ kŏrûṅ sŏkûṅ,* " I can do ;" p. 80, *mîṅ kŏrûṅ ichchhûṅ,* " I wish to do." We may here, on account of the frequent and pervading interchange of *r* and *l,* recall remembrance *en passant* to the remarkable similarity between the Marātha dative-accusative termination *lâ* and the modern Persian *râ.* Compare, for example, the just-mentioned *mŏlâ,* " to me, me," with the Persian *merâ;* and *tulâ,* " to thee, thee," with *turâ; âmhâlâ* (from *ŏsmâlâ,* see §. 166.), ἡμῖν, ἡμᾶς, with *mârâ; tumhâlâ,* ὑμῖν, ὑμᾶς, with *shumârâ.*

853. At the beginning of compounds, the infinitive in *tum,* according to the universal principle of the formation of compound words, loses its case-sign, and then arises the bare theme in *tu ; e.g.,* Nal. IX. 31., *nachâ 'han tyaktukâmas tvâm,* "nor also am I of the will to leave thee" ("having a quitting-wish"); where it is to be remarked, that in Sanscrit the first member of a compound may be treated, in respect to syntax, as an independent member of the sentence, wherefore *tyaktu* here governs the accusative (*tvâm*) just as much as if *tyaktum* stood there alone.

854. The Vêda dialect generally employs the dative to express the causal relation of the dative ; and, indeed, either that above mentioned (§. 851.) in *tavê* or [G. Ed. p. 1218.] *tavâi,** from the proper infinitive base in *tu,* or the dative

---

* The form in *tavâi* is the more rare: it accents, beside the radical syllable, also the case-termination ; *e.g. yámitavái,* " in order to bridle" (Rigv. I. 28. 4.); *kártavái,* " in order to make" (Naigh. II. 1.). In combination

FORMATION OF WORDS.

of abstract radical words, or of an abstract feminine base terminating in *dhi* or *dhî*, of which only the dative in *dhyâi* has been retained; so that this form has gained a still more genuine infinitive appearance through the lack of other cases from the same base. The termination *dhyâi* is always preceded by *a* or *aya*, by, therefore, the theme of the special tenses of the 1st or 6th class, with *a* as class-vowel; or by that of the 10th class, or causal form, with the character *aya*. Compare, *e.g.*, *píb-a-dhyâi* (strictly *piba-dhyâi*, cf. §. 508.), "in order to drink" (Rigv. I. 88. 4.), with *píbati*, "he drinks;" *kshár-a-dhyâi*, "in order to flow" (l. c. 63. 8.), with *kshár-a-ti*; *sáh-a-dhyâi*, "in order to conquer" (S. V. ed. Benf., p. 154), with *sáh-a-ti*; *vand-á-dhyâi*, "in order to praise," with the accusative, Rigv. I. 61. 5.; *víram . . . . vandádhyâi*, "in order to praise the hero," with *vánd-a-tê*; *char-á-dhyâi*, "in order to drink" (l. c. 61. 72.), with *chár-a-ti*; *mâd-ayá-dhyâi*, "in order to gladden or rejoice," with *mâdáyati* (causal of the root *mad*, "to rejoice," Yajurv. 3. 13.); *iśayadhyâi*, "in order to enjoy, to the enjoyment" (Rosen, "Rig-Vêdæ Specimen," p. 8), with *iś-ayati*.*

[G. Ed. p. 1219.] The *iśadhyâi*, "in order to stride through," cited by Westergaard (Radices, p. 278), belongs probably to the Vêdic *iś*, cl. 6., and answers, therefore, to *iś-á-ti*, "he goes" (Naigh. II. 14.). Among the infinitives in *dhyâi*, the

---

combination with prepositions the first accent, and in other forms from the infinitive base in *tu* the only one falls on the preposition; *e.g. ánvêtavâi*, "in order to follow" (from *ánu* and *êtavâi*, Rigv. I. 24. 8.); *prátidhâtavê*, "in order to place, to support" (from *práti*, "against," and *dhâtavê*, l. c.).

* A denominative from *iś*, "wish, food;" hence it signifies also "to wish" (so Rigv. I. 77. 4.). I have already, in the "Journal for Lit. Crit." (Dec. 1830, p. 949), explained the form *iśayadyâi*, which Sâyana regards as an instrumental plural, and explains by *êshanîyâih*, as Rosen does by "*exoptatas*," as an infinitive, but I then found a difficulty in the *i*, in that I presupposed a verb of the 10th class, which would lead us to expect *êshayadhyâi*. Cf. Lassen, Anthol., p. 133.

FORMATION OF WORDS. 1181

form *vâvṛidh-á-dhyâi,* " in order to make grow" (Rigv. I. 61. 3.), stands hitherto quite isolated, and may be regarded as a first attempt to form infinitives out of the themes of other tenses than the present, or also as a remnant of a lingual period, where, perhaps, from all or most of the tenses of the indicative, infinitives in *dhyâi* might have been formed. Westergaard (Radices, p. 189) takes the said form as the infinitive of the perfect, with which, in form too, it admirably corresponds, as the root *vardh* (*vṛidh*), " to grow," also " to make to grow, to augment, to extend," in the Vêda dialect, everywhere exhibits *vâ* for *va* in the syllable of reduplication. The fact of *vâvṛidh-á-dhyâi* belonging, according to its meaning, which Sâyana explains by the causal infinitive *vardhayitum,* to the present, cannot be impugned by its derivation from the perfect base, as in the Vêdas the participles also of the reduplicated preterite very often appear with a present signification; *e.g.* Rigv. I. 89. 8., *tushṭuvânsas,* "*laudantes.*" The *a* inserted in *vâvṛidh-á-dhyâi* is evidently the conjunctive-vowel *a,* which belongs to the perfect, and which, in several places of the indicative, has been weakened to *i* (see §. 614.); compare also, with regard to the accentuation, the dual forms *vâvṛidh-á-thus, vâvṛidh-á-tus.* Just, however, as this *a* of the indicative is referred by the Indian Grammarians to the personal terminations, so Pânini (III. 4. 9.) regards the *a* of the forms in *a-dhyâi* as really a mem- [G. Ed. p. 1220.] ber of the formative suffix.* It may be left to further ex-

---

* Pânini gives, l. c., the suffix spoken of in six different forms, viz. *adhyâi, adhyâin, kadhyâi, kadhyâin, śadhyâi, śadhyâin.* The final *n* negatives the accentuation of the suffix (cf. p. 1202, G. ed.), and the initial *ś* points out that the root appears in the form of the special tenses; hence, *e.g.* the above-mentioned *píbadhyâi,* according to Sâyana (ed. Müller, p. 712), contains the suffix *śadhyâin;* while *mádayádhyâi,* since it has the accent on the *a,* which is reckoned to belong to the suffix, according to Mahîdhara contains the suffix *śadhyâi.* Compare the suffix *śa,* i.e. *a*
according

amination of the usances of the Vêdic dialect to decide whether we have not to assume also aorists of the infinitive in *dhyái*, but with present signification, as in the potential (see §. 705.). It is certain that when, as by Benfey (Glossary, p. 216), the potential forms like *huvéma, huvémahi, huvéya*, and the participles *huvát, huvâná* (from the form *hu*, which is a contraction of *hvé*, "to call"), are ascribed to the aorist, we may with equal justice regard the infinitive *á-huvádhyâi*, "to invoke" (Yajurv. 3. 13.), as the aorist. For the present I prefer, however, to assume that the form *hu*, which is contracted from *hvé*, is, in the Vêda dialect, inflected according to three different classes, and refer the said potential forms to the 6th class, the participles *huvát, huvâná*, and the plural middle *húmáhê* (the latter with irregular lengthening of the *u*), to the 2d, [G. Ed. p. 1221.] and forms like *hávatê*,* "he calls," to the

---

according to Wilson ("Introduction to the Grammar of the Sanscrit Language," 2d Ed., p. 327), by which adjectives like *pibá*, "drinking;" *paśyá*, "seeing;" *párayá*, "filling." By *k* is pointed out the pure, devoid of Guna or weakened form of the verbal theme; and hence, *e.g.*, to the form *áhuvádhyai*, "to invoke" (Yajurv. 3. 13.), from the form *hu*, which is contracted from *hvé*, is the suffix *kadhyâi* assigned. *Adhyâi*, or, without accent, *adhyâin*, is the suffix when it is appended to the form of the root strengthened or incapable of the Guna-increment; *e.g.* in *kshâradhyái* (Rigv. I. 63. 8.), "in order to flow," from the root *kshar*, Cl. 1.

* I believe I may venture to trace back to *hu*, Cl. 1., the Zend *du*, "to speak," which as yet has not been satisfactorily compared with the Sanscrit (see Burnouf, Études, p. 309); while another *du*, which signifies "to run," evinces unmistakeably its affinity with the Sanscrit roots of motion: *dhu, dhû*, and *dhâv* (the latter likewise "to run"). I look upon the transition of ह *h* to द *d* in this light, viz. that the former has first become य *j*, and thence *d*, since of the *dṣh* sound only the first element remains. In the former respect, compare the relation of جن *jan*, "to slay," to the Sanscrit हन् *han*; in the latter, that of the Old Persian *adam*, "I," to अहम् *ahám*; and of the New Persian *dest*, "hand," to हस्त *hásta*; *dânem*, "I know," to जानामि *jânâmi*.

1st. The 1st person singular *huvê*, which occurs at the end of the Śloka quoted, might as well be referred to the 2d as to the 6th class, and just so the active participle *huvát*: I prefer, however, to assign the latter to the 2d rather than to the 6th class, because, as participle of the 2d class, it answers to the middle participle *huvâná*. Then *á-huvádhyái, gámadhyái,* " to go" (Yajurv. VI. 3.), would have greater claim to be regarded as the infinitive of the aorist (*ágamam*), as *gam* in the special tenses substitutes *gachh;* if, however, the hitherto uncitable form *gámati,* which Yâska (Naigh. II. 14.) assigns to the Vêda dialect, be established, then *gámadhyái,* too, may hold good as the infinitive of the present. It would be a convincing proof of the existence of an infinitive of the aorist could we anywhere point out the form *vôchadhyai* (cf. §. 705.).

855. As infinitives of the third formation of the aorist (not, however, of the form in *dhyái*) may be regarded the forms, mentioned by Pâṇini (III. 4. 10.), *rôhishyái* and *avyathishyái* (the latter with *a* privative). The root *ruh*, "to grow," would, according to the third formation of the aorist, form *árôhisham;* and from *vyath*, middle, "to tremble," is really to be found the aorist *ávyathishi*. After deducting the augment and the personal termination, there [G. Ed. p. 1222.] remain *rôhish, vyathish,* as temporal bases; whence, through the feminine form *î* of the suffix *a*, might easily arise as abstracts *rôhishî, vyathishî,* the datives of which must be *rôhishyái, vyathishyái*. These datives might also be derived from feminine bases in short *i*, which, therefore, would be appended to the aorist theme *rôhish, vyathish,* in the same way as, *e.g.* that of *ránhi,* "quickness," to the primitive root *ranh.* In this case, instead of *ái* we might expect also *ay-ê* in the dative. But if the said infinitives really belong to the third formation of the aorist, then those in *sê,* with the general dative termination *ê,* may be referred to the 2d (Greek 1st) (see §. 555.); where we should have to

assume that the conjunctive vowel, which enters between the appended verb substantive and the personal termination, does not extend itself to infinitives like *vakshê*, "to drive," *jishê*, "to conquer." The first example occurs in the Schol. to Pân., III. 4. 9., the latter Rigv. I. 112. 12., *anaśván yábhí rátham ávatam jiśé*, "by which ye help the courserless chariot to conquer" ("on account of conquering"). Sâyana calls the termination of this infinitive form *ksê*,* because the radical vowel has no Guna. The gunised infinitives in *sê* (euphon. *shê*, on account of the preceding *i, ê, k*), like the l. c. adduced *mêshê*, "to cast, to cast down" (root *mi*), answer better to the 1st aorist formation, viz. to the middle of roots ending in a vowel, which reduce the Vriddhi augment of their active, on account of the too great weight of the middle terminations, to that of Guna; while the roots ending in a consonant renounce all increase to the vowel in the middle. We might therefore refer all [G. Ed. p. 1223.] infinitives in *sê*, whether with Guna or not, to the 1st aorist formation. But whether the infinitives in *sê* are to be considered as formed from the 1st or 2d aorist, their agreement is remarkable with that of the 1st aorist in Greek; as, λῦ-σαι, τύπ-σαι, δεῖκ-σαι; for which, in Sanscrit, if *lû*, "to cut off," *tup*, "to smite, to wound," *diś* (from *dik*), "to shew," had formed an infinitive of this kind, we should have expected *lû-shê*, *tup-shê*, *dik-shê*: to θῦσαι would correspond *bhû-shê*; where we may recall attention to the fact, that the Vêda dialect has in the imperative also retained aorists of this kind; and, indeed, from the root *bhû*, the forms *bhû-sha* = φῦσον, *bhû-shatam* (*upa-bhûshatam*) = φύσατον, without our being able to trace the analogous indicative form.

---

* The grammatical technical language decides, with respect to the accent and the stronger or weaker form of the root, according to Pân. l. c. *sé*, *sen*, and *ksé*.

856. The Vêdic infinitives in *sê*, and their analogous Greek forms in σαι, conduct us to the Latin in *re*, which, in the "Annals of Oriental Literature," p. 58, I have already endeavoured to compare with the Greek infinitives of the 1st aorist. It is certain that in the Latin infinitives in *re* (from *se*), just as in the Greek 1st aorist, and the four first formations of the Sanscrit aorist, the verb substantive is contained. This is clearly seen in *pos-se* (for *pot-se*), as *possum*, throughout its conjugation, exhibits the combination of *pot* (by assimilation *pos*) with the verb substantive (regarding *pot-ui* from *pot-fui*, see §. 558.). *Es-se* for *ed-se* (with *ed-e-re*) most accurately corresponds with the said Sanscrit infinitives; and if, in the Vêdas, an infinitive of this kind should occur from the root *ad*, it must, in accordance with the well-known law of sound, be no other than *at-sê*. In *fer-re* from *fer-se*, and *vel-le* from *vel-se*, the sibilant of the auxiliary verb has become assimilated to the preceding consonant. For *fer-re* we should have expected in the Vêda dialect *bhri-shê*, or *bhar-shê*. To the Latin infinitives *da-re*, *stâ-re*, *î-re*, would, in Vêdic Sanscrit, [G. Ed. p. 1224.] correspond *dâ-sê*, *sthâ-sê*,* *i-shê* (according to the analogy of *ji-shê*),† or *ê-shê* (after the analogy of *mê-shê*). Observe, that only those Latin verbs which absolutely, or in some persons by the direct annexation of the personal terminations to the root, are based on the root of the Sanscrit 2d class (see §. 109ª. 3.), may or must also annex this suffix of the infinitive directly, while all others retain the class-vowel, and, indeed, in the third conjugation *e* (for *i*, from *a*), on account of the following *r* (see §. 707.); hence *veh-e-re* corresponds to the above-mentioned Sanscrit *vak-shê* (euphonic

---

* If not *sthi-shê*, with the *â* weakened to *i*, as in *sthi-tá* (p. 1118, Note *) and in *sthi-ti* (§. 844.).

† In the Schol. to Pân. l. c. we actually find *prêshê* as compounded of *pra-ishê*.

for *vah-sê*). Perhaps, also, we ought to look upon the *a* of the infinitives mentioned by Pâṇini (III. 4. 9.) in *asê* as the class-vowel;* and so the often-occurring *jīv-á-sê*,† "in order to live" (cf. *jīv-a-ti*, "he lives") would answer to the Latin *viv-e-re*. Another example of this kind is *riñjásê*, "in order to adorn," which, in a passage cited by Benfey (Glossary, p. 34) of the 5th book of the Rigv., runs parallel to the dative *stótavê* of the common infinitive: *vémi tvá púshann riñjásê vémi stótavê*, "I come, O Pûshhan, thee to glorify! I come (thee) to praise!" Thus, Rigv. I. 112. 8., *chákshasê* stands beside the dative of the common infini-
[G. Ed. p. 1225.] tive *étavê*: "by which deeds ye enable the blind (Rijrásvas) to see, the Śrónas to go."

857. We cannot overlook the possibility that the *a* of the Sanscrit infinitives in *asê* might also be the radical vowel of the verb substantive, though the latter is lost in compounds, and in many simple formations (see §. 480.). Then *-asê* would correspond to the Latin *esse*, inasmuch as *esse* is not to be divided into *es-se*; and here, therefore, the root of "to be" would occur twice, which we have admitted as possible above, in the subjunctive *essem*.‡ Be that, however, as it may, the forms in *asê* and *sê*, if they really contain the verb substantive, accord, as regards the principle of formation of the final infinitive expression, with the simple infinitives, which exhibit the dative of bare radical words; as, *driśé*, "in order to see." These always express a genuine dative relation; as, *e.g.*, Rigv. I. 23. 21., *súryan driśé*, "in order to see the sun;" 13. 7., *idán nó barhír ásádê*, "in order to repose on this our straw;"

---

* Cf. *e.g. pát-a-tra-m* (p. 1108. 2. 5.), *ára-ti-s*, "fear" (§. 847.).

† *E.g.* Rigv. I. 37. 15., where it governs the accusative: "We are to them (belonging or devoted to Maruts), in order to live the whole life (life's duration)" (*viśvañ chid áyur jīvásê*).

‡ See §. 708., and Curtius "Contributions," p. 352.

FORMATION OF WORDS. 1187

105.16., *atikrámê*, "to step beyond, to slight." The last-named passage deserves especial notice, since here the dative of the infinitive appears to hold the place of the nominative of a future passive participle, exactly in the same way as we use, for the same end, the infinitive with the preposition "*zu*," in such sentences as "*er ist zu loben*" (*laudandus est*), *i.e.* "he is fitted for praise." Moreover, in the said passage in the Sanscrit text the substantive verb is, in spirit, present, but, as is very common, not formally expressed. I annex Wilson's translation: "The sun, who is avowedly made the path in heaven, is not to be disregarded, Gods, (by you)."* Perhaps the Latin also was [G. Ed. p. 1226.] not wanting in infinitives which correspond to the Vêdic like *drishê, â-sâdê, ati-krâmê*: they would be to be looked for in the 3d conjugation, where, by the side of passive infinitives like *dici* (older form *dici-er*), must stand active forms like *dice*, in case the passive infinitive terminations *í, i-er,* are not abbreviations of *eri, erier*; for from *dicere* must have come *diceri, dicerier,* as *amari, amarier, moneri, monerier, audiri, audirier*, from *amare*, &c. As regards the origin of the Latin passive infinitives, the form in *i* is evi-

---

* *Asâú yâh pánthâ âdityô diví pravâchyaṅ kritáh* | *ná sá dêvâ atikrámê*. Pânini, in constructions of this kind, appears really to regard the infinitive datives in *ê*, with those in *taváí* (see §. 851. p. 1165), as Vêdic representatives of the future passive participles in *ya, tavya*, and *aníya* (called in the technical language of grammar *kritya*); for (III. 4. 14.) he puts them on the same footing with two real participial suffixes capable of declension, when he says that the suffixes *tavái, ê, ênya,* and *tva,* in the Vêdas, are used in the sense of *kritya*. In the following Sûtra *avachakshê* (root *chaksh*, prep. *ava*) is expressly represented as a participle of this kind; and in the Commentary he explains *nâ 'vachakshe* by *nâ 'vukhyâtavyam,* "*non narrandum.*" In the passage referred to above, Sâyana regards the form under discussion as a future passive participle, since he paraphrases *nâ 'tikrámê* by *nâ 'tikramituṅ śakyah*, and cites Pânini's Sûtra here quoted.

dently an abbreviation of the older *i-er* (*laudarier, viderier, credier*, see p. 662). The transition of the active *re* into *ri* before the appended *er* of the passive can scarcely arise in aught else than in the avoidance of the cacophony which would be occasioned by two successive *e* in forms like *laudareer*. We cannot be surprised that the *e* of the active infinitive termination is short, when, as the representative of the Sanscrit and Greek diphthong *sê*, σαι, it ought to be long, as vowels at the end of a word are, for the most part,

[G. Ed. p. 1227.] subject to abbreviation, or to entire suppression,* The length of the *î* of the passive infinitive may be regarded as a compensation for the *er* that has been dropped.†

---

* Observe, *e.g.*, the short final *e* in *benĕ, malĕ;* while in adverbs from adjectives of the 2d declension a long *ê* is found, in which I believe I recognise the Sanscrit diphthong *ê* ($=a+i$) of the locative of bases in *a* ($=$ Latin *u* of the 2d declension). Compare, *e.g.*, *novê* with the Sanscrit locative *navê*, from the base *nava*, "new." Observe, also, the occasional shortening of the *ê* of some imperatives of the 2d conjugation (*cave*, &c.), and the regular abbreviation of the *ê* of Old High German conjunctives at the word's end; as, *bĕre*, "he may carry"$=$Sanscrit *bhárêt*, Gothic *bairai* (§. 694. p. 922).

† I should not wish to have recourse to the rule which is set forth in the prosody of Latin grammars, that *i* at the end of a word, exclusive of certain well-known exceptions, is long, since in all cases in which, in Latin, the final *i* is long, there is a reason for it at hand; *e.g.* in the genitive singular and nominative plural of the 2d declension (see pp. 215, 244). I now refer the dative termination *î* rather to the real dative termination in Sanscrit *ê* ($=ai$), than to the locative termination *i;* as in the plural also the termination *bus* evidently answers to the Sanscrit dative ablative ending; while in Greek the dative singular and plural equally well admit of being compared with the Sanscrit locative (see §§. 195. 251.). The length of the *i* of *tibî* (*ibî, ubî*), *mihî*, contrasted with the Sanscrit datives *túbhyám, máhyam* (§. 215.), may be looked upon as compensation for dropping the personal termination *am:* without this loss, from *bhyam, hyam*, we should find in Latin *bium, hium*. In the 1st person singular of the perfect, the length of the *î* may be looked upon as compensation

858. It remains for us to mention the infinitive of the Latin perfect. Here we see, in such forms as *amavi-sse, monui-sse, legi-sse, audivi-sse,* the infinitive of the verb substantive, as plainly as, in the pluperfects like *amaveram,* we discover the imperfect, with the loss, there- [G. Ed. p. 1228.] fore, of the vowel of the auxiliary verb which I assume in *amave-ram* also (see §. 644.). But if the said perfect infinitives are, just as the pluperfects, evidently modern formations, still forms like *scrip-se, consum-se, admis-se, divis-se, dic-se, produc-se, abstrac-se, advec-se* (see Struve "On the Latin Declension and Conjugation" p. 178), which are of frequent occurrence in the older dialect, have every claim to be regarded as transmitted from an ancient period of language, and to be placed beside Greek aorist infinitives; and, indeed, with so much the more right, as all the Latin perfects are very probably, in their origin, nothing else than aorists (see §. 546.). We may, consequently, compare *scrip-se, dic-se,* with the Greek γράπ-σαι, δεῖκ-σαι, and *advec-se* with the Sanscrit *vak-shê* mentioned above (p. 1222 G. ed.). It is here important to remark, that, for all the perfect infinitives of the 3d conjugation quoted by Struve l. c., there are also analogous perfects (aorists) of the indicative as points of departure, just as there are for the Greek infinitives in σαι (ξαι, ψαι), indicatives in σα (ξα, ψα); only *invas-se, divis-se* (by assimilation from *invad-se, divid-se,* cf. §. 101.), are more perfectly preserved than *invâ-si, diví-si,* which have lost the final consonant of the root; in compensation for which, in *diví-si,* the

---

compensation for dropping the personal termination (see §. 552. Conclusion): in the 2d person the *î* of the termination *sti* represents, if the explanation given in §. 549. be correct, the long *â* of the Sanscrit ending *thâs*. In a similar way, the *î* of *uti* is based, as I now assume, in departure from §. 425., on the long *â* of Sanscrit pronominal adverbs in *thâ*; *e.g. utî* corresponds to the Vêdic *ká-thâ*, "how?" (Pâṇ. V. 3. 25.).

short radical vowel is lengthened. The future perfects* like *faxo, capso, axo, accepso*,† which in appearance are analogous to the infinitives in *se*, as also the perfect and pluperfect [G. Ed. p. 1229.] subjunctives, as *axim, ausim, objexim, excessis, dixis, induxis, traxis, sponsis, amissis, injexit, extinxit, ademsit, serpsit, incensit, faxem, extinxem, intellexes, recesset, vixet, traxet* (see **Struve**, l. c., p. 175), can hardly be put on the same footing with the infinitives in *se;* first, because the least of these have an indicative perfect in *si* (*sci* = *c-si*) corresponding to them; and secondly, because, even if this were the case, still, *e.g. capso, axim, extinxem,* could not, perhaps, have been derived from the to-be-presupposed *capsi, axi,* and the actually existing *extinxi,* by the termination of the future perfect and of the perfect and pluperfect subjunctive being substituted for the terminations of the perfect. The said three tenses and moods are comparatively modern formations, and are formed by combining the future and the present and imperfect subjunctive of the verb substantive with the perfect base‡ of the attributive verb; and the affinity of their concluding portion with the *si* of perfects like *serp-si* consists, consequently, not only in this, that in the latter also the verb substantive is contained, but in primeval relationship, which extends beyond the time of the separation of languages, if I am right in identifying such perfects with the Sanscrit 2d and Greek 1st aorist formations (see §. 551.). We gain, therefore, nothing towards the explanation of the forms under dis-

---

* In departure from what has been remarked at §. 664., I now regard *faxo*, and similar forms, as real future perfects.

† The *e* for *i* in *accepso*, and similar forms, is based on the principle laid down in §. 6.; whence *accepso, abjexim*, like *acceptus, abjectus*, for *acciptus, abjictus.*

‡ *Amave-ro* from *amavi-ero,* cf. §. 644.; *amave-rim* from *amavi-sim*, according to §. 710.; *amavi-ssem* from *amavi-essem.*

FORMATION OF WORDS. 1191

cussion, unless we presuppose non-existing perfects like *axi, faxi, sponsi;* for we must then first put aside the auxiliary verb of the perfect indicative, in order to replace it with the auxiliary of the new formation here spoken of (*so, sim, sem*); or we cannot explain, *e. g., faxo,* from the to-be-presupposed *faxi,* by means of the hence theoretically-to-be-formed *faxero,* by presupposing an [G. Ed. p. 1230.] overspringing of the letters *er.* Why is it, however, that we do not occasionally find, together with the really existing future perfects, contractions of this kind? Why do we not, for instance, find, together with *fēcero* a *fēco;* with *cēpero, cēpo;* with *tetigero* a *tetigo?* Or must, *e. g., fac-so* have been formed from a to-be-presupposed *facero,* in such wise that the *r* formed from *s* has again returned to its original state, and been joined directly to the final consonant of the root after the *e* has been rejected? Or was *faxo* formed from *faceso* at a time when *s* between two vowels did not regularly become *r* (see §. 22.)? I should now prefer deriving the obsolete future perfects, and the perfect and pluperfect conjunctives in *sim, sem,* connected with these, from a lost stock of real perfects, since the existing preterites called perfects, of all gradations, are originally aorists. There might, *e. g.,* have existed, together with the aorists *fēci, cēpi* (see §. 548.), *dic-si, duc-si, spopondi,* (see §. 579.) perfects like *fefaca* (or *pefaca*), *cecapa,*[*] *didica, duduca, spoponda,* which we might well assign to the Latin in an earlier period of the language, at the time of its close connection with the Greek. It may remain undecided whether the Latin afterwards dropped the syllable of reduplication

---

[*] The existing law, according to which the heaviest vowel *a* is, in consequence of the incumbrance of the reduplication, weakened to *i* (see §§. 6. 579.), must have had its beginning, and may not, perhaps, have obtained, in a time to which we are here endeavouring to look back. Observe that the Oscan *fefacust* is, in sense, = *fecerit.*

[G. Ed. p. 1231.] at once in the perfect indicative,* as it laid aside the augment in the imperfect and aorist: or whether this renunciation first took place when the verb was encumbered with the addition of the auxiliary verb substantive, just as the reduplicated aorists (perfects) in composition with prepositions for the most part dispense with the syllable of reduplication,† while the analogous Sanscrit reduplicated aorists (as *ádudruvam*) throughout retain it in composition also. Be that, however, as it may, at some time or other reduplicated future perfects, too, will have existed; thus, *e.g. fefaxo* (or *pefaxo*), *cecapso*, which, in essentials, would correspond to the Greek future perfects, as, λελύ-σομαι, τετύπ-σο-μαι, to which will have originally corresponded also active future perfects, as, λελύ-σω, τετύπ-σω, whose offshoots they properly are. Should this not be the case, we have nothing left but to abide by the opinion expressed above (§. 664.), and still earlier in my "Conjugation-System" (p. 98.), viz. that, as is also assumed by Madvig,‡ the future perfects under discussion are formally, as also partly as regards their meaning, primary futures. In fact, *axo* is as like the Greek ἄξω as one egg to another. Madvig fitly compares forms like *levasso* with those in Greek like γελάσω. The doubling of the *s* would consequently be purely phonetic, without etymological meaning, as, *e.g.* in the Greek ἐγέλασσα, mentioned by Madvig, and like ἐτέλεσσα, mentioned with a similar object above (§. 708.).

---

* Then, perhaps, *faca, capa, sponda*, would have the same relation to *fefaca*, or *pefaca*, &c., as, in Gothic, *e.g. band* to the Sanscrit *babandha* (see §. 589.); and those preterites which have still retained the reduplication in Gothic, as, *e.g. gaigrôt*, "I, he wept"=Sanscrit *chakránda*.

† It is probably to the weak form of the roots, and their terminating in a vowel, that *do* and *sto* owe the pervading retention of the reduplication in composition.

‡ "De formarum quarundam verbi Latini naturâ et usu" (Solemnia academica etc., Hauniae, 1835, p. 6.

Moreover, if *levasso* be regarded as an abbreviation of *lelevasso*, and as an actual future, it cor- [G. Ed. p. 1232.] responds, in respect to its denoting the future relation to γελάσω, just as, exclusive of the passive personal termination, to the Greek future perfect like τετιμήσομαι. This opinion is especially favoured by the old infinitives in *ssere* (Struve, p. 180) with the signification of the primary future, *impetrassere, reconciliassere, expugnassere, averuncassere, depeculassere, deargentassere*. They correspond, irrespective of the infinitive suffix, which throughout, in Latin, is that of the aorist, and of the doubling of the *s*, which cannot surprise us, to the Greek future infinitives like γελάσειν. We might reasonably expect that such infinitives not only originally existed in the 1st conjugation, but that there were such forms also as *habessere, axere* (= ἄξειν), *faxere, capsere*. It may be proper here to consider also the future perfects of the Oscan and Umbrian languages, as both these dialects, in several other grammatical points, present us with older forms than the Latin. It is important here to notice, that the Umbrian, in most of the future perfects which have remained to our time, exhibits the combination of the future perfect of the verb substantive with the present base, or the simple root of the principal verb, but in such wise, that, after consonants, and also, in one instance given by Aufrecht and Kirchhof (Umbr. Language, p. 146), after a vowel (*i-ust iverit*), the *f* of the root *fu* is rejected; hence, *e.g. fak-ust*, signifying "he is making to have been," while the Latin *fecerit* means, "he is having made to be." Other examples are, *covort-ust*, "*converterit*," *ampr-e-fus*, "*ambiverit*" (cf. *fus*, also *fust*, "*fuerit*"), *ambr-e-furent*, "*ambiverint*" (cf. *furent*, "*fuerint*"), *fak-urent*, "*fecerint*." The Oscan follows the same principle, only it is wanting as to the perfect retention of *fu;* but also in the simple *u*, *e.g.* in *dikust*, "*dixerit*," *pruhibust*, "*prohi-* [G. Ed. p. 1233.] *buerit*," *fefakust*, "*fecerit*" Mommsen ("Oscan Studies," p. 62) has recognised the root *fu* before the light was thrown upon it by the Umbrian. As the root *fu* in the conjugation of the verb substantive regularly makes its appearance in the perfect tense first, it has hence won for itself the capacity of expressing the relation of past time, which, however, is no obstacle to the "*fust*" in Oscan signifying also "*erit*" (see Mommsen, l. c. p. 61), the latter being in excellent agreement with the Zendian ܒܘܣܝܥܝܬܝ *búsyéiti*, and Lithuanian *bus* (see p. 918 G. ed.). Wherefore, also, *fefakust* may be literally taken to mean, "he is having made to be," since here the principal verb expresses past time by reduplication: the like may be the case with some reduplicated future perfects in the Umbrian (l. c. p. 146).

859. We return to the infinitive, in order to remark next, that, in the Vêdic dialect also, accusatives of abstract radical words are used as infinitives, and, indeed, in the genuine accusative relation, only, however, where the infinitive is governed by *śak*, "to be able." According to Pânini (III. 4. 12.) they are divided into two classes, of which the one strengthens the radical vowel, the other leaves it without extension. The Commentary furnishes as examples, *agniṅ vâi dêvâ vibhâjan* (*an* euphonic for *am*) *nâ 'śaknuvan*, "the fire could the gods not distribute;* *apalupan*(-*am*) *nâ 'śaknuvan*, "they could not destroy." To these we add, also, out of the Rigvêda (I. 94. 3.), *śakêma* [G. Ed. p. 1234.] *tvâ samídham*, "would that we could kindle thee;" and a passage from the Atharva-Vêda, cited by Aufrecht ("Umbrian Language," p. 148), *mâ śakan pratidhâm iśum*, "they cannot dispose the arrow." Though these infinitives may scarcely have been limited originally

---

* In this passage, which is detached from the context, I cannot answer for the exact meaning of *vibhâjam*. As regards the lengthening of the vowel of the root *bhaj* in this infinitive form, compare the feminine substantive *bhâj*, "portion, fortune, homage."

FORMATION OF WORDS. 1195

to the construction with *śak*, yet it is probable they can never have had a very extensive use, since, in general, the bare radical words are the most rare kind of abstract substantives. I therefore prefer comparing the Oscan and Umbrian infinitives in *um* (which Aufrecht and Kirchhof refer to this class) with the very numerous class of abstract substantives which are formed by the suffix अ *a*, and which, as has been shewn, are also occasionally substituted for infinitives, and to the accusatives of which the Umbrian-Oscan infinitives correspond better, as regards form, than to those of bare radical words; as bases ending in a consonant, especially the words of the 3d declension in Oscan, terminate in the accusative in *im*, and in Umbrian, after the analogy of the Greek, have lost the nasal of the termination, and end in the masculine or feminine with *u* or *o*. On the other hand, the accusatives of the 2d declension, which are based on the Sanscrit class of words in *a*, end universally in Oscan in *um* or *om* and in Umbrian the nasal of the termination *um* or *om*, is frequently suppressed (Aufr. and Kirchh., p. 116); and just so in the infinitive, *e.g. aferu* and *afero*, "*circumferre;*" *erum* and *ero*, "*esse.*" The following are examples of Oscan infinitives: *deikum*, "*dicere;*" *akum*, "*agere;*" *moltaum*, "*multare.*"* The last example is that which most resists identification with the accusatives of the Sanscrit radical words; and one sees plainly that here the *u* is a formative suf- [G. Ed. p. 1235.] fix which has been added to the theme of the 1st conjugation. As this corresponds to the Sanscrit 10th class (see §. 109ª. 6.), we may compare *molt-â-um*, exclusive of the masculine termination opposed to the Sanscrit-Zendian feminine one, with the Sanscrit and Zend infinitives mentioned above (§. 619.), like चोरयाम् *chôr-ay-âm*, ⟨zend⟩ *raôdh-*

---

* Mommsen, l. c. p. 66. These forms are distinguished from the common accusatives of the 2d declension only by the unmarked *u*.

ay-aṅm. Especial notice ought to be given to the form *trübarakavum*, if it, as Mommsen conjectures, is really a perfect infinitive; in which case *v-um*, euphonic for *u-um*, from *fu-um*, is the infinitive of the root *fu* with past signification (cf. p. 1232 G. ed. *dik-ust*, "*dixerit*," from *dik-fust*). Curtius* has compared with the Oscan present infinitives in *um* the Latin *venum*.† If this comparison be, as I think it is, correct, then this word, of which only the dative (*veno, venui*) and ablative *veno* are preserved, may originally belong only to the 2d declension: moreover, the *u* of the 4th declension, as formative suffix of an abstract in Latin, would stand quite isolated, while that of the 2d is frequently represented by the Sanscrit suffix *a* as a means of formation of masculine abstracts. These, for the most part, accent the radical vowel, and Gunise it when capable of Guna; while a radical *a* before a simple consonant is lengthened. The following are examples, in addition to those already mentioned: *bhḗda-s*, "cleaving" (root *bhid*), *chhḗda-s*, id. (root *chhid*); *yṓga-s*, "combining" (root *yuj*); *krṓdha-s*, "anger" (root *krudh*); *hā́sa-s*, "laughter" (root *has*); *kā́ma-s*, "wish, love" (root *kam*). In Greek, abstracts like πάλο-ς, φόβο-ς, δρόμο-ς, βρόμο-ς, τρόμο-ς, φόνο-ς, πλό(F)ο-ς, [G. Ed. p. 1236.] πόνο-ς,‡ ἔλεγχο-ς, ἵμερο-ς, correspond both in the suffix and in the accent. The Lithuanian, on account of the retention of the original *a* in abstracts of this kind, resembles the Sanscrit more than the Greek and Latin, which latter, with the exception at least of the base *venu*, already spoken of,

---

* "Journal of Archæology," June 1847, p. 490.

† *Venundo*, properly, "I give to sell;" *veneo*, for *venum eo*, "I go to the selling."

‡ As *o* is a heavier vowel than ε, the choice of this vowel in place of the ε, which elsewhere prevails in the roots referred to, reminds us of the vowel increment which appears in the corresponding Sanscrit abstracts, although *o*, as also ε, is only a corruption of an original *a* (see §. 3. p. 4, and cf. §. 255. a.).

presents for comparison only *ludu-s*, and perhaps *jocu-s* (the latter from an obscure root). The following are examples in Lithuanian: *miĕga-s*, "sleep" (*mĕgmi*, "I sleep"); *uź-mata-s*, "reproof, accusation,"* (*metù*, "I cast"); *báda-s*, "hunger" (*bádù*, "I hunger," cf. Sanscrit *bádh* or *vádh*, "to vex"); *jŭka-s*, "laughter" (cf. Latin *jocu-s*); *kára-s*, "strife, war;" *mena-s*, "understanding" (*menù*, "I think," *meno-s*, "I am skilful in something"); *maina-s*, "exchange;" *vĕda-s*, "order, regulation;" *róda-s*, "advice."

860. To this class in the Old Sclavonic belong those masculine abstracts, of which Dobrowsky says (p. 267) that they contain the pure radical syllable: they contain, however, in fact, the suffix *o*, corrupted from *a* (see §§. 255. a. 257.), which, in the nominative and accusative, is suppressed, or, more correctly, replaced by ъ, which Dobrowsky does not write. The following are examples: ловъ *lov'*, "the seizing" (Sanscrit *lábha-s*, "obtaining"); токъ *tok'*, "the flowing" (текѫ *tekuṅ*, "I run"); бродъ *brod'*, "passage, forth;" исходъ *isxod'*, "exit;" гладъ *glad'*, [G. Ed. p. 1237.] "hunger;"† стоудъ *stûd'*, "shame;" страдъ *strad'*, "fear;" from the bases *lovo, toko*, &c. Observe the agreement evinced by the Sclavonic with the Greek in the choice of the stronger radical vowel, so that *e.g.* токъ *tok'*, has exactly the same relation to *tekuṅ*, "I run," that, in Greek, δρόμο-ς, has to δρέμω, φόβο-ς to φέβομαι, &c. The relation of стоудъ *stûd'*, "shame," to стыд *styd*, in стыдѣти сѧ *stydyeti saṅ*, "to be ashamed" (see Micklos. Rad. p. 88) resembles that of Sanscrit abstracts like *yóga-s*, "joining;" to their

---

* This word deserves notice on account of the retention of the old *a*, which, in the verb and most of the other formations of this root, has been corrupted to *e*. *Metù*, "I cast," *uź-mata-s*, "reproof," *at-mota-s*, "outcast" (also *at-mata-s*), bear the same relation to one another as, *e.g.* in Greek, τρέπω, ἔτραπον, τρόπος.

† Sanscrit *gṛidh*, "to crave," from *gardh* or *gradh*, Gothic *grêdôn*, "to hunger," see Glossarium Sanscr. (Fasc. I. a. 1840), p. 107.

roots with *u,* for оу *û* is in Sclavonic the Guna of ы *y* (see §. 255. f.).

861. In German, too, the masculine abstracts which belong to this class have, by suppressing the final vowel of the base in the nominative and accusative, acquired the semblance of radical words. As, however, the bases in *a* and *i* are not distinguishable in the singular, it remains uncertain whether *e. g.* the Gothic *thlauh-s*, "flight," stands for *thlauha-s*, or for *thlauhi-s* (see §. 135.): in the former case it answers to the Sanscrit formations like *yóga-s*, "combination;"* but

---

* The root of the said Gothic abstract is *thluh;* whence *thliuha, thlauh, thlauhum*, the latter euphonic for *thluhum* (see §. 82.). The fact, that *thlauh-s* corresponds, as regards its vowel, better to the preterite than to the present, must not induce us to derive it from the preterite instead of from the root: otherwise we should have almost as much ground for deriving *e. g.* the Sanscrit *yóga-s* from *yuyója* ("I or he joined"); *bhéda-s,* "rupture," from *bibhéda;* and, in Greek, δρόμο-ς from δέδρομα. The truth is, that, in the formation of words, recourse is had sometimes to the pure, sometimes to the incremental radical vowel; and, moreover, in Greek and German, at times to the original radical vowel, at times to it in a form more or less weakened. Had, in Greek, δράμος been said for δρόμος, still the abstract would not have been to be derived from the aorist (ἔδραμον); but it would have had only this advantage in common with the latter, the retention, namely, of the radical vowel in its original form; while the ε of δρέμω is the greater, and the ο of δέδρομα the lesser weakening of the old *a*. In Gothic, *u* is the least (see §. 490.) and *i* the extreme weakening of the *a;* wherefore *run(a)-s,* "course, stream," from the root *rann,* "to run, to flow" (*rinna, rann, runnun*), stands on the footing of Greek abstracts like δρόμο-ς: so far, in reality, the said Gothic word belongs to the *a*-declension. We can, however, on account of the form of its radical vowel, just as little derive it from the plural of the preterite, as we could derive *e. g. anafilh,* "delivery" (neut.) from the same, because it exhibits the vowel of the present instead of that of the root itself (*falh*). Neither, too, can we derive *drus*, "fall," for *drusa-s* or *drusi-s* (the nominative sign is dropped in bases in *sa* and *si*), from the plural of the preterite; but, like the latter, it contains the pure radical vowel, which, in the present *driusa,* is Gunised by *i* (see §. 27.), and, in the singular preterite *draus,* by *a*. That the class of words under discussion is not wanting in Zend also is proved by

FORMATION OF WORDS. 1199

the Gothic diphthong in *thlauh-s*, can [G. Ed. p. 1238.] hardly be a consequence of Guna, but must rather result from the *h* following. That *slêp-s*, "sleep," belongs to this class, and is therefore for *slêpa-s*, not for *slêpi-s*, may be deduced from the cognate dialects.

862. To return to the Sanscrit infinitive suffix *tu*, it is further to be remarked, that the forms which are contracted by means of it occur in the Vêdas also in the ablative and genitive, which two cases are not formally distinguished from one another. Their use, however, is rare, and the ablative appears in the examples mentioned, and in the Schol. to Pân., III. 4. 16., quite in the character of a common abstract substantive; and we might *e.g.* regard the Latin *ortus*, everywhere that it occurs, as an infinitive, equally as well as the ablative *ud-étôs*, go- [G. Ed. p. 1239.] verned l. c. by *purâ*, "ere, earlier, before" (*purâ sûryasyô 'détôh̆* (-*ya ud*), "before the rising of the sun"). In the other examples, too, given l. c., the ablative of the abstract in *tu* is governed by a preposition, and, indeed, either by *purâ*, "before," or by *â*, "to;" so also in a passage of the 1st book of the Rigvêda (41. 9.), which has been already pointed out by Böhtlingk (Commentary on Pân., p. 152), *ấ nídhâtôh̆*, "to the casting (the dice)." Pâṇini, however, limits the kind of infinitive under discussion to the roots *sthâ, kar (kri), vad, char, hu, tam,* and *jan*; and therefore it is, probably, that Sâyana sees in *ní-dhâtós* no so-called *tôsun*, but a common abstract with the suffix *tu-n* (cf. p. 1220, Note, G. ed.). Perhaps, too, *ní-dhâtu* has a perfect declension, and thereby, in the opinion of the Indian

---

by the bases ⵡⵡⵡ *zaôsha*, "wish, will" (Sanscrit root *jush*, "to love, to wish"); ⵡⵡⵡ *frasa*, "query;" ⵡⵡⵡ *nâsa*, "destruction" (see p. 995, G. ed., §. 724.); ⵡⵡⵡ *fra-vâka*, "announcement;" ⵡⵡⵡ *raôdha*, "growth;" ⵡⵡⵡ *maga*, "greatness" ("growth," see Burnouf, Yaçna p. 72).

Grammarians, divides itself from the infinitive and its Vêdic representatives.

863. The form in *tôs*, according to Pâṇini (who nevertheless does not regard it as a genitive, but as an indeclinable (I. 1. 40.), as in the gerund in *tvâ*, and in the genitive of abstract radical words, where it stands for the infinitive*) occurs only in construction with *îśvara*, "lord, capable" (III. 4. 13.). The Scholiast gives as example, *îśvarô 'bhicharitôh̃*, "capable of affronting (lord of affronting)." Another genitive of this kind, though not recognised as an infinitive, and also not limited to the construction with *îshvara*, is *kártôs*, " of the doing, making, transacting," which Naigh., II. 1., mentions with the infinitive dative *kártavâi*, and the gerund *kritvî́* (see p. 1205, G. ed.), under the words signifying *karman* ("deed"), and which, Rigv. I. 115. 4., is governed by *madhyấ*, "in the midst."† As regards the relation of the gerund

---

* The genitive termination *as* is looked upon by the Indian Grammarians in this case, not as a case-termination, but as a formative suffix, which is called in the technical language *k-as-un* (cf. p. 1220, Note, G. ed.), and is therefore unaccented, though, in general, the monosyllabic base words have the accent only in the strong cases on the base syllable (see p. 1085, G. ed., §. 785. Remark). We may ascribe the accentuation of the radical words, where their genitive represents the infinitive, to the circumstance, that the infinitive outbids the common abstracts by greater power of life and action; and it will be well to recall what has been before (§. 814.) said regarding the double kind of accentuation of the forms in *târ* (*tṛi*), according as they, as participles, govern the accusative, or stand as more inactive nouns of agency. The datives, too, of abstract radical words have, where they stand as infinitives, in general the more powerful accentuation, at least in the cases in which, according to Pâṇini (III. 4. 14.), the infinitive in *ê* (in the technical language *k-ê-n*) takes the place of the future passive participle, as in the above-mentioned (§. 855.) example *ati-krámê*, in opposition to the oxytonised *dṛiśế* (Pân. III. 4. 77.; Rigv. I. 23. 21.).

† *Madhyấ kártôs*, "in the midst of doing (of work)." *Madhyấ* is an abbreviation of *madhyế* (= *madhyai*, see §. 196.), where the suppression
of

or the instrumental *kritvá*, "after," or "with," or "through making," to the accusative, which springs from the base *kartu*, or to the common infinitive *kártum*, as also to the datives *kártavê, kártavâi*, and to the genitive *kártôs*, and, in general, the relation of the gerunds in *tvâ* to the infinitives of the same root, it must be observed that the gerund in roots which admit of increment or weakening always exhibits the weaker form of the root, and has the accent, without exception, on the case-termination. Compare, *e.g.*

INFINITIVE.	GERUND.	ROOT.
váktum,	*uktvá,*	*vach,* "to speak."
sváptum,	*suptvá,*	*svap,* "to sleep."
práshtum,	*prishtvá,*	*prachh,* "to ask."
yáshtum,	*ishtvá,*	*yaj,* "to offer."
gráhîtum,	*grihîtvá,*	*grah,* "to take."
śrótum,	*śrutvá,*	*śru,* "to hear."
bhávitum,	*bhûtvá,*	*bhû,* "to be."
yóktum,	*yuktvá,*	*yuj,* "to join."
bhéttum,	*bhittvá,*	*bhid,* "to cleave."
sthátum,	*sthitvá,*	*sthâ,* "to stand."
hántum,	*hatvá,*	*han,* "to slay."

[G. Ed. p. 1241.]

864. This distinction in the form of the root and of the accentuation does not prevent the assumption, that the gerund and the infinitive originally had the same theme and the same accentuation, that, *e.g.*, together with *yóktum*, "to join," a *yóktvâ*, "after," "with," or "through joining," may have existed, just as the distinction which exists in the participle present between the strong and weak cases

---

of the case-termination is compensated by lengthening the final vowel of the base, in which respect compare Latin datives like *lupô* from *lupoi* (see §. 200., and compare वसन्त *vasanta* for वसन्ते *vasantê* in the Schol. to Pân. VII. 1. 39.).

cannot have been an original one; and, *e.g.*, to the accusative *tudántam* an instrumental *tudántá* must have corresponded; for which, in the language as it has remained to us, the oxytone *tudatá*, which has also lost the nasal, is left (cf. p. 1051). As the weakening of the gerund occurs in the root, and not in the suffix, I further recall attention to the declension of *pathín*, "way," from whence spring only the middle cases, while the strong strengthen the root by the insertion of a nasal, and, at the same time, accentuate it; and, moreover, exhibit the suffix also in a stronger form (*pánthán* compared with *pathán*); while the weakest cases suppress the suffix, as also the nasal of the root, and let the accent sink down on the case-termination: hence, *e.g.*, in the instrumental we find *pathá* opposed to [G. Ed. p. 1242.] *pánthánam*, "viam" and *pathíbhyas* "viis." The declension of *váh*, "bearing" (at the end of compounds) also presents a great agreement with the formal relation of the gerund in *tvá* to the infinitive; that is to say, with those gerunds which, in roots beginning with *va*, suppress the *a* and vocalise the *v*; only in compounds in *váh* the long syllable *vá* is contracted in the weakest cases to long *ú*, while the short syllable *va* of the gerunds is contracted to short *u*: in other respects *sály-úhá*, "through the rice-carrying," has the same relation to its accusative *sáli-váham*, as, *e.g.*, *uktvá* has to *váktum*. A short *u* is exhibited by *anad-váh*, "ox (wagon-drawer"),[*] in the weak cases: hence, *anad-uhá*, *e.g.*, stands exactly in the same relation to *anad-váham*, as *uktvá* does to *váktum*. With regard, however, to the circumstance that the feminine bases in *tu*, from which the gerund and the infinitive spring, have

---

[*] *Anad-uh* is assumed to be the theme; but it admits of no doubt that *vah* is the true base of the final member of this compound, and that hence *uh* has arisen by contraction. The nominative is *anad-ván*, and presupposes a theme with a nasal *anad-vánh* (cf. §. 786., suff. *váns*).

undergone a weakening only in the instrumental, *i.e.* in the gerund, but not in the other weak cases, we may perhaps look for the reason of this in the extremely frequent use of the instrumental of the gerund, as the forms most used are also most subject to detrition or weakening; for which reason, *e.g.*, the root of the verb substantive *as* loses its vowel before the heavy terminations of the present, while no other root beginning with a vowel undergoes such an abbreviation in any form whatever. Should the formal relation of the gerund in *tvâ* to the infinitive in *tum* be independent of the, as it were, moral principle which operates in the separation into strong and [G. Ed. p. 1243.] weak cases, I would assume, and I have already elsewhere alluded to it,* that the weight *tvâ* laid on the termination *tum* has had a similar influence on the preceding portion of the word, both with respect to the weakening of the form and the removal of the accent, as that exercised in the 2d principal conjugation by the weight of the heavy personal terminations. In that case, therefore, the relation of, *e.g.*, *i-tvâ* to *étum*, *dvish-tvâ* to *dvésh-tum*, *vit-tvâ* to *véttum*, *dat-tvâ* to *dâ-tum*, *hi-tvâ* to *hâ-tum*, would answer more or less to that of

i-más, " we go,"	to	*é-mi* " I go,"
dvish-más, " we hate,"	to	*dvésh-mi,* " I hate,"
vid-más, " we know,"	to	*véd-mi,* " I know,"
dad-más, " we give,"	to	*dádâ-mi,* " I give,"
jahí-más, " we quit,"	to	*jáhâ-mi,* " I quit."

Be that, however, as it may, it is certain that the gerund in *tv-â*, and the infinitives in *tu-m*, *tô-s*, *tav-ê*, *tav-âi*, have a common formative suffix, and in essentials are only distinguished by their case-termination; and that the abstract substantive base formed by *tu* is feminine, which before

---

* Smaller Sanscrit Grammar, §. 562.

could only have been inferred from the instrumental in *tv-â*,* but now is also apparent from the Vêdic dative forms in *tav-âi*. The Greek abstracts in τύ-ς, as βοητύ-ς, βρωτύ-ς, ἐδητύ-ς, ἐπητύ-ς, ἐλεητύ-ς, γελα-σ-τύ-ς, ὀρχη-σ-τύ-ς, which were first brought into this province of formation in my treatise on the "Influence of Pronouns on the formation of Words" (p. 25), [G. Ed. p. 1244.] testify in like manner for the feminine nature of the Sanscrit cognate words: they, however, testify also, and this is well worth notice, that it was after the separation of the Greek from the Sanscrit that this class of abstract substantives raised itself in Sanscrit to the position of infinitives and gerunds, while they still moved in Zend also in the circle of common substantives. Under this head is to be brought ⟨⟩ *pĕrĕ-tu*, the feminine gender of which is proved by the accusative plural *pĕrĕtûs;* but its abstract nature has been changed into concrete. It, perhaps, originally signified "passage, crossing,"† but has, however, assumed the signification "bridge." Perhaps, too, ⟨⟩ *zantu*, "city" (originally, perhaps, "production, creation"), the gender of which is not to be deduced from the forms that now occur, is to be classed here. The instrumental ⟨⟩ *zanthwâ*, "through production," mentioned above (§. 254. Rem. 3. p. 280), as also ⟨⟩ *janthwa*, "through smiting, slaying,"‡ and the ablative *zanthwât*, I now rather refer to the suffix *thwa* = Sanscrit *tva*, as in the Vêda dialect the said suffix also forms primitive abstracts (see §. 829.), and, indeed, from the strong form of the root; so that from जन् *jan* and हन् *han* might be expected the bases जन्त्व *jantva* and हन्त्व *hantva*. I am led to this opinion particu-

---

* From a masculine or neuter base, in classical Sanscrit at least, would come *tunâ*.

† Root *pĕrĕ*=Sanscrit *par* (*pṛi*), see Brockhaus, Glossary, p. 376.

‡ See §. 160. p. 178, where *janthwa* should be read for *zanthwa*. In the Ger. ed. §. 159 is here wrongly given for §. 160.

larly by the ablative 𐬰𐬀𐬧𐬚𐬎𐬎𐬁𐬝 *zanthwât*,* which answers better to a theme *zanthwa* than to *zantu*, as from bases in *u* no other ablatives in *ât* have elsewhere been found, but only such as have short *a* before the *t*, or those [G. Ed. p. 1245.] that append the ablative sign direct to the theme. The instrumentals in *thwa* (or *thwâ*, see §. 254. Rem. 3. p. 281) admit of being deduced from feminine bases in *tu* quite as well as from neuter or masculine in *thwa*. But it is decidedly from a base in *thwa* that the accusative *raêthwĕm*, " defiling,"† comes, from the theme of which *raêthwa* proceeds the denominative *raêthwayêiti*, " he defiles." The primitive verb does not occur, whence it is uncertain whether *raêthwa* is really a primitive abstract.

865. It is clear that the Latin supines are identical in their base with the Sanscrit infinitive bases in *tu*, although the analogous abstracts with a full declension, as *or-tu-s, inter-i-tu-s, sta-tu-s, ac-tu-s, duc-tu-s, rap-tu-s, ac-ces-su-s* (from *ac-ces-tu-s*, see §. 101.), *câ-su-s* (from *cas-su-s* for *cas-tus*), *cur-su-s, vom-i-tu-s*,‡ have, like their analogous forms in

---

* V. S. p. 83, 𐬰𐬀𐬧𐬚𐬎𐬎𐬁𐬝 ... 𐬞𐬀𐬭𐬀 𐬥𐬀𐬭𐬱 *para nars* ... *zanthwât,* " *ante hominis generationem*," see Gram. Crit., p. 253.

† Cf. Spiegel, " The 19th Farg. of the V. S.," p. 82.

‡ The Sanscrit also frequently joins the suffix under discussion to the root by means of a conjunctive vowel *i;* and forms, *e.g.*, from *vâm*, " to vomit," the base *vamitu;* whence the infinitive *vám-i-tum* (=sup. *vom-i-tum*), and the gerund *vam-i-tvâ*. With regard, however, to the infinitive and gerund not universally agreeing as to the insertion or not of the conjunctive vowel, and to our finding by the side of the infinitive *bhâv-i-tum*, " to be," *e.g.*, a gerund *bhû-tvâ*, I would recall attention to the circumstance that the suffix *váns* of the perfect participle, when it is appended to the root by a conjunctive vowel *i*, rejects this conjunctive vowel in the weakest cases (instr. *pêch-úsh-â*, opposed to the acc. *pêch-i-váns-am*), which does not prevent me from assuming, that in this participle all cases originally came from the same base. We do not require to explain the absence of the conjunctive vowel in the weakest cases by the circumstance, that here the formative suffix begins with a vowel, as *pêch-y-úshâ* (for *pêch-i-úshâ*)

[G. Ed. p. 1246.] Greek, not remained true to the feminine gender. How exactly in other respects, in many roots, the accusative of the Latin supine agrees with that of the Sanscrit infinitive, exclusive of the gunising of the latter, may be inferred from the following examples:—

SANSCRIT.	LATIN.
sthá-tum, "to stand,"	státum.
dá-tum, "to give,"	datum.
dhmá-tum, "to blow,"	flátum.
jñá-tum, "to know,"	nótum.
pá-tum, "to drink,"	pótum.
é-tum, "to go."	itum (cf. ἴτυς).
sé-tum, "to sleep,"	quiétum.
yó-tum, yáv-i-tum, "to join,"	jútum.
sró-tum, "to flow,"	rutum (cf. rivus).
stár-tum, "to strew,"	strátum.
pák-tum, "to cook,"	coctum.
ánk-tum, "to anoint,"	unctum.

pêch-i-úshá) could as little surprise us, as, e.g., ninây-i-tha (with ninê-tha), from the root ní, "to lead," which prefixes a conjunctive vowel i at pleasure to the personal termination tha, and necessarily to the personal endings va, ma, sê, vahê, mahê, dhvê; hence niny-i-vá, niny-i-má, niny-i-shé, &c. The verbs of the 10th class, and the causal forms which are analogous to them, have all of them, as well in the infinitive as in the gerund, the conjunctive vowel i after the character ay (for aya of the special tenses), and gunise radical vowels which are capable of Guna; hence, e.g., chôr-ay-i-tum, chôr-ay-i-tvá, from chur, "to steal." To the ay corresponds the Latin á or î, from forms like am-á-tum, aud-î-tum (see §. 109². 6.). On the other hand, verbs of the Latin 2d conjugation, though they are based in like manner on the Sanscrit 10th class, relinquish their conjugational character, and add the suffix either direct to the root, or by means of a conjunctive vowel i (doc-tum, mon-i-tum, for doc-ê-tum, mon-ê-tum, cf. §. 801. Note †, p. 1115 Note **, G. ed.): flê-tum, plê-tum make a necessary exception; dêl-ê-tum makes a voluntary one.

FORMATION OF WORDS.

SANSCRIT.	LATIN.
bhánk-tum, "to break,"	fractum. [G. Ed. p. 1247.]
bhrásh-ṭum, "to roast" (r. bhrajj),	frictum.
yók-tum, "to join,"	junctum.
át-tum, "to eat,"	ésum (see §. 101.).
chhét-tum, "to cleave,"	scissum.
bhét-tum, id.	fissum.
tót-tum, "to knock,"	tûsum (from tus-sum for tus-tum, see §. 101.).
rát-tum, "to rend,"	rôsum.
vét-tum, "to know,"	ví-sum,(from vis-sum, vis-tum).
ián-i-tum, "to beget, to bring forth, to become,"	gen-i-tum.
svá́n-i-tum, "to sound,"	son-i-tum.
lóp-tum, "to break,"	ruptum.
sárp-tum, "to go,"	serptum.
vám-i-tum, "to vomit,"	vom-i-tum.
désh-ṭum, "to shew,"	dictum.
pésh-ṭum, "to bruise,"	pistum.
dóg-dhum,* "to milk,"	ductum.
mé-dhum,† "mingere,"	mictum.
vó-dhum, "to ride,"	vectum.

866. The form which, in the Lithuanian and Lettish Grammars, is called "supinum," corresponds remarkably with the accusative of the supine in Latin, in that it is used only after verbs of motion, in order to express the object towards which the motion is directed, *i.e.* the purpose for which it takes place (cf. p. 1209 G. ed.). [G. Ed. p. 1248.] The accusative-sign, the nasal of which is elsewhere in Lithuanian marked on the preceding vowel (see §. 149.), is

---

* Euphonic for dóh-tum, from the root duh=Gothic tuh (tiuha, "I draw," tauh, "I drew").

† For méh-tum, whence next comes méḍ-dhum.

altogether lost in this form, though it is preserved in its original shape in the already before-noticed composites like *butum-bime* (see §. 685. p. 913, and §. 687.), under the protection of the following labial. I annex a few Lithuanian supine constructions out of the translation of the Bible: *iszẽyo sẽyẽyas sẽtu*, "A sower went forth to sow" (Matt. xiii. 3); *kad nuẽyen in miestelus, saw nusipirktu walgin*, "that they may go (going) into the villages to buy themselves victuals" (xiv. 15); *nuẽyens yeszkotu paklydusen*, "going to seek that which is gone astray" (xviii. 12); *yus iszẽyote .... sugáutu mannen*, "are ye come out for to take me?" (xxvi. 55). Nevertheless, the use of this supine in the received condition of the Lithuanian after verbs of motion is not exclusively requisite; but we find in the translation of the Bible, in such constructions, more frequently the common infinitive in *ti*, or with *i*, suppressed *t'*; e.g., Matt. ix. 11, *asz atẽyau grieszmůsus wadinti*, "I am come to call sinners" (cf. Sanscrit *vad*, "to speak"); x. 34, *asz ne atẽyau pakayun susti*, "I am not come to send peace;" v. 17, *ne atẽyau panukint', bet iszpildit'*, "I am not come to destroy, but to fulfil." On the other hand, the Old Prussian—a language which approaches the Lithuanian very closely—has two forms for the common infinitive, of which the one corresponds to the accusative of the Sanscrit infinitive and Latin supine, as also to the Lithuanian supine; and, indeed, as in the common declension, retaining the sign of the accusative in the form of *n*; e.g., *dâ-tun* or [G. Ed. p. 1249.] *dâ-ton*, "to give" = Sanscrit *dâtum*, *pû-ton*,* "to drink" = *pâ-tum*, *gem-ton*, "to bear a child" = *ján-i-tum*; and the other, with the termination *twei*, presents a remarkable similarity to the above-mentioned (§. 854.) Vêdic infinitive dative in *taväi* (for *tvâi*), of which no trace is left in any other cognate language of Europe. It has, however,

---

* *Ton* from *tun*, cf. §. 77.

FORMATION OF WORDS. 1209

unconscious of its origin, in like manner an accusative signification; where I would remind the reader, that in the Vêdas also the infinitives in *dhyâi*, discussed above (§. 854.), in spite of their dative form, occasionally suppress the accusative relation; thus, Yajurvêda VI. 3., *uśmasi gámadhyâi*, "we will go."* As regards, then, the Prussian form in *twei*, if we deduce *twei* from *tu-ei, ei* answers as the feminine case-termination to the pronominal datives in *ei*; as, *ste-ssi-ei*, "this" = Sanscrit *ta-sy-âi*, Gothic *thi-z-ai* (see §. 349. p. 485). It might, however, be, that the *ei* of the said infinitive form may be based on the Sanscrit *ê* (=*ai*) of the Vêda forms in *tav-ê*, so that, *e.g.*, *dâ-twei*, "to give," would have the same relation to its accusative *dâ-tu-n*, that, in the Vêda dialect, the to-be-presupposed *dâ-tav-ê*, which, without Guna, would be *dá-tv-ê*, has to *dâ-tum*. The Rigvêda furnishes us with *pâ-tav-ê*, the sister form to *pû-tw-ei*, "to drink" (I. 28. e.). The other Prussian forms which belong to this class, and which Nesselmann, p. 65, has collected, are: *biâ-twei, bia-twi*,† "to fear" (Sanscrit *bhî*, "to fear," *bhayá*, "fear"); *stâ-twei*, "to stand;" *at-trâ-twei*, "to answer;" *billi-tweî*, "to say" (Sanscrit *brû*, "to speak"); [G. Ed. p. 1250.] *en-dyrî-twei*, "to regard" (Sanscrit *darś, driś*, "to see"); *pallaps-i-twei*,‡ "to covet" (Sanscrit *lilaps*, infinitive *lilaps-i-*

---

* In another passage of the Yajurvêda (III. 13.) the infinitives *âhuvâdhyâi*, "to summon," and *mádayâdhyâi*, "to rejoice," are governed by a verb (according to the Schol., *ichchhâmi*, "I wish, 1 will"), and have, in like manner, an accusative meaning: *ubhâ vâm indrâgnî âhuvâdhyâ ubhâ râdhasah sahá mâdayâdhyâi*, "Ye both, Indra and Agni, (will I) call, both will together gladden on account of riches."

† For *twei* occur also *twi, twey,* and *twe*, see Nesselm., p. 65.

‡ *Pa* is a prefix, and the initial consonant of the root doubled, according to the inclination peculiar to the Prussian to double consonants. Compare the Sanscrit root *labh*, "to attain" (λαμβάνω, ἔλαβον), the desiderative of which would regularly be *lilaps* (see §. 750.), for which *lips*. From *labh*, "to attain," appears, too, through mere weakening of the vowel,

tum, "to wish to attain, r. *labh*); *kirdî-twei*, "to hear;" *madli-twei*, "to ask;" *au-schaudî-twei*, "to trust;" *schlûsi-twei*, "to serve;" *turrî-twei*, "to have;" *wacki-twei*, "to allure;"* *gallin-twei*, "to slay;" *leigin-twey*, "to direct;" *smunin-twey*, "to honour;" *sundin-twei*, "to punish;" *swintin-twei*, "to hallow;" *menen-twey*, "to think, to mention" (Sanscrit *man*, "to think);" *gir-twei*, "to praise" (Vêd. *gir*, "song of praise;" *gri-nâ-mi*, "I praise"); *gun-twei*, "to drive;" *lim-twei*, *lemb-twey*, "to break" (Sanscrit *lump-â-mi*, "I break"); *ranc-twei*, *ranck-twey*, "to steal;"† *is-twei*, *is-twe*, "to eat;"‡ *tiens-twei*, "to fascinate;" *wes-twei* (from *wed-twei*), "to conduct."

867. More frequent than the infinitives in *tum*, *ton*, and *twei*, are, in the Old Prussian language, the infinitives in *t;* as, *da-t*, "to give;" *sta-t*, "to stand;" *bou-t*, "to be;" *giw-i-t*, "to live;" *teick-u-t*, "to procure" (Sanscrit *taksh*, in the Vêda dialect, "to make"). These have, as I doubt not, lost a final *i*, and answer to the Lithuanian infinitives in *ti*, the *i* of which is also frequently apostrophised (see p. 1248 G. ed.), and in Lettish, as in Prussian, is utterly lost.§ Here also are to be ranked the

---

vowel, the root *lubh*, "to covet," to have sprung. The Prussian root *lap*, "to command," appears to belong to the Sanscrit *lap*, "to speak."

* *En-wackêmai*, "we invoke," cf. Sanscrit *vach* (from *vak*), infinitive *vaktum*, "to speak."

† Akin to this is, among other words, the Lithuanian *rankà*, "hand," as "taking," Old Prussian accusative *ranka-n*, plural accusative *ranka-ns*. In Sanscrit the as-yet-unciteable root *rak* (also *lak*) means "to obtain."

‡ Euphonic for *id-twei*, *id-twe* (see §. 457.), cf. Sanscrit infinitive *at-tum* from *ad-tum*.

§ The following are examples in Lettish: *yah-t* (=*jâ-t*), "to rule" (cf. Sanscrit root *yâ*, "to go"); *see-t*, "to bind" (Sanscrit root *si*, id.); *ee-t*, "to go;" *bih-t* (=*bî-t*), "to be afraid" (Sanscrit root *bhî*); *buh-t* (=*bût*), "to be" (Lithuanian *bu-ti*, Sanscrit *bhû-ti*, "the being"); *wem-t*, "*vomere*" (Sanscrit root *vam*).

FORMATION OF WORDS. 1211

Old Slavonic infinitives, which, however, have constantly preserved the *i* of the suffix; hence, *e.g.*, ꙗсти *yas-ti* (euphonic for *yad-ti*), "to eat," as compared with the Lithuanian *ĕs-ti*, and Prussian *is-t*. The source of these infinitives is most probably, as has been already elsewhere remarked,* the Sanscrit feminine abstracts in *ti* (see §. 844.), with whose theme the Lithuanian and Old Sclavonic infinitives are, as regards their suffix, identical: compare *buti*, быти *byti*, "to be," with the Sanscrit *bhûti*, "*existentia;*" *eiti*, ити *iti*, "to go," with इति *iti*, "the going" (only retained in *sam-iti*, "fight," properly, "coming together"). As, however, such base words, except at the beginning of compounds, do not occur in the languages, it becomes a question what case is represented by the Sclavonic-Lithuanian infinitive forms in *ti*. I believe the dative; for the accusative, which, according to sense, would be more suitable, would lead us to expect, in Lithuanian *tiṅ*, and in Sclavonic ть *ty* (cf. кость *kosty*, from the base *kosti*, p. 348), but in the dative and the locative, which is of the same form with it, the Old Sclavonic *i*-bases are not distinguished from their theme (see §. 268. and p. 348); and in Lettish also the bases in *i* exhibit in the dative, and at the same time also in the accusative, the bare primary form, of which the *i* in the nominative and genitive is suppressed: hence, *e.g.*, *aw'-s* as nominative and genitive for Sanscrit *avi-s*, *avê-s*, Latin *ovi-s*, *ovi-s*, but dative and accusative *awi;* and in the Lithuanian, in the common declension of bases in *i*, the dative is probably dis- [G. Ed. p. 1252.] tinguished from the base only in this, that it reaches into another province of declension.† If now the Sclavonic and Lithuanian infinitives are properly datives, in spite of the accusative relation which they generally express, they

---

* "Influence of Pronouns on the formation of Words," p. 35.
† See p. 48 Note †, and §. 193.

resemble in this respect the Prussian infinitives in *tw-ei* explained above (see p. 1249 G. ed.); and, amongst others, also the Greek infinitives, which I regard, where they are not mutilated (as those in μεν, εν, ειν, from μεναι), universally as datives. Of this more hereafter. But we have here further to recall notice to the fact, that in Zend, also, the dative of abstract substantives in *ti* is used as representative of the infinitive, yet only to express a genuine dative relation, viz. the causal one; thus, Vend. Sad. p. 198, *karstayaê-cha hictayaê-cha para-kantayaê-cha*, "in order to plough, and to water, and to dig," from the bases *karsti, hicti, para-kanti*; l. c. p. 39, ⟨zend⟩ *kharĕteê*, "in order to eat, on account of eating" (see p. 959). However, it is further necessary to inquire whether datives of this kind anywhere else in the Zend-Avesta as genitive infinitives govern the case of the verb, for which, in the passage quoted, there is no occasion.

868. I regard as accusatives, though in like manner without case-termination, and as originally identical with the Sanscrit infinitive accusatives in *tum*, and their Latin and Lithuanian sister-forms, the Old Sclavonic infinitives in тъ *t'* called "supines," which are governed only by verbs of motion as the object of the motion; but from such constructions also are expelled in the more modern MSS. and printed books by the common infinitives in ти *ti* (see Do-[G. Ed. p. 1253.] browsky, p. 646). Taken as accusative, the termination тъ *t'* has the same relation to the Sanscrit *tum* that сынъ *syn'*, "*filium*," has to सूनुम् *sún'm*.* In the dative we should expect *tovi* after the analogy of сынови *synov-i*, "*filio*" = Sanscrit *súnav-ê*, Lithuanian *sunu-i*. The examples given by Dobrowsky (pp. 645, 646), are: моучитъ *múchit'* ("art thou come hither to torment us?" Matt. viii. 29); оучитъ *úchit'*; проповѣдатъ *propovyedat'*, ("He departed thence to teach and to preach," xi. 1.); видѣтъ *vidyet'* ("what

---

* Lithuanian *sunu-ṇ*, Gothic *sunu*, see §. 262.

FORMATION OF WORDS. 1213

went ye out to see?" xi. 7.), сѣатъ *syeyat* ("a sower went forth to sow," iii. 3.); възовѣститъ *v'zoryestit'* ("they did run to bring word," xxviii. 8). In respect of syntax, it deserves notice that the Old Sclavonic supines can be also used in construction like common substantives with the genitive; so, Matt. viii. 29, *múchit' nas*, "to torment us," instead of *ny*.

869. We return to the Latin supine, in order to consider more closely the form in *tû*. As ablative, it answers, at least in respect of signification, to the Vêdic ablative of the infinitive in *tôs* (=*taus*), which, however, has not hitherto been found in its strict ablative function, but only governed by prepositions (see §. 862.), while the corresponding Latin form in *tû* avoids the construction with prepositions. Its ablative nature, however, is clearly shewn where the ablative of another abstract stands beside it in a similar relation; as Terence: *parvum dictu, sed immensum exspectatione;* Liv.: *pleraque dictu quam re sunt faciliora.* As the 4th declension also admits datives in *û* for *ui*, we might regard the supine in *tû*, when it stands by adjectives which govern the dative, as a dative; thus, *e.g., jucundum cognitu atque auditu* as = *cognitui, auditui.* I would rather, [G. Ed. p. 1254.] however, not concede to the suffix a 3d case, and believe that the form in *tû* may everywhere be taken as an ablative, and, indeed, in most cases, as an ablative more closely defined, which can be paraphrased by "on account of," "in respect to," as above, "*dictu quam re faciliora.*" The assertion, however, that it is possible to express the relation of removal by the ablative of the supine I now retract, since, in a passage in Cato R. R. (*primus cubitu surgat, postremus cubitum eat*), I no longer agree with Vossius (see also Ramshorn, p. 452) in recognising the supines of *cumbo*, but only the common ablative and accusative of the concrete *cubitus* "couch, bed," therefore "Rise the first from bed, go last to bed." Moreover, in *obsonatu redeo* (Plaut.) and *redeunt*

pastu oves, I cannot, with G. F. Grotefend (p. 347, see also Ramshorn p. 452), recognise the ablative of the supine; as the ablative of *obsonatus* and *pastus*, with which the said supine is, in its origin, certainly identical here, suffices very well. It is, however, certain, that the Latin supines, in respect to syntax, stand very near to the common abstracts of the 4th declension; and I do not think that the Latin brought its supines with it as such, or as infinitives, so early as from the Asiatic progenital land, but I now only assume a formative affinity with the Sanscrit infinitives in *tu-m*, as with the Greek abstracts in τυ-ς; but I admit of the syntactical individualization of the Latin supines first shewing itself on Roman soil, as, indeed, in the older Latinity also, the abstracts in *tio* have obtained the capacity, like infi-

[G. Ed. p. 1255.] nitives, of governing the accusative* which the more modern language has again resigned. The case is different with the forms of the Lithuanian and Sclavonic supines, which correspond to the Latin supines and the Old Prussian infinitive (§§. 866. 466.), which stand in the said languages isolated, and without any support on a class of words provided with a full declension, and shew themselves to be transmissions from the time of identity with the Sanscrit and the earlier, as the said languages, through several other phenomena, point to the fact that they were first separated from the Sanscrit at a time when the latter language had already experienced sundry corruptions, with which the classic and German tongues are not yet acquainted.†

---

* The following are examples in Plautus: *Quid tibi hanc digito tactio est? quid tibi istunc tactio est? quid tibi hanc notio est? quid tibi hanc aditio est? quid tibi huc receptio ad te est meum virum? quid tibi hanc curatio est?* This idiom therefore appears to have been retained, or generally to have been adopted, in questions only.

† I have expressed myself more fully on this subject in a treatise read before the Academy several years ago, but still unprinted, "On the Language

870. We ought not to ascribe a passive [G. Ed. p. 1256.] signification to the ablative of the supine, at least it cannot

---

guage of the Old Prussians;" and I have there appealed in particular to the palatal *ś*, which has arisen from *k*, for which the classical languages exhibit the original guttural tenuis, the German languages *h* (according to the rule for the permutation of sound, see §. 87.), while the Lettish and Sclavonic languages, in most of the words which admit of comparison, give likewise a sibilant. Compare, *e.g.*, Sanscrit *áśva-s*, "a horse," *áśvá*, "a mare," with the Lithuanian *aszwa*, contrasted with the Latin *equus, equa*, Old Saxon *ehu ; śvan* (th.), nom. *śvâ*, "dog, with the Lithuanian *szů* (nom.), gen. *szun-s*, contrasted with the Greek κύων, Latin *cani-s*, Gothic *hund(a)-s ; śatá-m*, "a hundred," with the Lithuanian *szinta-s*, (masc.), Old Sclavonic *sto* (neut.), contrasted with the Latin *centum*, Greek ἑ-κατόν (p. 445); *śákhá*, "bough," with Lithuanian *szakà*, Russian *suk*, contrasted with the Irish *geag*. By another process, Kuhn (see Weber's Indian Studies, p. 324) has arrived at the opinion, that the Sclavonic languages "have continued longer united with the Indian, or, still more probably, longer with the Zend and the Persian, than with the others of the Indo-Germanic family." I cannot, however, assume a special affinity between the Sclavonic (and Lettish) and the Arian languages (the Zend, Persian, Kurdish, Afghān, Armenian, Ossetish); and in the forementioned treatise regarding the Old Prussian I have drawn attention to the fact, that an especial peculiarity of the Arian languages consists in this, that they have all of them before vowels, and the most part before semi-vowels also, as well at the beginning as in the middle of words, changed the original or dental *s* (स) into *h*, or entirely suppressed it. This token, however, fails in the Sclavonic and Lettish languages, which, in this respect, have maintained themselves on a level with the Sanscrit. Compare, *e.g.*, the Lithuanian *septyni*, Sclavonic *sedmy*, with the Zend *hapta*, Persian *huft*, the Armenian *yevthn, yefthankh*, Ossetish *awd*, and Afghān *óva*. When, however, the Sclavonic-Lettish languages at times accord with the Arian, in that they contrast with the Sanscrit स *h* a sibilant, as, *e.g.*, in the nominative singular of the pronoun of the 1st person (see p. 471), I regard it in so far as casual, inasmuch as I believe that the two groups of languages (the Lettish-Sclavonic and Arian) in these, on the whole, but rare coincidences, have reached a common goal by separate routes; as the Greek, through its rough breathing, frequently coincides with the Arian *h* (cf. *e.g.* ἑπτά with the Zend *hapta*), without, however, the change of the original *s* into the rough breathing

at

[G. Ed. p. 1257.] be assigned with more right to it than to other abstract substantives, in which it can be inferred only

at the beginning of words having become a principle; for the Greek contrasts, *e.g.*, σύν, for Sanscrit *sam*, with the Zend *ham*. The Sanscrit ह *h* is properly an aspirated *g* (*gh*), and, in pronunciation, has the same relation to घ *gh* that the Greek χ has to the Sanscrit *kh* (*k* + *h*), in which, as generally in the Sanscrit aspirates, an *h* is clearly heard after the said tenuis or medial. The Sanscrit *h* is therefore, as it were, a weak χ, and leads us, in the Lettish-Sclavonic languages, which have no aspirates, to expect a *g*, which we here also frequently find in the place of the Sanscrit *h*; as, *e.g.*, in Lithuanian *degu*, "I burn"=Sanscrit *dáhámi;* and in the Sclavonic могѫ *moguṅ*, "I can," which is based on the Sanscrit root *manh*, *mah*, "to grow," whence महत् *mahát*, "great" (cf. *magnus*, μέγας), to which the Zend 𐬨𐬀𐬰𐬋 *mazô* is radically akin, with *z*, therefore, contrasted with the Sanscrit *h* and Sclavonic, Greek, and Latin *g*. Where, however, the Lithuanian contrasts a *ż* (= French *j*, Sclavonic Ж) and the Sclavonic a з with the Sanscrit *h*, there I regard the sibilant of the said languages, not as a corruption of the Sanscrit *h*, but of a *g*, in the same manner as, in Italian, the *g* before *e* and *i* has, in pronunciation, become *dsch* (English *j*): moreover, in this case the Lettish and Sclavonic languages, in spite of their near relationship, no longer invariably agree with one another; since, *e.g.*, the Russian contrasts with the Sanscrit *haṅsa*, "goose," the form гусь *gusy*, and the Lithuanian the form *żasis*. In the Zend this word would, in its theme, be either 𐬰𐬀𐬢𐬵𐬀 *zaṇha* or 𐬘𐬀𐬢𐬵𐬀 *jaṇha* (see §§. 56ᵃ. 57.), the *h* of which the Lettish-Sclavonic languages would have scarcely conducted back to its point of departure, *s*. I would also recall attention to the fact, that in the Lettish and Sclavonic languages occasionally weak sibilants occur for the Sanscrit *g* or the *j* ज, which was first developed out of the *g* after the separation of languages. Thus the Lithuanian *żada-s*, "speech," and *żodi-s*, "word," lead to the Sanscrit root *gad*, "to speak;" for which, in Zend, we have 𐬘𐬀𐬛 *jad*, "to require." To the Sanscrit root जीव् *jív*, "to live," corresponds the Sclavonic root жив *schiv;* while the Lithuanian in this root has preserved the original guttural (*gywas*, "living," *gywenn*, "I live"), which is a proof that the corruption of the original guttural in this root, in Sanscrit and Sclavonic, first made its appearance after the separation of the Lettish-Sclavonic languages from Sanscrit. The divergence of the Lettish

FORMATION OF WORDS. 1217

from the general sense whether the action passes from the subject or to it, as in general the abstract substantives ex-

---

tish and Sclavonic languages in the word "God" deserves notice; for while the Lithuanian *diewa-s*, and Prussian *deiwa-s*, are based on the Sanscrit *dêva-s*, "God" (Zend *daêva*, "evil spirit"), the word *bog* (theme *bogo*), which is common to perhaps all the Sclavonic languages, leads us to the Old Persian *baga*, with which Kuhn also, l. c., has compared it, while I, at a time when I was as yet unacquainted with the Old Persian expression (Glossarium Sanscr., Fasc. II. a. 1841, p. 242), compared it with भगवत् *bhagavat* (from *bhaga*, "*felicitas, beatitudo*"), "*felix, beatus, venerabilis*" (applied only to gods and saints); and under भग *bhaga* I have mentioned the Lithuanian *bagota-s*, and Russian *bagotyi*, "rich" (cf. Mikl. "Radices," s. v. богъ *bog'*, "*deus*"). The Sanscrit root *bhaj*, from *bhag*, signifies, "to worship, to adore, to love;" and as the suffix *a* has also a passive signification, the old Persian and Sclavonic term for "God" might originally have also signified "worshipped, adored," the possibility of which, with regard to the Sclavonic word, is also admitted by Pott (E. I., I. p. 236). I would, however, by no means found an argument for a special affinity between the Sclavonic languages and the Old Persian on their agreement in the designation of "God" (in Persian, "gods"), as the Sanscrit itself supplies a very satisfactory root for that; and, moreover, two languages might very easily have fallen upon the same method, quite independently of each other, so as to have designated "God," or "gods," from "adoration;" as, too, the New Persian ایزد *ized*, "God," is based on another root for "to pray," viz. on यज् *yaj* (Zend *yaz*), whence the perfect passive participle is, by contraction, *ishtá-s*. Though the opinion expressed above (§§. 21. 50.), and supported also by Burnouf (Yaçna, p. 173), be correct with regard to the original identity of the Lithuanian *swanta-s*, "holy," Old Sclavonic свать *svant'*, id., *svantiti*, "*sanctificare*," see Mikl. Rad. p. 79, Prussian *swint-s*, "holy," acc. *swinta-n*, *swintint*, "to hallow," it is nevertheless important to observe, that in this word also the Lettish and Sclavonic languages have thereby diverged from the Arian, or Medo-Persic, in that they have not changed the Sanscrit group of sounds, *śv* into *sp*, but have left the old semi-vowel unaltered. The Sanscrit supplies, as the original source of the word under discussion (see Weber, V. S. Sp. II. 68.), the extremely fruitful root *śvi*, "to grow," in the contracted form *śu*, if this be not the old form, and *śvi* an extension of it. From *śvi* we might expect *śvayanta*, according to

[G. Ed. p. 1258.] press in no degree whatever the relation of activity or passiveness. Moreover, the Sanscrit infinitive is wanting in a passive form; and where it has, or appears to have, a passive signification, this is discoverable only from the context, as, *e.g.*, in a passage of the Sâvitri (5. 15.), of which I annex the translation: "this man, bound by duty .... deserves not to be summoned by my servants," more literally, "is not deserving the summoning" (*nâ 'rhô nêtum*), where the circumstance that *nêtum* can be rendered by a passive infinitive does not justify us in assigning to it a passive signification. It has, if one will so view it, an active meaning with reference to the servants of Yama, and a passive with reference to *Satyavân*, while in

[G. Ed. p. 1259.] point of fact it denotes neither activity nor passiveness, but the abstract "summoning, leading away," which is itself irrespective of doing or suffering. So also in the Hitôpadêśa (ed. Bonn. p. 41), *abhishêktum*, "to sprinkle," has no passive signification, which Lassen (II. 75.) would make this infinitive borrow from the passive participle *nirûpita*. In my opinion, *nirûpita* retains its passive meaning for itself, and does not consign it to the infinitive. That however, l. c., the sprinkling (the kingly inauguration by sprinkling) is not performed by the elephant of the said person, but by another, is clear from the context. In order to leave the active or passive relation as undefined as in the original, I translate *aṭavîrâjyê 'bhishêktum bhavân nirûpitaḥ* by "to the sprinkling for the forest-sovereignty your honour is chosen."

871. We sometimes find the Vêdic dative also of the infinitive base in *tu* with an apparent passive infinitive signification; as, *e.g.*, S. V. (ed. Benfey, p. 143), *índrâya sóma*

---

the analogy of *jayantá* (n. pr., originally "conqueror"), and from *śu*, *śavanta;* and, without Guna, *śvanta;* to which the Sclavonic свать *svanť*, theme *svańto*, would correspond admirably.

pátavê vritraghnê paríshichyasê, "for Indra, O Sôma, for drinking (in order to be drunk) for the slayer of Vritra, thou art poured around;" Rigv. 28. 6., *indráya pátavê sunu sômam*, "for Indra, for drinking,* express the Sôma." Thus, also, at times the above-mentioned (§. 857.) dative form of abstract radical words appears to supply the place of the passive infinitive; *e.g.* Rigv. 52. 8. *ádhárayô divyá súryan drishé,* "thou hast placed the sun in the heaven to see."† As a practical rule, we may lay down the [G. Ed. p. 1260.] proposition for classical Sanscrit, that where an instrumental of the person accompanies the infinitive in *tum*, the former may, in languages which possess a passive infinitive, be translated by it. Thus, in the passage cited above (*ná 'rhô nêtum matpurusáih*); so also Mah. II. 309., *na yuktas tu avamánô 'sya kartun tvayá*, "It is not, however, fitting for thee to shew contempt for this one (=that contempt be made)." In another passage, which is in essentials similar (Mah. I. 769.), the passive participle *yukta*, "beseeming, fitting" (properly "joined"), is not governed by the subject, but stands impersonally in the neuter, *na yuktam bhavatá 'ham anritênô 'pacharitum*, "not beseeming (is it) that I, by thee with falsehood serve (=be served)."‡ There is also an interesting, and hitherto, in its kind, unique passage in the Raghuvansa (14. 42.), *yady arthitá . . . . pránán mayá dhárayituñ chiran vah.* Irrespective of *mayá*, "by me,"

---

* ="in order to be drunk." Sâyana explains *pátavê* by *pátaum;* but here, in classical Sanscrit, I should expect another abstract in the dative, rather than the accusative of the infinitive.

† ="to be seen." The Scholiast explains *drisé* by *dráshtum*, and then more closely by *sarvêshám asmákan darsanáya*, "on account of the seeing of us all."

‡ Compare a passage in Sâvitrî (II. 22.), where *sakyam*, "possibile," refers, according to the sense, to *dôsha*, masc., "fault:" *sacha dôshah prayatnéna na sakyam ativartitum*, "and this fault it is impossible to overpass without utmost endeavour."

the literal translation would be, "if your wish to retain life long," and then the obtaining of life would refer to the persons addressed; but by the appended *mayâ*, "by me," the sense is essentially altered, and the retention of life referred to the speaker, though the life might be that of those addressed if the context allowed of this; but *dhâra-*
[G. Ed. p. 1261.] *yitum*, "to receive," remains, however, in so far, a genuine active infinitive, as it governs the accusative (pl.) *prânân* "*vitam*." In order to imitate as closely the grammatical complexion of the original in translating it into German, we might perhaps render it thus, "if to you the wish (is) for the long retention of life through me;" only here the word that signifies "to retain" must be rendered as the common abstract with the genitive,* instead of as verbal with the accusative; and instead of the adverb "long" the corresponding adjective must be prefixed to it, while the proper infinitive is importantly distinguished from the common abstract by this, that it admits of no epithet.

872. It is worthy of notice, moreover, how the Sanscrit, being deficient in a passive infinitive, shifts for itself in cases where such an infinitive was to have been expected after verbs which signify "to be able" in such sentences as *vinci potest*. The Sanscrit then, in such cases, expresses the passive relation by the auxiliary verb शक् *śak*, "to be able," to which it has lent a passive, perhaps especially with a view to constructions of this kind, which, however, is only used impersonally; *e.g.* Mah. I. 6678., *yadi śakyatê*, "if it is possible" (literally, "if it is could");† on the other

---

* *I.e.* the infinitive in Sanscrit, which in the German is rendered by "*Erhalten*," must be regarded as a substantive "retention," not as verbal "retaining."—*Translator*.

† The reader will pardon this expression, which must be coined in order to render "*wird gekonnt:*" I had only the choice between it and "is been able."—*Translator*.

FORMATION OF WORDS. 1221

hand, *e.g.*, Nal. 20. 5., *nâ "hartuṅ śakyatê punaḥ*, "it (the garment) cannot be recalled," (literally, "is not can-ed to recall"); as if one could say in Latin, "*afferre nequitur*," instead of "*afferri nequit.*" The Latin language, however, allows of the doubled expression of the passive relation, both in the infinitive and in the negative auxiliary verb "*nequeo;*" hence, *e.g.*, *comprimi nequitur* (Plaut. Rud.), *retrahi nequitur* (Plaut. apud. Fest.), *ulcisci* (pass.), *nequitur* (Sall.), *virginitas reddi nequitur* (Apul.). Observe, also, the way in which the passive of the infinitive future in Latin is paraphrased by the accusative of the supine [G. Ed. p. 1262.] with *iri;* where, therefore, the auxiliary verb has, exactly as in the Sanscrit *śakyâtê*, "is could," taken upon itself the denoting of the passive relation, which the accusative of the supine, like its cognate form in Sanscrit, is incapable of expressing; thus, *amatum iri*, literally, "gone to love (in love)," instead of "to go to be loved." That, too, the indicative of *iri* can be used in constructions of this kind, is proved by a passage in Cato (apud Gell. 10. 14.), *contumelia per hujusce petulantiam mihi factum itur*, "Insult is gone to do to me," instead of "goes to be done to me."*

---

* I first drew attention to the peculiarity of Sanscrit idiom, as regards the construction of the passive of *śak*, "to be able," with the infinitive, in my review of Forster's "Essay on the principles of the Sanscrit Grammar" (Heidelberg Ann. Reg., 1818, No. 30, p. 476), and afterwards in a Note on Arjuna's journey to Indra's heaven, p. 81; and I believe that it was desirable, to express a meaning on this subject, as the singularity of a passive to a verb which signifies "to be able;" and the circumstance that *śak* admits also of being used as a middle of the 4th class (*e.g. śakyasê*, "thou canst," N. XI. 6.) might also induce the opinion that the Sanscrit infinitive in *tum* has both a passive and an active meaning; and that, therefore, *e.g.*, *hantuṅ śakyatê* literally signifies nothing else than "*occidi potest.*" This is, however, opposed by the passages in which infinitives are dependent on the decidedly passive participles of the preterite *śakitâ* (see p. 1118 Note ‡), and of the future *śakya*; *e.g.*, Râm. I. 44. 53., *punar na śakitâ nêtun gaṅgâ prârthayatâ*,

[G. Ed. p. 1263.]   873. Let us now turn to the German infinitive; and we will, in the first place, call attention to the remarkable agreement which the Gothic shews to the Sanscrit in this, that in the want of a passive infinitive in the cases in which this form, did it exist, would be placed after the auxiliary verb signifying "to be able" (*mag*, "I can," "I am able") it expresses the passive relation in the auxiliary verb. As, however, *mag*, "I can," is a preterite with a present signification (cf. §. 491.), and as the Gothic is not in a position to form a passive, except out of present forms (see §. 512.), and not, like the Sanscrit and Greek, out of other tenses also, it has recourse to the passive participle *mahts, mahta, maht*, which, like the formal indicative preterite *mag*, has always a present signification;[*] on which account the temporal relation, if it be a past one, can be denoted only by the appended verb substantive, while

---

"the Gangâ (would) not be able (possible) to bring back by the wisher;" Hidimba, I. 35., *kin tu śakyam mayâ kartum* "what, however, (is) to be able (possible) to do by me" (=what, however, can be done by me). Lassen (Hitôp. II. 75.) remarks that constructions of this kind can in nowise be limited to *śak*, "to be able," but it is nevertheless certain that the construction of the active infinitive with the passive of a verb which signifies "to be able" is the most original and most deserving of special notice; for that verbs which signify "to begin" have in Sanscrit, as in other languages, a passive, is just as little surprising, as that the action which is begun is expressed in Sanscrit, as in German, by the active infinitive, as it is not necessary that the passive relation should be expressed both at the beginning and in the action which is begun, though constructions occur in Latin like *vasa conjici coepta sunt* (Nep.); while we in German say, *e.g., das Haus wird zu bauen angefangen*, "the house is begun to build (to be built);" and in Sanscrit (Hit., ed. Bonn. p. 49, 1. 10.), *têna vihârah kârayitum ârabdhah*, "by this one (would) a temple be begun to be built." It is self-evident that, in constructions of this kind, the action expressed by the infinitive does not stand in an active relation to the subject.

[*] Cf. Grimm, IV. pp. 59, 60.

the Sanscrit *śakitá*, has already a past meaning, both in and for itself. For the feminine *śakitá* mentioned above (p. 1262 G. ed., Note) Ulfilas would have said *mahta was*, not *mahta ist;* while in Sanscrit, if the usually [G. Ed. p. 1264.] omitted verb substantive were actually expressed in the passage quoted l. c., we should have *śakitá 'sti*, in the manner of the Latin periphrasis of the lost perfect passive, as *amata est*. Though, in Gothic also, the circumlocutive for the passive infinitive by the participle preterite passive with the auxiliary verb "to be" (*vairthan*) already occurs (Grimm, IV. 57.) and, *e.g.*, Matt. viii. 24. καλύπτεσθαι is rendered by *gahulith wairthan*,* nevertheless Ulfilas rejects this periphrasis in the cases in which, in the Greek text, the passive infinitive is dependent on a verb signifying "to be able." Hence, Mark xiv. 5, *maht vêsi . . . . frabukyan*, ἠδύνατο πραθῆναι ; Luke viii. 43, *qvinô . . . . ni mahta* (nom. fem.) *was fram ainômêhun galeikinôn*, γυνὴ οὐκ ἴσχυσεν ὑπ' οὐδενὸς θεραπευθῆναι ; John iii. 4, *hvaiva mahts ist manna gabairan*, πῶς δύναται ἄνθρωπος γεννηθῆναι ; x. 35, *ni maht ist gatairan thata gamêlidô*, οὐ δύναται λυθῆναι ἡ γραφή ; 1 Tim. v. 25, *fithan ni mahta sind*, κρυβῆναι οὐ δύναται.

874. Like *mahts, skulds* (*skal*, "I must") also has the meaning of the present passive participle, while in form it

---

* The preterite participle passive is well suited, with the auxiliary verb "to be," for a periphrasis of the present infinitive, because the auxiliary takes, as it were, the temporal power from the expression of the past, and places the past or perfect nature of the action in the future, whereby the whole is, by this means, adapted to express the present. Compare the periphrasis for the future active in Old High Prussian by the perfect active participle and the auxiliary verb "to be" (see p. 1061 Note *). On the other hand, the perfect passive participle with *visan*, "*esse*," analogously to the Latin, expresses the perfect passive infinitive; and this is well worthy of notice. So in the subscription to 1 Cor., *mêlida visan* ("*scripta esse*"). Cf. 2 Cor. v. 11, *svikunthans visan*, "*cognitos esse*" (πεφανερῶσθαι), with iv. 11, *svikuntha wairthai* (φανερωθῇ).

corresponds to the perfect passive participle of the Sanscrit and Latin. This *skulds* (fem. *skulda*, neut. *skuld*), receives [G. Ed. p. 1265.] in like manner the expression of the passive relation, which the language is incapable of expressing in the accompanying infinitive: hence, *e.g.*, Luke ix. 44, *skulds ist atgiban in handuns mannê*, as it were, "he is being compelled to deliver into the hands of men," instead of, "he must be delivered" μέλλει παραδίδοσθαι). Moreover, in Gothic it often happens that it can be known only from the context and the accompanying dative (alone or with *fram*, "from"), which, in Gothic, frequently represents the Sanscrit instrumental, that the infinitive has not the common active meaning, but a passive one.* Thus, in Matt. vi. 1, it appears from the dative *im*, "by them," that the preceding infinitive has a passive signification, and that *du saihvan im*, which we, in order to imitate the construction, must translate by "to the seeing by them," translates the Greek πρὸς τὸ θεαθῆναι αὐτοῖς, where the infinitive has, through the prefixed article, the form of a concrete. Without, however, the *im*, which shews what is the proper meaning, *du saihvan*, "to see," for "seeing," could not well be otherwise taken in this passage than as active, and the preceding words, which lead us to expect a passive expression, would not justify us in taking the said infinitive as passive.—Von Gabelentz and Löbe (Gramm. p. 140 c.), remark, that, by a Germanism, the Gothic active infinitive after the verbs "to command, to will, to give" occurs with a passive signification. I cannot, however, perceive any passive signification of the infinitive in the examples adduced l. c., except in *du ushramyan*, "to crucify" (="to the crucifying, to be crucified"). Among others, the following are cited as examples: Matt. xxvii. 64, *hait vitan thamma hlaiva*, "command to watch the grave," exactly as,

---

* Cf. the analogous Sanscrit constructions, p. 1258 G. ed.

FORMATION OF WORDS. 1225

in Latin, *jube custodire sepulcrum;* only that [G. Ed. p. 1266.] the Gothic verb *vita,* "I watch," and therefore, also, its infinitive, instead of the dative, governs the accusative, while the Latin *jubere* also admits of the passive infinitive, as in the Greek text, κέλευσον ἀσφαλισθῆναι τὸν τάφον ("command the being watched with respect to the grave"); Luke viii. 53, *anabaud izai giban* (*dare,* not *dari* δοθῆναι) *mat,* "He commanded to give her (*actionem dandi ei*), meat," *jussit ei dare cibum,* compared with the Greek διέταξεν αὐτῇ δοθῆναι φαγεῖν, "He commanded the being given to her (*actionem τοῦ dari ei*) to eat (with reference to eating);"* a construction which cannot be imitated in Gothic, but to which Ulfilas, in Mark v. 43, (*haihait izai giban matyan*) thereby approximates, in that he renders φαγεῖν by an infinitive, which, however, here stands as the object of *giban,* "to give," in the common accusative relation, and does not, like the Greek, express the relation "in reference to" (as πόδας ὠκύς). Most common is the representation of the Greek passive infinitive by the Gothic active infinitive with a passive signification to be deduced from the context, in cases in which the infinitive expresses the causal relation, and the Vêda dialect uses the dative in *tu,* or another infinitive form (see §. 854.), while the Gothic employs the infinitive with the preposition *du,* or, also, the simple infinitive, but the latter almost only after verbs of motion, where it, irrespective of its possible passive signification, corresponds to the accusative of the Latin supine; *e.g.,* Luke v. 15, *garunnun hiuhmans managai hausyan* [G. Ed. p. 1267.] *yah leikinôn fram imma,* "great multitudes came together to hear and to healing (= to be healed, θεραπεύεσθαι) by

---

* By this un-German rendering I merely wish to shew that the Greek passive infinitive stands in the accusative relation. The case-relation of the infinitive φαγεῖν is likewise accusative, and corresponds to that of τάφον in the preceding example.

him;" Luke ii. 4, 5, *urran than yah ïosef* . . . . *anamêlyan mith mariin*, "and Joseph also went up to the taxing (to be taxed) with Mary;" 2 Thess. i. 10, *qvimith ushauhyan*, "he cometh to the glorifying (to be glorified," ἐνδοξασθῆναι). But above (p. 1265 G. ed.), for *du saihvan*, "to the seeing (to be seen"), *saihvan* alone could scarcely stand, as no verb of motion precedes: for the same reason, at Matt. xxvi. 2 also (*atgibada du ushramyan*, "is betrayed to be crucified," εἰς τὸ σταυρωθῆναι), the preposition *du* could not be removed. On the other hand, the strictly active infinitive is occasionally also found in the causal relation without *du*, and without being preceded by a verb of motion; *e.g.*, Eph. vi. 19, *ei mis gibaidau vaurd* . . . . *kannyan runa aivaggêlyôns*, "that utterance may be given unto me . . . . to make known the mystery of the gospel" (see Gabel. and Löbe, Gramm. p. 250).

875. In German, and indeed so early as in Old High German, the infinitive often apparently receives a passive signification through the preposition *zu* (Old High German, *za, ze, zi, zo, zu*. With it, for the most part, is found the verb substantive; and we render the Latin future passive participle, when accompanied by the verb substantive, by the infinitive with *zu*; *e.g. puniendus est* by "*er ist zu strafen*," "he is to punish" (*i.e.* "he is for the punishing fitted thereto"): on the other hand, in English we have, "he is to be punished" (= "*er ist gestraft zu werden*"). J. Grimm, IV. 60, 61, gives examples of the Old and Middle High German, from which I annex a few: *ze karawenne*[*] *sint* ("*præparanda sunt*"), Ker. 15ᵃ.; *ze kesezzenne ist* ("*constituenda est*"), Ker. 15ᵇ.; *za petônne ist* [G. Ed. p. 1268.] ("*orandum est*"), Hymn 17. 1.; *ist zi firstandanne* ("*intelligendum est*"), Is. 9. 2.; *daz er an ze sehene den frouwen wære guot*, Nib. 276. 2. But even without the accompaniment of

---

[*] Regarding the dative form, see §. 879.

the verb substantive, we give, in appearance, to the infinitive a passive signification in sentences like *er lässt nichts zu wünschen übrig,* " he leaves nothing to be desired ;" *er gab ihm Wein zu trinken,* " he gave him wine to drink." Such constructions answer to those in which, in the Vêda dialect, the dative of the infinitive stands apparently with a passive signification (see §. 871.); since, *e.g.,* पातवे *pátavê* may very well be translated by " to be drunk," though it signifies nothing else than " on account of drinking," exactly like our *zu trinken (zum Trinken)* in the sentence cited above (cf. pp. 1225, 1226 Note, G. ed.). Our infinitives have also the appearance of a passive signification, and the capacity of representing the real passive infinitives of other languages, after *hören,* " to hear," *sehen,* " to see," *lassen,* " to leave," *heissen,* " to be called," *befehlen,* " to command," in sentences like *ich höre erzählen, (audio narrari); ich sah ihn mit Füssen treten (calcari),* " I saw him trampled under foot ;" *ich kann kein Thier schlachten sehen (mactari),* " I cannot see an animal slaughtered ;" *lass dich von ihm belehren,* "let thyself be taught by him ;" *er befahl ihn zu tödten,* " he ordered him to be slain" (see Grimm, IV. 61). Yet, when such expressions arose, the want of a real passive infinitive was hardly felt, and it was scarcely intended to give to the active infinitive a passive signification; for the active meaning of the infinitive is here quite ample, and in the cases in which an accusative is governed by the infinitive *(ich sah mit Füssen treten ihn,* &c.) it is even more natural than the passive. Undoubtedly, in the sentences quoted above the infinitives are still more strictly active than the Sanscrit *nêtum* in the sentence previously (p. 1258 G. ed.) discussed, " he is not deserving the summoning by my people," because here there is no accusative governed by *nêtum,* " to summon," which allows the active expression to appear in its full energy. The circum- [G. Ed. p. 1269.] stance, that many languages in such kinds of expression arrive at the same method independently of each other, proves that it is very natural. I further recall attention, with J. Grimm (l. c.), to French sentences, such as, *je lui ai vu couper les jambes ; il se laisse chasser ;* and, moreover, to the fact, that in certain verbs the Latin admits both the active and passive infinitive, which, however, proves that the former is perfectly logical and correct, as it is not necessity, *i.e.* the actual want of a passive form, which occasions its use.

876. As regards the form of the German infinitive, it appears to me beyond all doubt, that, as has already been elsewhere ("The Caucasian members of the Indo-European Family of Languages," p. 83.) remarked, the termination *an*, afterwards *en*, is based on the Sanscrit neuter suffix *ana*, the formations of which in Sanscrit also very frequently supply the place of the infinitive,* and on which, too, are grounded also the Hindūstānī infinitives, as also the South Ossetish in *in*, the Tagaurish in *ün*, and very probably, also, the Armenian, in the final *l* of which I think I recognise the very common corruption of an *n* (see §. 20.), as is the case, among other words, in այլ *ail*, "the other," compared with the Sanscrit *anya-s*, Latin *aliu-s*, Greek ἄλλος, and the Gothic base *alya* (see §. 374.). The vowel which precedes the *l* of the Armenian infinitives belongs, however, not to the suffix, but to the verbal theme, which we may learn from its changing according to the difference of the conjugations; hence, *e.g.* բերել *ber-e-l*, "to carry,"† (Sanscrit [G. Ed. p. 1270.] *bhar-aná*, "the carrying, supporting") = Gothic *bair-a-n*, after the analogy of բերեմ *ber-e-m*, "I bear,"

---

* See pp. 1211, 1213, G. ed.

† I write the Armenian consonants in the Latin character, according to their parentage, and the pronunciation which is assigned to them by the order of the alphabet (see Petermann, p. 16). The vowel ե *e*, which is often pronounced like *ye*, corresponds etymologically to the Greek ε, and, as the latter generally does, to the Sanscrit *a*.

FORMATION OF WORDS. 1229

բերես ber-e-s, "thou bearest;" տալ ta-l, "to give" (Sanscrit dâna, "the giving, gift") with տամ ta-m, "I give," տաս ta-s, "thou givest" (Sanscrit dádâ-mi, dádâ-si); մնալ mn-a-l, "to remain," with մնամ mn-a-m, "I remain," մնաս mn-a-s, "thou remainest;" մեռանիլ merhan-i-l, "to die," with մեռանիմ merhan-i-m, "I die," մեռանիս merhan-i-s, "thou diest." In the German languages also the vowel preceding the final n of the infinitive does not belong to the infinitive suffix, but to the class-syllable. In the weak conjugation ($=$ Sanscrit Cl. 10., see §. 109^a. 6.), it is tolerably clear, that, e.g., the syllable ya of satyan, "to place" (see §. 741.), the a of which, according to an universal rule of sound (§. 67.), is weakened before a final s and th to i, is identical with the same syllable in sat-yu, "I place;" sat-ya-m, "we place;" sat-ya-nd, "they place." I therefore divide the infinitive thus, sat-ya-n. In forms like salb-ô-n, "to salve" (pres. salb-ô, salb-ô-s, salb-ô-th, &c.), it is still more clear that the simple n is the suffix of the infinitive. In Grimm's 3d conjugation of the weak form, the i of the diphthong ai is dropped before the n of the infinitive, as generally before nasals, thus, hab-a-n, "to have," so, too, hab-a-m, "we have," hab-a-nd, "they have," contrasted with hab-ai-s, "thou hast," hab-ai-th, "he has, ye have:" on the other hand, in Old High German, hab-ê-n, "to have," as also hab-ê-m, "I have," hab-ê-nt, "they have." In the strong verbs, which, with the few exceptions in ya (see §. 109^a. 2.), belong to the Sanscrit 1st class, it might have been before assumed that the a preceding the n in the infinitive is identical with the Sanscrit first a of the suffix ana; that therefore, e.g., bairan, "to bear," qviman, "to come," bindan, "to bind," beitan, "to bite," grêtan, "to weep," correspond [G. Ed. p. 1271.] also, with respect to the 1st a of the suffix, to the Sanscrit neuter abstracts which are akin in formation, bhar-aṇa, "the bearing, supporting," gam-ana, "the going," bandh-ana, "the binding," bhêd-ana, "the separating," krand-ana, "the weeping;" and this was formerly my opinion. As, however, the verbs which correspond to the Sanscrit 4th class retain the character *ya* in the infinitive, and, *e.g.*, the infinitive of *vahs-ya*, "I grow" (pret. *vôhs*), is *vahs-ya-n* (not *vahs-an*), and that of *bid-ya*, "I pray" (pret. *bath*, pl. *bêdum*), *bid-ya-n* (not *bid-an*), I now regard the *a* of forms like *bair-a-n*, *bind-a-n*, &c., as the class-vowel, and therefore as identical with that of *bair-a*, *bair-a-m*, *bair-a-nd*, *bind-a*, *bind-a-m*, *bind-a-nd*; and I derive in general the German infinitive from the theme of the special tenses, with which it always agrees in respect of the form of the radical vowel; since, *e.g.*, *bind-a-n*, "to bind," *biug-an*, "to bend," correspond in this respect to the present *binda*, *biuga*, but not to the true root *band*, *bug*, or to the singular of the preterite *band*, *baug* (plur. *bundum*, *bugum*). Consequently the German infinitive stands in exact accordance with the Armenian, if I am right in viewing in the *l* of the latter the corruption of an *n*, and therefore in the before-mentioned բերել *ber-e-l*, a form exactly analogous to the Gothic *bair-a-n*, Old High German *bër-a-n*.

Remark.—As the Armenian ե *e*, like the Greek ε, is the most common representative of the Sanscrit *a*; so the Armenian 1st conjugation, in the great majority of its verbs, viz. in those which interpose a simple ե *e* between the root and the personal terminations, corresponds to the Sanscrit 1st and 6th classes (see §. 109ª. 1.), which two classes cannot be distinguished in Armenian, a language in which Guna is unknown. The inserted ե *e*, therefore, of forms like բերեմ *ber-e-m*, "I bear," բերես *ber-e-s*, "thou bearest," բերեմք *ber-e-mkh*, "we [G. Ed. p. 1272.] bear," բերեն *ber-e-n*, "they bear," corresponds to the Greek ε of forms like φέρ-ε-τε, φέρ-ε-τον, ἔφερ-ε-ς, ἔφερ-ε, and to the Sanscrit *a* of forms like *bhár-a-si*, "thou bearest," *bhár-a-ti*, "he bears," *bhár-a-nti*, "they bear." The lengthening of the Armenian ե *e* to է *ê* in բերէ *ber-ê*, "he bears," բերէք *ber-ê-kh*, "ye bear," I regard as compensation for the dropping of the personal expression after the class-vowel;* for the *kh* of the last-named form is, to a

---

* As the 3d person *berê*, for *beret*=Sanscrit *bharati*, Gothic *bairith*, has

FORMATION OF WORDS. 1231

certain extent, only the expression of plurality, as, in the 1st person, *ber-e-mkh* (*mkh*=Sanscrit *mas*). In the 2d person the to-be-presupposed *tkh* or *takh*, like the Latin *tis* (*fertis*), would correspond rather to the Sanscrit dual (*bhár-a-thas*) than to the plural (*bhár-a-tha*). In the 1st Armenian conjugation occur also verbs, which add, not a simple *e*, but *ne* to the root, in which it is easy to recognise, as in the Latin *ni*, *e.g.*, in *ster-ni-s*, *ster-ni-t* (see §. 496.), the character of the Sanscrit 9th class, with *nâ*, *nî*, as class-syllable. Here belongs, *e.g.*, the root ｟ɯɯռ_ χarh, " to mix;" whence ｟ɯɯռեմ χarh-ne-m, "I mix," infinitive ｟ɯɯռել χarh-ne-l. The corresponding Sanscrit root *kar* (कृ *kṛi*), "to strew," with the preposition *sam*, also "to mix," follows the 9th class, not, indeed, in this signification, but in another ("to slay"); and it admits of no doubt that the Armenian χarh-ne-m corresponds to the Sanscrit *kṛi-ṇā-mi* (from *kar-ṇā-mi*) and Greek κίρ-νη-μι. Probably, also, the Armenian verbs in *ane-m* and *ana-m*—as ՀարցանեմЃ *harzanem*, "I ask" (Sanscrit root *prachh*); լուանամ *lovanam*, "I wash" (Sanscrit root *plu*, "to swim," causal "to wash," Greek πλύνω—belong to the Sanscrit 9th class, with the insertion, therefore, of an *a* between the root and the original class-character, in the same way as, at times, in Old High German, an *a* is prefixed to the formative suffixes beginning with a consonant (see §. 799.). Before the passive character *i*, which Petermann (p. 188) [G. Ed. p. 1273.] aptly compares with the Sanscrit *ya*, verbs of this kind, whether actually existing or presupposed, drop the vowel of the class-character. In this manner at least I think that we must explain deponents like մեռանիմ *merhanim*, "I die," for which we must suppose in Sanscrit *mṛi-ṇā-mi* (from *mar-ṇā-mi*), but not so as to identify the syllable *ni* of *merhanim*, and similar forms, with the *nî* which appears in Sanscrit before the heavy personal terminations (*yu-nî-más* compared with *yu-nắ-mi*). The Armenian 2d conjugation, which adds *a* to the root, as *e.g.*, որսամ *orhs-a-m*, "I hunt," would, if this *a* were based, like the *e* of the 1st conjugation, on the syllable of insertion of the Sanscrit 1st and 6th class, have retained

---

has lost a *t*, I think, too, that in the ablative in *é*, which Fr. Windischmann, in his valuable academical treatise on the Armenian (p. 28), calls a mysterious phenomenon, we have to assume the dropping of a *t*, and, indeed, the rather, as the original final *t* has become unendurable in many Indo-European languages. Hence the Armenian ablatives like *himan-é*, from the base *himan*, may be compared with the Zend like *chaṣhman-aṭ* (see p. 197), and the է *é* for ե *e* may be viewed as a compensation for the dropping of the *t*.

the character of its Indian prototype still more truly than the 1st conjugation. As, however, the Armenian *ա a* more frequently corresponds to the Sanscrit long *â* than to the short, it would also be possible that the *ա a* under discussion, like the Latin *â* of the 1st conjugation, with which Fr. Windischmann compares it,* is based on the Sanscrit *aya* of the 10th class (see §. 109ᵃ. 6.) The circumstance, however, that the Armenian *a*-conjugation contains many neuter verbs, while the Sanscrit *aya* is principally devoted to the formation of causal and denominative verbs, makes the deduction of the Armenian 2d conjugation from the Sanscrit 10th class little probable, and favours rather the derivation from the 1st or 6th class, or from the 4th, containing scarce any but neuter verbs, which in Armenian might easily have sacrificed the semi-vowel of their character *ya* (cf. Petermann, p. 188). In the Armenian 3d conjugation there are many verbs which add *nu* to the root, and thereby at once remind us of the Sanscrit *nu* of the 5th class (see §. 109ᵃ. 4.), with which Petermann also has compared them. Those which add a simple *u* have probably, like the Sanscrit verbs of the 8th class, lost an *n* (see §. 495.).

877. The Hindūstānī infinitive also has dropped the first vowel of the Sanscrit suffix *ana;*† and, on the other hand,

---

* "Foundation of the Armenian in the Arian Family of Languages," in the treatises of the 1st class of the Bavarian Academy of Lit., B. IV. Part I., in the special impression, p. 44.

† The *â* by which transitives like *jŏl-â-nâ*, "*urere*," is formed from intransitives like *jŏl-nâ*, "*ardere*," I derive from the Sanscrit causal character *aya*, in the same way as the Latin *â* of the 1st conjugation (§. 109ᵃ. 6.). By this *a* causatives also are formed from active transitives; e.g., *bidh-â-nâ*, "to cause to bore," from *bêdh-nâ*, "to bore" (= Sanscrit [1] *bhêd-ana-m*, "the cleaving," root *bhid*; (Gilchrist, "A Grammar," &c., p. 147). With regard to the causal here exhibiting a weaker vowel than the primitive verb, while in Sanscrit the causals usually experience an increment to the vowel, it is probable that the Hindūstānī finds a reason for weakening the radical syllable in the incumbrance of the causal by the affix *â*. Where, however, the causal or transitive loses the proper causal character, it often exhibits a stronger vowel than the primitive; *e.g*

---

[1] Shakespear, with more probability, compares the word वेधन *vedhan* from व्यध् *vyadh*, "to pierce." In the original, Professor Bopp writes *bid-â-nâ* and *bêd-nâ*, which do not occur in our dictionaries.—*Translator*.

lengthened the final *a*, in case we are not to [G. Ed. p. 1274.] suppose that it is derived from the feminine form of the suffix आन *ana*, which is used in Sanscrit for the formation of abstract substantives much more rarely than the neuter. The following are examples: आसना *ásaná*, "the sitting;" याचना *yáchaná*, "the request;" वन्दना *vandaná*, "the praising." Herewith agree, in respect of accentua- [G. Ed. p. 1275.] tion, also the Greek αὐονή and ἡδονή; while ἀγχόνη and δαπάνη, in this latter respect, differ; but the latter has retained the Old *a*-sound of the suffix. To this head, too, have

---

már-ná, "to slay" (Sanscrit *maráyámi*, "I make to die"), from *mŏr-ná*[1], "to die" (ŏ=Sanscrit ă, *mŏr-ná*=मरण *marana*, "the dying").—In the *w* of Hindūstānī, causals like *chŏl-wáná*, "to make to go" (*chŏl-ná*, "to go"), I recognise a corruption of the *p* of the causals like *jiv-áp-áyá-mi*, discussed above (§. 749.). The transition of the *p* into *w* appears, however, to have taken place at a time when one more vowel preceded the labial; as, *e.g.*, in the numerals *ĕkáwŏn* 51, *báwŏn* 52, *sŏtáwŏn* 57, in contradistinction to *tirpŏn* 53, *pŏchpŏn* 55, where it admits of no doubt that both *wŏn* and *pŏn* are based on the Sanscrit *panchásat* 50, and therefore *ĕkáwŏn* on *ĕkapanchásat*, *tirpŏn* on *tripanchásat*, the nasal of which is lost in the Hindūstānī *pŏchás* 50, while the simple پانچ *pánch* has retained it. The length of the *á* of پانچ *pánch*, compared with the Sanscrit short vowel, may perhaps serve as a compensation for the dropping of the syllable *an* (*panchan*), for short ă appears in Hindūstānī regularly as short *o*, which Gilchrist, according to English pronunciation, writes *u*. The Hindūstānī is most extremely sensitive with regard to the weight of the vowel, and therefore weakens the long *á* of *pánch* again to ŏ when the overloading the word by composition gives occasion for this, *e.g.* in *pŏndrŏh* 15; thus, *sŏtrŏh* 17, opposed to *sát* (from *saptan*) 7.

---

[1] The vowel here given as ŏ by Professor Bopp is undoubtedly ă, and the word مرنا is universally written *marná*. More than that, the sound ŏ does not exist in the language, except before *r*, any more than it does in Marāṭhī, as has been noticed before. It is true that in Bengālī short *a* is pronounced like ŏ; and hence Dr. Carey has imagined this to be the case in Marāṭhī, but there is no foundation for such a belief.—*Translator*.

4 L

already been referred (§. 803. sub. f.), as conjectural cognate forms, the Old High German abstracts in *unga*, while those in New High German have lost their final vowel. It does not, however, appear probable to me, that the Hindūstānī infinitives are based on these feminine abstracts, but I regard their *â* as the lengthening of the Sanscrit short *a*, which in general, in Hindūstānī, when final, is either entirely suppressed or lengthened; the latter, among other words, in the names of male animals, while those of females terminate in *í*, and the generic name has lost the original final vowel (see Gilchrist "A Grammar," &c., p. 52). Thus, *e.g.*, the general term for the buffalo (Sanscrit *mahisha*) in Hindūstānī is ميهك *maihik*,* while the male buffalo is *maihikâ*, and the female *maihikí*, the latter = Sanscrit *mahishí* (see §.119.). As the Hindūstānī has lost its neuter, the Sanscrit neuters, which in their theme are not to be distinguished from masculine bases, have in the said language become masculines, and we may therefore unhesitatingly compare the Hindūstānī infinitives in نا *nâ* with the Sanscrit abstracts in *ana;* thus, *e.g.*, *jŏl-nâ*, "to burn" = Sanscrit *jvalaná-m*, "the burning," or rather = *jvalaná-s*, as the Sanscrit neuters have, in Hindūstānī become masculines. The oblique case in *ê* of the Hindūstānī infinitive points to a Sanscrit base in *a*, in which we easily recognise the Sanscrit locative of bases in *a* (see §. 196.): therefore, *e.g.*, in *jŏlnê*, "to burn," † we perceive the Sanscrit *jvalanê*, "in the burning."

---

* The common term for a male buffalo in Hindūstānī is بهينسا *bhaiṅsā*, and for a female بهينس *bhaiṅs*; and in Marāṭhī, म्हैसा *mhaisā* and म्हैस *mhais*. ميهك *maihik*, in which a mere provincial pronunciation changes *sh* to *k*, is comparatively seldom used.—*Translator.*

† This form in *ê* usually expresses in the Hindūstānī infinitive the accusative relation, as is also occasionally the case in Sanscrit. I recall attention to the passage of the Râmâyana cited above (§. 852.), in which
grahaṇê

878. The dropping of the final *a* of the [G. Ed. p. 1276.] Sanscrit neuter suffix *ana* in the German infinitives accords

grahaṇé, "to take, to receive," is governed by *śćkur* (euphonic for *śćkus*), "they could." So in Hindūstānī, in an example given by Yates ("Introduction," &c., p. 65), *maiṅ bólné nŏhīṅ sŏktā*, "I cannot say," "I to say (in the saying, for the saying, acc.) not being able." Where, however, the infinitive stands in the nominative relation, as *sunnā*, "to hear" (the hearing), in the example given by Yates l. c., "hearing is not like seeing," we find the form in *nā*. As the adjectives also, the participles included, end, in the masculine singular nominative, in *ā*, I regard the lengthening of the originally short *a* as a compensation for the suppressed case-sign, and I therefore derive *ā* from *a-s*, just as in Marāṭhī. In the masculine plural nominative of both languages the termination *é* corresponds to the Sanscrit pronominal declension (see §. 228.): hence, in Hindūstānī, *maiṅ mārtā*, "I strike," properly "I (am) striking," fem. *maiṅ mārtī* "I (am) striking," pl. *hŏm mārté*, "we (are) striking." Compare *vé*, "they" (pl.), which belongs either to the Zend and Old Persian base *ava*, or, as is more probable, to the Sanscrit reflexive base *sva* (§. 341.), on which also the Old Persian *huva* (euphonic for *hva*), "he," is based, and from which we might have expected a masculine plural nominative *své*. The Sanscrit diphthong *é* plays throughout an important part in Hindūstānī Grammar; and thus we find also, in the subjunctive forms like *tū māré*, "thou mayest strike," *vŏh māré*, "he may strike," *hŏm māréṅ*, "we may strike," *vé māréṅ*, "they may strike," a good remnant of Sanscrit Grammar, since the *é* of those forms is evidently based on that of the Sanscrit potential of the 1st principal conjugation, and, indeed, so that the final *s* and *t* of the 2d and 3d person singular have been lost (thus, *māré* for *māré-s* and *māré-t*, cf. *bhāré-s*, *bhāré-t*, p. 946); and of the termination *ma* of the 1st person plural only the *m* has been left in the form of a weakened nasal; thus, *māré-ṅ* for *māré-ma* or *-mŏ*: in the 3d person plural we have *māré-ṅ* for *māré-nt* (see §. 462. p. 645), which approximates very closely to the Old High German forms like *bëré-n*, "*ferant.*" On the Sanscrit potential also is based, in my opinion, the Hindūstānī future, just like the Latin of the 3d and 4th conjugations (according to §. 692.), only that, in Hindūstānī, to the subjunctive mentioned above, where it represents the future indicative, a syllable has been added, in which I recognise the above-mentioned (p. 1104, Note †) Sanscrit enclitic *ha*, Véd. also *gha* or *ghā*, which, however, in Hindūstānī, just

[G. Ed. p. 1277.] with the phenomenon, that, in general, neuter bases in *a* have lost this vowel in the nominative

just as in Afghān, has become declinable (see Preface to the 5th Part, p. viii[1]), and also distinguishes the genders; hence, *e.g.*,

wŏh mârê-gâ, "he will strike;"
wŏh mârê-gî, "she will strike;"
hŏm mârên-gê, "they will strike."

After

---

[1] The Preface here referred to is as follows:—" I have, in the part now laid before the public, not yet been able to finish my Comparative Grammar, but give here preliminarily the conclusion of the formation of moods, the locative of the derivative adverbs, and a part of the formation of words, viz. the formation of participles, and of those substantives and adjectives which stand in close connection with any participle through the derivative suffix. Since the publication of the 4th Part of this book, Comparative Grammar has acquired a new region for research in Sanscrit accentuation which hitherto had remained almost unknown, and which Böhtlingk's academical treatise, "A first attempt regarding the accent in Sanscrit," opened out to us.[a] Aufrecht, in his pamphlet, " De accentu compositorum Sanscriticorum" (Bonn, 1847), treats of the accentuation of compounds. Benfey and G. Curtius have been the first to draw attention to detached instances of agreement between the Sanscrit and Greek accentuation, the former in his notice of Böhtlingk's treatise (Halle Journal of General Literature, May 1845), the latter in his brochure, "The Comparison of Languages in their relation to Classical Philosophy" (2d Ed. pp. 22, 23, 61). I believe I recognise a common fundamental principle in the system of accentuation in both languages in this, that in Sanscrit, as well as in Greek, the

---

[a] Some very valuable corrections, which have since been confirmed by the accentuated Vêda-text, are given by Holtzmann in his brochure "On the Ablaut" (Carlsruhe, 1844), p. 9. Thus Holtzmann has been the first to shew, or rather to understand rightly, the rule of Pâṇini on this head, concealed in an obscure, technical language, that the plural of *bódhâmi* is not accented *bô-dhâmás* but *bódhâmas*; that of *dvéshmi* not *dvishmas* but *dvishmás*. Hence it is clear that the division of the personal terminations in §. 480. into heavy and light, is also of importance for the theory of accentuation, and that the heavy terminations here, too, principally act on the next preceding syllable, since they can remove from it its accent as well as the Guna.

accusative singular, together with the case-sign. As, therefore, e.g., the Gothic base word *daura*, "door," con-

---

After what has been said, it hardly need be remarked that the Hindūstānī imperative also, in most persons of both numbers, is identical with the Sanscrit potential and the corresponding moods in the cognate European languages; so that, therefore, e.g., *mârê*, " let him strike," for *mârê-t*, corresponds to the Old High German forms like *bërê*, " let him carry,"

---

the accenting of the beginning of a word, or the throwing back of the accent as far as possible, is considered the most emphatic, and that which imparts the greatest animation to the whole word (see p. 1084 G. ed. 1052 E. Tr.). Hence follows a very pervading, though hitherto almost overlooked, agreement of the two languages in the accentuation of that part of speech which is formally and significantly the richest, viz. the verb (see p. 1086 G. ed., 1054 E. Tr.). A most convincing proof of the emphasis given by accenting the first syllable is furnished by the Sanscrit in this, that it withdraws this species of accent from the passive, but allows it to the middle of the fourth class, though in sound the two forms are identical; thus, *súchyátê* '*purificatur*,' compared with *súchyatê* '*purificat*:' it also deserves especial notice, with reference to this point, that the oxytone nouns of agency in *tár* (nom. *tá*), when they are found as participles governing the accusative, and therefore, to use an expression employed by Chinese Grammarians, are changed from dead words to living ones, then receive also the most animated accentuation; hence, e.g., *dátá maghâni*, '(he is) giving riches,' opposed to *dâtâ maghânâm*, 'the giver of riches' (see §. 814.). A similar contrast it to be found in the Greek paroxytone abstracts in τος, as compared with the verbals in τός, which correspond to the Sanscrit perfect passive participle; e.g., πότος, 'the drinking,' opposed to ποτός=Sanscrit *pîtás*, 'drunk' (see §. 817.). The two languages, when they accent the suffix in the case before us, do not intend to lay an emphasis on the suffix, but rather to remove from the whole word the emphasis, which lies in accenting the first syllable. In accordance with the theory here laid down is also the circumstance that the Greek gives the paroxytone accent to the interrogative τίς upon the number of its syllables being increased, as in a question there is an increase of animation which we also mark by raising the voice; while it oxytonises the indefinite pronoun of the same sound, in agreement with the Sanscrit weak cases of monosyllabic base words (see p. 1085 G. ed., 1053 E. Tr.). I cannot allow of a logical

trasts with the Sanscrit nominative accusative *dvâra-m* [G. Ed. p. 1278.] the form *daur;* so instead of the Sanscrit

carry," the Gothic like *bairai*, and Greek like φέροι. But in the 1st person singular *mârûṅ*, "let me strike" (at once future and subjunctive), I think I recognise the Sanscrit imperative termination *âni*, with *û* therefore for *â*, as above (p. 1215 G. ed.) in the Marāṭha present. The Hindūstānī fails to distinguish the Sanscrit terminations *âmi* and *âni*, as both have

logical accent either to the Sanscrit (in simple words), nor to the Greek,[a] and I cannot see a reason for the proparoxytonising of *bódhâmi,* 'I know,' *bódhâmas,* ' we know,' and the oxytonising of *imás,* ' we go ' (in disadvantageous contrast to ἴμεν), in this, that in the first-named forms the radical syllable, and in the latter the personal syllable, should be brought prominently forward as the most important, but I think it rather owing to the fact that the most animated accent belongs to the verb ; but of this the form *imás* is, as it were, cheated through the influence which, in Sanscrit, in disadvantageous contrast to the Greek, the heavier personal terminations exercise, in certain conjugational classes, on the removal of the accent. In forms like *striṇómi,* 'I strew,' *yunâmi,* 'I bind,' the length of the last syllable but one has, in disadvantageous contrast to the analogous Greek forms (στόρνῡμι, δάμνημι) exercised a similar influence in attracting the accent as that which a long penultima exercises in Latin in words of three or more syllables (see p.1090 G. ed., p. 1057 E. Tr.), while in Greek it is only in the first syllable that the quantity has gained a disturbing influence on the original accentuation ; so that, *e.g.*, ἡδείων stands in disadvantageous contrast when compared alike with the Sanscrit *svâdîyán* (see p. 1091 G. ed., p. 1058 E. Tr.), and with its own neuter ἥδιον, as in the dual of the imperative φερέτων, compared with the Sanscrit *bháratâm*, and the 2d person φέρετον (=Sans. *bháratam*).

"Besides the Greek, no other European member of our great lingual family has remained constant to the old system of accentuation, in which the accent forms an essential part of grammar, and does its part in aiding to decide the grammatical categories. In Latin the kind of accentuation, which

---

[a] Benlöw is of a different opinion, who, in his work, " De l'accentuation des langues Indo-Européennes " (Paris, 1847), p. 44, " En Sanscrit l'accent a une signification purement logique, et il porte sur toute syllable que la pensée veut mettre en évidence et faire ressortir du reste du mot, quelle que soit sa distance du commencement ou de la fin de celui-ci."

FORMATION OF WORDS. 1239

bandhana-m, "the binding," we may expect in Gothic only *"bindan."* With the dative बन्धनाय *bandhanâya,* should be

have lost the final *i*, and *m* like *n*, at the end of the word, has become anusvâra (*n*). With respect to the use of the 1st person singular of the imperative in the sense of the future, I would draw attention to a similar use in Zend (see §. 722. sub. f.). In the 2d person plural the form *mârô*, "ye strike," or "ye may strike" (*mârô-gê*, "ye will strike"), occasions a difficulty

which in Sanscrit and Greek is the most emphatic, viz. the farthest possible casting back of the accent, has become, under certain known restrictions, universal, and therefore the accent here is no more of service in Grammar; and when forms like *véhimus, véhitis, véhunt,* exhibit an external agreement in respect to accent with the Sanscrit *váhâmas, váhatha, váhanti,* the coincidence is so far fortuitous, that the reason of the accentuation is different in the two languages. So also, among other words, the agreement in the accentuation of *datórem* with *dâtáram* and δοτῆρα is accidental, since the Latin does not accent the suffix because the accent belongs to it from old time, but because the last syllable but one is long. Remarkable, if not resting on affinity, is the agreement of the Latin system of accentuation with the Arabian. The latter, in words of two and three syllables, accents the first, in polysyllables the third; but so that, as in Latin, a length of vowel or of position in the last syllable but one draws the accent to that syllable, while a long final syllable has no influence in removing the accent; thus, *e.g., kátala,* 'he slew,' *kátalú,* 'they slew,' contrasted with *katálta,* 'thou slewest,' *maktúlun,* 'slain,' *kátilúna,* "the slaying" (pl.). In Lithuanian perhaps some isolated remnants of the old accentuation occur. Much information, however, cannot be gleaned from the grammars and lexicons, which seldom mark the accented syllable. I preliminarily draw attention to the agreement which the adjective bases in *u* present with the Sanscrit and Greek in *u, v,* since they likewise accent this vowel; hence, *e.g., saldùs,* 'sweet,' as in Sanscrit *svâdús* (see §. 20), in Greek ἡδύς; *drasùs,* 'bold,' as in Greek θρασύς. The throwing back of the accent, too, which occasionally occurs in the vocative of the dual, compared with the nominative of the same sound, is also deserving of notice; *e.g.,* in *géru pónu,* compared with the nominative *gerù ponù,* 'two good masters' (Mielcke, p. 45). The vocative of *szwiesù dangù,* 'two light heavens,' is left by Mielcke unmarked (*szwiesu dangu*), probably because it is not oxytone but paroxytone. In Sanscrit, according

to

contrasted, in Gothic, according to §. 356. Rem. 3., *bindana;* and we should have looked for forms of this kind after the

---

difficulty on account of its final *ô*. For it the Marāṭhī exhibits in the imperative the form *mârâ*, which I think may be explained from Sanscrit forms like *bódh-a-ta*, "know ye," so that, after dropping the *t*, the two *a*-sounds have coalesced; as I also, in the 3d person singular of the present, derive इच्छे *ichchhê*, "he wishes," from the Sanscrit *ichchh-á-ti*, by casting out the *t*, and contracting the *a-i* to *ê*, according to Sanscrit rules. Cf. Greek

---

to a fixed rule, *sûnú*, 'two sons' (Lithuanian *sunù*), forms the vocative *súnû* (see p. 1086 G. ed., 1054 E. Tr.). At the end of the next Part I shall have much to supply regarding Sanscrit accentuation; for in the remark at §.785. I would not go back to all the former parts of the Grammar, but only lay down the fundamental principle, on which the most remarkable agreements between the Sanscrit and Greek accentuation rest, and at the same time draw attention to the grounds which have occasioned one or other of the said languages to diverge from the original path, in which, in my opinion, the Sanscrit and Greek meet. I shall also have some supplementary remarks to offer on some points of grammar and the doctrine of sounds, as I have already, in the present Part, pointed out some alterations in former views. In addition to what has been remarked at p. 1138 Rem. ** G. ed., p. 1104 Note † E. Tr., regarding the *ch* of our pronominal accusatives *mi-ch, di-ch, si-ch*, and the Old High German *h* of the accusative plural *unsi-h, iwi-h*, I have since found a very interesting analogy in the Afghān, where, however, the *h* referred to, which I think I recognise in *hagha*, 'the, this,' as sister-form of the Sanscrit *sáha*, Vêdic *ságha* or *sághâ*, Greek ὅγε, has become declinable; hence, in the plural, *haghû*, and in the feminine singular nominative, *haghê*, the latter like *dê*, 'she,' contrasted with the masculine *da*, 'he,' being a softening of the Sanscrit base *ta*. In the syllable *ga*, too, of *mûnga*,[a] 'we,' I think I recognise the said particle, and in the remaining part of the word the Sanscrit accusative *asmân*, ἡμᾶς, with the loss of the first syllable, which is also dropped in the New Persian *mâ*, 'we,' which, just like *shumâ*, 'ye,' is based on the theme of the Sanscrit oblique plural cases (*yushmán*, ὑμᾶς)."

---

[a] J. Ewald, in the "Journal of Eastern Intelligence," IV. 300. Klaproth "Asia, Polygl." p. 56, writes *mongha*.

FORMATION OF WORDS. 1241

preposition *du,* "to," which governs the dative; but we find in this position also only the form in *an,* e.g., *du sairan,* "to sow," *du bairan,* "to give birth to;" whether it be that the preposition *du* originally governed the accusative, like the Latin *ad* of cognate meaning, and the infinitive, at this more ancient epoch, remained unchanged, or that it had lost its capability of declension in Gothic earlier than in the other German dialects.

879. In the Old and Middle High German, as also in the Old Anglo-Saxon dative of the infinitive, the doubling of the *n* is surprising;* yet I cannot thereby see cause to derive the datives, and the analogous [G. Ed. p. 1279.] genitives of the Old and Middle High German,† from another base than that of the nominative accusative of the infinitive, and to see in it a different suffix from the

---

Greek forms like φέρει from φερ-ε-τι=Sanscrit *bhár-a-ti* (see §. 456.). In the 2d person the form इच्छेस् *ichchhês=ichehhais,* compared with the Sanscrit *ichchh-á-si,* is formed, in my opinion, by transposition, just as, in Greek, φέρεις from φερ-ε-σι=Sanscrit *bhár-a-si* (see §. 448.). So also, in the 3d person plural, *ichchhêt* from *ichchh-ánti,* with, at the same time, rejection of the *n*. If the Maráthí can be held to throw light on the Hindūstání, which closely resembles it, we might regard the *ô* of Hindūstání forms like *márô,* "beat ye," as the corruption of *á,* just as, in Sanscrit, पोडशन् *shôḍaśan* 16 for *sháḍaśan, sôḍhum,* "to carry," for *sáḍhum* (see "Abridged Sanscrit Grammar," §§. 102. 228. Rem. 1.).

* See the examples mentioned above (§. 875.). Old Saxon examples are, *faranne, blidzeanne, thôlonne;* Anglo-Saxon, *faranne, rêcenne, gefremmanne,* see Grimm, I. 1021. In Gothic the form *viganna* (*du viganna,* εἰς πόλεμον, Luke xiv. 31), even though not an infinitive, would be remarkable on account of the doubled *n,* if the reading were correct. It is most highly probable, however, that we ought to read *vigana* (see Gabel. and Löbe on l. c.). The word belongs, however, in respect of its suffix of formation, to the Sanscrit class of words in *ana,* and is probably a neuter, therefore nominative accusative *vigan.*

† *E.g.,* Old High German *topônnes,* "of raging;" Middle High German *weinennes,* "of weeping."

Sanscrit *ana*, of which we have just treated. I hold the doubling of the *n* to be simply euphonic, *i.e.* a consequence of the inclination for doubling *n* between two vowels; hence, also, *e.g.*, in Old High German *kunni* (or *chunni*), in Old Sclavonic *kunni*, in Middle High German *künne*, corresponds to the Gothic *kuni*, "sex." The word is radically akin to the Greek γένος, Latin *genus*, and Vêdic *jánus* (gen. *jánuṣh-as*), "birth;" and its formative suffix is *ya* (dat. pl. *ya-m*), which is contracted in the nominative accusative singular to *i* (see §. 153.). It is impossible, however, that the doubling of the *n* in this *kunni*, *künne*, &c., should give occasion to those forms to assume a different formative suffix from *ya*, of which more hereafter.*

880. The original destination of the preposition *zu*, "to," before the infinitive, is to express the causal relation, which is done in the Vêda dialect by the simple dative termination of the infinitive base in *tu*, or of some other abstract substantive supplying the place of the infinitive; and for which, in classical Sanscrit, the locative of the form in *ana* is also frequently employed, as, in general, the locative in Sanscrit is very often used for the dative. The Gothic, in its use of the infinitive with *du*, keeps almost entirely to the stated fundamental destination of this kind of construction, in sen-

[G. Ed. p. 1280.] tences like "he went out to sow" (*du saian*); "he that hath ears to hear" (*du hausyan*); "who made ready to betray him" *du galêvyan ina*). It is, however, surprising that Ulfilas too at times expresses the nominative relation by the prepositional infinitive; *e.g.*, 2 Cor. ix. 1., τὸ γράφειν

---

* That the Gothic, also, is not free from the inclination to double the *n* between two vowels is shewn by forms like *uf-munnan*, "to think;" *ufar-munnôn*, "to forget" (Sanscrit *man*, "to think"); *kinnu-s*, "jawbones"=Greek γένυ-ς, Sanscrit *hanú-s*. In Sanscrit the final *n* after a short vowel, in case the word following begins with any vowel whatever, is regularly doubled; *e.g.*, *ásann iha*, "they were here."

by *du mêlyan;** Philip. i. 24, τὸ μένειν by *du visan*. It is possible even for the nominative neuter of the article to precede the infinitive with *du;* thus, Mark xii. 33, *thata du friyôn ina* (τὸ ἀγαπᾶν αὐτόν); *thata du friyôn nêhvundyan* (τὸ ἀγαπᾶν τὸν πλησίον). Usually, however, Ulfilas translates the Greek nominative of the infinitive by the simple infinitive, and, indeed, without the article, even where the Greek text has the article; as, *e.g.*, Gal. iv. 18, *aththan gôth ist alyanôn in gôdamma sinteinô* (καλὸν δὲ τὸ ζηλοῦσθαι ἐν καλῷ πάντοτε); Philip. i. 21, *aththan mis liban Christus ist yah gasviltan gavaurki* (ἐμοὶ γὰρ τὸ ζῆν Χριστὸς καὶ τὸ ἀποθανεῖν κέρδος).

881. Where the infinitive is the object of a verb governing the accusative the Gothic translation of the Bible exhibits almost universally the simple infinitive; so that constructions like "he began," or "he commenced to go," to which, to a certain extent, analogous forms occur so early as in Sanscrit (see pp. 1211, 1212 G. ed.), are still tolerably remote from Gothic. Where, however, Ulfilas, in Luke iv. 10, renders ἐντελεῖται τοῦ διαφυλάξαι σε by *anabiudith du gafastan thuk*, he wished here probably to approximate more closely to the Greek text, and to paraphrase the genitive of the infinitive, which is wanting in Gothic, by the preposition *du*, or to fill out with that preposition the place which is occupied in the original text by the genitive of the article; since he elsewhere expresses the object of the verbs which signify "to command, to order," by [G. Ed. p. 1281.] the simple accusative of the infinitive; *e. g.*, Luke viii. 31, *anabudi galeithan*, ἐπιτάξῃ ἀπελθεῖν.

882. In the use of the Gothic infinitive, those constructions merit especial attention in which an accusative accompanies the infinitive, which is governed, as the case of

---

* *Ufyô mis ist du mêlyan izvis*, "it is superfluous for me to write to you" (=the writing).

the object, neither by the verb nor by the infinitive, but which, as in the Greek text, expresses the relation "in respect of," which relation is very frequently denoted by the Greek accusative (πόδας ὠκύς, ὄμματα καλός), but is strange to the Gothic, except in the construction with the infinitive. I regard the infinitive in such sentences in both languages as the subject, and therefore as nominative; and the verb, not as Gabelentz and Löbe do (Gram. p. 249, 5.), as impersonal, though we might translate it by "it happened, it befel, it became," &c., but just as much personal as when we, *e.g.*, say, "to sit is more pleasant than to stand;" "the rising up is seasonable, is now becoming;" "to enter is easy." That which is peculiar in the Greek and Gothic constructions referred to is only that the infinitive cannot, like an ordinary abstract, govern the genitive; that therefore, in Greek, *e.g.*, it cannot be said, τοῦ οὐρανοῦ καὶ τῆς γῆς παρελθεῖν, nor in Gothic *himins yah airthôs hindarleithan*, but that in both languages the person or thing to which the action which is expressed by the infinitive refers, must be placed in the accusative, since the infinitive admits not of the nearer destination either by an adjective or by a genitive, not even there where the Greek infinitive, by prefixing the article, is made more of a substantive than of itself it is. Of the examples collected by Gabel. and Löbe, l. c., the first, *varth afslauthann allans* (Luke iv. 36), must appear the most surprising, since the Greek text (ἐγένετο θάμβος ἐπὶ πάντας) furnishes no motive for a construction unusual in Gothic. In fact, the Gothic translation would appear very forced if *varth* here correspond in sense to our *ward*, so that it would be requisite to translate literally, " there was amazement (with reference to) all," or "amazement was (with reference to) all." As, however, the Gothic *vairthan*, as the said learned men have shewn in their Glossary, also

[G. Ed. p. 1282.]

signifies "to come,"* I here take *allans* as the accusative, governed by a verb of motion (which, too, the Greek ἐγένετο in this passage is), and I translate literally, "there came amazement (over) all," or "amazement fell upon all." Moreover, in another quite similar passage, Ulfilas finds it suitable to translate the Greek ἐπὶ πάντας by *ana allaim*, viz. Luke i. 65, *yah varth ana allaim agis* (καὶ ἐγένετο ἐπὶ πάντας φόβος), "and there came fear upon all." It would therefore be wrong in this passage to translate *varth* by "*factus est.*" Of the Gothic examples, therefore, collected by Gabelentz and Löbe,† of the infinitive with the accusative, let us dispense with the 1st, which has just been discussed, and also with the 5th (John xviii. 15), because in it the Gothic construction differs from the Greek, in that, as I doubt not, the accusative *ainana mannan* is governed as the objective case by the transitive infinitive *fraqvistyan*, "to destroy, to slay,"‡ so that we have only four examples left which belong here. These are, Col. i. 19, *in imma galeikaida alla fullôn bauan* (ἐν αὐτῷ εὐδόκησε πᾶν τὸ πλή- [G. Ed. p. 1283.] ρωμα), "it pleased the dwelling in him (in respect of) all fulness (of all fulness);" Luke xvi. 17, *ith azêtizô ist himin yah airtha hindarleithan thau vitôdis ainana vrit gadriusan*, (εὐκοπώτερον δέ ἐστι τὸν οὐρανὸν καὶ τὴν γῆν παρελθεῖν ἢ τοῦ νόμου μίαν κεραίαν πεσεῖν), "but it is easier to pass away (the passing away) with respect to heaven and earth (=of heaven and earth) than to fall (the falling) with reference to one tittle of the law;" Rom. xiii. 11, *mêl ist uns yu us slêpa urreisan*§ (ὥρα ἡμᾶς ἤδη ἐξ ὕπνου ἐγερθῆναι), "It is time (in

---

* Remark the connection of the Gothic root *varth* with the Sanscrit root *vart, vrit*, "to go," and the Latin *verto* (see Pott, E. I., I. 241.).

† Gramm., p. 249. 5.

‡ "It is better to put one man to death for the people."

§ This passage is, in Gothic, so far ambiguous, that *uns* may be both dative and accusative, especially as the dative more frequently occurs in constructions

reference to) for us now to rise (the rising) from sleep;" Skeir. (ed. Massmann, p. 38. 10.); *gadôh nu vas thanzuh ... gaqvissans vairthan*, "it were therefore fitting, in respect of this (the) being agreeing." It becomes a question, then, is this kind of construction as it were indigenous in the Gothic, or only an imitation of the Greek?* I believe the latter; and, indeed, because in Gothic the accusative elsewhere never expresses the relation "in respect of." Moreover, Ulfilas gladly avoids this kind of construction, as he shews, by frequently changing the infinitive construction of the original text into a verbal with the conjugation *ei*, "that," or by using, instead of the accusative of the person, the dative, whether the relation be the proper dative one or the instrumental. In the latter case he follows, indeed, the Greek text word by word, but, by the change of the accusative into a dative, the construction becomes essentially altered, and such that we, in New High German, also can, without much constraint, imitate it; *e.g.*, Luke xviii. 25, *rathizô allis ist ulbandau thairh thairkô nêthlôs thairhleithan thau gabigamma in thiudangardya guths galeithun* (εὐκοπώτερον γάρ ἐστι κάμηλον .... εἰσελθεῖν &c.), "for it is easier for the camel (the) passing through the eye of a needle, than for the rich (the) entering into the kingdom of God;" Luke xvi. 22, *warth than gasviltan thamma unlêdin* (ἐγένετο δὲ ἀποθανεῖν τὸν πτωχόν), "there was, however, dying through the poor man;" Luke vi. 1, *varth gaygan imma thairh atisk* (ἐγένετο διαπορεύεσθαι αὐτὸν διὰ τῶν σπορίμων), "there was going through him through the corn-field." On the other hand, the Greek constructions in which the Greek text exhibits the accusative with the infinitive.

* As regards the example in the Skeireins, I must recall attention to the fact, that these were hardly composed originally in Gothic, but most probably were translated from the Greek.

text, too, 1 Cor. vii. 26, has the dative: καλὸν ἀνθρώπῳ τὸ οὕτως εἶναι, *gôth ist mann sva visan*, "good is it for a man so to be." So Mark ix. 45, καλὸν ἐστί σοι εἰσελθεῖν εἰς τὴν ζωὴν χωλὸν, ἢ τοὺς δύο πόδας ἔχοντα βληθῆναι εἰς τὴν γέενναν, *gôth thus ist galeithan in libain haltamma, thau tvans fôtuns habandin gavairpan in gaiainnan*, "better (good) is it for thee to go into life lame (for thee lame), than having two feet (for thee having) to cast (the casting = to be cast) into hell."* Ulfilas employs the periphrasis by *ei*, "that;" *e.g.*, Eph. i. 4, *ei siyaima veis veihai yah unvammai* (εἶναι ἡμᾶς ἀγίους καὶ ἀμώμους), "that we should be holy and without blame;" iv. 22, *ei aflagyaith yus* . . . *thana fairnyan mannan* (ἀποθέσθαι ὑμᾶς . . . . τὸν παλαιὸν ἄνθρωπον).

883. When the accusative of the person, [G. Ed. p. 1285.] in like manner as that of the infinitive, is governed by the verb, the case is different from that of the constructions imitative of the Greek which have been noticed in the preceding paragraph, and in which the accusative of the person expresses only a secondary relation, which we must paraphrase by "in reference to," or "touching." At least I do not believe that sentences like *Ich sah ihn fallen*, "I saw him fall," *Ich hörte ihn singen*, "I heard him sing," *Ich hiess ihn gehen*, "I bade him go," *lass mich gehen*, "let me go," analogous cases to which occur in Sanscrit (see p. 1209 G. ed.), can be taken otherwise than so that the working of the operation of seeing, hearing, &c., falls directly upon the person or thing which one sees, hears, charges, &c., and then upon the action expressed by the infinitive which one in like manner sees, hears, &c. The two objects of the verb are

---

* The Gothic syntax agrees with the Sanscrit in this, that in the above sentence the adjective "lame," which is used adverbially, and the participle "having," appear in Gothic as epithets of *thus*, "to thee:" thus in Sanscrit one can say, *e.g.*, *tavâ 'nucharêṇa mayâ sarvadâ bhavitavyam*, "it is always to be by me following of thee" (lit., "by me following").

co-ordinate, and stand in the relation of apposition to one another (I saw "him" and "falling," "*actionem cadendi*"). It appears, however, from the context, but is not formally expressed, that the action expressed by the second object is performed by the person or thing expressed by the first object ("I saw the stone fall"). To this head belong, for the most part, the examples collected by Gabelentz and Löbe, p. 249, un-
[G. Ed. p. 1286.] der 1.), 2.), 3.), 4.),* of which I annex a few: John vi. 62, *yabai nu gasaihvith sunu mans ussteigan*, "if ye shall see the Son of man ascend up" (ἐὰν οὖν θεωρῆτε τὸν υἱὸν τοῦ ἀνθρώπου ἀναβαίνοντα); Matt. viii. 18, *haihait galeithan sipônyôns hindar marein*, "he bade the disciples go over the sea;" Mark i. 17, *gatauya iqvis vairthan nutans mannê*, "I will make you to become fishers of men," (ποιήσω ὑμᾶς γενέσθαι ἁλιεῖς ἀνθρώπων); John vi. 10, *vaurkeith thans mans anakumbyan*, "make the men sit down," (ποιήσατε τοὺς ἀνθρώπους ἀναπεσεῖν); Luke xix. 14, *ni vileim thana thiudanôn ufar unsis*, (οὐ θέλομεν τοῦτον βασιλεῦσαι ἐφ' ἡμᾶς). In the last-quoted example, and the others l. c., n. 3.), we cannot, indeed, follow the Greek-Gothic construction; we cannot say, *wir wollen nicht diesen herschen über uns*, "we will not this to reign over us;" but I doubt not, that here

---

* The following are to be excepted from No. 2.: Eph. iii. 6, where *visan*=εἶναι, stands in the nominative relation, and the accusative of the person expresses the relation "in respect of;" and 1 Tim. vi. 13, 14, where, indeed, the infinitive *fastan* (τηρῆσαι) stands in the accusative relation, but the accusative *thuk* (σε) lies beyond the direction of the verb, and likewise expresses the relation "in respect of." Although *anabiuda*, like the Greek παραγγέλλω, governs the dative, nevertheless Ulfilas skips the Greek σοι, although, in order not to express the 2d person twice, he might as well have omitted the less important σε, which accompanies the infinitive to express a secondary idea, which is of itself tolerably patent. Ulfilas, however, appears to find a truer imitation of the Greek construction in saying, "I give thee charge to keep (the keeping) in respect of thee the commandment," than in saying, "I give thee charge to keep the commandment."

here also the accusative of the person, like that of the infinitive, stands as object of the verb signifying " to will, to seek, to mean, to believe, to hope, to know," &c. The Old High German still accords to this kind of construction a tolerably extensive use (see Grimm, IV. 116.); *e.g.*, Notker, *er sih saget kot sín* (" *se deum esse dicit*"); Tat., *ih weiz megin fon mir úz gangan* (" *novi virtutem de me exiisse*"); Hymn., *unsih erstantan kelaubamês* (" *nos resurgere credimus*").

884. We now turn to a nearer examination of the Greek infinitive, and must therefore first of all recall to remembrance the point of comparison, which we have already obtained (p. 1223 G. ed.) between the Vêdic infinitives in *sê* and the Greek in σαι. If this comparison be based on a sure foundation, we have, in the termination αι [G. Ed. p. 1287.] of forms like λῦσαι, τύψαι, a genuine, and, as it were, Sanscrit dative termination, while the common Greek datives are based on the Sanscrit locative (see §. 195.). It is the more important to remark this, as all other Greek infinitives, partly in their common form, and partly in their oldest form, end in αι, and therefore may be regarded as old datives which are no longer conscious of their derivation and their original destination to express a definite case-relation, and hence can be used as accusatives and nominatives, and, in combination with the article, as genitives also. Exactly in the sense of Sanscrit datives (which most usually express the causal relation), and, as it were, as representatives of the Vêdic infinitive datives like *pátav-ê*, "in order to drink, on account of drinking," appear the Greek infinitives in sentences like ἔδωκεν αὐτὸ δούλῳ φορῆσαι; ἄνθρωπος πέφυκε φιλεῖν; ἦλθε ζητῆσαι, (" on account of the searching"); ἐμοὶ θυομένῳ ἰέναι ἐπὶ τὸν βασιλέα οὐκ ἐγίγνετο τὰ ἱερά (Xen. Anab. II. 2. 3.). As regards the formal development or gradual defiguration, we must antedate the form in ἐ-μεναι (*e.g.* ἀκου-έ-μεναι, εἰπ-έ-μεναι, ἀξέ-μεναι), as a point of departure for the infinitives in ειν, and that in μεναι

4 M

for the forms in ναι (as διδό-ναι, τιθέ-ναι). By dropping the case-termination αι, which had become unintelligible, there arose from ε-μεναι, first ε-μεν (ἀκου-έ-μεν, εἰπ-έ-μεν, ἀξέ-μεν), and hence, by casting out the μ, ειν (Æol. ην, ἄγην, Dor. εν, ἄγεν) for ε-εν. The conjugation in μι shews also, in the common dialect, by forms like τιθέ-ναι, ἱστά-ναι, διδό-ναι, δεικνύ-ναι, that the termination αι is essential to the infinitive: thus the perfect infinitives (τετυφ-έ-ναι), and the passive aorist infinitives, which, according to their form, belong to the active (τυφ-θῆ-ναι, τυπ-ῆ-ναι), exhibit however, in the epic language, for the most part the full form μεναι.

[G. Ed. p. 1288.] 885. As regards the origin of the forms in μεναι, I formerly thought ("Conjugations-system," p. 85) of deriving this μεναι from the suffix μενο=Sanscrit *mâna* of the participle middle and passive, so that αι would have taken the place of the ο of μενο like an adverbial termination. The derivation of an abstract substantive, which the infinitive is, from a participle, could not be a matter of surprise; but it would be strange, in the case before us, that the infinitives in μεναι, &c., should be entirely excluded from the middle and passive, with the exception of the aorists with active form. If the infinitives in μεναι, μεν, ναι, ν, belonged to the middle or passive, their connection with the participles μενο would, in my opinion, be placed almost beyond doubt: as active infinitives, however, I now prefer to derive them from the Sanscrit suffix *man*, which forms abstracts (see §. 796.); and I place them as sister-forms over against Latin abstracts like *certa-men, sola-men, tenta--men, regi-men* (see p. 1083, §. 801.), the *n* of which, in the Greek formations in ματ, is corrupted to τ, which, however, does not hinder a particular branch of this family of words, viz. the infinitives, from asserting its right to a more ancient place by a firm retention of the old *n*, while the vowel has undergone the favourite weakening to ε. In Greek, therefore, the originally identical suffixes ματ, μον (§. 797. 801.), μεν, which flow from one and the same source, have the same relation to one another, as regards their vowel, that forms like ἔτραπον, τέτροφα, τρέπω, have to each other with reference to their radical vowel. That this class of abstract substantives has been originally far more numerous in Sanscrit than in the condition of the language which has been bequeathed to us from the classic period, is proved by the circumstance, that, both in the Vêdic dialect and in Zend, formations of this sort occur which are wanting in common Sanscrit: in the Vêdic dialect, e.g., háv-í-man, "the calling;"* [G. Ed. p. 1289.] yá-man, "going;" dhár-man, "support" (Yajurv. 9. 5.): in Zend ⟨⟩ staôman, "the praising" (Sanscrit root stu, "to praise"); and Burnouf, Journ. As. 1844, p. 468, translates its dative ⟨⟩ staômainê,† by "pour célébrer." The Celtic languages also testify to a very extensive use of the forms in मन् man in the sense of pure abstracts, at a time anterior to the separation of languages. To them correspond Irish abstracts in mhain or mhuin (see Pictet p. 103); e.g., geun-mhuin, "engendering, begetting;" gein-ea-mhuin, "birth, conception" (Sanscrit ján-man, ján-i-man, "birth"); geall-a-mhuin, "a promise, vow" (geall-a-mhna, "a promise, promising"); gaill-ea-mhuin, "offence;" lean-mhain, lean-a--mhain, "following, pursuing;" olla-mhain, "instruction" (oil-i-m, "I instruct"); scar-a-mhain, scar-a-mhuin, "separation." The abstracts of this kind are brought nearer to the Greek infinitives in μεν, μεναι, in that some of them are actually used in Scottish-Gaelic as infinitives, at least Stewart cites among the rarer infinitive forms two also in mhuin, viz. gin-mhuin, "to beget," and lean-mhuin, "to follow." There are in the Gaelic dialects also infinitives in mh; e.g.,

---

* With î for i as conjunctive vowel, root hu from hvê, see p. 1221 G. ed.

† Another reading for the staomaêni, mentioned above (§. 518. p. 737, Note *), which I looked upon as an erroneous reading for the locative.

seas-a-mh, "to stand," where the *a* is the class-vowel, but the *mh*, as has been already elsewhere remarked,* very probably an abbreviation of *mhuin*, as the bases in *n* in [G. Ed. p. 1290.] the Gaelic languages in the nominative frequently suppress the *n* (cf. §. 139.), and, indeed, not unusually together with the vowel preceding.†

886. Should the Greek infinitives in μεν not be abbreviations of μεναι, but have originally co-existed as different case-relations, we must assume that the datives in μεναι, which are formed according to Sanscrit-Zend principles, have been simply designed to express the causal relation (cf. §. 854.), and that the forms in μεν, as naked neutral bases, were appropriated to the designation of the accusative and nominative relation; that, however, after the meaning of the termination in μεν-αι had been forgotten by the language, the forms in ν and ν-αι have been used indifferently by the language. I here recall attention to the displacement of personal terminations, and their appearance in places which do not belong to them, *e.g.*, in the Gothic passive (see §. 468.‡), as also of the exaltation of the accusative plural to the universal plural termination in Spanish; while in Italian the nominative termination plural has been extended to all cases, but in Umbrian the ending of the dative ablative plural, which is more to the point here, has become the termination of the accusative, which hence in the said dialect terminates in *f* (=Sanscrit *bhyas*, Latin *bus*).§ In English the pronominal forms "him" and "whom," which, in their origin, are datives, and, by their *m*, correspond with the Sanscrit *smâi* of *tásmâi, yásmâi*, &c.

---

* "The Celtic Languages," p. 59.

† Thus there exists, together with the above-mentioned *oll-a-mhain*, "instruction," a concrete *oll-a-mh* (genitive *oll-a-mhan*) "a doctor."

‡ In the German §. 466., but it will be seen that this is a wrong reference.

§ See Aufrecht and Kirchhof, p. 113; and cf., *e.g.*, the accusative *tri-f bu-f* with the Latin dative *tribus bobus* and Sanscrit *tri-bhyas gô-bhyas*.

FORMATION OF WORDS. 1253

(see p. 485) have assumed an accusative meaning, and, in order to express the dative relation, require the help of the preposition "to." As regards the infini- [G. Ed. p. 1291.] tive in particular, it must further be remarked, that the Vêdic infinitives in *dhyâi*, which usually denote the causal relation which belongs to their evidently dative termination (see §. 854.), occasionally occur also with an accusative signification. Thus we read in the Yajurv. 6. 3. *uśmasi gámadhyâi*, "we will go." In Latin the infinitives in *re*, if the explanation given above (§. 856.) be correct, have become altogether untrue to their original destination, and appear only in the accusative or nominative relation; while the Old Prussian infinitives in *twei*, which are likewise known as dative forms, express only the accusative relation (see p. 1249 G. ed.).

887. In favour of the opinion, that the difference between the Greek infinitives in ν and ναι is organic, so that both forms, which in the present condition of the language are of the same significance, originally belonged to different case-relations, we must allow weight to the circumstance, that in no other place of Greek Grammar do we meet with an entire abolition of the diphthong αι at the end of a word; as in general, in other languages also, the diphthongs do not admit of being discharged so easily as the simple vowels, because, before their utter absorption, the path is open to them to surrender one of the two elements of which they are composed. Universally, where the Sanscrit Grammar exhibits an *ê* (= *ai*, see §. 683. p. 917) at the end of the inflexions, the Greek preserves either αι, for example, in the medio-passive personal terminations (μαι, σαι, ται, νται=*ê*, *sê*, *tê*, *ntê*), or οι, as in the plural nominatives of masculine bases in *o* (*e.g.* Dor. τοί=Sanscrit *tê*, Gothic *thai*, see §. 228.), and in one single termination α, viz. in the personal termination μεθα=Sanscrit *mahê* from *madhê*, Zend *maidhê* (§. 472.). In general, the Greek per-

[G. Ed. p. 1292.] tinaciously retains the final vowels, and has not allowed the removal of any of the simple vowels but the lightest of all the primary ones, viz. i, and this, too, but very seldom, perhaps only in the 2d person singular of the principal tenses (δίδω-ς = dádâ-si, see §. 448.); while in Latin and Gothic the i has disappeared from the personal terminations: the Gothic, indeed, has even dropped the entire diphthong αι in the dative singular, since the Gothic singular datives, with the exception of those of the feminine pronouns, as has been pointed out above (p. 500, §. 356. Remark 3.), are in fact void of termination, so that, e.g., sunau, "filio," corresponds to the Sanscrit súnáv-ê; auhsin (theme auhsan) "bovi," to the Sanscrit úkshan-ê.

888. It remains for me only further to explain the Greek infinitives of the middle and passive in σθαι, which I think I was before (p. 659, §. 474.) wrong in explaining. They share the termination αι with the active infinitives like λῦ-σαι, τύψαι, τιθέ-ναι, τιθή-μεναι, ἀκου-έ-μεναι, τετυφ-έ-ναι. I recognise the base of the passive or middle signification in the σ, which I now look upon as the reflexive, the original σ of which has, in οὗ, οἷ, ἕ, become the rough breathing (see §. 341. p. 476), but before θ it occupies such a position that it could retire into a weak aspirate. But if the sibilant of forms like λέγ-εσ-θαι, τίθε-σθαι, belongs to the reflexive, these forms are, in this respect, based on the same principle as the Latin like amari-er, legi-er (see §. 477.). In general, a passive or middle infinitive, which was unknown to our great family of languages in its primæval period, would have been the easiest and most natural to acquire by affixing the reflexive, as the Lithuanian, too, transfers to the infinitive also the s appended to its reflexive verbs, e.g., wadin-ti-s, "to name oneself" (see §. 476. p. 662). Similar is the procedure of the

[G. Ed. p. 1293.] Northern languages, in which the reflexive, in forms like the Swedish taga-s, "to be taken" (from taga, "to take"), is quite as unmistakeable as in the indicative *tage-s* (in the three persons singular, see Grimm, IV. p. 46). In Greek forms like λέγεσθαι, the reflexive lies the more hidden, because it is not appended to the termination of the active infinitive; and, moreover, there exists no active infinitive in θαι or ται from which σθαι might have sprung, as above (§. 474.), *e.g.*, δίδοσθον from δίδοτον. Moreover, in the infinitive no personal termination can be looked for; and we durst not, therefore, in respect of the θ in forms like δίδοσθαι, search for any analogy with such as δίδοσθον, δίδοσθε, διδόσθω. Moreover, we cannot regard the θ of the middle passive infinitives as a formative suffix; for it would be unnatural to interpose between the root and the formative suffix of an abstract substantive a pronominal element to express a reflexive or passive relation; which would be as though from the Sanscrit infinitive and Latin supine *dâtum, datum*, we should look for a reflexive *dâstum, dastum*. Hence, therefore, in departure from the conjecture I before expressed, I now recognise in the syllable θαι of the infinitives under discussion an auxiliary verb, and, indeed, the same that we recognised above (§. 630.) in the aorists in θη-ν and futures in θή-σο-μαι, with which are connected our *thun* and the Gothic *da, dêdum*, of forms like *sôkida*, "I sought (made seek"), *sôkidêdum*, "we sought (made seek") (see §. 620.). In Old High German, an infinitive *suoh--tuan* ("to make seek"), together with the actually existing *suoh-ta* (for *suoh-teta*), "I sought (made seek"), could not surprise us; and just as little strange would it be if the Greek ζητεῖσθαι were, according to the explanation which has been given, to signify literally "to make to seek oneself" (= "to be sought"). It may here remain undecided whether the reflexive be appended after the theme of the said tense of the principal [G. Ed. p. 1294.] verb, or inserted before the auxiliary verb; whether, therefore, we should divide thus, *e.g.*, τύπτεσ-θαι, τύπ-σασ-θαι, τετύφ(σ)-θαι,* τύπ-σεσ-θαι, or τύπτε-σθαι, &c. The root θη = dhâ of the auxiliary verb is in these compounds represented simply by its consonant; for the diphthong αι is, as in the active infinitive, a case-termination, where we must recall attention to the circumstance, that the Sanscrit root also, dhâ, "to set, to make," which corresponds to the Greek θη (from θᾱ), as also all other roots in â when they appear without a formative suffix as adjectives of common gender at the end of compounds, drop their final vowel before case-terminations beginning with a vowel; and hence, from dhâ, "placing, making," comes the dative dhê (= dhai, Greek θαι). The root dhâ appears as an abstract substantive of the feminine gender in śrad-dhâ, "belief," properly, "belief-placing," or "belief-making," the dative of which, according to the universal principle of feminine bases in long â, is śrad-dhâyâi. In compounds with prepositions other naked roots in â also occur as abstract substantives, e. g., â-jñâ and anu-jñâ, "command," prati-jñâ, "promise," pra-bhâ, "lustre." Dhâ, in the Vêdic dialect, with the preposition ni, forms nidhâ (see Benfey Gloss.), which should properly signify "laying down," but has become an appellative with the meaning "net." As the root dhâ enters combinations more easily than other roots, and is suited for use as an auxiliary,† the conjecture [G. Ed. p. 1295.] is not far fetched that it also has its share in the formation of the Vêdic infinitives in धै dhyâi discussed above (§. 854.); whether it be that this dhyâi be

---

* The accumulation of consonants dislodged this reflexive σ, according to the analogy of §. 543.

† Cf. Zend yaôsch-dá, "to make purify" (§. 637.), śnâdha, "to make wash" (p. 993), Latin ven-do (§. 633.), Greek πλή-θω (Pott, E. I., p. 187), πέρ-θω. The first part of πέρ-θω answers to the Zend pĕrĕ, "to annihilate" (see Burnouf, Yaçn. p. 534, and Benfey, Gr. R. L. II. p. 362), whereto belong also the Latin per-do and per-eo (as ven-do compared with ven-eo).

FORMATION OF WORDS.

an abbreviation of *dhây-âi*, as dative of *dhâ*, or that the *â* of the root in this composition has been weakened to *i*, for which the weight added by compounding may easily have given occasion.* The strictly feminine dative termination *âi*, of infinitives like *píb-a-dhyâi* would be better established according to this, than if, according to an earlier attempt at explanation, *dhi* were taken as formative suffix, and the *dh* as a distortion of *t;* as the feminine bases in short *i*, in the dative, more frequently exhibit *ay-ê* than *y-âi*, while polysyllabic feminine bases in *í*, and in general those in a long final vowel, never exhibit *ê*, but only *âi*, as the dative character. But if in the Vêdic infinitives in *dhyâi* is involved the root *dhâ*, and in the Greek in σ-θαι the corresponding root θη, there arises hence a remarkable affinity of formation between यज्ञध्यै *yaj-a-dhyâi*, " in order to venerate," and ἄζ-ε-σθαι, which is also radically identical with it (cf. Ind. Bibl. III. 102.), which, however, could not induce me to recognise, with Lassen, in the Vêdic forms the infinitive of the middle; for in the first place they want the sibilant, which is so important an element [G. Ed. p. 1296.] in the Greek medio-passive infinitives; and secondly, the Vêda-texts which have intermediately appeared have not furnished us with the means of perceiving any nearer relation of the forms in *dhyâi* to the middle. I should prefer to regard the possible affinity of formation of the Sanscrit and Greek infinitives in *dhyâi*, σ-θαι, in no other

---

* Cf. the passives, as *dhi-yâtê*, *pi-yâtê*, for *dhâ-yâtê*, *pâ-yâtê*. I here further call attention to the Vêdic *dhî*, "work, action," which occurs, Naigh. 2. 1., under the words signifying *karman*, "action," and perhaps, as such, is to be referred, not like *dhî*, "understanding," to the root *dhyâi*, "to think," but, as an anomaly of another kind, to *dhâ*, "to make." Although, then, this *dhî*, as a monosyllabic word, forms, in the dative, *dhiyê* or *dhiyâi*, this does not prevent the supposition that it, in a primæval, as it were privileged composition, may follow the principle of the polysyllabic feminine bases in *î*, and may, after the analogy of *nadyâi*, form also *dhyâi*.

light than this, that the two languages, after their separation, accidentally coincided in an analogous application in the infinitive of a mutually common auxiliary verb; which can little surprise us, as this verb is well fitted in signification to enter combinations with other verbs, and to obtain the appearance of inflexions; and hence it occurs also in other members of our great family of languages in compounds more or less obscured. If, however, this auxiliary verb was once gained in Greek for the infinitive of the middle and passive, and, in its obscured nature, had once assumed the function of an inflexion, then the root ΘΗ combined itself with itself in combining with σ-θαι, just as, in the aorist and future, with θη-ν, θη-σομαι.

889. We have one more Sanscrit gerund to speak of, which indeed, as such, stands isolated in Sanscrit, but, with respect to its formation, presents many coincidences with the European sister-tongues; I mean, the gerund in ya.* Its signification is the same with that in tvâ, but it occurs almost only in compound verbs; while in the present condition of the language, as it appears to me, tvâ, on account of its heavier form, avoids verbs encumbered with [G. Ed. p. 1297.] prepositions. The following are examples of gerunds in य ya: ni-dháya, "after (with, through) laying down;" anu-śrútya, "after hearing;" nir-gámya, "after going out;" ni-víśya, "after going in;" prati-bhídya, "after cleaving;" â-túdya, "after impinging." I also consider these gerunds as instrumentals, and, indeed, according to the Zendian principle (see §. 158.); so that, therefore, e.g., nidháya stands for nidhâyâ, from ni-dhâya-â. I have already expressed this opinion in the Latin edition of my Sanscrit Grammar (p. 250), and found it confirmed since then through Fr. Rosen's edition of the first book of the Rig-

---

* Roots with a short final vowel receive the affix of a *t*. The accent rests on the radical syllable.

vêda, in so far that there instrumentals from bases in *a* actually occur, which are distinguished from their base only by the lengthening of the final *a*;* so that, according to this principle, one would have to expect from a base *nirgamya*, "the going out," an instrumental gerund *nirgamyá*, while before, with regard to the non-insertion of a euphonic *n*, I could only refer to the Vêdic *svapnayá* (for *svapnêna*), analogously to which, for *nirgamya* the form *nirgamyayá* would be required.

890. If one assumes that the abstract substantives which are to be presupposed for the gerund under discussion were neuter, then they would have an exact counterpart in the Latin *od-iu-m*, *gaud-iu-m*, *stud-iu-m*, *diluv-iu-m*, *dissid-iu-m*, *incend-iu-m*, *excid-iu-m*, *obsid-iu-m*, *sacrific-iu-m*, *obsequ-iu-m*, *colloqu-iu-m*, *praesag-iu-m*, *contag-iu-m*, *connub-iu-m*, *conjug-iu-m*; as in Sanscrit, therefore, [G. Ed. p. 1298.] nearly all compounds. In Greek, ἐρείπ-ιο-ν, ἀμπλάκ-ιο-ν, ἁμάρτ-ιο-ν belong to this class.

891. The Sanscrit forms also, by the neuter suffix *ya*, abstracts out of nominal bases, the final vowel of which is suppressed, with the exception of *u*, which receives Guna; while the initial vowel is usually augmented by Vriddhi (see §. 26.), and accented; *e.g.*, *mádhur-ya-m*, "sweetness," from *madhurá-s*, "sweet;" *náipun-ya-m*, "skill," from *nipuná-s*, "skilful;" *śáukl-ya-m*, "whiteness," from *śuklá-s*, "white;" *cháur-ya-m*, "theft," from *chórá-s*, "thief." Hereto admirably correspond, with respect, also, to the suppression of the final vowel of the primitive base, the Gothic neuter

---

* *E.g.*, *mahitvá* (Rigv. I. 52. 13.), "through greatness," from *mahitvá* (Vêd. *máhi*, "great," suffix *tva*); *mahitvaná* (85. 7.), id. (*mahi*, suffix *tvana*, see p. 1216 G. ed.); *vrishatvá* (54. 2.), "through rain" (abstr. from *vrishan*, "rainer"). This analogy is followed also by the Vêdic *tvá*, "through thee" (see Benf. Gl. p. 155, and cf. the Marāṭhī *tvá*, see p. 1162 G. ed.) for *tváyá*.

bases of abstract substantives like *diub-ya*, "theft," from *diub(a)-s*, "thief" (see §. 135.); *unlêd-ya*, "poverty," from *unlêd(a)-s*, "poor;" *galeik-ya*, "resemblance," from *galeik(a)-s*, "like;" *unvit-ya*, "ignorance," from *unvit(a)-s*, "foolish;" *hauhist-ya*, "height," from *hauhist(a)-s*, "the highest." In the nominative accusative, according to §. 153., the *a* of the suffix *ya* is suppressed, and *y* vocalised to *i;* hence, *diubi, unlêdi,* &c. The following are Latin abstracts of this kind: *mendac-iu-m, artific-iu-m, princip-ium, consort-iu-m, jejun'-iu-m, conviv'-iu-m.* This class of words is more scantily represented in Greek by forms like μονομάχ'-ιο-ν, θεοπρόπ'-ιο-ν. There belong, however, also to this class, though with their meaning perverted, words like ἐργαστήρ-ιο-ν, δικαστήρ-ιο-ν, ληστήρ-ιο-ν, ναυπήγ-ιο-ν; and from bases in ευ such as τροφεῖο-ν, κουρεῖο-ν, with, as it appears, digamma suppressed, for τροφέϜ-ιο-ν, κουρέϜ-ιο-ν.

892. In Old Sclavonic corresponds the neuter suffix ик *iye* (euphonic for *iyo*, see §. 255. n., p. 325), so that the vowel corresponding to the semi-vowel is also prefixed to it, while, however,

[G. Ed. p. 1299.] in Russian it is wanting; веселик *veseliye*,* "joy," (Russian веселіе *veselie*) from веселъ *vesel'*, "joyful." Abstracts in аник *aniye*, еник *eniye*, ѣник *yeniye*, тик *tiye*, are formed with the suffix under discussion from the perfect passive participle in a similar manner as in Old High German are formed; *e.g. farlâzanî,* "abandonment," *erweliti,* "choice," with the feminine form of the suffix я *ya*, out of the participle belonging to the conjugation of the verb referred to; *e.g.,* чаяник *chayaniye*, "expectation," from чаянъ *chayan'*, "he expects;" ѩвленик *yavleniye*, "unveiling," from ѩвленъ *yavlen'*, "he discovers;" питик *pitiye*, "the drinking," from питъ *pit'*, "drunken." With this suffix are formed also collectives in the Sclavonic languages as in Sanscrit; *e.g.* in

---

* See Miklos., Radices, p. 8. Dobrowsky (p. 283) writes веселіе, and similarly in the other examples given p. 282 of this class of words.

Russian древїе *drevie,* "many trees," from древо *drevo,* "a tree." So in Sanscrit *káisya-m,* "hairs," from *késás,* "hair."

893. In Lithuanian, which has lost the neuter gender of substantives, the class of words under discussion has become masculine; and then, according to §. 135, the syllable *ya* is contracted before the nominative sign *s* to *i,* and the final vowel of primitive bases, as in the sister-languages, is suppressed; and thus, with regard to the nominative, it appears as though the simple change of *a* or *u* into *i* could form an abstract from an adjective. Cf. *e.g.,*

yód'-i-s, "blackness,"	with *yóda-s,* "black;"	
ilg'-i-s, "length,"	with *ilga-s,* "long;"	[G. Ed. p. 1300.]
karszt'-i-s, "heat,"	with *karszta-s,* "hot;"	
szalt'-i-s, "coldness,"	with *szalta-s,* "cold;"	
auksztʼ-i-s, "height,"	with *áukszta-s,* "high;"	
rúgszt'-i-s, "sourness,"	with *rúgsz-tu-s,* "sour;"	
daug-i-s, "multitude,"	with "*daug,*" "many," indecl.	

In several of the oblique cases the *a* of these abstracts, which is suppressed in the nominative, is, by the euphonic influence of the preceding *i,* changed to *e* (cf. §. 157. p. 174, Note*); hence, *e.g., ilgie-ms,* "*longitudinibus,*" compared with *ilga-ms,* "*longis.*" Primitive abstracts also are formed in Lithuanian by the suffix *ia,* euphonic *ie,* nominative *i-s:* these correspond, therefore, exclusive of their vocalisation of the semi-vowel to *i,* tolerably well to the Sanscrit gerundial bases in *ya*; *e.g., púl-i-s,* "fall" (*púlu,* "I fall"); *musz-i-s,* "blow" (*muszu,* "I smite"); *kandi-s,* "bite" (*kandu,* "I bite").

894. The feminine form of the suffix य *ya,* viz. या *yâ,* forms primitive abstracts with the accent on the suffix; *e.g. vrajyá,* "travelling;" *vidyá,* "knowledge;" *śayyá,** "the

---

* From *śé-yâ,* with irregular Guna; as, *e.g.,* in *śé-té'=κεῖ-ται.* The *y* of the suffix acts like a vowel, hence *ay* for *é=ai.*

lying." Hereto admirably correspond Gothic abstract feminine bases in *yô* (*ô*=*â*, §. 69.), nominative *ya* or *i*;* for example, *vrakya*, "pursuit" (gen. *vrakyô-s*), corresponds also radically to the before-mentioned व्रज्या *vrajyâ*, with a tenuis for a medial, according to §. 87. The other abstracts of this formation which have been retained to our time are, *brakya*, "strife," (properly, "breach"); *hrôpi*, "clamour;" *haiti*, "command;" *usvandi*, "environs." Observe, that *vrakya*, *brakya*, and *us-vandi* (gen. *usvandyô-s*), have retained the true radical vowel, and hence correspond, not to the weakened present (*vrika*, *brika*, *vinda*), but to the [G. Ed. p. 1301.] monosyllabic forms of the preterite. So *bandi*, "band, fetter;" *fôtu-bandi*, "leg-iron;" on the other hand, *ga-bindi*, "band," with the extremest vowel-weakening of the present, and *ga-bundi*, id., with the middle vowel-weight of the polysyllabic forms of the preterite and perfect passive participle. An inorganic extension of the base with *n* (see §. 142.), is found in *rath-yô* (gen. *yôn-s*), "reckoning, account;" *sakyô*, "strife;"† *vaih-yô*, "contest" (*veiya*, "I contend"); *ga-run-yô*, "overflowing" (*rinna*, *rann*, *runnum*).

895. In the Sclavonic languages the class of feminine abstracts, which in Sanscrit is formed direct from the root by the suffix या *yâ*, is pretty numerously represented: it ends in old Sclavonic in the nominative in ꙗ *ya*; *e.g.*, волꙗ *volya*, "will;" желꙗ *schelya*, "mourning;" коуплꙗ *kúplya* (л euphonic), "business." In Lithuanian the *a*-sound

---

* The contraction of *ya* to *i* occurs, if preceded by a naturally long vowel, or one long by position, or if one simple word of more than one syllable precedes (cf. §. 135. &c., Gabel. and Löbe, p. 61). The latter case, however, does not occur in the class of words under discussion.

† Cf. the Gothic root *sak*, from *sag*, according to §. 87., with the Sanscrit सञ्ज् *sañj*, "*affigere*," with *abhi* (*abhishañj*), "*maledicere*, *objurgare*;" *abhishanga-s*, according to Wilson, 1. "a curse or imprecation," 2. "an oath," 3. "defeat," 4. "a false accusation," &c.

FORMATION OF WORDS. 1263

of this suffix has been usually changed by the euphonic influence of the semi-vowel to *e*, but the semi-vowel is itself dropped (cf. p. 174, Note *, and §. 137.), except in the genitive plural in *iû* or *yû* (see Ruhig's 3d declension). Here belong, for example, feminine abstracts; as, *srowé*, "flood" (sraŭyu, "I bleed," Sanscrit *sráv-á-mi*, "I flow," Greek ῥέω); *źinne͂*, "the knowing, knowledge" (*źinnau*, "I know"); *paine͂*, "entangling" (*pinnu*, "I plait"); *naktigone͂*, "the keeping watch by night" (*ganau*, "I watch"). On the other hand, *ia* is found in *pradźia*, "beginning" (*pra-de-mi*, "I begin"), for which, in Sanscrit, *pra-dhâ-yâ* would be to be expected.*

896. The Latin formations of this class [G. Ed. p. 1302.] of feminine verbal abstracts in *ia* or *iê* (see §. 137.) like the neuter in *iu-m*, and the Sanscrit gerunds in *ya* are for the most part compounded (see §. 890.); *e.g.*, *inedia*, *invidia* (if not from *invidus*), *vindemia*, *desidia*, *insidiæ*, *excubiæ*, *exsequiæ*, *diluviê-s*, *perniciê-s*,† *esuriê-s*. The following are examples of formations of this kind: *pluvia*, *scabiê-s* (properly, "the itching"), *rabiê-s*. With the inorganic affix of an *n*, and the substitution of an *ó* for *â*—as, *e.g.*, in the suffix *tôr* = *tár*, τηρ, §. 647., and in *môn* = *mán*, μων, §. 797.— the Sanscrit suffix *yâ*, in some abstract feminine bases, has been modified to *iôn*; and these, therefore, correspond to

---

* The Lithuanian form has suppressed the radical vowel before the suffix, otherwise it would be *pra-de-ya*, as the semi-vowel *y* between two vowels in Lithuanian, as in Latin, has remained, but after consonants, excepting *p*, *b*, *w*, *m* (Mielcke, p. 4), has been changed to the vowel *i*. *D* before *i*, with a vowel following, becomes *dź* (=*dsch*, Sanscrit ज *j*): the *i*, however, is scarcely pronounced.

† Without a base verb, for it has hardly sprung from *perneco*, as verbs of the 1st conjugation have produced no abstracts of this kind. The radically-cognate Sanscrit *náśyami*, "I go to ruin," would lead us to expect a Latin verb of the 3d conjugation, as *nacio*, *necio*, or *nocio* (cf. *nex*, *noceo*).

the above-mentioned (§. 894.) Gothic bases in *yôn*, nominative *yô*; thus *con-tagiô, -iôn-is, suspiciô, obsidiô, ambagiô, capiô*, as in Gothic *rathyô*, genitive *rathyôn-s*, &c. In Greek ιᾱ corresponds as exactly as possible to the Sanscrit या *yâ*, but is, however, in the primary formation, but rather weakly represented. The following are examples: πενία, μανία, ἁμαρτία, ἀμπλακία. In verbs in ευω (see §. 777.), which especially favour this kind of formation of the abstract, the υ is lost before the suffix, but probably first passed, on account of the vowel following, into F; thus, *e.g.*, ἀριστεία from ἀριστεϜία. More frequent is the appearance of the suffix ιᾱ (ε-ιᾱ̆) as a means of formation of denominative abstracts, in forms like εὐδαιμον-ία, ἡλικ-ία, μακαρ-ία, ἀνδρ-ία, σοφ'-ία, κακ'-ία, δειλ'-ία, ἀγγελ'-ία, ἀναγωγ'-ία, στρατηγ'-ία, ἀλήθεια,*

[G. Ed. p. 1303.] ἄνοια (ἀνο'-ια). To these denominative abstracts correspond in Latin, such as *capac-ia, feroc-ia, infant-ia, præsent-ia, inert-ia, concord-ia, inop-ia, perfid'-ia, superb'-ia, barbar'-ia; pauper-iê-s, barbar'-ie-s; un'iô(n), tal'-iô(n), commun'-iô(n), rebell'-iô(n)*.

897. The Old High German has in all cases, except the genitive plural (*heilô-n-ô* for *heilyô-n-ô* see §. 246.), dropped the vowel of the Sanscrit bases in *yâ*, which the Gothic has surrendered only in the nominative singular under the circumstances stated above (§. 894., Note *), and has changed

---

* The bases in ες (see §. 128.) lose their final consonant, as in the oblique cases; thus, ἀλήθεια from ἀληθεσ-ια, as ἀληθέ-ος from ἀληθεσ-ος. The combination of the ι of the suffix with the preceding ε or ο of the base word is the occasion of shortening the final *a*. The Homeric ἀληθείη also testifies to the original length of the *a* of such formations. In analogy with the phenomenon that bases in *s* suppress this consonant before the suffix ια, is the phenomenon that bases in *n*, in Sanscrit, suppress not only this consonant, but also the preceding vowel before vowels and the *y* of a derivative suffix; hence, *e.g.*, *râj-ya-m*, "kingdom" (Gothic *reik-i*, theme *reik-ya*, "dominion," from *reik(a)-s*, "ruler, supreme one"), for *râjan-ya-m*, from *râjan*, "a king."

the semi-vowel into the corresponding long vowel (see Grimm's 2d strong decl. fem.), to which, in the dative plural, the case-sign *m* (or *n*) is attached.* To this class belong nearly all the words of Grimm's 2d declension feminine of the strong form (I. p. 618), which, like the Gothic 3d weak declension feminine, with the exception of the formations in *nissi*, contains almost only abstracts, which have been formed from adjectives (participles included), with the suffix corresponding to the Sanscrit या *yá*; as, *e.g.*, [G. Ed. p. 1304.] *chaltˊ-î*, "cold," *warmˊ-î*, "warmth," *hôhˊ-î*, "height," *huldˊ-î*, "grace," *nâhˊ-î*, "nearness," *scônˊ-î*, "fairness, beauty," *suozˊ-î*, "sweetness," *stillˊ-î*, "stillness," *tiufˊ-î*, "depth," *rôtˊ-î*, "redness," *suarzˊ-î*, "blackness," from the adjective bases *chalta*, "cold," *warma*, "warm,"† &c. I call especial attention to the abstracts arising from passive participles, corresponding to the Sanscrit in *ta* and *na*, and formed with the suffix under discussion, which, irrespective of gender, accord with the Sclavonic abstracts mentioned above (§. 892.); as, питиѥ *pitiye*, "the drinking;" чаѩниѥ *chayaniye*, "expectation." The following are examples of Old High German abstracts of this kind: *er-welitˊ-î*, "choice," *vîr-wehsalôtˊ-î*, "alternation," *vir-terhinêtˊ-î*, "pretext," *varlâzanˊ-î*, "abandoning," *ar-habanˊ-î*, "elevation," *êrist-poranˊ-î*, "primogeniture," from the participial bases *erwelita* (nom. *-têr*), &c., *varlâzana* (nom. *-nêr*), &c. The formations in *nî* (Grimm, II. 161. 62.) are much more numerous than those

---

* I conjecture that the *i* is long also in the dative plural, thus *heilî-m*, as the long vowels maintain themselves better before a final consonant than at the end of a word. Compare the conjunctive forms like *âzi*, opposed to *âzis*, *âzît*, *âzîn* (see §. 711. p. 944.).

† Nom. masc. *chaltê-r*, *warmê-r*, with the pronominal affix of the strong declension (see p. 368, §. 288. Rem. 5.). At the beginning of compounds stands either the true base in *a*, or, and indeed more generally, the base mutilated by the removal of *a*; *e.g.*, *mihila-mot* and *mihhilˊ-mot*, "magnanimous" (Graff. II. 694.). Of this more hereafter.

in *tí* (Grimm II. 261.), but both spring from scarce any source but compound participles. It also deserves notice, that such formations are limited to the Old and Middle High German, with the exception, perhaps, of the Old Northern *um-géngni*, "*conversatio*," mentioned by Grimm (p. 162). I should not wish the above-mentioned remarkable coincidence between the German and Sclavonic to be so interpreted as that any should found on it the conjecture of a special affinity between those languages; for since the Sanscrit suffix य *ya*, feminine या *yâ*, as a means of formation of denominative abstracts in the European languages [G. Ed. p. 1305.] has been universally diffused, it is not in the least surprising that the Sclavonic and High German usually coincide in this point, that they have used this suffix also for the derivatives from passive participles. It might be possible that the Latin abstracts also in *tiôn, siôn,* were not formed, as has been before remarked (see p. 1195 G. ed.), by an extension of the suffix *ti*, but have been derived from the passive participle with the aid of the *iôn* discussed above; thus, *e.g., coct'-iô(n)* from *coctu-s, mot'-iô(n)* from *motu-s, miss'-iô(n)* from *missus, orbât'-iô(n)* from *orbâtu-s*, as above (p. 1303 G. ed.), *commun'-iô(n)* from *communi-s, un'-io(n)* from *unu-s*, as in Old High German *erwelit'-i* from *erwelita*.

898. It scarcely needs mention that the *e* of our abstracts like *Kälte*, ("cold"), *Wärme*, ("warmth"), is the corruption of the *i* of the analogous High German abstracts, as in general nearly all vowels in the final syllables of polysyllabic words have, in New High German, and the majority so early as in Middle High German, been weakened to *e*. Without attention, however, to the intermediate stages, it would have been impossible, in words like *Kälte, Grösse, Länge*, ("cold, greatness, length"), to recognise an affinity of formation with the Sanscrit *banijyâ*, "traffic" (from *banij*, "trader"); and collectives like *gavyâ*, "a number of

cows" (from *gó*); *pâsyá*, "a number of cords" (from *páśa*); to which correspond the Greek ἀνθρακ-ιά, μυρμηκ-ιά, σποδ'-ιά. In High German this class of collectives has become neuter, as in Sclavonic (see §. 892.); and hence the suffix *ya* in Old High German has, in the nominative and accusative, been contracted to *i* (cf. Gothic, §. 159), while in New High German it is either suppressed or turned into *e*. Before the base word is prefixed the preposition *ge*, "with," (Old High German *ga, gi*, &c.): hence, *e.g.*, Old High German *gafugil'-i* (for *-ali*), "*complexus avium*," from *fugal*, theme *fugala*, "a bird" (Middle High German *gevügele*, New High German *Gevögel*); *gabein'-i*, "bone, *ossa;*" *gabirg'-i*, "mountain, mountains;" *gafild'-i*, "fields," (properly, "many fields," "*agri, arva*"); *gadarm'-i*, "entrails;" [G. Ed. p. 1306.] *gistein'-i*, "stones;" *gistirn-i*, "stars." As regards the relation of the *e* of our abstracts like *Kälte* to the Sanscrit *yâ*, this corruption answers exactly to that in the conjunctive of the preterite, where, *e.g.*, *ässe* corresponds to the Old High German *âzi* and Sanscrit *ad-yâ-m, ad-yâ-t* (see §. 711. p. 944.): on the other hand, the Old High German *î* of *chalti* coincides with the contraction which the Sanscrit itself experiences in the middle of the potential, where, *e.g.* *ad-î-máhi* (from *ad-yâ-mahi*, see §. 675.), corresponds to the Gothic *êt-ei-ma*, and Old High German *âz-î-mês*. The Anglo-Saxon has, in the class of denominative abstracts under discussion, dropped the semi-vowel of the Sanscrit *yâ*, and weakened the vowel to *o*[*]; hence, *e.g.*, *hælo*, "health," *hyldo*, "grace," *yldo*, "age," compared with the Old High German *heili, huldi, alti*. The Gothic has further added an inorganic *n* to the या *yâ* contracted to *ei* (=*î*, see §. 70.), which, in the nominative, is laid aside, according to

---

[*] Probably from an earlier *u;* as, *e.g.*, in the final syllable of *sëofon*, 7, for Gothic *sibun*, Sanscrit *saptan;* and in the plural of the preterite, *e.g.*, *föron*=Gothic *förum*, 3d person *förun*.

§. 142.* Hence, *e.g.*, *hauh'-ei(n)*, "height;" *diup'-ei(n)*, "depth;" *lagg'-ei(n)*, "length;" *braid'-ei(n)*, "breath;" *manag'-ei(n)*, "multitude;" *magath'-ei(n)*, "virginity," παρθεν'-ία, from the bases *hauha* (nom. m. *hauhs*), &c., and the substantive base *magathi* (nom. *magaths*). Moreover, from weak verbal themes in *ya* (Grimm's 1st conjugation) spring abstract bases in *ein*, in which the verbal derivative in *ya* (= Sanscrit *aya*) is dropped before the abstract suffix *ein*; hence, *e.g.*, *ga-aggv-ei(n)*, "hemming in," from *ga-aggvya*, "I narrow;" *bairht'-ei(n)*, "announcement," from *bairhtya*, "I an-

[G. Ed. p. 1307.] nounce;" *vaia-mêr-ei(n)*, "burthening," from *vaia-mêrya*, "I burthen."† The inorganic *n* of this class of words occurs also occasionally in Old High German, but has here at the same time found its way into the nominative (see Grimm, I. 628.).

899. With the suffix *ya*, feminine *yâ*, future passive participles also are formed in Sanscrit, which, for the most part, accent the radical syllable, but some the suffix, with the weaker accent (Svarita). The latter kind of accentuation occurs only in roots which terminate in a consonant (including the syllable *ar*, which is interchanged with ऋ *ri*),

---

* In departure from §. 142., I now think that the cases in which the Gothic *ein* corresponds to the Sanscrit feminine character *î* ought to be limited to the classes of words mentioned in §. 120., since in the *ei* of the class of words here discussed we must recognise a contraction of *yâ*, after the analogy of the conjunctives; such as *êt-ei-ma*, "we ate"=Sanscrit *ad-yấ-ma*, Latin *ed-î-mus* (§. 711. p. 944).

† There are in Old High German also verbal abstracts of this kind, only that the inorganic *n* is dropped; *e.g.*, *mend'-î*, "joy," from *mendiu*, "*gaudeo*" (cf. Sanscrit *mand*, "*gaudere*"); *touf'-î*, "baptism," from *toufiu*, "I baptize." Observe, that in Sanscrit also the character of the 10th class and of the causal forms is suppressed before certain formative suffixes, while properly only the final *a* of *aya* ought to be suppressed (see §. 109ᵃ. 6.); *e.g.*, before the gerundial suffix *ya*, with which we are here most concerned, *ay* is usually suppressed; *e.g.*, *ni-véd-ya*, "after the giving up," for *ni-véd-ay-ya*.

FORMATION OF WORDS. 1269

and which are either long by nature (length by position included), or are in this class of words, to which also belong appellatives, which, according to their fundamental meaning, are future participles, augmented by Guna or Vṛiddhi.* At least *â*, *i.e.* the heaviest of the simple vowels, before two consonants in this class of words admits a different kind of accentuation; whence it is clear that the language here seeks to avoid the combination of the greatest vowel-weight with that of the strongest accent in one and the same syllable. The following are examples: *gúhya-s*, "*celandus;*" *gúhya-m*, subst. "a secret;" *idya-s*, "*cele-* [G. Ed. p. 1308.] *brandus;*" *śánsya-s*, "*laudandus;*" *dóhya-s*, "*mulgendus*" (root *duh*); *driśya-s*, "*spectandus*" (root *darś*, *driś*, see §. 1.); *chéya-s*, "*colligendus*" (root *chi*); *stávya-s* and *stávyà-s*, "*laudandus;*" *bhôjyà-s*, "*edendus;*" *bhôjyà-m*, subst. "food" (root *bhuj*); *páchyà-s*, "*coquendus*" (root *pach*); *ni-váryà-s*, "*arcendus*" (root *var*, *vṛi*, cl. 10.); *vákyà-m*, "discourse," as "to be spoken;" *káryà-m*, "business," as "to be done" (root *kar*, *kṛi*); *bháryâ*, "a spouse," as "to be supported, to be cherished" (root *bhar*, *bhṛi*); Zend ؤﺟﯽﻮﺟﻮ *vahmyô* (theme -*ya*), "*invocandus.*"† To these admirably correspond some Gothic

---

* In the technical language of grammar this participial suffix, in case it accents the Svarita, and provided the radical vowel is augmented, is called ण्यत् *nyat*.

† From the denominative *vahmayêmi*, with the suppression of the character of the 10th class; as in Sanscrit, *e.g.*, *ni-váryà-s*, "*arcendus*," from *ni-vâr-áyâ-mi*. No formal objection can be raised to the explanation given by Burnouf (l. c. p. 575), according to which *vahmya* would come direct from the base *vahma*, "*invocatio.*" I prefer, however, that a form which evinces itself by its signification to be a future passive participle should be also formally so explained, in which, as is shewn by the analogous forms in Sanscrit, there is no difficulty. Neriosengh, too, regards ؤﺟﯽﻮﺟﻮ *vahmya*, as also the *yaśnya* which accompanies it, of which hereafter, as the future passive participles (Burn., p. 572), and translates the former by *su-namaskaranîya* ("*bene adorandus*"), and the latter by *árádhanîya* ("*venerandus*").

adjective bases in *ya*, which, as has been already elsewhere remarked, are to be sought in Grimm's 2d adjective declension of the strong form (in Gabel. and Löbe, p. 74). Here we find the bases *anda-nêm-ya*, "agreeable," properly, "*accipiendus;*"* *unqvêth-ya*, "inexpressible" (root *qvath, qvitha, qvath, qvêthum*); *anda-sêtya*, "contemptible, horrible" (root *sat*, "to sit," *sita, sat, sêtum, and-sat*, "to be bashful"); *skeir-ya*, "clear, plain, intelligible" (*gaskeir-ya*, "I explain");

[G. Ed. p. 1309.] *un-nut-ya*, "useless," properly, "unenjoyable" (root *nut*, "to obtain, to enjoy," *niuta, naut, nutum*); *brûk-ya*, "serviceable;" *un-brûk-ya*, "unserviceable;" *riur-ya*, "destructible, perishable, transitory" (φθαρτός); *un-riur-ya*, "imperishable, ἄφθαρτος (*riurya*, "I mar"); *sût-ya*, "mild," properly, "*gustandus*" is identical with the Sanscrit *svâd-yà-s* of *â-svâd-yà-s*, "*gustandus*," "*jucundi saporis*,"† and akin to *svâdú-s*, "sweet" (Greek ἡδύ-ς, Old High German *suozi*, "sweet," in the uninflected form), theme *suozia* = Gothic *sûtya*. Among substantives, the neuter base *basya*, "berry" (n. a. *basi*), belongs to this class, if it corresponds, as I conjecture it does, to the Sanscrit *bhákṣh-ya-m*, "food," properly, "to be eaten" (from *bhakṣh*, "to eat," Greek φάγω), and has lost the guttural of the root, in the same way as, *e.g.*, in Zend, the Sanscrit *akṣhi*, "eye," has been abbreviated to *ashi*. In the Old High German *beri* (theme *berya*), the *s* has become *r*, as, *e.g.*, in *wârumés*, "we were" = Gothic *vêsum*.

Remark.—The theory of the nominative singular of the adjective bases in *ya*, feminine *yô*, admits, now that we have before us the remains of the Gothic translation of the Bible in von Gabelentz and Löbe's edition, and, moreover, the Skeireins edited for the first time by Massmann, of

---

* From the root *nam* (*nima, nam, némum*). With regard to the lengthening of the radical *a* to *ê* (=Sanscrit *â*, see §. 69.) in this and analogous forms, compare Sanscrit forms like *páchyà-s*, "*coquendus*."

† Root *svad* (seemingly from *su*, "well," and *ad*, "to eat"), "*gustare*," middle "*jucunde sapere*."

FORMATION OF WORDS. 1271

a more exact survey than was before possible; and so in the masculine, instead of the one form in *i-s*, which, following Grimm, I gave in §. 135., we possess in all four different gradations; for which Gabelentz and Löbe (Gramm., p. 74) give as examples, *sûtis*, *hrains*, *niuyis*, and *viltheis*. The more perfect form *yi-s*, for the, according to §. 67., impossible *ya-s*, occurs when any vowel, or a simple consonant with a short vowel preceding it, goes before; hence, *niu-yi-s*, "new;" *sak-yi-s*, "quarrelsome." Hence, also, from the base *midya*, the nominative masculine, which cannot be cited, can only be *midyi-s* (=Sanscrit *mádhya-s*, Latin *mediu-s*), not *midi-s*, as was assumed above (§. 135.), as the contracted form of an earlier *midyis*. As, then, *midyi-s* corresponds to the [G. Ed. p. 1310.] Sanscrit *mádhya-s*, so does *niu-yi-s* to the Sanscrit *náv-ya-s* and Lithuanian *nau-ya-s*, which are equivalent in signification; and thus, therefore, *niuyi-s* shews itself to be a future passive participle; for नव्यस् *náv-ya-s*, according to its derivation, can only be regarded as such, as it, like the more current *náva-s*,* on which the Latin *novu-s*, Greek νέ(F)ο-ς, and Sclavonic *novo* (theme and n. a. neut.), are based, springs from the root *nu*, "to praise," and originally signifies "*laudandus*." Formally it corresponds to the above-mentioned *stávya-s*, from *stu*. If the syllable *ya* in Gothic adjective bases be preceded by a long syllable terminating in a consonant, it is contracted in the nominative masculine either to *ei*, as in similarly constituted substantive bases (see §. 135.), or to *i*, or it is, as is most commonly the case, entirely suppressed. Instances of the first kind are forms like *alth-ei-s*, "old," and *vilth-ei-s*, "wild;" of the second, *sût-i-s*,† "mild," and *airkn-i-s*, "holy;" of the third, *hrain-s*, "pure," *gamain-s*, "common," *gafaur-s*, "fasting," *brûk-s*, "serviceable," *bleith-s*, "kind," *andaném-s*, "agreeable." To this class belong *alya-kun-s*, ἀλλογενής (Luke xvii. 18); for which, on account of the indubitable shortness of the *u*, *alya-kun-yi-s* might be expected: it appears, however, that the loading of the word by composition, or, generally, the circumstance, that in the entire word more syllables than one precede the

---

* This is the accentuation at least in the Vêda dialect: according to Wilson, however, who gives this word the suffix *ach* (*ch* denotes the accentuation of the suffix), this adjective would, in the common language, be oxytone, as most of the adjectives formed with *a* (see Wilson's Grammar, 2d Edition, p. 310).

† Grimm assuredly, with correctness, deduces the length of the *u* from the Old High German *suozi*. If it were short the nominative would most probably be *sutyis*.

suffix *ya*, has occasioned the suppression of the suffix in the nominative (cf. §. 135.)*.

[G. Ed. p. 1311.] 900. The Lithuanian also has some remains of the future passive participle under discussion, but

---

* V. Gabelentz and Löbe (Grammar, p. 74) assume, in the class of adjectives here spoken of, bases in *i*, though, with respect to the corresponding substantive declension, they agree with me that the same contains bases in *ya*. With regard to the adjectives, however, the cognate languages, and the oblique cases of the Gothic itself, speak just as emphatically in favour of the proposition that the bases of Grimm's 2d declension of the strong form end in the masculine and neuter in *ya*, and in the feminine in *yô* (=Sanscrit *yâ*), whence, according to §. 137., we should have *ya* in the nominative. The agreement of *niuyi-s*, "*novus*," *niuya*, "*nova*," with the Sanscrit *návya-s*, *návyâ*, and the Lithuanian *nauya-s*, *nauya*, and that of *midyi-s*, *midya*, with the Sanscrit *mádhya-s*, *mádhyâ*, and Latin *mediu-s*, *media*, speaks very decidedly against the opinion that the *y* of the Gothic forms is an insertion (l. c. p. 75, d. e.). Just so the *y* of the base *alya* (nominative, most probably, *alyi-s*) is identical with the Sanscrit *y* and Latin *i* of *anyá-s*, *aliu-s* (§. 374.). I cannot allot to this class feminine nominatives in *s*, as the feminine bases, which in Sanscrit terminate in *á*, have, from a period so early as that of the identity of languages, lost the nominative sign (see §. 137.). I regard, therefore, the forms *brûks*, "serviceable," *séls*, "good," and *skeirs*, "clear," although in the passages where they occur they refer to feminine substantives (1 Tim. iv. 8, 1 Cor. xiii. 4, Skeir. IV. b.), as masculine nominatives, which, in consequence of a peculiarity of syntax, represent adverbially, as we use uninflected adjectives (*er ist gut, sie ist gut*, "he is good, she is good"), the nominative of that gender, whatever it may be, to which the substantive referred to belongs. Thus, as has been elsewhere shewn (Nalus, 2d Edit., p. 214), in Sanscrit the masculine nominative singular of the present participle may, by an abuse, refer to any gender or number, in sentences like *bhâimî sântvayan . . . uvâcha*, "Bhaimî spake flattering" (for *sântvayantî*); and, in like manner, in Ulfilas (Rom. vii. 8.), the masculine participial base *nimands*, "taking," refers to the feminine substantive *fravaurhts*, "sins," to which, in the very same passage, also the masculine *navis*, "dead," refers: *inu vitôth fravaurhts vas navis*, "without the law sin was dead." The actual feminine nominatives of *brûks*, &c., could scarcely be aught else than *brûhi*, *sêli*, *skeiri*, according to the analogy of substantive forms,

with

only in a substantive form. To this class [G. Ed. p. 1312.] belong *walg-i-s* (from *walg-ya-s*, see §. 135.), "food," as "to be eaten" (*walgau*, "I eat"); *źod-i-s* "word," as "to be spoken" (cf. *źad-a-s* "speech," *źadu* "I promise," Sanscrit *gad*, "to speak"). In Latin, *ex-im-iu-s*, properly = *eximendus*, is, according to its signification, the truest remnant of this class of words. Formally, *gen-i-us* also, and *in-gen-iu-m*, belong to this class. To the latter corresponds, in root and formation, the Gothic neuter base *kun-ya*, nominative *kuni*, "sea." In Greek, ἄγ-ιο-ς (originally akin to ἄζω) corresponds to the Sanscrit *yáj-yà-s*. "*venerandus*." From a Greek point of view the following are more plain: στύγ-ιο-ς, φρύγ-ιο-ς, πάγ- -ιο-ς. Πάλλα, "ball" as "to be thrown," is to be derived, I conjecture, from παλγα, by assimilation,* in the same way as πάλλω from παλγω, but with this difference, that while the 2d λ of πάλλω is based on the Sanscrit character *ya* of the 4th class,† and hence is excluded, *e.g.*, from the abstract πάλο-ς, the λ of πάλλα corresponds to the य़ *y* of the participial suffix under discussion. Πάλλα, therefore, and πάλλω, with regard to the consonant which follows the root, have just as little in common as, *e.g.*, in Sanscrit, *lóbh-ya-s*, "deside-

---

with a long penultima, as *hrópi*, "clamour" (see §. 894. Note). Such a form have we then actually existing in the, of its kind, unique adjective form *vóthi*, "*grata*" (nom. masc. probably *vóths*), where it is important to remark, that, in the single passage where it occurs (2 Cor. ii. 15), it does not stand, like the masculines *brúks*, *séls*, *skeirs*, which represent in the before-mentioned passages the feminine, as predicate, but as epithet, "we are unto God a sweet savour of Christ" (*Christaus dauns siyum vóthi goda*). I do not believe that Ulfilas could here have written *vóths* for *vóthi;* and I consider the latter form as feminine nominative in the said passage entirely free from suspicion, provided the unciteable masculine nominative be *vóths*, or, according to the analogy of *sútis*, *vóthis* (cf. Gabelentz and Löbe, l. c.).

* See p. 414, G. ed., §. 300.
† See §. 501.

randus," and *lúbh-ya-tê*, "*desiderat*." I agree with G. Curtius ("*De nominum Græcorum formatione*," p. 61) in referring to this class also φθί-δ-ιο-ς and ἀμφά-δ-ιο-ς, as also ἑκτά-δ-ιο-ς. The inserted δ may be compared with the *t* which, after short vowels, is prefixed to the Sanscrit gerundial suffix य *ya*, or, which is here more to the purpose, with that of some ap-
[G. Ed. p. 1313.] pellatives, which, according to their fundamental meaning, are future passive participles; as, *chí-t-ya-m*, "funeral-pile," properly "*colligendum*" (from *chi*, "to collect"); *bhrí-t-ya-s*, "servant," as "to be supported," from *bhar*, *bri*, "to bear, to support, to nourish." To this class, according to its formation, belongs, although with active signification, the Greek στά-διο-ς, properly "standing" (cf. στα-τός = *sti-tá-s*).

901. The Greek ιο is of more common occurrence as the formative suffix of denominative adjectives (Buttmann, §. 119. 67.) than in the primary formation of words; and here, likewise, has its Sanscrit prototype in the secondary (Taddhita) suffix of words like *dív-ya-s*, "heavenly," from *div*, "heaven;" *hríd-ya-s*, "amiable, agreeable," from *hrid*, "heart;" *ágr'-ya-s*, "the most excellent" ("standing on the summit"), from *ágra-m*, "summit;" *dhán'-ya-s*, "rich," from *dhána-m*, "wealth;" *śún-ya-s*, "canine," from the weakened base *śun* = Greek κυν; *ráth'-ya-s*, "car-horse" ("belonging to the car"); *ráth'-ya-m*, "car-road," from *rátha-s*, "car;" *yaśasyà-s*, "famous," from *yaśas*, "fame;" *rahas-yà-s*, "secret," from *ráhas*, "mystery;"* *nâv-yà-s*,

---

* In the two last examples the demission and weakening of the accent is occasioned by the circumstance that the suffix is preceded by more than one syllable; with which may be compared the phenomenon, that, in Gothic, the same suffix, under the same circumstances, experiences in the nominative a contraction or suppression (see §. 135.). In *nâv-yà-s* (Pan. VI. 1. 213.) the long *â* has the same influence in weakening the accentuation that, in Gothic, *e.g.*, the *û* of *sût-i-s*, has in weakening the suffix.

"navigable," from *nâu-s*, "ship." The following are examples in Zend: ᴀᴊᴊ/ᴊᴡϛ/ *nmân'-ya*, "domesticus," from *nmâna*, "house"; ᴀᴊᴊ᾿ᴊ᾿ᴡᴊᴡ *âhuir'-ya*, "regarding the Ahura" (with Vriddhi), from *ahura*; ᴀᴊᴊ᾿ᴊᴡᴄ *yâir-ya*, "yearly," from ϛ᾿ᴀᴡᴄ *yârĕ*, "a year;" ᴀᴊᴊ᾿ϭᴀᴡᴀᴇʙᴠ᾿ᴀᴡᴄ *gaôschdâthr'-ya*, "purifying, purifier," from ᴀ᾿ϭᴀᴡᴀᴇʙᴠ᾿ᴀᴡᴄ *yaôschdâthra*, "means of purification" (§. 817.); *gaêith'-ya*, "earthly," from *gaêthâ* (nom. *gaêtha*, see §. 137.), "earth." [G. Ed. p. 1314.]
So in Greek, *e.g.*, ἄλ-ιο-ς, ἀγών-ιο-ς, ἡγεμόν-ιο-ς, πάτρ-ιο-ς (=Sanscrit *pítr-ya-s* "fatherly"), σωτήρ-ιο-ς, φιλοτήσ-ιο-ς, (from -τητ-ιο-ς), θαυμάσ-ιο-ς (from θαυμάτ-ιο-ς), ἑκούσ-ιο-ς (from ἑκόντ-ιο-ς), τέλειο-ς (from τελέσ-ιο-ς, see §. 128.), ἐπιτήδειο-ς (from ἐπιτηδέσ-ιο-ς), ὄρειο-ς (from ὀρέσ-ιο-ς), γέλοιο-ς (from γελώσ-ιο-ς for γελώτ-ιο-ς), ἐτήσ-ιο-ς (for ἐτέσ-ιο-ς, from the base ἔτες, whence also ἔτειο-ς), οὐράν'-ιο-ς, ποτάμ'-ιο-ς, θαλάσσ'-ιο-ς, κόν'-ιο-ς, λύσ'-ιο-ς, φύξ'-ιο-ς, ἀσπάσ'-ιο-ς (from the to-be-presupposed verbal abstract ἀσπασι-ς), πῆχυ-ιο-ς, τριπῆχυ-ιο-ς, δίκαιο-ς, ἀκμαῖο-ς, ἁμαξαῖο-ς, ἀμοιβαῖο-ς. The four last examples, as most of the derivatives from words of the 1st declension, depart from the original principle in this, that they retain the final vowel of the base (always as α, as in the nom. pl.) before the suffix. The diphthong which grows up in this manner occasions, in most cases, the displacement of the accent, in which respect I recall attention to a similar phenomenon in Sanscrit (see §. 899.). The retention of the υ of πήχυιος and τριπήχυιο-ς answers to the retention of the *u* in Sanscrit (§. 891.), *e.g.* in *ritav-yà-s*, "annual," from *ritu-s*. Here belong also gentilia like Σαλαμίν-ιο-ς, Κορίνθ'-ιο-ς, Μιλήσ'-ιο-ς (from -τ'-ιο-ς), Ἀθηναῖο-ς; proper names, as Ἀπολλών-ιο-ς, Διονύσ'-ιο-ς; neuter appellations of temples and sanctuaries called after the god to whom they are dedicated, as Ἀπολλώ-νιον; names of feasts in the plural, as Διονύσ'-ια; and perhaps feminine names of countries derived from the names of their inhabitants, as Αἰθιοπ-ία, from Αἰθίοπ-ς, Μακεδον-ία, from the base Μακεδον. To the proper

names correspond Sanscrit patronymics like *káurav-yá-s,* "Kuruide" from *kuru,* in which the first vowel of the primary word receives the Vriddhi augment, while the accent has sunk down upon the final syllable.

902. In Latin this class of words is less numerous than in Greek; yet to it belong, both various adjectives and [G. Ed. p. 1315.] appellatives, and also proper names. The following are examples: *egreg-iu-s, patr-iu-s, imperator-iu-s, prætor-iu-s, censor-iu-s, soror-iu-s, nox'-iu-s, lud'-iu-s,* (from *ludu-s,* not from *ludo*), *Mar-iu-s, Octav'-iu-s, Octav'-ia, Non'-iu-s, Non'-ia.* As regards the appellatives of countries in *ιᾱ* in Greek, and their relation to the names of the inhabitants, attention must be recalled to the circumstance, that above (§. 119.) we have recognised the Greek *ια* as the simple extension of the Sanscrit feminine character *î,* among other words, in feminines in τρια (ὀρχήστρια) compared with the Sanscrit in *trî* (*dâtrî,* "female giver," see §. 811.): accordingly, the names of countries in *ια* might also be taken as simple feminine formations of the base words expressing the names of the inhabitants; so that, therefore, *e. g.*, Μακεδονία would appear in a Sanscrit form as *Makadan-î,* and would properly signify "the belonging to," not to say "the spouse," of the Macedonian, or, too, "the mother" of all the Macedonians. This view would receive emphatic support from the circumstance, that there are also names of countries with feminine themes in *ιδ,* the *ιδ* of which,=Sanscrit *î,* has the same relation to the primary word denoting the inhabitant, as above (§. 119.) ληστρ-ιδ (for ληστηρ-ιδ) has to ληστήρ, or as, *e.g.*, ἡγεμον-ιδ to the masculine base ἡγεμον, and much the same as, in Sanscrit, *mahatî,* "the great," (fem.) has to *mahát.* The following are examples of this kind: 'Αβαντίδ from Ἄβαντ ('Αβαντ-ες); Περσ-ίδ, "Persia," from Πέρση-ς, "Persian man," feminine Περσίς. If, however, the Greek names of countries in *ια* are only the feminines of the names of the inhabitants, and if their ter-

FORMATION OF WORDS. 1277

mination is only an inorganic extension of the Sanscrit feminine character *í*, we might also explain in the same manner the Latin, as *Gallia, Germania, Italia, Græcia*, and assume that the *n* (= Sanscrit *a*, Greek *o*) of the masculine bases *Gallu, Germanu, Italu, Græcu*, is suppressed before the feminine character *i*, extended to *ia*, according to the same principle as that by which, in Sanscrit, the *a, e.g.*, of *dêvá*, "God" (nom. *dêvá-s*), is suppressed [G. Ed. p. 1316.] before the *í* of *dêví*, "goddess," and as, in Greek, the *o, e.g.*, of the base Δακο is lost before the feminine ια of Δακ'-ία. We can, even in the names of towns, *Florentia, Valentia, Placentia*, recognise feminine participles, the special form of which has been lost in the proper participles, as, in general, the adjective bases ending in a consonant have transferred to the feminines also the form which originally belongs only to the masculine and neuter. Feminine participial forms like *ferentia, tundentia*, compared with the Sanscrit *bháranti, tudánti*, and Greek φέρουσα, from φεροντια, cannot surprise us in Latin. Observe, also, the affix which, in Lithuanian, the feminine participle has gained in the oblique cases (see §. 157., Note*, p. 174, and §. 980.).

903. To the Sanscrit denominative adjective bases in *ya*, as *dív-ya*, "heavenly" (§. 901.), correspond most exactly some Gothic bases in *ya*, feminine *yô*; viz. *alêv'-ya*, "*olivifer*," from the primitive base *alêva* n., nom. *alêv*, "oil ;" *alth'-ya*, "old," from *althi* f., nom. *alth'-s* ; *nau'-ya*, "dead" (nom. m. *navis*), from *navi* m., nom. *naus*, "dead" (m.) ; *ana-haim'-ya*, "homely ;" *af-haim'-ya*, "absent," from *haimô* f., nom. pl. *haimô-s* ; *reik'-ya*, "chief," from *reika* m., nom. *reiks*, "supreme, chieftain ;" *uf-aith-ya*, "sworn," from *aitha* m., nom. *aith-s*, "oath ;" *in-gard-ya*, "homely, domestic," from *garda*, nom. *gards*, "house ;" *un-kar'-ya*, "careless," from *karô* f., nom. *kara*, "care." The definitions laid down above (p. 1309 G. ed., Rem.), hold with respect to the nominative masculine of these adjective bases. To the Sanscrit denominative

appellative bases like *ráth'-ya,* m. "car-horse," n. "car-wheel," correspond in Gothic such as *leik-ya,* "doctor" (nom. *leik-eis,* see §. 135.), from *leika* n., nom. *leik,* "the body;" *haird'-ya,* "herdsman," from *hairdô* f., nom. *hairda,* "herd;" *blôstr'-ya,* "worshipper," from the unciteable primitive base *blôstra* (see §. 818.); *faurstass'-ya,* "superintendant," from [G. Ed. p. 1317.] the unciteable *faurstassi,* "the superintendence" (from *-stas-ti, s* from *d,* according to §. 102.), nom. *faur-stass* (cf. *us-stass,* "resurrection"); *ragin'-ya,* "counsellor," from *ragina* n., (nom. *ragin,* "counsel"). The Gothic marks also with the favourite extension of the base by *n* masculine bases like *fisk'-yan,* "fisher" (nom. *fiskya,* according to §. 140.), *gud'-yan,* "priest," *vaurstv'-yan,* "labourer," *aurt'-yan,* "planter, gardener," *vai-dêd'-yan,* "malefactor," from the primitive bases *fiska,* m. "fish," *guda,* m. "God," *vaurstva,* n. "work," *aurti,* f. "plant," and the to-be-presupposed *vai-dêdi,* f. "misdeed" (*dêdi,* nom. *dêds,* "deed," see §. 135.). There are also some primitives, *i.e.* substantive bases, in *yan,* springing from verbal roots, which, according to their signification, are nouns of agency; viz. *af-êt-yan,* "eater, devourer" (root *at : ita, at, êtum*); *af-drugk-yan,* "drinker, tippler;" *vein-drugk-yan,* "wine-drinker" (root *dragk = drank: drigha, dragk, drugkum*); *dulga-hait-yan,* "creditor," (literally, "debt-namer"); *bi-hait-yan,* "boaster;" *arbi-num-yan,* "heir," literally, "inheritance-taker" (root *nam : nima, nam, nêmum, numans*); *faura-gagg-yan,* "intendant" (root *gagg,* "to go," see §. 92.); *ga-sinth-yan,* [G. Ed. p. 1318.] "companion," properly, "goer with."*

---

* Root *santh,* whence we should expect an unciteable verb *sintha, santh, sunthum* (see Grimm, II. p. 34); and whence, also, is formed by the suffix *an* (nom. *a*), *ga-sinthan,* of equivalent meaning, which answers to Sanscrit bases like *rájan,* "king," as "ruler." The causal *sandya,* "I send" ("make to go," see §. 740.), has the same relation, with regard to its *d,* to *santh,* that *standa,* "I stand," has to *stôth,* "I stood." Yet the *d* of *sandya* is more organic than the *th* of *santh,* at least *sand* can be

more

From weak verbs, too, spring some formations of this kind, and, indeed, so that the conjugational character is rejected before the formative suffix (cf. p. 1308 G. ed.): hence, *svigl-yan,* "piper," from the verbal base *svigló,* "to pipe;" and *timr'-yan* (scarcely to be divided *timry-an*), "carpenter," properly, "*ædificator,*" from *timrya,* "to build." To the bases in *yan* which spring from roots of strong verbs correspond in Sanscrit, exclusive of the appended *n,* besides some adjective bases, as *rúch-ya,* "pleasing, agreeable," *sádh--yà,* "complete," also some masculine or neuter appellative bases in *ya,* which, according to their fundamental meaning, are nouns of agency or present participles, and accent, some the radical syllable, some the suffix. The following are examples, of which I annex the nominatives: *súr-ya-s,* "the sun," as "shining;"* *bhíd-ya-s,* [G. Ed. p. 1319.]

---

more easily compared with the Sanscrit than *santh,* whether we betake ourselves to the root *sádh,* "to go, to attain," or to *sad,* "to go;" for for *dh* we find, in Gothic, regularly *d,* and the pure medial, which, according to §. 87., becomes *t,* might well have maintained itself in the case before us under the protection of the annexed liquids (cf. §. 90.).

* The Indian Grammarians assume a root *sur,* "to shine," which I regard as a contraction of *svar,* which is contained entire in the radical word *svàr,* "heaven" (as "shining"), on which is based the Zend *hvarĕ,* "sun." According to this, in *súrya* the syllable *va,* or its lengthened form *vâ,* would be contracted to *û.* If, however, *sur* were the old form of the root, its vowel would have become lengthened in *súrya.* The Greek ἥλιο-ς (from σϜήλιος) favours, however, the supposition that the form *súrya-s* is an abbreviation of *svárya-s.* As regards form, there would be nothing to prevent the derivation of *súrya* from *svàr,* "heaven:" from *svar* then would be formed, first *svarya* (as *dívya,* "heavenly," from *div*), and thence *súrvya-s;* I gladly, however, abandon this explanation, which has been already elsewhere proposed, as it appears to me more natural to represent the sun as "shining," than as "heavenly." The Lithuanian feminine *sáulĕ* exhibits correctly, according to rule, *ĕ* for *ia* or *ya:* I explain the Gothic neuter base *sauila* (nom. *sauil*) as formed by transposition from *saulia,* and this latter from *svalya;* and thus, also, the Lithuanian *au* of *saulĕ* may have arisen from *wa.* If any one, however, will follow

FORMATION OF WORDS.

"river," as "cleaving, breaking through;" *śal-yá-s*, "javelin, arrow," as "moving itself." To these are to be added some

---

follow Weber (V. S. Sp. I. p. 57) in deriving the Sanscrit *sū́rya* from *sū́ra* of equivalent meaning, and the latter, according to Indian Grammarians, from *sû*, "to bear, to bring forth" (Uṇâd. II. 35.), then *sū́rya-s* and *sū́ra-s* would originally signify, "bringer forth, producer." I, however, prefer, as has been already elsewhere done (Glossar. Scrt. a. 1847, p. 379) to refer *sū́ra*, though there is no formal impediment to the deriving it from *sû*, to the root *svar* (*sur*), "to shine;" and I recall attention to the fact, that in Zend, too, ⟨Zend⟩ *hvarĕ* (euphonic for *hvar*, see §. 30.), the syllable *va* has been contracted to *û* in perhaps all the weak cases, of which, however, only the genitive *hûr-ô* can be cited, which hereby stands in a relation to its nominative accusative and proper theme similar to that which the Greek κυν-ός holds to κύνω, and cannot possibly be derived from a different root from that to which the nominative accusative *hvarĕ* belongs. On स्वर् *svàr* is based also the Latin *sol* (from *suol* for *suar*, as *sopio* from *suopio*, from the Sanscrit root *svap*) and the Greek σείρ, from σϜερ with that favourite affix before liquids, ι, which occurs also in Σειρήν, which, with the Latin *ser-mo*, belongs to the Sanscrit root *svar*, *svṛi*, "to sound," whence comes the Vêdic *sûayá*, "speech," as "spoken," or "to be spoken," and in which likewise occurs the contractraction of *va* or *vâ* to *û*. The opinion that *sū́ra-s*, "sun," springs from *sû* or *su*, "to bear, to produce," finds confirmation in the fact, that another appellation of the sun, viz. *sav-i-tā́r* (-*tṛî*), has decidedly arisen from the root *su* or *sû*. This word occurs frequently in the Vêdic hymns: I would not, however, from the circumstance that the Vêdic poets delight in extolling the sun-god as "producer" (of the produce of the fields), as also as "supporter" (*pûṣhan*), deduce the inference that the proper designation of the sun, which existed so early as the time of the unity of the languages, must have pointed towards this image; for it certainly approximates more to the primary view of people to designate the sun as "lighting," or "shining," than as "producing," or "nourishing." To the Sanscrit names of the sun belongs also the hitherto unciteable *súvana-s* (Uṇâd. II. 78.), which, as a derivative from the root *su* or *sû*, is perhaps only a poetical and honorific title of the sun. It may, however, be possible, that the root which lies at the base of the word *súvana-s* is not the well-known root of "to bear," but an abbreviation of *svar* or *sur*, "to shine;" as, *e.g.*, together with *hu*, "to offer," exists also a root *hu*, "to call," abbreviated from *hvê* (=*hvai*), together with *śvi*, "to grow," a form

FORMATION OF WORDS.

feminine oxytone bases in *yá*; *e.g.*, *kanyá*, "a [G. Ed. p. 1320.] maid," as "shining" ("in the lustre of youth"), from *kan*, "to shine;" *jáyá*, "spouse," as "having children" (for *janyá*, root *jan*). The following are examples in Zend: ⟨⟨⟨⟩⟩⟩ *bĕrĕz-ya*, "growing," or, with a causal signification, "making to grow;"* ⟨⟨⟨⟩⟩⟩ *mair-ya*, "slaying" (making to die), [G. Ed. p. 1321.]

---

form *śu*; and in Zend, together with ⟨⟩ *zan*, "to strike," a form *za*, whence ⟨⟩ *upâ-zôit*, "let him strike" (cf. §. 699.); and together with ⟨⟩ *jiv*, "to live," the forms ⟨⟩ *ji*, ⟨⟩ *zi*, and ⟨⟩ *jyâ*. Might we assume, together with *svar*, *sur*, "to shine," a root *su*, of the same meaning, I should derive from it the appellation of the moon too, *sṓ-ma-s*, which would therefore develope a radical in affinity with the Greek σελ-ήνη (from σ(F)ελ-ήνη); while another *sṓ-ma* (the Sôma-plant) belongs to a different root *su*, which signifies "to express." If *súvana-s* be a genuine appellation of the sun, it will admit of comparison with the Gothic base *sunnan* (nom. *sunna*), by assimilation, from *suvnan*, for *suvanan*. But if the Sanscrit *súvana-s* originally signify "producer," I would rather derive the Gothic base *sunnan* (also *sunnôn*, fem.) from *svarnan* or *surnan*; and this, in like manner, by assimilation, so that it would be based on the root सर् *svar*, *sur*, "to shine, to be light," and *nan* for *na* would be the formative suffix, the feminine form of which is contained in the Latin term also for the moon (*lu-na* from *luc-na*).

* Root *bărĕz*, *bĕrĕz* (cf. *barĕz-nu*, "great") =Sanscrit *varh*, *vrih*, "to grow" (see Burnouf, Yaçna, p. 185). I have no scruple in assigning, with Anquetil, to this root, in the passage referred to (V. S. p. 4), a causal signification; and I recall attention to the fact, that in Sanscrit too, especially in the Véda dialect, the root *vardh*, *vridh*, with which *varh*, *vrih*, is originally one, is often used in its primitive form with a causal signification. Above (p. 118, §. 129. L. 19.), the Zend root *bĕrĕz*, *barĕz*, is erroneously placed beside the Sanscrit root *bhráj*, "to shine;" the participle *bĕrĕzant*, of which l. c. mention is made, signifies properly "growing," and hence "great, high," like the Sanscrit *vrihát* (strong *vrihánt*), which corresponds to it, and by which it is also occasionally rendered by Neriosengh, whose translation I was unable to procure, and of which, even up to the present time, I only know the passages published by Burnouf (see Burnouf's Review of the First Part of this Book in the "Journal des S.," 1833, p. 43, of the special impression, and Brockhaus, Glossary, p. 381. 82.).

"murder;"* ﻛﺌﻴﻨﯽ *kainê* from *kainyá,* "maid," as "shining." In Lithuanian to this class belong, first, several masculine bases in *ia* (nom. *is* or *ys* for *ia-s*, see §. 135.); *e.g., gaid-y-s* (gen. *gaidzio,* euphonic for *gaidio*), "cock," as "singing" (*gied-mi,* "I sing," Sanscrit root *gad,* "to speak"); *rysz-y-s,* "band" (*riszu,* "I bind"); *tek-y-s, tek-i-s,* "ram," ("leaper"); *źyn-y-s,* "sorcerer," ("knower," *źynnau,* "I know"): secondly, feminine bases, and, at the same time, nominatives in *ẽ,* from *ia,* as *źynẽ,* "enchantress, witch," as "knowing;" *saulẽ,* "sun, as "shining," though obscured from the point of view of the Lithuanian. From the Old Sclavonic we refer here, медвѣдь *medv-yedy,* "bear," literally, "honey-eater" (theme *-yedyo,* see §. 258.), which, in Sanscrit form, would be *madh-vadya-s,* (*madhu,* "honey," before vowels *madhv*), and вождь *voschdy,* "guide" (euphonic for *vody*): орь *ory,* "horse," leads to the Sanscrit root *ar, ṛi,* "to go, to run," whence *ára,* "fast."

904. We return to the Sanscrit future passive participle, in order to notice two other formative suffixes of the same, which likewise find their representatives in the European sister-languages, viz. *tavya* and *aníya*. They both require Guna, and the former has the accent either on the first syllable or on the second; in the latter case the *svarita.* The suffix *aníya* always accents the *í;* hence, *e.g., yóktávya-s* (or *-yà-s*) and *yójaníya-s, "jungendus,"* from *yuj.* To the suffix *tavya* corresponds, in my opinion, in Latin, *tivu* (*sivu*), in Greek τέο: the former has preserved the form, the latter the signification, more correctly; yet the

---

* *Mairya* is, according to its formation, identical with the Sanscrit *márya,* "*occidendus*," from the causal of the root *mar, mṛi,* "to die" (*máráyámi,* "I slay," Russian *moryu,* see §. 741.), but has, in both the passages explained by Burnouf ("Études," pp. 188, 240, *passim*), as decidedly an active signification as the only, in signification, causal *běrězya,* "making to grow."

FORMATION OF WORDS. 1283

passive signification at least is not entirely lost in the Latin formations, and is visible, e.g., in captívu s, nativu-s, abusívu-s (from abus-tivu-s, see §. 101.), adjectívu-s, coct.'vu-s. The most true Latinization of tavya possible would be taviu, whence, perhaps, came next tíviu (by the favourite weakening of a to i), and thence tívu; so that either the i preceding the v would be lengthened, in compensation for dropping the i, or the second i removed into the preceding syllable, and united with its ĭ to long í. Compare, irrespective of the direction of the meaning which the Latin suffix has taken,

<pre>
datívu-s,   with dâ-távya-s, " dandus ;"
(con)junc-tívu-s, with yôk-távya-s, "jungendus ;"
coc-tívu-s,   with pak-távya-s, " coquendus ;"
gen-i-tívu-s,   with jan-i-távya-s, "gignendus."
</pre>

According to its formation, mor-tuu-s, too, might be referred to this class, as it answers better to the Sanscrit mar-távya (neut. impers. mar-távya-m) than to mṛi-tá-s, from mar-tá-s. The Greek suffix τέο from τεϜο (for τεϜιο), as νέο from νέϜο= नव náva, novu, answers also, with respect to its accent, to the Sanscrit paroxytone forms of the participle under discussion ; e.g., δο-τέο-ς to dâ-távya-s, " dandus," θε-τέο-ς to dhâ-távya-s, "ponendus."

905. As, in Latin, the suffix tívu has, for the most part, assumed an active signification, and in Sanscrit the suffix य ya, which is contained in the suffix तव्य tavya, forms not only future passive participles and abstract substantives, but also appellatives, which, according to their fundamental meaning, are nouns of agency, and correspond to Gothic nouns of agency in yan (§. 903. p. 1318 G. ed.), so we might, perhaps, recognise in the Lithuanian suffix toya (nom. toyi-s, see §. 135.), which forms nouns of agency, [G. Ed. p. 1323.] a sister form of the Sanscrit tavya, and look on toya as an abbreviation of tavya. To this class belong, e.g., the bases

ar-tóya, "plougher" (*arù*, "I plough," Latin *aro*, Greek ἀρόω); *at-pirk-tóya*, "redeemer, ransomer;"* *gelb-ĕ̃-toya*, "helper" (*gelbmi*, "I help," fut. *gelb-ĕ̃-su*); *gan-y-toya*, "protector" (*ganau*, "I protect," fut. *gan-y-su*); *gund-i-toya*, "attempter" (*gundau*, "I attempt," fut. *gund-i-su*); *mokiṅ--toya*, "teacher" (*mokinù*, "I teach"); *pra-dĕ̃-toya*, "beginner" (*pra-de-mi*, "I begin"); nom. *artoyis*, *atpirktoyis*, &c. In Old Sclavonic correspond nouns of agency in атай *a-taĭ* (Dobr. p. 299), theme *a-tayo* (see §. 259.); *e.g.*, дозоратай *do-zor-a-taĭ*, "*inspector;*" возатай *voz-a-taĭ*, "*auriga*" ("driver"; прелагатай *pre-lag-a-taĭ*, "*explorator.*" These forms presuppose verbs in *ayuṅ*, infinitive *ati* (see §§. 766. 767. regarding the *ṅ*, p. 1047.).

906. I think I recognise in Gothic some interesting remains of the Sanscrit participial formation in *aníya*, as *bhêd-a-níya-s*, "*findendus*," in which remains the vowels surrounding the *n* are suppressed; thus, *nya* for Sanscrit *aníya*, in remarkable agreement with the Zend *nya*, from ᠊᠊᠊᠊᠊ *yêś-nya*, or ᠊᠊᠊᠊᠊ *yaśnya*, "*venerandus*, "*adorandus*" (see p. 1308 G. ed., Note) = Sanscrit *yajaníya.*† To this

---

* *Perku*, "I buy," pret. *pirkau*, cf. Greek πρίαμαι, πέρ-νη-μι, Sanscrit *kri-nâ̂-mi*, "*emo*," Irish *creanaim*, "I buy, purchase," Welsh *pyrnu*, "to buy," see Gloss. Sanscr., a. 1847, s. r. *kri*.

† The Sanscrit root *yaj* is, in Zend, either ᠊᠊᠊ *yaz* or *yaś*, before ᠊ *n* always *yaś*, as the combination *zn* was generally avoided in Zend; hence the Sanscrit *yajña*, "sacrifice," is in Zend *yaśna*; and from this Burnouf (Yaçna, p. 575) derives the above-mentioned *yaśnya*, which, as regards form, would suit very well. In support, however, of my view, I refer to what has been said above (p. 1308 G. ed., Note) regarding *vahmya*, and believe that if *yaśnya* came from *yaśna*, it would rather have the signification of the present active participle than that of the participle future passive, which Neriosengh, too, gives to it. The form *yêśnya* rests on the common euphonic influence of the preceding and following *y* (cf. p. 963, Note *), which, however, has not penetrated throughout in this word, but the original *a* has, on the contrary, very often kept its place in it (see Brockhaus Index, under *yaçnya*, *yaçnyanãm*, *yaçnyácha*).

class belong in Gothic the masculine neuter [G. Ed. p. 1324.] bases *ana-laug-nya*, "to conceal," *ana-siu-nya*, "visible," and *airk-nya*, "holy," properly, if my conjecture be rightly founded, "worthy of veneration"=Sanscrit *arch-aníya*, "*venerandus*" (root *arch* from *ark*),* as above (§. 900.) the Greek ἅγ-ιο-ς=Sanscrit *yâj-yà-s*, "*venerandus*." The base *ana-laugnya* is arrived at through the secondary base *ana-laugnyan* of the weak declension, which has proceeded from it, whence come the plural neuter *ana-laug-nyôn-a* (1 Cor. xiv. 25), dative *ana-laug-nya-m* (2 Cor. iv. 2). On the other hand, the strong neuter *analaugn*, which occurs twice as nominative and once as accusative, is in so far ambiguous, as a base *ana-laugna* would have the nearest claim on it (see §. 153.). As, however, the suppression of the syllable *ya* in the nominative masculine, mentioned above (p. 1310 G. ed.), is possible, under the same circumstances, also in the nominative accusative neuter (see Gab. and Löbe, p. 75.ᵃ), so the forms that have [G. Ed. p. 1325.] been mentioned in *yôn-a*, *ya-m*, leave no room for doubt that *ana-laug-n* stands for *ana-laug-ni*, and has *ana-laug-nya* for its base. Just in the same way the weak neuter *anasiu-nyô*, "*visibile*" (Skeir. ed. Massmann 40. 21.), proves

---

* Graff, too (I. 468.), refers, with respect to the Old High German *erchan*, "*egregius*," to the Sanscrit root *arch*: in Anglo-Saxon *eorcnan-stan* signifies "precious stone." According to the law for the mutation of sounds, we should expect in Gothic *airh-nya* for *airk-nya*, but it has retained the original tenuis; as, *e.g.*, in *slêpa*=Sanscrit *svâp-i-mi*, "I sleep" (see §§. 20. 89.). Regarding the radical vowel *ai*, for *i* from *a*, see §. 82. The nominative *airkni-s* admits of being quoted, but the reading is not quite sure (see Gab. and Löbe on 1 Tim. iii. 3). If we ought to read *airkns*, this might as well come from a base *airkna* as from *airknya* (see p. 1310 G. ed.). The circumstance that the compound *un-airkn'-s*, by the plural *un-airknai* (2 Tim. iii. 2), dative *un-airknaim* (1 Tim. i. 9.), clearly refers itself to the base *un-airkna*, affords no certainty that the theme also of the simple word ends in *na*, as it often happens that words are subjected to mutilation in composition.

that the strong neuter nominative *anasiu-n** is an abbreviation of *ana-siu-ni*, and belongs to the base *ana-siu-nya*, which is also confirmed by the adverb *ana-siu-ni-ba*. At the base of all these forms lies *siu* as root, which appears to have been formed from *saihv*, by casting out the *h* and vocalising the euphonic *v* (see §. 86.) to *u*,† while the *a* of the diphthong *ai* was dropped, together with the *h*, to which it owed its existence (see §. 82.). To the abbreviated root *siu* belongs also the above-mentioned (§. 843.) abstract *siu-n(i)s*, "the looking, the regarding," which corresponds to Sanscrit formations like *lú-ni-s*, "the cutting off." From the abstract base *siu-ni*, "the seeing," is found, by the suffix *ya* (see §. 903.), the derivative masculine base *siun'-ya*, "seer," nominative *siunei-s*, in the compound *sitba-siuneis*, "eye witness," literally, "self-seer," αὐτόπτης. In Lithuanian we refer to the passive participle under discussion *kans-ni-s*, "a bit," from *kans-nya-s* (from the root *kand*, "to bite"); as also some words which, in the nominative, terminate in *iny-s* (from *inya-s*); *e.g.*, *randiny-s*, "the found" (*randù*, "I find"); *plěsziny-s*, "the fresh-ploughed field" (*plěszu*, "I split, plough"); *pa-suntiny-s*, "envoy" ("*mittendus*," from *sunchiu* from *suntiu*, "I send"); *kretiny-s*, "the

[G. Ed. p. 1326.] fresh manured field" (*krechiu* from *kretiu*, "I manure"), *měziny-s*, "dunghill" (properly, "cleansed out," *měžu*, *měžiu*, "I cast out the dung"). The *i* preceding the *u*, if it does not belong to the class-syllable, so that throughout a present in *iu* would be to be presupposed, may be taken as the weakening of the *a* of the Sanscrit *aníya*.

---

* See Gab. and Löbe, Grammar, p. 75. 2.) a.

† With respect to the phenomenon, that of the *hv*, for which the Gothic writing has a peculiar letter, only the unessential euphonic affix has remained, compare the relation of our interrogative *wer* ("who") to the Gothic *hva-s* (Sanscrit *ka-s*).

907. As regards the origin of the suffixes *ya, tavya,* and *aníya,* I hold *ya* to be identical with the relative base *ya* (see, "Influence of the Pronouns on the formation of Words," p. 26); so that, where *ya* forms the future passive participle, the passive and future relation is just as little expressed by the suffix, as the relation of passive past time or completion by *ta, na.* It cannot, therefore, surprise us if the suffix *ya* be also applied to the formation of nouns of agency and abstract substantives. Were it limited to the formation of passive participles, it would be more suitable to recognise therein the passive character *ya,* and to regard, *e.g.,* the syllable *ya* of भिद्यते *bhid-yá-tĕ,* "*finditur,*" and भेद्यस् *bhéd-ya-s,* "*findendus,*" as identical, though the difference of accentuation might give some cause for doubt. I agree with Pott (E. I., II. 239. and 459.) in looking upon the future passive participles formed with the suffix *tavya* as offshoots from the infinitive base in *tu;* and accordingly derive, *e.g., kartávya-s,* "*faciendus,*" from the base *kartu;*[*] as I have already before this (see p. 728) explained the suffixes *tavat, navat,* which are represented by Indian Grammarians to be present active participles, as arising out of the combination of the suffixes *ta, na,* with the possessive suffix *vat.* Pott l. c., in my opinion with justness, regards the participles in *aníya* as springing from the abstracts in *ana,* which so frequently supply the place of the infinitive. Consequently, the secondary suffix *íya* would be contained therein, which, just like the shorter *ya,* sometimes has the meaning "worthy," as, therefore, *dakshin´-íya-s* or *dákshin´-yà-s,* "worthy of reward," from *dakshiná,* ("reward," especially of Brahmans after the performance of a sacrifice); so, *e.g., bhédan´-íya-s,* "*findendus,*" from *bhédana,* "the cleaving;" *pújan´-íya-s,*

---

[*] Cf. *ritavyà-s* from *ritú,* p. 1314, G. ed., and §. 891.

"*honorandus, honore dignus,*" from *pújana*, " the honouring." The suffix *íya* is perhaps only an extension of *ya*, so that the long vowel which corresponds to the semi-vowel *y* is further prefixed to it. Still more certain is, in my opinion, the proposition that the secondary suffix *vya* set forth by the Indian Grammarians is to be identified with the suffix *ya*, as in the words which are apparently formed with *vya* the *v* easily admits of being explained as a portion of the primary word. Thus, for example, we may suppose a transposition of *bhrâtur, pitur*—as weakened forms of *bhrâtar, pitar*, as in the uninflected genitive of this class of words— to *bhrâtru, pitru;* and hence, by vocalization of the *r* to *ri*, and change of the *u* into its semi-vowel, on account of the *y* following, deduce *bhrâtriv-yà-s*, "brothers' offspring," *pitriv-yà-s*, "father's brother ;" just as, in Gothic, the plurals of the terms of relationship in *tar, thar*, spring from bases in *tru, thru* (transposed and weakened from *tar, thar*); so that, *e. g., bróthriv-ê, "fratrum"* (cf. *suniv-ê, "filiorum,"* from the base *sunu*), in the portion of it which belongs to the base, approaches very closely the Sanscrit *bhrâtriv-yà-s*. To *pitriv-yà-s* corresponds (with a diverted signification), as regards the form of the primary word, the Greek πατρυιό-ς "stepfather," and, with respect to formation, also the feminine μητρυιά, for which, in Sanscrit, we should have to expect *mâtriv-yà*. Just as, in Sanscrit, we separate the *v* from the suffix, and assign it to the primary word, so we must di-
[G. Ed. p. 1328.] vide, too, the analogous Greek words into πατρυ-ιό-ς, μητρυ-ιό-ς, and derive them by transposition from πατυρ-ιο-ς, μητυρ-ιο-ς (from παταρ-ιο-ς, μηταρ-ιο-ς), as above (§. 253. p. 269, Note †), πατρά-σι, μητρά-σι, from παταρ-σι, μηταρ-σι. The Zend has, in the above-mentioned (§. 137.) ⁂ *brâtur-yê*, avoided transposition. I doubt not, however, that this word, with those in Sanscrit in *triv-ya*, and the Greek in τρυ-ιο, -ια, belong to one class: moreover, the ⁂ *tûiryê*, a female relation in the 4th degree (=San-

FORMATION OF WORDS. 1289

scrit *tur-íyá,* "*quarta,*" see §. 323. p. 452, Note [2].)* supports the conjecture mentioned before, that the Sanscrit suffix *íya* is only a phonetic extension of the suffix *ya,* and therefore the participial termination *aníya* also an extension of *anya* (Zend *nya,* and Gothic *nya*). I do not lay any stress for the support of this view on the, in classical Sanscrit, isolated *varénya,* "*eligendus*" (for *varaṇiya-s*), with which some other analogous Vêdic forms class themselves, as it scarce admits of any doubt that *varénya,* = *varainya,* is a transposed form of *varaṇíya,* just as, in Greek, ἀμείνων is a transposition of ἀμενιων (see §. 300. p. 402).

908. After having considered the participles, infinitives, supines, gerunds, and some formally-connected classes of substantives and adjectives, we now turn to the description of the remaining classes of words, while we treat, in the first place, of the naked radical words, then of the words formed with suffixes, and indeed, as regards the Sanscrit, according to the following arrangement of the primary suffixes, some of which, however, are at the same time used as secondary, *i.e.* for derivations from nominal bases.

                    PRIMARY SUFFIXES.†   [G. Ed. p. 1329.]

a, fem. *â* or *í*	*vya,* see *ya,* p. 1327 G. ed.
i	*na,* fem. *nâ,* §§. 836., 838., 842.
u	*ni,* §§. 843., 851.
an	*nu, snu*

---

* In the original a misprint occurs here which might give some trouble to the German reader. We have §. 462. for p. 462. Owing to mistakes of this kind I have in several places been unable to verify the references.— *Translator's Note.*

† I admit into this catalogue the suffixes of the participles also, which have been already discussed with a reference to the paragraphs adverted to. Such suffixes, however, as neither reappear in the European sister languages, nor are of importance as regards the Sanscrit itself, I leave unnoticed.

in	nt, ant, t, at, §§. 779., 782.; anta,
ana	§. 809. p. 1094, Note.
aníya, see ya	ma, §. 805.
âna, §§. 791., 792.	mi
as	man, §. 795.
us	mâna, §§. 791., 792.
is	ka, aka, âka, ika, uka
ya, tavya, aníya*	ta, fem. tâ, §§. 820., 829., tâti, §. 832.
ra, ira, ura, êra, ôra	târ, tri, §. 810.
la, ala, ila, ula	ti, §§. 843., 844., 849.; a-ti, §. 849.
va	tu f., §. 851.; tu, m. n., atu, athu
van	tra, fem. trâ, a-tra, i-tra, §. 818.
vas, vâṅs, vat, uṣh, §. 788.	tva, §§. 834., 835.

909. Naked radical words appear in Sanscrit—
a) as feminine abstracts; e.g., anu-jñấ, "command;" bhî́, "fear;" hrî́, "shame;" tviṣh, "lustre;" yudh, "strife;" kṣhudh, "hunger;" mud, "joy;" sam-pâd, "luck;" bhâs, "lustre." To this class belong the above-mentioned (§§. 857., [G. Ed. p. 1330.] 859.) Vêdic infinitives with a dative or accusative termination from bases which otherwise have left behind no case. A medial a is, in some formations of this kind, lengthened; hence, e.g., vâch, "the speaking," "speech," from vach. So also in Zend ⁧𐬬𐬁𐬗⁩ vâch, "speech," and frâs̀, "question" (Sanscrit root prachh).
b) At the end of compounds in the sense of the present participles, where the substantive preceding usually stands in the accusative relation; or simply as appellatives, which, according to their fundamental meaning, are nouns of agency. The following are examples: dharma-víd, "acquainted with duty;" ari--hán, "slaying foes;" duḥkha-hán, "removing pain;"

---

* See §§. 889, 891., 894., 899., 901., 906.

nêtra-músh, "stealing the eyes;" *sôma-pā́,* "drinking Sôma;" *sênâ-nī́,* "army-guiding" ("leading the army"); *víra-sū́,* f. "bearing heroes;" *jala-múch,* f. ("pouring out water") "cloud;" *dvish,* m. "foe," as "hating;" *dris̓,* f. "eye," as "seeing." A passive signification belongs, in Sanscrit, to *-yuj,* "joined, yoked;" hence, *e.g., hari-yúj,* "yoked with horses." In this class of words, too, radical *a* is sometimes lengthened; *e.g.,* in *pari-vrā́j,* "beggar," literally, "wandering around" (root *vraj*); *ava-yā́j,* "adoring ill." So in Zend ڊاۊیاج *daêvayâj,* "adoring the Daêvas;" اشانس *ashanâs̓,* "attaining purity," "vouching" (root نس *nas̓* = Vêdic नश् *nas̓,* see Benf. Gloss.). To roots with a short final vowel in compounds of this kind a *t* is added; hence, *e.g., visva-jít,* "conquering every thing;" *pari-srút,* "flowing around."

910. In Greek, the feminine radical words which formally belong to *a*) appear partly with a concrete meaning as appellatives, after the manner of the Sanscrit *dris̓,* f. "eye," as "seeing," which belongs to *b*). So, in Greek, ὄπ id. (from ὀκ), φλογ, "flame," as "burning," ὄπ, "voice" (from Foκ), as "speaking." The abstract [G. Ed. p. 1331.] signification has, on the contrary, remained in στυγ, "hate," ἀϊκ, "violent motion." In Latin, to this class belong the feminine bases *luc* (= Sanscrit *ruch,* "lustre," Zend راوچ *raôch,* "light"); *nec,* "death;"* *prec,* "request" (cf. Zend فراس *frâs̓,* "inquiry," Sanscrit root *prachh,* "to ask," *â-prachh,* "*valedicere*." To the Sanscrit and Zend *vâch,* "speech," corresponds, as regards the lengthening of the radical vowel, the Latin *vôc* (opposed to *vŏco*); and the Greek exhibits a similar lengthening in ὤπ, "eye," "face, as "seeing," which corresponds radically to the Sanscrit

---

* The base verb is lost, for *neco* is either a denominative or a causal.

akshi,* "eye," and Latin *ŏculus*. *Pâc*, "peace," from a lost root, probably means originally "joining," as a derivative of the Sanscrit root *paś* (from *pak*).

911. To the class of words (*b*) in §. 909. correspond Greek bases like χέρ-νιβ (properly, "washing hands"), ἀρχυρο-τριβ, παιδο-τριβ, πρός-φυγ, ψευσι-στυγ, κορυθ-αϊκ, βου-πλήγ, γλαγο--πήγ. In the two last examples, and other combinations with πληγ, the length of the final syllable appears to have thrust down the accent from its former position, and thus to have occasioned an accidental agreement with the Sanscrit accentuation of this class of words (*dharma-víd*, &c.), which I do not regard as original; so in -ῥωγ (διαῤῥώγ, καταῤῥώγ, περιῤῥώγ), with a passive signification, whereby, too, -ζυγ (in δίζυγ, νεοζυγ, μελανοζυγ, &c.), and the Latin base *jug* (*conjug*) answers to the Sanscrit *-yúj*, "yoked." To the simple base दिष् *dvish*, "foe," as "hating," corresponds τρωγ, "gnawer, devourer," and the Latin *duc*, as masculine, "guide," as feminine, "she that guides;" as also *rêg*, "king," as "ruling," the Sanscrit sister form of which, *ráj*, appears only in [G. Ed. p. 1332.] compounds, as *dharma-ráj*, "king of righteousness." Observe the lengthening of the radical vowel in the Latin *rêg* (opposed to *rĕgo*), after the analogy of the Sanscrit *pari-vrâj*, "beggar" ("wanderer around"); while the radical vowel of the Sanscrit *ráj* is, from its origin, long. We mention further, as examples of Latin radical words at the end of compounds, *arti-fic, carni-fic, pel-lic, in-dic, jû-dic, ob-ic, Pol-lûc, for-cip, man-cip, prin-cip, au-cup, præ-sid, in-cûd.* The latter answers, by its passive signification ("anvil," as that which is struck upon), to *jug* in *con-jug*, Greek -ζυγ, and Sanscrit *-yuj*, "yoked." In most of the remaining examples the *i* rests on the weakening of an original *a*, and the *e*, which enters into the

---

* I regard the verbal root ईक्ष् *íksh*, "to see," as a corruption of *aksh*.

nominative in its stead, on the principle laid down in §. 6. *Sid*, in *præ-sid*, is identical with the Sanscrit *shad* in *divi--shád* (euphonic for *-sad*), "sitting in heaven," "dwelling there," "*cœlicola*," a so-far anomalous compound, inasmuch as the first member of it is provided with a case-termination.* *Au-cup* exhibits the intermediate weakening of the vowel, which otherwise only occurs before *l* (cf. §. 490. Rem. 1.), and which therefore finds a more suitable place in *præ-sul, consul* (from *salio*, Sanscrit *sal*, "to move oneself").

912. With the *t*, which in Sanscrit (according to §. 909. *b*.) is added to roots with a short final vowel, the Latin *t* of *-it*, "going," and *stit* (as weakening of *stat*) in *super-stit, anti-stit*, has been already (§. 111. sub. fin.) contrasted; and since then Pott has also compared that in *pari-et*,† properly "going around, surrounding" (as above *pari-srút* "flowing around"), and Curtius that in *indi-get* (cf. [G. Ed. p. 1333.] *indi-gena*).‡ The Greek adds such a *t* to roots with a long final vowel (see Curtius l. c.) in compounds like ἀνδρο-βρώτ, ὠμο-βρώτ, ἀ-γνώτ, ἀ-πτώτ, λιμο-θνήτ. The terminations -βλήτ, -δμήτ, κμήτ, -τμήτ, -στρώτ (φυλλοστρώτ), have only a passive signification, which, in Sanscrit, does not occur in compounds of this kind, while -βρώτ and -γνώτ, are used both actively and passively. As regards the vowel of these formations, it rests, for the most part, on transposition, which

---

* The circumstance that the Latin *e*, corrupted from *a*, becomes *i* when the word is encumbered by composition, excepting when it stands under the protection of two consonants, or in a final syllable, proves that in Latin the *i* is held to be lighter than the inorganic short *e*.

† Euphonic for *pari-it*.

‡ "*De nominum Græc. formatione*," p. 10. With respect to the dropping of the *n* in the root *gen*, cf. the Sanscrit *j'-a* for *jan-a*, "born;" and with regard to the appended *t*, the phenomenon that, in Sanscrit, the roots in *an* and *am*, in case they reject their *n* before the gerundial suffix *ya*, then add, like roots with a short final vowel, a *t*; hence, *e.g.*, *ni-há-t-ya*, from *han*, "to slay."

1294 FORMATION OF WORDS.

is readily occasioned by liquids, and lengthening; where it is to be noticed that η and ω, according to their origin, = $\bar{a}$ (see §. 4.), and that in Sanscrit such transpositions occur, since, e.g., together with *man*, "to think," there occurs a root *mnâ*, "to mention" (cf. μιμνήσκω, fut. μνή-σω); together with *dham* "to blow" (only in the special tenses), occurs a form *dhmâ*, which the Grammarians assume to be the original one. The roots πτω (cf. πίπτω from πιπέτω), δμη (cf. δαμάω), θνη (cf. ἔθανον, θάνατος), κμη (cf. κάμνω), στρω (cf. στόρνυμι, Latin *sterno*), guide us to the Sanscrit roots *pat*, "to fall; *dam*, "to tame;" *han* (from *dhan*), "to slay;" *sram* (from *kram*), *klam*, "to be tired;" *star*, स्तृ *strî*, "to strew." If concrete bases then, like -βρῶτ, -γνώτ, with euphonic *t*, represent the Sanscrit naked radical words like -*pâ*, "drinking," then, irrespective of gender, the abstracts γέλωτ and ἔρωτ may be compared with the Sanscrit abstracts like *anu-jñâ*, "com-
[G. Ed. p. 1334.] mand;"* for though the ω of the said Greek bases is not radical, it nevertheless belongs to the verbal theme, and, like αο in ἐρ-άο-μαι, γελ-άο-μεν, represents the Sanscrit character *aya* of the 10th class (§. 109.ª· 6.). In departure, too, from a former opinion (§. 116.), I find this latter in the form of $\bar{a}$ or η in compounds like λογο-θήρᾱ-ς, ἱππο-νώμᾱ-ς, ὁπλο-μάχη-ς, πολυ-νίκη-ς, ἐλαιο-πώλη-ς. Compare the base -θήρᾱ with θηρᾱ́-σω, θηρᾱ́-τωρ; -νώμᾱ with νωμή-σω from νωμᾱ́-σω; -νίκη with νική-σω, νική-τωρ; -μάχη with μαχή-σομαι, μαχή-της, μαχή-μων. Τρίβης in παιδο-τρίβης, φαρμακο-τρίβης, can hardly spring from the root τριβ with a

---

* Here belongs the Latin *quiêt* (also *quiê*), which has remained true to the feminine gender, and the root of which, *qui*= Sanscrit *sî* (from *kî*), has united itself with the character *ê* of the 2d conjugation (=Sanscrit *aya, ay*, see §. 109.ª· 6.), for which I hold the *ê* of *qui-ê-vi, qui-ê-tus*. Cf. *im-pl-ê-vi, im-pl-ê-tus, im-pl-ê-s, im-pl-ê-mus, im-pl-ê-tis*. The three last forms, irrespective of the preposition, correspond to the Sanscrit *pâr-áya-si, pâr-áyâ-mas, pâr-áya-tha*, of the causal of the root *par* (पृ *prî*), "to fill," the vowel of which is passed over in Latin.

FORMATION OF WORDS. 1295

suffix η, but is rather a naked verbal base, and presupposes a derivative verb τριβέω, future τριβήσω. In the formations in ιᾱ-ς I think I recognise the Sanscrit root *yâ*, "to go,"* which actually occurs in the Vêda dialect in compounds of the kind described above (p. 1330 G. ed.); *e.g.*, in *dêva-yá*, nominative *dêva-yá-s*, "going to the gods;" *rina-yá-s*, "going into debt" = "taking guilt on oneself," "atoning," "freeing from guilt" (see Benfey's Glossary). In Greek, therefore, *e.g.*, ἀλωπεκ-ίᾱ-ς, "foxy," literally signifies, "approaching the nature of the fox," and λαμπαδ-ίᾱ-ς, "torch carrier," properly "going with the torch."

913. If we now proceed to consider [G. Ed. p. 1335.] the words formed with suffixes, we must, with reference to the secondary suffixes, which, by the Indian Grammarians, are called Taddhita, bring to remembrance the already frequently-mentioned circumstance, that the final vowels of primitive bases are, in all the Indo-European languages, under certain restrictions,† suppressed before suffixes beginning with vowels or the semi-vowel *y*. With reference to Sanscrit and Zend, it is to be remarked that certain secondary classes of words require the Vriddhi increment (see §. 26.) for the first vowel of the primary word; hence, *e.g.*, *dâsarath'-i-s* (from *dasarat'ia*),‡ "descen-

---

* Cf. ἵημι, with causal signification ("making to go"), probably a reduplicated form from γί-γημι, as ἵ-στημι from σί-στημι; so that the semi-vowel in the syllable of reduplication has become the rough breathing (cf. ὅ-ς=yá-s, §. 382.), and in the root itself is suppressed, as, *e.g.*, in the verbs in αω = Sanscrit *ayâmi*.

† See §. 891.

‡ *â* is held to be the Vriddhi of *a*, to which latter the Indian Grammarians assign no Guna. Moreover, *a*, as it is the heaviest vowel (see §. 6.), feels less occasion for increment, and remains, in most cases, unchanged, while other vowels are gunised: sometimes, also, *â* is found for *a* in places where other vowels experience the Guna increment. As both $a + a$ and $â + a$ are contracted to *â*, it might be said that *â* is both the

Guna

dant of Daśaratha;" and in Zend, ꞏꞏꞏ *âhuir'-ya* (from *ahura*, see §. 41.), "Ahurish" "referring to Ahura;" ꞏꞏꞏ *zâir'-i*, "golden," from ꞏꞏꞏ *zairi*, "gold." In Gothic, *-dôg'-s*, "daily" (theme *dôga*, see §. 135.), offers a similar relation to its primitive base *daga*, nominative *dag'-s*, "day," as *ô*, according to §. 69., is the most usual representative of the length of the *a*. According to the principles of Sanscrit, we must assume that the adjective base *dôga*, which occurs only in the compound *fidurdôga*, "of four days" (nom. *fidurdôg'-s*), is formed from the sub-
[G. Ed. p. 1336.] stantive base *daga*, in such wise that the final vowel of the latter is suppressed before the derivative suffix *a* in the same way as, *e.g.*, in Sanscrit, that of संवत्सर *sanvatsara*, "year," is suppressed before the Taddhita suffix *a* contained in सांवत्सर *sânvatsar'-á*, "yearly;" while apparently *sânvatsara*, "yearly," seems to be formed from *sanvatsara*, "year" by simply lengthening the first vowel of the primary word. The Lithuanian, too, the *o* of which is always long, and frequently represents the Sanscrit *â*, exhibits, in some derivative words, *o* in the place of the *a* of the primitive base; thus, *plót'-i-s*, "breadth" (theme *plotya*), comes from *platú-s*, "broad;" and *lób'-i-s*, "riches" (theme *lobya*), from *laba-s*, "rich;" in the same way as, in Sanscrit, *e.g.*, *mâdhur-ya-m*, "sweetness," from *madhurá*, "sweet."* As in Latin, also, *ô* frequently stands for original *â*, *e.g.*, *sorôrem* = Sanscrit *svásâram*, we might recognise in *ôv'-u-m* a remnant of the Vṛiddhi increment,

---

Guna and the Vṛiddhi increment of *a*, that, however, Guna takes place with *a* more seldom than with the lighter vowels *u* and *i*.

* See §§. 891., 893. If, in Lithuanian, in this class of words a primitive *a* of the base word does not pass into *o*, perhaps the length of position protects the original *a* : hence, in the examples mentioned above (§. 893.), *karsztis*, "best," *szaltis*, "cold," not *korsztis*, *szoltis*. In general, I know hitherto of no example in which *a* stands before a simple consonant in an abstract of this kind.

which the Sanscrit Grammar requires, when, with the suffix *a*, to which the *u* of the Latin 2d declension corresponds, a derivative is formed with the secondary idea of "springing from;" *e. g., sâmudr'-á-m*, "sea-salt," as that which springs from the sea (*samudrá*, nom. *-rá-s*). Therefore, as the neuter *sâmudr'-á-m* may be explained as coming from the masculine base *samudrá*, with the suppression of the final vowel before the derivative suffix *a*, so I think I may venture to explain *ôv'-u-m* as "offspring of the bird," from *avi-s*. In Sanscrit it would be quite regular, if *avi*, instead of *vi*, signified "a bird," to find an *âv'-á-m* coming from it as a term for "an egg." The Greek ὠόν from ὠϝ'-όν, which as respects its accentuation [G. Ed. p. 1337.] also answers to the Sanscrit class of words here spoken of, has lost its primitive :* on the other hand, exclusive of gender and accent, ὦα (from ὦϝα), "sheep-skin fur," stands in a relation to its primitive base ὄϊ from ὄϝι (Sanscrit *ávi* "sheep") similar to that which the Latin *ôv'-um* for *âv'-um* holds to *avi*.†

---

* In the form ὤϊο-ν for ὤϝιον I do not regard the ι as the retained final vowel of the primary word, but recognise in ιο the Sanscrit suffix *ya*, which, just like *a*, forms personal and neuter patronymics.

† In ἠνεμόεις I cannot recognise an accord to the Sanscrit Vriddhi increment of the secondary formation of words, as I do not derive it from ἄνεμος, but from ἤνεμος (in Hesych.), the base of which is also found in some compounds (ἠνεμόφωνος, ἠνεμόφοιτο-ς). Moreover, the Sanscrit suffix, which corresponds to the Greek εντ requires no Vriddhi increment. Just as little in Sanscrit, in compounded words, does a vowel lengthening of this kind occur, like that which the Greek exhibits in some compounds, especially in those with prepositions and monosyllabic prefixes and bases of words, or those which become monosyllabic by the suppression of their final vowel, and which takes place in order, perhaps, to bring forward more emphatically, after such weak preceding syllables, the principal part of the word in case it begins with a vowel; hence, *e. g.*, δυσήκεστος (ἀκεστός), δυσηκής (ἄκος), δυσήνυτος, δυσήνυστος (ἀνυστός), δύσηρις (for δύσερις), δυσώλεθρος (ὄλεθρος), δυσώνυμος (ὄνομα), εὐήρετμος (ἐρετμός), εὐήκης (ἀκή), εὐήνυστος

[G. Ed. p. 1338.] 914. The Sanscrit primary suffix *a*, which, as also the secondary, I hold to be identical with the demonstrative base *a* (see §. 366.), has, together with its sister-forms in the cognate languages, been already considered (see p. 1235 G. ed.) as the formative suffix of masculine abstracts. In Gothic, most of the abstracts which, in respect of their suffix, belong to this class, have become neuter, and terminate, therefore, in the nominative singular, with the final consonant of the root (see §. 135.). The following are nearly all of them: *anda-beit*, "blame"*; *anda-hait*, "avowal;" *bi-hait*, "strife;" *ga-hait*, "promise" (formally our "*Geheiss*, "behest"); *af-lêt*, "forgiveness;" *bi-mait*, "clipping;" *bi-faih*, "delusion;" *fra-veit*, "revenge;" *ana-filh*, "delivery," from the bases *anda-beita*, *ga-heita*, &c. As regards the radical vowel of these abstracts, what has been observed above (p. 1237, Note) holds good. We must not, therefore, derive the base *anda-nêma*, "acceptance," the gender of

---

εὐήνυστος (ἀνυστός), εὐήνωρ (ἀνήρ), εὐώδης (root ὀδ), εὐώνυμος, ἀνήκεστος ἀνηκής (ἄκος), ἀνήκουστος (ἀκουστός), ἀνώδυνος (ὀδύνη), ἐνήκοος (ἀκοή), ἐνήλατον (ἐνελαύνω), ἐνώμοτος (ὄμνυμι), προσήγορος (ἀγορεύω), περιώδυνος, τριήρης, μονήρης, ποδήρης, ποδώνυχος, πανήγορις, πανώλεθρος. I moreover recall attention to the fact, that in Sanscrit the Vriddhi increment of the secondary formation of words supplies the place of the Guna increment of the primary; thus as, *e.g.*, *bódh-a-s*, "the knowing," and *bódh-â-mi*, "I know," come from the root *budh*, so *bâuddh-á-s*, "Buddhist," comes from *buddhá*, "Buddha," as adjective, "knowing, wise." That the secondary formation of words, in as far as the class of words referred to in general requires an augment, calls for Vriddhi instead of Guna, may well arise from this, that the base words to which the secondary suffixes are attached are of themselves more heavily constructed than the naked roots, whence arise the primitive nouns or verbs. Hence, in the secondary formation of words, long vowels, and even Guna diphthongs and short vowels before two consonants, are augmented; for which the primary formation of words, except when the root ends in a vowel, feels no occasion.

* The base *anda-beita* is, after removing the preposition, identical with the above-mentioned (p. 1235 G. ed.) Sanscrit *bhéda*, "cleaving."

which, however, is not discoverable from the solitary genitive that can be quoted, *anda-nêmi-s* (see §. 191.), from the plural of the preterite (*nêmum*), but we must view it as coming, like the adjective theme *anda-nêm-ya* (see p. 1308 G. ed., Note), which corresponds to the Sanscrit future passive participle, from the root *nam*, the radical vowel being lengthened, in accordance with Sanscrit abstracts like *hása-s*, "the laughing," from *has*. I know in Sanscrit but one single neuter abstract of this class of words, viz. *bhay-á-m*, "fear," from *bhí*, "to fear," which, like the analogous masculine abstracts [G. Ed. p. 1339.] from roots in *i* or *í*, as, *e.g.*, *jay-á-s*, "victory," from *ji*, *kshay-á-s*, "ruin," from *kshi*, *kray-á-s*, "purchase," from *krí*, has allowed the accent to sink down on the suffix.

915. Oxytone, too, are for the most part the adjectives formed with अ *a* with the signification of the present participle; and the appellatives in *a* which belong to this class, and which, according to their fundamental meaning, are for the most part nouns of agency; *e.g.*, *nad-á-s*, "river," as "sounding, rushing;" *plav-á-s*, "vessel," as "swimming" (root *plu*); *danś-á-s*, "tooth," as "biting;" *dêv-á-s*, "God," as "shining" (root *div*, cf. θεός); *mûsh-á-s*, "mouse," as "stealing;" *chôr-á-s*, "thief" (root *chur*, "to steal"). The following are examples of adjectives: *chal-á-s*, "rocking, tremulous;" *char-á-s*, "going;" *tras-á-s*, "trembling;" *ksham-á-s*, "enduring;" *priy-á-s*, "loving," and "beloved" (root *prî*); *vah-á-s*, "carrying, bringing." This oxytone class of words in *a* = Greek o, in opposition to the abstracts which choose the more powerful accentuation, is also numerously represented in Greek, both by appellatives or nouns of agency, as, τροχ-ό-ς, "runner" (opposed to τρόχ-ο-ς, "course"); κομπ-ό-ς, "braggard" (opposed to κόμπ-ο-ς, "noise"); κλοπ-ό-ς, κομπ-ό-ς, μοιχ-ό-ς;* and by adjectives, as, φαν-ό-ς, τομ-ό-ς, θο-ό-ς, ἀρωγ-ό-ς,

---

* It corresponds in its root and primary meaning, as also in formation and accentuation, to the Sanscrit *mêgh-á-s*, "cloud," as "*mingens*" (root *mih*, "*mingere*").

ἀγωγ-ό-ς, στιλβ-ό-ς, and some with a passive signification, λοιπ-ό-ς, κυφ-ό-ς, πηγ-ό-ς, αἰθ-ό-ς. So the substantives λοπ-ό-ς, "shell," as "to be peeled off;" ὀδ-ό-ς, "way," as "to be gone, to be trod" (Sanscrit root *sad*, "to go," and "to seat oneself"). In Sanscrit, too, there are substantives of this kind with a passive signification; as, *e.g.*, *dar-á-s*, neut. *dar-á-m*, "a [G. Ed. p. 1340.] hollow," as "being cleft;" *lêh-á-s*, "food," as "to be licked;" *jan-á-s*, "man," as "born." The following accent the root: *édh-a-s* (opposed to the Greek αἰθ-ό-ς), "wood," as "to be burned" (root *indh*, properly, *idh*); *vés-a-s*, "house," as "place entered" (Greek οἶκ-ο-ς from Ϝοῖκ-ο-ς, Latin *vîc-u-s*, Old High German *wîh*, theme *wîha*, "village, borough," from an obsolete root). To the feminine bases of this class of words belong, in Greek, bases also in αδ, of which the δ is only an inorganic affix (see p. 108); *e.g.*, δορκ-άδ, "gazel," as "seeing" (also δόρκη); μοιχάδ (μοιχή), as feminine, from μοιχό; τοκάδ, "the bearing (female)"; πλο(ϝ)άδ, πλω(ϝ)άδ, "the swimming, the wandering around (female)"; τυπάδ, "hammer," as "striking."

916. In Sanscrit, as well as in Greek, adjectives of this kind of formation occur principally at the end of compounds, and in both languages have partly either not been retained in isolated use, or have, perhaps, never been used simply. Thus, in Sanscrit, *damá*, "taming," appears only in the compound *arin-damá-s*,* "foe-taming," and the corresponding Greek δαμο only in ἱππόδαμο-ς. So, in Latin, *-dic-u-s, -loqu-u-s, -fic-u-s, -fug-u-s, -sequ-u-s, -vol-u-s, -cub-u-s* (*incubus*), *-leg-u-s, -vor-u-s, -fer, -ger* (for *fer-u-s, ger-u-s*),

---

* *Arin*, euphonic for *arim*, is the accusative, which occurs also in many other compounds of this kind, in which the first member usually stands in the accusative relation instead of the naked theme which was to be expected according to the universal rules of composition; *e.g.*, in *puran-dará-s*, "towns-cleaving" (literally, "*urbem findens*"); *priyaṅ-vadá-s*, "amiably-speaking;" *bhayan-kará-s*, "fear-causing."

FORMATION OF WORDS. 1301

-*par-u-s* (*oviparus*), -*liqu-u-s* (*re-liqu-u-s* = Greek λοῖπ-ο-ς), -*frag-u-s* (*naufragus*). The following, perhaps, are the sole examples which occur simply: *sci-u-s*, *vag-u-s*, *fid-u-s*, *parc-u-s*. These substantives belong to this class: *coqu-u-s* (= Sanscrit *pach-á-s* from *pak-á-s*, "cooking"), *merg-u-s*, *proc-u-s* (cf. *precor*), *son-u-s*, as "sounding" = Sanscrit *svan*- [G. Ed. p. 1341.] -*á-s*, "tone," *jug-u-m*, *vad-u-m* (properly, "passed through," as above दरम् *dar-á-m*, "a hollow," as "cleft"); and perhaps *tor-u-s*, from *storus*, as "spread out."* To this class also are to be referred the feminines *mola*, "mill," as "grinding," and *toga*, as "covering."† The *a* of compounds like *parricida*, *cœlicola*, *advena*, *collega*, *transfuga*, *legirupa*, *indigena*, I now, in departure from §. 116., rather prefer viewing in such a way as to recognise in it a distinct feminine form, and therefore the Sanscrit long *â* of forms like *priyanvadâ*, "the amiably speaking (female)", which at the same time stands for the masculine, while, conversely, the Greek, at the end of compounds, by a mis-usage, transfers the masculine neuter *o* = Sanscrit short *a*, into the feminine also, and contrasts, *e.g.*, the form πολύκομος with the Latin *multicoma*; since, as it appears to me, the burthen of composition is an obstacle in the way of the free movement and liability to change of the entire word, on which account its concluding portion relinquishes the exact discrimination of the genders.‡

---

* With respect to the loss of the *s* of *ster-no*, στόρ-νυμι, cf. the relation of "*tonare*" to the Sanscrit root *stan*, "to thunder," and Greek στεν in Στέν-τωρ.

† In Latin the interchange of the sounds *e* and *o* in one and the same root occurs but seldom, and the etymology in the cases which occur is obscured, while in Greek it is self-evident that, *e.g.*, φόρος and φέρω are radically identical.

‡ The circumstance, that as well in the Greek as in the Latin 2d declension there are simple feminines, such as παρθένος, ὅδος, νῆσος, *alvus*, *humus* (Sanscrit *bhûmî-s*, fem., "earth"), *fagus* (= φηγός), does not impede the supposition that the Greek *o* and Latin inorganic *u* of the 2d declension

[G. Ed. p. 1342.] 917. The Gothic exhibits, in the class of words under discussion, (1) masculine substantive bases like *daura-vard-a*, "gatekeeper;" *vrak-a*, "persecutor;"* *vêg-a*, "wave," as "moving itself"†; *vig-a*, "way" (as "the place on which one moves"); *thiv-a*(nom. *thiu-s*), "servant"‡:

declension do not originally belong to the feminine; as also the corresponding Sanscrit, Zend, Lithuanian, and Gothic *a*, and Sclavonic *o*, never stand at the end of a feminine base. That, however, conversely, the Latin *a* at the end of compounds like *cœli-cola* does not correspond to the Sanscrit-Zend masculine neuter *a* may here be further supported by the consideration that compounds are most subject to weakening, and that, therefore, the retention of the Sanscrit masculine neuter *a* unchanged in Latin can least be expected in compounds. But if the feminine form in compounds like *parricida* has once found its way into the masculine, or attached itself to this gender alone (*cœlicola*), it cannot surprise us that, in an isolated case, a simple word appears in the feminine form as masculine, viz. *scrib-a* for *scrib-u-s*. The case is different with *nau-ta*, where *ta* stands for τη-s, as in *poëta*=ποιητής; and as in Homer, e.g., αἰχμητά, νεφεληγερέτα, ἱππότα, ἠπύτα, ἠχέτα, μητίετα, for αἰχμητής, &c. Here either the case-sign has been dropped, as in Old Persian is regularly the case with the final *s* both after short and long *a*; or, which I prefer assuming, these forms are based on the Sanscrit nominatives in *tâ*, Zend *ta* (see §. 144.), of bases in *târ*, on which rest, in Greek, not only the bases in τηρ and τορ, as has already been remarked in §. 145., but also the masculine bases in τη=τᾱ, which have lost an ρ (see also §. 810, and Curtius, "*De nominum Græc. form.*," p. 34). It is therefore no casual circumstance, that in the Homeric dialect nearly all the class of nouns of agency referred to exhibit masculine nominatives in *a*; and it is hence not improbable that εὐρύ-οπα, too, originally belongs to this class of words, and is therefore abbreviated from εὐρυοπτα, as, according to its meaning, it is a noun of agency.

* The nominative *vrak-s*, which can alone be quoted, might also belong to a base *vraki*.

† This answers, in respect of the lengthening of the radical vowel *a* to *ê* (=*â*, see §. 69.), to Sanscrit formations like *pâd-a-s*, "foot," as "going," from *pad*, "to go."

‡ In my opinion properly "boy," from a root *thav*=Sanscrit *tu*, "to grow;" as, *mag-u-s*, "boy," from *mag*=Sanscrit *mah, mank*, "to grow."

From

FORMATION OF WORDS. 1303

(2) the neuter substantive bases, as *ga-* [G. Ed. p. 1343.] *-baur-a*, "tax," as "that which is borne"(cf. φόρος); *faur-hah-a*, "curtain;" *ga-thrask-a*, "floor" (where they thresh); *ga-liug-a*, "idol," as "lying, false;" nominative *gabaur*, &c.: (3) feminine bases like *daura-vard-ô*, "portress;" *ga-bind-ô*, "band," as "binding" (root *band*, weakened to *bind, bund*); *grôb-ô*, "pit," as "dug" (root *grab*, lengthened to *grôb*); *grab-ô*, "trench;" *ga-bruk-ô*, "crumb," as "broken" (root *brak*, weakened to *brik, bruk*); *staig-ô*, "path" (root *stig*, "to mount," gunised *staig*); nominative *daura-varda*, &c.: (4) adjective bases like *and-vairth-a*, "present;" *ana-vairth-a*, "future;" *laus-a*, "loose, empty" (root *lus*); *siuk-a*, "sick" (root *suk*); *af-lêt-a*, "left free;" nominative masculine *and-vairth'-s*, &c.

918. In Lithuanian this class of words is less numerous, but is more correctly retained in the nominative singular than in any other of the sister languages of the Sanscrit. The following are examples: *sarg-a-s*, "warder" (*serg-mi*, "I protect,"); *prá-rak-a-s*, "seer, prophet"*; *prá-nasz-a-s* id.(*pra-neszu*, "I propose," *neszu*, "I bear,"); *laid-a-s*, "bail;" *draug-a-s*, "fellow, companion" (*drauga*, "I have partnership with another,"); *zwán-a-s*, "bell," as "sounding"

From तु *tu*, "to grow" (in Zend "to be able," see §. 520. sub. f.), comes, in the Véda dialect, among other words, *tuv-í*, "much;" and in Gothic, according to my opinion, also *thiu-da*, "people," as "grown;" parallel to which, in Umbrian, as feminine participle of the same root, stands the form *tuta*, afterwards *tota*, "town;" and with which, in departure from §. 343., I would now compare the Latin *to-tus*, "whole." To the causal of *tu* (*táv-áyá-mi*, "I make to grow, I make to thrive") belongs probably the Latin *tu-ê-ri* (see §. 109ª. 6.), and the Old Prussian *táwa-s*, "father," as "producer" or "bringer up," Lithuanian *tëwa-s*, "father." Parallel to the Umbrian *tuta*, "town," and as derivative from the same root, we find, in Prussian, *tauta* (acc. *tauta-n*), "land," as "cultivated." In Lithuanian, *tauta* signifies "Germany."

* The simple verb is wanting in Lithuanian; compare the Sclavonic рекѫ *rekuṅ*, "I say," see p. 626.

(*zwanú,* "I sound,"); *tăk-a-s,* "footpath" (*tekù,* "I run,"); *weid-a-s,* "face, visage," as "seeing" (*weizd-mi,* "I see," [G. Ed. p. 1344.] *waidino-s,* "I let myself see,"): *-nink-a-s,* which, at the end of compounds, has often a meaning tantamount to "maker, accomplisher," or one who is occupied with that which the first member of the compound expresses;* as, *balni-nink-a-s,* "saddler, saddle-maker" (*balna-s,* "saddle,"); *griĕki-nink-a-s,* "sinner, sin-committing" (*griĕka-s,* "sin,"); *lauki-nink-a-s,* "countryman, agriculturist, *agricola*" (*lauka-s,* "field,"); *miĕsi-nink-a-s,* "butcher, *carnifex*" (*miẽsà,* f., Sanscrit *mânsá,* m. n. "flesh,"); *darbi-nink-a-s,* "workman, doing work" (*darba-s,* "work,"); *remesti-nink-a-s,* "artisan, working at a craft" (*remesta-s,* "handicraft,"). Observe the weakening of the final vowel of the first member of all

---

* The base verb *ninku* does not occur in its simple form, but only in combination with the prepositions *in, ap, uz,* and *su* (see Nesselmann's Lexicon, p. 422), and probably meant originally "to go," then "to do, to make." Cf. the Old Prussian *neik-aut,* "to wander," and Russian *nik-nu,* "I bow myself." To the Lithuanian *-ni-ka-s,* in the compounds spoken of, corresponds, in Russian, никъ *nik*; *e.g.,* in седельникъ *syedelynik',* "saddler," *i.e.* "saddle-maker." The Old Prussian appears to form with *nika* (nom. *nix* for *nika-s,* acc. *nika-n*) nouns of agency from verbal bases (see Nesselmann, p. 76). I regard, however, all the words classed here as compounds, similar to the Latin *opifex, artifex;* for although, *e.g., waldnix,* "ruler," of which only the dative *waldniku* occurs, might be derived from the verbal root *wald,* "to rule," still nothing prevents the assumption that it properly signifies "using authority," and contains a lost or unciteable substantive *wald-s* or *walda-s* (theme *walda*), "dominion." *Crixti,* the substantive base of *crixt-nix,* "baptist" ("performer of baptism"), occurs in the compound *crixti-laiska-s,* "baptismal register;" and the substantive base *dila* (acc. *dila-n*), in *dil-nik-a-ns,* "workman, performing work" (acc. pl.); and for *daina-alge-nik-a-mans* (dat. pl.), "the day labourers, those working for daily pay," occur the substantive bases *deina,* "day" (Sanscrit *dina*), and *alga,* "pay" (gen. *alga-s*), but no verb of which the word referred to could be the noun of agency; and this is the case with most of the other formations which belong to this class.

these compounds to *i*, according to the principle of the Latin language, as, *cœli-cola, terri-cola, fructi-fer*, [G. Ed. p. 1345.] *lani-ger*, for *cœlu-cola, terra-cola, fructu-fer, lana-ger*.* The following are examples of adjectives of this kind of formation: *gyw-a-s*, "living;" *át-wir-a-s*, "open" (*at-weru*, "I open,"); *át--rak-a-s*, "unlocked" (*rak-inú*, "I lock," *atrak-inú*, "I unlock,"); *isz-tis-a-s*, "stretched out" (*tĕsiu*, "I erect"). To this class of words belong, in old Sclavonic, bases like токо *toko*, "river," as "flowing;" *pro-roko*, "prophet;" отрoко *ot-roko*, "boy," properly, "*infans*;" νήπιος, (Mikl. Rad. p. 74.) водоносо *vodo-noso*, "hydria," properly "water-carrier;" nom. токъ *tok'*, &c. The following are examples with a passive signification: градъ *grad'*, "town," as "enclosed" (*grad-i-ti*, "to enclose,"); милъ *mil'*, "dear (beloved), pleasant," as in Sanscrit *pur-á-m*, n., *pur-í*, f., "town," as "filled;" *priy-á-s*, "beloved" (root *pri*).

919. Between the Sanscrit and Greek there exists the remarkable coincidence, that the adjectives formed with the suffix under discussion in combination with the prefixes सु *su*, εὐ, "light," दुस् *dus*,† δυς, "heavy," most generally, if not in Sanscrit invariably, have a passive signification.‡ The accent in Sanscrit rests on the radical syllable; *e.g.*, *sukár-a-s*, "being lightly made, light to make;" *sulábh-a-s*, "being easily attained;" *dushkár-a-s*, [G. Ed. p. 1346.] "being made heavy, hard to do;" *durlábh-a-s*, "being with

---

* See §. 6., and "Vocalismus," pp. 139, 162, Note *. With respect to the Lithuanian *i* in *rótponis*, "senator," I must, however, in departure from §. 6. (conclusion), remark, that here the *i* is not the weakening of the *a* of *pona-s*, "lord," but the contraction of the suffix *ya* or *ia*, according to §. 135.

† Hence, according to settled laws of sound, and according to the measure of the letters following, *dush, dur, duḥ*.

‡ Those forms cannot be allowed to weigh as exceptions in which *su* does not signify "light," but has a meaning tantamount to "fair, good, pleasant;" *e.g.*, Rigv. I. 112. 2., *subhára*, "bringing fair (load)."

difficulty (heavily) attained;" *duḥsáh-a-s*, "being heavy to bear;" *durmársh-a-s*, id.; *durdhársh-a-s*, "being heavily pressed;" *duṣhpúr-a-s*, "being heavily filled;" *duṣhṭár-a-s* (euphonic for *dustár-a-s*), "being with difficulty (heavily) overstepped." So in Greek, *e.g.*, εὔφορ-ο-ς, εὐκάτοχ-ο-ς, εὐπερίγραφ-ο-ς, εὐέμβολ-ο-ς, εὐανάγωγ-ο-ς, δύσφορ-ο-ς, δύστροφ-ο-ς, δύστομ-ο-ς, δύσπλο-ο-ς, δυσπρόσμαχ-ο-ς, δυσανάπορ-ο-ς.

920. As secondary (Taddhita) suffix *a* in Sanscrit forms, usually with the accent and Vṛiddhi of the first vowel of the primary word: (1) Masculine substantives (with feminines in *î*,) which stand to the primary word in the relation of derivatives, or in any other relationship, as, *e.g.*, *vâsishṭh'-á-s*, from *vásishṭha*, "descendant of Vasishtha;" *mánav-á-s*, (from *manú*) "man," as "descendant of Manu;" *drâupad'-î*, (from *drupada*) "Drâupadî, daughter of Drupada;" *dáuhitr-â-s*,(from *duhitár*, *-tṛí*) "son of the daughter;" *nâishadh'-á-s*, "Naishadha," from *nishadha*, in the plural, "the country Nishadha;" *śâiv'-á-s*, (from *śíva*) "follower, worshipper of Śiva." (2) A kind of patronymics of things by which, *e.g.*, fruits are called after the trees on which they grow, and are represented, as it were, as their sons; *e.g.*, *áśvatth'-á-m*, (from *aśvattha*) "the fruit of the tree Aśvattha." To this class belongs also the already-mentioned *sámudr'-á-m*, "sea-salt," as "that which is produced from the sea" (*samudra*). (3) Abstract neuters, as, "*yáuvan-á-m*, "youth," from *yuvan*, "young." (4) Neuter collectives, as, *kâpót'-á-m*, "a flock of doves," from *kapóta*. (5) Adjectives and appellatives having various relationships to the primary word; *e.g.*, *rájat'-á-s*, "of silver," from *rajatá-m*, "silver;" *áyas-á-m*, "of iron," from *áyas* (theme and nom.=Latin *aes*, *aer-is*, [G. Ed. p. 1347.] from *aes-is*, Gothic *ais*, theme *aisa*); *sâukar'-á-s*, "porcine," from *súkara*, "swine;" *sânvatsar'-á-s*, "yearly," from *sanvatsara*, "year;" *dvâip'-á-s*, "a car covered with tiger-skin," as adjective, "made of tiger-skin," from *dvípa*, m. n. (*dvípa-s*, *-a -m*), "tiger-skin."

FORMATION OF WORDS. 1307

921. To class (1), and indeed to the feminine patronymics like *drâupadî'-î̆,* "Drâupadî" (from *drupada*); *dâuhitr-î̆,* "daughter of the daughter," (from *duhitár*); *pâutr'-î̆,* "son's daughter" (from *putra,* "son"); correspond (irrespective of the vowel-augment,) with regard to accent, also Greek words like Ταντάλ'-ιδ, Πριάμ'-ιδ, 'Ιναχ'-ιδ, Νηρεΐδ, Ion. Νηρηΐδ, the δ of which is only an inorganic prolongation of the base (see p. 138, and §. 119). Νηρεΐδ, Ion. Νηρηΐδ, from ΝηρεϜίδ, ΝηρηϜίδ, from the base Νηρεύ, corresponds to the Sanscrit forms like *mânav-î̆,* "woman," from *mânavá,* "man," as descendant of Manu, only that in Greek the Guna or Vriddhi vowel exists already in the primary word. With respect to the relation of accent, *e.g.*, of Ταντᾰλίδ to the primitive base Τάνταλο, compare that of *vásishth'-á,* "Vasishthide," to *vásishṭha*. To class (2) the Latin *óv'-u-m,* as derivative from "bird" (*avi-s*), and the Greek ὠ(Ϝ)'-ό-ν, have already been referred. To names of fruits, like *áśvatth-á-m,* correspond Latin words like *pom'-u-m* from *pomu-s, pir'-u-m* from *piru-s, prun'-u-m* from *prunu-s, ceras'-u-m* from *cera-su-s,* and Greek words like μῆλ'-ο-ν from μηλί(δ), κάρι'-ο-ν from καρία, ἄπι-ο-ν, from ἄπιο-ς. As the Greek and Latin, just like the Sanscrit, reject the final vowels of primitive bases before the vowels of derivative suffixes (see §. 913.), the possibility of the proposition cannot be contravened, that the names of fruits in both languages may have been formed from the names of the trees, not only by a change of gender, but by the addition of a suffix; that therefore, *e.g.*, the formal relation of *pirum* to *pirus,* of ἄπιον to ἄπιος, may be a different one from that of, *e. g.*, [G. Ed. p. 1348.] *bonum* to *bonus,* ἀγαθόν to ἀγαθός.* We should especially notice in this respect the relation of μῆλον to the base μηλίδ,

---

* Though the names of trees in the said languages are feminine, yet those in *us* and *os* are, according to their form, masculine (cf. p. 1341 G. ed.)

the δ of which is only an inorganic affix, which has been added to the originally long ι of μηλί (see §. 119.); so that the Greek word, put into Sanscrit form, would be nothing else but *mấlí*, whence, as from the name of a tree, we should have to expect, with the suffix under discussion, the name of the fruit, *mâl'-á-m*. But if in Greek and Latin we derive the names of trees from the names of fruits, after the same fashion as those of the inhabitants of countries, as above (§. 902.) we have endeavoured to represent the names of countries as the feminines of the names of the inhabitants, then, irrespective of accent, we might as easily arrive from a formally masculine neuter base μῆλο to a feminine base μηλίδ (for μηλί), as in Sanscrit, *e. g.*, from *áyas-á*, "the iron" (masc. and neut.) (nom., *áyasá-s*, *áyasá-m*), to *áyasî*. To class (5) correspond Latin adjectives which have been formed from substantive bases in *ôr* (originally *ôs*, Sanscrit, *as*), by the suffix *u* (from *a*), *e. g.*, *decôr-u-s*, *sopôr-u-s*, *honôr-u-s*, *sopôr-u-s*.

922. That in Zend, too, analogous forms to the classes of Sanscrit words discussed above (§. 915.) are not wanting, is proved by bases like ⸺ *csay-a*, "king," as "ruling" (v. ⸺ *csi*, "to rule"), ⸺ *gar-a*, "throat," as "swallowing," ⸺ *-gar-a*, "swallower," ⸺ *-yâz-a*, "worshipper," ⸺ *-ghn-a*, "slayer,". ⸺ *-yaôdh-a*, "combatant," at the end of compounds. Especial notice should be given [G. Ed. p. 1349.] to the compound *drujĕm-vanô* (theme *-vana*), "Druj-slaying," as analogous to Sanscrit compounds like *arin-damá-s*, "foe-taming" (§. 916.). I at least am of opinion that we cannot venture to assume that in Zend, in departure from Sanscrit, the adjectives which are formed with the suffix *a* govern also, in their simple state, an accusative; and that, therefore, *drujĕm* and *vanô*, which in the manuscripts are not, in writing, joined together, can be regarded as two independent words, as in the manuscripts of the Zend-Avesta the different portions

of a compound very often appear written separately.* An example of a Zend word, formed with the secondary suffix *a*, is to be found in ⲙⲱⳡⲱⳝⳝⲙ *ayanha*, "iron, an iron-vessel" (= Sanscrit *âyasa*), from *ayas*', "iron"(see Burnouf, l. c., p. 196).

923. The feminine of the suffix *a*, viz. *â*, forms, in Sanscrit, oxytone abstracts like *bhidá*, "cleaving;" *chhidá*, id.; *kshipá*, "the casting;" *bhikshá*, "the begging;" *kshudhá*, "hunger;" *mudá*, "joy."† So, in Greek, amongst other words, φορά, φθορά, κουρά, φαγή, τομή, φυγή. In Latin, beside *fuga*, it is probable that *cura*, the base word of *curare*, belongs to this class, which it seems to me has sprung from the Sanscrit root *kar*, *kṛi*, "to make" (*karômi*, "I make," *kurmás*, "we make," see §. 490.). The Gothic furnishes for this class of words the feminine bases *vrakô*, "persecution" (opposed to *vraka*, nom. *vraks*, "perse- [G. Ed. p. 1350.] cutor"); *bidô*, "request;" *bôtô*, "use"‡; *dailô*, "sympathy"§; *tharbô*, "want," *id-reigô*, "repentance;"‖ *saurgô*, "care;" *vulvó*, "plunder" (root *valv*: *vilva*, *valv*, *vulvum*),

---

* Burnouf ("Études," p. 250) is of a different opinion as regards the case before us, who, however, regards, and undoubtedly with justness, as a compound the expression *tbaêshô-taôurvâo* which immediately precedes, the members of which are, in the original manuscript, similarly separated, and translates it by "*triomphant de la haine.*"

† Remnants of this class of words, which, however, are not placed here by the Indian Grammarians, are the before-discussed (§. 629.) accusatives of the periphrastic preterite and the Zend infinitives in *anm*. *Mṛigayá*, "hunting," is an isolated word from a theme of the 10th class with a perfect declension.

‡ Root *bat* (presupposes a strong verb *bata*, *bôt*), whence *bats*, "good," English "better." In Sanscrit the root *bhand*, "to be fortunate," corresponds; whence *bhádra*, "fortunate, admirable," see Glossarium Sanscr., a. 1847, p. 243.

§ Root *dil* (=Sanscrit *dal*, "*findi*") presupposes a strong verb *deila*, *dail*, *dilum*, see Glossary, a. 1847, p. 164.

‖ From a lost root, which perhaps signified originally "to blush," then "to be ashamed," and appears to be connected with the Sanscrit root *rañj*, whence *raktá*, "red."

1310   FORMATION OF WORDS.

yiukô, "strife;" *hvôtô* "threatening;" nom. *vraka, bida,* &c., §. 137.). The following exhibit inorganic *n*: *reirôn*, "the trembling;" *brôthra-lubôn*, "brotherly love;" *trigôn*, "mourning" (see Grimm, II. p. 53, n. 555.); nom. *reirô*, &c. (§. 142.). The following are Lithuanian examples of this class of words: *maldà*, "request" (*meldżiu*, "I request"); *deyà*, "wailing" (whence *deyoyu*, "I lament, wail"); *ramszà*, "stopping" (*remszu*, "I stop"); *raudà*, "complaint" (Sanscrit root *rud*, "to weep"); *gĕda*, "shame" (whence *gĕdinu*, "I shame"); *pa-galba*, "help" (*gelb-mi, pa-gelb-mi*, "I help"); *priĕ-spauda*, "oppression" *spaudżiu*, "I press"); *pa-baiga*, "accomplishment" (*baigiu*, "I accomplish"). The following are examples in Old Sclavonic (in Dobrowsky, p. 276): млва *mlva*, "*tumultus*" (*mlv-i-ti*, молвити *molv-i-ti*, "*tumultuari*"); слава *slava*, "glory;" гоуба *gúba*, "*perditio*" (*gúb-i-ti*, "*perdere*"): мѣна *myena*, "*mutatio;*" побѣда *po-byeda*, "*victoria;*" оутѣха *ú-tyecha*, "*consolatio*."

924. The suffix *i* is either identical with the demonstrative base *i* (see §. 360.), or, as I now prefer to assume, a weakening of the suffix *a*, which made its appearance in a period before the separation of our stem of languages; in the same way as, in Latin, the bases in *u* of the 2d declension (= Sanscrit *a*), as also those in *a* (= आ *á*), have frequently permitted this vowel at the end of compounds to be corrupted to *i*, e.g., in *imbellis, imberbis, multiformis.* This suffix forms in Sanscrit, (1) feminine abstracts accenting the root, especially in the Vêda dialect; e.g., *ráṅh-i-s*, "quickness;" *kṛíshi-s*, "the ploughing;" *tvísh-i-s*, "lustre;" *sách-i-s*, "friendship," properly, "the following" (root *sach*, "to follow," cf. Latin *sequor* and *socius* with *sachiva-s*, "friend"); *líp-i-s*, "writing;" ‍‍‍ *věrĕidh-i-s*, "increase, fortune"*;

---

* Dative *věrĕidhyê*, gen. pl. *věrĕidhinanm*, see Burnouf, "Etudes," pp. 316, 324.

dâh-i-s, "creation"*; ܐܘܪܓܝܘ *raj-i-s*, "*institutio*."† The Gothic supplies for this class of words the feminine base *vunni*, "the suffering" (root *vann*: *vinna, vann, vunnum*), and from lost roots the bases *vrôhi*, "accusation," and *vêni*, "hope;" nom., *vunn'-s, vrôh'-s, vên'-s*. In Old Sclavonic to this class belong: рѣчь *ryechy*, "speech;" сѣчь *syechy*, "the smiting, flogging" (theme *ryechi, syechi*, ч *ch* euphonic for *k*); ѩдь *yady*, "food," properly, "eating" (theme *yadi*): in Greek, μῆν-ι-ς (cf. with respect to the root the Sanscrit *man-yû-s*, "wrath, dislike"), δῆρ-ι-ς (cf. the Sanscrit root *dar, drî*, "to tear asunder," δέρω, whence *vi-dâr-aṇá-m*, "war"), ἄγυρ-ι-ς, and with δ added (cf. §. 125. p. 138), the bases ἐλπιδ, ὀπιδ; with τ added, χαριτ. For the latter we should have to expect in Sanscrit *hrîsh-i* (from *hársh-i*), nom., *hrîsh-i-s*. In Latin to this class belong, perhaps, the bases *cæd-i, lábi*, and *ambá-g-i;* but in these and similar words the nominative singular in *ê-s* causes a diffi- [G. Ed. p. 1352.] culty, as it would furnish occasion for a comparison with Sanscrit bases in *as*, nominative masculine and feminine *ás;* e.g., *nubês* reminds us of the Sanscrit *nábhas*, both as masculine, meaning, among other things, "cloud," nom. *nábhâs*, and as neuter, on which the Greek neuter base νέφες (see §. 128.), and the Sclavonic *nebes* (nom. *nebo*, §. 264.), "heaven," are based.‡ *Sedê-s* answers to the Sanscrit

---

* Root *dâh*=Sanscrit *dâs*, "to give," see Burnouf, "Yaçna," Notes, p. ix. Rem. 16., whence it is clear that above (§. 180., p. 197), for ܕܐܘܢܗܐܘܬ *dâonhaôt* we ought to read, according to three other MSS., ܕܐܘܢܗܘܝܬ *dâonhôit*, which *dâhi*, according to §§. 180. and 56ª., must form in the ablative. The accusative *âhîm* of the same base is confirmed by the authority of V. S., p. 83.

† See §. 180. I now regard the ablative ܪܐܓܘܝܬ *rajôit*, which is ambiguous as regards its gender, as feminine.

‡ In Lithuanian *debesi-s*, f. (from *nebesi-s*, cf. §. 317.), "cloud," regarding which it may remain undecided whether, according to its origin, it belongs to *nábhas* m., or to *nábhas* n.

सदस् *sádas*, "assembly" (perhaps originally "sitting"), and Greek ἕδος, ἕδε(σ)-ος. Consequently the *i* of *cædi, labi, nubi, sedi*, &c., which lies at the base of the oblique cases as theme, might have been deprived of a following *s*, or *r* for *s* (see §. 22.), and so the whole have migrated into the *i*-declension; where I recall attention to the exactly similar abbreviation which *munus, muner-is* (from *munis-is*), has experienced in the compounds *immuni-s*, and *opus, operis*, from *opis-is* (= Sanscrit *ápas, ápas-as*), in *opi-fex* for *operi-fex*. (2) Nouns of agency, and appellatives which, according to their primary meaning, are nouns of agency, or denote instruments. They are for the most part masculine, and accent, some of them the root, some the suffix. The following are examples: *chhíd-i-s*, "cleaver;" *yáj-i-s*, "sacrificer;" *pách-i-s*, "fire," as "cooking;" *áh-i-s*, "snake," as "moving itself" (root *anh*); *péṣh-i-s*, "thunderbolt," as "crushing;" *vas-í-s*, "garment;" *dhvan-í-s*, "sound;" *kav-í-s*, "poet," as "speaking" (root *ku*, "to sound"); *chhid-í-s*, f. "axe," as "cleaving;" *ruch-í-s*, f. "beam of light." Also some adjective bases, as *śúch-i*, "pure;" *bódh-i*, "knowing, wise;" *tuv-í*, "much"[*]; and, with reduplication, *jágm-i*, [G. Ed. p. 1353.] "quick" (root *gam*, "to go," Vêd.); *gághn-i*, "slaying" (root *han*, Vêd.), with the accusative (S. V. Benfey, p. 74); *sásn-i*, "giving," with the accusative (Vêd. l. c.); *sásah-i*, "enduring" (Vêd.), with the accusative (l. c. p. 127). To the paroxytone nouns of agency, as *yáj-i-s*, "sacrificer," corresponds, in Greek, τρόχ-ι-ς, "runner:" with *áh-is*, "snake," in Zend ‏az-i-s, the etymologically obscure ἔχ-ι-ς is identical; and so, too, the Latin *angu-i-s*, the *u* of which (=*v*) is only a favourite affix after gutturals. To the oxytone feminine formations like *chhid-í-s*,

---

[*] In the Vêda dialect, root *tu*, "to grow." From the same root comes the Old Prusian *toú-la-n*, "much" (neut.), and the adverb *touls*, "more" (properly a comparative with *s*=Sanscrit *íyas, yás*, cf. §. 301.).

FORMATION OF WORDS. 1313

"axe," as "cleaving," belong, probably, Greek feminine bases like ῥαφ-ίδ, "needle," as "sewing;" γραφ-ίδ, "style," as "writing;" κοπ-ίδ, "hanger, sword," as "smiting;" σφαγ-ίδ, "butcher's knife," as "slaughtering;" and, with passive signification, λεπ-ίδ; with both active and passive, λαβ-ίδ. In Sanscrit the masculine *as-í-s* (cf. *ensi-s*), "sword," as "being whirled" (root *as*, "to cast"), has a passive meaning. The Greek termination ίδ, the δ of which is undoubtedly an inorganic affix, is, however, in so far ambiguous, that its ι is frequently the abbreviation of a Sanscrit *í*; and as the Sanscrit suffix *a* =Greek *o* (see §. 915.) frequently forms its feminine by *í*, and, *e.g.*, parallel with the masculine *nadá-s* stands a feminine *nadí*, likewise "river," as "making a rushing noise," so we might also regard the said Greek formations in ίδ as corresponding to the Sanscrit formations in *í*, and therefore derive, *e.g.*, γραφίδ from a to-be-presupposed masculine base γραφό or γράφο, in the same way as, *e. g.*, στρατηγ'-ίδ, "female leader of an army," comes from σταρατηγό; κορων'-ίδ, from κορωνό. Beside the Sanscrit adjective bases like *súch-i*, "pure," *bódh-i*, "knowing," the Greek τρόφ-ι places itself as analogous. In Gothic, to this group of words belong the masculine substantive bases *yugga-laudi*, "young man, youth" (root *lud*, "to grow"=Sanscrit *ruh* from *rudh*), nominative *lauth'-s* ; *nav-i*, "slayer,"* [G. Ed. p. 1354.] nominative *nau-s; muni*, "thought;" *saggvi*, "song" (with euphonic *v*, see §. 388.), and the feminine bases *daili*, "portion" (Sanscrit root *dal*, "to cleave"); *qvêni*, "woman," as "bearing" (Sanscrit root *jan*, "to bear"). The Lithuanian remnants of this class of words are all feminine, and their origin lies beyond the consciousness of the Lithuanian lingual intelligence. To this class belong, as ancient transmis-

---

* From *nahv-i*, with euphonic *v* (see §. 388.). It, with the Latin *nec*, Greek νέκυ, νεκρό, belongs to the Sanscrit root *nas*, from *nak*, "to be ruined."

sions from the time of the unity of language, *ang-i-s,* "adder" = Sanscrit *áh-i-s,* Zend *az-i-s,* Greek ἔχ-ι-ς, Latin *angu-i-s; a'.-i-s,* "eye"=Sanscrit *áksh-i* (neuter), Zend ﺍﺵ *ash-i,* (see §. 52. conclusion): *us̆-i-s,* "ash," accords well with the Sanscrit root *vaksh,* Zend ﻭﺱ *ucs,* Gothic *vahs,* "to grow." Perhaps *kand-i-s,* "moth," has grown up on Lithuanian ground (cf. *kandu,* "I bite," Sanscrit खाद् *khand,* "to bite," खद् *khad,* "to eat." In Zend the adjective bases ﺩﺭﺷﻲ *darshi,* "courageous," and ﻧﺎﻣﻲ *námi,* "flexible, tender," belong to this class of words. The following are examples of substantives: *ashi,* "eye," as "seeing" (see §. 52.): ﺩﺭﻭﻱ *driwi,* "beggar" (see §. 45. p. 42, and cf. the Sanscrit root *darbh, dribh,* "to fear"); ﺍﺯﻱ *azi,* "snake" (=Sanscrit *áhi*); ﻭﺍﺋﺮﻱ *vairi,* probably, "harness," as "covering" (Sanscrit root *var, vri,* "to cover."* With respect to the secondary suffix *i,* in which the European languages have no share, the example quoted above (§. 913.) may suffice.

925. The suffix *u,* in which I think I recognise a demonstrative base, whence come the prepositions *ut, úpa,* and *upári,* forms, in Sanscrit, (1) adjectives from desiderative themes with the signification of the participle present. They, like the latter, govern the accusative, and retain also [G. Ed. p. 1355.] their energy by the accentuation of the first syllable, *i.e.* in the case before us, of the syllable of reduplication; *e.g., dídrikshuh pitáráu* "wishing to see the parents" (Sâv. 5. 109.). (2) Adjectives which, in agreement with the Greek in *v,* and Lithuanian in *u,* for the most part accent the suffix; *e.g., tanú,* "thin" (properly, "stretched out," root *tan,* "to stretch out"), Greek τανυ-, "stretched," "long;" *svádú,* "sweet" ("savoury," root *svad,* "to taste well"), Greek ἡδύ, Lithuanian *saldù,* from *sladù* for *swadù* (see §. 20.); *laghú,* "light" ("moveable," root *langh,* "to spring

---

* See Burnouf, "Yaçna," p. 444.

over"), Greek ἐ-λαχύ; *mṛidú*, "soft, tender" (properly, "fine, pounded," from *mardú*, root *mard, mṛid*, "to crush"), Greek βραδύ, from μραδύ; *áśú*, from *ákú*, "quick,"* (root *a'*, "to attain," originally, perhaps, "to be quick, to run," hence *áśva*, "steed," as "runner"), Greek ὠκύ; *purú*, from *parú*, "much" (root *par*, पृ *pṛī*, "to fill," *píparmi* "I fill"), Greek πολύ, from παλύ for παρύ, Gothic *filu*, indeclinable; *pṛithú*, "broad," from *prathú* (comparative *práthíyas*, root *prath*, "*extendi, expandi*"), Greek πλατύ, Lithuanian *platù; gurú*, "heavy,"† Greek βαρύ (as βίβημι compared with *jágámi*); *urú*, "great" (probably from *varú*, from *var, vṛi*, "to cover"), Greek, εὐρύ; *bahu*, "much," probably from *badhú*,‡ Greek βαθύ, "deep." To the Greek θαρσύ, θρασύ, corresponds the Lithuanian *drasù*, "bold, courageous."§ In Gothic, besides the already-mentioned indeclinable *filu*, there belong to this class‖ *thaursu*, nom. m. f. *thaursu-s*, neuter *thaursu* (root *thars* = Sanscrit *tarsh*, [G. Ed. p. 1356.] *tṛish*, "dry," and *qvairru* "soft, quiet, mild" (our *kirr*). The following are examples in Zend: ⟨⟩ *póuru*, "much" = Sanscrit *purú*; ⟨⟩ *ĕrĕzu*, "direct" = ऋजु *riju* (root *rij*,

---

* In classical Sanscrit only an adverb; in the Vêda dialect also an adjective.

† From *garú*, whence compare *gáríyas*, superlative *gárishṭha*, see p. 1058, p. 1091, G. ed.). I do not know a root suitable to this adjective as regards its signification.

‡ Root *banh*, "to grow," from *bandh*, as *vṛih*, "to grow," from *vṛidh*, see §. 23.

§ Sanscrit root *dharsh*, "to dare," to which also belongs our *dreist*. Regarding other cognate affinities, see Glossarium Sanscr., a. 1847, p. 186.

‖ That *qvairru-s* is radically identical with *qvair-nu-s*, "millstone," may appear strange: I therefore recall notice to the connection of the above-mentioned Sanscrit *mṛidú*, "tender," with the root *mard, mṛid*, "to crush." The root of the Gothic *qvairr-u-s* (with inorganic doubling of the liquid) and *qvair-nu-s* is to be found in the Sanscrit *jar*, जॄ *jrî*, "to triturate, to be ground."

from *arj* or *raj*); ژسو *áṡu*, "quick,"* whence the superlative اپسيسترو *áṡista*; وڼهو *vanhu*, "good,"= Sanscrit *vasú* (see §. 56ª.). The reason that, in Latin, adjectives corresponding to this class of words are wanting, is, as has been already elsewhere remarked,† that that language has added to all the words which, according to their origin, belong to this class, the inorganic affix of an *i*. In this way, from the Sanscrit *tanú* has been formed *tenui*, and *gurú*, for *garú*, has become *gravi* (transposed from *garui*); from *laghú* has come *levi* (for *legui*); from *svâdú, suavi* (for *suadui*); from *mṛidú*, for *mardú*, *molli*, as it seems by assimilation from *molvi* (cf. §. 312., pp. 428, 429), where the *l* corresponds either to the Sanscrit *r* or *d*. (3) Appellatives; *e.g.*, *dấru*, n. "wood," as "to be cleft;"‡ *íshu*, m. f. "arrow," as "moving itself;" *bándhu*, m. "kinsman," from *bandh*, "to bind;" *rájju*, m. "cord," as "bind- [G. Ed. p. 1357.] ing" (cf. Latin "*ligare*"); *kấrú*, m. "artificer," as "making;" *bhidú*, m. "thunderbolt," as "cleaving;" *tanú*, f. "body," as "stretched out;" also in Zend (see §. 180. p. 197). So, in Greek, beside the already-mentioned δόρυ, perhaps also the bases γῆρυ, f. (Sanscrit root *gar*, ऋ *grī*, whence *gir*, f. "voice"); νέκυ (Sanscrit root *naś*, from *nak*, "to be ruined" (= Zend ژسڼو *naṡu*, "a corpse" (see §. 247.), στάχυ, "ear of corn," as "raised

---

* To the superlative *áṡista*, which Neriosengh translates by *végavattama* (see Burnouf, "Vahista," p. 14, "Études," p. 211), corresponds admirably the Greek ὥκιστος. In Sanscrit we should have expected *áṡishṭha*.

† "Influence of the Pronouns on the formation of Words," p. 20.

‡ Cf. δόρυ, in the oblique cases δόρατ, as, γόνατ, together with γόνυ, Sanscrit *jánú*, n. The Gothic lengthens the two neuter bases by the affix of an *a*, which is again removed from the nominative and accusative, according to §. 153.; hence, *triva*, "tree," *kniva*, "knee," nom. acc. *triu*, *kniu* (dat. pl. *kniva-m*, *triva-m*).

up" *; πῆχυ=Sanscrit *báhú* " arm," Zend ڪسو *bázu* (Sanscrit root *báh* or *váh*, "to strive"); in Latin *curru*, "car," as " running;" perhaps *acu*, if it belongs to the Sanscrit root अश् *aś*, from *ak*, in the signification "to penetrate"†; whence also has come the Sanscrit *aś-áni-s*, "thunderbolt," as "penetrating." The Gothic furnishes us with several masculine bases for this class of words, which, except *lith-u*, "limb," as "moving itself" (root *lith* "to go"), *mag-u*, "boy" (root *mag*, originally "to grow," then "to be able"), come from lost roots; viz. *airu*, "messenger" (Sanscrit root *ar, ṛi,* "to go"); *fôt-u*, "foot," as "going" (Sanscrit *pad,* "to go," whence *pad* and *pád-a-s,* "foot"); *auhs-u*, "ox," (Sanscrit *uksh,* "to wet," "to sow," whence *úkshan* "bull"); *grêd-u,* "hunger." ‡ In Lithuanian, *dangu-s,* [G. Ed. p. 1358.] "heaven," as "covering" (*dengiu,* "I cover") probably belongs to this class.

926. The Sanscrit suffix *an*, in the strong cases *án*, forms appellatives which denote the person acting, and, like the

---

* In so far as it is connected with στείχω (root στιχ=Sanscrit *stigh*, "to mount") the *a* is only the Guna vowel, like the *o* of στόχο-s.

† In this case *acuo* is a denominative from *acu*, as in Greek, *e.g.*, γηρύ-ω from γηρυ (see §. 777.). Against a former conjecture, which I agreed with Pott in encouraging, that *acuo*, and similar words in the European sister languages, belonged to the Sanscrit root *śô* (from *kô*), "to sharpen," with the preposition *á,* speaks the circumstance, that in Sanscrit itself this preposition does not occur in combination with *śô;* and that in the Greek forms, which are most probably connected with the Latin *acuo*, viz. ἀκή, ἀκωκή, ἀκμή, ἀκρός, &c., as also the Lithuanian *asz-tru-s,* "peaked, sharp," *asz-mů,* "sharpness," and the Sclavonic оstrъ *os-tr',* "sharp," in all of these the initial vowel belongs to the root. As अश् *aś* is a compound of *ak,* the Sanscrit *ág-ra-m,* "peak," may also be assigned to this root, and an anomalous mutation of the tenuis to the medial be assumed.

‡ The gender is uncertain: *grêdô,* "I hunger," is a denominative. The Sanscrit supplies the root *gridh*, from *gradh*, "to wish, to require," whence also the Sclavonic *glad',* "hunger."

majority of the analogous Greek formations in αν, εν, ον, ην, ων, accent the radical syllable. The following are examples: *snéhan*, "friend," as "loving;" *rájan*, "king," as "ruling;" *tákshan*, "carpenter," as "cleaving, forming;" *úkshan*, "bull," as "impregnating;" *vríshan*, an appellation of Indra, originally, "causing to rain," also "bull," as "impregnating with seed." To the latter, from the root *varsh*, *vrish*, ("to rain, to rain over, to besprinkle, to sow"), whence, also, other names of male animals, corresponds, in root, suffix, and accentuation, the Greek base ἄρσ-εν (from Ϝάρσεν), by assimilation, ἄρρεν, from an obsolete root. The suffix under discussion further exhibits itself in Greek in the same form in the base εἶρ-εν, "youth," as "speaking." This suffix, however, diverges from its original destination in the adjective base τέρ-εν, in which εν has a passive signification, like the ον of πέπ-ον, "ripe," properly, "cooked," which is originally identical with it. The suffix ον appears, in its original destination in τέκτ-ον, contrasted with the above-mentioned तक्षन् *táksh-an*, "a carpenter," and with demitted accent in σταγ-όν, ("drop," as "trickling"), τρυγ-όν, ἀρηγ-όν, ἀη-δόν, εἰκ-όν. The original α, with the genuine accentuation, has remained in τάλαν. As regards the bases in ην and ων,

[G. Ed. p. 1359.] it is to be observed that the Sanscrit suffix *an* forms the strong cases in *án* (see §. 129.), with the exception of the vocative singular, and this latter is probably the older form of the suffix, which appears to me to have arisen from *ana*, so that the dropping of the final *a* has been compensated by lengthening the first. The shortening of the vowel of the suffix under discussion, and its entire suppression in the Sanscrit weakest cases (see §. 130.), have, however, probably entered into the different languages independently of one another, and probably for the first time after the separation of languages. Compare, *e.g.*, the plural nominatives σκήπων-ες, ("staves," as "supporting"), κλύδων-ες, ("billows," as "laving"), αἴθων-ες, εἴρων-ες, τρίβων-ες, (the latter, contrary to the Sanscrit principle, with a passive signification), with the plural nominatives of the above-mentioned (p. 1358 G. ed.) Sanscrit bases, *snéhân-as, rájân-as, tákshân-as, vríshân-as*,* In genitives like *snéhnâm,* "*amicorum*," sing. *snéhn-as,* as generally in the weakest cases, the Sanscrit stands in very disadvantageous comparison with Greek forms like σκηπών-ων, σκήπων-ος; while, on the other hand, it surpasses the Greek in this, that in the classical language it has nowhere allowed the length of the vowel of the suffix to be lost in the strong cases (with the exception of the vocative singular and the anomalous *púshan,* "the sun," as "nourisher," in all the strong cases); and hence, *e.g.,* it contrasts the forms *tákshân-am, tákshân-ân, tákshân-as,* with the Greek τέκτον-α, τέκτον-ε, τέκτον-ες.† . Moreover, the Sanscrit, in this class of words, has never suffered the accent to sink [G. Ed. p. 1360.] down on the suffix, like, *e.g.,* in the Greek, πενθήν, ἀπατεών.

927. The Latin exhibits the suffix under discussion in the form *ôn,* and therefore likewise favours the supposition that its vowel was originally pervadingly long. To this class belong, *e.g.,* the bases *ed-ôn, ger-ôn, combib-ôn, prædic-ôn, err--ôn,* the accusatives of which, *ed-ôn-em, ger-ôn-em,* &c., corre-

---

* *ṇ* for *n* in the two last forms, through the euphonic influence of the preceding *sh*.

† With regard to the τ for Sanscrit *sh,* τέκτων has the same relation to the Sanscrit *tákshâ* (see §. 139.) that ἄρκτο-ς has to *ṛikshâ-s,* "bear" (from *arkshâ-s*), the sibilant of which is preserved by the Latin *ursu-s* as original. In the Vêda dialect the suffix under discussion admits after *sh* in the strong cases, at option either *â* or *a* (Pân. VI. 4. 9.); *e.g., tákshân-am* and *tákshaṇ-am*=τέκτον-α, *tákshân-as* and *tákshaṇ-as*=τέκτον-ες. I cannot, however, regard this agreement with the Greek, with respect to the shortening of the vowel, as merely accidental, as in the Vêda dialect it is bound up with the condition of *sh* preceding, which shews itself also in the above-mentioned *púshan,* and as the Vêda dialect admits also of several other forms, which can only have arisen in the progress of corruption.

spond well to the Sanscrit, like *snéh-ân-am, râg-ân-am.* A weakening of the original *â* to *i* is found in *pect-in,* nominative, *pect-en* (according to §. 6.), the *i* of which for *ô* resembles that of the base *ho-min,* the nominative of which belongs to a base *ho-mân* (see §. 797. p. 1077.). In Gothic the suffix spoken of has throughout in the singular, in the cases which, in Sanscrit, are weak, just like the suffix *man* (§. 799.), experienced the weakening of the *a*-sound to *i* (see §. 132.). To this class belong the bases (some of which have sprung from lost roots) *han-an,* "cock," as "singing" (Latin *cano,* Sanscrit *śans* from *kans,* "to say"); *stau-an,* "judge" (Sanscrit root *stu,* "to praise"); *faura-gagg-an,* "superintendant" (literally, "preceder"); *ar-an,* "eagle," as "flying" (Sanscrit root *ar, ri,* "to go"); *ah-an,* "sense, understanding" (cf. *ah-man,* "spirit," §. 799., *ah-ya,* "I think, I mean"); *liut-an,* "hypocrite;" *nut-an,* "catcher;" *ga-sinth-an,* "companion;" *skul-an,* "debtor" (root *skal,* "to owe, to be obliged"); *veih-an,* "priest," as "consecrating;"
[G. Ed. p. 1361.] *spill-an,* "announcer;"[*] *auhsan,* "ox," =Sanscrit *úkshan* (see §. 82.), nom. *auhsa=úkshâ* (see §. 140.). In Old High German the Gothic *a* of this suffix and of the suffix *man* has been corrupted to *o* or *u*: in the genitive and dative plural, however, we find inorganic *ô,* while the Gothic *an-ê, a'-m* (for *an-m*), would lead us to expect a short *o* (see Grimm, I. p. 624). The *i* of the Gothic genitive and dative singular has remained, or been further corrupted to *e,* which latter, in the Middle and New High German, has extended itself through all the cases. The Old High German bases in *on, e.g., bot-on,* "messenger," as "announcing"[†] *ox-on,* "ox," *has-on,* "hare," as

---

[*] *Spillô,* "I announce, I relate." The *s* is probably a phonetic prefix or an obsolete preposition. Compare the Old Prussian *billu,* "I say," Lithuanian *biloyu* id., Irish *bri,* "word," and the Sanscrit root *brû,* "to speak."

[†] Properly, "offering." The root *but,* "to offer," is based on the Sanscrit

"springing (Sanscrit *śaś*, "to spring," *śaśá*, "hare"), *hlouf-on*, "runner," *trink-on*, "drinker," *fah-on*, "seizer," *heri-zoh-on*, "leader of an army," correspond excellently to Greek bases like ἀρηγ-όν, and the nominatives which drop the *u*, like *bot-o* (our *Bote*, "messenger," from the base *Boten*), to the Latin like *edo*, *combibo*. The English language exhibits a remarkable remnant of the Sanscrit suffix *an* in the plural "oxen," which, according to form, is nothing but the form of the Sanscrit base *úkshan* a little altered, which appears in German in the form *Ochsen*, not only in the plural, but also in all the oblique cases of the singular. Through its limitation to the plural, the ancient formative suffix has, in English, obtained the appearance of an expression of plurality; and just so in "brethren" (Sanscrit base *bhrâtar*, *bhrâtrí*), "chicken," and "children," where the original state of our stem of languages gives no occasion for it. In modern Netherlandish this suffix has fixed itself in the plural of all regular words, and has [G. Ed. p. 1362.] hence become a distinct mark of plurality for the practical use of language. Regarding a similar abuse of another Sanscrit suffix in the oldest period of High German (see §. 241.).

928. The suffix under discussion does not form in Sanscrit regular neuter bases; but some anomalous neuters in *i* form their weakest cases (see §. 130.) from bases in *an*, *e.g.*, *áksh-i*, "eye" (as "seeing"), from *akshán*, which may, perhaps, have originally had a perfect declension, and on which, perhaps, *áksha*, which, at the end of compounds, takes the place of *ákshi*, is based, with the loss of an *n*, as also *râj-an*, which is the word most in use of this class, is regularly replaced as the final element of a compound by *râja*. Con-

---

scrit *budh*, "to know," and has assumed a causal signification; so that *boton*, as "making to know," approaches nearer to the old meaning than the verb *biutu*, "*offero*."

1322   FORMATION OF WORDS.

versely, in German, several bases of words, which, in their simple state, terminate in a vowel, assume, at the end of compounds, the suffix *an*, e. g., in Gothic, *ga-dailan*, "sympathiser" (from *ga*, "with," and *daili*, nom., *dails*, f. "part"); *ga-hlaiban*, "companion" (*hlaiba*, nom., *hlaifs*, m., "bread"); *us-lithan*, "palsied" (*us*, "from," and *lithu*, n., *lithu-s*, m., "member"). In Old High German the appellation of "day" (simple theme *taga*, nom. *tag*) has, in several compounds, by extending itself to *tagon*, re-approached its conjectural Sanscrit sister word *áhan*,* Zend (𐬀𐬴𐬀𐬥 *aṡan*), (see §. 253. p. 270). To return to the Sanscrit neuter base *akshán*, "eye," whence, in the Vêda dialect also, the middle [G. Ed. p. 1363.] cases spring—at least the instrumental plural *akshábhis*—the Gothic base *augan*† corresponds to it in root, suffix, and gender. As the nominative, accusative, and vocative plural of neuters in Sanscrit belong to the strong cases, we should here expect from *akshán* the form *akshā́ni*, from *akshā́n-a* (see §. 234.); and to this the Gothic *augón-a*, "eyes," admirably corresponds (see §. 801. p. 1083, Note). In Gothic, however, the nominative, accusative, and vocative singular of neuter bases in *an* also prove themselves to be strong; hence, *augô* for the *akshā́* to be expected in San-

---

* I regard *áhan* as an abbreviation of *dáhan* (root *dah*, "to burn," here, "to give light"), see Gloss. Scr., a. 1847, p. 26, where, however, as in my Sanscrit Grammar, this anomalous word, which forms the middle cases in *áhas*, is erroneously given as masculine. It is neuter, and therefore forms in the nominative, accusative, and vocative plural *áhâni* (the Vêda form *áhá* belongs to the base *áha*), dual *áhnî*, or Vêdic *áhanî*, see Benf. Gloss.

† The sibilant of the Sanscrit root may be a later affix, and is wanting in the Gothic, as in the Latin *oculus*, the Lithuanian *aki-s*, and Greek root ὀπ, from ὀκ. For the *g* in *augan* we might expect *h*, according to §. 87., and therefore *auhan*, which form probably preceded *augan*. In that case we should regard the *u* as the weakening of the old *a*, and explain the *a* of the diphthong *au* according to §. 82. With the Sanscrit *aksha* at the end of compounds the Gothic base *iha* or *aiha*, of *haiha*, "one-eyed," has been already compared (see §. 308. p. 418.).

FORMATION OF WORDS. 1323

scrit. With the Gothic neuter base *vatan*, "water" (for which, in Lithuanian, where, in substantives, the neuter is in general wanting, we find the masculine base *wanden*, (nom. *wandü*, see §. 139. p. 151), the Sanscrit compares the base *udan*, which, however, can only be inferred from its derivatives, *udan-vat*, "ocean" (literally, "gifted with water"), and *udan-yâ*, "thirst" (*i.e.* "craving for water"), and whose gender, therefore, cannot be decided. Perhaps *udan* is also contained in the compounds which begin with *uda*, "water," as final *n* is regularly suppressed in such a position: a simple *uda*, however, has hitherto not been discovered. The corresponding verbal root is *und* ("to be wet"), the nasal of which has remained in the Latin *unda* and Lithuanian *wandü*. In Lithuanian we must further, in respect of its suffix, refer to this class the base *rud-en*, nom. *rudü*, "autumn," and radically, perhaps, to the Sanscrit *ruh*, [G. Ed. p. 1364.] from *rudh*, "to grow," to which, also, *inter alia*, belongs the Sclavonic *rod-i-ti*, "to bear young."

929. I look upon the Sanscrit accented suffix *in* as a weakening of the suffix *an*. After augmenting the radical vowel, it forms words like *vâdín*, "speaking" (root *vad*), *kârín*, "making" (root *kar*, *kṛi*), *hârín*, "taking, rubbing," *êshín*, "wishing," *yôdhín*, "striving" (root *yudh*), *sâvín*, "squeezing out," which occur only at the end of compounds; *e.g.*, *rita-vâdín*, "speaking truth," Yajurv. V. 7.; *manyu-sâvín*, "zealously squeezing out" (the Sôma), S. V., I. 3. 1., 4. 1.). We find in the simple form, as substantive, कामिन् *kâmín*, "loving, lover." With respect to the weakening of the *a* to *i*, these formations correspond to the above-mentioned (§. 927.) Latin bases *pect-in*, and the Gothic genitives and datives like *stau-in-s*, "*judicis*," *stau-in*, "*judici*," in contrast to the more organic *a* of the other cases, *e.g.*, of the accusative *stau-an*, "*judicem*," and of the nominative and accusative plural *stau-an-s*, "*judices*." The Sanscrit itself presents some remarkable words in which the suffixes *an* and *in* occur to-

gether, and indeed so, that *an*, or rather *án* (see §. 926.), occurs only in the strong cases, and *in* extends over all those weak cases which do not, as is done in the said words by the weakest cases, entirely divest themselves of the suffix, and, beyond these, also to the vocative, which especially inclines to a weakening of the vowel. Moreover, the accent in the words spoken of is so divided, that the cases with the suffix ·*an* (*án*) follow the accentuation of *rájan*, "king, ruler," and similar words, and those with the suffix *in* (excepting the vocative, §. 785. Rem. p. 1054), that of -*kárín*, "making." -*vádín*, "speaking," and similar formations in *in*. Thus, *e.g.*, from the root *manth*, "to shake," comes the base *manthan*, "a churn," as "shaker" [G. Ed. p. 1365.] (accented like *rájan*); and hence, by weakening the root, the suffix, and the accentuation, the base *mathín*, which is found also at the beginning of compounds, and is therefore viewed by the grammarians as the proper theme. The analogy of *mánthan*, *mathín*, is, moreover, followed by the already-mentioned *pánthan*, *pathín*, "way," where the suffix under discussion has a passive signification; a circumstance which has already been remarked of the Greek τριβών, which is, in formation, akin to it. The root is *path*, "to go," perhaps originally *panth*: the signification, therefore, of *pánthan*, *pathín*, is tantamount to "gone upon, trodden." In the Vêda dialect the accusative singular *pánthánam*, and the nominative plural *pánthánas*, allow the *n* to be cast out, after which the two *a*-sounds coalesce; whence *pánthám*, *pánthás*, a remarkable though fortuitous coincidence with the Greek εἰκώ, εἰκοῦς, εἰκούς, for εἰκόνα, εἰκόνος, εἰκόνας.

930. The suffix *in* is used in Sanscrit also for the formation of derivative words, and then denotes the person gifted with the thing which is expressed by the primitive; and has, therefore, a passive meaning like the primitive *pathín*, "way," as "trodden." This *in* has likewise the

accent; *e.g., dhanín,* " rich, endowed with riches" (nom. m. *dhanî,* according to §. 139.), from *dhaná,* " wealth ;" *kèśín,* "covered with hair, having beautiful hair "(from *kèśá*, "hair "), and as substantive masculine "a lion" ("the maned"); *hastín* and *karín,* "the elephant," properly, " having a trunk," from *hastá, kará,* " hand, trunk." It appears to me to admit of no doubt that the secondary *in,* too, is a weakening of *an,* or rather *án,* which, in Greek and Latin, has remained in the form of ων, ôn, in possessives to which the use of language has imparted a partly amplified signification, in like manner as several of the Sanscrit formations under discussion may be regarded as ampliatives; since, *e.g., kèś-ín,* as "lion" is "the shaggy ;" [G. Ed. p. 1366.] *dant-ín,* ("gifted with teeth") as "elephant" is "the large-toothed ;" *dánshṭr'-ín* (from *dánshṭrá,* "tooth "), as "boar" is "the tusk-endowed." So in Greek, *e.g.,* the bases, and, at the same time, nominatives, γνάθ-ων, " thick-cheeked" (properly only "having cheeks"); κεφάλ'-ων, "thick-head ;" γάστρ-ων, "thick-belly, having a great paunch ;" Πλούτ-ων, properly, "having great riches ;" in Latin, *e.g., nas-ôn,*[*] *capit-ôn, front-ôn, ped-ôn, bucc'-ôn, labi'-on, gul'-ôn. Cæs'-ôn,* from a lost base, is perhaps, together with *cæsaries,* connected with the Sanscrit *kèśá* (nom. *kèśá-s,* "hair "), although the Sanscrit *ś* (from *k*) would lead us to expect in Latin *c.* But if, notwithstanding the connection which Pott (E. I., p. 588) conjectures should be well founded, we may recognise in the name *Cæs-ôn* a cognate formation of the abovementioned Sanscrit appellation of the lion *(kèś'-ín* from *kèś'-án),* and of the proper name of a Dânava, which we meet with in Kâlidâsa's Urvaśî, while the feminine form of the said word *(kèś'-íni)* in the Nalus appears as the name of a female attendant of Damayantî. As regards the ac-

---

[*] In Sanscrit we should have to expect from *nâsá,* "nose," a *nás'-in,* formed with *in*

centuation, the Greek possessives correspond to the Sanscrit nouns of agency in *an*, *ân*: compare *e.g.*, the plural γάστρων-ες with *râjân-as*. The feminine formation ῥύγχαινα (for ῥυγχανια) is remarkable: it corresponds to τάλαινα, μέλαινα (see §. 119.), and therefore presupposes a masculine neuter base ῥυγχαν, and represents the Sanscrit feminine possessives like *kêśinî*, "having (fine or much) hair," for *kêśânî*. So, according to its form, θεράπαινα is based, not on θεραποντ, but on a to-be-presupposed base θεραπαν and [G. Ed. p. 1367.] represents the Sanscrit feminines like *râjñî* ("she that rules," "queen") for *râjanî*, and this for *râjânî*.

931. It is important to observe, that where the Greek possessive suffix ων refers not to persons but to rooms, which are gifted with the thing expressed by the base name, the accentuation which has been recognised above (§. 785. commencement of Remark) as the more energetic and animated is replaced by the weaker, since the accent sinks down from the first or second syllable of the word to the suffix; thus, *e.g.*, ἱππών, properly, "gifted with horses," with the to-be-supplied secondary idea of room, and thus "stall for horses;" so ἀνδρ-ών, γυναικ-ών, πιθ'-ών, οἰν'-ών, ἀμπελ'-ών, σιτ'-ών, μελισσ'-ών, περιστερε-ών,* in opposition to the living possessors of the things denoted, as Γνάθων, Πλούτων, Χείλων, Κεφάλων, Τύχων. The accented

---

* I regard the ε of περιστερε-ών as the thinning of the final vowel of the base of the primary word, which in περιστερ'-ών, according to the prevailing principle (see §. 913.), is suppressed. So ἀμπελε-ών together with ἀμπελ'-ών, οἰνε-ών together with οἰν'-ών, ῥοδε-ών with ῥοδ'-ών; χαλκε-ών, λυχνε-ών. There is no source for the ε of κωνωπεών in the primitive base κωνωπ; and it is probably introduced through analogy with the forms in which the ε is founded on the final vowel of the primitive base, and the origin of which is now lost sight of by the language. With respect to the weakening of ο to ε compare vocatives like λύκε from λύκο (§. 204.).

FORMATION OF WORDS. 1327

suffix ων, transferred from that which possesses room to time, forms also names of months, in which the preceding ι everywhere belongs to the primitive, where this really admits of being traced; hence, e.g., ἐλαφηβολι'-ών, properly, "gifted with the hunting-feast," and hence, "month of the hunting-feast." The Sanscrit forms with the feminine of the suffix *in* (=Greek ών) words which express the place provided with the thing denoted. At least, from all the appellatives of the lotus-flower come words in *iní*, [G. Ed. p. 1368.] which denote "lotus-field," "lotus-pond;" as, e.g., *padm-iní* from *padma*. Hereto remarkably correspond Greek feminines like ῥοδ'-ωνιά, properly, "gifted with roses," hence, "rose-garden," where, as in the above-mentioned (§. 119.) forms in τρια=Sanscrit *trí*, to the feminine character *í* there has been further added an inorganic α, thus -ωνια= *iní* from *ání*.

932. The suffix अन *ana*, fem. *aná*, and *aní*, which we have already taken cognizance of as a means of formation of abstract substantives, as *gám-ana-m*, "the going," and on which the infinitives of various Indo-European languages are based,* I regard as identical with the demonstrative *ana* (see §. 372. passim). This suffix forms in Sanscrit, *inter alia*, proparoxytone appellatives neuter or masculine, as *náy-ana-m*, "eye," as "guiding" (root *ní*, with Guna); *lóch-ana-m*, id., as "seeing" (root *lóch*); *vád-ana-m*, "mouth," as "speaking;" *láp-ana-m*, id., (root *lap*, "to speak," cf. Latin *loquor* and *labium*); *dás-ana-m* and *dás-ana-s*, "tooth,"

---

* See §§. 851. (p. 1211 G. ed.), 852., 876., 877. To the feminine abstracts in अना *aná*, like *yách-aná*, "the begging" (§. 877.), I have further to assign the Gothic base *ga-mait-anôn* (nom. -*anô*), "the cutting in pieces," as an analogous form which stands alone in Gothic, which is distinguished from its Sanscrit prototypes (see §. 142.) only by the *n*, which in German is so frequently added to bases terminating originally in a vowel.

as "biting" (root *danś* from *dank* = Greek δακ); *váh-ana-m*, "car," as "carrying"*; *táp-ana-s*, "sun," as "burning;" *dáh-ana-s*, "fire," as "burning;" *dárp-ana-s*, "mirror," as "making proud" (root *darp, dṛip* in the causal); *tár-aṇa-s*, [G. Ed. p. 1369.] "boat," as "ferrying over." Hereto well correspond, with respect to accentuation also, Greek bases in ανο, and indeed to the neuter, such as δρέπ-ανο-ν ("sickle," as "cutting off"), γλύφ-ανο-ν, κόπ-ανο-ν, ὄργ-ανο-ν, τήγ-ανο-ν (for τήκανον), ὄχ-ανον (as "means of holding"), σκέπ- -ανο-ν.† The following are examples with a passive meaning: πλόκ-ανο-ν, πόπ-ανο-ν, τύμπ-ανο-ν. To the masculine forms like *dáh-ana-s*, "fire," as "burning," correspond στέφ- -ανο-ς, χό-ανο-ς, χόδ-ανο-ς. In Lithuanian, to this class belong most probably words like *tek-ûna-s*, "runner," where the first vowel of the suffix is weakened as regards quality, but lengthened as regards quantity, and has drawn to itself the accent. The following are other examples: *bĕg-ûna-s*, "fugitive;" *klaid-ûna-s*, "wanderer;" *pa-klaid-ûna-s*, "rover" (*klys-tu*, "I wander," pret. *klyd-au*); *lep-ûna-s*, "weakling;" *mal-ûna-s*, "mill;" *riy-ûna-s* or *ryy-ûna-s*, "devourer" (*ryy-ú*, "I swallow, I devour"). In Gothic, perhaps the base *thiud- -ana*, nom. *thiudan'-s*, "king," if it originally signifies "ruling," belongs to this class‡. In Old High German the masculine

---

* The following have a passive signification: *e.g.*, *śáy-ana-m*, "couch, bed," and *ás-ana-m*, "seat." To the former corresponds the Zend ꬉꬉꬉꬉꬉ *śay-anĕ-m*. Another example in Zend is ꬉꬉꬉꬉꬉ *khar- -anĕ-m*, "sustenance," as "being eaten" (Burnouf, "Yaçna," p. 550):

† As in Sanscrit the *ay* of causals and verbs of the 10th class, which has its influence in the formation of words, is dropped before the suffix *ana* (*dárp-aṇa-s*, not *darpayana-s*); so in Greek the *a* of the corresponding verbs in άω falls off: hence σκέπ-ανο-ν, the *a* of which has nothing to do with that of σκεπ-άω.

‡ The lost root *thud* is perhaps an extension of the Sanscrit *tu*, "to grow" (whence *táv-as*, "strength"), which we have already recognised in Gothic in the form in *tav* (see p. 1342 G. ed., S. 917., 3d Note).

base *wag-ana,* "wagon," nom. acc. *wag-an,* irrespective of gender, accords admirably with the above-mentioned Sanscrit *váh-ana-m*. The suffix under discussion forms in Sanscrit adjectives also with the accent on the final syllable of the suffix, as *śóbh-aná,* "fair" (*śóbh-aná-s, -aná, -aná-m*), properly, "shining"(root *śubh,* "to shine"); [G. Ed. p. 1370.] *jval-aná,* "flaming;" *chal-aná,* "tottering, trembling."* So in Greek, σκεπ-ανό-ς, " covering ;" ἱκ-ανό-ς, " sufficient."

933. Let us now examine somewhat closer the Sanscrit suffix *as,* the dative of which we have already recognised as the termination of Vêdic infinitives (see §. 856.), and whose origin we have sought in the root *as* of the verb substantive (see §§. 855., 857.). The Indian grammarians, however, recognise as infinitives, *i.e.* as representatives of the form in *tum,* only those forms which have no other case from the same base accompanying them, as is the case, *e.g.*, with *jívás-ê,* "in order to live," the sole remnant of the base *jívás*. On the other hand, *chákshas-ê,* which above (at p. 1224 G. ed., §. 856.), in a passage there quoted from the Rig-Vêda, we have seen standing beside a dative of the common infinitive in a similar relation, is looked upon by the Scholiast Sâyana as no infinitive, clearly because *chákshas,* "the seeing," is retained with a complete declension, and for example has a nominative, which is wanting in the Vêdas in the form in *tu* in the simple word.† The simple suffix, called *asun*

---

* To this class of words I refer the Zend 𐬰𐬀𐬎𐬎𐬀𐬥𐬀 *zav-ana,* "living" (cf. Burnouf, "Yaçna," Notes, pp. 81 and 88, n.), from the contracted root *zu,* for *ju* (cf. §. 109 b) 2. p. 119, and §. 58.).

† *Jivâtu,* "*vita,*" which occurs in the nominative, I should agree with Benfey in regarding as an infinitive, were it found in sentences like *na saknóti jivâtum,* "he cannot live," or like *jivitañ jivâtum,* "*vitam vivere.*" In the passages, however, quoted by Benfey (Glossary, p. 72), the signification "*vita*" is sufficient; moreover, *jivâtu* is not, like the infinitives in *tu,* a feminine, but a masculine and neuter (see Unâdi, I. 75.), and signifies, like the Latin word, akin to it in root and formation, *victus,* besides

[G. Ed. p. 1371.] or *asi* by the Indian grammarians, with reference to the difference of accentuation forms:

[G. Ed. p. 1372.] *A*) Abstract neuters with the accent on

sides "living," also "nourishment, food, means of living (cooked rice, &c."), and, moreover, "medicine," as "making to live." When, however, Benfey, in his recently-published "Complete Grammar of the Sanscrit Language," p. 431, says that *jivâtum* appears in the Vêdas distinctly as an infinitive, I am unable to perceive this distinctness, at least from the passages quoted in the Glossary to the S. V., just as I am unable to deduce, with Benfey, the masculine nature of these infinitives from the Vêdic infinitive datives in *tavê;* as, indeed, as the said learned man himself says in §. 727. V., which is adduced as proof, the feminines in *u* optionally form the dative in *avê*, while the masculines do so necessarily. Now the Vêdic infinitive datives actually avail themselves of the option of using in the dative both the termination *ê* with Guna, and also the termination *âi*, inasmuch as they employ both the one and the other form, with this peculiarity, that before the heavier and exclusively feminine termination *âi* they gunise the *u* of the suffix. I will not here, in support of my views, refer to the gerund in *tvâ*, as Benfey (l. c., p. 424) pronounces no opinion whatever on it as to its gender and case, and especially as to the grammatical category to which it belongs: as, however, he remarks (p. 426, §. 911.) that *alan kritvâ* signifies "do not," properly, "enough done," it might be imagined that the form in *tvâ*, in construction with *alam*, is a perfect passive participle; while I am convinced that *alan kritvâ* properly means "enough with doing," and *kritvâ* here clearly shews itself to be an abstract substantive in the instrumental (see p. 1204 G. ed., §. 851., Note). It may appear strange that one should find this gerund, or rather the equivalent form in *ya* (on account of the weight of composition), in constructions where, instead of it, a preposition might be used; but even here, too, if we view the said form as the instrumental of an abstract substantive or gerund there is no difficulty; for *atikramya parvatan nadî*, according to Benfey, "the river behind the mountain," means properly, "the river after crossing the mountain (of the mountain)," *i.e.* "the river at which, after crossing the mountain, one arrives;" *amaratvam apahâya* (Arj. 3. 47.) may be aptly rendered by "except immortality," but *apahâya* does not thereby become a preposition, for it properly signifies "with abandonment," *i.e.* "with exception (of immortality"); and the instrumental termination of the gerund (see §. 889.) expresses here, as is very usual, the relation "with."

the radical syllable, and commonly with Guna of the vowels capable of receiving that augment; e.g., téj-as, "lustre" (root tij, "to sharpen"); várch-as, id.; sáh-as, "might," ránh-as, "quickness;" áñj-as, id.; táras, id. (root tar, तृ trí, "to step over"); sáv-as, "strength :" Zend ɯʌɯʌɯ sav-as̀, "use" (root śu, from śvi, "to grow"); táv-as, "strength" (Vêd. tu, "to grow"); ráh-as, "secret" (root rah, "to leave"); máh-as, "greatness" (root mah, manh, "to grow"); nám-as, "bending, reverence, adoration :" Zend ɯʌɢɕʝ němas̀ ; táp-as, "penitence," properly, "the burning;" díw-as, "transformation, reverence," Vêd., properly, "going" (root du, "to go").

B) Neuter appellatives, with an active, and some of them with a passive signification, and with accentuation of the root and Guna; e.g., sár-as, "pond," Vêd. "water," as "flowing" (root sar, sri, "to move itself"); śráv-as, "ear," as "hearing;" Zend ɯʌɯʌɯʌ śravas̀, id. (root śru), formally the Greek κλέ(F)-ος; cháksh-as, "eye," as "seeing"*; ródh-as, "coast," as "hemming in ;" chét-as, "spirit," as "thinking" (root chint, chit); mán-as, id.: Zend ɯʌʝʌɢ man-as̀, "spirit, thought" (Greek μέν-ος, root मन् man, "to think"); sró-t-as, "stream," as "flowing"†; páya-s, "water, milk,"

---

* Like the abstract चक्षस् chákshas only in the Vêda dialect, where chaksh means "to see."

† Root sru, with t inserted (Unâdi, IV. 203.); so also rét-a-s, "seed," from ri, "to flow." An inserted th is found in på-th-as, "water" (l. c. 205.), as "being drunk." N, too, or n is inserted; viz. in áp-n-as, "operation, work," together with áp-as and áp-as (root âp, "to obtain," with prep. sam, "to complete"); ár-n-as, "water," root ar, ri, "to move oneself." Compare chatur-n-âm, τεσσάρων, from chatur. In Latin, pig-n-us (root pag), faci-n-us, and perhaps mû-n-us, belong to this class, if the latter, with respect to its root, is connected with the Sanscrit mâ, "to measure" (with prep. nis, nir—nir-mâ, "to make, to produce"). In Greek to this class belong words like δά-ν-ος, κτῆ-ν-ος, δρᾶ-ν-ος, τέρχ-ν-ος, Dor. τρέχ-ν-ος (cf. τρέχω, τρίχ, θρίκ-s, Sanscrit drih, from darh or drah, "to grow"),

[G. Ed. p. 1373.] as "being drunk" (root *pí*, "to drink"); *édh'-as*, "wood," as "about to be burnt" (root *indh*, "to kindle"); *vách-as*, "speech," as "spoken;" Zend ᚖᚖᚖᚖ *vach-aś*, id. Here must be ranked some masculine bases in the Véda dialect like *vákṣhas*, "ox," as "drawing," if it springs, as the Grammarians assume (see Böhtling, Uṇâdi-suffixes IV. 220.), from the root *vah*, with the affix of a sibilant. It might, however, as I prefer supposing, come from *vakṣh*, "to grow," so that it would properly signify "the great," like the term for a buffalo, *mahiṣhá*, from another root "to grow." An isolated form is the oxytone feminine *uṣh-ás*, "aurora," as "shining;" Zend ᚖᚖᚖᚖ *ush-aś*, id., likewise feminine, acc. ᚖᚖᚖᚖ *ushâonhĕm* = Véd. *ushâsam* (root उष् *ush*, "to burn," here "to shine"). This word deserves especial notice, because in the Véda-dialect it exhibits a long *â*,* not only in the nominative singular, but occasionally also in other strong cases, and indeed even in the genitive plural (*ushấ-sâm*, see Benfey's Glossary) and thus as it were prepares the Latin form

[G. Ed. p. 1374.] *aurôr-a* (*ô* = *â*), which, through the appended *a*, has the same relation to the Sanscrit *ushâs*, that

---

grow"), τέμε-ν-ος. The latter contains, like the Latin *faci-n-us*, the class-vowel of the verbal theme. In Zend to this class belongs ᚖᚖᚖᚖ *khărĕ--n-aś*, "lustre" (nom. acc. *kharĕnô*, according to §. 56ᵇ., gen. *kharĕnanh-ô*, according to §. 56ᵃ.), from the root *khar* = Sanscrit *svar*, "to shine" (see §. 35. and §. 815. last Note), the ε of which is explained by §. 30. With Sanscrit formations which insert a *t*-sound, like *sró-t-as*, *pá-th-as*, we might compare the Greek μέγε-θ-ος, in case it does not come from μέγας, but, like the latter, from the obsolete root (which, too, has lost its verb) μεγ = Sanscrit *mah*, *maṅh*, "to grow."

* The form *ushâs-â*, at the beginning of copulative compounds, shews itself to be the Vêdic dual termination of the base *ushâs*, as the Vêda dialect, as has already been elsewhere remarked, admits also, in the first member of such compounds, the dual termination.

oper-a has to *oper*, the theme of the oblique cases of *opus* = Sanscrit *áp-as*, "work."*

C) Adjectives with the signification of the present participle, which, in combination with the substantive preceding, and standing in the accusative relation, appear partly as appellatives, but in the Vêda dialect, which is here of special importance to us, retain in composition too their adjective natures. The following are Vêdic examples: *nri-chákshas*, "seeing men;" *nri-mánas*, "thinking of men;" *nri-váhas*, "bearing man or men;" *stóma-váhas*, "bringing hymns of praise;" *visvá-dhá-y-as*, "bearing all" (with euphon. *y*, see §. 43.), *risádas* (*risa-adas* "consum- [G. Ed. p. 1375.] ing the foes." To this class belongs the Zend ᴊᴊᴊᴊᴊᴊᴊᴊ *ash-aój-as*, "destroying purity," if Burnouf's analysis of

---

* From the Vêdic instrumental *ushád-bhis*, for which probably the form *ushád-bhyas* will occur as dative and ablative, and *ushátsu* as locative, I should not choose to infer, with Benfey (Grammar, p. 149), that *as* has arisen from *at* of the present participle, as *s* in Sanscrit, in the common language too, is changed, according to fixed laws, into *t;* hence, *e.g.*, from *vas*, "to dwell," the future *vat-syámi*, and aorist *ávát-sam*. Moreover, the *s* of our suffix proves itself, by the cognate Greek, Latin, German, Lithuanian, and Sclavonic forms, to be a sibilant, existing there before the period of the separation of languages; and which, in the Vêdic Sanscrit in the word under discussion, at the beginning of compounds, passes over into *r* (*ushar-búdh*, "waking early"). I likewise recall attention to the fact that the base word *ap*, "water," allows its *p* before the *bh* of the case-terminations to be changed into *d*, without its being possible to thence infer that *ap*, on which are based the Latin *aqua* and Gothic *ahva*, "river," has proceeded from *ad* or *at*. I would rather assume, with Weber (V. S. Sp. 1. 18.), that only the forms with *d* belong to a base *at* (root *at*, "to move oneself"). However suitable this root, to which the said learned man has, l. c., assigned a numerous family, may be for an appellation of "water," I nevertheless prefer assuming that the circumstance, that in forms like *ab-bhyas* the base separates itself less sharply from the termination than if the termination were preceded by a mute of a different organ, has given occasion for the change of the *p* into *d*.

this word is right ("Études," p. 167). In the Vêda dialect there are also simple adjectives of this kind with the accent on the suffix; *e.g.*, *tar-ás*, "quick," properly "hastening," contrasted with *táras*, "quickness;" *tavás*, "strong," properly, "grown," contrasted with *táv-as*, "strength;" *mahás*, "great," likewise, originally, "grown"*; *apás*, "acting" (as "warrior, sacrificer," see Benfey's Glossary to the S. V. s. v.), contrasted with *ápas*, "work;" *ayás*, "going, hastening, quick" (see Benfey l. c.). The latter lengthens the *a* of the suffix in the same way as *ushás*. *Yaś-ás*, "famed" (contrasted with *yáśas*, "glory"), has a passive signification, properly, "praised" (cf. Zend *â-yêsê*, "I praise, I glorify," see §. 28.).

934. To *A*) correspond Greek abstracts in ος, ε(σ)-ος†; *e.g.*, ψεῦδ-ος, μῆδ-ος, γῆθ-ος, λῆθ-ος (=Sanscrit *ráh-as*, see §. 933. *A*), κῆδ-ος, φλέγ-ος, (Vêd. *bhárg-as*, "lustre," for *bhráj-as*, root *bhráj*, "to shine," from *bhrâg*), ἕδ-ος ("the sitting")‡, πάθ-ος,
[G. Ed. p. 1376.] μάθ-ος, θάρσ-ος. A feminine base in ος, with a pervading *o*-sound, and lengthening of the same in the nominative, is αἰδ-ός, whence αἰδώ-ς, αἰδό(σ)-ος. As secondary suffix, also, ος, ες appears in Greek as a means of formation

---

* Cf. *mahát*, "great," from the same root, properly a present participle with the signification of the perfect participle, and with the anomaly that the strong cases lengthen the *a*, and thus exhibit *mahânt* for *mahant*.

† See §. 128. The difference in vowels between *os* and ε(σ)-ος, &c., probably rests on this, that in loading the base with the case-terminations, the language prefers the lighter substitute of the old *a* to the heavier, in remarkable agreement with the Old Sclavonic, where, *e.g.*, the Sanscrit *nábhas* and Greek νέφος are paralleled by the form небо *nebo*, but the genitive *nábhas-as*, νέφε(σ)-ος by the form небесе *nebes-e* (cf. the somewhat different view at §. 264.).

‡ The corresponding Sanscrit *sád-as* has, in common Sanscrit, assumed the signification "assembling," but occurs in the Vêdas also with that of "seat" (so Yajur-Vêda, 19. 59.). Regarding the Latin *sedê-s* (see p. 1352 G. ed. §. 924.).

FORMATION OF WORDS. 1335

of neuter abstracts, and occasionally with a vowel-increment, in compensation for the abbreviation of the adjective base words (cf. p. 396); hence, *e. g.*, γλεῦκ'-ος, from γλυκύ-ς, ἔρευθ'-ος, from ἐρυθρό-ς, μῆκ'-ος, from μακρό-ς. Perhaps, also, the Zend neuter abstracts ᚱᚢᚱᚨ *frathas̀*, "breadth," *baǹz--as̀*, "length," *mazas̀*,"greatness," ᚱᚢᚱᚨ *bĕrĕz-as̀*, "height,"* are of adjective descent, and, like the said Greek forms, have dropped the suffix of the base word before the formative of the abstract. Very remarkable is the almost literal agreement between ᚱᚢᚱᚨ *frathas̀* and the Greek πλάτος; *baǹz-as̀* corresponds to βάθ-ος, and radically to the Sanscrit *bahú* (probably from *badhú*), "much," and still more to the comparative बंहीयस् *báǹhíyas*, and superlative बंहिष्ठ *báǹhishtha*, which are, indeed, derived from *bahula*, but which may, with equal justness, be assigned to बहु *bahú*. The root is *baǹh*, "to grow." ᚱᚢᚱᚨ *maz-as̀*, "greatness," answers to μῆκ-ος, the κ of which, as also that of μακ-ρό-ς, is probably only a mutation of γ; and I have scarce a doubt that these two words belong to one and the same root with μέγας, which root is, in Sanscrit, *maǹh*, and signifies "to grow." The Vêdic sister word to ᚱᚢᚱᚨ *maz-as̀* and μῆκος is *máh-as*, which certainly signifies, not only "brightness" (see Benfey's Glossary), but also, and indeed primitively, "greatness ;" and I believe that this abstract proceeds not directly from the root, but, just like *mah-i-mán*, of equivalent signification, from *mahát*, or another adjective of the same root signifying "great." To the Zend *frathas̀*, [G. Ed. p. 1377.] "breadth," there may still be found in the Vêdas a corresponding *práth-as* of similar meaning, as derivative from *prithú*; and for *bĕrĕz-at* (strong, *bĕrĕz-ant*), "height," we actually find the corresponding Sanscrit sister word in the first member of the compound name *bṛíhas-páti* (in the common language, *vṛihas*), in as far as it signifies, as I be-

---

* See Burnouf, "Yaçna," Notes, pp. 12, 14, 99.

lieve it originally does, "lord of greatness." The Latin exhibits the Sanscrit neuter suffix *as* in four shapes, but principally in that of *us, er-is*.* The other forms are *us, or-is, ur, or-is*, and *ur, ur-is*, For the class of words under discussion (§. 933. *A.*), the Latin neuter suffix furnishes but a few remnants, obscured as to their root; viz. *rŏb-ur* (cf. *rŏb-us-tus*, see §. 827.), which, like the Vêdic *táv-as*, "strength," comes from a root which signifies "to grow"†; as *fœd-us*,‡ and *scel-us* (*sceles-tus*).§ In Latin, in case of the suffix under discussion as a formative of abstract substantives, the neuter is replaced by the masculine, and, indeed, with a lengthening of the vowel (*ôr*, from *ás*), which, however, in the nominative, through the influence of the final *r*, is again [G. Ed. p. 1378.] shortened. With respect to the vowel length of the true base word, compare the strong cases and the genitive plural of the above-mentioned (pp. 1373, 1375, G. ed.) forms *ushás* and *ay-ás* in the Vêda dialect; *e.g.*, the accusative singular *ush-ás-am, ay-ás-am*, with *flu--ôr-em, langu-ôr-em, rud-ôr-em, frem-ôr-em, trem-ôr-em, ang--ôr-em, pud-ôr-em, sap-ôr-em, od-ôr-em* (Greek root ὀδ), *fulg-ôre-m, sop-ôr-em, son-ôr-em, am-ôr-em*, &c. The *s* of the old nominatives like *clamôs* is, perhaps, not the original final consonant of the base, but the nominative sign before

---

* See §. 22. The *e* of the oblique cases, for *i*, which might be expected according to §. 6., owes its origin to the following *r* (cf. §. 710.).

† Sanscrit root *ruh*, "to grow," from *rudh*, and *ṛidh*, id., from *radh* or *ardh* (see §. 1.). With *ruh*, from *rudh*, compare the Irish *ruadh*, "strength, power, value," as adjective "strong, valiant;" see Glossarium Sanscr. a. 1847, and Ag. Benary, "Doctrine of Roman Sounds," p. 218. With reference to the Latin *b* for *dh* we must note the relation of *ruber* to the Sanscrit *rudhirám*, "blood," and Greek ἐ-ρυθρός.

‡ From *foidus*, from the root *fid*. With regard to the Guna, compare the Greek πέποιθα.

§ Cf. Sanscrit *chhalá-m* (see §. 14.), "guile, deceit," probably from *chhad*, "to cover," with *l* for *d* (see §. 17.).

FORMATION OF WORDS. 1337

which the base has dropped its final consonant (see §. 138.). This suffix forms, in Latin, abstracts from adjective bases also, hence, *e.g., amar'or, nigr'-or, alb'-or.*

935. The Gothic has added an *a* to the sibilant, which has become incapable of declension, and has weakened the preceding vowel to *i*. As in the uninflected nominative and accusative singular neuter the final *a* of the base is dropped, we obtain here the forms *hat-is,* " hate ;" *ag-is,* " fear" * ; *rim-is,* " rest" † ; *sig-is,* " victory ;" *riqv-is,* " gloom." ‡ Perhaps the *s* of *hulistr* (theme *hulistra*), [G. Ed. p. 1379.] is not, as has been conjectured above (see §. 818. p. 1113), a euphonic insertion, but *hulis* is a lost abstract with the suffix *is* and the suffix *tra* appended. Moreover, some neuter bases in *sla* appear to me to have abstracts in *is,* with *i* suppressed, as primitive bases for their foundation : I mean the forms *hun-s-l* (theme *hunsla*), " sacrifice," from *hun-is-l,* from a lost root *han* or *hun; svum-s-l,* " pond," as " place

---

* Root *ag,* whence *ôg,* "I feared," according to form a preterite. The Old High German *ekiso,* theme *ékison,* has exchanged the neuter with the masculine, and further added to the base an *n,* but preserved the old sibilant, in which it surpasses the suffix *ira,* which, in §. 241, is compared with the Sanscrit *as.*

† Sanscrit root *ram,* with prep. *á (á-ram),* "to rest," Lithuanian *rimstu,* "I rest," Lettish *rahms (=râms),* "tame, quiet, sedate." The Greek ἠρέμα, ἠρεμέω, &c., answer, in their η, to the Sanscrit compound *áram.* It is not improbable, that in the adverb ἠρέμας (before vowels) the suffix under discussion is contained in its original form. Moreover, the ες of the comparative ἠρεμέσ-τερος appears to me to belong to the suffix *as,* as σ, according to regular rule, has its etymologically established place before the suffixes τερο, ταто, and is dislodged in some places only by a mis-use, and driven where it does not belong.

‡ It has already been compared, in my Glossary, with the analogous Sanscrit *ráj-as.* This word, from the root *rañj* (*"adhærere, tingere"*), signifies, indeed, not "darkness," but "dust ;" but from the same root is derived, by another suffix, a term for night (*rajanî*), and *rajas* is contained in the compound *rajô-rasa,* "gloominess."

of swimming" (root, *svamm*, weakened to *svimm, svumm*). *Svart-is-l*, " blackness," presupposes a more simple abstract *svart-is*, which would correspond to the Greek secondary abstracts like βάθ-ος, and, irrespective of gender, to Latin like *nigr'-or, alb'-or*. More important appears to me the deduction, that most probably the Sanscrit suffix *as* has been preserved in Gothic in combination with another suffix assigned to abstracts, and, indeed, with the retention of the old *a*-sound. I believe, viz. that the Gothic masculine abstracts in *as-su-s*, as, *e.g.*, *drauhtin-as-su-s*, " military service" (*drauhtinô*, " I do military service "), *frauyin-as-su-s*, "lordship" (*frauyin-ô*, " I rule "), *leikin-as-su-s*, " healing" (*leikinô*, " I heal"), may be explained by assimilation from *as-tu-s*, as, *e.g.*, *vis-sa*, " I knew," from *vis-ta* for *vit-ta*, and, in Latin, *quas-sum*, from *quas-tum* for *quat-tum* (see §. 102.). Most of the formations of this kind are based on weak verbs in *in-ô*,* the analogy of which is followed, also, by *thiudin--as-su-s*, " government, dominion," though the base word [G. Ed. p. 1380.] *thiu-danô* has an *a* before the *n*, which, however, without reference to the verbs in *in-ô*, might have been weakened to *i* on account of the incumbrance of the heavy double suffix (cf. §. 6.). Irrespective of the newly-appended suffix *su*, from *tu*, *leikin'-as-sus* has the same relation to *leikinô*, with reference to the suppression of the *ô* of the verbal theme, that in Latin, *e.g.*, the abstracts *am'-or*, *clam'-or*, have to the verbal themes *amâ, clamâ*, where the *â* corresponds to the Gothic *ô* = Sanscrit अय *aya* (see §. 109.ᵃ· ₆.). Further, from adjective bases are derived, in Gothic, some abstracts in *as-su-s*, viz. *ibn'-as-sus*, " similarity," from *ibna*, nom. m. *ibns*, " like," and *vanin-as-sus*, " want." The latter, however, springs, not from the strong adjective bases *vana*, nom. m. *vans*, " wanting," but from the weak base *vanan*, the *a* being weakened to *i*, as in the genitive and dative *vanin-s*,

---

* See Grimm, II. 175. 321., and Gabelentz and Löbe, Grammar, p. 118.

FORMATION OF WORDS. 1339

vanin. From the preposition *ufar,* " over" (Sanscrit *upari*), comes *ufar-as-su-s,* "overflowing," a form remarkable as being the only one in which the abstract double suffix is not preceded by an *n* of the primitive base. In the more modern dialects the *n*, which belongs in Gothic to the base word, has, by an abuse, completely passed over into the derivative suffix, which hence begins universally with *n*, distinguishes the genders, and has changed the Gothic *n* of the second part of the double suffix into *a* or *î* (Grimm, II. 323). To this class belong, *e.g.*, the Old High German feminines *arauc-nissa,* or *-nissî,* " *manifestatio* " (our *Ereigniss,* or, more properly, *Eräugniss,* " occurrence"); *drî-nissa,* and *drî-nissî,* " *trinitas* " (Anglo-Saxon, *dhre-ness*); *milt-nissa,* " *misericordia* " (English, mild-ness); *ki-hôr-nussî,* " *auditus* ;" *peraht-nissî, beraht-nessî,* " *splendor* " (English, bright-ness); the neuters *got-nissi* (theme *nissya*), " *divinitas* ;" *fir-stant-nissi,* " *intellectus* " (our *verständniss,* " understanding"); *suaz-nissi,* " *dulcedo* " (English, " sweet-ness").

936. Some Old High German bases in [G. Ed. p. 1381.] *us-ta, us-ti,* or *os-ta, os-ti,* appear to contain a combination of two suffixes,* viz. *us* or *os* (= Sanscrit *as*), and *ta* or *ti*. The following are examples: *dion-us-ta,* nom. *dionust,* in Otfr. *thionost,* our *Dienst,* " service," in Old High German neuter; *ang-us-ti,* f. " anxiety," nom. *ang-us-t; ern-us-ta,* n. and *ern-us-ti,* f. " earnest," nom. *ern-us-t* (see Graff, I. 429.). *Ang-us-ti* is connected in its first suffix with the first of the Latin adjectives *ang-us-tu,* as also with that of the abstract *ang-or*. The Lithuanian, too, exhibits some abstracts with two suffixes combined, of which the first is connected with the *as* under discussion, and the latter with the *ti* discussed above; *e.g., gyw-as-ti-s,* m. " life," and *rim-as-ti-s,* m. " rest."†

---

* See Grimm, II. 368. and 371. β.

† Also the Lithuanian abstracts mentioned at p. 1192, G. ed., §. 844., are masculine, and have extended the suffix by an inorganic *a*, which is suppressed

The former, after withdrawal of the second suffix, answers to the base of the Sanscrit infinitive *jîv-ás-ê*, "in order to live;" the latter to the above-mentioned (§. 935.) Gothic *rim-is* (theme *rim-isa*), "rest." In *ed-esi-s*, "food" (theme *edesia*, see §. 135.), perhaps originally "the eating," and in *deg-esi-s*, "the month August," as "burning," I recognise the Sanscrit suffix *as* with the affix *ia*, which, in general, the Lithuanian loves to append to suffixes which originally terminate with a consonant. With reference to this I recall attention to the participles of the present and perfect (§. 787.).

937. To the Sanscrit appellatives mentioned in §. 933. under *B*), correspond some of their literatim analogous appellatives in Greek, as ἕλ-ος, ἕλε(σ)-ος (§. 128.) = Sanscrit *sára-s*, "pond, water," as "flowing;" μέν-ος = *mán-as*, "spirit," as "thinking;" φλέγ-ος = Vêdic abstract *bhárg-as*, "shining;"
[G. Ed. p. 1382.] ῥέ-ος = *srŏ-t-as*, "river" (see p. 1372, Note 2, G. ed., §. 933. *B*) Note); σκῦ-τ-ος, "skin," as "covering"*; στῆ-θ-ος, (see Curtius l. c., p. 20 and cf. εὐστα-θ-ής); ὄχ-ος (cf. Sanscrit *váh-as*, "driving, drawing"); ἔπ-ος, from Fέκ-ος = Sanscrit *vách-as*, from *vák-as*; τέκ-ος, γέν-ος. In Latin to this class belong, *e.g.*, *ol-us*, *ol-er-is*, from *ol-is-is*, "greens," as "growing;" *gen-us*, *fulg-ur*, *corp-us*, "body," as "made" (see p. 1069, Note †); *pec-us*, *pecor-is*, "beast," as "tied up" (Sanscrit *paśú-s*, root *paś*, from *pak*, "to bind"); *vell-us*, *op-us* (= Sanscrit *áp-as*, "work"). To the *u* arising from *a* of the uninflected cases corresponds accidentally the corruption which the Sanscrit suffix *as* has experienced in the form *us*, by which neuter appellatives are formed which, for the most part, accent the root (Uṇâdi, II. p.113). The following are examples: *chákṣh-us*, "an eye," as "seeing" (op-

---

suppressed in the nominative. In the genitive the words mentioned l. c. are *smerchio*, &c.

* Latin *cu-ti-s*, Sanscrit root *sku*, "to cover," see Benf., Gr. Root-Lex., p. 611; and cf., with respect to the inserted τ, the abstract χῆ-τ-ος.

posed to the Vêdic *cháksh-as*); *yáj-us*, "sacrifice;" *dhán-us*, (also masc.) "bow," as "slaying" (root *han*, from *dhan*, "to slay," *ni-dhána*, "death"); *tánus*, "body," as "extended;" *jánus*, "birth,"* in the Vêdic dual (*jánushí*), "the two worlds," as "created" (S. V. II. 6. 2. 17. 3.), in admirable agreement with the Latin *genus* (Greek γένος) of cognate formation. The Vêdic adjective *jay-ús*, "conquering," irrespective of the weakening of the vowel, corresponds to the above-quoted (§. 933. under C) adjectives like *tarás*, "quick." I regard, too, the suffix *is*, which forms some abstracts and appellatives, for the most part oxytone, as a weakening of *as*. Examples are, *sóch-ís*, n. "lustre" (root *such*); *arch-ís*, f. id.; *hav-ís*, n. "clarified sacrificial butter" (root *hu*, "to sacrifice"); *chhad-ís* (optionally masc.), "roof" (root *chad*, "to cover"); *jyót-is*, n. "sheen, [G. Ed. p. 1383.] star" (root *jyut*, "to shine"). Observe the accidental coincidence, as respects the weakening of the vowel, with the Gothic suffix *isa* from *agis*, "fear," &c. (§. 935.). Perhaps the Latin *cinis*, *cin-er-is*, from *cin-is-is*, belongs, in respect of its suffix, to this class, in which case its original signification would be "the glowing ashes," and it would be radically akin to कन् *kan*, "to shine."

938. To the Vêdic formations mentioned in §. 933. under C), like -*chákshas*, "seeing," -*mánas*, "thinking," at the end of compounds, correspond, irrespective of their accentuation, the numerous class of Greek bases like -δερκές (ἀδερκές, ὀξυδερκές), -αγές (εὐαγές), -δεχές (πανδεχές), -λαβές (εὐλαβές, μεσολαβές), and with a passive signification, *e.g.*, -βαφές (πολυβαφές, &c.), -δρυφές (ἀμφιδρυφές). In Greek, as well as in Sanscrit, we must distinguish from this class of words the possessive compounds, the last member of which is, in its simple state, a neuter substantive base in अस् *as*, ες; as, *e.g.*,

---

* In the Vêda dialect, in this meaning, also masculine, see Weber, V. S., Sp. II. 74.

सुमनस् *sumánas*, "having a good spirit, well-intentioned" = Greek εὐμενές, nom. m. f. *sumánás*, εὐμενής (see §. 146.). To the simple oxytone adjectives mentioned in §. 933. *C*) as *tarás*, nom. m. f. *tarás*, "hastening, quick," corresponds in Greek ψευδές, ψευδής, which stands to the corresponding abstract ψεῦδος, in a similar relation as regards accent to that occupied by the *tarás* mentioned above to *táras*, "quickness."

939. The suffixes *ra* and *la*, fem. *rá, lá*, I consider, on account of the very common interchange between *r* and *l* (see §. 20.), as originally one; and I regard as class-vowels, or vowels of conjunction,* the vowels which precede these liquids, as also the mutes *k*, *t*, and *th*, in several [G. Ed. p. 1384.] suffixes given by the Indian Grammarians, *ara, ura, êra, ôra, ala, ila, ula, aka, âka, ika, uka, atra, itra*,† *utra, athu*. With *ra, la, a-la, i-la, u-la, i-ra, u-ra*, are formed base words like *díp-rá*, "shining," *śubh-rá*, "dazzling, white;" *bhád-ra*, "happy, good;" *chand-rá*, m. "moon," as "giving light‡; *śuk-la*, "white" (Vêd. *śuk-rá*, "giving light, shining") (root *śuch*, from *śuk*, "to shine"); *chap-a-lá*, "tremulous, shaking" (root *champ*, "to move"); *tar-a-lá*, "shaking" (root *tar*, *trí*, "to overstep," "to move oneself"); *mud-i-rá*, m. "voluptuary," *chhid-i-rá*, m. "axe, sword" (root *chhid*, "to cleave"); *an-i-lá*, m. "wind" (*an*, "to breathe," cf. Irish *anal*, "breath"); *path-i-lá*, m.

---

* The *ê* and *ô* of a small number of rare words, *e.g.*, *pat-é-ra*, "moving itself" (as subst. masc. *pat-é-ra-s*, "bird"), *sáh-ô-ra*, "good" (root *sah*, "to endure"), are perhaps the Gunas of the vowels *i* and *u*, which are often found inserted as copulatives.

† Regarding *a-tra, i-tra*, see p. 1108. The *u* of *var-ú-tra*, "upper garment," as "covering," is either only a weakening of the *a* of *a-tra*, or the character of the 8th class, which is merely an abbreviation of the syllable *nu* of the 5th, to which *var, vri*, belongs. It is certain that the *v* of the radically and formally cognate Greek ἔλυ-τρο-ν belongs to the verbal theme. Cf. the Sanscrit root *val*, Cl. 1., "to cover."

‡ Cf. Latin *candeo, candê-la*, the latter also as respects the suffix.

"traveller" *panth*, "to go"); *vid-u-rá*, "knowing, wise;" *bhid-u-rá*, m. "thunderbolt" (*bhid*, "to cleave"); *harsh-u-lá*, m. "lover, antelope" (*harsh, hrish*, "to rejoice").

940. To this class of words belong in Zend 𐬌𐬎𐬭𐬀 *suw-ra*, "shining,"=सुभ्र *subh-rá* (see §. 45.); 𐬯𐬎𐬗𐬭𐬀 *suc-ra*, "shining, clear"=Vêd. *suk-rá*; 𐬘𐬀𐬟𐬭𐬀 *jafra*, "mouth," as "speaking" (cf. जफ्नु *janfnu*, §. 61.); 𐬯𐬭𐬀 *sû-ra*, "strong" (San. *sû-rá*, "hero," root *svi*, contracted *su*, "to grow"). In Greek this class of words is more numerous than in Sanscrit. To adjectives like *díp-rá-s*, correspond, [G. Ed. p. 1385.] as regards accent also, such as λαμπ-ρό-ς, λιβ-ρό-ς, λυγ-ρό-ς, νεκ-ρό-ς (cf. νέκυς, Latin *nec-s*, Sanscrit *nas*, "to be ruined"), ψυχ-ρό-ς, ψηχ-ρό-ς, θεω-ρό-ς. In Latin to this class belong: *gna-rus, ple-ru-s, pu-ru-s* (Sanscrit *pú*, "to purify"); *ca-ru-s* (San. *kam*, "to love"); *pig-er*, theme *pig-ru*; *in-teg-er*, theme *integ-ru*. In the Gothic a remnant of this class of words is found in the masculine base *lig-ra*, nom. *lig-r'-s*, "couch." The *a* of the Old High German neuter theme *lëgar-a* is probably a later insertion (cf. p. 1112), but if not, the suffix belongs to the Sanscrit *as* (see §. 933.), whither, most probably, *dem-ar* (likewise neuter), "twilight," compared with the Sanscrit *támas*, "gloom," is to be referred. To Sanscrit adjectives like *díp-rá*, "giving light," correspond the bases *bait-ra*, "bitter," properly, "biting," and *fag-ra*, "suitable, good" (cf. *fullafahyan*, "to satisfy, to serve"). I refer the Greek suffix λο, as originally identical with ρο, rather to the Sanscrit *ra* than to *la*, and therefore to the oxytones mentioned above (§. 939.), *díp-rá-s, subh-rá-s*, I refer the Greek δει-λό-ς, αὐ-λό-ς, βη-λό-ς, δα-λό-ς, στρεβ-λό-ς, ἔκπαγ-λο-ς, σιγη-λό-ς, φειδω-λό-ς.* In Latin to this class belongs *sel-la*, from *sed-la* (=Greek ἕδ-ρα), with a passive signification; so Gothic *sit-la*, m., nom. *sitl's*, "rest," as "place

---

* The η and ω of σιγη-λό-ς, φειδω-λό-ς, belong to the verbal theme (cf. σιγή-σω), and for the latter we may presuppose a verb φειδόω.

where sitting takes place," *fair-veit-la*, n. (nom. acc. *fair-veit-l*) "stage." The Old High German, in order to avoid the harshness of two final consonants coming together, inserts an *a* in the nominative and accusative singular, which theme has often made its way into the oblique cases (cf. p. 1112), and often assumes the weaker form of *u, i, e*. To this class belong, *e.g.*, the masculines *sez-a-l* or *sezz-a-l*, "a chair," [G. Ed. p. 1386.] *sat-a-l*, "a saddle," also *sat-u-l, sat-i-l, sat-e-l; huot-i-l*, "warder," *mûr-huot-i-la*, "*custodes murorum*" (Graff, IV. 803.); *fôzkengel*, "foot-traveller" (Grimm, II. 109., Graff, IV. 104.); *bit-e-l*, "*procus*," *pit-al-a*, "*proci, nuptiarum petitores*" (Graff, III. 56.); *stein-bruk-i-l*, "stone breaker;" *sluoz-i-l*, "key," as "locking," accusative plural *sluoz-i-la*; *stôz-i-l*, "pestle." The following are examples of Old High German adjectives of this order of formation (Grimm, II. 102.): *scad-a-l*, "*noxius*," *slâf-a-l*, "*somnulentus*, *sprunk-a-l*, "*exultans*," *suik-a-l*, "*taciturnus*."

941. To the Sanscrit formations like *chap-a-lá-s, tar-a--lá-s*, "trembling" (see §. 939.), correspond, in Lithuanian, *dang-a-la-s*, "covering" (*dengiu*, "I cover"); *draug-a-la-s*, "the companion," masc., *draug-a-la*, fem. (*drauga*, "I have communion with another"); and, with passive signification, *myz-a-lai*, (pl.) "urine" (*myzù*, "*mingo*"), *wĕm-a-laí*, (pl.) "the discharged;" in Greek, forms with α inserted, or with ε which has proceeded therefrom, as, τροχ-α-λό-ς, τραπ-ε-λό-ς, στυφ-ε-λό-ς, αἴθ-α-λο-ς, διδάσκ-α-λο-ς, μεγ-α-λο (Gothic *mik-i--la*, nom. *mik-i-l'-s*, Sanscrit root, *mah*, "to grow"), εἴκ-ε-λο-ς, and the reduplicated κεκρύφ-ε-λο-ς, δυςπέμφ-ε-λο-ς, εὐπέμπ-ε-λο-ς. To *vid-u-rá-s*, "knowing," correspond φλεγ-υ-ρό-ς, ἐχ-υ-ρό-ς; to forms like *harsh-u-lá-s*, "lover, antelope," properly, "rejoicing," correspond, irrespective of accentuation, εἴδ-υ-λο-ς (cf. *vid-u-rá-s*), καμπ-ύ-λο-ς. The weakening, however, of the vowel of conjunction *a* to *ŭ*, appears to have been arrived at by the two languages independently of each other; so the Latin, in analogous formatives like *trem-u-*

FORMATION OF WORDS. 1345

-lu-s, ger-u-lu-s, strid-u-lu-s, fig-u-lu-s, cing-u-lu-m, vinc-u-lu-m, spec-u-lu-m, teg-u-lu-m, teg-u-la, reg-u-la, mus-cip-u-la, am-ic--u-lu-m, where the *l* may have had its influence in producing *u* from *a*. As from *a-la* in Sanscrit we may deduce *a-ra*, we may here call attention to Greek forms like στιβ-α-ρό-ς, φαν-ε-ρό-ς, λακ-ε-ρό-ς, and to Latin like [G. Ed. p. 1387.] *ten-e-r, gen-e-r* (theme *ten-e-ru, gen-e-ru*), if the *e* of the latter does not, on account of the *r* following, stand for *i*. To the form इल *i-la* (*an-i-lá-s*, "wind," as "blowing") belongs, perhaps, the Latin *i-li*, in adjectives like *ag-i-li-s, frag-i-li-s, fac-i-li-s doc-i-li-s* (see §. 419. sub. f.), for which, if the connection be justly assumed, we should have expected *ag-i--lu-s*, &c. I would draw attention to forms like *imberbis, inermis*, for the more organic *imberbu-s, inermu-s* (see §. 6.).

942. As secondary suffixes, र *ra*, ल *la* (*i-ra, i-la, ír-a, í-la*) form a small number of oxytone adjectives; as, *e. g.*, *aśma-rá*, "stony," from *áśman*, "stone;" *madhu-rá*, "sweet," properly, "gifted with honey," from *mádhu*, "honey" (cf μέθυ); *śrí-lá*, "fortunate," Zend ⁕⁕⁕⁕ *śrí-ra*, from *śri*, "luck;" *pánśu-lá*, "dusty," from *pánśu*, "dust;" *phêna-lá*, "foaming," from *phêna*, "foam;" *mêdh'-i-rá, mêdh'-i-lá*, "intelligent," from *mêdhâ*, "understanding."* In Greek this secondary formation also of words is more numerously represented than in Sanscrit. I refer the vowel which precedes the ρ in all cases to the base word, and take the ε of words like φθονε-ρό-ς, νοσε-ρό-ς, κρυε-ρό-ς, νοε-ρό-ς, φοβε-ρό-ς, δολε-ρό-ς, σκιε-ρό-ς, βλαβε-ρό-ς, according to the measure of the termination of

---

* Perhaps the words would be better divided thus, *mêdhi-rá, mêdhi-lá*; and we might recognise in the *i* the weakening of the *a* of the primitive base, in the same way as, in Latin, the final vowels of the primitive bases are weakened to *i* before various derivative suffixes; *e.g.*, cari-tas, amari--tudo. The *u* of words like *danturá*, "having a projecting tooth," is probably likewise only a weakening of the final vowel of the base word (*dánta*, "tooth"), a weakening which the Gothic *tunthu-s* also has undergone in its simple state.

4 s

the base word, as the thinning or shortening of ο, α, or η.*

[G. Ed. p. 1388.] Conversely, lengthenings of ο to η (= ω, see §. 4.) also occur; hence, *e.g.*, νοση-ρό-ς, μοχθη-ρό-ς (cf. μοχθή--εις), οἰνη-ρό-ς. The old α, of which ο, ε, are the most common corruptions, has maintained itself in μυσα-ρό-ς (later μυσε--ρό-ς), λιπα-ρό-ς, σθενα-ρό-ς—the latter from the base σθένος, σθένες, the suffix of which corresponds to the Sanscrit *as* (see §. 934.)—and in λαμυ-ρό-ς. ἀργυ-ρό-ς, has been weakened to υ.† A vowel of conjunction is found in αἱματ-η-ρό-ς, ὑδρ-η--ρό-ς. To *pâṅsu-lá-s,* "dusty," *phêna-lá-s,* "foamy," correspond forms like ῥιγη-λό-ς (scarcely from ῥιγέω, but from ῥῖγος, as above σθενα-ρό-ς from σθένος), χαμα-λό-ς, στωμύ-λο-ς (for στωμα-λο-ς). I would now, too, in departure from §. 419., rather refer to this class those Latin formations in *li*, which spring from substantives. Consequently the *â* after bases ending in a consonant in forms like *corn-â-lis, augur-â-li-s,* &c., would be to be regarded as a vowel of conjunction equally with the Greek η of the αἱματ-η-ρό-ς, ὑδρ-η-ρό-ς, just mentioned. The vowel relation of *li* to ऌ *la,* λο, is the same as, *e.g.*, in the genitive singular that of *ped-is* to *pad-ás,* ποδ-ός.

943. To the Sanscrit primary suffix *ri*, which occurs only in a few words of rare use, *e.g.*, in *áṅh-ri-s,* and *áṅgh--ri-s,* masc. "foot," as "going" (root *aṅh* and *aṅgh,* "to go"), corresponds the Greek ρι of ἴδ-ρι-ς, ἴδ-ρι, for which, in Sanscrit, *víd-ri-s, -ri,* would be expected. The Latin has prefixed to the suffix *ri* a vowel of conjunction in *cel-e-r,* theme *cel-e-ri,* the *i* of which, together with the case-sign, has been suppressed in the nominative masculine. The obsolete root *cel* (*ex-cello, præ-cello*) corresponds to the Greek κελ (κέλλω), whence κέλης, "runner," and to the Sanscrit *śal* (from *kal*), "to go, to run" (as yet not found as a verb).

---

* Cf. p. 1367, Note, G. ed.

† Cf. νύξ, contrasted with the Sanscrit *naktam* (adv. "by night") and Latin *nox*, and ὄ-νυξ with the Sanscrit *nakhá*.

FORMATION OF WORDS. 1347

To this class, moreover, belong, in Latin, [G. Ed. p. 1389.] *put-e-r*, theme *put-ri*, and *ac-er**, theme *ac-ri*, which limit the inorganic *e* to the nominative masculine, where it cannot be dispensed with after the *i* of the base is dropped. The cause of the retention of the inserted *e* throughout the word *cel-e-r* is the awkwardness of the combination *lr*.

944. Of the words in Sanscrit formed with the suffix *ru*, (they are collectively but few) there are only two in common use, viz. the adjective *bhí-rú-s*, " fearing, fearful," fem. likewise *bhí-rú-s*, or *bhí-rǘ-s*, neut. *bhí-rú*, and the neuter substantive *áś-ru*, " a tear," which I look upon as a mutilated form of *dáś-ru*, and derive from *danś*, from *dank*, " to bite " (Greek δακ). In Greek, δάκ-ρυ corresponds to it, and in Gothic, as far as the root is concerned, the masculine *tag-r̃-s*, theme *tag-ra* = Sanscrit *áś-ra*, neut., also " a tear." For भीरु *bhí-rú*, " fearful," there exists also the form *bhí-lú*, to which answers, in respect of its suffix, the Gothic *ag-lu-s*, " heavy, cumbersome." To *bhí-rú-s*, " fearing, fearful," correspond the Lithuanian adjectives *byau-rù-s*, " ugly "(cf.*biyau*, "I fear," *bai-mẽ*, " fear "); *bud-rù-s*, " watchful " (*bundu*, " I watch," Sanscrit *budh*, " to know," caus. " to wake "); *ĕd-rù-s*, " gluttonous;" and some others from obsolete roots.

945. The Sanscrit suffix *va*, fem. *vá*, forms appellatives, which express the agent, and also a few adjectives; most of them with the accent on the radical syllable. The most current word of this class is *áś-va-s*, " horse," as " runner,"† which has been widely diffused over the [G. Ed. p. 1390.]

---

* The original meaning of *acer* appears to be " penetrating;" and, like *ac-u-s*, it seems to belong to the Sanscrit root *aś*, from *ak* (see §. 925, p. 1357, G. ed., Note †). Cf. the Sanscrit *aś-ri-s*, fem., " the sharpness of a sword," which I would rather derive from *aś*, with the suffix *ri*, than, with the Indian Grammarians, from *śri*, " to go," with the prefix *á* shortened.

† Cf. the radically cognate *áś-ú*, " quick," see p. 1355 G. ed.

4 s 2

cognate languages too: Latin *equu-s*, Lithuanian *ász-wa*, "a mare," Greek ἵππο-ς, from ἵκκο-ς (by assimilation from ἴκ-Ϝο-ς), Old Saxon *ehu*, in the compound *ehu-scalc*, "*servus equarius*," * Zend ᴧᴏᴊᴊᴧ *aś-pa* (see §. 50.). The following are other examples in Sanscrit of extremely rare use: *khát-vâ*, f. "bed" (root *khaṭṭ*, "to cover"); *pád-va-s*, "car," as "going;" *prúsh-va-s*, "sun," as "burning." We find an example of an adjective in *rísh-va*, "affronting," as also in the oxytone *pak-vá*, with a passive signification, "cooked," "ripe." In Gothic the adjective base *las-i-va*, nom. *las-i-v'-s*, "weak," from an obsolete root, appears to belong to this class of words. In Latin, *v* must, after consonants, except *r*, *l*, and *q* (*qu* = *cv*), become *u*; therefore *uu* = व *va* in adjectives like *de-cid-uu-s*, *oc-cid-uu-s*, *re-sid-uu-s*, *vac-uu-s*, *noc-uu-s*, *con-tig-uu-s*, *as-sid-uu-s*. On the other hand, *de-cli-vu-s*, *tor-vu-s*, *pro-ter-vu-s*, *al-vu-s* (properly, "the nourishing"). An *i* as vowel of conjunction is found in *cad-í-vu-s*, *recid-í-vu-s*, *vac-í-vu-s*, *noc-í-vu-s*. To पक्व *pak-vá-s*, "cooked," "ripe," correspond, in respect to their passive signification, *e.g.*, *per-spic-uu-s*, *in-gen-uu-s*, *pro-misc-uu-s*. In Greek the suffix ευ, in which I formerly imagined I recognised a Guna form of the suffix *v*, may be explained by transposition from *va*, Ϝo, with the thinning of the *o* to ε; thus, *e,g.*, δρομεύς, γραφεύς, instead of the impossible δρομ-Ϝό-ς, γραφ-Ϝό-ς; and in the secondary formation, *e.g.*, ἱππεύς, properly, "gifted with horses," from ἱππ-Ϝό-ς. The Greek ευ might also be deduced from the Sanscrit *va*, regarding *v* as the contraction of *va*; as, *e.g.*, in ὕπνος = *svápna-s*, and the ε as the vowel of conjunction, whether it stand for α or for ι. In the latter case, δρομ-ε-ύς would answer to the above-mentioned (p. 1390 G. ed.) Gothic [G. Ed. p. 1391.] base *las-i-va*, and to the Lithuanian for-

---

* See Schmeller, "*Glossarium Saxonico-Latinum.*" The genitive would be *eh-ua-s* or *eh-ue-s*; so that the suffix has been retained very correctly in this word.

FORMATION OF WORDS. 1349

mations like *stêg-i-u-s*, "thatcher;" *źindź-i-u-s*,* " who sucks much and long" (*źindu*, " I suck"); *péch-i-u-s*, "baker's oven"; *czisch-i-u-s*, "purgatory" (*chist-iu*, " I purify").† For this class of words, and the Greek in ευ, there is, however, another source in Sanscrit to which we may betake ourselves for their explanation. I mean the suffix *yu*, which, like the Greek ευ, has the accent, and forms a small number of words (see Böhtlingk's Unâdi Affixes, p. 32), among which are *tas-yú-s*, "thief"‡; *jan-yú-s*, " a living creature," as "producing" or "begotten" (cf. *jan-tú-s*, id.); *śundh-yú-s*, "fire," as "purifying." It also forms some abstracts, as, *bhuj-yú-s*, " the eating;" *man-yú-s*, " hate" (Zend *main-yu-s*, "spirit," as "thinking"); and, with *t* inserted, *mri-t-yú*, m. f. n. "death." To this would correspond in Lithuanian *skyr-iu-s*, " separation" (*shirru*, " I separate"). In Gothic, perhaps *drun-yu-s*, "clang," belongs to this class.§

946. As regards the origin of the suffix व *va*, I believe I recognise in it a pronominal base, which occurs in the enclitic *vat*, " as" (according to form a nominative and accusative neuter, see §. 155.), as also in *vâ*, " or," " as," and, besides these, only in combination with other demonstrative bases preceding, *inter alia*, in the Zend *ava*, " this " (see §. 377.). Perhaps, also, the reflexive base *sva* (§. 341.), on which the old Persian *huva*, " he" (euphonic for *hva*), is based, is nothing but the combination of *sa* with [G. Ed. p. 1392.] *va*, the final vowel of the former being suppressed, as in *s-ya*, from *sa-ya*, " this " (§. 353.).

947. The suffix *van* forms, *a*) adjectives with the signification of the participle present, which occur only at the

---

* *Dź* for *d*, on account of the *i* following.

† Pott, too (E. I., II. p. 487), notices a possible relationship between the Greek suffix ευ and the Lithuanian *iu*.

‡ The root *tas*, " to take up," which has not yet been met with as a verb, here probably signifies " to take."

§ Cf. the Sanscrit *dhvan*, " to sound," and see §. 20.

end of compounds, especially in the Vêda dialect; *e.g.,* *suta-pá-van,* "drinking the Sôma;" *vája-dá-van,* "giving food." *b*) Nouns of agency, like *ṛík-van,* "extoller;" *yáj--van,* "sacrificer." *c*) Appellatives, *e.g., rúh-van,* "tree," as "growing;" *śák-van,* "elephant," as "powerful, strong." The Zend furnishes a remarkable word of this class, viz. ᚠᚢᚱᚲᚨᚾ *zar-van,* "time," in which I recognise a word radically akin to the Sanscrit *har-i-mán,* which signifies "time," as "carrying away, destroying" (see §. 795.). The Greek χρόνο-ς* is referable, in my opinion, with equal facility, to the Sanscrit root *har, hṛi,* with which, in Greek, obsolete root, χείρ, "the hand," as "taking," is also most probably connected. The omission of the radical vowel in χρόνος, if we refer the *o* to the suffix, can occasion no doubt; while the suffix *ovo* admits of ready comparison with the Sanscrit-Zend *van.* With respect to the necessary dropping of the digamma, compare the relation of the suffix εντ to the Sancrit *vant;* and with reference to the vowel added to the final consonant of the suffix, the relation of the Latin *lentu* (with *lent*) to the same suffix (see §. 20.).

948. The Sanscrit suffix *nu* (see §. 851.) forms oxytone adjectives and substantives; *e.g., gṛidh-nú-s,* "wistful, eager;" *tras-nú-s,* "trembling, fearing;" *dhṛish-nú-s,* "venturing, bold" (*ṇ,* on account of the preceding *sh*); *bhâ-nú-s,* "the sun, as "giving light;" *dhê-nú-s,* f. "milch-cow," as "giving [G. Ed. p. 1393.] to drink" (root *dhê,* "to drink," with causal signification); *sû-nú-s,* "son," as "born." So, in Zend, ᚠᚢᚱᚲᚨᚾ *taf-nu-s,* "burning" (see §. 40.); ᚠᚢᚱᚲᚨᚾ *raś-nu-s,* "straightforward, true"†; ᚠᚢᚱᚲᚨᚾ *bareśh-nu-s,* "high, great," as substantive, "summit"‡; *janf-nu-s,* "mouth," as

---

* Cf. Burnouf, "Études," p. 197.

† Root ᚱᚨᛉ *raz*=Sanscrit *ṛij* (from *raj*), whence *ṛijú,* "direct," see Burnouf, "Yaçna," p. 195.

Bĕrĕz=San. *vṛih,* Vêd. *bṛih,* "to grow," see Burnouf, "Études,"p. 194.

FORMATION OF WORDS. 1351

"speaking" (see §. 61.); in Lithuanian, mostly from obsolete roots, *drung-nù-s* (also *drung-na-s*), "lukewarm;" *gad-nù-s*, "fit;" *mac-nù-s*, "powerful" (cf. *maci-s*, "might," Gothic *mah-ts*, Sanscrit *mańh, mah*, "to grow," Latin *mag-nus*); *szau--nù-s*, "able, doughty" (cf. Sanscrit *śáv-as*, "strength," *śû-ra*, "a hero" (from *śu* from *śvi*, " to grow"); *sû-nù-s*, "son" = Sanscrit *sû-nù-s* (सु *sû*, "to bear"). In Greek, compare λιγ-νύ-ς, which I have already elsewhere referred to the Sanscrit root *dah* (infin. *dág-dhum*, "to burn," to which the Latin *lig-num* also belongs (see p. 1179 G. ed.). As feminine, it answers to the Sanscrit *dhê-nù-s* and the Latin *ma-nu-s*, in so far as the latter, together with *mu-nu-s*, belongs to the Sanscrit root *mâ* (see p. 1372 G. ed., Note**). And θρῆ-νυ-ς, too, in spite of the difference of accent, belongs to this class.

949. The suffix *snu* (euphonic *shṇu*) given by the Indian grammarians appears to me essentially identical with *nu*, and I regard the sibilant as an extension of the root, and, in some cases, as an affix to the vowel of conjunction *i*. Compare the relation of *bhás*, "to shine," *dás*, "to give," *más*, "to measure," to the more simple, more current, and, in the cognate languages, more diffused roots, *bhâ, dâ, mâ*, and that of *dhiksh, dhuksh*, "to kindle," to *dah*, "to burn." Similar is the relation of the adjectives *glâ-s-nú-s*, "withering," *ji-sh-nú-s*, "conquering," *bhû-sh-ṇu-s*, or *bhav-ish-ṇú-s*, "being." Hereto corresponds the Lithua- [G. Ed. p. 1394.] nian *dús-nù-s*, "giving" (*dů-mi*, "I give").

950. There is a weakened form *mi* of the suffix म *ma* discussed in §. 805.: it forms oxytone appellatives; *e.g.*, *bhû-mí-s*, fem. "earth," as "being" (Latin *hu-mu-s*, cf. p. 1077); *úr-mí-s*, m. f. "wave"*; *dal-mí-s*, m. "Indra's thunderbolt," as "cleaving;" *raś-mí-s*, m. "beam of light,

---

* Either from *ar, ṛi*, "to go," with *û* for *a* (see Unâdi, IV. 45.), or from *var, vṛi*, "to cover," with the contraction of *va* to *û*.

bridle."* Under this class of words is to be reckoned the Gothic *hai-m(i)-s*, f. (theme *hai-mi*), "village," from the obsolete root *hi* with Guṇa = Sanscrit *śi*́, from *kí*, "to lie, to sleep;" the plural, *hai-mós*, belongs to a base *haimô*.†

951. The suffix क ka (*a-ka, â-ka, i-ka, u-ka, û-ka,* see §. 939.) I regard as identical with the interrogative base *ka*, which, however, as suffix, must be taken in a demonstrative or relative sense, as indeed its representative also in New Persian and Latin has both a relative and interrogative meaning. In direct combination with the root, *ka* is not of frequent occurrence in Sanscrit. The most current word of this kind of formation is *śush-ká-s*, "dry," the Latin sister form of which *siccu-s* has probably arisen by assimilation and weakening of the *u* to *i* from *sus-cu-s*. That the *ś* of the Sanscrit root, for which, in Latin, *c* were to be expected, has arisen from the dental स *s*, and not from *k*, is proved [G. Ed. p. 1395.] by the Zend ۦۮ۠ۮ۬ۮ۫ۦ *hush-ka*, "dry." The χ *ch* of the Sclavonic ϲογχъ *súch'*, "dry," is based on the Sanscrit *sh* of the root (see §. 255. m.). The Lithuanian form of this adjective is *saus-a-s*. With *a-ka, â-ka, i-ka, u-ka,* are formed adjectives, and nouns of agency or appellatives, which accent the root; *e.g., nárt-a-ka-s,* "dancer," fem. *nárt-a-kí,* "female dancer;" *náy-a-ka-s,* "guide" (root *ní* with the Vṛiddhi); *khán-a-ka,* "digging," fem. *-ká; jálp-â-ka,* "loquacious," fem. *kí* (Am. Ko., III. 36.); *khán-ika-s,* "digger;" *mush-i-ka-s,* "mouse," as "stealing" root *mush*); *kâm-u-ka,* "longing;" *ghát-u-ka,* "destroying" (root *han,* "to slay," causal *ghátáy*). *Ú-ka* forms paroxytone adjectives from frequentatives and *jágar, -gri,* "to watch,"

---

* Akin, in the first signification perhaps, to the roots *arch, ruch* (from *ark, ruk,* as *raś* from *rak*), "to shine," or to *las,* "to shine." There is no root *raś*.

† Regarding the European cognates of the Gothic word, see Glossarium Sanscr., a. 1847, p. 350.

thus only from reduplicated roots, which, as it appears, support their heavy build by a long vowel; hence, *e.g.*, *vávad-ú-ka*, "loquacious," *jágar-ú-ka*, "watchful." Hereto correspond, irrespective of the reduplication, in Latin, *cad-ú-cu-s* and *mand-ú-cu-s*. *Fid-ú-cu-s*, presupposes a primitive *fid-ú-cu-s* or *fid-ú-c-s*. As *ú-ka*, *ú-cu*, is only a lengthening of *uka*, *ucu*, so perhaps, the Latin, *í-cu* of *am-í-cu-s*, *pud-í-cu-s*, is a lengthening of the Sanscrit *i-ka*, while *med-i-cu-s*, *vom-i-cu-s*, subs. *vom-i-ca*, *pert-i-ca* (if it comes from *partio*), have preserved the original shortness*. The bases *vert-i-c*, *vort-i-c*, *pend-i-c*, *append-i-c*, *pŏd-i-c* (from *pédo*), have lost the final vowel of the suffix. Under आक *â-ka*, is to be ranked the Latin *â-c*, with the final vowel suppressed in bases like *ed-â-c*, *vor-â-c*, *fall-â-c*, *ten-â-c*, *retin-â-c*, *sequ-â-c*, *loqu-â-c* (as above *jálp-â-ka*, "loquacious"); so too *ô-c*—as *ô = â*, see §§. 3., 4.—in *cel-ô-c*, *vel-ô-c* (for *vol-ô-c*), *fer-ô-c*. In Greek, φύλ-ακο-ς from a lost root (φυλάσσω springs from φυλακ), corresponds as exactly [G. Ed. p. 1396.] as possible to the Sanscrit formations like *nárt-a-ka-s*, "a dancer," and φέν-ᾱκ-ς, for φεν-ᾱκο-ς (cf. φενάκη), to such as *jálp-âka-s*, "loquacious, chatterer," and, in Latin, such as *loqu-âc-s*. The base κήρ-ῡκ for κηρ-ῡκο, likewise from an obsolete root, corresponds to the Sanscrit bases in *úka*, and Latin in *ú-cu*. To the above mentioned feminine *nárt-akí*, "dancer" (also nom.), corresponds, in point of formation, the Greek γυν-αικ, in which I recognise a transposition of γυνακι (see §. 119.); for which, in Sanscrit, *jánakí*, as "bearing children," would be to be expected, as feminine to the actually existing *ján-aka-s*, "father," as "begetter."—The Sanscrit formations like *khán-i-ka-s*, "digger," are most truly represented in Lithuanian, of all the European members of our family languages, by nouns of agency like *deg-i-ka-s*, "incendiary" (*degu*=Sanscrit *dáh-â-mi*, "I burn");

---

* See Düntzer, "The Doctrine of the Formation of Latin Words," p. 37.

leid-i-kha-s, "wood-floater*" (*léid-mi*, "I float wood");
kul-i-kha-s, "thresher" (*kullù*, "I thresh, pret. *kulau*). The
Gothic places as parallel to the Sanscrit *a-ka*, of *khán-a-ka*,
"digging," the suffix *a-ga*† in *grêd-a-ga*; n. m. *grêd-a-g'-s*,
"hungry," properly, "desiring" (Sanscrit root *gridh*) from
gradh, "to crave."

952. It is probable that the *n* of the forms in *ng* (theme
nga) which occurs in all the German languages, with the
exception of Gothic, with a vowel preceding (*i* or *u*), is an
unessential insertion, just as, according to §. 56.ª, in Zend
forms like *mananha*, for *manaha* = Sanscrit *manasâ*. If this
be the case, we may compare Old High German forms like
[G. Ed. p. 1397.] *kun-ing*, "king" (also *kun-ig*), theme *kun-*
-inga, with Sanscrit formations in *a-ka* (*nárt-aka-s*, "dancer,"
p. 1395 G. ed.), and Greek in α-κο-ς, (φύλ-α-κο-ς, l. c.), which
I prefer to do, rather than regard the *i* as existing even
from the time of the unity of languages; and I therefore
compare *i-nga* with the Sanscrit *i-ka*, e.g., in *khán-i-ka-s*,
"digger" (l. c.). The original meaning of *kun-in-g* was
probably "man," κατ' ἐξοχήν, as the English "queen" is, properly, merely "woman" (cf. Gothic *qvein(i-)-s*, "woman"
= Sanscrit जनिस् *jáni-s*, "woman," as "bearing children"),
and corresponds in root and suffix to the above-mentioned
(p. 1396 G. ed.) Sanscrit *ján-a-ka-s*, "father," as "begetter."
Should, too, in the often-mentioned abstract substantives in
unga‡, the guttural be the principal letter, and the last
syllable, therefore, the most important part of the suffix,
then *unga*, e.g., in *heil-unga*, "healing" (Grimm, II. 360.),
must be compared with the Sanscrit feminines in *a-kâ*, e.g.,

---

* The doubling of the consonants very commonly serves in Lithuanian
only to mark the shortness of the preceding vowel, see Kurschat, "Contributions," II. p. 32.

† Regarding the medial for the original tenuis, cf §. 91. p. 80.

‡ See §. 803. and p. 1275 G. ed.

FORMATION OF WORDS. 1355

in *khán-a-kâ,* " the digging," and we must assume that this feminine adjective form has raised itself in the German languages to an abstract; as, *e. g.*, in Greek, κάκη comes from the adjective κακό-ς, κακή, and, in Latin, forms like *fractura, ruptura,* are evidently nothing but the feminines of the future participle. In English, as is also frequently the case so early as the Anglo-Saxon, *ing* represents our *ung* as a formative of abstract substantives; and since adjectives are formed in *ing,* this termination has, in New English, utterly and entirely dislodged the old participle in *end,* while in Middle English the forms in *end* and *ing* still co-exist (Grimm, I. p. 1008.). I therefore am not of opinion that, as Grimm, in the second part of his Grammar (p. 356), assumes, the New English participles are [G. Ed. p. 1398.] corruptions from *end,* as *e* does not readily become *i,* whence it has often itself been, by a corruption, derived.

953. As a secondary suffix, *ka (i-ka, u-ka)* forms, in Sanscrit, words of multifarious relations to their primary word. To forms like *mádra-ka-s, síndhu-ka-s,* " native of the land Madra, Sindhu," *bála-ka-s,* " boy," from *bála,* of equivalent meaning, *síta-ka-s,* " cold weather," "the cold season of the year," "a slothful man," from *sítá,* " cold," correspond, as regards formation, the Gothic adjective bases *staina-ha,* " stony," *vaurda-ha,* " literal," *un-barna-ha,* " childless," *un-hunsla-ga,* " without offering, not distributing" (*hunsl'-s,* theme *hunsla,* " offering"), *aina-han,* " sole" (the latter with inorganic *n*)*; and, with *g* for *h* (see §. 951., conclusion), *móda-ga,* " ireful," *auda-ga,* " happy " (*aud,* theme *auda,* "treasure"), *handu-ga,* " dextrous, skilful, clever," in the nominative masculine, *handa-g(a)-s.* The last example answers well to the above-mentioned Sanscrit *síndhu-ka-s,* and it might, therefore, be expected, that also from the

---

* So the substantive base, occurring only in the plural *bróthra-han* (transposed from *bróthar-han*), nom. *bróthra-han-s,* "brother."

bases *grêdu*, "hunger," *vulthu*, "splendour," not *grêda-g'-s*, "hungry," *vultha-g'-s*, "famed," would come, but only *grêdu-g'-s, vulthu-g'-s*. Perhaps, however, the preponderating number of the adjective bases in *a-ga*, nom. m. *a-gs*, which come from substantive bases in *a*, has had an influence on the formation of the adjectives derived from *grêdu, vulthu*, and given them, by an abuse, *a* for *u;* or the said adjectives come from lost substantive bases *grêda, vultha* (cf. §. 914.), which, perhaps, for the first time after the production of the adjectives referred to, have been weakened to *grêdu, vulthu*, just as the Sanscrit bases *páda*, "foot," *danta*, "tooth,"
[G. Ed. p. 1399] have become, in Gothic, *fôtu, tunthu*. The Gothic substantive bases in *i* lengthen their final vowel before the suffix *ga* to *ei;* hence, *e.g., anstei-ga*, "favourable," *mahtei-ga*, "powerful," *listei-ga*, "subtle," from the feminine primitive bases *ansti*, "grace," *mahti*, "might," *listi*, "subtilty." Feminine bases in *ein*, nom. *ei*, produce, in like manner, derivatives in *ei-ga;* as, *e.g., gabei-ga*, from *gabein*, n. *gabei*, "riches;" and so, too, the neuter base *gavairthya*, "peace" (nom. *gavairthi*), whence *gavairthei-ga*, "pacific." As several abstract feminine bases in *ein* come from adjective bases in *a* (see p. 1306 G. ed.), so, perhaps, from *sina*, nom. *sin(a)-s*, "old," may have come an abstract *sinein*, "age;" and hence *sinei-ga*, "old," *i.e.* "having age;" and for *thiudei-ga*, "good," I presuppose a feminine base *thiudein*, "goodness" (from *thiuda*, n., nom. *thiuth*, "good"). Of verbal origin is *lais-ei-ga*, "teaching" (from *lais-ya*, "I teach," pret. *lais-ei-da*); and so, *andanêm-ei-ga*, "accepting," may have sprung, not from the above-mentioned (§. 914.) base *andanêma*, "acceptance," but from a to-be-presupposed weak verb *anda-nêmya*. In New High German the *i* of words like *sternig*, "starry," *günstig*, "favourable," *kräftig*, "powerful," *mächtig*, "mighty," has won for itself the appearance of an important portion of the suffix, the more, as it has kept its place without reference to the primary

word; and hence, *e.g.*, we equally find *steinig*, "stony," *muthig*, "mettlesome," answering to the Gothic bases *staina- -ha*, *môda-ga*, and, with more exactness, *mächtig*, corresponding to the Gothic *mahtei-ga*.

954. The Gothic adjective bases in *iska*, our *isch*, I should be inclined to derive from the genitive singular, although this case does not correspond universally with exactness to the adjectives under discussion; *e. g.*, the anomalous genitive *funins*, "of the fire," does not correspond to *funisk(a)-s*, "fiery," in the same way as *gudis*, "of God," *barnis*, "of the child," to *gudisk(a)-s*, "godlike," *barnisk(a)-s*, "childish." The circumstance, however, that also in Lithuanian, Lettish, Old Prussian, and Sclavonic, there [G. Ed. p. 1400.] are adjectives in which a sibilant precedes the *k* of the suffix under discussion, induces me to prefer looking on this sibilant as a euphonic affix, on account of the favour in which the combination *sk* is held, that we may not be compelled to assume for the said languages a suffix *ska*, *szka*, ско *sko*, which would meet with no corroboration in the Asiatic sister languages. The following are examples in Lithuanian : *diew'-i-szka-s*, "godlike," from *diewa-s*; *wyr'-i- -szha-s*, "manly," from *wyra-s*; *lĕtuw'-i-szka-s*, Lithuanian, from *lĕtuwà*; *dang'-i-skza-s*, "heavenly," from *dangu-s*: in Old Prussian, *deiw'-i-ska-s*, "godlike," from *deiw(a)-s;* *taw'- -i-ska-s*, "paternal," from *tan(a)-s;* *arw'-i-ska-s*, "veracious," from *arwi-s*, "true" (Nesselmann, p. 77): in Old Sclavonic, женскый *schen'-skyĭ* (nom. m. of the definite declension, see §. 284.), *"femininus,"* from жена *schena*, "woman;" морскый *mor'-skyĭ*, "marinus," from море *more*, theme *moryo* (§. 258.), "sea;" мирскый *mir'-skyĭ*, "mundanus," from миръ *mir'*, theme *miro*, "world" (see Dobrowsky, p. 330). The suppression of the final vowel of the primitive base points to the circumstance, that in the Sclavonic formations also of this kind a vowel universally preceded the suffix. It is most probable, too, that the σ of the Greek diminutive formation

in ι-σκο, ι-σκη (παιδ-ί-σκο-ς, παιδ-ί-σκη, στεφαν-ί-σκος), is only a phonetic prefix. In support of this view we may refer to the euphonic *s*, which, in Sanscrit, is inserted between some roots beginning with *k* and certain prepositions*, *e.g.*, in *parishkar, -kri*, " to adorn," properly, "to put around." Compare, also, the Latin *s* in combinations like *abscondo, abspello, abstineo, ostendo* (for *obstendo*).

[G. Ed. p. 1401]. 955. In Latin I regard the *i* of words like *belli-cu-s, cœli-cu-s, domini-cu-s, uni-cu-s, auli-cu-s*, as a weakening of the final vowel of the base word, like the *i* before the suffixes *tát* and *túdin* and at the beginning of compounds. I compare here the said word with the Sanscrit like *mádra-ka-s, bála-ka-s, síndhu-ka-s*, and Gothic like *staina-h(a)-s, móda-g(a)-s, handu-g(a)-s*. In words like *civi-cu-s, classi-cu-s, hosti-cu-s*, the *i* demonstrates itself to belong to the primitive base, while the *i*, which is appended to bases terminating in a consonant, *e.g.*, in *urbi-cu-s, patri-cu-s, pedi-ca*, and that, too, in the Latin ablative plural (*pedi-bus*=Sanscrit *pad-bhyás*), and in compounds like *pedi-sequus*, have been first introduced in Latin to facilitate the combination with the following consonant, on which account I am unwilling to place such words, with respect to the *i* before their suffix, on the same footing with Sanscrit words like *háimant'-i-ká-s*, " wintry, cold," from *hémantá*, " winter ;" *dhárm'-i-ká-s*, " virtuous, devoted to duty," from *dhárma*, " duty, right ;" *áksh-i-ká-s*, " diceplayer," from *akshá*, " dice." To these, however, correspond, with respect to accentuation also, Greek derivatives like πολεμ'-ι-κό-ς, ἀδελφ'-ι-κό-ς, ἀμπελ'-ι-κό-ς, ὡρ'-ι-κό-ς, ἀστ'--ι-κό-ς, ῥητορ-ι-κό-ς, δαιμον-ι-κό-ς, ἀρωματ-ι-κό-ς, γεροντ-ι-κό-ς. To Sanscrit forms in which the suffix is appended without the intervention of any vowel, as above *síndhu-ka-s*, corresponds, irrespective of the accentuation, ἀστυ-κό-ς. Re-

---

* See my "Smaller Sanscrit Grammar," 2d Edition, p. 62.

FORMATION OF WORDS. 1359

garding the Greek formations in τι-κό-ς, from to-be-presupposed abstract bases in τι, see p. 1198 G. ed., Note.

956. The Sanscrit suffix *tu*, with its cognates in the European sister languages, has already been considered as a formative of the infinitive*. The cor- [G. Ed. p. 1402.] responding Gothic abstracts, like the Latin (§. 865), have exchanged the feminine gender with the masculine, and preserved the original tenuis under the guard of a preceding *s* or *h*, but, after other letters, changed it to *d* or *th* (cf. §. 91.). The suffix is either added direct to the verbal root, or to the theme of a weak verb terminating in *ô*, or to an adjective base in *a*, lengthening this vowel to *ô* (see §. 69.). To this class belong *vahs-tu-s*, "growth;" *kus-tu-s*, "proof;" *lus-tu-s*, "desire"†; *thuh-tu-s*, "prejudice;" *vratô--du-s*, "journey;" *auhyô-du-s*, "noise;" *mannishô-du-s*, "humanity" (from *manniska*, nom. *mannisk'-s*, "human"); *gabauryô-dus*, "desire, pleasure" (cf. *gabaurya-ba*, adverb, "willingly, voluntarily"). *Dau-thu-s*, "death," properly, "the dying;" is radically connected with the Greek θάνατος, and the Sanscrit *han*, from *dhan*, "to slay" (*ni-dhaná*, "death"); and has vocalised the *n* of the obsolete root to *u* (cf. §. 432.). In Sanscrit, *a-thu*, the *th* of which I regard as a mutation of *t*, forms some masculine abstracts from verbal roots; *e.g., vam-a-thú-s*, "*vomitus;*" *vêp-a-thú-s*, "the trembling;" *nand-a-thú-s*, "joy;" *śvay-a-thú-s*, "the tumefying" (*śvi*, "to grow").

957. With the suffix *tu* in Sanscrit are formed also nouns of agency and appellatives, some of which accent the root, and some the suffix; *e.g., gán-tu-s*, "traveller" (*gam*, "to go"); *tán-tu-s*, "thread" (*tan*, "to stretch"); *bhâ-tú-s*, "sun" (*bhâ*, "to shine"); *yâ-tú-s*, "traveller" (*yâ*, "to go");

---

* See §§. 852., 853., 862., 863., 865., 866., 868.

† Probably from *lus* (= Greek λυ, Sanscrit *lû*); so that it properly signifies "loosening," or "letting go."

[G. Ed. p. 1403.] *jan-tú-s*, "animal," as "producing," or "produced." So in Gothic, *hlif-tu-s*, "thief," as "stealing" (cf. κλέπ-τω); *skil-du-s*, "shield," as "covering"*: in Greek, μάρπ-τυς in Hesych., if the form is genuine, and μάρ-τύ-ς, which Pott, as it appears to me rightly, traces back to the Sanscrit root *smri* (*i.e. smar*), "to recall," to which the Latin *memor*, and Old High German *mâriu*, also belong.† With the above-mentioned (§. 933., Note †) Vêdic *jîv-á-tu-s*, m. "life," might be compared, as regards the inserted *â*, the abstracts from nominal bases in Latin like *princip-â-tu-s*, *consul-â-tu-s*, *patron'-â-tu-s*, *triumvir'-â-tu-s*, *tribun'-â-tu-s*, *sen'-â-tu-s*. These, however, are, as it were, only imitations of the abstracts, which spring from verbs of the first conjugation‡; as also *sen-â-tor* answers to nouns of agency like *am-â-tor;* and *jan'-i-tor* (from *janua*, with the suppression of the two final vowels), *ol'-i-tor* (for *oler-i-tor*, just like *opifex* for *oper-i-fex*), to those like *mon-i-tor*. So in Greek, ἀκρω-τήρ from ἄκρο; and as τη-ς and τηρ are originally one (see §. 810.), numerous denominative formations in τη-ς, like δημό-τη-ς, ἱππό-τη-ς, πολῖ-τη-ς, κωμή-τη-ς, Σιβαρῖ-τη-ς, Πισᾶ-τη-ς, Αἰγινή-τη-ς. I believe, too, that I may refer to this class patronymics in ι-δη-ς or δη-ς, as Κεκροπ-ί-δη-ς, Μεμνον-ί-δη-ς, Κρον-ί--δη-ς, Ἱπποτά-δη-ς, Βορεά-δη-ς, as I assume a change of the tenuis to the medial, as in the Latin forms like *tim-i-du-s* (see §. 822.). It may here be observed, that the Greek patronymics in ῐ-ων (theme ῐ-ων or ῐ-ον), too, stand, in respect to their [G. Ed. p. 1404.] suffix, if we regard ων, ον, as the important part of it, combined with a class of words, which is originally destined for the formation of nouns of agency (see §. 926.), which is also the case with the feminine pa-

---

* Cf. *skal-ya*, "*tegula*," and the Sanscrit root *chhad* (see §. 14.), "to cover," *l* therefore from *d* (see §. 17.).

† See Glossarium Sanscr., a. 1847, p. 392.

‡ Cf. Pott, II. p. 554.

tronymics in *ιδ*, since the corresponding Sanscrit *í*, as feminine of *a*, forms both feminine nouns of agency and appellatives with the fundamental meaning of a participle present (*e.g.*, *nadí*, "river," as "purling," from *nadá*, id.), and feminine patronymics like *bhâimí* (see §. 920.).

958. Some few suffixes still remain to be discussed, which occur only in the secondary formation of words: among them is the Sanscrit *êya*, fem. *êyâ*, which is used for a purpose similar to that of *ya*, according to §. 901. In its origin, too, *êya* appears identical with *ya*, and to be only a phonetic extension of the latter. The accent in formations in *êya* rests either on the final syllable of the suffix, or on the first syllable of the entire word; *e.g.*, *âtr'-êyá-s*, "descendant of Atri;" *dâs'-êyá-s*, "son of a slave," from *dâsa*; *gâir'-êyá-m*, "bitumen," from *giri*, "a mountain;" *vrâih'-êyá-m*, "rice-field," from *vríhi*, "rice;" *mâh'-êyá-s*, "earthen," from *mahî*; *pâúrush'-êya-s*, "referring to men," "consisting of men," from *purusha*; *âh'-êya-s*, "*anguinus*," from *ahi*, "*anguis*;" *grâív'-êya-m*, "belonging to the neck," from *grîvâ*, "throat, neck." To the three last examples correspond also, in throwing back the accent as far as possible, Greek words like λεόντ-ειο-ς, λεόντ-εο-ς, αἴγ-ειο-ς, τράγ'-ειο-ς, σιδήρ-ειο-ς, ἀργύρ'-ειο-ς. To this class belong, in Latin, words like *pic-eu-s*, *ciner-eu-s*, *flor-eu-s*, *aer-eu-s*, *argent'-eu-s*, *aur'-eu-s*, *ign'-eu-s* (cf. Pott Etym. Inq., II. 502.). In these formations, therefore, and in the Greek in εο-ς, the Sanscrit diphthong of *ê*, which is contracted from *ai*, has left behind only its first element in the shape of ε, ἔ (as in ἑκάτερο-ς = *êkatará-s*, see §. 293.); on the other hand, [G. Ed. p. 1405.] in *pleb-êju-s*, the Sanscrit suffix *êya* (*y* = Latin *j*) has been retained with the utmost exactness, and so, too, in some proper names, as *Pomp'-êju-s*, *Petr'-êju-s*, *Lucc'-êju-s* (see Düntzer, "Doctrine of the Formation of Latin Words," p. 33).

959. The secondary suffixes *vat*, *mat*, in the strong cases *vant*, *mant*, which form possessive adjectives from substan-

tives, are perhaps simply phonetic extensions of the primary suffixes *van* and *man* (cf. §. 803.); and, on the other hand, *vin* and *min*, e.g., in *téjas-vín*, "gifted with light," *médhá-vín*, "intelligent," *svá-mín**, "lord, owner" ("gifted with his own (*sva*")), have been formed by weakening the vowel from *van* and *man*. It is most probable, too, that *vant* and *mant*, as also *van* and *man*, are originally one, as *v* and *m* are easily interchanged. A comparison has already been drawn between *vant*† and the Latin *lent*, extended to *lentu*. In Greek the suffix εντ (from Ϝεντ) corresponds, which, as is usually done by its Sanscrit sister-form *vant*, allows the accent to fall on the syllable which immediately precedes; hence, e.g., δολό-εντ, ἀμπελό-εντ, ὑλή-εντ, τολμή-εντ, πυρ-ό-εντ, μελιτ-ό-εντ, δακρυ-ό-εντ, μητι-ό-εντ, as in Sanscrit, e.g., *dhaná--vant*, "rich," from *dhána*, "riches;" *médhá-vant*, "intelligent," from *médhá*, "understanding;" *lakshmí-vant*, "fortunate," from *lakshmí*, "fortune."

960. The suffix तन *tana*, f. *taní*, forms adjectives from adverbs of time. They accent optionally the first syllable of the suffix or the syllable preceding, e.g., *hyas-tána-s* or *hyás-tana-s*, "hesternus," from *hyas*, "yesterday;" *śvas-tána-s* or *śvás-tana-s*,

[G. Ed. p. 1406.] "crastinus," from *śvas*, "to-morrow;" *sáyan--tána-s* or *sáyán-tana-s*, "vespertinus," from *sáyam*, "at evening" (properly an accusative); *saná-tána-s* or *saná-tana-s*, "sempiternus," from *saná*, "always." In Latin corresponds, as needs hardly be mentioned, *tinu* in *cras-tinu-s*, *diu-tinu-s* (cf. *divá-tana-s*, "daily," (?) from *divá*, "in the day"), *pris--tinu-s*; lengthened to *tínu* in *vesper-tínu-s*, *matu-tínu-s*.‡

---

* The Indian Grammarians refer the *á*, which I regard as the lengthening of the *a* of the primitive base, to the suffix.

† See §. 20., and "Influence of the Pronouns on the formation of Words," p. 7.

‡ *Mátú* (an adverbial ablative like *noctú*), which is to be presupposed as base word, is perhaps connected with the Sanscrit *bhátu*, "sun;" so
that

The forms *hesternus, sempiternus, æternus*, have either prefixed an inorganic *r* to the *n*, or they presuppose *hester, sempiter, æter (æviter)*, as primitives (cf. §. 293.), so that only *nu* would be the derivative suffix. The former view is favoured by the forms *hodiernus, nocturnus,* and some others, which have probably first appended the suffix *nu*, and then further prefixed an *r* to the *n* (cf. *alburnus* from *albus, lucerna* from *luceo*).

961. As regards the origin of the suffix *tana,* I look upon it as a combination of the pronominal bases *ta* and *na*, a combination which occurs in Old Prussian in the independent pronoun *tan'-s* (from *tana-s*), "he ;" fem. *tennâ* (for *ta-na*), "she." So the suffix *tya*, which forms paroxytone adjectives from indeclinables, as *ihá-tya-s*, "a man of this place," *tatrá-tya-s,* "a man of that place," is probably identical with the compound demonstrative base *tya* (see §. 353.), and therefore, in the said examples, denotes the person, who is here (*iha*), there (*tatra*). So, too, as has already been remarked (§. 400.), in Greek, ἐνθά-σιο-ς (in Hesych.), comes from ἔνθα (thus, -σιο-ς from τιο-ς); and in Latin, *propi-tiu-s*, from *prope ;* and in [G. Ed. p. 1407.] Gothic, the base *framathya* (nom. m. *framatheis,* "*alienus,*" "strange"), from the preposition *fram,* "from," whether it be that *frama* is the original form of the preposition, or that the *a* of the derivative is a vowel of conjunction. The base *ni-thya,* nom. *nithyi-s*, "cousin," as "*propinquus,*" I derive from the same preposition *ni* ("among"), whence, in Sanscrit, *ni-haṭá-s,* "*propinquus ;*" *ní-tya-s,* "*sempiternus.*" Another Sanscrit word of this class which has sprung from a preposition is *amâ-tya-s*, "counsel," properly, "*conjunctus,*" from *amâ*, "with :" I also refer here *ápa-tya-m*, "offspring, child," in spite of its different accentuation (see Nâigh.,

---

that the labial mute of the root *bhá*, "to shine," passes over into the nasal of its organ, as is also probably the case in *mâne*.

II. 2., and Benfey's Gloss. to the S. V.), as I derive it, as I formerly did, from the preposition *ápa*.

962. The demonstrative base *sya*, fem. *syâ* (see §. 353.), which is limited in classical Sanscrit to the nominative singular, with which, most probably, the genitive termination *sya* is connected (see §. 194.), has, in the secondary formation of words, likewise its presumptive equivalent, viz. in the now but seldom found *sya* (euphonic *shya*), through which *manu-shyà-s*, "man," is formed from *manú*, "Manu," and *dhênu--shyà*, "a cow tied up (to be milked)," comes from *dhênú*.* If words of this kind have originally been numerous, we might then refer to this class the Latin *riu*, which is always preceded by an *â*, and assume the favourite transition of *s* into *r*, thus, *e.g.*, *tabell'-â-riu-s, palm'-â-riu-s, arbor-â-riu-s, ær-â--riu-s, lign'-â-riu-s, actu-â-riu-s, contr'-â-riu-s, advers'-â-riu-s, prim'-â-riu-s, secund'-â-riu-s*, from *tabell'-â-siu-s*, &c. But if the *r* of these forms is primitive, *riu* might be regarded as an extension of the suffix *ri* = Sanscrit रि *ri* (see §. 943.), as together with *palm'-â-riu-s* there actually exists a form *palm'-â-ri-s*. The *â* can in neither case be referred to the proper suffix, but is to be regarded as that of forms like *princip-â-tu-s, sen-â-tu-s, sen-â-tor* (see p. 1403 G. ed.)

963. The Latin *â-riu* guides us to the Gothic suffix *arya*, to which, however, I can concede no affinity to the former, whether it be that the Latin *r* is primitive, or has arisen from *s*. The Gothic is unacquainted with any interchange between the *s* and *r*, and we must therefore allow the *r* of the said suffix to pass as original. It forms nouns of agency, and, in the secondary formation, words which denote the person who is occupied with the matter denoted by the base word. To this class belong the mas-

---

* The Indian Grammarians form both these words with the suffix *ya* with *sh* prefixed.

culine bases *lais-arya*, "teacher" (*lais-ya*, "I teach"); *sôk-arya*, "examiner" (*sôk-ya*, "I seek"); *liuth-arya*, "singer" (*liuthô*, "I sing"); *bôk'-arya*, "scribe" (*bôka*, theme *bôkô*, "letter," pl. *bôkôs*, "writings"); *môt'-arya*, "toll-gatherer" (*môta*, "toll, custom"); *vull'-arya*, "fuller" (*vulla*, "wool"). The nominatives are, *lais-areis, sôk-areis*, &c. (see §. 135.). A neuter is *vagg'-arya*, nom. *vagg-ari*, "pillow for the head" (Old High German, *wanga*, "cheek"). It is perhaps by an accident that the sources of Gothic literature which remain to us supply no nouns of agency from roots of strong verbs: these, however, are not wanting in the other Germanic dialects. The following are examples in Old High German, of which I annex the nominatives: *scrîb-eri*, "*scriba ;*" *bët-eri*, "*adorator ;*" *halt-âri*, "*servator ;*" *hëlf-âre*, "*adjutor ;*" *aba-nëm-âri*, "*susceptor ;*" *sez-ari*, "*conditor ;*" *troum-sceid-ari*, "*interpres somnii,*" "interpreter of dreams." The following are examples derived from nouns: *gart'-eri*, "*hortulanus ;*" *hunt'-eri*, "*centurio ;*" *muniz'-eri*, "*monetarius ;*" *havan'-ari*, "*figulus*" ("potter"); *satal'-ari*, "*ephippiarius*" ("saddler"); *wagin'-ari*, "*rhedarius*" ("cartwright"); *vran-hônô-vurt-ari*,"*Francofurtensis.*"* In [G. Ed. p. 1409.] New High German this class of words is very numerously represented by nouns of agency, as *Geber*, "giver;" *Seher*, "seer;" *Denker*, "thinker;" *Binder*, "binder;" *Springer*, "springer;" *Läufer*, "runner;" *Trinker*, "drinker;" *Schneider*, "cutter;" *Streiter*, "striver;" *Bäcker*, "baker;" *Fänger*, "seizer;" *Weber*, "weaver;" *Forscher*, "prover;" *Sucher*, "seeker;" *Dreher*, "turner;" *Brauer*, "brewer;" and denominatives, like *Gärtner*, "gardener;" *Schreiner*, "joiner;" *Töpfer*, "potter;" *Ziegler*, "tiler;" *Wagner*, "cartwright;" *Frankfurter*, "inhabitant of Frankfort:" *Mainzer*, "inhabitant of Mainz;" *Berliner*, "inhabitant of Berlin." The

---

* Regarding the difference of the vowel before the *r*, and especially as to this class of words, see Grimm, II. p. 125.

following are examples in English : " giver, singer, killer, bringer, seller, brewer; glover, gardener, wagoner." Perhaps the Gothic *arya* is on one side an extension, and on the other a mutilation of the Sanscrit suffix *târ*, *tṛi* (see §. 810.); an extension by adding the suffix *ya*, as above*, in *bêr-us-yós*, " parents," as " bearing children," we have seen the Sanscrit suffix *ush* (from *vas*) in combination with *ya*; and a mutilation by dropping a *t*-sound (*t*, *th*, or *d*, see §. 9.); thus, *e.g.*, *laisarya*, " teacher," from *laistarya*, just as, in French, the *t* of the Latin *frater*, *pater*, *mater*, has disappeared in the forms *frère*, *père*, *mère*, and that of the suffix *tor* in the nouns of agency in *eur*, in forms like *sauv-eur* (=*salvator*), *port-eur*, *vend-eur* (=*venditor*). If the form was once *arya*, and obtained from *târ*, which corresponds to it in the different German dialects, it might then easily have extended itself as well over roots as nominal bases, to which the perfect form with the initial *t*-sound had never been appended. A form like *Geb-ter* or *Gebder*, for *Geber*, " giver," could never have existed; perhaps, however, in Gothic, a base *gif-tarya* may have existed, the *f* of which for *b*, after dropping the *t*, became again *b* (as in

[G. Ed. p. 1410.] the pret. pl., *e.g.*, *gêbum* compared with the sing. *gaf*, *gaf-t*), therefore *gibarya*, to which our *Geber* would correspond.

COMPOUNDS.

964. In the Indo-European languages the verbs are compounded with scarce aught but prepositions, which in Sanscrit are always accented, and some of which, except in the Vêda dialect, never occur in the uncompounded state. I annex some Sanscrit verbs compounded with

---

* See §. 788., and, with reference to analogous extensions in Lithuanian, §. 787.

prepositions in the 3d. person of the present: *ádhi-gachchhati*, "he goes thither;" *antár-gachchhati*, "he goes under;" *ápa-kramati*, "he goes off;" *abhí-gachchhati*, "he goes towards, he approaches;" *áva-skandati*, "he descends;" *párá-vartaté*, "he returns;" *pári-gachchhati*, "he goes round;" *prá-dravati*, "he runs away;" *práti-kramati*, "he gives way;" *práti-bháshaté*, "he answers, he speaks against;" *práti-padyaté*, "he arrives;" *níṣh-kramati*, "he comes forth," *sán-gachchhati* (euphon. for *sam*), "he comes together." Compare, without reference to the verbal root, in Greek, ἀποβαίνει, ἀμφιβαίνει, περιβαίνει, προβαίνει, προς-βαίνει (πρός from προτί, see §. 152. p. 167), συμβαίνει: in Latin, *adit, interit, abit, ambit, obit, procedit, congreditur*: in Old High German, *umbi-cât, umbe-gât*, "he goes round;" *untar-gât*, "he goes under:" in Gothic, *at-gaggith*, "he goes to;" *af-gaggith*, "he goes away;" *bi-qvimith*, "he overtakes" (*qvimith*, "he comes"); *bi-gairdith*, "he girds;" *fra-létith*, "he abandons:" in Lithuanian, *isz-eiti*, "he goes out" (*isz* = निस्, *nis*); *par-eiti*, "he goes back;" *par-nesza*, "he brings back," *pra-nesza*, "he represents;" *priesz-tarauya*, "he contradicts;" *su-maiszo*, "he mingles:" in Old Sclavonic (see Dobrowsky, p. 401), обрѣзати *obriezati*, περιτέμνειν, "*circumcidere;*" изидѫ *iz-iduń*, "*exibo;*" пролити *pro-liti*, "*profundere;*" приидѫ *pri-iduń*, "*adveniam;*" приимѫ *pri-imuń*, "*accipio;*" приведе *pri-vede*, "*adduxit;*" принести [G. Ed. p. 1411.] *pri-neste*, "*afferre;*" приступити *pri-stúp-i-ti*, "*accidere;*" пришивати *pri-shiv-a-ii*, "*assuere;*" съристатиса *s-ristati--sań*, "*concurrere.*"

965. In the Véda dialect the prepositions are frequently found separated by intermediate words from the verb to which they belong: notwithstanding this, with respect to sense there continues the most intimate connection between the preposition and the verb; *e.g., sám agním indhaté nárah*, "*ignem accendunt viri*" (see Rosen's "Specimen," p. 20). Here *sam* taken alone has no meaning at all, but

in combination with the root *indh* it signifies "to kindle," which *indh* also means by itself. In Zend, too, such separations of the prepositions from the verbs often occur*; and in German many old combinations are so altered, that, in the proper verb (not in the infinitive and the participles, and especially not in the formation of words), we place the preposition that had been prefixed either directly after the verb, or separate it still farther from it by several intermediate words: we say, *e.g.*, *ausgehen, ausgehend, Ausgang*, "to go out," "going out," "egress;" but not *er ausgeht*, "he goes out," as in Gothic *usgaggith*, but *er geht aus*, "he goes out," *er geht von diesem Gesichtspunkte aus*, "he goes from this point of view out;" while, however, after the relative and most of the conjunctions we prefix the prepositions, since we say, *e.g.*, *welcher ausgeht*, "who goes out;" *wenn er ausgeht*, "if he goes out;" *dass er ausgeht*, "that he goes out." Moreover, in prepositions, whose meaning is no more clearly perceived, and also in those to which there are no correlative prepositions with an opposite meaning, as in *ein*, "in," opposed to *aus*, "out," *vor*, "before," opposed to *nach*, "after," *an*,

[G. Ed. p. 1412.] "on," opposed to *ab*, "off," or where the verbal motion has a decided preponderance over the prepositional, or where the significations of the preposition and the verb have blended completely together, the separation of the preposition from the verbal root is not allowed; hence, *e.g.*, *er begreift, beweist, vergeht, verbleibt, zerstört, zerspringt, umgeht, umringt, übersetzt, überspringt*, "he understands, proves, vanishes, remains, destroys, shatters, goes round, surrounds, translates, crosses." The phenomenon under discussion may be so regarded, as that only those prepositions which are accented, and whose signification

---

* For examples see §. 518., where the translation of *frâ . . . hunvanha* is to be corrected according to p. 960.

COMPOUNDS. 1369

is clearly retained, have the power of separating themselves from the verbs to which they belong, while in Vêdic Sanscrit and Zend those prepositons, too, the meaning of which has quite disappeared in the verbal notion, may be detached from the verb.

966. In Sanscrit there are but very few* verbs which enter into combinations other than prepositional, and even of these only the gerund in *ya* and passive participle in *ta* for the most part appear in multifarious combinations; *e.g.*, *kuṇḍalí-kṛita*, "made into a ring," *ékí-bhúta*, "become one;" which forms need not be regarded as derivatives from compound verbs like *kuṇḍalí-karômi*, *ékí-bhavámi*, but it is probable that here the participles *kṛita* and *bhúta* have, as already independent words, united with the first members of the compounds. In Greek, as is well known, the verbs which are compounded with other elements than prepositions are, with very few exceptions, not primitive combinations of the particular verb with the preceding word, but derivatives from compound nouns; as, *e.g.*, τοκογλυφέω from τοκογλύφο-ς (see Buttmann, §. 121. 3.). The same is the case with Old High German [G. Ed. p. 1413.] compounds, as *hanta-slagô*, "*plaudo*," from *hanta-slag*, "clapping the hands;" *rât-slagô*, "*consulo*," from *rât-slag*, "advice:" and in the New High German, as, *ich wetteifere*, "I vie;" *ich hofmeistere*, "I criticise;" *ich brandschatze*, "I put under contribution" (see Grimm, II. p. 583). In Gothic, *e.g.*, *vei-vôdya*, "I testify," comes from *veit-vôd'-s*, "witness," and *filuvaurdya*, properly, "I am loquacious," either from the substantive base *filuvaurdein*, nom. *-ei*, "loquacity," or with this latter word from a to-be-presupposed adjective base *filuvaurda*, "loquacious." The Latin, on the other hand, produces verbal compounds by direct combination of a

---

* See shorter Critical Grammar of the Sanscrit Language, 2d Edition, §. 585.

substantive, adjective, or adverb with a verb; *e.g., signi-fico, ædi-fico, anim'-adverto, nun-cupo* (cf. *oc-cupo,* and see §. 490.), *tali-pedo, magni-fico, æqui-paro, bene-dico, male-dico.* In Greek, from the participle δακρυχέων we may infer a lost verb δακρυχέω, and from the adverb νουνεχόντως the participle νουνέχων, and hence a verb νουνέχω. With respect to the accusative νουν, we may compare νουνεχόντως with the above-mentioned (§. 916.) Sanscrit compounds like *arindamá-s,* "subduing-foes," and the Zend *drujĕm-vanô,* "Drujslaying" (§. 922.). On the other hand, we need not, with Buttmann (§. 121., Rem. 1), regard δακρυ in δακρυχέων as an accusative, as in this word the accusative (and nominative) is not distinguishable from the theme. Compare Sanscrit compounds like *madhu-líh,* "bee," as "licking honey."

967. When Buttmann (§. 120. 6.), in Greek, assumes compounds, of which the first part must be a verb, which most usually terminates in σι, the ι of which, however, as vowel of conjunction, may also be elided, I am unable to agree with him in this. Should, however, in such compounds as δεισιδαίμων, ἐγερσίχορος, τρεψίχρως, δαμασίβροτος, φυξάνως, παυσάνεμος, [G. Ed. p. 1414.] ῥίψασπις, πλήξιππος, a verb be contained, we should have to define to what part of the verb, to what tense, to what number, and what person, these forms in σι or σ' belong. Having previously determined them to be verbs, I should explain them as obsolete presents in the third person singular, according to the analogy of the conjugation in μι, since σι or τι, as termination of the third person, originally belongs to all active present forms (see §. 456.); thus, δεισιδαίμων would properly signify "he fears the gods," and stands on the same footing with the French compounds like *tire-botte, tire-bouchon, porte-mouchettes, porte-manteau, porte-feuille.* I would rather, however, with Pott (E. I., p. 90), recognise in the first part of ἐρυσίχθων and similar compounds abstract substantive bases in σι (from τι, see §. 845.),

the ι of which is suppressed before vowels*, and which had, perhaps, originally a far wider diffusion than in the received condition of the language. It is, therefore, not necessary that the abstract of each of the compounds of that kind be retained in use as a simple word, or that the abstract which occurs in the compounds should in all cases answer exactly to that which is preserved in use in the simple state. I see no difficulty in the circumstance to which, e.g., G. Curtius (*De nominum Gr. form.* p. 18) has drawn attention, that the first part of στησί-χορος does not answer to στάσι-ς, nor that of προδωσ'-έταιρος to πρόδοσι-ς. The radical vowel of δίδωμι, ἵστημι, which is shortened before the heavy personal terminations (see §. 480.) and most of the formative abstracts is naturally long (cf. Sanscrit *dâ*, "to give," *sthâ*, "to stand"); and from the roots δω, στη, from στᾱ, the forms δω-σι-ς, στη-σι-ς, or στᾱ-σι-ς, might be expected as abstracts. The original length of the vowel may [G. Ed. p. 1415.] then have been retained in the compounds under discussion, or carried back in order to give more emphasis to this class of compounds, as above (p. 1337, Note † G. ed.) we have seen a lengthening accrue to the vowel of the last member of another kind of compounds, which does not prevent us from recognising, e.g., in ἀνήκουστος, the simple ἀκουστός. I recall attention, too, to the lengthening which the radical vowel of some abstracts in σι experiences in roots terminating in a vowel before the suffix ιο (= Sanscrit *ya*, see §. 901.), e.g., in στήσ'-ιο-ς (contrasted with ἐπιστάσ'-ιο-ς), λῦσ'-ιο-ς, and λῦσί-πονο-ς, λῦσί-ποθο-ς, &c., compared with λῠ-σι-ς (Sanscrit root *lû*, "to cut off"). If, then, in the first part of the compounds referred to we recognise abstract bases in σι, the whole must then be referred to the class of the

---

* In φερέσβιος, φερεσσάκης, also before a consonant. The to-be-presupposed abstract φέρ-ε-σι-ς answers to forms like γέν-ε-σι-ς, νέμ-ε-σι-ς (see §. 850. conclusion).

Sanscrit possessive compounds, and a transposition of the individual members of the compound must be assumed, as, *e.g.*, in the Vêdic compounds like *mandayát-sakha-s*, "friends-gladdening," *kshayád-víra-s*, "ruling men," *tarád--dvêsha-s*, "foes-conquering"*, where the first member of the compound, a present participle in the weak theme, should properly stand at the end, as the person expressed by the participle is subjected, in construction, to the alte- [G. Ed. p. 1416.] ration of the case-relations, while the word it governs, according to the sense, abides ever in the accusative relation; as, *e.g.*, in Greek, λυσί-πονος, "having the relaxation of toil"="relaxing toil," πόνος is not subjected to any alteration of the case-relation, and hence the order πονο-λυσις would be the more natural. In compounds like φυγόμαχος, φυγόπολις, λιπομήτωρ, λιπόναυς, λειπόγαμος, φιλόβοτρυς, φιλόγαμος, the prefixed adjectives answer, in respect to their formative suffix, to those which we have seen above (§. 916.) at the end of compounds; and as they, for the most part, have the meaning of the participle present, they may be compared with the above-mentioned Vêdic forms like *tarád-dvêsha-s*, "*superans inimicos.*" The ε of forms like ἀρχέπολις, δακέθυμος, φερέπονος, is probably only the thinning of an *s*, as in the vocative†; and therefore ἀρχε in ἀρχέπολις is the same word which forms the concluding portion of πολίαρχο-ς, and in the inflectionless voca-

---

* See Fr. Rosen, "Rigvêda-Sanhita," at H. VI. 6. In Zend, too, there are compounds of this kind; *e.g.*, ⟨zend⟩ *frâdhat-vîra*, "creating men." The compound ⟨zend⟩ *frâdat-vîspaṅm-hujâiti*, "creating prosperity," where *vîspaṅm* stands in the case governed by the participle, while the substantive is ruled by the position of the whole in the sentence, and therefore stands in the case governed by the verb; and in the case before us, according to three MSS. to the reading of which Burnouf ("Yaçna," p. 262) justly gives the preference, in the dative, while only the lithographed Codex gives *hujâitim* for *hujâiteê*.

† See §. 204.

tive appears likewise in the form ἄρχε. The prefixed adjectives make choice in the root, too, of the lighter vowel; hence φερε, in opposition to φορο, e.g., φερεστάφυλο-ς opposed to σταφυλόφορος. The ι, too, of τερπι and ἀρχι, in τερπι-κέραυνος, ἀρχι-κέραυνος, ἀρχι-θάλασσος, ἀρχί-ζωος, &c., cannot, perhaps, be regarded as aught else than the weakening of an o = Sanscrit a, Latin u, of the second declension, and therefore must rest on the same principle on which, in Latin, e.g., the relation of *cæli-cola* to *cælu-cola* or *cælo-cola* is based, as might be expected if the Latin did not love the most extreme weakening of the final vowel in the first member of compounds (see "Vocalismus," p. 132).

968. While the Latin, in its nominal compounds, regularly changes the final vowel of the base of the first member of the compound into the lightest [G. Ed. p. 1417.] vowel i^*, the Sanscrit, exclusive of a few anomalies, exhibits the first member of the compound (which, however, as also the second, may itself, too, be compounded) universally in its true theme, only that its final letter is subject to the euphonic laws, which, without the compounding too, obtain with respect to the initial and final consonants of two contiguous words. I annex a few examples of dependent compounds, of a class to be more closely examined hereafter: *lôka-pâlá-s*, "world-

---

* Hence, e.g., *cæli-cola* for *cælu-cola* or *cælŏ-cola*, *lani-ger* for *lanager*, *fructi-fer* for *fructu-fer*, *mani-pulus* for *manu-pulus*, cf. §. 6. and §§. 244. 829. In *albŏ-galerus*, *albŏ-gilvus*, *merŏ-bibus*, the final vowel of the base has been retained in the form which lies at the base of the dative and ablative singular and genitive and accusative plural; while *locu-ples*, lengthened *locû-ples*, is based on the form which has assumed the original *a* in the nominative and accusative singular. Before vowels the final vowel of the first member is suppressed; hence, e.g., *un'-animis*, *flex'-animus;* occasionally also before consonants, for example in *nau-fragus* for *navi-fragus*, *au--spex* for *avi-spex*, *vin'-demia* for *vini-demia* or *vinŏ-demia*, *puer'-pera* for *pueri-pera* or *puerŏ-pera*, *mal-luviæ* (with assimilation) for *mani-luviæ* from *manu-luviæ*.

protector;" *dharâ-dhará-s*, "earth-bearer;" *mati-bhramá-s*, "error of the mind;" *vîriṇî-tîrá-s*, "shore of Vîriṇî;" *madhu-pá-s*, "bee," as "honey-drinker;" *bhû-dhará-s*, "earth-bearer" ("mountain"); *pitṛi-bhrâtấ*, "father's brother" (see §. 214.); *gô-dhúk* (theme *gô-dúh*), "cowherd," literally, "milking-cows;" *nâu-sthá-s*, "standing, being in a ship" (Diluv. Śl. 32.); *marud-ganá-s*, "troop of winds" (euphonic for *marut-*); *râja-putrá-s*[*], "king's son;" *nabhas-talá-m*, "atmosphere."

[G. Ed. p. 1418.] 969. The Sanscrit does not use a vowel of conjunction to lighten the two members of the compound, and it must be regarded as a consequence of the effeminacy which has in this respect entered into Greek and Latin, that these two languages, in the composition of nouns, with the exception of some isolated cases, do not understand how to combine a consonantal termination with an initial consonant, but insert a vowel of conjunction, or, which is the same thing, extend the first member with a vowel affix; for which purpose the Greek regularly makes choice of ο, occasionally of ι, while the Latin invariably chooses the weakest vowel *i*. The σ alone, in Greek, has left itself pretty often free from the inorganic affix; hence, *e. g.*, σακεσ-φόρος (see §. 128.), τελεσ-φόρος, σακέσ-παλος, ὀρεσ--κῷος, ἐπεσ-βόλος, μυσ-κέλενδρον†, φωσ-φόρος (for φωτ-φόρος, cf. §. 152.). And ν, too, in the bases μελαν and παντ, the

---

[*] For *râjan-*; *n* is dropped at the beginning of compounds (see §. 139.).

† That the σ in this compound is not a euphonic affix, but belongs to the base, and that hence, in the genitive, μυ-ός stands for μυσ-ός, as, *e.g.*, μένεος for μένεσος, is plain, as well from the Latin *mus*, *mûr-is*, from *mûr-is*, as from the etymology of the Sanscrit *mûṣh-â-s*, "mouse," from *mûṣh*, "to steal," see Glossar. Scr., a. 1847, p. 268. In Latin the compounds *mus-cipula* and *mus-cerda* are deserving notice, as they have in like manner retained the original *s* without the addition of a vowel of conjunction. I must dissent from Buttmann (§. 120. Rem. 11.), as I can by no means recognise a euphonic or formative σ in Greek compounds.

latter with the loss of the τ, appears in some compounds before consonants without the copulative ο, in which case the ν adapts itself to the organ of the following letter, as final m does in Sanscrit; hence, e.g., μελάγχολος, μελάμπεπλος, μελάνδετος, contrasted with μελανόφρων, &c.; πάγκακος, παγχάλκεος, παμβασιλεύς, παμμῆτις, πανδαμάτωρ, παντελής, opposed to παντογόνος, &c. Among bases in ρ, only the monosyllabic πυρ dispenses in some compounds with the vowel of conjunction, hence, e.g., πυρβόλος opposed [G. Ed. p. 1419.] to πυρόβολος. Before vowels, the monosyllabic bases ποδ, παιδ, κυν, too, appear without a conjunctive ο; hence, e.g., ποδ-αλγής, ποδ-ένδυτος, ποδ-ήνεμος*, παιδ-αγωγός, παιδ-εραστής, κυν-αγωγός, κυν-αλώπηξ, κυν-όδους; so also φωτ in some compounds (φωτ-αγωγός, &c.), and the dissyllabic base κορυθ in κορυθ-άϊξ, κορυθ-αίολος. Proceeding from bases ending in consonants, the conjunctive vowel ο has been communicated also to bases of the third declension ending in a vowel; and while, e.g., πολί-πορθος, μαντι-πόλος, μεθυ-πλήξ, γηρυ-γόνος, βου-τρόφος, ναύ-σταθμος, correspond well to the above-mentioned (§. 968.) Sanscrit formations, mati-bhramá-s, madhupá-s, gô-dhuk, náu-sthá-s, there are no analogous forms to φυσι-ο-λόγο-ς, ἰχθυ-ο-φάγο-ς, βο(F)-ο-τρόφο-ς, νη(F)-ο-φόρο-ς, in Sanscrit and the other sister-languages. In words, however, like λογοποιός (see Buttmann, §. 120. 4.), I can neither recognise a declinational ending, nor a vowel of conjunction, but only the naked base λογο; and therefore consider, e.g., νε(F)ό-μην in its first member as identical with the first member of the Sanscrit nava-dalá-m, "young leaf," and Sclavonic новогрѧдъ novo-grad', "new town" (see §. 257.). In the o, too, of words like ῥιζο-τόμος, ἡμερο-δρόμος, δικο-γράφος, I cannot recognise a vowel of conjunction, but here, as generally in words of the first declension where they are found at the beginning of compounds, I take the o (=Sanscrit a) for the weakening or

---

* With transposition of the members of the compound, cf. p. 1415 G. ed.

shortening of the $\bar{a}$ or η (from $\bar{a}$, see §. 4.), both which vowels, in all feminines, correspond to the Sanscrit $\hat{a}$ (see §. 118.), even where the $\bar{a}$ has been shortened in the nominative and accusative singular. The change of $\breve{a}$, $\bar{a}$, or η, therefore, is like the shortening of the Sanscrit $\hat{a}$ to a in compounds like *priya-bhâryá́,* " dear spouse," where the feminine base *priyá́* [G. Ed. p. 1420.] is changed into the masculine-neuter base by being shortened to *priya.*

970. In remarkable coincidence with the Greek, the Sclavonic, too, at the beginning of compounds, weakens the feminine a = Sanscrit $\hat{a}$ (see §. 552.[a]) to the masculine-neuter o (= Sanscrit a, Greek o, see §. 257.); hence, *e.g.*, водоносъ *vodo-nos̄*, "*hydria,*" properly, "carrying water" for *voda-nos̄;* козодой *koz̄o-doĭ,*" *caprimulgus*" for *koz̄a-doĭ.* The latter would, in Sanscrit, be *ajâ-dhúk* (theme *-dúh*).* The Greek, however, admits also long vowels at the end of the first member of compounds; and so, *e.g.*, σκιᾱ-γράφος, νικη-φόρο-ς, resemble the Sanscrit compounds like *chhâyá́--kará-s,* "umbrella-carrier," properly, "shadow-maker." Γεω--γράφος has again lengthened the form γεο, which has been first developed from γέα, and νεη-γενής, λαμπαδ-η-φόρο-ς, exhibit $\eta = \hat{a}$ for $o = \breve{a}$, as, conversely, η is usually thinned to o. Forms like αἰγ-ί-πους, νυκτ-ί-βιος (=νυκτ-ό-βιος), answer, through their conjunctive ι, to Latin like *noct-i-color;* and so also in forms like μελεσ-ί-πτερο-ς, properly, "having long pinions," I can only recognise in the ι a means of composition in accordance with what has been remarked at §. 128; and in this I differ from Buttmann (§. 120. Rem. 11.). Compare, with reference to the first member of such compounds, and the inserted vowel of conjunction, Latin forms like *fœder-i-fragus.* In forms like ὀρειβάτης, the diphthong ει is explained by the dropping of the σ which belongs to the base; while in the Latin compounds *opifex, munificus, vulni-*

---

* коза *koza*=अजा *ajá,* as кость *kosty*=अस्थि *ásthi,* " bone."

COMPOUNDS.   1377

ficus, for *oper-i-fex*, &c. (cf. *fœder-i-fragus*), not only the *r* which corresponds to the Greek σ, but also the preceding vowel, appears to have been passed over.* [G. Ed. p. 1421.] So, too, *horr-i-ficus*, *terr-i-ficus*, may be regarded as abbreviations of *horrôr-i-ficus*, *terrôr-i-ficus* (cf. *sopôr-i-fer*, *honôr--i-ficus*). In accordance with the almost universal weakening in Latin of the final vowel to *i*, we find in Greek, beside the already mentioned ἀρχι and τερπι, also ἀργι in ἀργί-πους, ἀργι-όδους &c., χαλκι in χαλκί-ναος, χαλκί-οικος, μυρι in μυρί-πνοος, and φοξι in φοξί-χειλος.

971. The Gothic, in my opinion, never makes use of a conjunctive vowel in its compounds, and does not require one, as it has but few bases which end in a consonant, and these are principally such as terminate in *n*. These, however, as in Sanscrit, suppress (see §. 139.) the *n* at the beginning of compounds; hence, *e.g.*, *smakka-bagms*, "fig-tree" (theme *smakkan*, nom, *smakka*. "fig"), for *smakkan-bagms*; *auga-daurô*, "window," properly, "eye-door," for *augan-daurô*,† as above, *râja-putrá-s*, for *râjan-putrá-s*.‡ [G. Ed. p. 1422.] Bases in *r* avoid the harshness of the combination with a

---

* A somewhat different explanation of *opifex* has been attempted above (p. 1352 G. ed.).

† So in Latin, *homi-cida*, *sangui-suga*, for which might have been expected *homin-i-cida*, *sanguin-i-suga*. In Greek, in a similar way, the τ is often suppressed in the suffix ματ (from μαν, see §. 801.), and then the preceding α is generally weakened to ο; hence, *e.g.*, σπερμο-φόρος for σπερματ-ο-φόρος: on the other hand, ὀνομά-κλυτος, which in Sanscrit would appear in the form *náma-śrutá-s*. The Latin retains the *n* of *nomen* in *nomenclator* without appending a conjunctive vowel.

‡ The neuter nom. and acc. *augó* (see §. 141.) affords no ground for the supposition that *augón* is the theme (cf. Gabelentz and Löbe, Gramm., p. 129): we cannot, therefore, in this example, speak of the shortening of the final syllable. Such an abbreviation, however, occurs in inorganic feminine bases in *ôn* and *ein* (see §. 142.); hence, *qvina-kunds*, "having the sex of women" (theme *qvinôn*, nom. *qvinô*, "woman"); *mari-saivs*, "sea," literally, "ocean-sea" (theme *marein*, nom. *marei*).

4 U

following consonant by transposition; hence, *brôthra-lubô*, or *brôthru-lubô*, "brotherly love." *Fidur*, "four" = Sanscrit *chatur* (of the weak cases, and at the beginning of compounds), admits, on the other hand, of the combination of *r* with *dôgs* (see §. 913.); hence, *fidur-dogs*, "every four days," "quartan." As the Gothic, in the nominative and accusative singular, suppresses *a* and *i* of the base, it hereby comes to look as if the said bases properly terminated with a consonant, while the *a* or *i* which enters into the composition seems to be a compositional or conjunctive vowel. Such a compositional vowel, however, I can no more admit in the German languages than in the first and second declension of the Greek and Latin; and as I recognise in Grimm's first strong declension of masculines and neuters, bases in *a*, and in the masculines and feminines of the fourth, bases in *i*, I look upon the *a* of compounds like *guda-faurhts*, "god-fearing," *veina--gards*, "vineyard," and the *i* of such as *gasti-gôds*, "hospitable," *gabaur-di-vaurd*, "birth-register," as distinctly belonging to the first member of the compounds; and I regard the said examples as standing in perfect accordance with the above-mentioned (§. 968.) Sanscrit compounds like *lôka--pálá-s, mati-bhramá-s*.* Just so, in Grimm's third declension,

[G. Ed. p. 1423.] compounds like *fôtu-bandi*, "iron for the feet," *handu-vaurhts*, "prepared with the hand," correspond to Sanscrit like *madhu-pá-s*, "honey-drinking," and Greek like $\mu\epsilon\theta\upsilon\text{-}\pi\lambda\acute{\eta}\xi$. Bases in *ô* (=*â*, see §. 118.) shorten that letter to *a*, whereby there results an accidental agreement with the nominative and accusative singular; hence, *e.g., airtha-kunds*,

---

* I have already, in my review of Grimm's German Grammar (Journal of Lit. Criticism, 1827, p. 758, "Vocalismus," p. 132), shewn that a compositional vowel is altogether unknown in the German languages, and is limited in Latin to the cases in which the first member of the compound terminates with a consonant (*honôr-i-ficus*). In Greek it has by degrees extended itself over the whole third declension, but kept aloof from the first and second, where it is the least needed.

COMPOUNDS. 1379

"earthly" ("having earthly nature"), contrasted with Sanscrit words like *dharâ-dhará-s*, "earth-carrier," and Greek like γεο-φόρο-ς, γεο-ειδής. The originally short *a* of masculine and neuter base words is occasionally suppressed; for example, in *thiudan'-gardi*, "king's house;" *guth'-blôstreis*, "God-worshipper" (for *guda-*); *gud'-hus*, "God's house;" *hals'-agga*, "nape" ("nape of the neck"); *thiu-magus*, "servant," properly, "servant-boy" (for *thiva-*); *sigis'-laun*, (for *sigisa-*, see §. 935.) "reward of victory;" *gut'-thiuda*, "the Gothic nation; *midyun'-gards*, "terrestrial globe"*; *vein'--drugkya*, "wine-drinker;" and in some compounds, the first member of which is an adjective or pronoun, as, *hauh'-hairts*, "magnanimous" (literally, "having a high heart"); *laus--handus*, "having empty hands;" *anthar'-leiks*, "diverse," properly, "like to another." To *vein'-drugkya*, corresponds, with respect to the suppression of the final vowel of the first member, the Latin *vin'-demia* (cf. p. 1417 G. ed., Note). Those Gothic substantive bases in *ya* (Grimm's second declension) which, before this syllable, have a long syllable, or more syllables than one, suppress the *a*, and vocalise the *y* to *i* (cf. §. 135.); hence, *e.g.*, *andi-laus*, "endless," for *andya-laus; arbi-numya*, "heir" ("taker of [G. Ed. p. 1424.] inheritance"); on the other hand, *frathya-marzeins*, "deception of the intellect" (*frathya*, n., nom. *frathi*, see §. 153.); *vadya-bôkôs*, pl. "mortgage" (*vadya*, n., nom. *vadi*). The feminine substantive base *thusundyô*, too, in the compound *thusundi-faths*, χιλίαρχος, contracts its final syllable to *i*, for which its polysyllabicness, or the positional length of its penultima, may have given occasion. Adjective bases in

---

* As the first member of this compound does not occur in its simple state, it is uncertain whether its theme is really *midyuna;* in which case I should compare it, just as also the feminine base *midumi* (nom. *midums*), with the Sanscrit *madhyama*, "*medius*." In Sanscrit the earth is called, among other names, *madhyama-lôká-s* and *madhya-lôká-s*, *i.e.* literally, "the middle world" ("between heaven and the infernal regions").

4 U 2

ya retain, even when preceded by a long vowel, the full themal form; hence, *hrainya-hairts*, "having pure heart:" besides which I do not know another compound with an adjective base in *ya* as the first member, for in *midya-sveipeins*, "deluge," properly, "earth-inundation," *midya*, though identical with the adjective base *midya*, stands as substantive, while the Sanscrit sister word, *madhya* in the above-mentioned (p. 1423 G. ed., Note) *madhyalôká-s*, "earth," as "middle world," stands as adjective. The pronominal base *alya* = Sanscrit *anya*, "*alius*," corresponds in *alya-kuns* to the Greek ἄλλο in ἀλλο-γενής.

972. In Old High German, too, the final vowel of the bases of Grimm's first strong declension, masculine and neuter, has been pretty frequently retained, either unaltered, or weakened to *o* or *e*; hence, *e.g.*, *taga-rod*, "redness of morn" ("aurora"); *tage-lôn*, "daily pay;" *taga-sterno*, and *tage-sterno*, "lucifer" ("day-star"); *spila-hûs*, *spilo-hûs*, *spile-hûs*, "playhouse;" *grape-hûs*, "grave-house." Bases, too, in *i* have occasionally preserved this vowel, or corrupted it to *e*, *e.g.*, in *steti-got*, "loci genius;" *prûti-chamara*, *briute-chamara*, "bride-chamber;" *prûti-geba*, "bridal present;" *brûti-gomo*, "bridegroom" ("bride's-man"). The Lithuanian, exclusive of the obscure compounds in *ninka-s* discussed above (p. 1344 G. ed.), regularly rejects the final vowel, as also the termination *ia*, *ya* (nom. *i-s*, *yi-s*, see §. 135.) of the substantive, adjective, and nominal bases, which appear as the first member of compounds, when they have more than one syllable; *e.g.*, *wyn'-kalnis*, "hill planted with vines" (*wyna-s*, "wine"); *wyn'-médis*, "vine;" *dyw'-darys*, "wonder-worker" (*dywa-s*, "wonder"); *krau-leidys*, "one who lets blood" (*krauya-s*, "blood" = Sanscrit *kravya*, "flesh"); *griĕk-twanis*, *Sündflut**, "deluge;" *auks'-kalys*, *auksa-kalys*, "goldsmith" (*auksa-s*,

---

* *Griĕka-s*, "sin;" *twana-s*, "flood:" the German word, however, has avowedly nothing to do with "sin," and is in Old High German *sin-fluot,'sin-flüt*.

COMPOUNDS. 1381

"gold"); *auksa-darys*, "worker in gold ;" *barzd'-skuttis*, or *barzda-skuttis*, "razor," properly, "beard-shaving" (*barzdà*, f., "beard"); *did'-burnis*, "one that has a great mouth" (*diddi-s*, theme *didia*, euphonic *didźia*, "great"); *did'-galwys*, "he that has a great head;" *wien'-rágis*, "one-horned" (*wiena-s*, "one"): *saw'-redus*, "obstinate" (*sawa-s*, "*suus*").

973. The Zend, as has been already remarked, instead of the naked theme, places the nominative singular as the first member of its compounds, and I have already drawn attention elsewhere to a similar use in Old Persian*. It cannot surprise us if, in the European sister-languages also, isolated cases occur, in which the nominative singular takes the place of the theme; and I differ from Buttmann (§. 120., Note 11.), in that I do not hesitate to take the Greek θεος of θεόσ-δοτος in Hes. to be just as much the nominative as the Zend *daêvô* (from *daêvas*, see §. 56.[b.]) in the quite analogous compound *daêvô-dâta*, "produced by the Daêvas" (Sanscrit *dêva*, "God"). In θέσφατος, and some other compounds beginning with θες, one easily recognises a contraction of θεος. Perhaps, also, in the compounds beginning with ναυσι, as ναυσιβάτης (=ναυβάτης), Ναυσίθοος, Ναυσιθόη, Ναυσιμέδων, the nominative ναυς is con- [G. Ed. p. 1426.] tained as representative of the theme†, and to it an ι has been added as conjunctive vowel (cf. §. 970); if not, I should prefer to regard ναυσι as a derivative which has been formed from ναυ=Sanscrit *nâu*, with the suffix σι (from τι), and which has ceased to be used by itself. It appears to me less probable that it is the dative plural of ναῦς, and least of all would I take the σ here as euphonic. The Gothic *baurgs* of *baurgs-vaddyus*, "town walls," I take to be the genitive, as it stands in the genitive relation, and as this irregular word

---

* See Monthly Intelligence of the Acad. of Lit., March 1848, p. 135.
† I recall attention to the fact, that in Sanscrit only monosyllabic words carry the *s* of the nominative into the locative, to which a case-sign does not properly belong.

exhibits, as well in the genitive as in the nominative, the form *baurgs*. In Sanscrit we might take *divas* in *divas--pati-s* as the genitive of *div*, as I also formerly did: as, however, there is a compound *divas-prithivy-âu*, "heaven and earth," which is passed over in this explanation, and in which *divas* does not stand in the genitive relation, I now prefer to assume a base *divas*, to be found only in composition, which is also contained in the proper name *divô-dâsa* (see Benfey's Gloss.), and whence, too, has proceeded the extended base *divasa*, as in general the suffix *asa* is only an extension of *as*. To the base *divas*, which is only found at the beginning of compounds, corresponds well the Latin *dies* in *dies-piter*. The second part of this compound is indeed only a weakening of *pater*, to be explained according to §. 6., but here hardly signifies "father," but, in accordance with its etymology, "ruler" (see §. 812.). The Greek exhibits a real genitive, which, however, Buttmann (§. 120., Note 11.) will not recognise as such, in the compound νεώσ-οικοι, in which the singular surprises me as

[G. Ed. p. 1427.] as little as in our term *Schiffshäuser*, "ships' houses." Moreover, the first part of οὐδενόσ-ωρα I cannot take otherwise than as the genitive.

974. The Indian Grammarians divide compound words into six classes, which we will now examine separately in the order in which they follow one another in Vôpadêva.

FIRST CLASS.

Copulative Compounds called *Dvandva*.*

This class consists of the compounds of two or more substantives, which are co-ordinate to one another, *i.e.* which

---

* The Sanscrit term *dvandva-m*,, *i.e.* "pair," is a reduplicated form formed from the theme *dva*, "two" (cf. §. 756.).—*N.B.* I spell this word as it is found in the German, but व *v*, when compounded with another consonant in Sanscrit, is pronounced like *w*. See Wilson's Grammar, p. 5, l. 18.—*Translator*.

stand in the like case-relation, and are, according to the sense, joined together by "and." These compounds are divided into two classes; the first permits to the last member of the compound the gender which belongs to it, and puts it in the dual when only two substantives are joined together, of which each by itself stands in the singular relation; and in the plural when the compound consists of more than two substantives, or when one of the two members so united is in a plural relation. The accent regularly falls on the final syllable of the united base; hence, e.g., sûrya-chandramásâu, " sun and moon." In the Vêda dialect, however, one of the two words combined in Dvandva very often receives the accent which belongs to it in its simple state; and in the Dvandvas, which occur in the Vêdas, the first member often stands in the dual, at least I think in compounds like agnî-shômâu, "Agni and Sôma," índrâ-várunâu, "Indra and Varuna," mitrâ-várunâu, "Mitra and Varuna," índrâ-víshnû, "Indra and [G. Ed. p. 1428.] Vishnu," I may venture to regard* the lengthening of the final vowel of the first member of the compound, not as purely phonetic, but as the consequence of the dual inflection; as, too, I look upon the final á of dyávâ, "heaven," in combination with prithivî, " earth " (dyâvâprithivî), as the Vêdic dual termination, which has been added to dyâu (the strong theme of dyô), just like the â in the Vêdic compound pitarâ-mâtárâu, "father and mother." As dual, too, I regard the Zend âpa (theme âp) in the copulative ᚴᚢᛋᛦᚴᛋᚢ âpa-urvarê†, "water and tree" (V. S. p. 40). There occurs, l. c., one other Dvandva which we cannot leave unnoticed, as compounds of this kind have hitherto

---

* Cf. §.214., p.228, Note *, and see "Smaller Sans. Gram.," §.589., Note.
† Burnouf, to whom we owe an admirable disquisition on the greatest part of the 9th chapter of the Yaçna, does not declare his opinion as to the first member of the copulative compound âpa-urvarê ("Études," p. 147).

been but very seldom cited in Zend. I annex the conclusion of the passage referred to, according to Burnouf's corrected text: -ɛ̓ɛ̔ɢ̌ᴀ ᴘᴏᴍ⁄ᴏ̌ᴍᴘᴏ̌ᴏ̌ ᴘᴜᴡᴍᴀᴊᴘ ᴘᴏᴍᴊᴋ̌ᴊɛ̓ɛ̔ᴄ̌ ᴘᴏᴍᴄ ᴘᴏ⁄ᴀᴍ⁄ᴊᴏᴏᴍᴘᴏᴊᴍᴄ̌ᴀ̌ᴘᴘᴀᴄᴊᴡᴍᴀᴘ ᴀᴊ⁄ᴊᴊ»ᴊᴊᴀᴏᴏᴏ ᴀᴘᴏ̌ᴍᴀᴍᴘᴘ *yaṭ kĕrĕnôiṭ anhê cshathrâṭ amĕrĕshanta paṡu-vîra anhushamanê âpa-urvarê*, i.e., literally, "that he make under his dominion not dying beast and man, not drying up water and tree." Neriosengh translates pretty exactly, only with a different notion for the compound *paṡu-vîra: yaś chakâra tasya râjyê amarân paśuvîrân aśoshini udakâni vanaspatîn*, i.e., "who made in his kingdom undying the males among animals and not drying up the water, trees." Burnouf (l. c. p. 145) draws attention to the circumstance, that *yaṭ kĕrĕnôiṭ* properly sig-

[G. Ed. p. 1429.] nifies "*pour qu'il fît,*" nor has it escaped him that *paṡu-vîra* may also mean "*les troupeaux et les hommes*" (p. 140); he translates, however, in accordance with Neriosengh, "*car il a, sous son règne, affranchi de la mort les mâles des troupeaux, de la sécheresse les eaux et les arbres.*" I admit that *amĕrĕshanta** and *vîra* might also be plural accusatives, and I recall attention on this head to what has been remarked above (§. 231., Note) regarding the manner in which neuter forms have found their way into the plural of masculines. This does not, however, prevent me from letting, in the passage before us, the *a* of the said words, according to §. 208., stand for the dual termination, as, in my opinion, it gives a much more suitable sense, if, by taking *paṡu-vîra* as Dvandva, we place, not only the males of animals, but animals and human beings

---

* In the sibilant of this form I recognise neither any connection with the character of the future, nor with that of the desiderative, but simply a phonetic affix, and recall attention to the fact, that the Sanscrit, too, has several secondary roots which have appended a sibilant. In the case before us the Lithuanian *mirsz-tu*, "I die" (pret. *mirriau*, fut. *mir-su*, infin. *mir-ti*), fortuitously coincides with the Zend.

of both sexes under the protection of the government of Yima.

975. To return to the Vêdic Dvandvas, I must draw attention to the circumstance, that the dual termination, which is common to the nominative, accusative, and vocative, is retained also in that case, in which the whole word stands in another case-relation, and the last member, therefore, ends in *bhyâm* or *ôs; e.g., dyává-prithiví-bhyâm*, "to the heaven and to the earth" (Yajurv. XXII. 28.), *indrá-púshnóh*, "of Indra and the Sun" (l. c. XXV. 25.). This phenomenon may be explained by the language having become unconscious that the first member actually carries a case-termination, whereby remembrance may be drawn to the above-mentioned (§. 973.) [G. Ed. p. 1430.] Zend idiom, by which the nominative singular very commonly takes the place of the theme. If we should also actually recognise, in forms like *índrá, agní*, simply a phonetic lengthening of the *a* and *i* of the common language, we could not, however, by this mode of explanation, clear up *pitár-á, dyáv-á, púshán-á* and *kshám-á*. It is also important to remark, that, as Benfey has been the first to notice*, where the first member of the Dvandva is separated from the second, the former assumes the requisite termination of the oblique cases of the dual, but *á* only there where suitable for the connection with the other words. Thus, in a passage cited by Benfey l. c. of the Rigv. (IV. 8. 11.), we find the genitive, *mitráyôs ... várunayôs*, "of Mitra and Varuna;" on the other hand *dyává*, as accusative dual separated from *prithiví* (Rigv. I. 63. 1.). This phenomenon in expressing the numeral relation is owing to the speaker's, when he names each part of the compound thing which is usually thought of together, having

---

* In his Review of Böhtlingk's Sanscrit-Chrestomathy (Göttinger Learned Notices, 1846).

the other in his mind, and this latter thus ideally comprehended under the name of that he mentions (cf. §. 214. 1st Note), so that, therefore, *e.g.*, *dyává-prithiví**, properly signifies, "Heaven and earth, earth and heaven;" hence, too, the name of one member of the compound may be understood; and, *e.g.*, in a passage of the Sâma-Vêda (II. 3. 2. 8. 2. and 3.), the dual *mitrá* occurs in the sense of "Mitra and Varuṇa," and I am of opinion that the dual *ródasí*, which, in classical Sanscrit, also signifies "heaven and earth," denotes by its base *ródas* only "heaven," though the meaning "earth" [G. Ed. p. 1431.] has also been ascribed to it †. I draw attention here to a similar procedure in several Malay-Polynesian languages, since, *e.g.*, in the New Zealand *tá-ua* (lit. "thou two," therefore, as it were, the dual of the second person) signifies, "thou and I. ‡" Here, *ta* answers to the Sanscrit base *tva*, "thou," and *ua*, which, when standing by itself, is *dúa*, to *dva*.

976. Combinations of more than two substantives in one Dvandva appear not to occur in the Vêdic dialect and Zend; at least, I know of no example. Examples in classic Sanscrit are: *agni-váyu-ravibhyas*, "From fire, air, and sun" (Manu, I. 23.); *gíta-váditra-nrityáni*, "Song, instrumental music, and dance" (Arjuna's Journey to Indra's heaven,

---

* For *prithivyáù*, with the case-termination suppressed, cf. p. 1205 G. ed.

† Wilson, perhaps correctly, derives *ródas* from *rud*, "to weep," with the suffix *as;* "the heaven" therefore would be here represented as "weeping" ("raining"), and the drops of rain as its tears. This is certainly not more unnatural than when the cloud (*méghá*) is represented as "*mingens*." Moreover, the Greek οὐρανός admits of being derived from a root which, in Sanscrit, signifies "to rain," viz. from *varsh*, *vṛish*, with the loss, therefore, of a sibilant, as χαίρω from χαίρσω (Sanscrit root *harsh*, *hṛish*). Οὐρανός, therefore, would be a transposition of Ϝορανός. Regarding the suffix *avo*, see p. 1369 G. ed.

‡ See "On the connection of the Malay-Polynesian languages with the Indo-European," p. 87.

IV. 7.); *siddha-chârana-gandharvâis,* " by Siddhas, Châranas, and Gandharvas (l. c. V. 14.). In such cases the last member, if it does not already for itself stand in the plural relation, should evidently express, by its plural termination, the sum of the whole. In the second kind of copulative compounding, which is used especially in antithesis, or when speaking of the members of the body, or of abstract ideas, and generally of inanimate things or insects, the last member stands in the singular with a neuter termination; the separate members may stand by themselves in the singular, dual, or plural re- [G. Ed. p. 1432.] lation, *e.g., charâcharam (chara-acharam),* "the moveable and immoveable" (Manu, I. 57.); *hasta-pâdam,* " hands and feet" (1. c. II. 90.; *pâda,* masc.); *anna-pânam,* "food and drink" (Arjuna, 4. 11.); *chhatrôpânaham*,* " umbrella and shoes" (Manu, II. 246.); *yûkâ-makshika-matkunam,* " lice, flies, and bugs" (l. c. I. 40., *matkuna,* masc.).

977. In Sanscrit adjectives, too, which are in sense joined by "and," may be united in compounds, which are not indeed reckoned by the Indian grammarians as Dvandvas, but can be assigned to none of the six classes with more justice. The following are examples: *vritta-pîna,* "round and thick" (Arjuna II. 19); *hrishitasrag-rajôhîna,* "having garlands of flowers standing upright and free from dust" (Nal. V. 25.). So in Greek, λευκο-μέλας, " white and black." A substantive Dvandva base is βατραχομυο, in the compound, βατραχομυομαχία, " frog-mouse war." In Latin the derivative *suovitaurilia* is based on a Dvandva consisting of three members, which must have been, according to the first kind of this class of Sanscrit compounding (§. 974.), *su--ovi-tauri;* according to the second (§. 976.), *su-ovi-taurum* (" swine, sheep, and bull").

---

* From *chhatra* n., and *upânah* f., with *a* added.

SECOND CLASS.

Possessive Compounds, called *Bahuvríhi*.*

978. Compounds of this class denote as adjectives or [G. Ed. p. 1433.] appellatives the possessor of that which the separate members of the compound signify, so that the notion of the possessor is always to be supplied. For this reason I call them "possessive compounds." The last member is always a substantive, or an adjective taken as a substantive, and the first member may be any other part of speech but a verb, conjunction, or interjection. The final substantive undergoes no other alteration but that which the distinction of genders makes necessary; whence, *e.g.*, *chháyá*, f., "shadow," in the compound *vipulá-chchháya*,† has shortened its long feminine *á*, in order to become referable to masculines and neuters. So, in Greek, the feminine final vowel of the bases of the first declension becomes *o* (= Sanscrit *a*), and in Latin *u*, in possessive compounds like πολύσκιο-ς, πολύκομο-ς, αἰολόμορφο-ς, *multi-comus, albi--comu-s, multi-vius*. The procedure in Old High German is the same, when it places the feminine substantive *farwa* or *farawa*, &c., "colour," at the end of possessive compounds, and then furnishes the whole word, where it refers to masculines or neuters, with the terminations of the said genders; hence, *e,g.*, nom. m. *snio-varawar seo*, "sea having the colour of snow" (Graff, III. 702.) ; neut. *golt-varawaz*, "having the colour of gold." I see, therefore, no occasion to presuppose, for the explanation of such compounds, adjectives which do not exist; otherwise we might, with equal justice, assume in Greek and Latin adjectives like κομος,

---

* This word signifies "having much rice," and it is properly only an example of the kind of compounding here spoken of, as, in Greek and Latin, πολύκομος, *multicomus*, might be used to denote the same.

† *Chchh*, euphonic for *chh*, on account of the short vowel preceding.

comus, "hairy," and for Sanscrit an adjective *chhâya-s,* "shady." The Greek has forgotten how to re-transform into its feminine shape the ο which has arisen from α or η in compounds like πολύσκιος, πολύκομος, and contrasts, therefore, with Sanscrit feminines like *vipulâchchhâyâ,* "having a large shadow," and Latin like [G. Ed. p. 1434.] *multicoma, albicoma,* masculine forms like πολύσκιος, πολύκομος (see p. 1341 G. ed.): on the other hand, the Latin, according to the principle laid down in §. 6., has changed the final vowels of the bases of the first and second declension frequently into the lightest and most suitable vowel of the three genders.* Hence, *e.g., multi-formis, difformis, biformis, imbellis, abnormis, bilinguis, inermis;* so, also, the organic *u* of the fourth declension in *bicornis;* while, on the other hand, *manu-s,* in the compound *longi-manus,* has passed into the second declension.

979. Just as the neuter Sanscrit *hṛid,* "heart" (from *hard*), in the possessive compound *suhṛid,* "friend," properly, "having a good heart," has become masculine, and is therefore, in some cases, distinguished from the simple *hṛid,* so it happens with the Latin neuter base *cord* in the compound bases *miseri-cord†, concord, socord;* hence the accusatives *misericordem, concordem, socordem,* answer to the Sanscrit *suhṛidam,* while the simple *cor*(*d*), as nominative and accusative, corresponds to the Sanscrit *hṛid* (euphonic *hṛit*). The Gothic neuter base *hairtan* suppresses, in the undermentioned possessive compound, the final *n,* and ex-

---

* The final *e* of neuters like *difforme* is only a corruption of the *i* at the end of a word (see §. 251.).

† Properly, "for the unfortunate having a heart," not "*cujus cor miseret.*" So the Gothic *arma-hairts,* "pitiful," properly signifies "having a heart for the poor;" for in it the adjective-base *arma* is contained, as the base *miseru* in the Latin *misericors,* which base is weakened to *miseri,* according to §. 968.

hibits then *arma-hairta* as theme, and *arma-hairt-s* (Old High German *arme-herzer* in Notk.) for *arma-hirta-s*, (see §. 135.), as masculine nominative (pl. *arma-hairtai*); so *hrainya-hairts,* "having a pure heart;" *hauh-hairts* (for *hauha-hairts,* "high-minded," properly, "having a high heart." The Greek and Latin, too, oc- [G. Ed. p. 1435.] casionally drop a final consonant at the end of possessive compounds; hence, e.g., in Greek ὁμώνυμος, ἑπτάστομος, ἄναιμος, αὔθαιμος, in Latin, *exsanguis* (properly, "having the blood out," gen. idem., for *exsanguin-is*), *multi-genus*: for the latter we might have expected *multi-genor,* if the suffix of the simple word be contained therein uucurtailed, and also without affix, as *us, eris* = Sanscrit *as, asas,* has retained the old *s* only in the uninflected cases of the neuter (see §. 128.), but for it exhibits *r* in the masculine and feminine (see p. 1377 G. ed.); hence, *bicorpor,* opposed to the simple *corpus, corporis*. The base *gener (genus, gener-is)* appears with the inorganic affix of an *i* in *multi-generi-s*. The Greek occasionally appends an *o* to bases ending in a consonant, e.g., to πῦρ in ἄπυρο-ς, θεόπυρο-ς (properly, "having God's fire"), to ὕδωρ in εὔϋδρος, μελάνυδρος.

980. The Lithuanian uses its possessive compounds for the most part substantively, and adds to their last member as to that of almost all its compounds, the suffix *ia*, nom. m. *is**; hence, e.g., *did'-burnis,* "the large-mouthed" (*burna,* "mouth," cf. Sanscrit *brû,* "to speak"); *did'-galwis,* "great head" ("having a great head," *galwà,* "head"); *ketur-kampis,* "four-cornered" (*kampa-s,* "corner"); *trikoyis,* "three-footed, having three feet" (*kòya,* "foot"). The feminine of the Lithuanian possessive compounds, and other classes of compounds, ends, in the nominative singular, in *ĕ̆*, from *ia* †; hence, e.g., *na-bagĕ̆,* "the poor," properly, "not

---

* See §. 135., and p. 1345 G. ed., Note.
† See §. 895.

having wealth"*; *pus-mergḗ,* "the half-maid" (the latter a determinative compound; *mergà,* "maid"). [G. Ed. p. 1436.] To this belongs the phenomenon, that the Sanscrit, too, adds a derivative suffix to some of its possessive compounds, and, indeed, the same wherewith above (§. 953.) our *i-g,* Gothic *ha, ga,* has been compared. Our compounds, therefore, like *hochherzig,* "high-hearted," contrasted with the Gothic *hauh-hairts,* are in a measure already prepared through the Sanscrit by compounds like *angushṭhá--mátra-ka-s,* "having a thumb's length" (Nal. XIV. 9.); *mahóraska-s,* "great-breasted." Without the derivative suffix we can use our possessive compounds like *Dreifuss, Viereck, Rothbrüstchen, Langohr, Gelbschnabel, Dickkopf, Grossmaul,* "Three-foot," "Four-corner," "Red-breast," "Long-ear," "Yellow-beak," "Thick-head," "Great-mouth," only as appellatives, or as words of abuse.

981. The accent in the Sanscrit possessive compounds usually rests on the first member of the compound, and, indeed, on that syllable which receives it when the word stands uncompounded. This kind of accentuation approaches most closely to that of Greek, in which the principle prevails to cast back the accent in all kinds of compounds as far as possible, without reference to the accentuation of the separate members in their simple state; a procedure by which the compound gains much more of the character of a new ideal unity than if the retention of the accentuation of one of the combined elements preserved for that member its individuality, and made the other member subservient to it. In the other classes of compounds, the Sanscrit usually takes no notice of the accentuation of the single members in their simple state, yet

---

* The simple *baga-s,* "wealth," is wanting; cf. Sanscrit *bhaga-s* and *bhága-s,* "share," "luck." The masculine *na-bágas* has the suffix *ia* contained in it.

does not cast back the accent, but allows it to sink down on the final syllable of the whole base; hence, e.g., *mahá-báhú-s*, "a great arm," opposed to *mahá-báhu-s*, "great-armed," while in Greek the possessive compound μεγαλόπολις, "great-town [G. Ed. p. 1437.] forming," and the determinative Μεγαλόπολις, properly, "great-town," have the same accentuation.

982. The form *mahá*, in the just-mentioned compounds *mahá-báhu-s* and *mahá-báhú-s*, is an irregular abbreviation of *mahát*, "great" (theme of the weak cases), which, at the beginning of possessive and determinative compounds, drops its *t*, and then the lengthening of the *á* may be regarded as compensation for the consonant that has been dropped. Although in Sanscrit, according to §. 978., all the parts of speech, with the exception of verbs, conjunctions, and interjections, may stand as the first members of possessive compounds, still for the most part, as also in the European sister-languages, adjectives, including participles, appear in this place. I further annex some examples from the Mahâ-Bhârata: *chấru-lốchana-s*, "having beautiful eyes;" *bahú-vidha-s*, "of many kinds" (*vidhá*, m. or *vidhá*, f. "kind"); *tanú-madhya-s*, "having a thin middle;" *virûpa-rûpa-s*, "having a disfigured form" (*rûpá-m*, "form"); *tíkshná-danshtra-s*, "having pointed teeth" (*dánshtrá*, f. "tooth"); *lambá-jathara-s*, "having a swagging belly;" *sphurád-ôshtha-s*, "having trembling lips" (*sphurámi*, Cl. 6. "I tremble"); *jáyad-ratha-s*, proper name, signifying "having a conquering car;" *jitá-krôdha-s*, "having subdued anger;" *gatá-vyatha-s*, "having departed grief," *i.e.*, "free from grief." The following are examples in Zend: ﺟﺴﺘﻤﺠﺴﺘﻤ *sríraôcshan*, "having good oxen" (from *sríra* and *ucshan*); *kĕrĕsaôcshan*, "having thin oxen" (*kĕrĕsa*=Sanscrit *krísa*)*; *kĕrĕsáspa*, proper name, "having thin horses" (from *kĕrĕsa* and *aspa*); ﺟﺴﺘﻤﺠﺴﺘﻤ *cshaêtô-*

---

* See Burnouf, "Yaçna," p. 328, n. 185.

-*puthrî*, " who has bright (beautiful) children." The following are examples in Greek: μεγά-θυμος, [G. Ed. p. 1438.] μεγα-κύδης, μεγα-κλεής, λευκό-πτερος, δολιχό-σκιος, λευκ'-όφθαλμος, βαθύ-στερνος, πολύ-χρυσος, τανύ-πεπλος, μελάμ-βωλος, μελαν-ό-κομος, κλυτό-παις, κλυτό-βουλος. The following are Latin examples: *magn'-animus, multi-caulis, longi-pes, atri--color, açu-pedius*, versi-color, fissi-pes, flex'-animus.* Gothic examples are: *laus'-qvithr'-s*, " having an empty body, fasting" (for *lausa-*); *laus'-handus*, " having empty hands ;" *lausa-vaurds*, " having wanton, vain words, speaking unprofitably" (*vaurd*, n., theme *vaurda*, " word"); *hrainya--hairts*, " having a pure heart" (see §. 979.). Examples in Old High German are: *lang-lîper*, " having long life"†; *lanch-mueter*, " long-suffering ;" *milt-herzer*, " having a mild heart." For Lithuanian examples, see §. 980. Examples in Old Sclavonic are: милосердъ *milo-serd'*, " misericors," literally, " having a loving heart ;" черноокый *cherno-okyĭ*, " black-eyed ;" бѣлоглавый *byelo-glavyĭ*, " white-headed."‡ The following are examples in Sanscrit of possessive compounds, which have a substantive as their first member: *bandhú-kâma-s*, " having love to kindred ;" *tyáktu-kâma-s*, "having a desire to leave " (see §. 853.); *bála-putra-s*, "having a child as son" (Sâv. II. 8.); *mâtrí-shashtha-s*, " having the mother as sixth " (Hid. I. 1.): in Greek, κυν-ό-φρων, κυν-ο-θαρσής, βου-κέφαλος, ἀνδρ-ό-βουλος: in Latin, *angui-*

---

* This compound (according to Festus) should properly be *acu-pes*, in the theme *acu-ped*. Through the appended suffix *iu* it answers to the Lithuanian compounds (§. 980.). In Sanscrit the theme would be *âsú--pád* (from *âkú*), and in Greek ὠκύ-πους, ὠκύ-ποδ-ος. The first member of the Latin compound is therefore important to us, because adjective bases terminating in an original *u* have elsewhere, in Latin, universally received the inorganic affix of an *i* (see p. 1356 G. ed.).

† Graff (II. p. 46) unnecessarily assumes an adjective *lîb*, " lively," while we may be satisfied with the substantive *lîp*, *lib*, "life."

‡ The two last examples with the affix of the definite declension.

[G. Ed. p. 1439.] *comus, angui-pes, ali-pes, pudor-i-color*: in Lithuanian, *szuk'-dantis*, "having gaps in the teeth" (*szukkě*, "hole, gap"); *szun-galwis*, "dog's head" (an abusive word), properly, "the dog's headed" (cf. §. 980.). The following are examples in Sanscrit, with a numeral at the commencement: *dvi-påd**, "two-footed;" *trichakrá*, "three-wheeled" (Sâma-V.); *chátush-pád*, "four-footed" (l. c.): in Zend, ·ᛚᛰᛯᛝ·ᛝᛧᛞᛟ *bi-zanhra*, "two-footed;" ·ᛰᛝᚦᛝᛟᛝᛟ᛫ᛪᛝᛰ *chathru-chashman*, "having four eyes;" ·ᛰᚦᛝᚢᛝᛟᛟ»ᛪᛯᛟᛙ *cshvas-ashi*, "having six eyes;" ·ᛰᛪᛯᛙᛰᛝᛳᛝᛟᛯᛝᛰ *hazanhrô-ghaôsha*, "having a thousand ears:" in Greek, δίπους, διπόταμος, δίπορος, τρίπους, τετράκυκλος: in Latin, *bipes, bidens, bicorpor, tripes, tripectorus†, quadrupes, quadr'-urbs, quinquefolius*: in Lithuanian, *wien'-ragis*, "one-horned" (*ragas*, "horn," see §. 980.); *dwi-koyis*, "two-footed;" *tri-koyis*, "three foot;" *tri-kampis*, "three-cornered;" *tri-galwis*, "three-headed;" *ketur-koyis*, "four-footed:" in Sclavonic, кдиноѓогъ *yedino-rog'*, "one-horned;" четврѣногъ *chetvrye-nog'*, "four-footed" (*noga*, "foot"): in Gothic, *haihs*, "one-eyed" (see p. 418): in Old High German, *ein-hanter*, "one-handed;" *ein-ouger*, "one-eyed;" *zui-ekker*, "two-cornered;" *feor-fuazzer*, "four-footed." The following are examples of Sanscrit possessive compounds with a pronoun as the first member: *svayám-prabha-s*, "having lustre by itself" (*svayám*, "self," see §. 341., *prabhá*, "lustre"); *tád-ákára-s*, "having such appearance;" *mád-vidha-s*, "like me," properly, "having the kind of me." Examples in Greek are: αὐτόβουλος, [G. Ed. p. 1440.] αὐτόδικος, αὐτοθάνατος, αὐτόκομος, αὐτομή-

---

* In the weak cases *dvi-pád*. The numerals in this kind of composition retain the accent only under certain conditions: usually it falls on the final syllable of the whole word (see Aufrecht, "*De accentu compositorum Sanscr.*," pp. 12, 20.

† With an extension of the base *pector* (cf. *bicorpor*) by a vowel affix, as in Greek forms like θεόπυρος (§. 979. conclusion).

τωρ, αὐτόμοιρος. The following are examples with an adverb preceding them in Sanscrit: *táthá-vidha-s*, "so constituted," properly, "having its kind so;" *sadá-gati-s*, "always having going," an appellation of the wind; so in Greek, ἀείκαρπος, ἀειπαθής, ἀεισθενής. In Sanscrit the *a* primitive, before vowels *an*, very frequently appears at the beginning of this class of compounds, in which case the accent sinks down on the final syllable; hence, *e.g.*, *a-malá-s*, "spotless" ("not having spots"); *a-pád*, "footless;" *a-balá-s*, "weak" ("not having strength"); *a-bhayá-s*, "fearless;" *an-antá-s*, "endless" ("not having end"). Hereto correspond, irrespective of the accentuation, Greek compounds like ἄπαις, ἄπους (genit. ἄποδ-ος=Sanscrit *a-pad-as*), ἄφοβος, ἄνοικος. The Latin, which retains the nasal of the privative particle before consonants, also furnishes us with compounds like *inops, iners, inermis, insomnis, imberbis, imbellis*. So in Old Northern, *ó-hræsi*, "not having glory, gloryless" (*hrus*, "praise"); *ó-máli*, "not having speech," "child" (*mál*, "speech"): Old High German, *un-fasel*, "insect," literally, "not having seed" (*fasel*, "seed," Grimm, II. 776.). A Zend example of this class of words is *anaghra*, "beginningless," from *an* and *aghra* = Sanscrit *agra*, "point, beginning" (see p. 246).

983. For a purpose similar to that for which the privative particle *a* is applied, prepositions also, which express separation, are used in Sanscrit and its sister-languages as initial members of possessive compounds; *e.g.*, in Sanscrit, *ápa-bhí-s*, "fearless, having fear away" (*ápa*, "from, away," *bhí*, f. "fear"); so in Greek, ἀπόθυμος, ἀπόθριξ; in Latin, *abnormis;* in Gothic, *af-guds*, "godless" ("having God away"), in opposition to *ga-guds*, "pious," properly, "having God with." निस् *nis*, "out," before sonant letters *nir*, is found, *e.g.*, in *nír-mala-s*, "spotless," properly, "having the spots out;" as in Latin, *e.g.*, *ex-* [G. Ed. p. 1441.] *animis, exsanguis, expers;* in Gothic, *e.g.*, *us-véna*, theme

uz-vênan, "hopeless, having the hope out" (*vên(i)-s,* f. "hope"); Old High German, *ur-hërzêr,* "*excors;*" *ur-luzêr* (for *-hl.*), "*exsors;*" *ur-môt,* "spiritless;" *ur-wâfan,* "unarmed, defenceless." In a sense opposed to that of the privative prepositions, the preposition *sa,* "with"*, which occurs only as prefix, is employed in Sanscrit to express persons or things which possess that which the final substantive expresses; *e.g., sá-kâma-s,* "with wish," *i.e.* "being with the circumstance of the wish, having a satisfied wish;" *sá-ruj,* "sick, being with sickness;" *sá-rôga-s,* id. (*ruch* and *rôga,* "sickness"); *sá-varna-s,* "similar," properly, "*concolor*" (*varna-m,* "colour"); *sá-garva-s,* "proud, being with pride;" *sá-daya-s,* "sympathizing" (*dayâ,* "sympathy"). So in Latin, *e.g., concors, consors, concolor, conformis, confinis, commodus, communis* (for *con* and *munus,* cf. *immunis*); in Greek, *e.g.,* σύνορος, σύνταφος, συντελής, σύνορκος, σύνοπλος, σύνομβρος, σύνοικος, σύνοδος, σύγγονος, σύνθρονος, σύμμορφος, συγγάλακτος; the latter with the extension of the substantive base by *o* (see §.979. conclusion). On the Sanscrit *sa* is based the Greek ἁ (from ἁ for σα) in compounds like ἀγάλακτος, ἀγάλαξ, ἀδελφός, ἄλοχος. Mention has already been made elsewhere of the exact retention of the Sanscrit preposition *sa* in the Greek σαφής, properly, "with light, being with brightness." In Sanscrit, *bhâs,* "brightness," would regularly combine with *sa* into the compound *sá-bhâs,* and this, in like manner, would signify "clear, shining." In Gothic, *ga-guds,* "pious," properly, "being with God," belongs to this class of words, being the anti-
[G. Ed. p. 1442.] thesis to the above-mentioned *af-guds:* and also *ga-liugs,* "false"†; *ga-daila,* "sympathiser," "with

---

* When used alone, *sahá* ; as verbal prefix, *sâm.* The former appears also in the compound *sahádêva-s,* and the latter in some nominal compounds.

† Properly, "being with lying:" it presupposes a lost substantive *liugs,* "lie."

COMPOUNDS. 1397

portion having" (for *ga-dail(i)-s*, see §. 923.); *ga-hlaifa*, "companion, with bread having" (for *ga-hlaifs*, l. c.). If I have been wrong in comparing, in §. 416., the Gothic formations in *leik'-s*, and the forms analogous to them in German, with the Sanscrit in *dris̓a-a*, they must then be included in the class of compounds under discussion, and we must recognise in their concluding element the substantive *leik'-s*, "body;" then *ga-leiks*, "similar," signifies properly, "with body having," "having the body, *i.e.*, the form in common with another," and it would correspond in its formation to the Latin *conformis*, Greek σύμμορφος, and Sanscrit *sá-rûpa-s*.* The form *anthar-leik'-s*, "separate," deducible from *anthar-leikei*, "difference," would then literally signify "having another body," *i.e.* "another form," ἀλλόμορφος (cf. Sanscrit *anyárûpa-s*, "other shaped;" S. V. II. 8. 1. 4. 1.

984. The Sanscrit prefixes *su* and *dus* (before sonant letters *dur*, cf. §. 919.), like their sister forms in Greek, εὐ and δυς, stand in the class of compounds under discussion for adjectives, whereby *su* allows the accent which belongs to it to sink down on the final syllable of the base, or before words which are formed with the suffixes *as* and *man* on the penultima;" hence, *e.g.*, *su-pḗsas* (nom. m. f. *supḗsâs*), "having a good form;" *sumánas*, nom. m. f. *sumánâs*, "having a good spirit, well-intentioned," in opposition to *su-jíhvá-s*, "having a good [G. Ed. p. 1443.] tongue" (*jihvâ*, f. "tongue"); *su-parṇá-s*, "having good wings." The following are examples with *dus, dur*, "bad:" *dúr-âtman* (nom. *-mâ*), "having a bad soul;" *dúr-bala-s*, "having bad strength;" *dúr-mana-s* (nom. *-manâs*), "having a bad spirit." To the latter corresponds, irrespective of the accentuation, the Greek δυςμενής (see §. 146.), as

---

* Likewise "similar," from *sa*, "with," and *rûpa*, "form;" so *ánu--rûpa-s*, "similar," from *ánu*, "after," and *rûpa*, "form."

εὐμενής to *sumânâs*. Other Greek examples belonging to this class are: εὐμελής, εὐμεγέθης, εὔμορφος, εὔμηλος, δύςμορφος, δύςμορος, δυςπρόσωπος, δύςλεκτρος. Examples in Zend of this class of words are : 𐬵𐬎𐬐𐬆𐬭𐬆𐬞 *hu-kĕrĕp*, "having a handsome body," nom. 𐬵𐬎𐬐𐬆𐬭𐬆𐬞𐬯 *hu-kĕrĕf-s* (see §. 40.); 𐬵𐬎𐬘𐬌𐬙𐬌 *hu-jĭti*, "having a good life" (see §. 128.); *hu-puthra*, f. *hu-puthrî*, "having handsome children ;" 𐬛𐬎𐬴𐬨𐬀𐬥𐬃 *dus-manas̆*, "having a bad spirit;" 𐬛𐬎𐬴𐬯𐬐𐬌𐬈𐬊𐬚𐬥𐬀 *dus-skyaôthna*, "having a bad deed, acting badly;" 𐬛𐬎𐬴𐬬𐬀𐬗𐬀𐬵 *dusch-vachas̆*, "having bad discourse."

THIRD CLASS.
Determinatives called *Karmadhâraya*.

985. The last member of this class of compounds is a substantive or adjective, which is more closely defined or described by the first member. The first member may be any part of speech, excepting verbs, conjunctions, and interjections; the most usual, however, is the combination of an adjective with a following substantive. Adjectives, which have a peculiar theme for the feminine, use, if the concluding substantive be feminine, not the feminine base, but the primary form common to the masculine and neuter. The accent falls most commonly on the final syllable of the united base. The following are examples: *divya--kusumá-s*, "heavenly flower ;" *priya-bhâryá,* " dear spouse"
[G. Ed. p. 1444.] (not *priyá-bhâryá*); *saptarshâya-s*, " the seven Rĭshis ;" *a-bhayá-m*, " not fear, fearlessness "*; *ádhrĭshta-s*, "invincible ;" *án-rĭta-s*, " untrue ;" *suprîta-s*,

---

* Inseparable adverbs and prepositions have the accent at the beginning of these compounds: just so substantives which denote the thing with which the person or thing to which the compound refers are compared. To the numerous exceptions from the rules of accent in this class of compounds belong, *inter alia,* the compounds described in §. 919., like *su-lábha-s*, "being easily attained ;" *dur-lábha-s*, " being with difficulty attained."

COMPOUNDS. 1399

"much beloved;" *sú-púrṇa-s*, "very full;" *dúr-dina-m*, "storm," lit. "hard day;" *sú-níti-s*, "good behaviour;" *sámí-bhukta-s*, "half eaten;" *prá-víra-s*, "fore-man," i.e. "superior man;" *ádhi-pati-s*, "regent, lord;" *ví-sadṛik*, "dissimilar;" *ghána-śyáma-s*, "cloud-dark, black like a cloud;" *śyêná-patvá* (theme -*van*), "flying like a falcon." Examples in Zend are : ꟑꟑꟑ *pĕrĕnó-máo*, "full moon;" ꟑꟑꟑ *a-mara*, "undying" (theme); ꟑꟑꟑ *amĕrĕ-shańs*, "not dying" (see p. 1421 G. ed., Note); ꟑꟑꟑ *dusch-varĕstĕ-m*, "bad deed, bad action;" ꟑꟑꟑ *dus--matĕ-m*, "bad thought;" ꟑꟑꟑ *dusch-úctĕ-m*, "badly said;" ꟑꟑꟑ *hu-matĕ-m*, "well thought;" ꟑꟑꟑ *hu--fĕdhra*, fem. -*í*, "very fortunate, excellent."

986. To this class belong Greek compounds like μεγαλ'--έμπορος, μεγαλο-δαίμων, μεγαλο-μήτηρ, ἰσό-πεδον, εὐρυ-κρείων, ἄ-γνωτος, ἀν-ήμερος, εὔ-δηλος, εὐ-άνοικτος, δυς-άγγελος, δυς--άπιστος, ἡμι-κύων, ἡμί-κενος, πρό-θυμα, ἔξ-οδος, ἔφ-οδος. The following are examples of Latin compounds of this class : *merí-dies*, properly, "the middle day," from *medí-dies* (see §§. 17., 20.), for *medii-dies*, as *tibí-cen* for *tibii-cen*, from *tibia-cen* (see §. 968.), *albŏ-galerus* (see [G. Ed. p. 1445.] p. 1417, Note, G. ed.), *sacri-portus, quinque-viri, decem-viri* (as in Sanscrit *saptárshayas*, "the seven Ṛishis"), *pœn-insula, neg-otium, in-imicus, semi-deus, semi-dies, semi-mortuus, bene--dicus, male-ficus* (see §. 916.), *in-felix, in-sulsus* (see §. 490. Remark 1), *in-sipidus* (see §. 6.), *dif-ficilis, dis-similis, pro--avus, pro-nepos, ab-avus, ante-pes, ante-loquium, con-serva, inter-rex, inter-regnum, per-magnus, præ-celer, præ-dulcis, præ--durus*. In German this mode of forming compounds is still in full force in all its varieties. The following are examples : *Grossvater*, "grandfather;" *Grossmutter*, "grand-mother;" *Grösmacht*, "great potency;" *Grosshändler*, "wholesale dealer;" *Weissbrod*, "white bread;" *Schwarz-brod*, "black bread;" *Vollmond*, "full moon;" *Halbbruder*, "half-brother;" *haushoch*, "high as a house;" *federleicht*,

"light as a feather;" *himmelblau,* "sky-blue;" *dunkelblau,* "dark blue;" *Unschuld,* "innocence;" *Unverstand,* "indiscretion;" *unreif,* "unripe;" *uneben,* "uneven;" *Übermacht,* "overpowering force;" *Abweg,* "by-way;" *Ausweg,* "outlet;" *Beigeschmack,* "false taste;" *Unterrock,* "petticoat;" *Vorhut,* "vanguard;" *schwarzgelb,* "tawny;" *Vorrede,* "preface;" *Vorgeschmack,* "foretaste;" *Vormittag,* "forenoon;" *Nachgeschmak,* "after-taste;" *Miterbe,* "co-heir;" *Mitschuld,* "participation in guilt;" *Abgott,* "idol;" *Abbild,* "image." In Old High German only the compounds with *sâmi,* which are wanting in our dialect, will be here mentioned by me as analogous to the above-mentioned (p. 1399, l. 3.) Sanscrit *sâmi--bhuktas,* "half-eaten," Greek ἡμίκενος, Latin *sêmi-mortuus,* viz. *sâmi-heil,* "half well;" *sâmi-qvëe,* "*semi-vivus;*" *sâmi-wîz,* "*subrufus* ("half white"). The following are examples in Gothic: *yugga-lauths,* "young man, youth;" *silba-siuneis*,* "eye-witness, αὐτόπτης;" *afar-dags†,* "the other (following) day;" *anda-vaurd,* "answer" ("counter-word"); *anda--vleizn‡,* "face, countenance;" *ufar-gudya,* "high priest, ἀρχιερεύς;" *ufar-fulls,* "overfull." Examples in Lithuanian are: *pirm-gimmimmas,* "first-birth;" *pus-dêwis,* "demi-god;" [G. Ed. p. 1446.] *pus-sessŭ,* "half-sister;" *pus-gywis,* "half-dead" (literally, "semi-animate"); *pus-salĕ,* "peninsula;" *san-kareiwis,* "competitor;" *san-tewonis,* "co-heir;" *prybuttis,* "vestibule." Examples in Old Sclavonic are: новогрaдъ *novo-grad',* "new-town;" вьсеславный *vyse-slavnyĭ,* "entirely famous;" вьсеблагый *vyse-blagyĭ,* "quite good;" вьсецаръ *vyse-zar',* "παμβασιλεύς;" самовидецъ *samo-videz',* "eye-

---

* In case the last member of this compound occurred in its uncompounded state, and that the whole is not, which I consider more probable, a derivative from a to-be-presupposed *silba-siuns,* "self-seeing."

† In Sanscrit *aparâhṇa-m* (from *apara-ahna-m*) is called "the afternoon," but literally, "the other day" ("the other part of the day").

‡ *Vleizn* does not occur uncompounded.

witness, αὐτόπτης:" in Russian, полдень *pol-deny*, "noon"*; полночь *pol-nochy*, "midnight;" полубогъ *polu-bog*, "demigod;" свѣшлоѵеленый *svyetlo-chelenyi*, "light green;" совладѣшель *so-vladyetely*, "co-owner."

FOURTH CLASS.

Dependent Compounds called *Tatpuruṣha*.

987. This class forms compounds, of which the first member is dependent on, or is governed by, the second, and therefore always stands in some oblique case-relation. Examples, in which the first member stands in the genitive relation, are contained in §. 968. So in Zend, *e.g.*, ꬰꬰꬰꬰꬰꬰꬰ *nmânô-paiti-s*, "*loci dominus;*" ꬰꬰꬰꬰꬰ *nmânô-pathni*, "*loci-domina;*" ꬰꬰꬰꬰꬰꬰꬰꬰ *zantu-paiti-s*, "*urbis dominus:*" in Greek, οἰκό-πεδον, στρατό-πεδον, οἰνο-θήκη, οἰκο-φύλαξ, θεσαυρο-φύλαξ: in Latin, *auri-fodina*, *auri-fur*, *mus-cerda* (see p. 1418 G. ed., Note), *su-cerda*, *imbri-citor*, *Marti-cultor:* in Gothic, *veina-gards*, "vineyard;" *aurti-gards*, "kitchen-garden;" *veina-basi*, "grape;" *heiva-frauya*, "master of the house;" *smakka-bagms*, "fig-tree" (see §. 971.); *daura-vards*, "warder, keeper of the gate;" *daura-varda*, [G. Ed. p. 1447.] "portress, door-waitress;" *sigis'-laun*, "guerdon of victory" (for *sigisa-laun*): in Lithuanian, *wyn'-ŭgĕ*, "grape" (*ŭga*, "berry," see §. 980.); *wyn'-szakĕ*, "vine" (*szakà* = Sanscrit *śâkhâ*, "branch"); in Old Sclavonic, домостроитель *domostroitely*, "steward;" свѣтодавецъ *svyeto-davez'*, "light-giver;" богородица *bogo-rodiza*, "mother of God;" пѣтлоглашеніе *pyetlo-glashenie*, "*gallicinium*" (Dobrowsky, p. 458). Examples in which the first member of the dependent com-

---

* Lit. "half-day." If L. Diefenbach is right, as I think he is, in comparing the Lithuanian *pussĕ*, "half," with the Sanscrit *pârśva*, "side," the Sclavonic *pol* may also be referred to this class, and *l* may be regarded as the representative of the Sanscrit *r*, as is done by Miklosich, who traces back полъ *pol'* to पर *para*, "*alius.*"

pound stands in the accusative relation have been given on a former occasion.* In Sclavonic, водоносъ *vodo-nos'*, "*hydria,*" properly, "water-carrier," belongs to this class. In the instrumental relation the first member of the compound appears frequently in Sanscrit in combination with the passive participle in *ta*, and that member then receives the accent which belongs to it in its uncompounded state; hence, *e.g.*, *páti-jushṭâ,* "*a marito dilecta.*" Thus, *e.g.*, in Zend, irrespective of the accentuation, which is here unknown to us, [Zend] *zarathusthrô-frôcta,* "announced by Zaratusthra;" [Zend] *mazda-dâta,* "made by Mazda (Ormuzd): in Greek, *θεό-δοτος, θεό-τρεπτος*; in Gothic, *handu-vaurht'-s,* "made with the hand, *χειροποίητος*:" in Sclavonic, ржкотворенный *ruṅko-tvorennyi,* id. (*ruṅka,* "hand," see §. 970.). In the dative relation we find, *e.g.*, पितृ *pitṛí* and हिरण्य *híraṇya,* in the compounds *pitṛí-sadṛiśa-s,* "like the father;" *híraṇya-sadṛiśa-s,* "like gold"†; so in Greek, *θεοείκελος*; in Gothic, *gasti-gôds,* "hospitable," literally, "to the guest or guests good;" in Russian, богоподобный *bogopodobnyĭ,* "Godlike;" богопослушный *bogoposlyshnyĭ,* [G. Ed. p. 1448.] "obedient to God." In the ablative relation stands नभस् *nábhas,* "heaven," in the compound *nabhaś-chyutá-s,* "fallen from heaven." In the locative relation is *nâu,* in the above-mentioned *nâu-sthá-s,* "standing in the ship."

988. To the class of dependent compounds belong, too, our German formations like *Singvogel,* "singing-bird;" *Springbrunnen,* "well-head;" *Ziehbrunnen,* "draw-well;" *Schreiblehrer,* "writing-master;" *Singlehrer,* "singing-master;" *Fahrwasser,* "water-channel;" *Esslust,* "desire to eat;" *Lesezimmer,* "reading-room;" *Scheidekunst,* "analy-

---

* See §§. 916., 922.

† In combination with *sadṛiśa* and *pratirûpa* the first member takes its proper accent.

tical art, chemistry;" *Trinkglas*, "drinking-glass;" *Trinkspruch*, "drinking-speech, toast;" *Kehrbesen*, "broom, whisking-brush;" *Lehrmeister*, "instructor;" *Lebemann*, "worldly-man, epicurean;" *Lockvogel*, "decoy-bird." They have this peculiarity, that the first member is not used alone; but I can no more regard it as a verb than I can the first member of the Greek compounds like δεισι-δαίμων, discussed above (§. 967.). I rather look upon it as an abstract substantive, although, for some compounds of this kind, the signification of the present participle appears the more suitable; for *Singvogel* is "a singing-bird," *Springbrunnen*, "a springing-well;" but *Ziehbrunnen* is not "a drawing-well," but "a well for drawing;" *Trinkglas* not "a drinking-glass," but "a glass for drinking;" *Schreiblehrer* not "a writing-teacher," but "a teacher of writing," as *Tanzlehrer* is "a teacher of the dance;" and so, too, *Singvogel* may be taken as *Gesangsvogel*, *Ziehbrunnen* as *Zugbrunnen*, "well for drawing." The circumstance that many substantives occur in the manner cited only at the beginning of compounds can no more surprise us than another which has come under our notice, that in several members of our family of languages some classes of adjectives are limited, either solely and entirely, or principally, to the end of compounds.* In formation, the [G. Ed. p. 1449.] substantives of the class of compounds under discussion, and which do not occur so early as in the Gothic, are identical with the theme of the present, the class-syllable of which is for the most part suppressed in strong verbs, but retained in some, and, indeed, in the Old High German, either in its original form *a* (see §. 109.[a)] 1.), or in that of *e*; hence, *e.g.*, *trag-a-stuol*, "sedan" ("chair for carrying"), analogous to *trag-a-mês*, "we carry;" so *trag-a-betti*, "pa-

---

* See §§. 909.[b.], 911., 912., 916.

lanquin;" *trag-a-diorna*, "female supporter," "Caryatis;" *web-e-hús*, "web-house," "*textrina*." The few remnants of the Sanscrit 4th class (§. 109.[a] 2.) contract, in Old High German, the class-syllable *ya* (य *ya*) to *i*, of which *hef-i--hanna*, "midwife," appears to be a solitary example. As *wasku*, "I wash," and *slífu*, "I drag," do not belong to this class, the *i* of *wash-i-wazar* and *slíp-i-stein* (literally, "wash-water," "draw-stone"), may be regarded as the weakening of *a*. The syllable *ya* of the first weak conjugation is likewise contracted to *i* (see Grimm, II. p. 681), and this latter vowel is frequently weakened to *e*, or entirely suppressed; hence, *e.g.*, *wez-i-sten*, *wezz-e-sten*, *wez-stân*, "whetstone." The second and third weak conjugations afford, in Old High German, no examples of this class of compounds, which has continually extended itself in the course of time, and is most numerously represented in New High German. Since the weak conjugation, as I think I have proved, is based on the Sanscrit 10th class (see §. 109.[a] 6.), I would further recall attention to the fact that the character of this class is retained in the accusative forms in *ayâm* discussed in §. 619., and in the Zend infinitives in *ayanm*.

FIFTH CLASS.

Collective Compounds called *Dvigu*.

989. This class forms collectives, which are more closely defined by a numeral prefixed. The final substan-
[G. Ed. p. 1450.] tive, without reference to its primitive gender, becomes a neuter, for the most part in *a*, or fem. in *í*. The accent rests on the final syllable of the collective base. The following are examples: *tri-guṇá-m*, "the three properties" (*guṇa*, m.); *chatur-yugá-m*, "the four ages of the world" (*yuga*, n.); *pañchêndriyá-m*, "the five senses" (*indriya*, n.); *tri-khaṭvá-m* or *tri-khaṭvî́*, "three beds" (*khaṭvá*, f.); *tri-râtrá-m*, "three nights" (*râtra*, for the

simple *râtri*, f.); *pańchâgní*, "the five fires"*; *tri-lôkí*, "the three worlds." Examples in Zend are : ‏ﺑﯿﺎرۀ‎ *byârĕ*, "biennium," for *bi-yârĕ* (*ĕ*, according to §. 30.); ‏ﺛﺮىﭼﺸﭙﺎرۀ‎ *thri-csaparĕ-m*, "trinoctium;" ‏چﺘﺮﻣﺎﻫﯿﺎ‎ *chathru-mâhya*, "four months," acc. -*mâhîm* (see §. 312. and §. 42.); ‏نوچشپارۀ‎ *nava-csaparĕ-m*, "nine nights;" ‏پنچماهیا‎ *pancha-mâhya*, acc. -*hîm*, "five months;" ‏چشوشچشپارۀ‎ *csvas-csaparĕ-m*, "six nights." To these, viz. to the neuters, correspond in Latin *tri-viu-m*, "point where three roads meet," *bi-viu-m*, *ambi-vium*†, *quadri-vium*, *bi-duu-m*, *tri-duu-m*, for which we may presuppose a simple *duu-s*, or *du-a*, or *duu-m*, as an appellation of " day ;" for all three forms *duu-m*, according to the Sanscrit principle, must be employed in the compound. In Sanscrit, *divâ* appears as an appellation of " day," in the compounds *divâ-karâ-s*, " sun," as " day-maker ;" *divâ-maní-s*, likewise " sun," lit. "precious stone of day," and *divâ-madhya-m*, "noon " (" middle of day "). The adverb *divâ*, " by day," does not suit for these three compounds. From the base *divâ* in Latin, after suppressing the *i*, we must get *dua*. [G. Ed. p. 1451.] The Latin forms like *bi-noct-iu-m*, *tri-noct-iu-m*, *quinqu'-ert-iu-m* (see §. 6.), *bi-enn'-iu-m*, have quitted the original position of genuine compounds, by annexing a neuter suffix. The Greek prefixes the feminine form of the suffix to the neuter in *ιο-ν*, which latter, however, is not wanting. Examples are : τριημερία, τριοδία, τετραοδία, τετραόδιον (*quadrivium*), τετρανυκτία, τρινύκτιον (*trinoctium*). In exact accordance with the Sanscrit neuter compounds like *chatur--yugá-m* stands τέθριππον: on the other hand, the Sanscrit, too, can, from its copulative compounds, form with the neu-

---

* Viz. the sun and four fires kindled in the direction of the four quarters of the world, to which he who undergoes penance exposes himself.

† The *i* of *ambi* is the weakening of the final vowel of the base, which, in the nominative singular, would form, were it imaginable, *ambu-s*.

ter suffix *ya* derivations, which do not alter the meaning of the primary word. Thus, together with the abovementioned *tri-gunâ-m, tri-lôkí*, there exist, too, the forms *trâigun'-ya-m, trâilôk'-ya-m*, of equivalent meaning; so *châturvarn'-ya-m*, "the four castes," from *chaturvanâ-m*. These, therefore, irrespective of the Vriddhi augment, are the true prototypes of Latin forms like *tri-enn'-iu-m, quadri--enn'-iu-m*, &c., and of the Greek τρι-όδ'-ιο-ν, τρι-νύκτ-ιο-ν.*

[G. Ed. p. 1452.] SIXTH CLASS.
Adverbial Compounds called *Avyayíbhâva*.

990. The first member of this class of compounds is either, and indeed most commonly, a preposition, or the privative particle *a, an*, or the adverb *yáthâ*, "as;" and the last member is a substantive, which, without reference to its gender when uncompounded, always assumes the form

---

* The term "collective compounds" would be unsuitable for this class of compounds, if, with the Indian Grammarians, we included in this class also adjectives like *pañchagava-dhana*, "having the wealth of five bullocks," "five bullocks rich." If, however, we do not regard the having a numeral for the first member as the most important condition of these compounds, I do not see any reason for withdrawing adjectives like that above mentioned from the possessive class, and placing them in a class with the collectives, which are more narrowly defined by a numeral. The word which Indian Grammarians put forth as an example of this class of compounds, viz. *dvigu*, is likewise no collective, but an adjective of the class of compounds, with a trifling overplus of meaning beyond what literally belongs to it, "having two bullocks." It should, however, signify, "bought for two bullocks," but must originally have meant scarce aught else but "having the value of two bullocks" = "costing two bullocks." The peculiarity of this compound consists, therefore, only in this, that *dvigu* signifies, by and for itself, not "two bullocks," but "the worth of two bullocks." If *gô*, with a numeral, should form a real collective, its base receives the extension of an *a*; hence, *e.g.*, *pañcha-gavá-m*, "five bullocks." Cf., with respect to the *a* which is used to extend bases, Latin compounds like *multi-colôr-u-s, tri-pector-u-s*, and Greek like θεό--πυρ-ο-ς.

which belongs to the neuter in the nominative and accusative; hence, *e.g.*, the feminine *śraddhá*, "belief, faith," becomes *śraddham* in the compound *yathá-śraddhám**, "proportioned to faith," literally, "like faith." The following are other examples: *yathá-vidhí*, "like prescription, corresponding to prescription" (*vidhi-s*, f.); *a-sanśayá-m*, "not doubt, without doubt" (*sanśaya-m*, n.); *anu-kshaná-m*, "immediately" (*anu*, "after," *kshana-m*, "moment"); *ati--mátrá-m*, "beyond measure" (*mátra-m*, "measure"); *pratyahám*, "daily" (*prati*, "towards," *ahan*, n. "day," with *n* suppressed). Latin compounds of this kind are, *admodum, præmodum, obviam, affatim*, in which, however, the last member retains its original gender, while, according to Sanscrit principle, *obvium, affate*, must be said for *obviam, affatim*. The following are compounds of this kind in Greek: ἀντιβίην, ἀντίβιον, ὑπέρμερον, παράχρημα. Some similarity to these adverbial compounds is to be observed [G. Ed. p. 1453.] in the Old High German periphrases of superlative adverbs by neuter accusatives with prepositions prefixed, which elsewhere govern, not the accusative, but the dative (see Grimm, III. 106.); *e.g.*, Old High German *az yungist*, "tandem;" *az lázôst*, "demum;" *zi furist*, "primum." We write in one word *zuerst, zuletzt, zuvörderst, zunächst, zumeist*, &c. A certain likeness to this class of compounds is to be traced also in Greek adverbs like σήμερον, τήμερον (see §. 345.), in which ἡμέρα has appended a neuter form in the very same way as the Sanscrit *śraddhá* mentioned above.

INDECLINABLES.

ADVERBS.

991. Exclusive of the compounds described in the preceding §., adverbs are formed in Sanscrit,

---

* The accent ordinarily rests on the final syllable.

1) With particular suffixes, the most important of which have been already considered (see §. 420.). I must here further mention, that, in departure from §. 294. Remark 2, I now prefer to trace back the Gothic adverbs *hva-drê,* "whither," *hi-drê,* "hither," *yain-drê,* "thither, ἐκεῖ," to the Sanscrit pronominal adverbs' in *tra* (§. 420.). They will therefore have experienced an irregular transformation of the tenuis to the medial, *e.g., fadrein,* "parents," contrasted with the Sanscrit *pitárâu.* As regards the *ê* of the said Gothic adverbs, it would lead us to expect in Sanscrit, according to §. 69., *â* for *a.* This *â* occurs in the Sanscrit suffix when it is appended to certain substantives and adjectives. Thus we read in the Schol. to Pânini, V. 4. 36., *manushyatrâ vasati,* "he dwells among men;" *dêvatrâ gachchhati,* "he goes to the gods."*

[G. Ed. p. 1454.] 2) With case-forms; *e.g.,* the form of adjectives, which is common to the nominative and accusative singular neuter, represents also the adverb. I, however, of course consider the said form to be the accusative, as any oblique case is better adapted than the nominative to denote an adverbial relation. The following are examples: *madhurám,* "lovely, pleasant;" *síghrám, kshiprám, ású,* "quick;" *nítyam,* "ever" (*nítya-s,* "*sempiternus*"); *chirám,* "long;" *prathamám,* "first;" *dvitíyam,* "for the second time;" *bahú,* "much;" *bhúyas,* "more;" *bhúyishtham,* "most." So in Latin, *e.g., commodum, plerumque, potissimum, multum, primum, secundum, amplius, recens,*

---

* In classical Sanscrit I have not met with forms and constructions of this kind: they seem to be limited to the Vêda dialect. Böhtlingk cites, in his Commentary to Pânini, p. 230, two passages of the first book of the Rigvêda: in the one (32. 7.) occurs *purutrá,* "in many," *i.e.* "in many places" or "members" (Schol. *bahushv anvayavêshu*); in the other (50. 10.) *dêvatrá,* in the sense of "among the gods."

INDECLINABLES. 1409

facile, difficile. So, in Sclavonic, the adverbs in *o* are identical with the accusative (nom. also) neuter of the corresponding adjective; *e.g.*, малo *malo*, "little;" мнoгo *mnogo*, "much;" дoлгo *dolgo*, "long, a long time." To this class belongs, in Gothic, *filu*, "much," "very." Observe, too, the adverbial use of neuter adjectives in Greek, both in the singular and in the plural, as μέγα, μεγάλα, μικρόν, μικρά, καλόν, πλησίον, ταχύ, ἡδύ, which likewise must of course be regarded as accusatives. The adjective base word for δηρόν, "long," is wanting: it is probably, just like δολιχός, akin to the Sanscrit *dírgha* from *dargha* or *dragha*, "*longus*," whence the adverb *dírgham*. Some Sanscrit adverbs are, according their form, plural instrumentals, formed from adjective bases in *a; e.g., uchcháis,* "high," "loud," from *uchchá; nicháis,* "low," from *nichá; sandís,* "slow," from the unused *śana*. [G. Ed. p. 1455.] The Lithuanian, which forms instrumentals plural in *ais, eis* (from *iais*), from bases in *a* and *ia* (*diewais* = Sanscrit *dêvâis*, see §. 243.), exhibits, in remarkable conformity with the Sanscrit, adverbs also with plural instrumental terminations; *e.g., pulkais.* "frequent," from *pulka-s,* "heap;" *kartais,* "at times," from *karta-s,* "a time," "once;" *wakarais,* "in the evening," from *wakara-s,* "evening;" *nakti-mis,* "by night;" *pietu-mis,* "at noon." The instrumental singular occurs in Sanscrit likewise in some forms which pass for adverbs; *e.g.*, in *dákshinê--n-a,* "southern," from *dákshina; áchirê-n-a,* "soon," literally, "after not long:" *ahnâya,* "soon," literally, "this day," is a dative. The Old High German adverbs with a dative plural termination like *luzzíkêm*, "*paulatim;*" the Anglo-Saxon like *middum,* "*in medio,*" *miclum,* "*magnopere;*" the Old Northern like *löngum,* "*longe,*" *fornum,* "*olim*" (Grimm, III. p. 94), remind us of the Sanscrit and Lithuanian adverbs first discussed, with the plural termination of the instrumental. The following are examples in Sanscrit of adverbial ablatives: *paschât*, "hereafter;" *ârât*, "near," also "far;" *adhastât*, "under;" *purastât*, "before," from the lost bases *pascha*, &c.; *áchirât*, "swift," from *áchira*, "not long." To this class have already been referred the Greek adverbs in ως (from ωτ).* They enrich, to a certain extent, the declension of adjectives by one case; and Buttmann (§. 115. 4.) remarks that ως may still be regarded as a termination entirely devoted to the inflection of the adjectives. We [G. Ed. p. 1456.] must, however, here give up the simple rule, that the termination ος, nominative and genitive, passes into ως, as ως cannot possibly, as an independent case-termination, arise at one time from a nominative, and that of the masculine gender, and at another from a genitive. The agreement in accentuation, *e.g.*, of σοφώς with σοφός, of εὐθέως with εὐθύς, εὐθέος, corresponds with the phenomenon, that in Greek, as in Sanscrit, the accent regularly remains on the syllable on which the base or the nominative has it; thus, in Sanscrit, from the base *samá*, "like," comes the nominative *samá-s*, acc. *samá-m*, abl. *samá-t*, as in Greek from ὁμό come the analogous forms ὁμ-ός, ὁμό-ν, ὁμώ-ς. The following are Latin adverbs with an ablative form, *e.g.*, *continuo, perpetuo, raro, primo, secundo;* and in Gothic these have a genuine ablative signification, *e.g.*, *hva-thrô*, "whither?" *tha-thrô*, "therefrom" (see §. 294. Rem. 1); and the following have not an ablative meaning like the Greek in ως and Latin in *ô: sinteinô*, "always;" *sniu-*

---

* See §. 183. Since, then, Ahrens ("*De dialecto Dorico*," p. 376) has similarly explained the Doric adverbs in ῶ (πῶ, τουτῶ, αὐτῶ, τηνῶ), which, as representatives of the adverbs in θεν (see §. 421.), have a genuine ablative meaning. By their termination ω, for ω-τ, they correspond admirably to the Gothic adverbs, which are likewise strictly of an ablative nature, like *alyathrô*, "*aliunde*" (see §. 294. Rem. 1.).

INDECLINABLES. 1411

mundô, "hastily," &c. (l. c.). We have a Sanscrit adverb with a genitive form in *chirásya*, "finally," literally, "of the long;" so in Greek, *e.g.*, ὁμοῦ, ποῦ, ἄλλου, in Gothic, *allis*, "entirely;" *gistra-dagis*, "yesterday."* In Sanscrit, *prâhṇê*, "in the forenoon," is regarded as an adverb with a locative termination, as the said case-termination, without transgressing its original destination, as is frequently the case with adverbs, stands here quite in its place. The language, however, itself distinguishes *prâhṇê* from the common locative in this, that it forms from it, as from a theme, the derivative *prâhṇê-tana-s* (see §. 960.). From Latin [G. Ed. p. 1457.] we refer to this class, as has already been done (p. 1227, Note *, G. ed.), the adverbs of the second declension, and compare, *e.g.*, *novê* with the Sanscrit locative *navê*, "in the new," which is no obstacle to regarding the genitive also, *noví*, according to its origin, as locative (see §. 200.). As the Lithuanian forms locatives in *è* (see §. 197.) from bases in *a*, but occasionally contrasts *ai*, too, with the Sanscrit Guna diphthong *ê* (from *ai*) (see p. 997), so perhaps its adverbs in *ay*, *ey* (the latter from *ia*), and which spring from bases in *a*, are, according to their origin, locatives, since *ay*, *ey*, are not distinguished in pronunciation from *ai*, *ei* (see Kurschat, "Contributions," II. 9.). The following are examples: *gieray*, "good, well" (*giera-s*, "a good man"); *żinnomay*, "knowing" (*żinnoma-s*, "a male acquaintance"): *pirmay*, "before" (*pirma-s*, "the first"); *tenay*, "there" (Old Prussian *tan'-s*, from *tana-s*, "he," acc. *tenna-n*); *didey*, "very" (*didis*, "great," theme *didia*, euphonic *didżia*). Ruhig remarks, that, in Lithuanian, adverbs can be formed from

---

* Matt. vi. 30, "to-morrow," see Gabelentz and Löbe, l. c. Regarding the comparative adverbs, see §. 301. Remark; and as to High German adverbial genitives, see Grimm, III. 93.

verbs by adding the syllable *nay* to the infinitive; but I believe that the language has arrived in a different manner at adverbs like *laupsin-tinay*, "in a praiseworthy manner" (infin. *laupsinti*, "to praise"), than by appending the syllable *nay* to the infinitive suffix *ti*. I believe, viz. that in Lithuanian abstract bases in *tina-s* existed, which suffix might be added to the root or the verbal theme in the same way as the infinitive suffix *ti*. I presuppose, therefore, *e.g.*, abstracts like *laupsintina-s*, "the praising," *mylḗtina-s*, "the loving;" and I deduce therefrom the adverbs *laupsin-tinay*, *mylḗ-tinay*, in the same way as *gieray*, "bene," from *giera-s*, "bonus." I regard the suffix *tina* as identical with the secondary suffix *tvana* (see p. 1216 G. ed., Note), which forms abstracts in the [G. Ed. p. 1458.] Vêda dialect. With regard to the loss of the *v*, remark the relation of the Lithuanian *sapna-s*, "sleep," to the Sanscrit *svápna-s*. To the Vêdic suffix *tvana*, and in fact to its locative *tvanê* ($=tvanai$), I refer also the Old Persian infinitives or gerunds in *tanaiy*, if Oppert is right, as I think he is, in assigning the *t* of *chartanay* and *thastanay* to the suffix*; *char-tanay* then ranks itself under the Sanscrit root *char*, "ire," also "facere," "agere," "committere;" and *thas-tanay* under *thah*, which Rawlinson compares† with the Sanscrit root शंस् *śaṅs*, the final sibilant of which is protected by the *t* following. But if it be correct to divide *char-tanay* and

---

* Benfey refers the *t*, *e.g.* that of *chartanaiy*, "to make," to the root, and takes *ana* as the suffix.

† "Journal of the Royal Asiatic Society," Vol. XI. p. 176. I formerly thought (Glossar. Sanscr., a. 1847, p. v) of a connection of the Old Persian *thah* with the Sanscrit *chaksh*; but if we do not follow Benfey in referring *thastanay* (the original confirms also the reading *thastaniya*) to the Sanscrit root *chéṣht*, "to strive," other Persian forms are wanting with *th* for Sanscrit *ch*, though it is true that further instances may be quoted where the Persian 𐎰 *th* is substituted for sibilants.

t̠has-tanay, instead of *chart-anay, thast-anay*, in which, too, Rawlinson recognises gerunds, then the agreement with the Lithuanian verbal adverbs under discussion is very remarkable; and I think that *laupsin-tinay, mylĕ̃--tinay*, which Ruhig translates by "in a praiseworthy, loveable manner," signify, according to their origin, nothing else than "in the praising," "in the loving," "*in laudando*," "*in amando*."*

992. There are in Sanscrit also several ⌈G. Ed. p. 1459.⌉ adverbs which can be referred to no settled principle of formation. To this class belong, among others, the negative particles *a* (as prefix), *na* (see §.371.); the adverbs of time, *sanâ*, "ever†," *adya*, "to-day" ("on this day"), *śvas*, "to-morrow" (Latin *cras*), *hyas*, "yesterday," *parut*, "in the past year‡," *sadyas*, "simultaneously" (probably from *sa*, "this," and *dyas* from *divas*, "day"); the prefixes *su*, "well," "fine," and *dus*, "bad."

---

* As in Greek, together with the abstracts in συνη (see p. 1216 G. ed., Note), there exist adjectives in συνος (see Aufrecht, "Journal of Compar. Philol.," p. 482), *e.g.*, μαντόσυνος, together with μαντοσύνη; and as, in Sanscrit, the suffix *tva*, which is specially devoted to abstracts, and with which Pott (E. I., II. p. 490) compares the Greek suffix συνη, may, in the Vêda dialect, form also the future passive participle (see §. 835.); so, in Lithuanian, together with the to-be-presupposed abstracts in *tina-s* there exist also adjectives with the signification of the future passive; *e.g., bar-tina-s*, "*vituperandus*;" *biyo-tina-s*, "*timendus*;" *wes-tina-s*, "*ducendus*" (*wedu*, "I lead," cf. §. 102. conclusion). In my opinion, it cannot be denied that these formations, too, have much in common with those in *tvana* in Sanscrit; and if, in Lithuanian, where we ordinarily find masculines for Sanscrit neuter substantives, there never existed abstracts in *tina-s*, we must then derive the adverbs in *tinay* from those adjectives.

† Probably from the demonstrative base *sa* (cf. *sa-dá*, §. 422., and see Gloss. Sanscr., a. 1847, p. 367).

‡ From *par* for *para*, "the other" (see §. 375.), and *ut*, a contraction probably of the syllable *vat*, from *vatsara*, "year." Pott (E. I., II. p. 305) rightly compares the Greek πέρυσι.

CONJUNCTIONS.

993. The different members of the Indo-European family of languages agree in the construction of genuine conjunctions in this point, that they form them from pronominal roots (see §. 105.); but great difference prevails in specialities, *i.e.*, in the choice of the pronouns, whence conjunctions of the same meaning are formed in the various languages [G. Ed. p. 1460.] and groups of languages; so that, *e.g.*, our "*dass*," Old High German *daz*, answers neither to the Sanscrit *yat, yáthá*, nor to the Latin *quod, ut*, nor to the Greek ὅτι, ὡς, ἵνα, ὅπως, nor to the Lithuanian *yog, kad*, nor to the Russian *kto*, at least not to the last as an entire word, but only to the concluding portion of it (*to*) (cf. §. 343.). The Old High German *daz* is nothing else than the neuter of the article, and the difference in writing which we make between *das* and *dass* has no organic foundation, as the *s* in the neuter of the pronouns and strong adjectives is everywhere based on an older *z*, and properly should always be written ʒ. I see no sufficient ground for regarding, with Graff (V. 39.), the conjunction *daz* as the neuter of the relative, though the Gothic *thatei* contains the particle *ei*, which gives relative signification to the demonstrative; but for the conjunction *dass* the demonstrative meaning is more suitable than the relative; and when we say, *Ich weiss dass er krank ist*, "I know that he is sick," this is tantamount to *Ich weiss dieses: er ist krank*, "I know this: he is sick;" and I have, for this reason, already, in my Conjugational-system (p. 82), called the conjunction *dass* the article of the verbs. We cannot place a verb or a sentence in the accusative relation without prefixing to it a conjunction, *i.e.* a pronoun, which is the bearer of the case-relation in which the sentence appears. As neuter, too, *dass* is adapted to express the nominative relation: this it does in sentences like, *Es ist*

erfreulich dass er wieder gesund ist, " It is pleasing that he is well again," which is equivalent to *das Wiedergesundsein desselben ist erfreulich,* " the being well again of that person is pleasing." With *dass*, be it in the accusative or nominative relation, the grammatical sentence, the general grammatical scheme is in a manner completed; so that, after *Ich weiss dass* .... or *Es ist erfreulich dass,* " I know that," or " it is pleasing that," the logical import, whatever it may be, follows. As the accusative can express adverbially other oblique case-relations also, and, *e.g.*, the Sanscrit *tat* and *yat* express not only [G. Ed. p. 1461.] " this " and " which," but also, " on which account," " therefore," " wherefore," " since," *i.e.* the instrumental or causal relation, and may therefore be substituted for *téna* and *yéna*, so *dass* too is suited to assume the place of *damit*, " therewith," where the preposition *mit*, " with," takes the place of the instrumental termination, which is wanting: hence, *e.g., Nimm diese Arzenei, dass* (*damit*) *du wieder gesund werdest,* " Take this medicine, that (therewith) thou become well again." Like *dass*, most of the other conjunctions also always stand in some case-relation, though it be not formally expressed in the conjunction. Our *aber*, " but," properly, " other " (see §. 350.), like the conjunctions which correspond in sense to it in other languages, stands always in the nominative relation; as, *Er befindet sich nicht wohl, aber er wird doch kommen,* " He does not feel well, but he will come notwithstanding." With *aber*, therefore, the other thing, that is to be said, begins, as antithetical to the preceding. In Greek, ἀλλά, in spite of the difference of accentuation, is evidently identical with the neuter plural ἄλλα. The Sanscrit gives us *tú*, which, like the Greek δέ, never stands at the beginning of a sentence, and which, as it appears to me, is a weakening of the base *ta*, to which we have above (§. 350.) referred the Greek δέ also. For "*aber*" we also find in Sanscrit *kintu* from *kim*, "what?" and also for the *tu* just mentioned, to which the *kim* serves, in a manner, only as a fulcrum ; as *yádi*, "if," to *vá*, and, in Latin, *si* to *ve*, in *yádivá*, *sive*, "or," which *vá*, *ve*, by themselves signify.

994. The just-mentioned Sanscrit *yádi*, "if"*; has sprung, I doubt not, from the relative base *ya*, to which, too, the Gothic conjunction *ya-bai*, of equivalent signification, likewise belongs (see §. 383. p. 539): on the other hand, the *it* (see §. 360.) contained in चेत् *chêt*, "if," is to be classed under the demonstrative base *i*, and can scarcely be any thing else than the neuter of the said base, not occurring in use by itself, and identical with the Latin *id*. It may be left an open question whether the Gothic *iba* of *n'-iba*, "if not," be a contraction of *ya-ba* (cf. *thauh-yaba*), or whether its *i* belong to the base of the Sanscrit *it*, with which the Gothic *i-th*, "but," "if," is also connected in its base. The Latin *si* belongs evidently, like *se-d* and *si-c*, to the reflexive base (cf. *si-bi*). The Greek εἰ might be taken as an abbreviation of ἐδι, and so be compared with यदि *yádi*, to which it would bear nearly the same relation that, *e.g.*, φέρει does to *bhárati*, "he bears." Our *wenn*, "if," is identical with *wann*, "when," and the meaning "if" is still unknown to the Old High German adverb of time *hwanne*, *hwenne*. The Old High German expression for *wenn*, and also for *ob*, "whether," is *ibu*, *ipu*, &c. (formally = Gothic *iba*, English *if*), Middle High German *obe*, *ob*, on which our *ob* is based, which has lost the signification "if," the case-relation of which is always accusative, a relation expressed in the Latin *num* and *utrum* also by the form. The transition of the lightest vowel *i* in the Gothic *iba* and Old High German *ibu*, *ipu*, to the heavier *o* of the Middle and New High German *obe*, *ob*, is

---

* Zend ܝܙܝ *yézi*, ܝܐܝܕܗܝ *yêidhi*, see §. 520., §. 638. Note, §. 703. Rem. sub finem (for *yédhi*, better *yêidhi*).

so far remarkable, in that languages become defaced, in the course of time, usually only by the weakening, not by the strengthening, of vowels.* In Sanscrit the above-mentioned *yádi* signifies, like the Greek εἰ, and [G. Ed. p. 1463.] Old High German *i-bu, i-pu,* besides "if," also " whether." The Lithuanian *yey,* "if," answers, with respect to the diphthong *ey,* to the adverbs *ay, ey,* discussed above (p. 1457 G. ed.); but, with reference to its base, it is identical with that of the Sanscrit *yádi* (see §. 383.). In the syllable *gu* of *yey-gu,* "if, perhaps" (also *yei-g*), I believe I recognise the Sanscrit particle *ha,* Vêdic *gha, ghá, há,* Greek γε, discussed above (§. 814. p. 1104, Note); and in the *gi* of *yey-gi,* "albeit, although, notwithstanding," the particle हि *hi,* which occurs without any perceptible meaning, or signifies "for," and in the latter case, too, never appears at the beginning of a sentence.†

995. From the relative base *ya* spring also, in Sanscrit, the conjunctions *yát* and *yáthá,* "that;" the former in the

---

* To what has been observed above (§. 383., p. 539) regarding the syllables *ba, bai,* in the conjunctions referred to, and of the adverb in *a-ba,* which spring from strong adjective bases in *a,* one more attempt at explanation may be here added, according to which *ba* might be based on the Sanscrit *pa,* whereby, from the demonstrative bases *a* and *u,* the prepositions *á-pa* and *ú-pa* have arisen. The Gothic prefers between two vowels a medial instead of the tenues of the formative suffixes and the terminations; while, at the end of a word, an aspirate is preferred (cf. §. 823., p. 1120): hence the preposition *af,* contrasted with the Sanscrit *á-pa,* cannot hinder us from recognising also, in the conjunctions *ya-bai, n'-i-ba,* and in the adjective adverbs in *ba,* the Sanscrit suffix *pa* of *a-pa, u-pa, prati-pa, samî-pa*=the Latin *pe,* of *pro-pe, nem-pe, quip-pe* (from *quid-pe*), *sæ-pe.* Then, too, in Lithuanian, the pronominal adverbs *tai-po, tai-p,* "so," *kittai-p,* "otherwise," *kai-po, kai-p,* "as," *katrai-p,* "in which manner," *autrai-p,* "in another manner," and the conjunctive *yei-b,* "in order to," must be referred to this class, in respect to their labial, in departure from §. 383., p. 540.

† See §. 391., where, too, mention is made of the Greek γάρ.

sense of the Latin *quod*, and like it, according to form, the neuter of the relative; the latter in the sense of *ut*, and, like it, originally signifying "as."* In the Vêda dialect there is found, also, a conjunction of rare occurrence, *yát*, "that," as adverb, "as," a very interesting form, which was first regarded by Kuhn† as a conjunction, and, according [G. Ed. p. 1464.] to formation, as an ablative according to the common declension (for *yásmât*). We have, therefore, in this *yát*, as it were the prototype of the Greek ὡς, which corresponds to the said *yát* both in its base (see §. 382.) and in the significations "as" and "that," and as ablative, if I am right in taking the ς of the adverbs in ως as a corruption of τ.‡ As correlative to *yát*, and, as it were, as twin-brother to the Greek τώς, occurs also, in the Vêda dialect, the demonstrative adverb *tát*, with the signification "so," in a passage of the Fourth Book of the Rig-Vêda (VI. 12.), cited by Benfey (Glossary to the Sâma-Vêda, p. 75), where, in one verse, *yát* is found with the signification "as," and *tát* with that of "so."

996. Our *so*, where it answers to *wenn*, ought to be regarded as a conjunction, just as much as *wenn*; for in sentences like *Wenn er gesund ist, so wird er kommen*, "If he is well, then he will come," *so* "then" is as much the support of the following sentence, as *wenn*, "if," is of the preceding; and it is quite impossible to translate it in languages in which a corresponding expression is wanting, as they feel no occasion, in constructions of that nature, to introduce the following sentence with a conjunction, or to prefix, as it were, an article to its verb. In the later

---

* Regarding *yá-thá*, see §. 425.; and as to *ut* from *utí* for *cutí*, p. 1227 G. ed., Note †. Regarding the use of the Zend conjunctions ‎ *yat*, ‎ *yatha*, see §. 725., and p. 1428 G. ed.

† See Hoefer's Journal, II. p. 174.

‡ See §. 183., and p. 1445 G. ed.

lingual period of the Sanscrit, *tadá*, originally, "then" (see §. 422.), has taken on itself the part of this conjunction, which corresponds to *yádi*, "if;" and thus we read, *e.g.*, in Lassen's Anthology, p. 7, *yady éshâ mama bhárya bhavati tadâ jívámi, nô chên* (euphonic for *chét*), *marishyâmi*, "if this woman becomes my spouse, then I will live; if not, (then) I will die." The Lithuanian gives the neuter of its article, viz. *tai*, and the Sclavonic the corresponding то= Greek τό, Sanscrit *tát*, "this," as conjunction for our *so* (see Dobrowsky, p. 447). The following [G. Ed. p. 1465.] is an example in Lithuanian, *yey żmonẽms atléisite yû mussidẽyimus, tai atléis ir yums yusû tẽwas danguyeṅsis,* "if ye forgive men their trespasses, then your heavenly Father will also forgive you" (Matt. vi. 14).

PREPOSITIONS.

997. The genuine prepositions, and such adverbs as in form and meaning are connected with prepositions, admit universally of being derived with greater or less certainty from pronouns: according to their signification they are based on such antithetical terms as "this" and "that," "this side" and "that side." Thus, *e.g.*, we may take *über*, "over," in relation to *unter*, "under," *vor*, "before," in relation to *hinter*, "after," *aus*, "out," in relation to *in*, "in," as "this side," and the counter term as "that side," or conversely (see §. 293.). The pronominal origin is most clearly discerned in the Sanscrit preposition *áti*, "over;" for, according to its formation, it has the same relation to the demonstrative base *a*, that *iti*, "so," has to *i*. It was, however, the adjectives *á-dhara-s, a-dháma-s,* "the lower," or "lowest," that first led me to perceive the pronominal origin of the old prepositions.* It

---

* See "Transactions of the Historic-Philological Class of the Royal Academy of Literature for the year 1826," p. 91.

was later that I first represented the preposition *a-dhá-s* "under," as adverb, "below," as a derivative from the demonstrative base *a*.* To *á-dhara-s, a-dháma-s,* correspond, in Latin, *inferus, infimus* (see §. 293., p. 379), the former of which Voss derives from the verb *infero,* while [G. Ed. p. 1466.] the Sanscrit *adháma-s,* in the Uṇadi-book (V. 54.), is formed from the verbal root *av,* "to help," with the suffix *ama.* If we would divide the words thus, *á-dha-ra-s, a-dhá-ma-s,* we must then derive these adjectives from *a-dhás,* "under, beneath," the *s* being suppressed, as *áva-ra-s, avá-ma-s,* have clearly sprung from the preposition *áva,* "from, down from," though, l. c., *avámas-s,* is assigned to the verbal root *av,* "to help." The former derivation would not prevent us from deriving the prepositional and adverbial *adhás,* "itself," from the demonstrative base *a* by a suffix *dhas,* as a modification of *tas.*

998. To *áti,* "over," Zend ꝏ *aiti,* belongs probably the Latin *at* of *at-avus* (see §. 425.), as also the Lithuanian *ant,* "up," with a nasal inserted (cf. §. 293., p. 379), and without a nasal, but with altered meaning, *at,* according to Ruhig, "to, back," only as prefix; *e.g.,* in *at-eimi,* "I come here;" *at-dŭmi,* "I give back." The Greek ἀντί and Latin *ante* appear doubtful to me now as derivatives from *ati,* because ἄντα, which it is not possible to separate in its origin from ἀντί, cannot easily have come from ἀντί, though ἀντί might have come from ἄντα by a very common weakening of α to ι. But if ἄντα be the old form, then अन्त *anta,* "end," presents itself as the medium of comparison, at the root of which, as the opposite to "beginning," *i.e.* that which is before, lies a prepositional idea.† Our *ant* in *Antwort,* "answer," as

---

* See "On some demonstrative bases, and their connection with different prepositions and conjunctions," 1830, p. 9. Cf. C. G. Schmidt, "*De præpositionibus Græcis,*" 1829.

† I have literally translated this obscure passage, which means that अन्त *anta,* "end," as the opposite to what is first, or before, may very well be

"counter-word," has already been compared by Thiersch with the Greek ἀντί: the Gothic *anda-*, in *anda-vaurd, anda-nahti,* "evening" (properly, "fore-night," or "the time meeting night"), *anda-numfts*, "acceptance, the taking in front of," *anda-nêms*, "agreeable," opposed to *and'-nima*, "I accept," speak in favour of ἄντα as the older form. In its isolated state, and in most compounds, too, the Gothic preposition, on which our *ent*, in *entsagen, entsprechen,* &c., [G. Ed. p. 1467.] is based, has lost its final vowel. The. Sanscrit substantive base *anta*, "end," has been changed in Gothic to *andya*, nom. *andeis* (also *andi*, nom. *andis*), and the latter substantive has, in our *Ende,* kept itself free from the second alteration of sound (§. 87.), which *ant* and *ent*, in *Antwort, ent-sprechen,* &c., have undergone. In the Vêda dialect there is an adverb *ánti*, "near," which recurs, too, in the later language (see Benfey Gloss.), and from which, in the first edition of my Glossary, without being aware of its existence, but presupposing that such a form did formerly exist, I have derived the substantive *antika-m*, "nearness." It is probable that this अन्ति *anti* has been formed from the demonstrative base *ana*, with *a* suppressed, and with the same suffix as that which forms *á-ti* from *a*. The substantive अन्त *ánta*, "end," may, however, be regarded as the etymological brother of अन्ति *ánti*, "near," as it may be derived from the same pronominal root through another, but cognate suffix. A verbal root suitable for the derivation of *ánta*, "end," is not to be found; at least the root *am*, "to go," to which the Indian Grammarians have recourse (Unâdi, III. 85.), does not appear to me to be a dangerous competitor with the demonstrative base *ana*.

999. The suffix धि *dhi* of अधि *ádhi*, "over, up, towards," answers to the Greek θι of locative adverbs like πό-θι,

---

be the source from which ἄντα, "over against," has sprung, and may itself have a prepositional idea as its base, as there is a similar idea at the root of "beginning."—*Translator.*

ὄ-θι, οὐρανό-θι. The possibility that the Greek ἄγχι may have arisen from ἀνθι for ἀθι, and be akin to अधि *ádhi*, has already been noticed (see §. 294., Rem. 1., p. 388). I compare with more confidence the Latin *ad*, as also the Gothic *und*, "as far as, up to" (Old Saxon *unti, unt*), if this belong not to अन्त *ánta*, "end," and so be originally identical with *anda, and*. The great mobility in the transition of meanings in prepositions, combined with the facility of alteration [G. Ed. p. 1468.] in form, causes us here a difficulty in arriving at comparisons which can be entirely depended upon. For comparison with the Gothic preposition *at*, "near, at," we find in Sanscrit no other preposition than *ádhi*. To the Latin *ad* the Gothic *at* would correspond exactly, with regard to the law for the mutation of sounds, but the German languages do not stand in direct connection with the Latin.

1000. The Sanscrit preposition *á-pa*, "from," has already been mentioned (p. 1462 G. ed., Note) as an offshoot of the demonstrative base *a*, and as analogous, with respect to its termination, to *ú-pa*: the Greek ἀ-πό (like ὐ-πό to *úpa*), Latin *a-b* (like *su-b* to *u-pa*), Gothic *a-f* (according to §. 87.), English *o-f*, our *a-b*, correspond to it. The preposition अपि *á-pi*, "over, on," in *api-dhá*, "to cover," properly, "to lay upon" (as conjunction, "also"), as conjectural derivative of the base *a*, has, with regard to its termination, no analogous form elsewhere. Formally it has the same relation to *á-pa* that, in Greek, ἀν-τί has to ἄν-τα. To *ápi* corresponds the Greek ἐπί, but with respect to the vowel, and more restricted signification, the Lithuanian *ap* answers better; *e.g.*, in *ap-auksinu*, "I gild" ("I gild over"); *ap-denkiu*, "I cover" ("I cover over"); *ap-dumóyu*, "I reflect" ("I think over"); *ap-galu*, "I overpower" (*galù*, "I can"); *ap-si-immu*, "I take upon myself;" *ap-beriu*, "I spill" ("I over-fill"); *ap-twystu*, "I overflow;" *apipyaustau*, "I clip."*

---

* Nesselmann (Lexicon of the Lithuanian Language) remarks regarding

1001. The termination *bhi* of the preposition अभि *abhí*, "to, towards" (adv. *abhí-tas*, "near"), is connected with the case, and adverbial terminations beginning with *bh*, Zend and Latin *b*, Greek φ.* I recall attention [G. Ed. p. 1469.]

---

ing this preposition, that before roots which begin with *p* we sometimes find *api*, but rarely before other roots. I therefore leave it an open question, whether this *i* be the original *i*, or a euphonic affix.

* See §. 215. I know not why Spiegel has thought it necessary to compare the Zend termination *byô* of the dative and ablative plural with a Sanscrit termination other than that which corresponds in form and signification, *bhyas* (see §§. 215., 244.). He says, however, in Hoefer's Journal of Philology, I. p. 60, "So, *e.g.*, in the declension of words in *a* several Vêdic forms have taken firm root also in Zend; thus, the nominative plural *âoñha* (as I write it *âoṇha*), to which answers the Vedic in *âsah*, and thus the dative plural in *aêibyô*, to which corresponds the Vêdic in *êbhih*." I am fully persuaded that the Vêdas are altogether innocent of having aught to do with there being plural datives in *aêibyô* in Zend; for, in the first place, the Vêdic forms in *êbhis*, *êbhih*, are not datives at all, and were never regarded by any one else as such, but are distinct instrumentals (see §. 219.); secondly, even if the Vêdic forms in *êbhis* were actually datives, still the Zend datives in *aêibyô* could not be derived from them, as the Sanscrit termination *is* in Zend has never become *yô*, but has either remained unaltered, or has lengthened its *i*: thus, instead of the Sanscrit instrumental termination भिस् *bhis*, we find ᭄᭄ *bîs*, in Zend, of frequent occurrence. The datives in *aêibyô* may, at pleasure, be deduced from the Vêda dialect, or from classical Sanscrit, as in both these the form *êbhyas* is found in the dative and ablative plural of the *a*-bases; and this *êbhyas* is, in Zend, changed into *aêibyô* according to regular rule. That the Zend plural forms in *âoṇhô* are based on a peculiarity of the Vêdic dialect admits of no doubt; and I believe that I was the first to draw attention to this fact (see §. 229., and cf. Burnouf, "Yaçna," Notes, p. 73), and, indeed, at a time when but little was known of Zend forms, so as to admit of being brought together for comparison in my Comparative Grammar. In general, I believe I may, in contradiction to an assertion of Spiegel's (Weber's "Indian Studies," I. p. 303), maintain that the greatest part of what is adduced regarding Zend Grammar in this book, and in the Reviews mentioned in the Preface to the First Part (p. xiii), is based on my own observation; and I think I have
shewn

to the Greek locative adverbs αὐτό-φι, θύρη-φι (§ .217.), and the Latin datives and adverbs *ti-bi, si-bi, i-bi, u-bi, utru-bi* [G. Ed. p. 1470.] (§. 223.). To the preposition अभि *abhí*, the Greek ἀμφί, Latin *amb-*, Old High German *umbi* (our *um*) have the same relation, with respect to the inserted nasal, that ἄμφω, *ambo*, have to उभौ *ubhâú* (theme *ubha*). "both." Under the Sanscrit preposition *abhí* must also be ranked our *bei*, as prefix, *be*, Old High German *bí*, *bi*, Gothic *bi* (see §. 88., p. 77), with the suppression of the initial vowel, as in Sanscrit, for the above-mentioned (§. 1000.) *ápi*, as preposition *pi* is more commonly used than the full form *ápi*: this *pi*, however, would lead us to expect, in Gothic, rather *fi* than *bi*. In Latin, the *amb-* just mentioned need not deter us from bringing *ob* also under this head, as the division of one and the same form into several is nothing uncommon. For *amb*, we find also *am* (like our *um* for *umbi*) and *an*, e. g., in *am-plector, am-icio, un-fractus*. In Zend, likewise, the preposition under discussion appears in two forms, viz. in that of ‍‍ *aibi* and ‍‍‍‍‍‍‍‍‍‍‍‍‍‍‍‍‍‍‍‍‍‍‍‍‍‍‍‍ *aiwi*. To another preposition connected with the demonstrative base *a*, the Zend ministers this service, that it still uses its form in its original demonstrative signification with a full declension; I mean, the preposition *áva*, "from," "down" (see §. 377.). The prepositional meaning in the European sister-languages is most clearly represented by the Old Prussian inseparable *au*, e.g., in *au-mû-sna-n* (acc.), "ablution" (cf. Russian мою *moyu*, "I wash"); *au-luu-t*, "to die" (see §. 787., p. 1062, Note, and cf. Sanscrit *lû*, "*abscindere, evellere*," Lithuanian *lawonas*, "corpse"). In Old Sclavonic both оу *û* and о seem to be

---

shewn that Anquetil's traditional, but, in a grammatical point of view, most faulty, translation of the Zend books might lead to the developement of the grammatical system of the Zend language, even without the aid of the Sanscrit translation of the Yaśna by Neriosengh, which often follows the Zend text word for word.

assignable to this class, the latter, however, not in all compounds (see Dobrowsky, p. 401). The following are examples: оугѣзати *û-ryeζati*, "*abscindere;*" оумалити *û-maliti*, "*minorare, diminuere;*" оудалити [G. Ed. p. 1471.] *û-daliti*, "*elongare;*" оугаситиˊ *û-gasiti*, "*extinguere;*" оубогъ *û-bog'*, "pauper" ("not rich"); омыти *o-myti*, "*abluere;*" оставити *o-staviti*, "*dimittere;*" опровергати *o-provergati*, "*dejicere, abjicere.*"

1002. Besides अव *áva*, अभि *abhí*, too, lays claim to the Sclavonic preposition *o*, which appears in Polish in the forms *obe, ob,* and *o*, and, indeed, most frequently in the last (Bandke, §. 210.). The following are examples: *obe-zna-ch*, "to make known" (Sanscrit *abhí-jñá* like *jñá*, simply, "to know"); *obe-lz'wa-ch*, "to calumniate" (*lz'y-ch*, id.); *obe--lgna̢-ch*, "to adhere round;" *ob-cowa-ch*, "to go about, to associate with;" *ob-iazd*, "riding about;" *o-kaza-ch*, "to shew round about;" *o-garnia-ch*, "to embrace" (Sanscrit *grih-ṇá-mi*, from *grahṇámi* for *grabh-ná-mi*, "I take, I grasp"); *o-grycha-ch*, "to gnaw, to nibble round." To return to the preposition अव *áva*, I do not believe that the Latin *au* of *au-fugio, au-fero*, can be compared with it, but I hold to the common derivation of this *au* from *ab**: on the other hand, I believe, with Weber, that I recognise in *aver-nu-s* a sister-word of the Sanscrit *ávara-s*, "*inferus*" (see p. 1466 G. ed.), which springs from *áva*. As regards the addition of the suffix *nu* to the Latin form, I would recall attention to the relation of *infer-nu-s* (with *inferus*) to the Sanscrit *ádhara-s* (see §. 293., p. 379) of equivalent meaning. Should the Sanscrit preposition *áva*, "from," "off," be further retained elsewhere in the European languages, then, in my opinion, the Old High German privative *â* (Grimm,

---

* The assimilation to *af-fero, af-fugio* (like *of-fero* from *ob-fero*), must be avoided, because the form *af* has been claimed already by the preposition *ad* (cf. Pott, E. I., II. 153.).

II., p. 704) would have the next claim to it. As अप *ápa*, "from," and the corresponding European forms, are used [G. Ed. p. 1472.] for negative (see §. 983.), so, too, the preposition *áva* would be similarly employed, and, after dropping the semi-vowel, the two short *a* must have been contracted to *â*. But if *â* is, as J. Grimm (l. c., p. 705.) assumes, identical in its origin with *ar*, "out," Gothic *us* (cf. §. 983.) then the Sanscrit *ávís*, of which the original signification was probably tantamount to "out," "herefrom," hence "visible, evident," might perhaps have the next claim to the paternity of this preposition, with which, too, an Irish preposition, viz. *as*, likewise meaning "out," admits of comparison. If आविस् *ávís* be really a preposition, and therefore *ávir-bhúta* signify, with reference to the moon, "arisen," properly, "become forth," and *ávishrita* signify "disclosed," properly, "made forth," then the Latin and Greek *ex*, ἐξ, may also be compared with it, so that we should have to assume a hardening of the *v* to *k* (see §. 19.).

1003. From the demonstrative base *a* comes, in Sanscrit, the adverb *á-tas*, "thence," expressing separation from a place which might, as justly as *a-dhás*, "under" (§. 997.), be used as a preposition, and to which the signification "from" would be very suitable. This is the meaning in Sclavonic of the preposition отъ *o-t'*, which, as regards form, I hold to be identical with the above-mentioned *átas*, with the observation, that the Sclavonic ъ, almost as commonly as the Latin termination *us*, represents the Sanscrit termination *as*, the *s* of which, according to §. 255. k, must necessarily be dropped; hence, *e. g.*, новъ *nov'*=Sanscrit *navá-s*, Latin *novu-s;* везомъ *veẑ-o-m'*=*váh-â-mas*, *veh-i-mus*. I know, however, no termination in which Sclavonic ъ is based on a Sanscrit or Lithuanian *i*, but for that letter stands и *i* or ь (*y*); the former, *e. g.*, in даси *da-si*, "thou givest"=*dádâ-si;* the latter in дамь *da-my*, "I give"=*dádâmi;* томь *to-my*, "in that"=*tá-smin*. I cannot, therefore, with Miklosich (Radices, p. 60.), refer the said отъ *o-t'* to [G. Ed. p. 1473.] the Sanscrit preposition *áti*, "over," discussed above (§. 997.), although I see no objection in the meaning, which, in prepositions, is very changeable.

1004. From the indeclinable demonstrative base *u*, which supports itself as enclitic on other pronouns (see Gloss., a. 1847, p. 44), proceed probably the prepositions उप *ú-pa*, "to, towards," and *ú-t*, " up, upwards, aloft," the former being formatively akin to *á-pa*, "from" (see §. 1000.). As in Greek, ἀ-πό is related to *á-pa*, just so is ὑ-πό to *ú-pa;* only here the rough breathing may cause a difficulty, and the more, as the Latin *su-b* exhibits for it *s*. If, however, it is considered that with the Sanscrit *upá-ri*, "over," Gothic *ufa-r*, also, the Greek contrasts ὑπέ-ρ, and the Latin *supe-r*, we shall be readily inclined to regard the rough breathing in Greek and the *s* in Latin, in the preposition referred to, as purely a phonetic prefix. To this class belongs in Gothic, *uf*, "under," to which the Old High German *o-ba*, "over," our *ob* in *obliegen*, "to be incumbent," *Obdach*, "shelter," *Obhut*, "protection," adv. *oben*, "above," correspond, with an opposite signification (see Grimm, III. 253.). The Sclavonic, Lithuanian, and Old Prussian have lost the initial vowel, as in Sanscrit *pi* occurs together with *ápi*, §. 1000.; hence, in Old Sclavonic, *pa*, more frequently *po*, as prefix (Dobrowsky, p. 404), *e.g.*, in памать *pa-manty*, "memory;" помнѣти *po-mnye-ti*, "*meminisse;*" помазати *po-maζati*,"*inungere;*" полагати *po-lagati*,"*ponere;*" подати *po-dati*, "*præbere;*" постлати *po-stlati*, "*sternere*." From по, *po*, it would appear, proceeded подъ *po-d'*, "under," and so, too, надъ *na-d'*, "over," from *na*, пѓедъ *pre-d'*, "before" (*pred-iti*, "*præire*," пѓедъвидѣти *pred'-vidyeti*, "*prævidere*"), from пѓе *pre*, though the latter generally signifies "*trans*." The suffix *d'* may perhaps be identical with the Zend *dha* of locative pronominal adverbs (see §. 420.).

[G. Ed. p. 1474.]　　1005. In Lithuanian, *po*, as a separable preposition, signifies, among other things, "under," *e.g.*, *po dangumi*, "under the heaven:" where, however, it means "after," *e.g.*, *po pêtù*, "after noon," it springs, probably, from a different source, and is akin to the Sanscrit adverb *paschát*, an ablative form of *páscha**, which occurs in no other case, with the primary element of which the Latin *pos-t*, too, is to be compared, but in such wise, that the suffix *t* (from *ti*, cf. *pos-ticus*), has nothing to do with the Sanscrit *cha* (from *ka*), though, amongst other words, the Lithuanian *kuy*, may be connected with it, in *pas-kuy* (= *paskuy*), "hereafter," which is perhaps a dative (like *wilkui lupo*, §. 177.), from the base *paska*. In Old Prussian, *pans-dan*, with a nasal inserted, means "hereafter," as in the dative termination plural *mans* = Sanscrit *bhyas*, Lithuanian *mus* (§. 215.). With respect to the suffix *dan*, *pans-dan* answers to *pirs-dan*, "before," in the primary element of which the Sanscrit *purás* (from *parás*), "before," is easily recognised, of which hereafter. Without suffix, *pas* signifies, in Lithuanian, "near," with the accusative. The inseparable Lithuanian *pa* may partly be based on the Sanscrit preposition *ápa*, "from," *e.g.*, in *pa-bégu*, "I run away;" *pa-gaunu*, "I purloin, I take away;" partly on *úpa*, "to, towards," *e.g.*, in *pa-darau*, "I prepare" (*darau*, "I make"); *pa-giru*, "I praise" (Old Prussian, *gir-twei*, "to praise," *po-gir-sna-n*, "praise," accusative); *pa-żintis*, "acquaintance."

1006. Regarding the prepositions which have probably sprung from the base अन *aná*, "this," see §. 373. I formerly imagined† a relationship between the Latin and

---

* From *pas* (cf. Persian *pes*, "hereafter") and *cha*; as, *uchcha*, "high," from *ut*, "upwards;" *ni-cha*, "low," from *ni*.

† See "On the Demonstrative, and the origin of the Case-sign" in the Transactions of the Historic-Philological Class of the Royal Academy of Literature for 1826.

German preposition *in*, Greek ἐν, and the [G. Ed. p. 1475.] demonstrative base *i*; but the *i* of *in*, and the Greek ε of ἐν, may easily be regarded as a weakening of *a*, as in *inter* = Sanscrit *antár*; and the Gothic adverb *inna-thrô*, "from within" (see §. 294. Rem. 1. p. 384.), is much easier explained as coming from the base *aná*, by doubling the liquid (cf. §. 879.), than from the base *i*. By weakening the final *a* of the Sanscrit base *aná* to *u*, we get the preposition अनु *ánu*, "after," which has the same relation to *aná* that the interrogative base *ku* (§. 386.) has to the extensively used *ka*. The Sclavonic *na* and *na-d'*, "over" (cf. Greek ἀνά*, Old Prussian *na*, *no*, "up," Lithuanian *nů*, *nůg*, "from,†" appear, like *po*, *pod'*, *pa*, to have lost an initial vowel. The last part of the compound pronominal base *aná*, viz. *na* (see §. 369.), with the weakening of *a* to *i* becomes a preposition, with the signification "down," and is, too, the source whence our *nie-der*, Old High German *ni-dar* (see §. 294. p. 382.), has proceeded. There can, too, be scarce any doubt that the Sanscrit preposition नि *ni* lies at the root of the Sclavonic adverb ниэъ *ni-ζ'*, "under;" зъ ζ', consequently would be an appended suffix, as perhaps, also, in и-зъ *i-ζ'*, "out," for which, in Lithuanian, *isz* (= *ish*), in Old Prussian *is*, id. Perhaps the preposition signifying "out," has lost an initial *n*, as имѧ *imań* = Sanscrit *náman*, so that the said prepositions, at least with regard to their base, rank themselves under the Sanscrit *ni-s*, "out," which is evidently formed from *ni* by appending *s*, as *s* is frequently added to prepositions, and, indeed, without altering their meaning. But though, in Sanscrit, *nis* has assumed a meaning different from that of *ni*, still, in Zend, it has retained that of *ni*, "down." [G. Ed. p. 1476.]

---

* With regard to the *dh*, see §. 1003. conclusion.

† I hold the *g* for an enclitic (cf. §. 994. conclusion): *û* (*uo*) frequently represents a long *â*; *e.g.*, in *dûmi*, "I give"= *dádámi*.

also, since in this language *nis-had* or *nis-hidh*, *nis-hadh* represents the Sanscrit *ni-shad* (euphonic for *ni-sad*), in the special tenses *ni-shíd, e.g.*, V.S. p. 440: *yat ahmi, nmânê* .... *nâirika* .... *nis-hadât,* "when in this place a woman sits down." If, at the time when the Lettish-Sclavonic languages separated from the Sanscrit, the locative suffix ह *ha* in Sanscrit (from ध *dha*, see §. 420.), already existed in this abbreviated form, and, indeed, simultaneously with the more perfect ध *dha*, then the suffix зъ *ζ'* of the Sclavonic forms низъ *ni-ζ'*, изъ *i-ζ'*, might be derived from the suffix *ha* (cf. азъ *aζ'*, "I," Lithuanian *asz*, with the Sanscrit *ahám*), and, as has already been remarked, in the дъ *d'* of forms like подъ *pod'*, the elder form of the Sanscrit suffix, preserved in Zend, might be recognised, in spite of its corrupted form.

1007. From the above-mentioned (§. 1004.) *úpa* has been formed, as it appears, with the suffix *ri*, the Sanscrit *upá-ri*, and under it is to be classed the Gothic *ufa-r* of equivalent meaning, Old High German *uba-r*, *oba-r*, our *übe-r*, English *ove-r*, Greek ὑπέ-ρ, Latin *super*. To the Gothic *ufa-r* correspond as regards their suffix, several locative pronominal adverbs; *e. g.*, *hva-r*, "whither?" *tha-r*, "there;" *yaina-r*, "yonder;" *alya-r*, "elsewhere;" *hê-r*, "here." Should, too, the Gothic *iup*, "on," Old High German *úf*, our *auf*, come from the Sanscrit preposition *úpa*, so that the old tenuis would have remained in Gothic, as that of *svap*, "to sleep," has been preserved in the Gothic *slêpa*, we should then have to assume that the vowel *u* has, by the weaker Guna, become *iu* (see §. 27.), and the Guna been replaced in Old High German by lengthening the vowel. But from an older *ú* in New High German must come *au* (see §. 76.). It is impossible to compare in any other way the said German preposition with the Sanscrit. The Greek presents for comparison ὕπ-σι, in the suffix of which we easily recognise the corruption of *ti*, which appears in Sanscrit in the prepositions *á-ti*, "over," *prá-ti*, "towards," "against," (Greek προ-τί, πρό-ς), and the pronominal adverb *i-ti*, "thus." Observe, also, that the Sanscrit abstract suffix *ti* occurs in Greek, after labials, only in the form of σι; hence, *e. g.*, τέρπ-σι-ς, compared with the Sanscrit *tṛip-ti-s* (from *tarp-ti-s*), "contenting, satisfying."

1008. The Sanscrit preposition *út*, "up, upwards," might, according to its form, be taken as the nominative and accusative neuter of the base *u*, in analogy with *tá-t*, *yá-t*, *anyá-t*, &c. (see §§. 155., 156.). In Greek ὕσ-τερος, ὕσ-τατος, admit of being compared with this *ut* (see §. 102, conclusion), whence, likewise, are formed degrees of comparison: viz. *út-tara-s*, "the higher," as prototype of ὕσ-τερο-ς; and *ut--tamá-s*, "the highest," with which may be compared, in Latin, *in-timus*, *ex-timus*, *ul-timus*, and *op-timus*, as of cognate formation (see §. 291. conclusion). *Optimus*, likewise, probably contains an obscured preposition, and, indeed, a sister-form of the Sanscrit *ápi*, "on, over" (Greek ἐπὶ, §. 1000.), to which, as regards its vowel and the suppressed *i*, it would bear the same relation as *ob* to अभि *abhí* (§. 1001.). Consequently *op-timus* would properly signify "the highest." In Gothic, *út*, "out," Old High German *ûz*, our *aus*, English *out*, might be referred to the Sanscrit preposition *ut*, so that the long vowel would be just as inorganic or ungrounded as the Guna of the above-mentioned *iup*, "on" (see §. 1007.). If we compare *út* with *úta*, "without," "abroad," we perceive a sort of declension of a base *úta*, whence *út* would be the nominative and accusative (as, *e. g.*, *vaurd*, "word"), *úta* the dative (as *vaurda*), and *úta-na* the masculine accusative, according to the pronominal declension, like *tha-na*, "the," *hi-na*, "this." On the latter is based our adverb of place, *hin*, "towards." Moreover, from the base *úta* has arisen a secondary base *úta-thra*, whence comes [G. Ed. p. 1478.] the ablative *úta-thrô*, "from without," analogous to *inna-thrô*, "from within," and some similar formations (see §. 294.

1432

Rem. 1. p. 384). With respect to the retention of the old tenuis in the Gothic forms *ût, úta*, &c., in so far as they are really connected with the Sanscrit preposition *ut*, I recall attention to the relation of the Gothic *slêpa* to the Sanscrit *svápimi* (§. 89.), as also of the pronominal neuters like *tha-ta*, " this, the," to Sanscrit like *ta-t* (§. 155.). In Zend, the *t* of the preposition under discussion has been changed into ⟨⟩ *s̀*, or, especially before sonant consonants, into ⟨⟩ *z*; hence, *e.g.*, ⟨⟩ *us̀-i-hista*, " stand up, arise" (see §. 757.); ⟨⟩ *us̀-a-zayanha*, " thou wast born" (l. c.); ⟨⟩ *uz-dâta*, " held on high;" ⟨⟩ *uz-vazaiti*, " he bears on high."

1009. From the preposition *ápa*, "from," comes, in Sanscrit, most probably *ápara-s*, " the other" (see §. 375.), in the same way as *áva-ra-s*, " the lower," from *áva* (see §. 997.), and in Zend, *upa-ra*[*], " superior," " *altus*" (cf. Old High German *oba-ro(n)*, " the higher"), from *upa*. Observe, with respect to the signification, the derivation of the Gothic *framu-theis* (theme *frama-thya*) " *alienus*," from *fram*, "from." From *ápara-s*, came, by Aphæresis, the more current form *pára-s*, which, like *ápara-s, anyá-s*, and, in Latin, *alius, alter*, has been assigned by the language itself, through its declension, to the pronouns: moreover, in point of fact, the idea of " other" is not far removed from that of the remote demonstrative. The prepositions which, in my opinion, come from *pára*, are *prá, práti, párâ, purás, pári*. *Prá* (insep.), formed by a very ancient syncope from *para*, means " before, in front, forwards, forth." To it corresponds, in Zend, *fra* or *frâ*[†], in Greek πρό, in Latin *prô*, in Lithuanian *pra*

---

[*] *E.g.*, in the possessive compound *uparô-kairyô*, " having a high body," see Burnouf, " Études," p. 182.

[†] See §. 47. If we take *frâ* as the ancient form, we may recognise in it an instrumental, as in the Sanscrit *pra* (cf. p. 1207 G. ed.). I recall

(insep.), "before," *e. g.*, in *pra-dŭmi*, "I give provender beforehand;" *pra-dĕmí*, "I commence;" *pra-neszu*, "I represent;" *pra-rakas*, "prophet" ("foretelling"); *pra-stoyu*, "I quit"*; *pra-szok-ti*, "to dance away;" *pra-girti*, "to drink away," *i. e.* "by dancing, by drinking to squander one's money:" in Sclavonic пҏа- *pra-*, пҏо-; *e. g.*, in пҏадѣдъ *pra-dyed'*, "*proavus*;" пҏавноукъ *pra-vnŭk'*, "*pronepos;*" пҏамати *pra-mati*, "first mother;" пҏовидѣти *pro-vidyeti*, "*providere;*" пҏоповѣдати *pro-po-vyedati*, "*prædicare;*" пҏолити *pro-liti*, "*profundere;*" пҏоводити *pro-voditi*, "*deducere:*" in Gothic, perhaps, *fra-* (cf. §. 1011.), our *ver-* (Old High German *fra*, transposed *far, for, fir, fër*); *e. g.*, in *fra-lêtan*, "to leave free, to release (to let go)," &c.; *fra-kunnan*, "to despise" (*hunnan*, "to know"); *fra-qviman*, "to expend, to lay out" (properly, "to make proceed," *qviman*, "to come"); *fra-bugyan*, "to sell" (*bugyan*, "to buy"); *fra-qvithan*, "to curse, to execrate" (*quithan*, "to say"); *fra-vaurkyan*, "to sin" (*vaurkyan*, "to do, to make"). A weakening of *fra* is *fri*, in *fri-sahts*, "picture, example" (*sakan*, "to admonish, to interdict," *in-sakan*, "to indicate," "to describe"). Perhaps, too, the Lithuanian and Sclavonic *pri* is a weakening of *pra*.

1010. From *pra* may be derived the preposition *práti*, "towards," unless this, as I prefer assuming, just like *pra*, has come direct from *pára*, and is therefore an abbreviated form of *para-ti*, which made its appearance so early as in the time of the unity of language. Thus [G. Ed. p. 1480.] much appears certain, that the suffix of *prá-ti* is identical with that of *i-ti*, "thus," and *á-ti*, "on." In Greek, προτί, (Cret. πορτί), πρός (see §. 152. p. 167.), ποτί, corresponds.

---

call attention to the fact, that in Sanscrit, too, evident instrumentals occur as prepositions; *e.g.*, *parêna*, "over," from *para*.

* *Stowyu*, "I stand." In Sanscrit, *sthá*, "to stand," receives through *pra* (*prá-sthá*) the signification "to proceed."

1434 FORMATION OF WORDS.

The latter answers, with respect to the loss of the semi-vowel, to the Zend 𐬞𐬀𐬌𐬙𐬌 *paiti*, which, when isolated, signifies not only "towards," but also "on," "over;" *e.g.*, *barĕshnushu paiti gairinaṁm*, "on the summits of the mountain;" in combination with *vach*, "to speak," it signifies "towards," and the whole means "to answer" (see §. 536. Rem.). In Lettish correspond *pretti*, *prett'*, "towards, against," with the accusative, sometimes also with the genitive; in Slowenian, *proti*, "towards," with the dative; in Lithuanian, *priĕsz*, id., with the accusative. In Latin, *por-*, *pol-*, *pos-*, in forms like *por-rigo*, *pol-liceor*, *pos-sideo*, have arisen most probably, by assimilation, from *pot* ($=\pi o\tau i$) or *pod*, and perhaps *præ* has come from *prai*, for *prati* (cf. Pott, I. 92, Ag. Benary "Doctrine of Roman sounds," p. 185.).

1011. *Párá* (insep.) is little used in Sanscrit, and signifies "back, away, forth;" *e.g.*, *párá-vrit*, "to return back" (*vrit*, *vart*, "to go"); *párá-han*, "to strike back, to drive forth;" *pálây* (for *párây*), "to draw back, to flee" (*ay* "to go"); *parâñch* (*párá-añch*), in the weak cases *parâch*, adjective "turned back" (*añch*, "to go"); *párá-krish*, "to draw forth;" *párá-pat*, "to fly away;" *párá-bhû*, "to go to ruin" (*bhû*, "to be, to become"). In Lithuanian the corresponding word is *par*, 1. "back," 2. "down" (insep.); *e.g.*, in *par-eimi*, "I come back;" *par-wadinu*, "I call back;" *par-půlu*, "I fall down;" *par-si-klaupyu*, "I kneel down;" *par-dauźiu*, "I plunge down." In Zend the preposition *para* by itself has the meaning "before," in reference to time, and with the ablative*, and παρά corresponds [G. Ed. p. 1481.] in Greek. In Sclavonic the inseparable preposition *pre*, which generally means "through" or "over, across," might be referred to this class, provided

---

* See "Crit. Gram. linguæ Sanscr.," p. 253. According to form, the Sanscrit *párá* seems to be an instrumental as well as the Zend *para*.

it does not belong to पार *párá*, "the further shore" (cf. Greek πέραν), or to प्र *pra*, or has been derived from different sources according to the difference of its meanings. I annex some examples from the Slowenian, according to Ant. Janezich (Lexicon, p. 317.): *pre-bdeti*, "to watch through;" *pre-bechi*, "to outrun;" *pre-bernuti*, "to throw round;" *pre-bèrsnuti*, "to cast beyond;" *pre-biti*, "to beat to pieces;" *pre-bosti*, "to stick through, to pierce through;" *pre-bresti*, "to wade through;" *pre-buditi*, "to rouse up" (Sanscrit *pra-budh*, id.); *pre-bulati*, "to overfill;" *pre-hod*, "passing over, passage;" *pre-pád*, "abyss;" *pre-páditi*, "to be ruined;" *pre-pis*, "transcript;" *pre-pláviti*, "to overflow;" *pre-poditi*, "to expel, to drive away" (cf. Dobrowsky, p. 417). In Russian this inseparable preposition becomes пере *pere*; hence, e.g., перебіраться чрезъ рѣку *pere-biraty-sya chrez' ryeku*, "to go over a river;" перебітый *pere-bityĭ*, "mingled with one another, mixed;" перебрасываю *pere-brasyvayu*, "I cast over;" перебѣгъ *pere-byeg'*, "the outrunning;" перевалъ *pere-val'*, "the ferrying over from one shore to another;" переворачиваю *pere-vorachivayu*, "I turn round;" перегладываю *pere-gladyvayu*, "I see through, I examine." The Lettish has lost the final vowel of this preposition, and, on the other hand, retained the old *a*-sound of the first syllable unweakened, indeed lengthened, and uses *pâr* (*pahr*) both separate and in compounds; e.g., *sakkis pâr zellu tekk*, "the hare runs across over the way" (see "Rosenberger's Doctrine of Forms," p. 170); *pâr-kâpt*, "to overlook;" *pâr-lûkôt*, "overseeing;" *pâr-dôt*, "to sell" ("to give over"); *pâr-eet*, "to return home, to return back." In the meaning "back" this *pâr* (according to Lettish ortho- [G. Ed. p. 1482.] graphy, *pahr*) agrees with the Lithuanian *par*, and Sanscrit *párá*; on the other hand the Lithuanian also has a preposition *pér*, used only separated, which signifies "through, over, across," e.g., *pér tiltaṅważóti*, "to drive over the bridge;" *pér naktiń*, "through the night;" *pér buttań*, "through the house" (see Nesselmann Lexicon, p. 285). That the *e* of this *pér*, and the Russian *e* of *pere*, are corruptions of *a*, and that therefore *pér*, *pere*, and the Lettish *pâr*, "over, across," are originally one, is self evident: it is, however, impossible to decide with certainty whether the Sanscrit *párâ*, "back, forth, away," is the sole source of the Lithuanian, Lettish, and Sclavonic preposition under discussion, or whether, in accordance with its signification, in spite of the similarity of form, it is based at one time on परा *párâ*, at another with the Greek πέρᾱν, πέρην, on पार *párá*, "the further shore," which probably proceeds from *pára-s*, "*alius.*" In Sanscrit the neuter accusative, too, of *pára*, "*alius, remotior, ulterior,*" viz. *páram*, is used as a preposition, with the meaning, "on that side, behind," with reference to time, "after." There is also, in Sanscrit, a preposition *parás*, "over, across yonder, on that side," whence the adverb *paras-tât*; all of them bases of prepositions in the European sister-languages, of similar sound and similar signification. The Latin *per* must likewise be brought under this class, and must be compared especially with the Lithuanian *pér*. We have already noticed *peren-*, in *perendie*, as sister-form of *pára*, "*alius*" (see §. 375., p. 527). The Latin *re-*, before vowels *red-*, like *prod-*, euphonic for *pro-*, together with the Ossetish *ra-*, admits of being regarded as an abbreviation of परा *párâ* (cf. Pott, II. p. 156); for the surrender of the first syllable of a dissyllabic preposition is something so common, that two languages may well accidentally coin-

[G. Ed. p. 1483.] cide in that point in one and the same word. In Ossetish, *e.g.*, we have *ra-jurin*, "to answer."

---

* *Jurin* (infin. see p. 1269 G. ed.), "to speak;" cf. Sanscrit *gir* from *gar*, "voice;" and see G. Rosen's Ossetish Grammar, p. 39. In some other compounds occurring l. c., *ra*, or, transposed, *ar*, expresses, so far as
the

1012. In Gothic the inseparable *fair*, as far as its form is concerned, might as well belong to *pári*, "around," with which I have before (p. 68) compared it, as to *párâ*. In any case the *i* of *fair* is a weakening of *a*, and the preceding *á* a euphonic prefix according to §. 82. With regard to its signification or operation, however, *fair*, to which our *ver-* corresponds, answers, in the cases in which it is not based on *fra* (see p. 1479 G. ed.), better to *párâ* (with which I have also compared it in my Glossary, a. 1847, p. 210), than to *pári*. Perhaps *fair*, *faur*, *faura* and *fra* are originally one, and have all proceeded from *párâ* ; at least परा *párâ*, "back, forth, away," answers just as well for the compounds cited at p. 1479 (G. ed.), and for all our combinations with *ver*, and, in some respects, better than प्र *prá*. Thus, *e.g.*, the place of our *ver* in *verkommen*, "to perish," *verfallen*, "to go to ruin," *verleiten*, "to mislead," *verführen*, "to seduce," *verirren*, "to lead astray," *vergeben*, "to give away, to resign," *verschenken*, "to bestow," *verscheuchen*, "to scare away," *verbreiten*, "to divulge," *verjagen*, "to chase away," *verachten*, "to despise," *verthun*, "to squander," may very well be represented in Sanscrit by *párâ*, exclusive of the circumstance that this preposition, as has already been remarked, has become of but very rare employment. In the idea of separation, removal, the Sanscrit *párâ* and our *ver* coincide, and | G. Ed. p. 1484.] that which corresponds to the latter in the older dialects (see Grimm, II. 853.).

1013. The meaning of the Zend *para*, "before," is re-

---

the latter is not to be taken as $=(p)ar(\hat{a})$, "appropinquation," viz. in *ra-tzawin*, *ar-tzawin*, "to arrive," in opposition to *a-tzawin*, "to depart," the *a* of which can only be a remnant of a more full Sanscrit preposition, probably from *ápa* (cf. Latin *ab*, *a*); *ar-chasin*, "to bring to," opposed to *a-chasin*, "to carry forth." From Sjegrön's Lexicon I cite in addition, *ra-vadun*, "to leave off;" *ra-dtun*, "to give up, to deliver;" *ra-ζdaechun*, "to step aside, to retire."

presented in Gothic by *faura, faur*, the *u* of which I regard as the weakening of *a*, like that of the Sanscrit *purás*, "before." To the *u*, however, must, in Gothic, according to §. 82., an *a* be further prefixed; as, *e.g.*, in *baurans* for *burans*, "borne," from the root *bar* = Sanscrit *bhar, bhri*, "to bear." On the Gothic *faura, faur*, which signifies not only "before," but also "for," are based our *vor* and *für*. In the Old High German *fora, foro, for, furi, fori, fore*, &c., the meanings "before" and "for" are not firmly distinguished by the form (see Graff, III. 612.). The *i* of *furi* I take to be the weakening of the *a* of *fora*. As in Latin gutturals very often stand for labials, *e.g.*, in *quinque* for *pinque* (§. 313.), *coquo* for *poquo* (Sanscrit *pach*, from *pak*, "to cook"), so, perhaps, the *c* of *côram* might be taken as the representative of *p*, and the whole word be referred to the class of words which, in Sanscrit, Zend, and the German languages, signify "before." The Latin *ô*, like the Greek ω, stands very commonly for an original *a*, as, *e.g.*, in *datôrem* = *dátâram, sôpio* = *svâpáyâmi;* wherefore for *côram* we should have to expect in Sanscrit *pâram* (cf. Greek πέρᾱν πέρην), which occurs, not indeed as preposition, but as accusative of the above-mentioned (p. 1482 G. ed.) substantive *pârâ*, "further shore," as in general the lengthening of an *a* in the derivative forms is, in Sanscrit, of very common occurrence.

1014. The Sanscrit *pári*, "around," Zend ‍‍‍‍‍‍ *pairi*, ‍‍‍‍‍‍ *pairis*, may be taken either as an abbreviation of *apari*, and as a derivative from *ápa*, to which it would have the relation that *upá-ri* has to *úpa* (see §. 1004.); or we may presuppose, which appears to me less satisfactory, a base *par*, and look upon *pári* as its locative: so much [G. Ed. p. 1485.] seems certain, that *pári* is etymologically connected with other prepositions beginning with a labial. In Greek, περί corresponds, and in Latin, most probably, the *pari* (see §. 912.) which stands quite isolated in *pari-es*, and which surpasses περί in retaining the original vowel. In the same way, in Latin, another Sanscrit preposition is preserved in an obsolete compound, viz. the preposition *vi*, which expresses separation, and on which our *wi-der*, Old High German *wi-dar*, is based (see §. 294. p. 382.). This preposition occurs, viz. in the Latin *vi-dua*, which makes itself etymologically known through the Sanscrit sister-word *vi-dhavâ*, "widow," as "the woman robbed of her husband, the husbandless," for *dhava-s* means, in Sanscrit, "man, husband;" a rare word, which, however, in the term for "widow," has been widely diffused in the Indo-European department of languages. The Gothic form is *vi-duvô** (theme -*ôn*), the Sclavonic вдова *v-dova*. As regards the origin of the preposition *vi*, it may have sprung, by a weakening of the vowel, from the base *va*, which is preserved in the compound *á-va* (see §. 377.), as *ni*, "down," is most probably connected with the final portion of *aná* (see p. 1475 G. ed.) ; or it may also come from the demonstrative base *u*, whence, in Zend, the adverb *uiti*, "so" (for *u-ti*, according to §. 41.), analogously to *i-ti* (§. 425.) of equivalent signification.

1015. There remains further for discussion, among the conjectural derivatives of the Sanscrit *pára*, the Gothic preposition *fram*, "von," which is *fram*, likewise, in Old Saxon, Anglo-Saxon, and Old High German, and in English "from." I look upon *fra-m* as an abbreviation of *fra-ma*, whence the above-mentioned (§. 1009.) base *fra-ma--thya*, "*fremd*, foreign, ἀλλότριος." In connection with *fram* stands also the comparative adverb [G. Ed. p. 1486.] *framis*, "further, *ulterius*" (see §. 301., Remark). This might be rendered into Sanscrit by the above-mentioned (see p. 1482 G. ed.) *páram ;* but nevertheless the Gothic *m* of *fram, framis*, has nothing to do with the accusative sign

---

* Occurring once as *vidôvô* (Luke vii. 12).

of *páram*, but is connected with the derivative suffix of *paramá-s*, which springs from *pára*, "*alius, remotus*," and which, according to its derivation, might just as well signify "*remotissimus*," as "*eximius, altissimus, summus*." With this *paramá-s*, has been elsewhere compared also the Gothic *fru-ma* (theme *fruman*), "*prior, primus*," the Lithuanian *pir-ma-s*, "*primus*," and the Latin "*primus*,"* The comparative adverb *framis* has the same relation to the positive base *frama*, that, *e.g.*, *hauhis*, "higher," has to *hauha*; and the preposition *fram*, just like *faur*, has the form of a nominative and accusative neuter, but must of course be taken as an adverbial accusative.

1016. The prepositions which spring from the demonstrative base *sa* (see §. 345.) signify, all of them, in Sanscrit, "with." They are *sahá, sam, sa, sákam, samám*, and *sárdhám*. The former corresponds in its suffix, to *i-há*, "here" (from *i-dhá*, §. 420.), and occurs in the Vêdas also in the form of *sadhá*. The Zend in this preposition furnishes us with a powerful corroboration of the origin of prepositions from pronominal roots, since it uses ⲛⲟⲉⲩⲱ *hadhá*, which corresponds to the Vêdic *sadhá* not at all as a preposition, but as a pronominal adverb with the signification "here:" on the other hand, it employs another form, *hathra* (see §. 420.), which is formed from the base *ha* by a locative adverbial suffix, both as a preposition with the meaning "with," and as an adverb with the primitive signification "here, there." *Sam* and *sa* appear, in Sanscrit, only [G. Ed. p. 1487.] as prefixes,† but in Zend the feminine accusative form ⲅⲯⲩⲱ *hanm* occurs also as an isolated preposition governing the genitive.‡ On the Sanscrit *sam*

---

* See Gloss. Sanscr., a. 1847, p. 209.

† See §. 964., and p. 1441 G. ed.

‡ So in a passage of the Vend. Sad., p. 230, elsewhere cited ("Ann. Reg. of Lit. Crit.," Dec. 1831, p. 817): ⲅⲯⲩⲥⲗⲥⲱⲩⲅ ⲅⲯⲩⲱ *hanm náirinanm*, "with women."

are based the Greek σύν, the Old Prussian *sen*, the Lithuanian *san* in *san-dora*, "contract" (or *san-dora*), *san* in compounds like *san-têwonis*, "co-heir," *san-darbininka-s*, "co-labourer," *su* (separate with the instrumental), the Old Sclavonic съ *s'*, the Old High German *sin* in *sinflôt*, "*diluvium.*" To *sa-* corresponds the Greek ἁ-, σα-, of the compounds discussed above (p. 1441 G. ed.). With *sâkám*, of which I know examples only in the Vêda dialect (see Benfey's Glossary), the Latin *cum* may be compared, supposing the first syllable to be suppressed. And, further, the Gothic *ga-*, "with" (see p. 1441 G. ed., sub. f.), admits of being similarly compared with *sâkám*. The derivation from स *sa* is on that account doubtful, because one does not meet with other examples in which an original sibilant has been hardened in German to a guttural. It would be better to trace back the Latin *cum*, through the medium of the Greek ξύν, to *sam*. As regards the violation of the law for the mutation of consonants in the Gothic *ga-*, if we derive it from *sâkám*, I would recall attention to similar phenomena which have been mentioned before.* The Sanscrit *sâr-dhám*, or *sârddhám*, "with," I hold to be an adverbial compound, formed, according to §. 990., from *sa*, "with," and *ardha*, *arddha*, "half," so that the meaning of the substantive has been entirely lost in the whole compound. From the pronominal base, or which comes to the same thing, from the preposition *sa*, I derive, too, the Vêdic adverb *sáchâ*, "*simul*," which I regard as the instrumental of a to-be-pre- [G. Ed. p. 1488.] supposed adjective base, सच *sá-cha*, and as analogous, with respect to its formative suffix, to *nî-cha*, "low," from *ni*, and *uch-cha*, "high," from *ut*. In Old Persian, *hachâ* is used as a preposition with the meaning "out, from, without," with the ablative, just as, in Zend, 𐬵𐬀𐬗𐬁 *hacha*, which,

---

* See §§. 91., 823., 943., 951., conclusion.

1442 FORMATION OF WORDS.

with the ablative or instrumental, signifies "out," "from," and with the accusative "for."*

1017. In Zend ⟨Zend⟩ *maṭ* means "with," and governs the instrumental, and standing by itself, too, expresses the relation "with." According to its formation, it appears to be the accusative (and nominative) neuter of the demonstrative base *ma*, which, in combination with the base *i* (*i-ma*), produces the neuter *i-maṭ*, "this" (see §. 368.). Thus, therefore, *maṭ* would be, in its primary meaning, identical with सम् *sa-m*, समम् *sa-má-m*, &c. With its theme that of the Greek με of με-τά admits of being compared, which, in its formative suffix, coincides with that of κα-τά, the base of which is identical with that of the Sanscrit interrogative base *ka*. The interrogative signification might easily pass into the demonstrative, and thus κα be adapted to the developement of prepositions, as, too, our *hinter*, Old High German *hin-tar*, conducts us back to the Sanscrit interrogative; since the Gothic demonstrative base *hi* (see §. 396. and §. 293. Rem.), acc. masc. *hi-na*, is based on the Sanscrit *ki*, with which we have also to compare the Latin *hi-c* (see §. 394.). With the Zend [G. Ed. p. 1489.] *ma-ṭ*, our *mi-t*, Gothic *mi-th*, with the prepositions beginning with *v*, *w*, in other German dialects, have already been compared (see §. 294. p. 383, Note).

1018. The sole verbal root, which, so early as the time of the unity of our family of languages, at least at the

---

* For examples with the ablative, see §. 180. p. 198, and §.756., p. 1013; for examples with the accusative, see Brockhaus Glossar., p. 403. In the passages in which Benfey ("Glossary to the Cuneiform Inscriptions") makes the Old Persian *hachâ* govern the instrumental, I can only acknowledge the ablative, as the ablative of bases in *a*, on account of the regular suppression of the final *t*, is equivalent in sound to the instrumental. Regarding the form *aniyanâ*, "*hoste*," see Monthly Report of the Academy of Literature, March 1848, p. 133.

period when the Sanscrit and Zend were still one, produced prepositions, may, perhaps, be the root तर् *tar*, तृ *lṛī*, whence we have above (p. 375) derived the comparative suffix *tara*. This root already combines in itself the signification of a preposition with that of a verb, for it expresses motion with the secondary idea of "across," "through:" *tár-a-ti* means "he transports," *e. g.*, *nadím*, "over a river." From the root *tar* springs the preposition *tirás*, which is of such frequent occurrence in the Vêdas, governing the accusative, and signifying "across, through, *trans*."* The *i* is evidently a weakening of *a*, and the whole word originally an adverbial accusative neuter of an adjective belonging to the class of words described in §. 933. C. The Zend ⲯⲗⲱⲡ *tarô* (*e. g.*, *tarô haranm*, "over the mountain") of equivalent meaning has retained the old *a*.† In the Irish dialect of the Celtic correspond *tar*, *tair*, "beyond, over, through," &c.; and *tri*, "through, by," &c. Moreover, the Latin *trans* and Gothic *thair-h*, our "*durch*," are to be classed under this head, but are independent formations from the same root; and, indeed, *trans* for *terans* (cf. *terminus*, §. 478. sub. f.) is, according to its form, a participle present, and the Gothic *thair-h* corresponds in its formation to the classes of words discussed in §. 951. passim. Further, *thair-kô* (neuter theme *thair-kan*, "hole," "ear," might be referred to the root [G. Ed. p. 1490.] under discussion, which lies beyond the lingual consciousness of the German, so that it would properly signify "passage," πόρος, δίοδος.

---

* See Fr. Rosen on the Rigv., I. 19. 7., and Benfey's Gloss. to the S. V.

† See Burnouf, "Yaçna," p. 83, where, however, as it appears to me wrongly, the termination *as* of this and some other prepositions is represented as an ablative ending. We should then have to suppose for *tarô*, *tiras*, a base *tar*, *tir*.

SUPPLEMENT.

Since I wrote that part of my work which treats of the Formation of the Tenses, Shaffarik and Miklosich have brought to light some Old Sclavonic forms which were before unknown, and which are too important for me to conclude this work on the Comparison of Languages without a supplementary notice of them. They are as follows:—

1) Preterites which deviate from the ordinary formation, in that, instead of the *ch* of the 1st person singular and plural, which has been shewn (§. 255. *m.*) to come from *s*, they have retained the original sibilant, and thus afford a practical demonstration that the said tense is, without a doubt, essentially identical with those Sanscrit and Greek aorist forms which append the substantive verb to the principal root.* The 3d person plural exhibits the organic *s* for *sh*. To this class must be referred, *e.g.*, ꙗсъ *ya-s'*, "I ate," 1st person plural probably ꙗсомъ *ya-som'*, 3d person ꙗсѧ *ya-sań*, from the root *yad* = Sanscrit *ad*, the *d* of which must be suppressed before the *s* of the auxiliary verb, according to the same principle from which, in the 2d person singular, we find ꙗси *ya-si* for the Sanscrit *at-si*. Compare, also, Greek aorists and futures like ἔψευ(δ)-σα, ψεύ(δ)-σω, contrasted with Sanscrit like *átáut-sam, tót-syá--mi*, from *tud*, "to knock." The Sclavonic, as a general rule, does not admit of the combination of a mute with *s*, or the junction of two sibilants; hence, *e.g.*, погресѧ *po-gre-sań*, "they buried" (root *greb*); съꙇрѧсъ *s'-trań-s'*, "I terrified" (root *trańs*).

[G. Ed. p. 1491.] 2) Preterites which correspond to the Sanscrit aorists of the sixth formations, and to Greek aorists like ἔλιπ-ο-ν, ἔφυγ-ο-ν, ἔτυπ-ο-ν (see §. 575.). In verbs which are based on the Sanscrit 1st or 6th class (see §. 109. [a)] 1.), as the augment is lost in Sclavonic, a distinction from the present in this aorist formation is only possible in the persons, in which there exists a distinction between the terminations of the 1st and 2d persons. The 1st person singular ends in ъ, which corresponds to the Sanscrit *a* and Greek *o* of forms like *ábudh-a-m*, ἔφυγ-ο-ν: the 3d person plural ends in ѫ *u-ń*, agreeing with the Sanscrit *a-n* and Greek *o-ν* of *ábudh-a-n*, ἔφυγ-ο-ν. The 2d and 3d person singular end in є, as, according to §. 255. *l.*, the original final consonants are suppressed in Sclavonic; hence, *e.g.*, несє *nes-e*, "thou didst bear," and "he bore," contrasted with Sanscrit and Greek forms like *ábudh-a-s, ábudh-a-t*

---

* See §§. 561—575., and Miklosich, "Doctrine of Forms in the Old Slowenian," p. 50.

ἔφυγ-ε-s, ἔφυγ-ε. We may, to wit, now assume that the aorists in χъ, as неϲохъ *nes-o-ch'*, "I bore," are not used in the 2d and 3d person singular, but borrow these persons from the second aorist (see Miklos., l. c., p. 53). If this be the case, then бы *by*, "thou wast," "he was," belongs to the Sanscrit fifth aorist formation (see §. 573.), and answers in the 2d person as exactly as possible to the Sanscrit *ábhû-s* and the Greek ἔφῡ-s, in the 3d to *ábhû-t*, ἔφῡ. The analogy of these forms might also have had its influence on those conjugational classes in which the first aorist formation is altogether wanting in other persons; so that the *búdi* mentioned above (§. 561.) must be explained according to the selfsame principle as that on which rest forms like *nese*; and therefore not the verb substantive, but only the character of the 2d and 3d person has been dropped after the *i* of *búdi*. *Búdi*, therefore, would stand for *búd-i-t*, in the 2d person, *búd-i-s*, in the 3d, *búdit*. According to the first aorist formation we should have to expect *búd-i-she*.

3) Imperfects, which, like the first aorists, append the verb substantive to the theme of the principal verb, but so that the latter, without reference to the remaining tenses, always contains the character of the Sanscrit 10th class, and, indeed, for the most part, in the form of ѣ *ye**; but the *ch*, *sh*, or *s* of the auxiliary verb is always preceded by an *a*, or by its occasional representative ѣ *ye* (see Mikl. l. c. p. 35), in which I recognise the old *a* of the root अस् *as*, which is found still in an uncompounded state in Old Prussian (*asmu, asmai, as-mu,* "I am"). I divide, therefore, thus, e.g., вѣдѣахъ *vyed-ye-ach'*, from вѣмь *vye-my*, for [G. Ed. p. 1492]. *vyed-my,* "I know," according to the Sanscrit 2d class (वेद्मि *véd-mi*); while the first aorist вѣдѣхъ *vyed-ye-ch'*, the infinitive вѣдѣти *vyed-ye-ti*, and the participles preterite вѣдѣвъ *vyed-ye-v'* and вѣдѣлъ *vyed-ye-l'*, in like manner, follow the Sanscrit 10th class, or causal form. Compare, e.g., in the case before us, वेदयामि *véd-áyá-mi*, Prâkrit *véd-ê-mi,* "I make to know."† Perhaps ахъ *ach'* (from *as*), 2d and 3d person аше *ashe*, is the obsolete, in its simple form, imperfect of ксмъ *yes-my*, for есмь *es-my,* "I am;" and perhaps we ought to recognise the reason of the vowel difference between the imperfect and present in this, that *ach'* is based on the Sanscrit augmented *ásam*, as, in general, the Sclavonic *a* corresponds more frequently to the Sanscrit *â* than to the short *a*, which has commonly become е or о (see §. 255. *b*.). Compare—

SANSCRIT.	OLD SCLAVONIC.
ásam	ахъ *ach'*
ásîs	аше *ashe*

---

* Cf. §§. 505., 742.   † See §. 109. a) 6 , p. 110.

SANSCRIT.	OLD SCLAVONIC.
âsît	АШЕ *ashe*
âs-va	АХОВѢ *ach-o-vye*
âs-tam	АСТА *as-ta*
âs-tâm	АСТА *as-ta*
âs-ma	АХОМЪ *ach-o·m'*
âs-ta	АСТЕ *as-te*
âs-a-n	АХѪ *ach-u-ṅ*

I recall attention, moreover, to the fact, that in Sanscrit also the root *as* furnishes a tense, of occurrence in composition only, viz. the future *syâmi* (see §. 648.).

4) Remains of the Sanscrit auxiliary future, to which the Greek in σω, σίω (§. 656.), and Lithuanian in *su*, correspond. The Sclavonic forms of this kind which have been discovered up to the present time (in Mikl., p. 73) all occur in the 1st person singular; *e.g.*, ИЗМИШѪ *iẑ-mi-shuṅ*, "*tabescam*" (root *mi*). The other futures mentioned by Miklosich have, all but one, an *n* after the future character с *s*; *e.g.*, ОБРЪСНѪ *o-brysnuṅ*, "*tondebo*" (root *bri*); ВЪСКОПЫСНѪ *v's-kopysnuṅ*, "*claleitrabo*" (root *kop*); ПЛАСНѪ *plasnuṅ*, "*ardebo*" (root *pla*); ТЪКЫСНѪ *t'kysnuṅ*, "*tangam*" (root ТЪК *t'k*). These forms have probably thus arisen: the [G. Ed. p. 1493.] character of the verbs discussed in §. 496., p. 692, has been appended to the future base which ends in *s*, just as if, in Greek, λυσνω, τυψνω, were said for λύσω, τύψω. The form БѢГАСІАѨ *byegasyayuṅ*, from *byeg*, "to run," stands quite isolated. In case this form, which Miklosich translates by *curso*, is, according to its formation, a future, then in the syllable СІА *sya* we have exactly to the letter the Sanscrit future character *sya*; the *a* preceding answers to that of the infinitive *byeg-a-ti* and analogous forms; and the whole corresponds, as regards the syllable *yu* inserted between the base *byegasya* and the personal termination *ṅ*, to present forms like ЗНАѨ *ẑnayuṅ*, "I know."* The verb substantive has left us a future participle in the following forms of the definite declension: БЫШѪШТЕЇЕ *byshuṅshteye*, "τὸ μέλλον;" БЫШѪШТААГО *byshuṅshtaago*, "τοῦ μέλλοντος;" БЫШѪШТИИМИ *byshuṅstiimi*, instr. pl. (Mikl., pp. 69, 70). Cf. the Zend future participle ۔۔۔ *bûsyaṅs*, "*futurus*," acc. *bûsyantĕm*, and the Lithuanian *buseṅs*, acc. *busentiṅ* (see §. 784.).

5) Remains of the Middle. For *vye-my*, "I know" (abbreviated from *vyed-my* = Sanscrit *véd-mi*), occurs, as Miklosich remarks, in the older MSS. ВѢДѢ *vyedye*. This form is explained, correctly in my opinion,

---

* See §§. 500., 526., p. 746: respecting the nasal Ѫ, see §. 783. Rem. 1.

by the said learned man, as middle. It corresponds as exactly as possible to the Sanscrit vidé*, and, like the Sanscrit termination, has lost the personal character *m*, which, together with the reasons mentioned above (see p. 1255 G. ed.), points to a comparatively later separation from the Sanscrit (cf. §. 467.). Miklosich, however (p. 71), calls the above-mentioned вѣдѣ *vyed-ye* the sole remnant in Sclavonic of the Atmanê-padam (the middle), which isolation might raise some suspicion of the genuineness, or real middle nature of the said form. This mistrust must, however, disappear, when we find that several other Old Sclavonic forms have great claims to be regarded as middle. The conjugation given by Miklosich (l. c. pp. 71, 72) of the verbs without a conjunctive vowel, ꙗмь *ya-my* (from *yad-my*), "I eat," and дамь *da-my* (from *dad-my*, "I give"), supplies four forms, as regards sound only two, which I am of opinion must be assigned to the middle. I mean the aorist forms of the 2d and 3d person singular, ꙗстъ *yast'*, "thou didst eat;" [G. Ed. p. 1494.] *yast'*, "he ate;" дастъ *dast'*, "thou gavest;" *dast'*, "he gave." Miklosich refers the *s* of these forms to the root, and divides *yas-t'*, *das-t'*: if this division be correct, the *s* would be a euphonic alteration of the radical *d*, and I should then compare *yas-t'*, *das-t'*, in the 2d person, to the Sanscrit imperfect middle *ât-thâs*, *adat-thâs*, and in the 3d person to the Sanscrit *ât-ta*, *a-dat-ta*, Zend *daś-ta* (see §. 102. conclusion). The circumstance that the middle of the Sanscrit root *ad*, Cl. 2., is hitherto unciteable † need not prevent us from presupposing its former existence, as in the time of the unity of language the middle must have been much more extensively used than in the present condition of the different members of our lingual stem. The above-mentioned Sclavonic forms may, however, be so regarded, as that, instead of distributing them as Miklosich does *yas-t'*, *das-t'*, the sibilant may be separated from the root, thus, *ya-s-t' da-s-t'*. In this view of the subject, to which I give the decided preference, the roots *yad*, *dad*‡, have dropped their final consonant before the *s* of the aorist, as before that of the 2d person singular (*ya-si*, *da-si*, see §. 436.); and the *s* is, in its origin, identical with that of ꙗсте *ya-s-te* ("ye ate"), ꙗста *ya-s-ta* (2d and 3d per. dual), дасте *da-s-te*, ("ye gave"), даста

---

* Not *vêdê*, as the Guna is dropped before the heavy terminations (see §. 486.), while the Sclavonic *vyemy* retains the Gúna vowel (see §. 255. *e*.) also before the heavy terminations; and hence, *e.g.*, *vyes-te*, "ye know," stands for comparison with the Sanscrit *vit-tha*.

† The *ad-a-sva* which occurs in Mahâ-Bh. III. 2435. follows, like the corresponding Greek verb, the 1st class (see §. 109. ᵃ⁾).

‡ *Dad* is based, indeed, on reduplication, but nevertheless passes, as Miklosich assumes, for a root in Old Sclavonic.

da-s-ta; as also with the χ of ѩхъ *ya-ch'*, "I ate," ѩхомъ *ya-ch-o-m* "we ate," дахъ *da-ch'*, "I gave," дахомъ *da-ch-o-m'*, "we gave and with the *sh* of ѩшѧ *ya-shaṅ*, "they ate," дашѧ *da-shaṅ*, "they gave." All these forms belong to the Sanscrit first aorist formation (see §. 562. conclusion); and as *yad* and *dad*, by dropping the final *d*, put themselves on the same footing with the roots ending in a vowel, let a comparison be made between ѩстъ *ya-s-t'*, "thou atest," дастъ *da-s-t'*, "thou gavest," and the Sanscrit middle *a-yâ-s-thâs*, "thou wentest," and between ѩстъ *ya-s-t'*, "he ate," дастъ *da-s-t'*, "he gave," and *ayâ--s-ta*, "he went;" while ѩсте *ya-s-te*, "ye ate," дасте *da-s-te*, "ye gave," would correspond to the active *aya-s-ta*, if *yá*, or, in general, the roots in *â*, admitted the first aorist formation. We compare, therefore, more aptly, *a-nê-sh-thâs*, "thou leddest;" *a-nê-sh-ta*, "he led" (see §. 545.). To these forms corresponds also that mentioned by Miklosich,

[G. Ed. p. 1495.] p. 37, among other aorist and imperfect forms which, with respect to their personal terminations, are to be referred to this class, viz. быстъ *by-s-t'*, "ἐγενέθης, ἐγενέθη;" for which we should find, in Sanscrit, *ábhô-sh-thâs*, *á-bhô-shta*, if *bhû*, "to be, to become," followed this aorist formation. I cannot put faith[*] in a replacement of the secondary personal terminations, which belong to the aorists, by the primary, with the exchange of ь *y* and ъ (see §. 255. *k.*), and the removal of the 3d person into the 2d: otherwise we should have to charge the language in the case before us with three errors, while, according to my view of the Old Sclavonic, it retains the merit of having preserved, in accordance with the oldest German dialect, the old middle. The Gothic and Old Sclavonic make up one another's deficiencies with regard to the middle, inasmuch as the former has preserved the present, the latter the preterites (the aorists and the imperfect). The fact that the Russian, in the 3d person singular and plural of the present, contrasts a ъ with the Old Sclavonic ь *y*, *e.g.*, несешъ *nes-e-t*, несушъ *nes-u-t*, for Old Sclavonic несеть *nes-e-ty*, несѫть *nes-u-nty*, must be explained, in my opinion, thus, that the old *i* of the Sanscrit forms like *bár-a-ti*, *bár-a-nti*, which in Old Sclavonic has been weakened to ь *y*, has in Russian, as in several other modern languages, been entirely lost. As, however, the Russian orthography requires that the imperceptible ъ be added to the final consonants, *i.e.* to those which are not followed by a perceptibly-sounding ь *y*, the Russian forms, therefore, *nes-e-t* and *nes-u-t*, can, in the Russian character, be written no otherwise than несешъ, несушъ.

---

[*] Cf. Schleicher, "Doctrine of Forms of the *Church* (or Kyrillian) Sclavonic Language," p. 337, where, in discussing the personal terminations here spoken of, the middle has been quite unnoticed.

ALPHABETICAL TABLE OF CONTENTS.

A heavier than *i* §. 6.
A-, *an*-, privative §. 537., of pronominal origin §. 371.
Ablative singular §. 179., in Zend §. 180., in Latin and Oscan §. 181., in Greek §. 183, in Gothic §. 294. Rem. 1. p. 380., in Armenian p. 1272 G. ed. Note, dual §. 215., plural §. 244.
Ablaut, see vowel-increment, vowel-weakening, vowel-interchange.
Accentuation §. 785., p. 1052.
Accusative singular §. 149., in Old Sclavonic §. 266., of the pronouns of the first and second person, and of the reflexive in German p. 1113 Note ** G. ed.; dual §. 206., in Old Sclavonic §. 273.; plural §. 236., in Old Sclavonic §. 275.
Active §. 426.
Adjectives §. 281., pronominal and derivative §. 404., definite declension in Lithuanian and Old Sclavonic §§. 283., 285., in German §. 287.
Adverbs §. 324., pronominal §. 420., adverbial compounds §. 990.
Ampliatives §. 930.
Anusvâra §. 9., in Lithuanian §. 10., in Old Sclavonic §. 783., Rem. 1.
Aorist §. 542., in Latin §. 546., in Old Sclavonic §. 561. and p. 1490 G. ed., Supplement 1) and 2).
Arian Languages, affinity with the Sclavonic and other European languages not traceable p. 1215 Note.
Aspiration thrown back in Sanscrit and Greek §. 104.
Atmanêpadam §. 426.
Augment §. 537., derivation from the demonstrative base *a* §. 540.
Auxiliary future §. 648., in Old Sclavonic, Supplement 4).
Avyayîbhâva p. 1452 G. ed.
Bahuvrîhi p. 1432 G. ed.
-*bam*, of Latin Imperfects, from *fam* §. 526.
-*bo*, of Latin Futures, from *fo* §§. 526., 662.
Cases, formation of §. 112., division into strong, weak, and middle cases §§. 129., 130., difference of accentuation in strong and weak cases §. 785., Rem. p. 1053.
Causals §. 739., in German §. 740, in Old Sclavonic §. 741., in Lithuanian §. 743., in Latin §. 745. p. 999, in Old Persian §. 750., in Lasish §. 750. p. 1006., in Hindūstānī §. 877., Note †.
Collective Compounds §. 989.
Comparative degree §§. 291., 307., in Latin §. 299., in German §. 301. in Old Sclavonic §. 305., in Lithuanian §. 306.
Compounds 1410 G. ed.
Conditional §. 730.
Conjugational classification §. 109.ᵃ⁾ ¹· §. 493., Latin 1st, 2d, and 4th conju-

1450 ALPHABETICAL TABLE OF CONTENTS.

gations=Sanscrit 10th class §. 109.a)6. p. 111; Latin 3d conjugation= Sanscrit 1st, 6th, and 4th class §. 109.a)1., §. 500.; the German strong verbs=Sanscrit 1st class §. 109.a)1. p. 105, or 4th class 109.a)2.; the German weak conjugation=Sanscrit 10th class §. 109.a)6., Armenian conjugations p. 1271 G. ed.

Conjunctions p. 1459 G. ed.

Conjunctive in Sanscrit, Zend, and Greek §. 713., in Latin §§. 674., 690., of the imperfect §. 707., of the perfect §. 710. and p. 1228 G. ed., of the pluperfect §. 858. and p. 1229, G. ed., German conjunctive, preterite §. 756., present §. 694., Lithuanian conjunctive §. 684., Hindūstānī p. 1276 G. ed. Note

Consonants, permutation of §. 87.

Copulative compounds (*dvandva*) p. 1427 G. ed.

Dative Singular, in Sanscrit and Zend §. 164., in Lithuanian §. 177., in Old Sclavonic § 267., in Latin p. 1227 G. ed. Note †, in German §. 356. Rem. 3, in Greek §. 195., dual §. 215., in Lithuanian §. 215. p. 231, in Old Sclavonic §. 273., in Greek §§. 215., 221.; plural §. 244., in Lithuanian §. 215., in Old Sclavonic §. 276., in Greek §. 251.

Degrees of comparison §. 291.

Demonstratives §. 343.

Denominatives §. 761.

Dependent compounds (*tatpuruṣha*) p. 1446 G. ed.

Deponent of intensives §. 760.

Derivative verbs §. 732.

Desideratives §. 751.

Determinative compounds (*karmadhâraya*) p. 1443 G. ed.

Dual, its cases §. 206.

Dvandva p. 1427 G. ed.

Dvigu p. 1449 G. ed.

ê, in Sanscrit, Old High German, and Latin, from *ai* §§. 2., 5., 78., 688., in Greek (η), Gothic, Latin, from *á* §§. 4., 69., 137. p. 1445 G. ed., in Latin and Gothic, through reduplication §§. 547., 605., p. 827.

Feminine, character of §. 118.

Final consonants suppressed in Sclavonic §. 255.l.

Fruit, names of §§. 920., 921.

Future §§. 646., 692., in Old Sclavonic, Supplement 4), in Hindūstānī p. 1276 G. ed. Note.

Futurum exactum p. 1228 G. ed., in Umbrian and Oscan p. 1232 G. ed.

Genitive singular §. 184., §. 254. Rem. 3, in Old Sclavonic §. 269.; dual §. 225., in Zend §. 254. Rem. 1, in Old Sclavonic §. 273.; plural §. 245., in Old Sclavonic §. 278., §. 284. Note 6., §. 783. Note *, p. 1046

Gerunds, in Latin §. 809., in Sanscrit, in *tvâ* p. 1203 G. ed. Note *, p. 1240 G. ed., in य *ya*, p. 1296 G. ed., in Marāṭhī p. 1215 G. ed., in Prâkrit p. 1215 G. ed., p. 1277 G. ed. Note.

Guna, in Sanscrit §. 26., in Greek §. 26. p. 24, §. 491., in Gothic §. 27., in Zend §. 28., in Lithuanian §. 744. p. 997, in Old Sclavonic §. 255.b)f), §. 741.,

Heavy personal terminations, influence of §. 480.

ALPHABETICAL TABLE OF CONTENTS.

i lightest of the primary vowels §. 6.
Imperative §. 717., of the aorist §. 727., of the future §. 729.; Old Sclavonic, imperative §§. 677., 696., Carniolan §. 697., Lithuanian §§. 681., 695., Old Prussian §. 695., Lettish §. 682.
Imperfect §. 517.
Indeclinabilia p. 1453 G. ed.
Infinitive: Sanscrit, in *tum*, p. 1202 G. ed., in causal or dative relation p. 1209 G. ed., represented by forms in *áya, anáya, ané*, pp. 1211—1214 G. ed., by forms in *am*, p. 1214 G. ed., in *ám, ayám* §. 619., p. 1215 G. ed., in *tu*, at the beginning of compounds, (§. 853.) p. 1217 G. ed., Vêdic, in *tavê, taváe*, p. 1218 G. ed., in *dhyái*, p. 1218 G. ed., in *shyái*, p. 1221 G. ed., in *sê*, p. 1222 G. ed., in *asé*, p. 1224 G. ed., in *ê*, p. 1225 G. ed., in *am*, p. 1233 G. ed., in *tôs*, p. 1238 G. ed.; with an apparent passive meaning, p. 1258 G. ed.; periphrasis of passive infinitive, p. 1261 G. ed. Marāthī, pp. 1215, 1217 G. ed., Ossetish, p. 1269 G. ed., Armenian, p. 1269 G. ed., Hindūstānī, p. 1273 G. ed., Zend §. 619., Old Persian, p. 1458 G. ed., Latin, p. 1223 G. ed., of the perfect, p. 1227 G. ed., of the future, p. 1232 G. ed., of the passive participle, p. 1226 G. ed., Oscan and Umbrian, p. 1234 G. ed., Old Prussian, p. 1248 G. ed., Lithuanian and Lettish, p. 1250 G. ed., Old Sclavonic, p. 1251 G. ed., German, pp. 1263, 1271, 1276, 1286 G. ed., Greek, p. 1286 G. ed., middle and passive, p. 1292 G. ed.
Insertion of euphonic sibilant §§. 95., 96., of a labial §. 96., of a nasal §§. 158., 212., 234., 246., in Old High German, Old Saxon, and Anglo-Saxon §. 246., of a euphonic *y* §. 43.
Instrumental singular in Sanscrit and Zend §. 158., in the Veda dialect, p. 1297 G. ed., in Gothic §. 159.*, in Old High German §. 162., in Lithuanian §. 162. p. 180, in Old Sclavonic §. 266.; dual §. 215., in Old Sclavonic §. 273., plural §§. 216., 243., in Old Sclavonic §. 277.
Intensive §. 753.
Interrogative §. 386.
Karmadháraya, p. 1443 G. ed.
L, for other liquids and semi-vowels §§. 20., 409. p. 571, Note †.
Letters §. 1., sonant §. 25.
Light personal terminations §. 480.
Lêt=Greek Conjunctive §. 713
Locative singular §. 195., in Old Sclavonic §. 268.; dual §. 225., in Zend §. 254. Rem. 1. p. 276.; plural §. 250., in Old Sclavonic §. 279.
M, from *v* or *b* §. 63., §. 109.^{b)1}. p. 114.
Middle terminations §. 466., origin of §§. 470., 473., reflexive §. 426., in Gothic §. 426., in Old Sclavonic, p. 1493 G. ed., Supplement 5.

---

* What is said in §§. 160., 161., 171., regarding the Gothic dative must be corrected according to §. 356. Rem. 3.; and so, too, the dative plural in *m* is not to be compared with the instrumental termination in *bhis*, but with the real dative termination in *bhyas*.

1452 ALPHABETICAL TABLE OF CONTENTS.

Moods, formation of §. 672.
Neuter §. 113.
Nominative singular §. 134., of the bases in *n* §. 139., of the bases in *ar*, *ṛi* (ऋ) §. 144., of neuters §. 148., in Old Sclavonic §. 266.; dual §. 206., in Old Sclavonic §. 274.; plural §§. 226., 274.
Numerals §. 308.
Numeral adverbs §. 324.
ô in Sanscrit and Zend from *a+u* §§. 2., 33., Greek *u*, Gothic and Latin *ó*, from *â* §§. 4., 69., p. 1484 G. ed.
Optative §. 672.
Ordinal numbers §. 321.
Parasmâipadam §. 426.
Participles §. 779., future §. 784., perfect §. 786., middle and passive §. 791., perfect passive §§. 820., 836.
Passive §. 733.
Perfect §. 588.
Personal terminations §. 434., middle and passive §. 466., weight of §. 480.
Pluperfect §. 644.
Possessives §. 404.
Possessive compounds (*bahuvrîhi*) p. 1432 G. ed.
Potential §. 672.
Prepositions p. 1465 G. ed.
Present §. 507.
Preterite §. 513.
Precative §§. 701., 705.
Primary forms of nouns §§. 112., 116.
Pronouns §. 326., derivative pronominal adjectives §. 404.
Pronominal adverbs §. 420.
Ṛi (ऋ) from *ar*, *âr*, *ra*, *ri*, *ru* §§. 1., 811., and p. 1057 Note (*prichchhâmi*) 109.[b)2]., *tṛitîya* §. 322.*
R from *v* §§. 20., 409., Note †, §. 447., Table, Note [6].
Reduplication §. 109.[a)3]., §§. 546., 579., 589., 751., 753.
Relative §§. 382., 383.
Roots §. 106.
Radical words, p. 1329 G. ed.
S, changes of §§. 21., 22., 86.[5]., 136., 302., p. 1059, p 1374 G. ed. Note. rejected §. 128.
Sound, system of §. 1., Old Sclavonic §§. 255., 783., Rem. 1., Mutation of, *vide* Consonants.
Special Tenses §. 109.[a].
Strong cases §. 129.
Suffixes, Sanscrit *a*, pp. 1235, 1338 G. ed., Greek o, p. 1235 G. ed., Latin *u*, p. 1236 G. ed., Lithuanian *a*, pp. 1236, 1343 G. ed., Old Sclavonic *o*, p. 1236 G. ed., German *a*, pp. 1237, 1238; Sanscrit *a* §. 913., pp. 1339, 1345 G. ed., Greek o, pp. 1339, 1346 G. ed., αδ, p. 1340 G. ed., Lithua-

---

* *ṛi* from *ru*, in *śṛiṇómi*, "I hear," for *śṛuṇómi*, root *sru*.

ALPHABETICAL TABLE OF CONTENTS. 1453

nian *a*, p. 1343 G. ed., Latin *u*, p. 1340 G. ed., *a*, p. 1341 G. ed., Gothic *a*, p. 1342 G. ed.; Sanscrit * *a, p 1346 G. ed., Greek *o, p. 1347 G. ed., Latin *u, p. 1347 G. ed.; Zend *a*, *a, pp. 1348, 1349 G. ed.

Sanscrit *â*, Greek *a*, *η*, Latin *a*, Lithuanian *à*, Old Sclavonic *a*, Gothic *ô*, nominative *a*; *ôn*, nominative *ô*, p. 1349 G. ed.

Sanscrit *i*, Zend *i*, Gothic *i*, Old Sclavonic *i*, nominative ь *y*, Greek *ι*, *ιδ*, *ιτ*, Latin *i*, Lithuanian *i* §. 924.

Sanscrit *u*, Greek *v*, Lithuanian *u*, Gothic *u*, Zend *u* §. 925.

Sanscrit *an*, *ân*, Greek *αν*, *εν*, *ον*, *ων* §. 926.

Latin *ôn*, nom *ô*; *in*, nom. *en*, Gothic *an*, nom. *a*, Old High German *on*, nom. *o* §. 927.; Lithuanian *en*, nom. *ŭ*, p. 1363 G. ed ; Sanscrit *an* neut., Gothic *an*, nom *ô* §. 928.

Sanscrit *in* §. 929.; Sanscrit *in, Greek *ων, Latin *ôn, Sanscrit *inî §. 930.

Sanscrit *ana*, fem. *anâ*, *anî*, Zend *ana*, Greek *ανο*, Lithuanian *úna*, Gothic *ana*, nom. *an'-s*, *anôn*, nom *anô* §. 932.

Sanscrit *anîya* §§. 904., 906, 907.; Zend *nya*, Gothic *nya*, Lithuanian *nya*, *inya* §. 906.

Sanscrit *âna* § 791.

Sanscrit *as* § 933., Greek *ες* (nom. *ος*, *ης*, *ες*), *ες, Zend *aś, Latin *us*, *eris*; *us*, *or-is*; *ur*, *or-is*; *ur*, *ur-is*; *or*, *ôr-is*, *or, *ôr-is* §§ 934., 937., 938., Gothic *isa* neut. (nom. and acc. *is*) *is-tra*, *is-la*, *s-la*, *as-su* (*drauhtin--as-su-s*) §. 935., Old High German *us-ta*, *us-ti*, *os-ta*, *os-ti*, Lithuanian *as-ti* §. 936.

Sanscrit *us*, p. 1382 G. ed.

Sanscrit *is*, p. 1382 G. ed.

Sanscrit *ya* §. 889., Latin *in* neuter §. 890.; Sanscrit *ya neut., Gothic *ya, Latin *iu, Greek *ιο § 891.; Old Sclavonic *иѥ *iye* §. 892.; Lithuanian *ya §. 893.; Sanscrit *yâ*, Gothic *yô*, nom. *ya* or *i* §. 894., Old Sclavonic *ya*, Lithuanian *ia*, *ě* §. 895.; Latin *ia*, *iê*, *iôn*, *ia, *iê, *iôn, Greek *ια* § 896.; Old High German *i §. 897., New High German *e §. 898., Sanscrit *yâ, Greek *ια, Old High German *ya, neut. nom. *i*, Gothic *ein, nom. *ei* § 898 ; Sanscrit *ya* fut. pass. part., Zend *ya*, Gothic *ya*, Lithuanian *ia*, nom. *is*, Latin *iu*, Greek *ιο §§. 899., 900.; Sanscrit *ya, Zend *ya, Greek *ιο, *ια, Latin *iu, *ia §§. 891., 902.; Latin *ia* for Sanscrit *î*, Greek *ιδ* (?) §. 902.; Gothic *ya, fem. *yô, *yan, *yan*, Sanscrit *ya*, Zend *ya*, Lithuanian *ia*, fem. *ě̃*, Old Sclavonic *yo* §. 903.

Sanscrit *yu*, Zend *yu*, Lithuanian *iu*, Greek *ευ*, p. 1390 G. ed.

Sanscrit *íyâṅs, *íyas*, see Comparative.

Sanscrit *iyâ, see Possessives.

Sanscrit *êya, Greek *ειο, *εο, Latin *eyu, *eu §. 958.

Sanscrit *ra*, *la*, *a-la*, *i-la*, *u-la*, *i-ra*, *u-ra*, *ê-ra*, *ô-ra* §. 939., Zend *ra* §. 940, Greek *ρο*, *λο*, Latin *ru*, *la*, Gothic *ra*, *la*, Old High German *a-la*, *u-la*, *i-la*, *e-la*, nom. *a-l*, &c. §. 940.; Lithuanian *a-la*, Greek *α-λο*, *ε-λο*, *υ-ρο*, *υ-λο*, *α-ρο*, *ε-ρο*, Latin *u-lu*, *u-la*, *e-ru*, *i-li* (?) §. 941.

---

* The mark (*) prefixed distinguishes the secondary suffixes from the primary.

1454 ALPHABETICAL TABLE OF CONTENTS.

Sanscrit *ra, *la, *i-ra, *i-la, *í-ra, *í-la, Zend *ra, Greek *ρο, *λο, Latin *li (?) §. 942.
Sanscrit ri, Greek ρι, Latin ri, e-ri §. 943.
Sanscrit ru, Lithuanian ru §. 944.
Sanscrit va, Latin vu, uu §§. 945., 946.
Sanscrit van, Zend van §. 947.
Sanscrit *vant, vat, Zend *vant, vat, Latin *ntu, Gothic *lauda §§. 409., 410., Lithuanian *leta, linta, la, ant §. 411. ; Sanscrit *vant, vat, Latin *lent, lentu, Greek εντ §. 959.
Sanscrit vas, vâns, vat, ush, fem. ushî §. 786., Lithuanian eṅ (nom. eṅ-s), usia, nom. f. usi, Old Prussian wun-s, un-s, on-s, an-s (nom. m. usi) Zend vâonh, ush, úsh, fem. ushî, úshî §§. 786., 787., Gothic usia (nom. pl. m. bêrusiôs, "the parents," as "having begotten") §. 788., Greek οτ, υια, Latin úri (sec-uri-s), *ósu-s §.789., Old Sclavonic v'sh, fem. v'shi (after vowels) §. 790.
Sanscrit na, Zend na, Gothic na, Lithuanian na, Old Sclavonic но, Greek νο, Latin nu §§. 836., 837., 838. ; Sanscrit na, fem. nâ, Zend na, Greek νο,νη, Latin nu, na, Old High German na, f. nô, nom. n', na §.842.
Sanscrit *i-na, Greek *ι-νο, Gothic *ei-na, Old High German *î-na, Lithuanian *i-na, *i-nia, *y-na (=î-na), *o-na, Old Sclavonic *Е-НО §. 838. ; Latin *i-nu, *î-na, *ĕ-nu, *ê-na, *â-nu, *nu §. 839.; Sanscrit *î-na §. 839. p. 1185 G. ed.
Sanscrit *ânî, f. (indrâ-ṇî, mâtulâ-nî, &c.), Greek *αινα, *ω-νη, Latin *ó-na, *ó-nia, Lithuanian *ĕ̃-ně̃, Old Sclavonic *ынiа ynya, Old High German *inna, New High German in, inn, Old Northern *ynya §§. 840., 841.
Sanscrit ni, f., Greek νι, Old Sclavonic ni, nom. нь ny, Lithuanian ni, Gothic ni §. 843.
Sanscrit ni m., Latin ni, Old Sclavonic ni, Lithuanian ni f. §. 850.
Sanscrit nu, s-nu, Zend nu, Lithuanian nu, s-nu, Gothic nu, Latin nu fourth declension, Greek νυ §§. 948., 949.
Sanscrit nt, ant, t, at, see Participle present and future.
Sanscrit ma, Zend ma, Greek μο, Latin mu, Lithuanian i-ma, i-mma, Gothic ma, Old High German ma §§. 808., 809. ; Greek μη, Latin ma, Lithuanian mà, mě̃ §. 810., Gothic mô §. 950.
Sanscrit mi, Gothic mi §. 950.
Sanscrit man, mân, i-man, i-mân, Zend man §§. 796., 797., Greek μον, μων, μεν, Latin môn, min, môn-ia §. 797., Greek μῖν §. 798. ; Gothic man, Old High German mon, Lithuanian men, nom. mũ, Old Sclavonic мен, nom. мы my §§. 799., 800., Greek ματ, Latin men, min, Old Sclavonic мен neut. ; Sanscrit *i-man, Old High German *mon §. 799. conclusion.
Latin mentu, Greek μινθ, μιγγ, Old High German munda, nom. mund §. 803.
Sanscrit mâna, Old Prussian mana, Lithuanian ma, Greek μενο, Latin minu, mnu, Gothic monyô, f., Old Sclavonic mo, Zend mana, mna, mn §. 791—795.
Latin mulu §. 808.

ALPHABETICAL TABLE OF CONTENTS. 1455

Sanscrit *mara, vara* §. 808.
Sanscrit *mant, mat §. 959.
Sanscrit *ka, a-ka, â-ka, i-ka, u-ka, û-ka*, Latin *û-cu, î-cu, i-cu, i-c, â-c, ô-c*, Greek α-κο, ᾱ-κ, ῡ-κ, αικ (γυναικ), from ακι, Lithuanian *i-ka, i-kka*, Gothic *aga* §. 951., Old High German *i-nga*, nom. *ing, u-ngâ*, f., nom. *unga* (?) §. 952.; Sanscrit *ka §§. 404., 953., Gothic *ha, *ga, *i-g §. 953., Latin *cu, Greek *κο, *ι-κο, τι-κο §. 955.; Gothic, Lithuanian, Old Prussian *i-ska, Old Sclavonic *i-sho*, Greek ι-σκο, ι-σκη §. 954.
Sanscrit *t*, Latin *t*, Greek τ §§. 909. conclusion, 912.
Sanscrit *ta*, Zend *ta*, Lithuanian *ta*, Latin *tu*, Greek το §§. 820., 821., 821., 824.; Gothic *ta, da* §. 823., Latin *du* §. 822., Old Sclavonic *to, lo* §§. 825., 826., Marāṭhī *lá*, fem. *lī*, neut. *lo*, p. 1160 G. ed. (cf. Bengal. p. 1159. G. ed.).
Sanscrit *i-ta, Latin *tu, Greek *ro, Lithuanian *ta, Old Sclavonic **to, sto* §§. 827., 828.
Sanscrit *tâ, *tât, *tâti, Greek τητ, Latin *ta, tât, tût*, Gothic *thô*, nom. *tha*, once *dô, da* (p. 1169 G. ed.), Old High German *dô*, nom. *da*, English *th*, Old Sclavonic *ta* ´§. 829—834.
Sanscrit *ti*, f., Zend *ti*, Gothic *ti, thi, di*, Lithuanian *ti*, Old Sclavonic *ti* §§. 844., 867., Greek τι, σι, σια §§. 845., 846., Lithuanian *tẽ*, from *tia*, *y-stẽ, from *y-stia*, Old Sclavonic *sti §. 447., Latin *ti, si, tión, sión*, **tia, tiê*, p. 1195 G. ed.
Sanscrit *ti*, m. Lithuanian *ti*, Gothic *ti, di*, Lithuanian *ti, chia* (euphonic for *tia*), Old Sclavonic *ti*, Greek τι, Latin *ti*, *sti (?) §. 848.
Sanscrit *a-ti*, Greek ε-τι, Lithuanian *a-schia*, nom. *a-stis* §. 849.
Sanscrit *ti, Zend *ti*, Latin *t* §. 414.
Sanscrit *tîya*, Zend *tya*, Gothic *dyan*, Latin *tiu*, Sclavonic *tiyo*, nom. *tŭ*, Lithuanian *iyo*, from *tia* §§. 322., 323.
Sanscrit *tu*, f., (see Infinitive), Greek τυ, p. 1243 G. ed., Zend *tu*, p. 1244 G. ed., Latin *tu, su*, 4th declension m. §. 865., *â-tu, p. 1403 G. ed., Old Prussian *tu* (infin.), Lithuanian *tu* (supine), Old Sclavonic тъ *t'* (supine) §§. 866., 868., Gothic *tu, thu, du*, m. §. 956., Sanscrit *a-thu*, m. §. 956. conclusion.
Sanscrit *tu*, m., Gothic *tu, du*, Greek τυ §. 957.
Sanscrit *tár, tri* Zend *târ*, Greek τηρ, τορ, τη-s, Latin *tôr, tûru*, Sclavonic *tely* §§. 646., 647., 810., 811., 814, 815.; Sanscrit fem. *trî*, Latin *trîc*, Greek τριδ, τρια, τειρα, τιδ §§. 119., 811.; Latin **â-tôr, i-tôr*, Greek *τη-s, *δη-s, *ι-δηs §. 957.
Sanscrit *tar, tr, tri*, Zend *tar, thr*, Greek τερ, τρ, Latin *ter, tr*, Gothic *tar, tr, thar, thr*, Lithuanian *ter*, nom. *te*, Old Sclavonic *ter*, nom *ti* §§. 144. (p. 157), 265., 812.
Sanscrit *tra*, fem. *trâ*, Greek τρο, τρα, θρο, θρα, Latin *tru, tra*, Zend *tra, thra* §§. 816., 817., Gothic *tra, thra, dra*, Old High German *tra, dra*, nom. and acc. *tar, dar*, New High German *ter*, English *ter* §. 818.; Gothic *thlô*, f, nom. *thla*, Old High German nom. *dla, dila, dela, dal*, Greek τλο, τλη, θλο, θλη; Gothic *thrô*, nom. *thra*, Old High German *trô*, nom. *tra, tar, tera, ter* §. 819.

1456 ALPHABETICAL TABLE OF CONTENTS.

Sanscrit *tra*, Zend *thra* §. 420.
Sanscrit *trâ*, Gothic *drê* §. 991.
Sanscrit *tara*, Zend *tara*, Greek *τερο*, Latin *teru*, Gothic *thara*, Old High German *dara* §. 291.,, Old Sclavonic *toro*, *tero* §. 297.
Sanscrit *tama*, Zend *tĕma*, Latin *timu*, *simu*, Gothic *tuman*, tum'-ista, dum'-ista §§. 291., 292., 295.
Sanscrit *tas*, Latin *tus*, Greek *θεν*, Old Sclavonic *dû* §§. 293. (p. 379), 421.
Sanscrit *tana*, Latin *tinu* §§. 960., 961.
Sanscrit *tavya*, Latin *tǐvu*, Greek τεο §. 904., Lithuanian *toya*, Old Sclavonic *a-tayo*, nom. *a-taĭ* §. 905.
Sanscrit *tya*, Gothic *thya*, Latin *tiu*, Greek στο §. 961.
Sanscrit *tva*, Zend ꓭꓳꓵ thwa, Gothic *tva*, neut. nom. *tv*, *thvô*, fem. nom. *thva*, Old High German *don*, nom. *do*, Old Sclavonic *tva*, *ba*, Lithuanian *ba*, *bẽ* (?) §§. 835., 864., and p. 1244 G. ed.
Sanscrit *tva*, Old Sclavonic *stvo* §. 834.
Sanscrit *tvano*, Prâkrit *ttana*, Old Persian *tana*, Greek fem. *συνη*, adj. *συνο*, Lithuanian adj. *tina*, adv. *tinay* pp. 1216, 1457 G. ed.
Sanscrit *tha*, Greek το, Latin *tu*, Lithuanian *ta*, Sclavonic *to*, Gothic *tan*, *dan*, nom. *ta*, *da* §§. 322., 323., Sanscrit *tham*, Latin *tem* §. 425.
Sanscrit *thâ*, Zend *tha*, Latin *ta*, *tî* §. 425. and p. 1227 G. ed., Note.
Sanscrit *dâ*, Sclavonic *da*, *g-da*, Lithuanian *da* §. 422.
Sanscrit *dhâ*, Greek *χa*, §. 325.
Sanscrit *śas*, Greek κις §. 324.
Sanscrit *sya*, Latin *riu* (?) §. 962., Gothic *arya*, *arya* §. 963.
Sanscrit *ha*, Zend *dha*, Greek θa, Gothic *th*, *d* §. 420.
Superlative §§. 291., 298.
Supine in Latin, pp. 1245, 1253 G. ed., in Lithuanian and Lettish, p. 1247 G. ed., in Old Sclavonic, p. 1252 G. ed.
Tadhita suffixes, p. 1335 G. ed.
Tenses, formation of §. 507.
T-sound suppressed at the end of a word in Greek §§. 155., 456., in German §§. 294. Rem. 1. p. 385, 432.
U, middle vowel weight §§. 490., 584.
Umlaut §. 72.
Verb §. 426.
Vowel weakening §§. 6., 109.[a)] [1]., 272., 490., 605.
Vowel strengthening, *See* Guna.
Vowel interchange, in German §§. 68., 589., pp. 1335, 1338 G. ed , in Old Sclavonic §. 255., p. 1237 G. ed., in Lithuanian §. 744., pp. 1236 G. ed., Note, 1336, 1341, in Greek §. 589., in Latin p. 1336 G. ed.
Visarga §. 11.
Vocative singular §. 204., in Old Sclavonic §. 272.; dual §. 206., in Old Sclavonic §. 273.; plural §. 226., in Old Sclavonic §. 280. Table.
Vṛiddhi §§. 26., 27., p. 1335 G. ed.
Weak cases §. 129.
Words, suffixes used in formation of, *Vide* Suffixes.

CORRECTIONS AND ADDITIONS.

§. 2. Regarding ê from *ai* see §. 688. p. 917.
§. 3. Regarding ε and ο see also p. 1375 G. ed. Note †.
§. 3. 1. 19. Read αι, ει, or οι.
§. 6. Regarding *rótponis* from *rótponyas* see p. 1345 G. ed. Note.
§. 7. Regarding the weight of the *u* see §§. 490., 584.
§. 15. 1 16, for *never* read *seldom*.
§. 20. Mention should have been made here of the Cretan τρέ, "thee," from τϝέ=Sanscrit *tvá*.
§. 26. Regarding Greek οι as Guna of ι see §. 491.; regarding Guna in Old Sclavonic and Lithuanian see §§. 255.b), f), 741., 746.
§. 32. What is here said respecting ꬷ *o* is to be* corrected according to §. 447. Note.
§. 33. ꬷꬷ according to Burnouf, occurs occasionally as the termination of the genitive singular of the *u*-bases for the more common ꬷꬷ *eus*, e.g., ꬷꬷꬷ *bâzaôs*, "*brachii*."
§. 35. p. 32. The Zend *dâta* in *kha-dâta*, belongs to the Sanscrit root *dhâ*, "to place, to make," not to *dâ*, "to give" see §. 637.
§. 40. Last line but one, for ꬷꬷ *hufĕdris* read ꬷꬷ *hufĕdhris*.
§. 41. p. 37. l. 19. for ꬷꬷ *âhûirya* read ꬷꬷ *âhuirya*.
§. 42. To be completed according to p. 963 Note.
§. 42. p. 39, l. 7. for ꬷꬷ *y* read ꬷꬷ *ya*.
§. 42. p. 40. l. 4. 5. to be corrected according to §. 721.
§. 44. l. 14. for ꬷꬷ *âtharvan* read ꬷꬷ *âtarvan*.
§. 45. l. 17. for ꬷꬷ *dadhwâo* read ꬷꬷ *dadhvâo*. The root corresponds to the Sanscrit *dhâ* see §. 637.
§. 45. p. 42. l. 20. for ꬷꬷ *abi* read ꬷꬷ *aibi*.
§. 45. p. 42. l. 26. for ꬷꬷ *aové* read, according to Burnouf, *aôi* (*i.e.* "over"), and *yasnô* signifies "reverence."
§. 46 l. 12. for ꬷꬷ *âturuné* read ꬷꬷ *ataurunê*.
§. 46. l. 13. for तरुन *taruna* read तरुण *taruṇa*.
§. 48. l. 5. for ꬷꬷ *kĕrepĕm* read ꬷꬷ *kĕrĕpĕm*.

---

* I take this opportunity of cancelling what is said at p. 1155, Note *. Had I remembered the Note at §. 447. I should not have written my note, or changed the ꬷ in several places into ꬷ, which latter letter is reserved, it seems, for the final syllable.—*Translator*.

§. 49. p. 45. l. 1. omit ᚷ *th*.

§. 49. p. 45. l. 6. 7. for ᚼᚾᚷᛋᛋᚾ *asthanm* read ᚼᚾᛕᛋᛋᚾ *astanm*.

§. 61. last line. The termination *aṅn* from *án* belongs to the potential, precative, and subjunctive.

§. 65. l. 20. Also between *a* and *r* (*hazaṇra*, "thousand").

§. 77. l. 2. Regarding the Zend ᛋ *o* see §. 447. Note.

§. 90. p. 78. It is better to regard the phenomenon here discussed, so as to assume *d* in Gothic to be the proper character of the 3d person, and the Old High German *t* as the regular substitute for it. The *d* has maintained itself also in the Gothic passive (*bair-a-da*), and the active form *bairith* is to be deduced from *bairid*, as the Gothic prefers aspirates to medials at the end of a word. The same is the case with the passive participle, the suffix of which in Gothic is *da*, which in Old High German, in consequence of the second phonetic change, becomes *ta*, so that, by proceeding in the corruption, we recur to the original form.

§. 90. l. 16. *da* is an abbreviation of *dai*=Greek ται, Sanscrit *tê*, see §. 466.

§. 95. last line, is to be corrected according to §. 616. 2d Note. The *s* of *tars-t, tors-ta*, belongs to the root.

§. 99. p. 88. l. 4. add *ED*.

§. 100. p. 90. l. 4. Regarding *sêdi, vîdi*, from *sesedi, vividi*, see §. 547.

§. 100. p. 90. cf. §§. 547., 576., 579.

§. 102., concl., cf. Sclavonic and Lithuanian §. 457.

§. 109.^(a. 1.) l. 8. The accent distinguishes here the 1st class from the 6th, since, *e. g.*, for *pátati* we should have, did it belong to the 6th class, *patáti*.

§. 109.^(a. 3.) p. 107. l. 23. To the 2d class belong also *FLA, FA,* and *NA*.

§. 109.^(a. 4.) l. 11. I now consider the *v* of *saihva*, and similar verbs, as purely euphonic, cf. §. 86., and Latin forms like *coquo, linquo, stinguo*.

§. 109.^(b 1.) p. 113, l. 6. for §. 117. 2. read p. 107.

§. 109.^(b. 2.) p. 117, l. 24. for ᛋᚢᛃᚾᚼᛃᛠᛠᛖ *kĕerĕnoiti* read ᛋᚢᛃᛠᚾᛃᛠᛠᛖ *kĕrĕnaôiti*.

§. 109.^(b. 2.) p. 118, l. 20. To be corrected according to p. 1320, G. ed. Note.

§. 112. p. 125, l. 15. for *kimah* read *kimaḣ*.

§. 116. l. 25. To be corrected according to p. 1334 G. ed.

§. 119. p. 130, l. 26. for इन्द्रानी *indrâni* read इन्द्राणी *indrâṇi*.

§ 125. last line but one, for "in the oblique cases" read "in most of the oblique cases."

§. 135. Respecting the nominative singular of Gothic bases in *ya* see p. 1309 G. ed. Remark.

§. 139. p. 151, l. 19. I now prefer taking the *i* of *homin-is*, &c., as the weakening of the *o* of *homo*. The relation resembles that of Gothic forms like *ahmin-is, ahmin*, to the nominative and accusative *ahma, ahman*, which preserve the original vowel.

§. 141. p. 153. l. 9. for *namôn-a* read *namn-a* (p. 1083 Note).

§. 144. p. 157, l. 10. for τωρ read τορ, and at l. 14. τορ for τωρ (as termination of the base).

§. 148. p. 163, l. 2 for ᛞᚾᛋᛋᛕ *vachaô* read ᛞᛋᛋᛕ *vachô*.

CORRECTIONS AND ADDITIONS. 1459

§. 156. last line but one. The *â* of *â-děm* is the preposition corresponding to the Sanscrit *â*.

§. 157. 2d Note. Latter part to be corrected according to §. 386. p. 544.

§. 157. Table, p. 174, l. 1. for *patin* read *pátiṅ*.

§. 160. The German dative singular is, according to §. 356. Rem. 3., to be everywhere identified with the Sanscrit dative; and so, too, the dative plural, the *m* of which approaches as closely to the Sanscrit *bhyas*, Latin *bus*, Lithuanian *mus*, as the instrumental termination *bhis*, Lithuanian *mis*.

§. 163. l. 4. for *vriké-n-a* read *vriké-ṇ-a*, with *ṇ*, through the euphonic influence of the *ṛ*.

§. 164. p. 182, l. 25. To be corrected according to §. 254. p. 286, Note †.

§. 171. and §. 172. p. 190, l. 21. To be corrected according to §. 356. Rem. 3. p. 501, last line but seven.

§. 178. p. 194, l. 2. for *tanâv-é* read *tanav-é*.

§. 180. p. 196, l. 18. for ⸺ read ⸺ (see §. 447. p. 624, Note); for ⸺ *aôṭ* occurs also ⸺ *euṭ*; *e.g.*, ⸺ *mainyeuṭ* from *mainyu*.

§. 183. cf. the Gothic ablatives in *ô* adduced in §. 294. Rem. 1. p. 384.

§. 194. p. 210, l. 14. Gothic *handau-s*; l. 20. for *fiyand-s* read *fiyand-is*, see §. 254. p. 302, Note ‡.

§. 194. p. 210, l. 22. for *nâmn-ô* read *nâmn-as*; l. 23. 24. for *brât-ar-s* probably should be read *brâthr-ô*, after the analogy of *dâthr-ô*, *creatoris* (Burnouf "Yaçna," p. 363 Note). The genitive of *dúghdar* is probably *dughděr-ô* (see p. 194 Note†).

§. 195. and §. 203. I now refer the Latin dative to the Sanscrit dative, rather than to the locative; see p. 1227 G. ed. Note.

§. 214. p. 223, Note, last line but one, expunge the words "and which is entirely wanting in the genitive."

§. 216. l. 3. also ⸺ *bis*.

§. 222. l. 10. for अस्माभ्यम् *asmâ-bhyam*, युष्माभ्यम्म् *yushmâbhyam*, read अस्मभ्यम् *asmabhyam*, युष्मभ्यम् *yushmabhyam*.

§. 226. p. 243, l. 3. As to the Latin termination *ê-s* see §. 797., p. 1078, *passim*.

§. 235. l. 5. Zend *vĕhrkâonhô*, see §. 229.; and as to *hosté-s*, *messé-s*, *bové-s*, *você-s*, *ferenté-s*, *sermôné-s*, *fratré-s*, *matré-s*, *dator-és*, see p. 1078.

§. 236. l. 9. The Old Prussian, too, exhibits, in the accusative plural, *ns*, *e.g.*, *tâva-ns*, πατέρας. Respecting the Védic termination *ṅr*, from *r̄s* see §. 517. Remark.

§. 236. first Note, for *vidvaṅs* read *vidvâṅs*.

§. 239. l. 3. cf. Védic forms in *áṅ*.

§. 242. first line of Table, for *vulfan-s* read *vulfa-ns*.

—— twelfth line of Table, Lithuanian *sunù-s*, Gothic *sunu-ns*.

—— p. 260, l. 5. Gothic *fiyand-s*.

§. 243. l. 5. As to the German dative, see correction at §. 160.

—— Table, last line but one, for *nama'-m* read *namn-am*.

1460 CORRECTIONS AND ADDITIONS.

§. 248. l. 1. cf. Old Prussian *-son*, e g., in *stei-son*, τῶν.
§. 249. fifth line of Table, for *trí-n-âm* read *tray-â-ṇâm*, from the extended base *traya*.
§. 254. p. 274, l. 12. Lithuanian *wilkú*.
—— l. 17. *wilkùs* for *wilkú*.
—— Rem. 3, p. 281, l. 11. As to ꙁѫбъ *zańthwâ*, see p. 1244 G. ed.
—— p. 287, l. 9. Regarding *turrê-s* and similar forms see p. 1078.
—— p. 305, l. 6. for *brâtar-s* read *brâthr-ô*, according to the correction at §. 194. p. 210, l. 23.
§. 255. b) p. 311, l. 15. The suppression here noticed of final *i* refers to Dobrowsky's incorrect orthography. In point of fact, however, the final *i* in Old Sclavonic has either been retained unaltered, or has become ь y, e. g., that which Dobrowsky, l. c., writes *dadjat*, "they give," *sút*, "they are," should be corrected to ДАДѦТЬ *dadańty*, сѪТЬ *sunty*. Regarding the nasalized vowels, see §. 783. Remark.
§. 255. f) Here, according to §. 783. Remark, we must distinguish between оу *ú* and Ѫ *uń*.
—— p. 318, l. 13. for पान्दव *pándava* read पाण्डव *pâṇḍava*.
—— g) p. 319. cf. §. 783. Remark.
—— l) p. 323, cf. §. 783. Remark.
—— n) p. 324. The vowels mentioned here, preceded by *y*, are, with the exception of ѥ *ye* and ѣ *yě*, nasalized vowels (see §. 783. Remark); and hence, *pyaty*, "five," must be pronounced *panty* (in the original character ПѦТЬ).
§. 259. p. 329, l. 15. To be corrected according to §. 647., last Note.
§. 266. cf. §. 783. l).
—— last line but two, for *m* (according to Dobrowsky) we should read мь *my*.
§. 280. Table. In the instrumental, *my* is everywhere to be read for *m*.
§. 294. Rem. 2. Regarding *hi-drê* see §. 991.
§. 305. l) l. 2. for "better" read "best."
§. 306. p. 414. In the Lithuanian comparative adverbs like *daugiaus*, "more;" *mažaus*, "less," I regard the *u* as the vocalization of the *n*; thus, *daugiaus* from *daugians*, where *ians*=Sanscrit *íyâns* of the strong cases.
§. 315. l. 2. read ἑπτά (in the accentuation=Vêdic *saptá*).
§. 319. Rem. p. 440. J. Grimm, in his history of the German language, p 246, agrees with my explanation of *eilf, zwölf*, and analogous forms in Lithuanian and Sclavonic.
—— p. 441, Note †. I now prefer, with Benfey, to assign the Latin *linquo*, Greek λείπω, Gothic *af-lif-na*, to the Sanscrit *rich*, from *rik*, "to leave."
§. 338. Regarding the Old Sclavonic *naś, vas'*, see §. 788. first Note p. 1046.
§. 340. l. 3, 4 of Table. Respecting the *k* of the Gothic *mi-k, thu-k* (and that of *si-k*, "self") see §. 814. p. 1104, Note †. In Old Sclavonic we should read for *mya, tya*, according to §. 785. Rem. and 2), *mań, tań*.

CORRECTIONS AND ADDITIONS. 1461

§. 341. p. 476, l. 3. Respecting the origin of the Sanscrit *sva*, see §. 946.
§. 343. p. 478, l. 16. ть *t'* with the semi-vowel ь.
—— p. 479, l. 6. Regarding *totus*, see p. 1343 G. ed., Note.
§. 383. l. 4. for *yus* read *yas*.
pp. 539, 540, l. 8. As to the Gothic suffix *ba* and Lithuanian *p*, cf. p. 1462 G. ed., Note. l. 19.
§. 387. l. 15. Regarding *quæ*, as plural neuter, see §. 394.
§. 416. Regardiug *leiks*, see, too, p. 1442 G. ed.
§. 419. p. 587, l. 10. As to forms like *regâli-s*, see also §. 942. conclusion.
§. 421. p. 592, l. 7. to be corrected according to p. 1227 G. ed., Note.
§. 425. l. 9. cf. the Zend *utî*, "thus," from the base *u*; as to the Latin *utî*, see p. 1227 G. ed., Note †.
§. 436. p. 609, l. 17. and §. 442. p. 618, Table l. 3 and 7, for ઠ *û* should be written ઠ̃ *uṅ*, see §. 783. Remark [4)]
§. 455. p. 635, l. 14. For *dazdhi* read *dazdi*, and so, perhaps, *azdi*, *vischdi*, for *azdhi*, *vischdhi*, did the said forms actually occur, as the Sanscrit *dh* in Zend loses its aspirate after sibilants.
—— p. 636 [12)]. Regarding *azdhi*, &c., see the preceding correction.
§. 456. p. 638, l. 8. for §. 433 read §. 432.
§. 458. p. 640, l. 20. for *û* read *â*.
§. 460. To be corrected according to §. 783.5).
§. 463. Of the termination *ant* only the *t* has been dropped, but the *n* is contained in the preceding nasalized vowel (see §. 783. Remark), hence we should read *aṅ* for *a*, *uṅ* for ઠ.
§. 464. p. 646, Note, Respecting *vacsayatô* see §. 922.
§. 465. Table, p. 648. In the 3d person plural of the Old Sclavonic, for *ûty*, *aty*, we should read *uṅty*, *aṅty*, and for *a*, *aṅ*, see §. 783. Remark.
§. 466. p. 649, l. 1. 2. cf. § 473.
§. 470. p. 653, Note *. cf §. 719. p. 956, Note.
§. 472. last line but three, for "special forms" read "secondary forms."
§. 474. p. 659, l. 22. To be corrected according to §. 888 p. 1292 G. ed.
§. 480. p. 670, last line of Table, for *sûty* read *suṅty*.
§. 485. first line of table, for *krî-na-mi* read *krî-nâ-mi*.
§. 490. In the German preterite, the weakening of the vowel is produced by the polysyllabicness, see §. 420. Rem. 1.
§. 495. p. 691, l. 1. cf. p. 996.
§. 496. first line of Table, for *gyb-nû* read *gyb-nu-ṅ*.
§. 500. p. 695, l. 12. for *bhúvayâmi* read *bhávayâmi*.
§. 503. p. 700, l. 1. for αεκ(ον)-αζόμενος read ἀεκ(οντ)-αζόμενος.
§. 504. p. 701. From line 16. "In this point" to line 19. "The Pråkrit" expunge.
§. 505. l. 16. cf. §. 741. p. 992.
§. 506. Mielcke's 4th conjugation, too, belongs to the Sanscrit 10th class, see §. 698. Note.
—— p. 704, l. 4 for *sravayêshi* read *srávayêshi*.
§. 507. p. 712, for *veẓú*, *veẓuty*, read *veẓ-u-ṅ*, *veẓ-u-ṅty*, see §. 783.[4)] and [5)].
§§. 522. 523. The Lithuanian *bavau*, &c., and *kirtau*, are to be expunged.

§. 531. l. 8. for Krüger read Kühner.
§. 552. last line but three. cf. p. 1227, Note †.
§. 561. last line of Table, for *bûd-i-sha* read *bûd-i-shaṅ*.
§. 569. p. 792, Note †, instead of *f* for *h* read *f* for *p*.
§. 647. p. 878, l. 13. for τωρ read τορ.
—— p. 879, l. 5. To be corrected according to §. 818.
§. 664. first line of Table. Zend forms of the 1st person singular, like the theoretically formed *bûsyêmi*, are not quoteable; cf. §. 731, Remark.
§. 665. l. 2. cf. §. 731. Remark.
§. 668. l. 12. 15. for ꜱꜱ *zan* read ꜱꜱ *zaṅ*.
—— l. 9. 19. 30. for *zaṅhyamana* read *zaṅhyamana*. and from l 30. to end of §., expunge.
§. 724. p. 969, l. 8. for ꜱꜱ *nâsemnâi* read ꜱꜱ *nâsĕmnâi*.
§. 741. p. 993, l. 21. According to Kurschat, *o* in Lithuanian is always long.
§. 751. p. 1008. cf. §. 776. pp. 1037, 1038.
§. 770. p. 1027, l. 29. To be corrected according to §. 837.
—— p. 1030, l. 19. for *ufar-haf-ya-n(a)-s* read *ufar-haf-a-n(a)s*.
§. 785. p. 1053, last line Note, for 1845 read 1843. .
—— p. 1054, l. 30. In compound words I now ascribe the throwing back of the accent in the vocative to the circumstance that compounds in Greek regularly throw back the accent as far as possible. I therefore assume that the accent in vocatives like Ἀγάμεμνον, εὔδαιμον, rests on that syllable of the base word to which it originally belongs, and that, on the other hand, in Ἀγαμέμνων, Ἀγαμέμνονος, εὐδαίμων, εὐδαίμονος, it has sunk down from its original position on the base for well-known reasons.
§. 805. p. 1089, Note *, for *middu-mmas, middis*, read *diddu-mmas, diddis*.
§. 807. p. 1091, l. 8. cf. p. 1178 G. ed. l. 4.
§. 809. p. 1095, l. 23. cf. §. 447.⁶), p. 627.
P. 1462 G. ed. l. 16. *Ob*, and the conjunctions of equivalent meaning in other languages, appear also in the nominative relation in sentences like "*er ist ungewiss, ob er kommen wird, oder nicht,*" "It is uncertain whether he will come or not." The Latin *utrum*, as neuter, is adapted, by its case-termination, as well for the nominative as the accusative relation. The signification "if," is, moreover, claimed by our *ob*, in combination with *schon, gleich*, and *wohl* (*obschon, obgleich, obwohl*).

FINIS.

For EU product safety concerns, contact us at Calle de José Abascal, 56–1º, 28003 Madrid, Spain or eugpsr@cambridge.org.

www.ingramcontent.com/pod-product-compliance
Ingram Content Group UK Ltd.
Pitfield, Milton Keynes, MK11 3LW, UK
UKHW041313110326
11208UKWH00004B/1298